PRINCIPLES OF DATA PROCESSING

PRINCIPLES OF DATA PROCESSING

Robert A. Stern   Nancy B. Stern

John Wiley & Sons, Inc. New York London Sydney Toronto

This book was set in Helvetica Light with Laurel by York
Graphic Services, Inc.; printed and bound by Vail-Ballou.
Designed by Jules Perlmutter and Jerome B. Wilke; the
drawings were designed and executed by the Wiley
Illustration Department. The editor was Beverly N.
Nerenberg. Stanley G. Redfern supervised production.

Library of Congress Cataloging in Publication Data

Stern, Robert A
Principles of data processing.

1. Electronic data processing.   2. Electronic
digital computers.   I. Stern, Nancy B., joint
author.   II. Title.

QA76.5.S776   001.6′4   72-6849
ISBN 0-471-82324-4

Printed in the Unites States of America

10 9 8 7 6 5 4 3 2 1

To Melanie and Lori

Preface

Principles of Data Processing is an introductory text for:

1. Business students majoring in such areas as business administration, accounting, and marketing and retailing who wish to obtain a fundamental understanding of how data processing relates to the business world.

2. Data processing majors who wish to obtain an overview of data processing with respect to the business world.

This textbook differs significantly from the data processing texts currently in use. It introduces the concepts of data processing as they actually relate to the business world. The degree of communication and interaction between the businessman and the computer specialist is emphasized throughout in an effort to facilitate business information flow. We do not attempt to idealize data processing. The common pitfalls and problem areas of computer processing are presented in order to familiarize the student with all facets of this field. No emphasis is placed on obsolete concepts and terminology.

This combination text-workbook utilizes a step-by-step unit approach designed to effect an integration of material heretofore unattained. The approach is basic, neither all-encompassing nor encyclopedic, designed to provide the student with a working knowledge of data processing as it really exists, not to overwhelm him with independent and isolated topics.

The purpose of the text-workbook combination is to introduce the student to data processing and to provide him with the facility, in the workbook, to apply his understanding to any one of a number of business areas. In this way, the student comprehends both the nature of data processing and its relation to the business world. The workbook follows the text, chapter by chapter. It includes key questions designed to test the student's understanding of the text material. More importantly, it includes applications in specific business areas, designed as realistic illustrations of the use of data processing and as vehicles for classroom discussion.

The text-workbook is divided into three sections.

Section 1. "Fundamental Concepts of Data Processing." This section introduces the student to the basic concepts of data processing, such as the input/output forms, hardware, and data communications.

Section 2. "Concepts of Computer Programming." This section includes material on flowcharting and on each of the major languages. We do *not* attempt, however, to cram independent programming courses into each of these chapters. Instead, an effort is made to provide the student with enough information so that he can both read and understand simple business programs.

There are four primers available in each of the major languages that may be used at the instructor's discretion to supplement the text if a thorough, yet meaningful, approach to programming in any of these languages is desired. Primers are available in COBOL, RPG, BASIC, and FORTRAN. The text, in conjunction with one of these primers, is recommended for a full-year course in data processing.

Section 3. "Systems Analysis and Design." The basic concepts of systems analysis and design are presented as they relate to the business world.

We express special appreciation to Al Beckett, Jr., formerly of Wiley, and Gene Davenport, editor at Wiley, for their assistance and moral support. Also we express our special thanks to Barbara Fortgang for her patience and fortitude in typing the manuscript.

Robert A. Stern
Nancy Stern

Contents

° *The asterisk (°) indicates optional topics.*

ix

Section Three
Systems Analysis and Design   *461*

Appendix
Numbering Systems and Their Significance
in Computer Processing   *583*

PRINCIPLES OF DATA PROCESSING

Section One *Fundamental Concepts of Data Processing*

Chapter 1 *An Overview of Data Processing*

I. THE RELEVANCE AND PREVALENCE OF COMPUTERS

A. HANDLING MORE DATA AT A CHEAPER RATE
B. SPEED AND ACCURACY
C. PERFORMING MORE SOPHISTICATED OPERATIONS THAN
   COULD POSSIBLY BE PERFORMED WITHOUT
   A COMPUTER'S USE FOR
   1. The Manager
   2. The Customer

II. THE DEVELOPMENT OF COMPUTERS-TRACING THE HISTORY OF ELECTRONIC ACCOUNTING MACHINES

A. THE ABACUS
B. THE PASCAL CALCULATING MACHINE
C. THE JACQUARD TECHNIQUE FOR OPERATING A WEAVING LOOM
D. THE BABBAGE ANALYTICAL ENGINE
E. THE PUNCHED CARD—HOLLERITH AND POWERS
F. ELECTRONIC ACCOUNTING MACHINES
   1. Sorter
   2. Reproducer
   3. Interpreter
   4. Collator
   5. Accounting Machine
G. MODERN COMPUTERS

III. INTRODUCTION TO COMPUTER CONCEPTS

A. INPUT
B. OUTPUT
C. PROGRAM

3

How long does it take you to add the following two numbers?

$$998756 + 985769 =$$

It probably took approximately five to ten seconds. In the same time interval, a typical business computer could easily have performed between 50,000 and 100,000 such additions! There are some business computers that could have performed over 1,000,000 such operations in the same time period.

We have just observed one of the most compelling reasons for the use of computers—that is, speed. In addition, computers can perform these operations with greater accuracy than people.

Thus the relatively recent surge in computer technology is a result of the tremendous need in many companies to perform relatively simple arithmetic and clerical functions quickly and accurately. It is simply not feasible, for example, for a company with 75,000 employees to have a manual payroll system. It would be too costly and too cumbersome to hire enough clerks necessary to handle the calculation and creation of a weekly or semimonthly payroll check. In addition, because of the volume, the chances of manual errors would be very great, necessitating a thorough, costly, and prohibitive control procedure.

Fundamental Concepts of Data Processing

Thus tremendous growth and expansion in many companies would not be feasible without the advances made by computers. However, in one month alone we received bills processed by a computer that were in error by over $100. In addition, we know a fortunate individual who received a weekly payroll check for $600,000 (ultimately corrected, however). Recently, the president of one of the largest corporations in this country received an incorrect payroll check. The list of errors in computer processing goes on and on. It is because of such well-publicized errors that a businessman may be justifiably apprehensive of computers and may question their accuracy and usefulness. We will see, however, that the computer is almost always innocent and the people who are responsible for its control are the guilty ones. In data processing, the term GIGO reflects the manner in which computers operate—Garbage *In*, Garbage *Out*. If a time card is incorrectly processed by an operator as having an annual salary of $600,000 instead of $6,000 the computer will operate accordingly. Likewise, if the individual who instructs the computer does not provide for all possible contingencies in billing, it is possible that specified individuals will receive erroneous bills. Computers are designed to be technically precise and except in rare cases they function normally. They are not, however, rational entities and therefore they cannot, by themselves, determine if the information entered is reasonable or correct.

The primary purpose of this book is to allay misapprehensions about computers and to demonstrate how they can be successfully used in business applications. In addition, we will show how the businessman can achieve the greatest productivity and assistance from a computer in areas such as: accounts receivable, accounts payable, sales forecasting, marketing and retailing, inventory control, payroll, personnel record keeping and other areas, where repetitive clerical chores are required.

Perhaps one of the most astonishing discoveries to be made by a businessman in studying computers is that man is smarter than the computer. A computer is essentially a nonthinking machine. It does only what it is told to do, by man, in the form of written instructions. These instructions, known as a *program,* indicate exactly how to take information entered into the machine, to process that information by performing the required operations, and then to produce the desired results or *output.* The examples of computer errors listed above are in reality not the computer's fault. They are due to *human* error. Either the people who told the computer what to do were somehow remiss in their instructions to the machine or the incoming information, prepared manually, was incorrectly generated.

Our purpose in writing this text is essentially twofold. We will illustrate the potential of the computer and indicate how easy it is for the capabilities of the computer to be harnassed efficiently and economically. We will also impress upon the reader the necessity for close interaction between the businessman and the computer specialist in all areas of business data processing. By far the greatest cause of inadequate computer processing today, is the communications gap between computer specialists and the businessmen whose operations and procedures must be computerized. The computer staff is often not properly attuned to the needs of the businessmen within their company and, similarly, the businessmen are not properly aware of what they can realistically expect from a computer system. This text attempts to bridge that gap. It will provide the businessman or business student with enough familiarity with computers to effectively communicate his needs. It will provide the computer specialist or data processing student with enough familiarity with business needs to be able to function in a business environment.

Understanding the basic concepts and terminology of computers within a business environment will provide, in the end, more efficient processing by translating information processing needs into effective computer systems.

I. *The Relevance and Prevalence of Computers*

Computers have automated business operations at a phenomenal rate. The first commercial computer was a Univac installed in business in 1954. Today, there are over 60,000 computers in the United States.

At the time of this writing, United States business, government, and science are spending approximately $15 billion a year buying, renting, and operating general-purpose computer systems. This annual outlay is expected to increase greatly in the middle 1970s.

Hardly any facet of our lives today is unaffected by computers. With the widespread use of checks for financial transactions, for example, it is not surprising to find that the banking industry is the largest investor in computers. You may have already observed, for instance, the magnetic ink characters on the bottom of your check that facilitate processing by computer.

In many banks, when an individual wants to cash a personal check, the teller accesses the computer via a touch-tone phone. The person's account number and the amount of the check are then transmitted to the computer by pressing the appropriate keys. The computer checks the account and responds over the telephone with a voice response, indicating basically whether there are sufficient funds to cover the check. Note that it is merely a man's prerecorded response that is accessed by the computer—as of this writing no one has invented a computer that has its own larynx!

If you have ever had occasion to walk into a stock brokerage house you have probably noticed what appear to be small television sets on the brokers' desks. These *display terminals* are hooked into a central computer and allow instant retrieval of the latest stock quotations. One simply has to press the keys corresponding to the code of the particular stock, and the latest quotations are displayed on the terminal. Figure 1.1 illustrates a typical terminal used for this purpose.

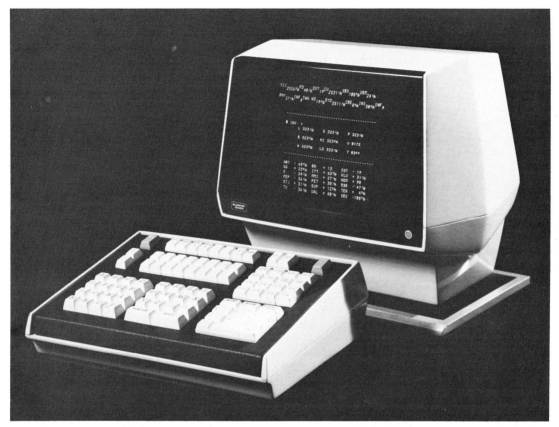

Figure 1.1
Bunker Ramo Market Decision System 7 provides brokers with simultaneous displays of data from three different sources, including tickers, newswires, computer and stock market data bases containing a variety of information on stocks, commodities and averages. In addition, these units perform all the functions of a programmable computer terminal enabling the user to perform trading computations, to transmit buy and sell orders, and to switch circuits at will to any of the many services to which the unit may be connected. Courtesy Bunker Ramo Corporation.

The same type of display is used by many of the airlines to supply information pertaining to airline reservations. You can walk into one of thousands of offices throughout the country and inquire about the availability of seats on a particular flight. If seats are available, this information is relayed from the computer, which may be hundreds or thousands of miles away. The agent then keys in such information as your name, address, and so on and the computer stores this data and updates, or changes, the figures on seat availability for that particular flight, while providing you with a flight ticket.

In this age of credit cards, it is natural to find that most large and medium-sized companies have computerized their accounts receivable system (which is responsible for billing customers), for example. You may have had the experience of buying something with a credit card and having the sales clerk put the card in a special machine for verification. The identification on the card, usually the account number, is transmitted directly to the computer, which determines if the card is valid. If, for example, the card was reported stolen, or the account is in arrears, the computer may indicate by lights on the machine, that the card should be confiscated or that the purchase be disallowed.

Many companies utilize computers for inventory control (which maintains records and control of available stock). As an example, one company utilizes terminals, similar to a typewriter, to communicate with the computer and to retrieve information concerning inventory on hand. These terminals are located in the various offices of the company. When a customer calls one of the locations and orders a particular part, an operator keys in the information on the terminal. The computer, in a matter of seconds, supplies data such as the availability and location of the parts.

Other applications that are commonly computerized in business include accounts payable, sales analysis, budget reports, personnel records, product scheduling, order processing, pricing, and financial planning.

There is virtually no limit to the types of information that a businessman can have processed and stored by a computer system. The degree of sophistication in processing information is a direct function of the money a businessman is willing to spend. Small-scale business computers rent from under $1000 per month, while more sophisticated ones such as those for airline reservation systems can rent for over $150,000 per month. These figures are for equipment rental alone. Supplies, personnel, overhead, and miscellaneous expenses are extra.

Most businesses with any clerical procedures that handle large volumes of data manually can usually be automated at an *eventual* savings to the company. This is not to say that employees currently performing the procedures manually will be fired. To allay a common misconception, layoffs are rarely, if ever, the result of an automated procedure. These employees, usually clerks, are generally reassigned, since computer installations also require clerical assistance. Although the acquisition of a computer center usually results in an *increase* in personnel, the long-term result is hopefully the stabilization of personnel growth. Another common misconception that should be dispelled is that computers must save money in order to be successful. The acquisition of computer equipment is *never* a money-saving venture, at the onset. In addition to the initial outlay, a computer center must be staffed with trained personnel. The expense of establishing a computer center is very costly. Ultimately, however, it is hoped that the procedures which take excessive time and handle large volumes of

Fundamental Concepts of Data Processing

data can be computerized with greater *efficiency*. Here, again, the cost of the computerized systems may not result in a tangible monetary savings but it will provide for the following.

A. HANDLING MORE DATA AT A CHEAPER RATE

Growth trends can easily be built into computer operations. Although more and more employees would be required each year to handle increased amounts of data in a manual procedure, the computer could process this increased data at minimal cost and manpower.

B. SPEED AND ACCURACY

There is little question that a computer, *when instructed properly,* can perform the tasks of large numbers of employees in relatively little time, with decreased error ratios.

C. PERFORMING MORE SOPHISTICATED OPERATIONS THAN COULD POSSIBLY BE PERFORMED WITHOUT A COMPUTER'S USE

We have seen that desired reports and results from computerized operations can be more precise and can provide more extensive information than without a computer. This can serve two major users of a company's operations: the manager and the customer.

1. The Manager
Decision-making functions required of managers become easier and more reliable if a computer is used to integrate the operations of all procedures to determine future requirements, goals, and so on.

2. The Customer
A customer who can go to an airline and, in an instant, obtain flight information and even get an airline ticket is more apt to return to that airline than to go to one that performs operations manually, requires more time to process, and is more likely to make errors.

Thus people who say: "My company has had a computer for three years and it still costs the same to perform the operations" are not perceiving the situation properly. Perhaps the operations now handled by the computer process 20% more records. Or perhaps the customer complaint ratio or error ratio is reduced by 5%.

Since many small companies do not feel they can justify the expense of a computer system, the use of *time-sharing* has been expanding rapidly. Through time-sharing, a company does not need its own computer. Instead, the company can rent computer time from a rental company and access the computer via terminals. This concept of sharing computer time with others has several advantages, the main ones being low equipment cost and low personnel cost, since there is no need to fully staff a computer center.

Businesses have also found other ways to avail themselves of computer systems. One is by leasing computer equipment from computer leasing companies, which buy them from the manufacturer and then make profits by leasing them to individual companies. Another way is to utilize one of the many service bureaus or facilities management organizations that will process a company's information for a negotiated fee. In addition, they will design new systems, or procedures, for the company, and/or write the necessary computer programs, or instructions, that are required for processing. In this way, the small-scale company need not hire a full computer staff to perform these operations.

A recent study claims that computers, on the average, are used only 64% of the time they are available, and only during *48% of that time* are they used productively. Thus, although computers result in many positive effects for companies, they are not always utilized effectively or efficiently. This is almost always a result of an improperly trained computer staff. It is the task of the computer specialist to maximize computer efficiency. It is the businessman's task to assist the computer specialist in obtaining the greatest productivity and increased profits from a computer. A computer that rents for $150/hour which is idle for several hours a day is not being used properly. It is the task of the computer specialist and the businessman to work closely in order to computerize systems in a manner that will increase overall company productivity.

It is thus our perspective in writing this book to insure that the businessman and computer analyst will have the facts, the techniques, and the understanding of computers needed to make sure that the best decisions are made when the specific systems are computerized. With this background, we envision more productive and economical computer systems.

II. The Development of Computers—
Tracing the History of Electronic Accounting Machines

Although many have characterized the current era as the "Age of the Computer," the ideas and concepts for computers have materialized over a period of centuries. This section and the following one provide a perspective on the growth of data processing equipment over the years. We will present several innovations that have resulted in more sophisticated calculating machines and ultimately in computers.

A. THE ABACUS

The abacus is a device first used in China about 2000 years ago. Still in use today in some parts of the world, this device was one of the original calculators or tools used for performing simple addition and subtraction operations with speed and accuracy. It consists of beads that can slide on wires. Five beads below a wooden bar represent units. Each bead above the bar represents five. The wires represent columns, and have positional values familiar to us; that is, the rightmost column is for units, the next is for tens, and so on. By pushing appropriate beads next to the wood bar, various numbers can be established. In some Chinese areas, we can still see businessmen using the abacus, to perform arithmetic operations, at speeds that often surprise and even awe the onlooker (see Figure 1.2a).

B. THE PASCAL CALCULATING MACHINE

In 1642, Blaise Pascal, a French mathematician and philosopher, devised a calculating machine that was operated by dialing a series of wheels. Around the circumference of each wheel were the numbers zero to nine. Sums or totals appeared above the dials on indicators (see Figure 1.2b).

C. THE JACQUARD TECHNIQUE FOR OPERATING A WEAVING LOOM

In 1804, Joseph Marie Jacquard developed a method for controlling the operation of a weaving loom from coded information punched into paper cards. It was found that different punched cards could produce various patterns with a high degree of accuracy. This basic idea of the punched card is still in use today (see Figure 1.2c).

D. THE BABBAGE ANALYTICAL ENGINE

During the nineteenth century, Charles Babbage, an English mathematician, developed the idea for an analytical engine that could perform any kind of computation automatically. His idea was to have the engine powered by steam. It would operate from a set of instructions coded on punched cards, and would be capable of storing information and printing desired results. The idea of the analytical engine eventually materialized in the twentieth century.

E. THE PUNCHED CARD—HOLLERITH AND POWERS

In the 1880s, Herman Hollerith, who was working for the United States Census Office, devised *electrical* tabulating equipment (Figure 1.2d) that was used in amassing data for the 1890 census. The essence of his contribution was a method of representing information by a series of punched holes in paper cards. He also developed the electrical equipment to tabulate information from these cards and to sort the cards by particular categories, such as age, sex, or place of birth. Hollerith eventually left the Census Bureau and formed his own company to produce this equipment. In time, his company merged with others, and the result was the birth of IBM, which today has approximately 70% of the computer market in the United States.

At the same time that Hollerith was working for the Census Bureau,

Abacus used for rapid calculation in
the Orient since the 13th century.

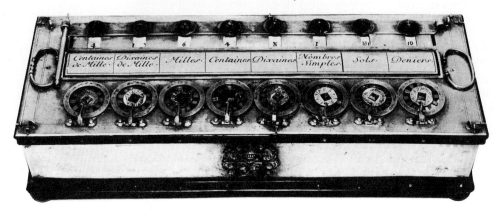

Pascal's calculator invented in 1642.

A nineteenth century jacquar
loom controlled with punched cards.

Figure 1.2
The history of data processing.

Electrical tabulator and sorter devised by Herman
Hollerith to speed processing of data for 1890 census.

James Powers was also employed there. Like Hollerith, he too devised electrical tabulating equipment and a scheme for coding information in the form of punched holes on cards. His scheme for coding the information and his development of the associated tabulating equipment differed from those of Hollerith's. Powers formed his own company and through a series of mergers the Sperry Rand Corporation was founded, which installed the first commercial computer, the Univac, in 1954.

F. ELECTRONIC ACCOUNTING MACHINES

Punched-card equipment, based on the machines developed by Hollerith and Powers, was introduced to business in the early part of this century to process such things as payroll, billing, sales, and accounting data. This equipment has been commonly referred to as Electronic Accounting Machines (EAM equipment), since many companies have utilized it primarily for the accounting function. It is also commonly called *unit-record* equipment, since each card is handled as an individual unit or record. There are still some companies that use this equipment today, although the machines are rapidly becoming obsolete.

These punched cards (Figure 1.3) can be punched by an operator

Figure 1.3
The punched card.

Figure 1.4
Keypunch machine. Courtesy IBM.

who uses a device called a Keypunch Machine (Figure 1.4) to produce the holes. The Keypunch Machine has a keyboard, not unlike a typewriter, where a letter or digit is depressed by the operator and a corresponding hole or holes are punched onto the card. In this way, *files* of cards can be keypunched with data relating to a specific system such as Accounts Receivable and Inventory. A keypunch operator uses a document, such as a sales ticket, and keypunches the *fields* of data, such as customer name, account number, date of transaction, or amount of purchase onto the punched card. In addition, the machine can imprint the letter or digit on the card. The format of a punched card will be discussed in more depth in Chapter 3. Let us consider the more widely used unit-record machines that utilize the punched card for any of the above-mentioned applications.

Notice that each EAM or unit-record machine serves a specific and somewhat limited function.

Fundamental Concepts of Data Processing

Device	Function	Typical Uses
1. SORTER Figure 1.5 Courtesy IBM.	Sorts cards into an alphabetic or numeric sequence by sensing the holes punched into cards. Cards may be sorted into ascending or descending sequence. A group of cards, called a file, must be arranged in a specific sequence so that individual cards can be extracted, when required, and so that reports produced from these cards will have some order. Most files utilize a specific field such as social security number, account number, etc. for their sort fields.	Accounts Receivable or Billing Cards may be sorted into account number sequence, as a major sort, and into date sequence within each account number. Payroll cards may be sorted into an alphabetic sequence, by employee name. Inventory cards may be sorted by part number.
2. REPRODUCER Figure 1.6 Courtesy IBM.	Duplicates punched cards or duplicates specific items of a punched card.	A Payroll system may require the duplication or *gang-punching* of a specific date into each employee's time card. A major banking firm may require each branch office to use cards as transactions records. It would be advantageous for each branch to duplicate or gang-punch the individual branch office number onto all of its transaction cards. In this way, costly key-punching of each card is not required. For companies with a shipping *and* a receiving department, it is sometimes necessary to maintain two sets of records. Where records are maintained on punched card, all may be reproduced or duplicated and thus two groups can be obtained.
3. INTERPRETER Figure 1.7 (next page). Courtesy IBM.	Prints on top of the card the data that has been punched onto the card. There are 80 positions on a card. Using a keypunch machine, it is possible to *print* the corresponding punched information on the face of the card:	A utility company, such as a gas or electric company, uses a computer to produce customer bills onto punched cards. The punched data, although useful for eventual reentry to the computer system when the bills are paid, must be interpreted so that the customer can read them.

Device	Function	Typical Uses
 Figure 1.8 Printing performed by keypunch machine Figure 1.9 Interpreted card	If cards were punched by the computer there would often be no facility for printing. In this case, an interpreter may be used to make the cards serviceable for manual reading. A typical interpreter can print punched data on either of two lines in any position, but can only print a total of 60 positions on each line. Thus to print all 80 punched positions, two lines of printing are required. Figure 1.9 illustrates an example of interpreted output. Notice that the printed data is not directly above the punched data as in Figure 1.8, where data was imprinted by a keypunch machine.	A college, utilizing a computerized registration system produces course registration punched cards. These computer-produced punched cards must be interpreted so that students and faculty members can read them.
4. COLLATOR  Figure 1.10 Courtesy IBM.	The collator can perform four basic functions. a. Merging—taking two separate files, each sequenced in the same order, and combining them to form one sequenced merged file, as shown in Figure 1.10a. b. Sequence checking—checking to determine if cards are in the proper order. If cards are not in the proper sequence, the machine can be made to stop, so that resequencing can be performed or so that the cards that are out of order can be selected into an error "pocket" or stacker.	A banking firm has many branch offices. Each day sorted transaction cards from each branch office are sent to the EAM staff. The entire deck of cards from all branch offices, can be merged using a collator. An inventory department has a master file of all parts on hand in sequence by part number. A check must be performed to insure that there are no duplicate part numbers in the master file. The collator can perform this check. Note that duplicate part numbers for a single item (that

Device	Function	Typical Uses
Figure 1.10a Example of a merging operation 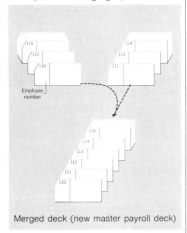 Merged deck (new master payroll deck)	c. Matching—determining, for two independent decks, whether the cards from each *match* on some field. That is, two decks of payroll cards can be matched on employee number. Cards that do not match from either deck can be selected into an error pocket or stacker or the machine can be made to halt until a matching card is placed in the deck. d. Selection—selecting cards with specially coded fields. Cards with a blank social security number, for example, can be selected into an error pocket or stacker.	is, two records of the number of nails on hand, for example) would make it extremely difficult to determine what was really in stock.
5. ACCOUNTING MACHINE OR CALCULATOR  Figure 1.11 Courtesy IBM.	This is the only EAM device that is capable of printing a report. It uses cards as input and produces a printed document as output. It can perform simple addition and subtraction. It can print one line for a group of cards by sensing a change in control numbers. It can be wired to the REPRODUCER to *summary punch* control cards, with total or summary information. The REPRODUCER must be used here since the ACCOUNTING MACHINE is not capable of punching cards.	An accounting system can use an ACCOUNTING MACHINE to produce bills. Punched cards sorted into account number sequence can be entered as input. The machine can total all charge slips (which are in the form of punched cards) totals for each customer and then produce a bill on a preprinted bill form. An inventory system can use an ACCOUNTING MACHINE to produce a weekly status report of items on hand. Each time an item is transmitted to a specific department, a card is punched with the item number and the number of items delivered. At the end of the week, these cards are sorted along with the master file of items on hand into part number sequence. The ACCOUNTING MACHINE can then produce a listing of parts with their current availability. That is, the items transmitted during the week are subtracted from the number on hand.

The sorter, as indicated, can sort into various sequences, depending essentially on the manner in which the dials are positioned. The other devices are *wired* in order to perform the specific tasks required. The control panel with corresponding wires for a typical EAM device is illustrated in Figure 1.12. Note that most control panels are *not* as complex as indicated in the figure. Using a REPRODUCER to reproduce the *first* five positions of a card onto 100 additional cards will require wiring that is different from that required to reproduce the *last* five positions. To merge two decks of cards using a collator will require wiring different from that required for checking the sequence of the cards. In short, the specific operation required from any EAM device (except a sorter) is obtained by first wiring the control panel of that machine. Although the word wiring denotes sophisticated

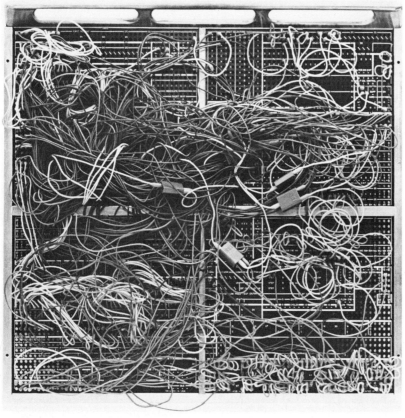

Figure 1.12
Control panel. Courtesy IBM.

Fundamental Concepts of Data Processing

electronic ability, it is a relatively simple task to wire these devices. Each machine has a booklet that indicates how to wire the machine for any operation required. Most companies have prewired control panels for the more frequently used tasks. For example, almost all companies that have a REPRODUCER also have a prewired control panel that will reproduce all 80 columns of a card onto successive cards, since this is the most frequently required operation of a REPRODUCER. When a specific operation is required for which a prewired control panel is not available, then a data processing employee must prepare the panel, using the specification booklet as a guide.

As indicated, each device has a specific function. Thus, for relatively complex tasks, more than one machine is often needed. That is, to produce bills from Accounts Receivable cards, it is usually necessary to sort and/or collate the cards, and reproduce them, in addition to using an accounting machine.

Let us examine the following systems and see how they effectively utilize several machines to achieve a given purpose.

EXAMPLE 1

An Accounts Receivable Department of a large company maintains records and prepares bills for all charge account customers. This department, with the assistance of the data processing staff, makes use of EAM equipment in order to eliminate excessive manual effort. One of the procedures that utilizes unit-record equipment is the processing of new charge accounts so that they can become part of the master file for standard billing operations.

1. Keypunching
One copy of the Approved Charge Account Application is sent to the Keypunch Unit. There cards are punched into standard punched card format while the approved charge account applications are filed. The punched cards comprise the *NEW NAME AND ADDRESS FILE* for new customers.

2. Sorting
This *NEW NAME AND ADDRESS FILE* is created from the approved charge applications, which enter the keypunch unit in a random manner. They must be sorted into account number sequence. Once sorted, the deck is referred to as the *SORTED NEW NAME AND ADDRESS FILE*.

3. Collating
The *SORTED NEW NAME AND ADDRESS FILE* must become part of the *MASTER NAME AND ADDRESS FILE* that contains *all* charge account data, which is also maintained in account number sequence. To merge two decks of cards that are both in the same sequence, the

collator is used. If an account number from the *SORTED NEW NAME AND ADDRESS FILE* matches an account number from the *MASTER NAME AND ADDRESS FILE* then an error exists and both cards are rejected by the collator. A match would indicate that a new account has the same account number as an existing record. The merged file, which contains only the unmatched or correct records, is called the *UPDATED MASTER NAME AND ADDRESS FILE*.

4. Accounting Function

The *UPDATED MASTER NAME AND ADDRESS FILE* is used by the Accounting Machine to prepare a current CUSTOMER NAME AND ADDRESS REPORT. The CUSTOMER NAME AND ADDRESS REPORT is used by the Accounts Receivable Department for validation and for customer inquiries. The *UPDATED MASTER NAME AND ADDRESS FILE* is also used for the preparation of bills for the current month, until a new updated file is created the following month.

A pictorial representation of the above procedure, called a SYSTEMS FLOWCHART (Figure 1.13) can be used to illustrate the processing required, without using as much narrative. We shall discuss flowcharts in more depth later in the text.

EXAMPLE 2

The daily processing of sales slips, credit slips and payment memos is required to prepare a Transaction File and a Daily Accounts Receivable Register.

Each day, the Accounts Receivable Department receives sales slips for all charge account purchases, credit slips for all returns, and payment forms or memos, denoting receipt of a payment.

1. Keypunching

All forms (sales slips, credit slips, and payment forms) are keypunched as received, and at the end of the day a *TRANSACTION FILE* is created from these cards.

2. Sorting

The *TRANSACTION FILE* is sorted into account number sequence and the result is a *SORTED TRANSACTION FILE*.

3. Accounting

The *SORTED TRANSACTION FILE* is entered into an Accounting Machine to produce a *DAILY ACCOUNTS RECEIVABLE REGISTER REPORT* which is maintained by the Accounts Receivable department.

The *SORTED TRANSACTION FILE* is maintained so that at the end of the month all such daily files are sorted and a cumulative bill can be prepared.

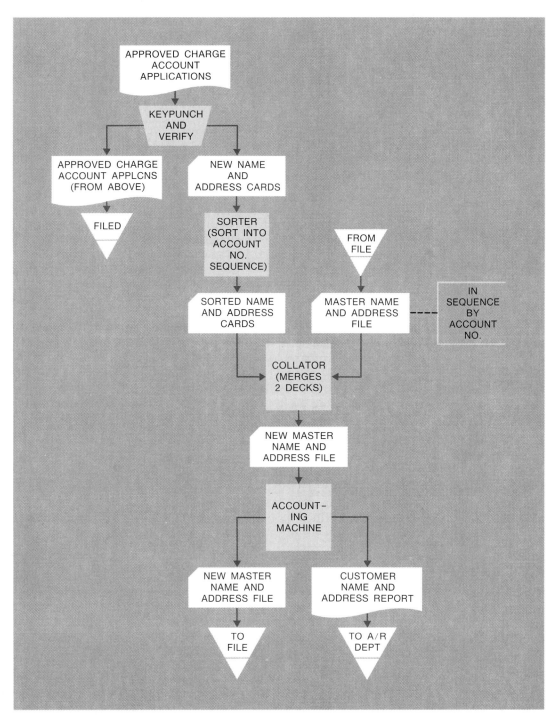

Figure 1.13
Processing of approved applications for new charge accounts.

21

There are several major reasons why these Electronic Accounting Machines are becoming obsolete.

1. Electronic Accounting Machines consist of several different physical units, each one serving a different function. Thus, processing information to produce a single report requires the use of many machines, which is a time-consuming procedure. A computer, although more costly, can do the work of several EAM machines. For example, suppose that in a department store information pertaining to balances due by customers is coded on punched cards. There is one card for each customer with information such as his account number, name, and balance due coded on it. Suppose the cards are currently in sequence by account number, and we wish to add cards for new accounts and then produce a report in alphabetical order by customer name showing the balances due. We might perform the following: We would first put both sets of cards into a *collator* to merge or combine both sets into one deck of cards. We would then put the cards through a *sorter* to arrange them in alphabetical order. We would then take the cards and put them into an *accounting machine* (or tabulator) in order to produce the report. We would then probably put the cards into the sorter again to return them to the original sequence by account number. We will see later that a computer, when programmed accordingly, can perform most of the above operations by itself.

2. Electronic Accounting Machines (or punched-card machines) are limited to processing of information on punched cards. We will see later that processing of punched cards is not only slow but results in other problems such as warped or damaged cards. A computer can handle information on many types of media—not just punched cards. We have already seen illustrations of display devices, audio devices, and so on that serve specified needs far better than punched cards.

3. Most of the Electronic Accounting Machines perform specific tasks through the use of specially wired panels. Every time we want to process information on a particular machine in a slightly different manner from the way it was previously processed, we must first remove the panel with the circuits presently wired on it. We replace it with a panel that has the appropriate circuits to accomplish the new task desired. These panels, which look like pegboards, thus require special knowledge of how the circuits are completed to perform specific functions. It is not unusual to find that some companies which use Electronic Accounting Machines have hundreds of these panels prewired and ready for use. Even in these cases, it is still necessary for people to know how to wire the machines, in case their information processing requires even a slight change.

The above discussion has served as a brief introduction to EAM equipment. Note that such devices fall into the category of historical data processing equipment, since they are rarely used as major contributors to a data processing center. Although some smaller companies still use such devices as their chief data processing tools, EAM equipment is most often employed as a supplement to a computer to assist with card processing.

G. MODERN COMPUTERS

The 1940s saw the development of machines that were faster and had greater capability than Electronic Accounting Machines. In 1944, the Mark I was completed. It consisted of 78 devices linked by 500 miles of wiring. With 3304 electromechanical relays, it was controlled by a sequence of instructions punched into a roll of paper tape. Once a problem was started, no further human intervention was required until the next problem was to be solved. That was a major improvement over accounting machines that required frequent operator intervention and supervision.

In 1946, the ENIAC was developed. Instead of electromechanical parts, vacuum tubes were incorporated that could process information thousands of times faster than previously possible.

During the 1940s, John Von Neumann developed the idea that instructions which constitute a *program,* as well as data, could be stored inside the computer. This idea, known as the *stored program concept,* laid the foundation for present day computers. The program instructs the computer as to how to read in data, process it, and produce desired results. The first computer installed in business that utilized the stored program concept was the UNIVAC in 1954.

The last 25 years have seen such rapid development of computers that we speak of different generation computers, as follows:

Generation	Basic Characteristics
First	Used vacuum tubes in its circuits.
Second	Replaced vacuum tubes with transistors.
Third	Replaced transistors with microelectronic circuits.
Fourth	Improved upon solid logic technology of third generation.[1]

[1] *Since fourth-generation computers are still in the developmental stages, this text will concentrate on third-generation computers because they are the ones most prevalent in business today.*

Essentially, the progression from vacuum tubes to transistors to microelectronic circuits resulted in faster and more reliable computers. It is interesting to note that computers are operated in an air conditioned environment due to the heat given off by its electrical components.

III. Introduction to Computer Concepts

At this point, it would be helpful to introduce some of the basic concepts of computers in order to enhance the business and data processing students' understanding of how a computer system operates. In addition, we shall attempt to eliminate the mysticism that most people associate with computers.

The following diagram indicates the essential aspects of any business computer operation.

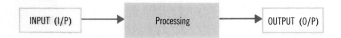

That is, we put information or *input* into the computer to be processed so that we can produce the desired results or *output*. Since the primary function of the computer is to process information, the main unit of the computer system is known as the Central Processing Unit (CPU).

There are many ways that information can be transmitted to the CPU as input to be processed. Data may be on punched cards, or it may be stored on a reel of magnetic tape similar to that used in tape recorders. Information may also be on magnetic disks that resemble long-playing records. We may also feed input into a computer via a typewriter-like terminal device. Each form of input requires a specific device that is linked by cables to the CPU.

The primary purpose of the Central Processing Unit is to process data. Since much processing involves arithmetic computation, it is interesting to note that the computer basically performs all arithmetic operations by addition. In other words, the computer is, in a sense, like a giant adding machine. It can be shown that multiplication is really a process of addition. For example $2 \times 5 = 2 + 2 + 2 + 2 + 2$. Likewise, it can be shown that computers perform subtraction by a process of addition known as complementation. Finally, division is really a process of subtraction, which in turn can be performed by addition.

In order to process information, the computer must be told exactly what to do in a series of instructions known as a *program*. This program will be inside the computer to direct its actions at the time the information is to be processed. Hence, we say a computer requires a stored program. A modified sketch of a computer system now looks as follows:

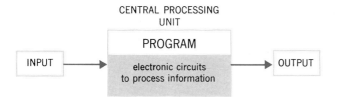

CENTRAL PROCESSING
UNIT

PROGRAM

INPUT → electronic circuits
to process information → OUTPUT

Included in the program will be instructions indicating what should be done with the results after processing; that is, what form the required results or output should take. For example, we may instruct the computer to print out certain reports. Or we may require that it punch out cards to be sent to customers, as is done by many utility companies. We may also instruct the computer to extract an audio response from a master file of responses and project it over a speaker or telephone, as was indicated previously in the example of audio-response units in banks. In addition, the output may be stored on such media as magnetic tape and magnetic disks for future processing. For example, it is common to store payroll information such as number of dependents, gross earnings to date, federal taxes withheld to date, state taxes withheld to date, and so on for each employee on magnetic tape or disk. This information, which was originally created as output, eventually serves as input when the payroll is processed the next time, and these figures are then updated to reflect any changes in earnings, deductions, and so on. Here, again, each form of output requires a specific device that is linked to the CPU by a cable. Figure 1.14 illustrates a sample computer center with

Figure 1.14
Typical computer system. Courtesy Burroughs Corp.

typical equipment. This discussion on computer concepts was meant to serve as a cursory exposure in order to facilitate your understanding of what a computer is and perhaps to dispel any misconceptions you may have. The remaining chapters will introduce business students to data processing functions in hopes that the students can more effectively communicate with the computer specialists. We shall also introduce data processing students to the use of computers in business areas. We wish to expose the business student to the area of data processing so that he can work with the computer specialist to effectively automate procedures. Too often the businessman understands nothing about the computer and what is required to effectively instruct it. Similarly, the computer specialist knows too little of what a businessman requires for his specific operation. As a result, computerized procedures can become ineffectual and can often produce erroneous results. Hence, the employee receives checks for the wrong amount or the customer receives an incorrect bill. Ultimately, then, the fault lies with both the businessman and the computer specialist. Both performed their jobs poorly, since somewhere a misunderstanding or misconception between them occurred and it was not discovered until operations were computerized. It is the aim of this book to bridge this communications gap.

SELF-EVALUATING QUIZ

At the end of each chapter in this text, there will be a series of review questions that test the student's understanding of the information therein presented. Solutions will be provided.

The purpose of this quiz is to provide the student with a method of evaluating his understanding of the chapter, hence the term, as above, SELF-EVALUATING QUIZ. These tests should be a critical part of the student's study. It provides him with a method of determining those areas within the chapter that need review.

There will be more review questions in the workbook and more thought-provoking analytical problems, for which no solutions are provided. These will enable the student to integrate all material learned and will provide a basis for classroom discussion.

1. Computers are required in commercial organizations to perform _____ .
2. When a computer produces erroneous results, it is most often because of _____ .
3. (T or F) A computer is capable of far more complex "thinking" or computing than man.
4. (T or F) Computers are most often rented by companies that want to fire personnel.
5. (T or F) Computers can handle more data at a less expensive rate than can be handled by manual methods.

6. The two major groups that benefit from the use of a commercial computer are _____ and _____ .
7. _____ is used by companies, often too small to rent computers, who buy computer time from rental companies.
8. (T or F) Companies that have computer centers use their computers approximately 98% of the available time.
9. EAM is an abbreviation for _____ .
10. Name and describe the functions of 4 EAM devices.
11. Except for the sorter, EAM devices must be _____ .
12. State two major disadvantages of EAM equipment.
13. Incoming information is called _____ .
14. Outgoing information is called _____ .
15. The main unit of a computer system is called the _____ .
16. The series of instructions to the computer is called the _____ .

SOLUTIONS

1. arithmetic and other clerical functions
2. the communications gap between data processing personnel and businessmen
3. F—a machine can only do what it is instructed or "programmed" to do.
4. F—computer centers usually result in an *increase* in company personnel.
5. T—its chief asset.
6. the manager for decision-making, the customer for quick service
7. Time-sharing
8. F—it should be 98% of the time but it is much lower than that.
9. Electronic Accounting Machines
10. SORTER—sorts cards
    INTERPRETER—prints punched data onto the face of the card
    REPRODUCER—duplicates card data
    COLLATOR—collates, merges, sequence checks cards
    ACCOUNTING MACHINE—prints reports
11. wired
12. They need to be wired.
    They can operate on cards only.
    Most processing requires extensive use of many of these machines which can be performed more easily and efficiently by a single computer system.
13. input
14. output
15. Central Processing Unit (CPU)
16. program

Chapter 2 *Business Organizations and the Role of the Data Processing Department*

Electronic Data Processing, often abbreviated EDP or called just data processing, is defined as the use of automated procedures to enter information, to operate upon it, and to produce desired results. Traditionally, electronic data processing has included the processing of data by EAM (Electronic Accounting Machines) equipment *and* computers. Keep in mind, however, that the use of EAM equipment has become stagnant and recent advances in EDP techniques have been almost exclusively in the computer area. Thus, although many texts and periodicals utilize the phrase electronic data processing, they often mean computer processing.

I. Business Organization

The development and utilization of EDP has followed two distinct courses: business and science. Most modern computers are capable of performing *either* business or scientific functions. The procedures, processing, and total EDP approach, however, is critically different, depending on whether business or scientific applications are to be computerized. Only recently has there been an attempt to manufacture computers that are capable of performing both functions.

As we have indicated, the purpose of this text is to explore the significance, advantage, and general usage of computers in the *business* area. To do this, however, the reader must be aware of the structural organization and the flow of information in typical businesses. It is no simple task to present an overview of business organization in a computer text. First, the diversity of businesses makes a general approach to business structure, at best, difficult. Businesses may fall into one of three broad categories, as shown in Figure 2.1.

Each will have a different structure. We will, however, generalize our approach so that the organizations illustrated could basically apply to any of the three.

Second, business organization is a variable item and is not consistent, even for typical business fields. That is, typical production firms, for example, could have substantially different structures.

The purpose of this section is to familiarize the reader with the *fundamental* business structure that will be illustrated throughout the text. Each computer or business student must be cognizant of departmental organization. Each company's structure may differ, however, and must therefore be evaluated independently. Similarly, we will outline the functions of major departments within typical businesses so that we can observe, generally, the intricacies of information flow.

We shall see, later, that all business functions can be described with regard to their flow of information. That is, each function operates on information and alters it in some way. The relationship between the Data Processing Department and the various Business Departments lies in this information flow. The role of data processing in any business is to *optimize information flow*.

Businessmen, as well as data processing personnel, must understand both the organizational structure and the flow of information within their specific company. It is imperative that both groups realize that a department, whether it be the Accounting Department or the Marketing Department, does not function independently. Each facet of a company must be considered in relation to the business as a whole. The businessman who is a Manager of the Sales Department must understand the relation of his Department to the Inventory and Accounts Receivable Departments, for example. He must be aware that decisions which he makes for his department could affect other departments. Similarly, the EDP staff cannot attempt to

EXAMPLES	PRODUCTION	DISTRIBUTION	SERVICE
	MANUFACTURING CONSTRUCTION	RETAILING	BANKING HOTELS

Figure 2.1

automate procedures for a given department without being cognizant of how such changes will affect other departments. For example, a narrow-minded computer specialist may redesign an input document without realizing that the original is utilized by another department that will not approve the alterations.

A. A REVIEW OF TYPICAL DEPARTMENT FUNCTIONS WITHIN BUSINESSES

In an effort to provide a general frame of reference for the reader, we will discuss the *fundamental* objectives of typical departments within a company. In this way, the reader will obtain a general understanding of the functions of each department. He can then relate the data processing functions subsequently discussed to each department's needs. In this way, data processing techniques, illustrated throughout the text, which apply to specific departments, will be meaningful.

There are six departments that are usually part of most organizations, as shown in Figure 2.2. Sometimes the Accounting function is handled by *two* departments: ACCOUNTS PAYABLE, which processes monies owed by the company for products, equipment, and supplies; and, ACCOUNTS RECEIVABLE, which processes monies owed to the company by customers. Similarly, MARKETING AND SALES may be handled by two distinct departments. Note that the PRODUCTION DEPARTMENT is applicable only to those manufacturing companies that produce a product.

Keep in mind that there is no attempt to be complete and thorough in our discussion of business organizations. There are entire texts that devote themselves to an explanation of most business structures. We have only attempted to illustrate the basic organization that is applicable to most firms.

Chapter 2 of the workbook discusses each of these departments in depth in an effort to present all pertinent facets of a hypothetical company. That discussion of the departments will serve as a review for students who possess minimum knowledge of business organization.

We shall see that for each of these departments the computer may be used for two broad categories of operations.

1. TO AUTOMATE PROCEDURES IN INDIVIDUAL DEPARTMENTS IN ORDER TO ACHIEVE INCREASED EFFICIENCY AND PRODUCTIVITY
For example:
a. Prepare payroll checks from time cards.
b. Prepare accounting ledgers from ticket transactions.
c. To maintain records on stock for inventory.
2. TO ASSIST MANAGEMENT IN ITS DECISION-MAKING ROLE.
A computer may be used to prepare forecasts or projection statistics, for example, that will assist management in its decision-making functions. Often these operations are not currently performed, even manually, but with the use of a computer, they could prove extremely beneficial to management. For example:

PRODUCTION (Where Applicable)
Produces Items to be Sold

INVENTORY	SHIPPING & RECEIVING
Controls Stock in Warehouse and on Sales Floor	Receives Goods from Vendors, Inspects Them, Ships to Customers; Receives Returned Merchandize

PAYROLL	PERSONNEL
Maintains Employee Pay Records and Produces Payroll Checks	Hires Personnel Needed to Maintain Company Operations; Maintains Employee Records for Statistical Personnel Reports

ACCOUNTING	MARKETING & SALES
Maintains and Processes Records on Company Transactions—Money Owed by Company and Money Owed to Company; Processes Financial Dealings with Customers and Vendors	Determines Best Combination of Products to Merchandise in Order to Maximize Profits, and Advertises Accordingly; Maintains Sales Force; Performs Sales Forecast

Figure 2.2
A review of business departments and their functions.

    a. Economic Order Quantities may be computed so that management can determine what items to buy and in what quantity.

    b. Sales Forecasts may be prepared so that management can be made aware of expected profits in the near future.

    c. Personnel turnover studies may be performed so that management can determine how many new employees to hire.

This second category of assisting management in its decision-making role can result in the creation of a Management Information System. This is the sophisticated, high-level computerization of *all* pertinent facets within a company's organization to assist top level management in making key decisions about the company as a whole. An MIS (Management Information System) system can utilize a computer in determining, for example, at any moment the company's profit or loss position for a given period. Similarly, an MIS System can be used to predict growth factors, project production growths, and so on.

Remember that MIS requires a highly sophisticated process of computerization. Before we can meaningfully discuss this use of automated equipment, we must first discuss how *each* department within a company can effectively utilize computers. The major portion of this text will illustrate this latter use of computers. The purpose of this discussion on MIS, however, is to indicate that computers can also be employed on a much higher plane. (MIS is discussed later in the text). The business and data processing students who perceive accurately the overall potential of computers in industry have a real future in most companies.

In short, a computer is most often used to automate functions within specific departments or to assist management in its decision-making role by compiling data from all departments. Thus we see that although each department may function as an entity, it is part of the total organization and is, therefore, not independent.

B. THE FLOW OF INFORMATION WITHIN A TYPICAL COMPANY

Thus far, we have been exposed to the fundamental operations of each department. Let us see how all departments are integrated into the total company.

To achieve a proper understanding of how EDP techniques are used in various companies, we must consider how the functions of one department may affect the operations of another department. The term *INFORMATION FLOW* is used to indicate that data, or information, flows through a company and can have resounding effects on more than one organizational element or department.

EXAMPLE 1

A customer wishes to purchase an item and phones in a request. The following departments are affected by the flow of this information:

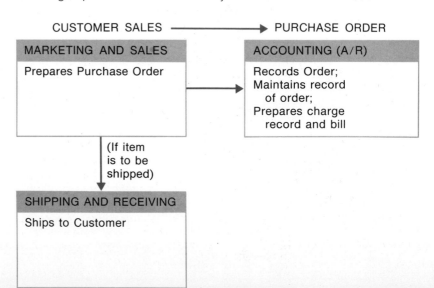

34

EXAMPLE 2

A new employee is hired for the production department. The following departments are affected by the flow of this information:

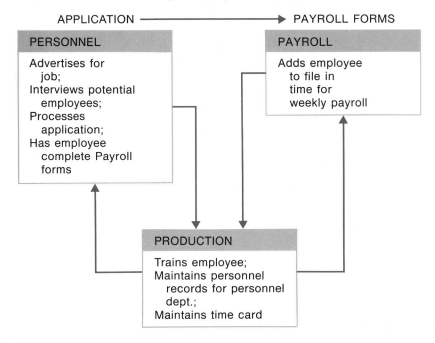

APPLICATION ⟶ PAYROLL FORMS

PERSONNEL
Advertises for job;
Interviews potential employees;
Processes application;
Has employee complete Payroll forms

PAYROLL
Adds employee to file in time for weekly payroll

PRODUCTION
Trains employee;
Maintains personnel records for personnel dept.;
Maintains time card

Thus we have seen that departments do not function independently. Activities that are performed by one are often of major concern to another. Although each department must fulfill its specific objective, as stated in Figure 2.2, the overall objective of every company, as a whole, is to increase profits while minimizing costs. It is the responsibility of each department to work toward this ultimate end. That is, although a specific procedure employed by the inventory department to meet its objectives may result in increased efficiency, if it is excessively costly or is not responsive to the needs of the other departments, it will not result in increased profits or minimized costs. Thus it is an unsound procedure and must be eliminated. Similarly, an EDP Department which, in the narrow view, usually results in increased cost expenditures for the company, must, in the broader or long-range view, result in increased profits, or it should be eliminated from the organization.

C. ORGANIZATIONAL STRUCTURE IN TYPICAL BUSINESS

The organization of a business indicates how each element, or department, relates to the company as a whole. The last section

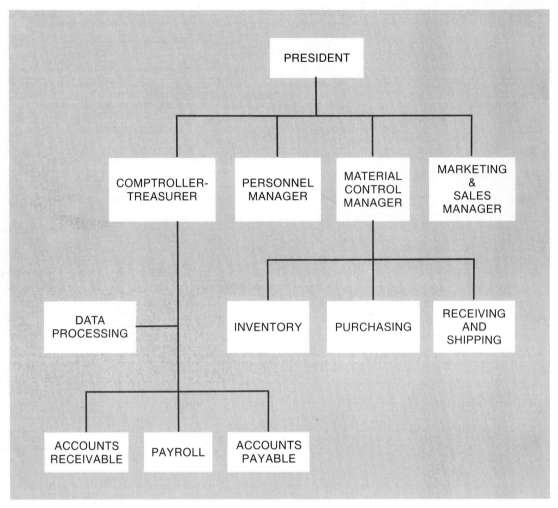

Figure 2.3
Organization chart for retail firm.

depicted the fundamental operations of each department. We must now discuss the integration of departments to determine how the proper flow of information between them is achieved.

An *organization chart,* which is a pictorial representation of the hierarchy of company departments, is a critical document that is most often used to evaluate structural organization.

Figure 2.3 illustrates a sample organization chart for a retail firm. Figure 2.4 illustrates a sample organization chart for a manufacturing firm.

Fundamental Concepts of Data Processing

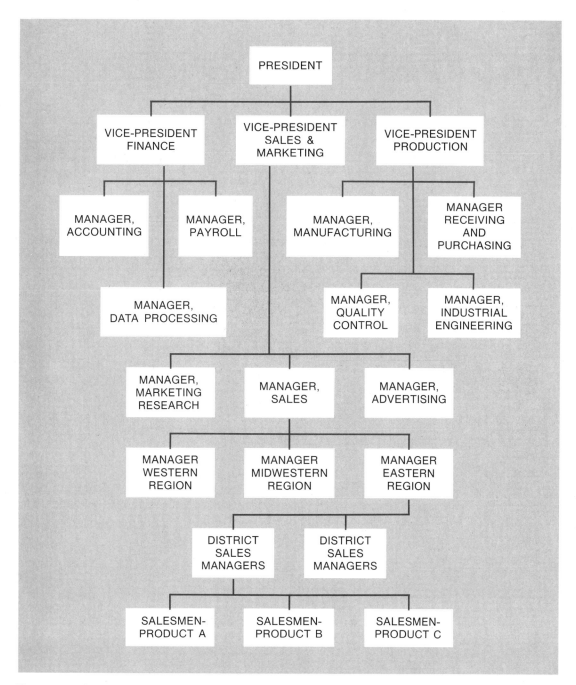

Figure 2.4
Organization chart for manufacturing firm.

Note that from an organization chart we can determine the relation of each department to the company as a whole. Also note that the executive level management personnel, the president and vice presidents, are ultimately responsible for making major policy decisions on the company as a whole. Although management generally has top-level personnel managing each individual department, it is the task of the top executives to integrate departments so that a meaningful, productive, and profitable organization is evolved.

Keep in mind that a data processing center is often employed to achieve this end. While extremely useful in automating manual procedures, a computer, if used properly, can be of invaluable aid in the overall decision-making function that is based on the integration of departmental objectives.

A company's departmental structure generally focuses on two separate functions: line and staff. *Line functions* are those that are directly responsible for achieving the company's goals. That is, these functions *directly* result in producing company profits. *Staff functions* are primarily those that offer advice or service in an effort to *indirectly* enhance company profits.

In a typical business, sales is a line function since its direct and primary goal is the sale of goods that results in increased profits. Production is also a line function, since it directly influences company profits. The resulting figures, sales records, and productivity levels are used directly in producing profit statements.

Typical staff departments within a company include personnel and accounting. The Personnel Department is responsible for hiring employees. There is no concrete measure for productivity. How well the staff of this department performs its function cannot be measured directly against company profits. That is, Personnel is a service department that can *indirectly* enhance profits.

Similarly, the Accounting Department maintains financial records. If the employees perform their record-keeping poorly, the company will certainly lose customers. But we can only measure the department's effectiveness or productivity indirectly.

We shall see that the Data Processing Department is also strictly a *staff* function. The Data Processing Department is maintained generally as a service to other departments. Let us now consider the relationship of the Data Processing Department to other departments within a typical company.

In many companies, the Data Processing Center is *strictly* a service department. That is, it is a *separate* entity that serves other departments. In this way, its primary function is to computerize company operations and, by so doing, make them more efficient. The staff within a Data Processing Center is called upon by managers to analyze operations for each department. The DP staff must then become familiar with each department's operations and how they relate to the company as a whole.

In other companies, the Data Processing installation is a subdivision of the department that utilizes computer facilities the most. In this way, computer specialists become well-versed in the procedures of that one department and, thus, they require less time to analyze each job for that department. When the Data Processing installation reports to a specified department, other departments that require computerized functions must wait until the needs of this "priority" department are met.

Still other companies have the Data Processing Center report directly to the company Controller, who supervises all accounting operations. With the onset of electronic data processing, when the potential of computers was being tested, it was logical to assume that these electronic "brains" would be utilized mostly, if not solely, by the Accounting Department. Thus, the newly organized Data Processing unit initially became a subdivision of the Accounting Department. Even though many other departments currently utilize the computer center as a service organization, such companies simply have not found it necessary to reorganize their Data Processing installations.

Remember that some companies are too small to absorb the cost of a Data Processing Center. They simply cannot afford to rent adequate equipment and maintain a full-time data processing staff. Yet such companies often have operations and procedures that could be efficiently computerized. Still other companies need a computer for five or ten hours a week and cannot, therefore, justify rental of such equipment, since most manufacturers require rentals on the basis of a minimum of 40 hours per week.

Time-sharing is a concept that will allow such firms to utilize computer equipment. A time-sharing organization buys or rents full-scale computer equipment, employs a staff to operate the equipment, and then rents or leases computer time on an hourly basis to other companies. Time-sharing is then a method by which small firms can utilize another company's computer and pay essentially for the time used. In this way, any business can employ such equipment on a part-time basis.

Time-sharing eliminates excessive rental costs for those companies that cannot justify full-time utilization of computers. For companies that cannot afford a computer staff or that cannot maintain one on a full-time basis, there are *service bureaus* or *facilities management* organizations which, for a given fee, will computerize any company's operations. If a firm wishes to computerize just a few procedures, it is usually not feasible to hire a full Data Processing staff. Instead, a service bureau can be contracted to analyze and design these new procedures.

Thus it is possible for some companies to utilize computerized operations with no Data Processing installation. They employ outside consultants to perform the necessary programming and they utilize computers and operators on a time-sharing basis.

Keep in mind, however, that both the use of time-sharing and service bureaus can be very costly if employed to excess. That is, such outside contracting is economical only if used on a limited basis.

Before deciding to employ outside firms, a company should consider its own growth factor and future potential. It may be that the expense of a computer center could be offset by increased efficiency and decreased expenditure in other areas. Similarly, if the company's growth will necessitate a data processing facility in future years, it might be more economical, in the end, to acquire one initially rather than to utilize outside assistance.

SELF-EVALUATING QUIZ

1. (T or F) Some businesses do not have Production Departments.
2. (T or F) A banking organization would have a Production Department.
3. (T or F) All business organizations have the same structure.
4. (T or F) The role of data processing in any business is to optimize information flow.
5. EDP is an abbreviation for _____ .
6. Name six typical departments within a business.
7. (T or F) The function of the Payroll Department, generally, is to hire employees.
8. (T or F) Some companies function with a single Accounting Department while others have an Accounts Receivable and an Accounts Payable Department.
9. State the two broad categories of operations that a commercial computer can perform.
10. The term _____ is used to indicate that data flows through a company and can have resounding effects on more than one organizational element or department.

SOLUTIONS

1. T
2. F
3. F
4. T
5. Electronic Data Processing
6. Production; Payroll; Personnel; Accounts Receivable, Accounts Payable; Marketing; Sales; Shipping; Receiving; Inventory

7. F
8. T
9. automate clerical operations for individual departments and assist management in its decision-making role
10. information flow

For proper analysis and successful computerization of business operations, businessmen and data processing personnel must be fully cognizant of each other's functional responsibilities and capabilities. Improper communications between these two departmental representatives is a major cause for inadequately automated procedures.

The businessman, who requires the assistance of the EDP department to computerize some functions, must specify his requirements in the utmost detail. Data processing personnel must extract from the businessman *all* relevant data so that the computer output is exactly what is required. Unfortunately, however, the transfer of all pertinent data from the businessman to data processing personnel is no simple task. Information is sometimes omitted by the businessman and/or misunderstood by the computer specialist. Errors in computer output are often the result of these omissions and misconceptions.

Most of us are familiar with the results of poor communications between these two departments, having been victims of inadequate or erroneous computerization. Some of us have witnessed computerized registration procedures that have caused gross scheduling errors. Similarly, many of us have been billed for goods not purchased, because of computer problems in an Accounts Receivable Department. More dramatically, there are those who have had to wait for outstanding checks that are long overdue, because of computer foul-ups. The computer, which is often not responsible, is usually blamed for these problems.

Be advised, however, that in the great majority of cases the errors or inadequacies are caused by poor communications between the major business representatives and the appropriate data processing personnel. In such cases, both must share the blame. The data processing personnel were not adequately familiar with the requirements of the job, and the businessmen failed to communicate their needs properly.

This chapter (indeed, this entire text) is aimed at familiarizing the business and data processing students with the requirements of data processing personnel so that business functions can be properly computerized.

With an understanding of computer concepts and basic terminology the businessman can thus actively interact with data processing personnel. Note that the businessman is not required to fully understand the intricacies of computer operations. He should, however, know enough of computer processing to effectively communicate his needs to the data processing staff. Similarly, the computer specialist is not required to be expert in business areas, although he should be cognizant of how data processing is most effectively utilized by various departments.

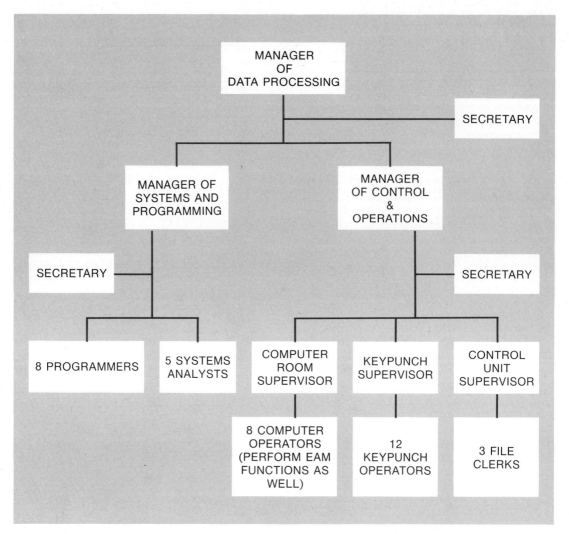

Figure 2.5
Organization chart for a data processing department.

Prior to any discussion of computer operations, it is imperative that the business and data processing students understand the organization within a Data Processing Center. In this way, they can be fully cognizant of each individual's role and how it relates to the entirety.

Consider the organization chart in Figure 2.5, which represents the relationships within a typical Data Processing Center or installation. Note that there are three distinct groups for which the data processing manager is responsible.

A. THE SYSTEMS AND PROGRAMMING STAFF

1. The Systems Staff

a. Performs a Systems Study to determine the feasibility of computerizing a specific system

A system, in the business sense, is an organized method of accomplishing a business function.

The systems analyst analyzes the elements of the present system, determines the requirements of the job, and decides if a computerized set of procedures is monetarily justifiable.

If computerized operations can save the company money, then they are considered feasible. If they are, the systems analyst then:

b. Designs a more efficient, computerized system

This design includes *all* elements, operations, and procedures to be utilized in the new system. It is the analyst, therefore, who has initial contact with the businessman. In order for the analyst to fully understand the latter's job requirements, he must be aware of *all* facets of the present system. Similarly, the businessman must be fully cognizant of the analyst's requirements and the computer's capabilities in order to provide a smooth transition from the old system to the new one.

Let us consider an illustration.

EXAMPLE 1

An Accounts Receivable manager has six full-time clerks who are employed to extend accounting tickets (multiplying a unit price of an item by the quantity sold to obtain a total). These clerks may work with calculators. It is estimated that 10,000 tickets are extended each week. Including employee and supply costs, this procedure costs the company $60,000 a year. The manager wishes to determine if a computerized system would be more economical.

The systems analyst performs a systems study. He studies the present system, in detail, so that he can make judgments on what is required and how to eliminate its problem areas. He determines that a computerized operation to do the extensions would only cost $10,000 a year. Upon receiving an approval from executive-level management, he then designs the new operations and procedures that will require a single computer run to extend the tickets each week. The clerks currently assigned to this task are either retrained to assist in the new tasks required or are reassigned to other departments.

Note that during all phases, the analyst and the business manager must work closely to insure that the new system incorporates all operations of the old. The slightest omission or misconception can cause major errors in the new system.

2. Programming Staff

Once a system has been designed, the Programming Staff is then called on to write the set of computer instructions (programs) that are required within the system. Again, the programmer must be fully cognizant of each program's requirements to insure proper conversion.

He must often communicate with both the analyst and the business manager to clarify details necessary for writing efficient programs. Frequently, he is called on prior to programming, in the design phase, to assist the analyst and the businessman.

Once the programs are written, they must be tested to make certain that no errors or "bugs" exist. Once the programs are tested and are executing properly, the businessman in conjunction with the analyst and programmer is responsible for insuring a smooth conversion to the new system.

In some installations, the programming staff reports directly to the systems staff. In this way, the analysts can assign programs to their subordinates, according to the strong points of each. Similarly the analyst can insure that proper priorities are placed on all assignments.

In other installations, the programming staff is a separate division. In this way, programmers are not subtly restricted in their discussions; that is, they are free to question analysts without being conscious of an employer-employee relationship.

In still other installations, the systems and programming staff includes programmer-analysts who perform *both* systems and programming functions. This further reduces the communications problem, since a single programmer-analyst can perform all aspects of the job.

B. OPERATIONS STAFF

When design and programming efforts have been completed, the system is ready for conversion. During this phase, the systems and programming staff turns the job over to the operations staff, which is responsible for implementing it. The operations staff consist of keypunch operators, EAM operators, and computer operators.

Keypunch operators are usually required to convert incoming or source documents to a machine-readable form such as punched cards. Electronic Accounting Machine (EAM) operators are required to prepare card inputs for computer processing. That is, they do such things as sort, merge, and reproduce cards when necessary. Computer operators must then feed input into the computer and transmit the output produced, according to specifications supplied by the systems and programming staff.

Ordinarily, the programming and systems staff gives directions to the computer operators. Operators are given schedules indicating when they can expect inputs and when outputs must be completed. They are also provided with a set of procedures that they must follow. Note that the analyst is usually responsible for preparing the above schedules and instructions for operations.

Consider Example 1 again. The keypunch operators may be given the following schedule for Accounts Receivable Tickets:

Fundamental Concepts of Data Processing

KEYPUNCHING SCHEDULE

1. Receive tickets (approximately 2000) by 10:00 A.M. each day.
2. Keypunch tickets onto cards as indicated on instruction sheet.
3. Transmit tickets and cards called A/R cards (with count of cards produced) to Control Unit by 3:00 P.M. each day.

The computer operators may be given the following schedule.

COMPUTER SCHEDULE

1. Receive weekly A/R cards by 4:00 P.M. each Friday.
2. Use Program No. 608 to extend amounts on cards and create a printout with the extended figures.
3. Transmit output along with A/R cards to Control Unit.

For the initial run, the steps are followed systematically under the supervision of the systems and programming staff. If proper output is achieved, then "cut-over" begins, which means that the operations staff takes charge and proceeds with the job on a weekly basis.

C. CONTROL UNIT STAFF

Once implementation is complete, the Control Unit insures that all steps are followed systematically. This group is responsible for maintaining control of data as it proceeds through the data processing installation. Similarly, the staff maintains various totals to insure that data is not lost.

In Example 1, the Control Unit must:

CONTROL UNIT SCHEDULE

1. Insure that tickets are received daily by 9:30 from the A/R department; if not, those in charge must be contacted.
2. Count tickets.
3. Transmit tickets to keypunching.
4. Insure that tickets and A/R cards are received daily by 3:30 from keypunching.
5. Count A/R cards to insure that they equal the total number of tickets—if not the error must be found.
6. Transmit total A/R cards each Friday to Computer Center at 3:30.
7. Insure that cards and printout are received by 5:00 P.M. on Friday.
8. Count print lines to insure total agrees with the number of cards—if not, the error must be found.
9. Transmit printouts to A/R Dept by 9:00 A.M. on the following Monday morning.

You will note that the businessman maintains contact primarily with the systems analyst and the programmer. These are the two professional positions, requiring extensive training and expertise. Because of its complexity, the analyst's job generally requires even more background than that of the programmer. The businessman is rarely in contact with the operations staff, which receives its instructions from the systems and programming unit.

Business and data processing students should be aware of the general background required of analysts and programmers. An individual can become a Programmer Trainee generally in one of four ways:

1. Graduate from a four-year college.

    This position generally requires little prior programming knowledge and consists of a six-month to one-year extensive training program. A college graduate with no background in computers may be required to attend company computer courses and/or read computer reference manuals or programmed instruction texts to obtain a general understanding. He then works with an experienced programmer and writes and debugs programs under the latter's supervision. The more experience one has, however, the greater the responsibility and salary one can expect. Companies are eager to hire college graduates for these positions since they hope to promote programmers into higher positions within the company. Most companies require that their executives have at least a four-year college degree.

2. Graduate from a two-year or junior college with a major in data processing or computer science.

    Although these individuals do not have a four-year degree, their expertise in the data processing field is a distinct asset. Many junior colleges have extensive data processing courses that prepare the student for advanced work in systems analysis and programming.

3. Graduate from a certified data processing institute.

    This offers the individual, for a fixed fee, a concentrated course in data processing. This course does not, however, receive college credit.

4. Possess experience in the operations phase of data processing.

    Often when jobs are scarce, individuals accept jobs in the computer operations fields in hopes that they will be "promoted" to the programming staff. Note that this would not constitute an actual promotion, since these two groups are on separate organizational planes.

Positions in systems analysis, because of their complexity, require more training. They often require classroom training in combination with several years in business and programming, or a related data processing position. In most companies, a programmer with adequate experience can eventually be promoted to a systems analyst position. Because of the high degree of business experience required, few companies hire analysts who have not had several years in data processing or in business.

It should be noted that many programmers and analysts have taken such courses in college as introductory accounting and marketing to facilitate their understanding of business needs. However, a businessman must still recognize the fact that he will have to supply the minutest details to data processing personnel.

The businessman should never assume that data processing personnel comprehend all of the inner workings of a particular system. To dramatize this point to the business student, we will discuss below one of many actual case histories that highlight how problems sometimes arise in computerized systems.

Recently, the president of a large corporation called the data processing department in his company to inform them that his paycheck had an error in it. It seems that although the check was issued at the end of June, such figures as the year-to-date gross earnings figure on the check stub were printed in error, as zero. An investigation of the problem quickly revealed an error in the recently computerized payroll system. The president is the only company executive who earns $200,000 a year. At the end of June, his year-to-date earnings, for example, are $100,000. However, when the computer was instructed in the payroll program to print out such figures, room was only left for printing out up to five whole number digits and two decimal places. Hence, in effect $100,000.00 became zero, since the "1" was "lost." Who was responsible for such a catastrophe? Several people.

1. The systems analyst, who never investigated or considered such a "minute" detail as the largest salary earned within the company.
2. The programmer, who never questioned the analyst and/or businessman on this detail.
3. The businessman, who did not properly work with the data processing staff to check out the new payroll system before it was fully implemented.

This text will concern itself with the relationship between the businessman and the programmer, and the businessman and the analyst. We will consider the programmer's role initially since his is a more concrete and specific job. Once the programmer's role is understood, we will then consider the systems analyst's primary responsibilities, which are less specific, but more all-encompassing.

SELF-EVALUATING QUIZ

1. More data processing jobs are deemed inadequate because of poor _____ than for any other reason.
2. Communications between _____ and _____ must be adequate to insure proper computerization.
3. (T or F) The responsibility of failures in computerization of jobs generally rests with the businessman and the data processing staff rather than with the computer.
4. Name the three basic elements within a Data Processing Center.
5. Who is in charge of a Data Processing Center?
6. Name two major functions of the programming staff.
7. Name two major functions of the systems staff.
8. How are the systems and programming staff related?
9. Name the types of operators within the operations staff.
10. Who is usually responsible for writing the procedures to be followed by the operations staff?
11. State what is meant by a conversion procedure.
12. What is the purpose of the control group?
13. Who is responsible for writing the set of procedures to be followed by the control staff?

SOLUTIONS

1. communications
2. businessmen; data processing personnel
3. T
4. operations staff; systems and programming staff; control staff
5. Data Processing Manager
6. Write programs and debug programs.
7. Study present system to determine problem areas; design new, more efficient systems.
8. They are under the supervision of a single manager—they may be separate entities, or a systems analyst may supervise several programmers, or the entire unit may consist of programmer-analysts who handle both tasks.
9. keypunch operators; EAM operators; computer operators
10. Programming and systems personnel
11. A conversion procedure is the process of transferring from the old system to a new one.
12. The purpose of the control unit is to maintain control over the data entered into a data processing department and the output data that is sent to the requesting departments.
13. The systems staff, in conjunction with the businessman.

Chapter 3 *The Punched Card and the Printed Report*

I. Characteristics of the Punched Card

This chapter will familiarize business and data processing students with the most common form of computer input, the punched card, and the most common form of computer output, the printed report. With some knowledge of the fundamental nature of these media, business and data processing students can begin to understand how data processing functions are performed.

It is assumed that these students have had some exposure to both the punched card and the printed report in their daily routines. This chapter, however, will discuss the technical nature of these media, in a data processing sense.

The punched card is the most basic form of computer input. It is still the most widely used form in small computer organizations.

A. THE PUNCHED CARD AS A DATA RECORD

A brief history of the punched card in Chapter 1 served to illustrate its uses and advantages. Data is recorded on this card in the form of punched holes used to represent a code. Vast amounts of records are converted to these cards. Historically, machines were constructed to mechanically sense the holes, and then sort, merge, or otherwise

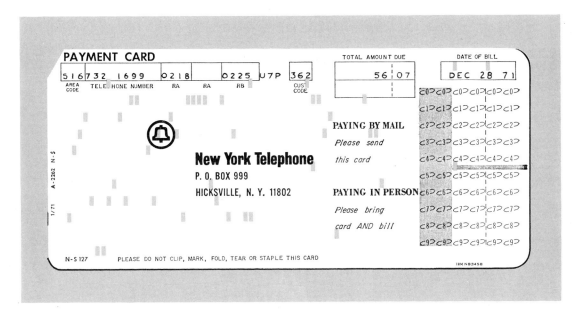

Figure 3.1
Sample utility punched card.

compile the data. In this way, the manual method of amassing data gave way to a mechanical, more reliable, and more economical method. Today both electronic accounting machines *and* computers make widespread use of the punched card.

Most businesses today utilize the punched card in some phase of their operations. Consumers often see these cards in bills and orders that they receive. Utility companies, for example, supplying gas, electric, and telephone services, often bill customers with the use of punched cards, as shown in Figure 3.1. Some companies also prepare stock dividend checks on punched cards.

This chapter will discuss the method used to record data onto a punched card.

Consider the time card illustrated in Figure 3.2. You will note that the card represents a *record,* or a unit of information. All such time card records constitute a *file* of information, which is the collective group of related records. The record consists of *characters,* which make up information referred to as *data.* The illustrated record serves to indicate an employee's name, hours worked at his job for a specific week, and additional payroll data. A *character* of information consists of a letter, a digit, or a symbol such as $, +, −, *. Thus data is the combination of characters consisting of letters, digits, and symbols that result in meaningful information. The punched card represents characters of information with the use of punched holes.

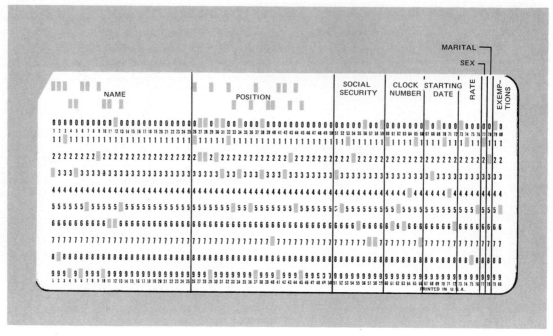

Figure 3.2
Time card.

B. HOLLERITH CODE

Consider the blank card in Figure 3.3. Notice at the very bottom of the card there are small digits that are numbered 1 to 80. Note also that below the first horizontal group of numbers (zeros) there are the same 80 numbers. Each of these numbers refers to a *column,* or vertical section of the card. Thus there are *80* card columns. *Columns 34 to 56* on the illustrated card are shaded.

The code used for representing data on an 80-column card is referred to as the *Hollerith Code,* named for the man who developed it, Herman Hollerith.

Each column is used to represent one character of data. Thus each column can contain one letter, digit, or special character. A card, then, can store or hold 80[1] characters. Notice that columns 1 to 25 in Figure 3.2 are referred to as NAME. NAME, then, will consist of 25 characters.

There are 10 horizontal sections of a card, numbered 0 to 9, which

[1] *Most cards contain 80 columns. There are, however, 90-column and 96-column cards, for example, which are utilized on some computer systems. We will discuss these later on in the text.*

Fundamental Concepts of Data Processing

contain imprinting. Each *horizontal* section is referred to as a *row*. Thus we have the 0-row, 1-row, 2-row . . . 9-row. For numeric characters, or numbers, we punch a hole in the corresponding row of a specific column. Thus, if we wish to punch a 3 in the 51st position of a card, we would punch a hole in the 3-row of column 51, and this would represent the digit 3.

In Figure 3.2 we see a 3 punched in column 51, a 5 in column 52, a 1 in column 53, etc.

To represent alphabetic data, we must use a digit punch in conjunction with another punch. Consider the card illustrated in Figure 3.4. There are, you will note, 10 numbered rows (0 to 9) and 2 without printing, called the 11- and 12-rows. We use the 0-, 11-, and 12-row in conjunction with a digit punch, in a *single* column, to represent the letters of the alphabet. Thus, the 0-, 11-, 12-rows are referred to as the *zone* rows and the 0 to 9 as the *digit* rows. For convenience, the 0-row is considered both a zone and a digit row. When used as a digit, alone, it is a digit row; when used with another digit to form a letter, it is called a zone row. The card in Figure 3.5 illustrates the coding of alphabetic characters. Letters A to I are coded as 12-1 through 12-9 punches, respectively. Letters J to R are coded as 11-1 through 11-9 punches,

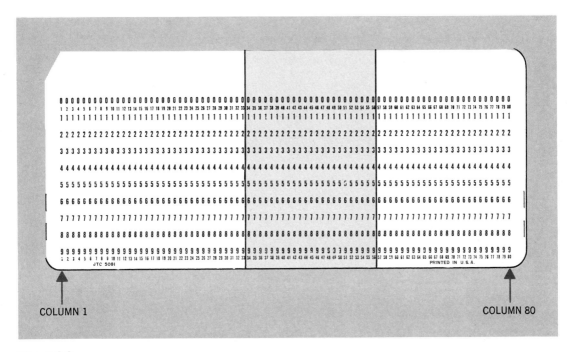

Figure 3.3
Sample punched card (columns 34 to 56 shaded).

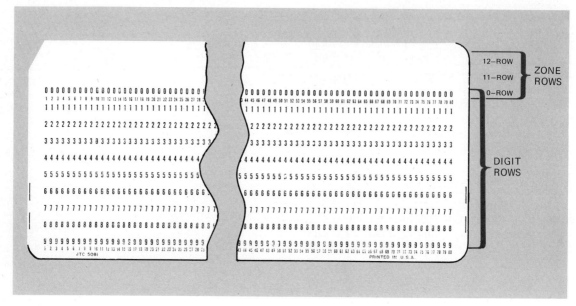

Figure 3.4
Illustration of zone and digit rows on a punched card.

respectively. Letters S to Z are coded as 0-2 through 0-9, respectively. Thus, all alphabetic characters are represented with two punches, a zone punch and a digit punch, in a single column.

Figure 3.6 illustrates significant facts about the punched card. The top of the card is called the *12-edge,* since the 12-row is located there. Similarly, the bottom of the card is called the *9-edge,* since the 9-row is at the bottom. Some punched card equipment requires cards to be entered 9-edge first; others require the cards to be entered 12-edge first.

The special characters that can be represented on a card are indicated in columns 51 to 76 of Figure 3.6. They each utilize 1, 2, or 3 punches in a single column. An asterisk, * for example, (column 60) is represented by the 11-4-8 punches. An ampersand, &, is represented by a 12-punch alone (column 50). Note that the standard special characters are accepted by almost all computers, while the extended set is recognized only by the more modern ones.

C. FIELDS OF DATA

Let us reconsider Figure 3.2, illustrating a time card. Note that consecutive card columns that represent a unit of data are called a *field.* In other words, a field is a set of adjacent positions reserved for a specific purpose only. The consecutive card columns 1 to 25 in the

Fundamental Concepts of Data Processing

figure represent the NAME field. Card columns 26 to 50 represent the POSITION field, and so on.

Each field consists of characters. The NAME field has the character C in its first column (12-zone and 3-digit punches), an H in column 2 (12-8 punches). Note that if a person's name does not fill the whole field, the remainder of the field is left blank.

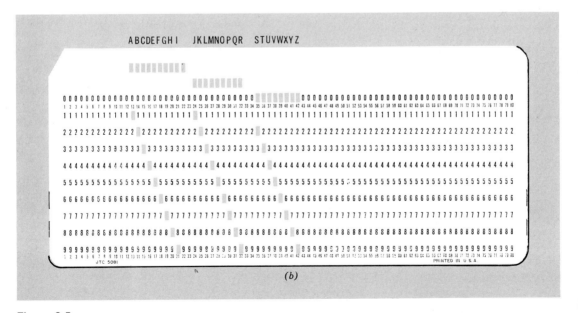

HOLLERITH CODE

		DIGIT PUNCHES								
		1	2	3	4	5	6	7	8	9
ZONE PUNCHES	12	A	B	C	D	E	F	G	H	I
	11	J	K	L	M	N	O	P	Q	R
	0	/	S	T	U	V	W	X	Y	Z

(a)

ABCDEFGHI JKLMNOPQR STUVWXYZ

(b)

Figure 3.5
(a) Codes for alphabetic letters. (b) The alphabet punched on a card.

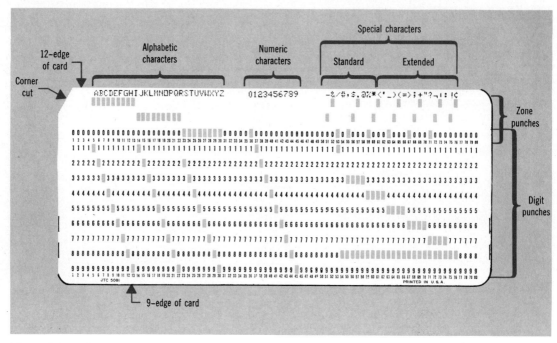

Figure 3.6
Review of punched card codes

II. *The Recording of Data on Punched Cards*

Punched card data is a form of input to the computer as well as to EAM equipment discussed earlier, such as a sorter, collator, or accounting machine. A punched card is sometimes referred to as a *Unit Record,* because a card typically represents a unit of information.

A. USE OF KEYPUNCH MACHINES

Generally, data is initially recorded on punched cards from information supplied in a printed report, called a *source document*. A device called a *keypunch machine* is used to convert written documents to punched cards. This device, not unlike a typewriter, needs an operator to press the appropriate keys representing characters so that the machine can punch corresponding holes in the card. (See Figure 3.7.) Using a keypunch machine, data is punched on the card according to the Hollerith code and, if desired, the corresponding characters are printed on the top edge.

To insure that data is correctly transcribed by the keypunch operator onto a punched card, a card verifier device is used. This

Fundamental Concepts of Data Processing

device resembles the keypunch machine. The operator uses the keypunched cards instead of blank cards. She then depresses the verifier's keys, as in normal keypunching. If she depresses a key that has not, in fact, been punched on the card, an error light goes on.

Correctly keypunched cards are typically notched on the right side, while incorrectly keypunched ones are notched *above* the column in error. Therefore all cards with right-side notches have been verified and ones with notches on top are in error. (See Figure 3.8.)

Some keypunch machines are equipped with verifying ability so that a single machine may be used first to keypunch data and then to verify the keypunching.

B. CHARACTERISTICS OF FIELDS

Data fields can be classified in three ways:

numeric-digits only
alphabetic-letters and blanks only
alphanumeric or alphameric-combination of letters, digits, and
special characters; such as an ADDRESS field

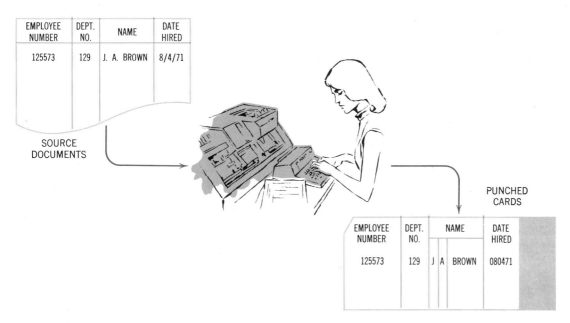

Figure 3.7
The keypunching of data.

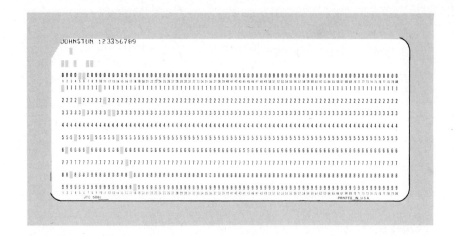

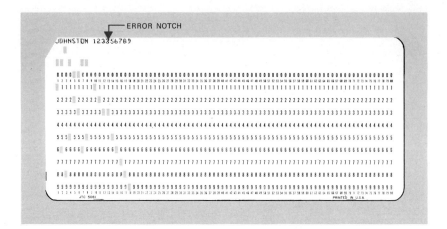

Figure 3.8
Verification of punched cards. (1) Card is keypunched. (2) Card is verified and an error is detected in column 13, causing an error notch. (3) Card is rekeypunched and successfully verified, resulting in a final "OK" notch on right side.

Figure 3.9 is another sample data card. Columns 1 to 5 represent an AMOUNT, which is a *numeric* field. Columns 6 to 25 are used for an *alphabetic* NAME field. Data is represented differently in numeric and alphabetic (or alphanumeric) fields, when fill characters are required.

Field sizes are generally established to accommodate the longest number of characters. That is, a LAST NAME field may be 25 characters in length because the longest name is that size. Since most names are shorter than this, part of the field will remain blank. Similarly, numeric fields, consisting of only numbers, are *right-justified* with leftmost positions generally *zero-filled*. That is, to represent 383 in an AMOUNT field in positions 1 to 5, 383 is put in the rightmost positions, (columns 3, 4, 5) with leftmost positions (column 1 and 2) filled with zeros. (See Figure 3.9.) Thus 00383 has been placed in the field. The right-most positions are sometimes referred to as *low-order* or units positions, and leftmost as *high-order* positions.

Alphabetic or alphanumeric data is placed in the *leftmost* or *high-order* positions with low-order positions filled with blanks or spaces. Consider the LAST NAME field in columns 6 to 25 in Figure 3.9. The field size is 20 characters. The data is SMITH consisting only of five characters. The data is placed in the high-order positions with low-order positions left blank.

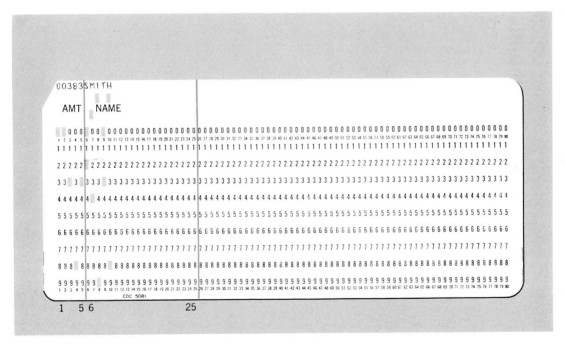

Figure 3.9
Sample data card—I.

C. ELEMENTS OF CARD DESIGN

As we have seen, the punched card is generally coded from information supplied on a source document. This source document is usually an established report that has been used successfully in a business area. When a procedure is automated, the source document is usually converted to a machine-readable form, such as a punched card. Time Sheets, Purchase Orders, Sales Slips, Credit Return Slips, Applications for Credit Cards, and Stock Transfer Sheets are examples of source documents that are generally converted to a punched card or to some other form of input for computer processing.

We have thus far seen that there are typically 80 positions on a card. This limits the size of most card records to 80 characters.

When designing card records, every effort must be made by the systems analyst, who is normally responsible for card design, to limit record size to 80 positions. If more characters per record are required, then two or more cards per record will be necessary. This, in essence, defeats the purpose of the unit-record concept and, where possible, should be avoided.

Since 80 characters per record is often a limiting factor, several design plans, discussed below, are generally implemented to insure a concise card record. The businessman will be required to work closely with the computer specialist to determine that these design plans are appropriate for the specific system.

Where source document fields are not really useful or required, they are eliminated from the card format. The businessman together with the computer specialist must determine which fields are really unnecessary. By eliminating these fields from the card, a monetary savings may be realized. Concise card records that do not include unnecessary source document fields reduce the time required to keypunch cards and the time it takes the computer to process them.

Edit symbols such as a dollar sign, decimal point, or comma, and superfluous blanks are not entered on input cards. Consider the NAME field on the card illustrated in Figure 3.10.

The LAST NAME field appears *first* in many data cards, since it is better form to have major fields before minor ones, for identification and sorting purposes.

You will note that the initials are adjacent to the LAST NAME field, *with no spaces or periods in between*.

No blanks appear between initials on a card document, since such superfluous *blank columns* would utilize extra positions of the card. These additional positions are often not available, where card records have many fields of data. Although printed output will incorporate these blanks or periods between initials for ease of reading, card input need only be read by unit-record devices, or computers, which readily accept concise data.

Thus the elimination of blanks, as superfluous characters, helps to insure that most card records will fit the 80-character limit, making additional cards per record unnecessary.

Fundamental Concepts of Data Processing

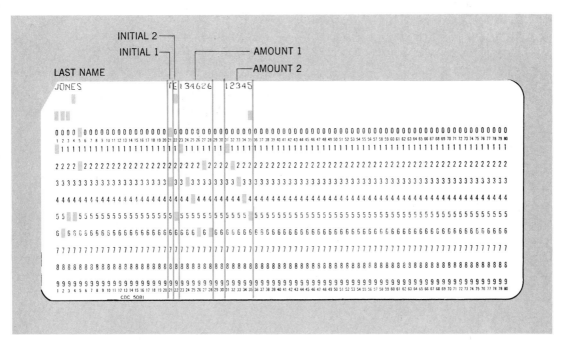

Figure 3.10
Sample data card—II.

The elimination of edit symbols, such as a dollar sign, comma, or decimal point, will result in a similar savings.

The programmer need only indicate to the computer that the amount represents four integers and two decimal positions. The above AMOUNT 1 field results in a savings of three positions, since the dollar sign, comma, and decimal point are eliminated.

Thus an amount of $1,346.26 would be represented on a card as shown above. In addition, the computer cannot usually perform arithmetic operations if fields have special characters such as a dollar sign or comma included in the field.

Consider the DATE field (columns 52 to 57) on the card in Figure 3.11.

This represents a date of 01/20/73, with the slashes omitted to save space. This is another conventional method for eliminating edit symbols.

Operational signs are often noted in the units or low-order position of a field. That is, they do not occupy a separate position. If a negative numeric field is to be printed it would generally print as −12345 or 12345−, for example. To indicate negative amounts on a card, however, such representation of five positions for the amount and one for the operational sign would be wasteful.

The Punched Card and the Printed Report

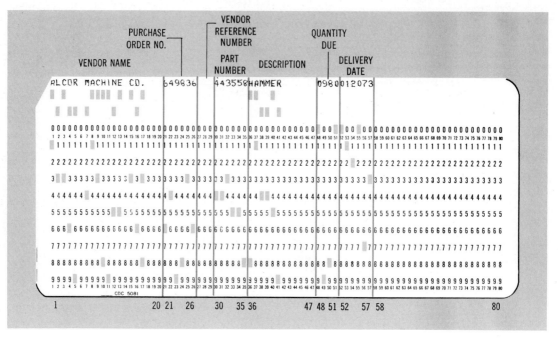

Figure 3.11
Sample data card—III.

The convention for input cards is usually to place an operational sign, if needed, in the low-order position of the field, *along with* the units digit.

That is, an AMOUNT field would be indicated as $1234\bar{5}$. A minus sign is a special character, coded as an 11-zone. Thus, the field would appear as indicated in columns 31 to 35 of Figure 3.10.

In this way, a position would be saved for each signed numeric field. An 11-5 punch in a single column can also be considered as the letter N. Thus 1234N in a *numeric* data field means -12345 to the computer and to unit-record devices. That is, all arithmetic operations on this amount field will result in proper calculations. The computer is designed to treat 1234N in a numeric field as a negative 12345.

Similarly, 12J would be considered as -121 when coded in a numeric field. To program the computer to add 100 to this number would result in a sum of -21 or 2J.

Sometimes an operational plus sign, represented by an ampersand (12-punch) is placed over the units position of a field to represent a positive quantity. Note that the *absence* of a sign also implies a positive quantity.

The use of a plus sign, however, insures that a sign was not inadvertently or incorrectly omitted. That is, in fields where many items

Fundamental Concepts of Data Processing

have negative quantities, plus signs are used to denote positive amounts. In this way, all items are signed; thus negative quantities are less likely to be incorrectly coded as positive or unsigned amounts.

Plus signs are represented, in their low-order position, as a 12-punch in conjunction with the units digit. Thus 423 might be a positive quantity in an AMOUNT field. This can also be coded as 42C (12-3 punches in units position).

Coded fields are often used to make data more concise. The use of codes on a card is an effective method of saving positions. Suppose, for example, that a retail establishment has 5000 customer accounts. The card could be designed with a 20-position field for customer name. Each customer could, however, be given a coded ACCOUNT NUMBER, by which he will be known within the data processing department. Thus, a 4-position coded ACCOUNT NUMBER representing accounts from 1 to 5000 would save 16 card columns. Similarly, certain payroll procedures often utilize an assigned MAN NUMBER or a SOCIAL SECURITY NUMBER instead of NAME. This saves many storage positions and also is a more reliable identification field. Although two employees may have the same name, all man numbers and social security numbers are unique.

Control punches or fields are often used to save space. Sometimes it is possible to conserve space on a card by utilizing the same positions for two mutually exclusive fields. Suppose, for example, that a Transaction card can have *either* a 5-position AMOUNT OF CREDIT field or a 5-position AMOUNT OF DEBIT field. By using *six positions* on the card, we can provide for both these fields. That is, we can include a 5-position AMOUNT field with a sixth position as a CONTROL field. If the sixth position is a 1, for example, then AMOUNT is really equal to AMOUNT OF CREDIT. If it is a 0, then AMOUNT = AMOUNT OF DEBIT. In this way, we need only provide a *single* 5-position field.

To eliminate the need for a sixth position, we can incorporate that control punch into the AMOUNT field itself. An 11-punch, sometimes called an *X*-punch, over the units position can be used for control purposes and *not* to denote a sign. Thus $1387\overline{2}$ would be AMOUNT OF CREDIT equal to 13872, while 13872 in the same positions would indicate an AMOUNT OF DEBIT equal to 13872.

In short, every effort must be made to limit a card record to 80 positions so that multiple cards per record are not required. The above 5 methods of (1) eliminating unnecessary fields (2) eliminating edit and superfluous symbols, (3) placing operational signs in the low-order position of a numeric field, (4) using coded fields, and (5) using control punches are the most frequently used methods for conserving space on a card and thereby insuring a concise record.

Data is also represented on a card in a logical sequence. That is, fields are *not* haphazardly arranged. The beginning fields on the card are usually those that identify card data or that serve as sort fields. The businessman is not likely to find the date or an amount as the first field of a card, for example. NAME, ACCOUNT NUMBER, TRANSACTION

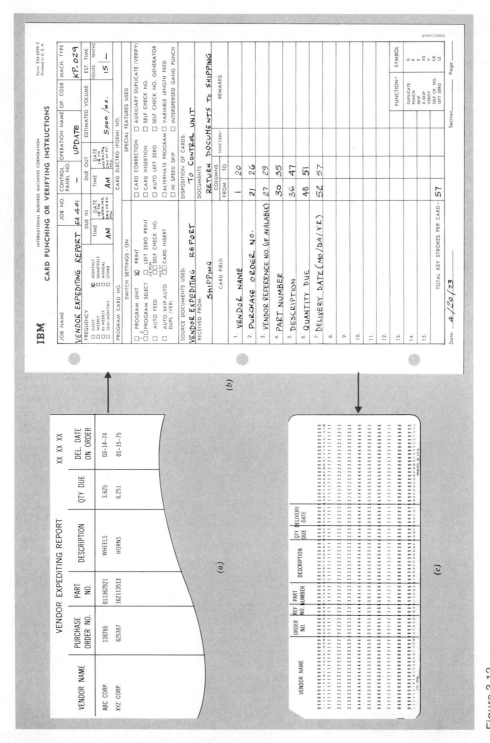

Figure 3.12
Conversion of source document to punched card.

NUMBER, SOCIAL SECURITY NUMBER are more likely fields which serve to identify the card or are used for sorting purposes.

After major fields are indicated on a card, the remaining fields are generally arranged as they appear on the original source document so that keypunch operators are not required to visually skip over fields. Figure 3.12 illustrates a conversion from a source document to a punched card. The included CARD PUNCHING OR VERIFYING INSTRUCTIONS sheet is the document that is sent to the keypunch supervisor to insure that the keypunching staff is provided with the information necessary to punch cards with data in the correct format and sequence.

At this point, we will indicate the hierarchy in which data is represented. We have thus far seen that records are composed of related fields. For example, an Employee Time Card is a *record* of information containing a NAME field, HOURS WORKED field, and so on. A collection of related records is called a *file*. Thus, a collection of *all* Employee Time Cards would constitute a file. (See Figure 3.13.) These definitions of fields, records, and files apply to any type of input/output medium.

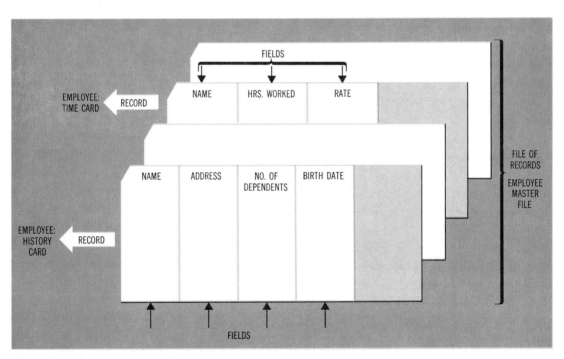

Figure 3.13
Related fields in records within a file.

D. ILLUSTRATIVE CARD RECORDS

Let us consider some cards designed for specific systems, as shown in Figures 3.14, 3.15, and 3.16.

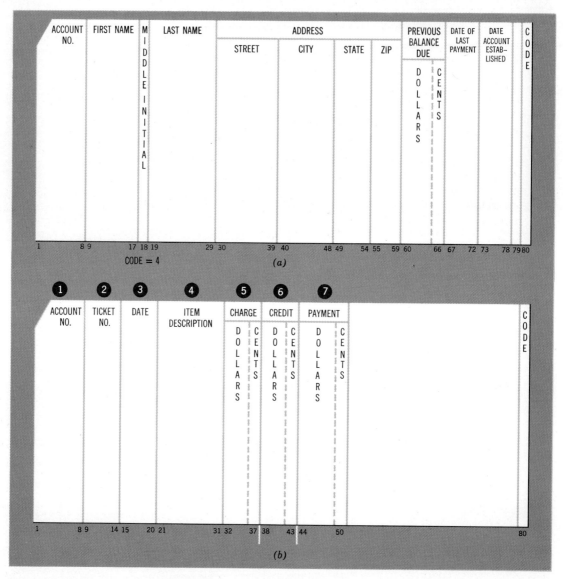

Figure 3.14

Accounts Receivable card records. (a) Name and address card. (b) Transaction card—for sales slips, credit slips payment notices, memos. (The following fields are keypunched, depending on the source document, as follows:

Sales slip: fields 1,2,3,4,5,8 are filled; Code = 1
Credit slip: fields 1,2,3,4,6, are filled; Code = 2
Payment memo: fields 1,3,7,8, are filled; Code = 3)

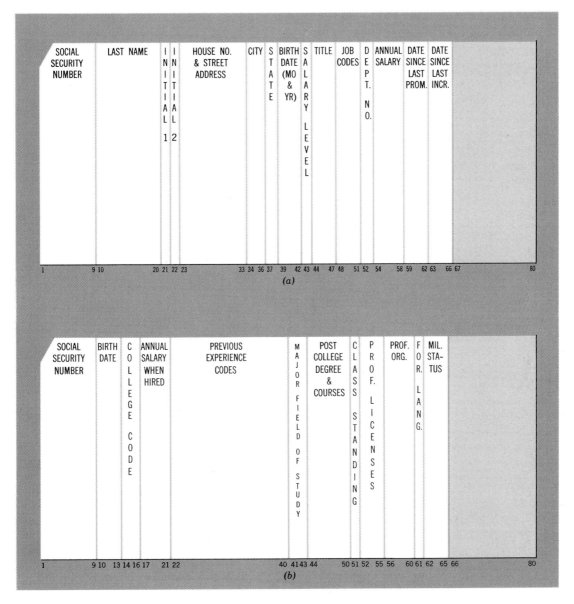

Figure 3.15
Personnel card records for salaried employees. (a) Change in status
personnel card. (b) New employee personnel card.

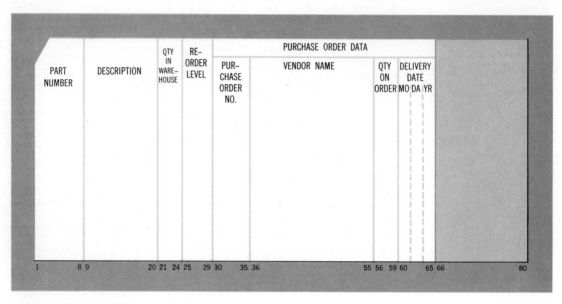

| PART NUMBER | DESCRIPTION | QTY IN WARE-HOUSE | RE-ORDER LEVEL | PURCHASE ORDER DATA | | | | |
| | | | | PUR-CHASE ORDER NO. | VENDOR NAME | QTY ON ORDER | DELIVERY DATE MO DA YR | |

```
1        8 9              20 21 24 25    29 30    35 36                    55 56 59 60    65 66              80
```

Figure 3.16
Inventory card record.

III. Uses of a Card

A. TYPES OF CARDS

The major use of the input punched card is for computer or EAM processing. That is, these cards are meant to be machine-read and interpreted, and thus are designed for ease of processing. They are also machine-prepared, usually with the use of a keypunch machine. Often they are not very "readable," since the coded fields and elimination of edit symbols reduce their readability. They do, however, usually contain the printed equivalent of the punched holes.

Some cards serve as *output* as well as machine-readable input. That is, a card can also be created as *output* from a computer or from specific EAM devices such as a REPRODUCER. A typical example is a utility bill created on a punched card by a computer, which serves as output to be read and interpreted by a customer, as in Figure 3.17. The customer is instructed to return this card, or bill, with the payment. He

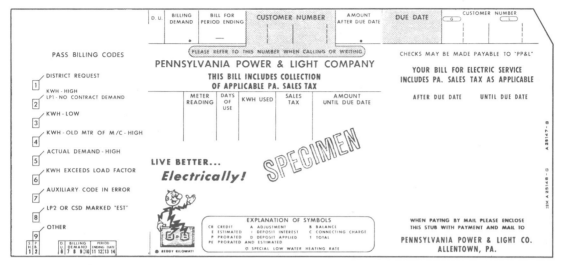

Figure 3.17
Utility bill on a punched card. Courtesy IBM.

is also urged not to "bend, fold, staple, or mutilate" the card, since it will later serve as input to the computer to update the customer's account.

Time cards are also often created by a computer with just EMPLOYEE NAME and NUMBER. These cards are then additionally punched by special machines to denote the hours worked for each employee.

In short, a punched card can be created or keypunched from a source document to serve as *input* to a computer or EAM device. In addition, a punched card can serve as *output* from a computer or EAM device. When a card is created as output, it will usually be reentered into the data processing flow at some later date as input. Thus the utility bill or the time card is only an intermediate form of output, since it will eventually serve as input again.

Some cards are punched *manually* by a hand device, and are called Port-A-Punch cards (Figure 3.18). Other cards are manually marked by a special electrographic pencil. These marks on the card can then be interpreted by a special machine and converted to conventional punched cards. These cards are called Mark-Sensed cards (Figure 3.19). Many students have used these for taking multiple-choice tests. The answers are mark-sensed by the student with the special pencil. They are then converted into the appropriate Hollerith configuration on the same card, by a special machine. Both Port-A-Punch and Mark-Sensed cards eliminate the need for a conversion from a source document to a machine-readable form, thereby saving a data processing cost. That is, the card itself serves as

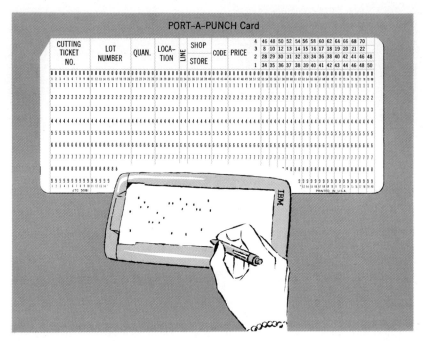

Figure 3.18
Punching a Port-A-Punch card.

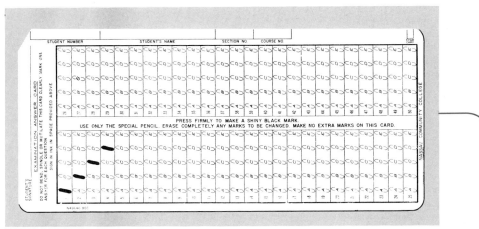

(a) Mark-sensed card

(b) Reproducer
(Courtesy IBM)

(c) Same mark-sensed card with punches

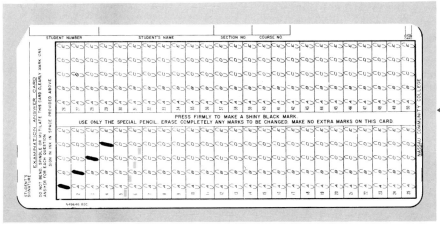

Figure 3.19
Marked sensing and the reproducing punch.

a source document. An employee from a water company, for example, can use either Port-A-Punch or Mark-Sensed cards to punch or mark water meter figures that he obtains from each home meter. In this way the cards can serve as input to a data processing machine.

B. ADVANTAGES AND DISADVANTAGES OF PUNCHED CARD PROCESSING

Thus, we can see that the punched card has numerous uses in industry. As indicated, it is the most widely used storage medium in small-scale computer installations.

Its basic advantages include the fact that data recorded on cards is machine-accessible *and* manually accessible as well. That is, computers and EAM devices can utilize card data, while manual methods can still be utilized to extract specific records since the data punched on the card may also be printed on the face of the card. (Most keypunch machines have printing facility, but most card punch devices do not.)

Another important consideration is the relatively economical method by which cards can be processed.

There are, however, several inherent disadvantages to card processing that must be realized by all business and data processing students. The relative convenience of card processing decreases with increased numbers of cards. That is, large numbers of cards are cumbersome to process. Cards within a file can often be lost, misplaced, dropped, or missorted. Operator time is greatly increased with large numbers of cards. Operators must constantly feed these records into the appropriate machines. Magnetic tapes and disks discussed in the next chapter do not have these disadvantages.

The card reader of a computer and the EAM devices utilize essentially mechanical methods for sensing holes in a card. Mechanical devices often jam, causing the loss of many hours of machine time. These devices, then, are not as efficient as others that rely solely on electronic equipment. Similarly, mechanical devices are notoriously slow. Some card readers, for example, can read *an average* of 1000 cards per minute. This speed, although seemingly fast for a layman, is very slow compared to the *billionths* of seconds in which the computer can process the data, once it is read. We shall see that other computer forms are much faster.

Thus, while cost is minimal, efficiency is limited with punched cards. Similarly, physical limitations often adversely affect card processing. The previously mentioned factor of 80 positions per record is a distinct disadvantage. Some records do not lend themselves to 80-character formats. Also, humid weather conditions result in warped cards, which causes mechanical devices to jam.

In short, the punched card is the basic form of input. Most computer centers utilize the card as input, often to be converted to a more efficient medium at some later date.

Only small computer centers, however, utilize the punched card as a *primary* form of input. Such small companies usually have limited amounts of data, and for these the card remains the most economical and efficient medium. In larger companies, the disadvantages and inefficiencies of the punched card make other storage media more desirable.

SELF-EVALUATING QUIZ

Use Figure 3.20 to answer questions 1 to 14.
1. The punched card illustrated has _____ columns.
2. Each column can hold one _____ of data.
3. A character of data consists of a _____ , _____ , or _____ .
4. A field is a _____ .
5. The first three columns of the illustrated card represent the _____ field.
6. The data in the above field is _____ .

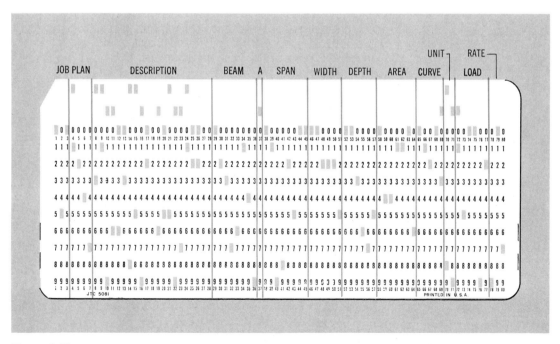

Figure 3.20
Illustration of a punched card.

7. The _____ punches are called the digit punches and the _____ punches are called zone punches.
8. A numeric field consists of _____ punches.
9. An alphabetic character consists of a _____ punch and a _____ punch in a single column.
10. An alphabetic field on the illustrated card is the _____ field.
11. An alphanumeric field is one that consists of _____ .
12. _____ is a *general* example of an alphanumeric field.
13. The CURVE field is a numeric field with a _____ sign in its _____ position.
14. The high-order position of the RATE field contains a _____ .

15. Punched cards can be punched by operators using a _____ machine, transcribing from a _____ .
16. To check the cards for accuracy, a _____ is used.
17. Punched cards can also be created by the _____ , as output.
18. Such output cards are usually reentered into the computer cycle as input at some later date. Examples of these types of cards include _____ and _____ .
19. Two advantages of card processing are _____ and _____ .
20. Three disadvantages of card processing are _____ , _____ , _____ .
21. Coded fields are sometimes used on a card to _____ .
22. An example of a coded field is _____ .
23. (T or F) Edit symbols such as dollar signs and commas are rarely used on a card.
24. The most common code used to represent data on a card is called the _____ code.

SOLUTIONS

1. 80
2. character
3. letter; digit; symbol
4. group of consecutive card columns used to indicate a unit of data, for example, JOB field, DESCRIPTION field
5. JOB
6. 050
7. 0 to 9; 0-, 11-, 12-
8. digit
9. zone; digit
10. DESCRIPTION
11. a combination of letters, digits, or special characters
12. ADDRESS
13. negative; low order or units
14. 9
15. keypunch; source document
16. verifier
17. computer
18. utility cards (gas, electric, telephone); time cards

19. they can be processed by machine and also used for manual retrieval; the cost is relatively low.

20. cards warp easily, are easily dropped, misplaced, bent, etc.; card records are restricted to 80 columns or multiples of 80;

cards are processed relatively slowly.

21. conserve card space.

22. an ACCOUNT NUMBER as opposed to CUSTOMER NAME

23. T

24. Hollerith

IV. Printed Output

The printed report is the primary form of computer output. It is the form of output that is most commonly distributed to nondata processing businessmen.

The printed document is generally used *exclusively* as an end product. It is the final result of a computer run, often to be viewed by high-level management. It is prepared by the computer device called a Printer. (See Figure 3.21.)

Other forms of output are generally intermediate products, having the ultimate function of being reentered into the computer flow as input to another job. These types of outputs are designed to be as efficient as possible. Fields and records of this type are condensed to make maximum use of the computer and its storage capabilities. The printed report, however, is written with the businessman in mind. Since many computer-generated reports are read by company executives, such forms must be clear, neat, and easy to interpret. The businessman should keep in mind that output reports must provide him with the *precise* information he requires within, of course, cost limitations. He should not be persuaded to settle for something less when he can obtain exactly what is needed.

A. CHARACTERISTICS OF PRINTED OUTPUT

Several characteristics applicable to only printed output must be considered:

1. Printing of Headings
Headings generally supply identifying information such as job name, date, page number, and field designations. These items are essential for clearness of presentation when creating printed output. In Figure 3.21 the lines above the actual data indicating TRIAL BALANCE and the field delineations are called headings.

2. Alignment of Data
Reports do not have fields of information adjacent to one another, as is the practice with cards. Printed output is more easily read and interpreted when data is spaced neatly and evenly across the page.

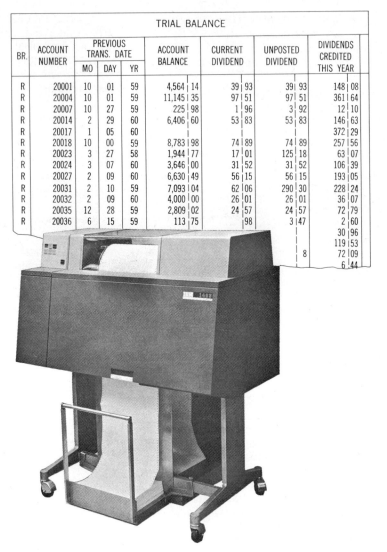

TRIAL BALANCE								
BR.	ACCOUNT NUMBER	PREVIOUS TRANS. DATE			ACCOUNT BALANCE	CURRENT DIVIDEND	UNPOSTED DIVIDEND	DIVIDENDS CREDITED THIS YEAR
		MO	DAY	YR				
R	20001	10	01	59	4,564 14	39 93	39 93	148 08
R	20004	10	01	59	11,145 35	97 51	97 51	361 64
R	20007	10	27	59	225 98	1 96	3 92	12 10
R	20014	2	29	60	6,406 60	53 83	53 83	146 63
R	20017	1	05	60				372 29
R	20018	10	00	59	8,783 98	74 89	74 89	257 56
R	20023	3	27	58	1,944 77	17 01	125 18	63 07
R	20024	3	07	60	3,646 00	31 52	31 52	106 39
R	20027	2	09	60	6,630 49	56 15	56 15	193 05
R	20031	2	10	59	7,093 04	62 06	290 30	228 24
R	20032	2	09	60	4,000 00	26 01	26 01	36 07
R	20035	12	28	59	2,809 02	24 57	24 57	72 79
R	20036	6	15	59	113 75	98	3 47	2 60
								30 96
								119 53
							8	72 09
								6 44

Figure 3.21
The Printer. Courtesy IBM.

3. Editing of Printed Data

As we have indicated, a punched card does not usually contain any edit or fill characters, since these occupy valuable card columns, not necessary for machine readability. A printed document, however, must be as clear as possible, since it is designed to be read by individuals. While 12450 is a typical AMOUNT field on a card, $12,450.00 is more meaningful as a printed field.

Fundamental Concepts of Data Processing

4. Spacing of Forms

Printed documents, unlike other kinds of output, must be properly spaced for ease of reading. Certain entries must be single spaced, others double spaced. The printed output must have adequate margins at both the top and bottom of the form. This requires the computer to be programmed to sense the end of a form and thus to transmit the next line of information to a *new* page.

Remember that the computer-generated output report can contain any type of information. It can be an individual listing of specific records or it can be a summary report indicating only totals. It can be broken down into specific categories with control totals. It can be a statistical survey. In short, it can be compiled in any manner that is recommended by the computer specialist and deemed appropriate by the businessman.

You will recall that most cards contain 80 characters of information. The printed report typically contains 132 characters on each line, although some printers can only print 100 characters per line. Note that all positions need *not* be filled with significant characters; *many* positions on a printed line are filled with blanks or spaces. To align data on a page, we must leave numerous blank fields between significant ones. To assist in aligning printed data, a Printer Spacing Chart sometimes called a Print Layout Sheet (Figure 3.22) is often used. It maps out those areas of a form that are to be filled with data. Often, the computer specialist reviews these charts with the businessman prior to programming to confirm that the format is acceptable.

B. CONTINUOUS FORMS AND THE PRINTER

Printed reports that serve as computer output are sometimes referred to as *continuous forms* since they are connected together, separated only by perforations. (See Figure 3.23.) They are fed into a PRINTER as one continuous form so that constant aligning of forms is not required. After an entire report has been printed, it is *burst* by machine into individual sheets (see Figure 3.24) for binding or circulating separately. Each page must have its own heading and usually a page number so that misplaced documents can be properly arranged.

Continuous forms can have additional carbon copies prepared by the computer. Standard stock continuous forms can usually be obtained as follows: 1-part (no copies) 2-part, 3-part, 4-part, or 5-part paper (4 copies). There are machines that burst the forms called Bursters and others that *decollate* them, or remove the carbons called Decollators. (See Figure 3.24.)

Most standard stock continuous forms are 12 inches long. Usually, 6 lines of data may be printed per inch. That is, most continuous forms may contain 72 lines of information. Sometimes, however, to condense a report, 8 lines per inch are utilized. (See Figure 3.25.) This is not as popular as the density of 6 lines per inch, since it is not as readable.

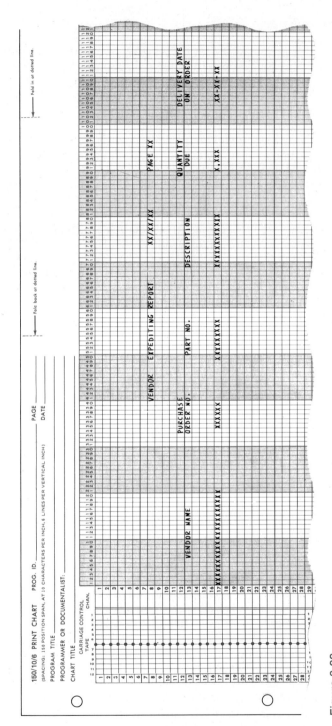

Figure 3.22
Print layout sheet.

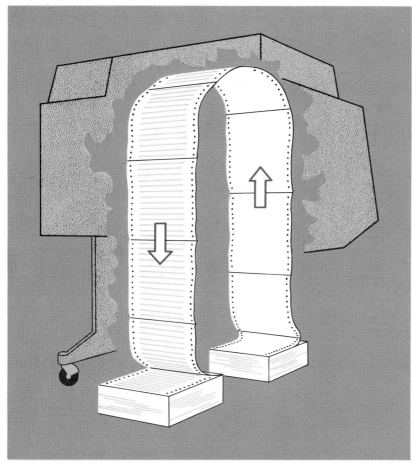

Figure 3.23 Continuous forms. Courtesy IBM.

Note, however, that reports usually contain much less than 72 or 96 lines per page. Generally, there are both top and bottom margins; that is, several blank lines are included at the top and bottom of each form. Similarly, many reports utilize double or triple spacing as well as single spacing to separate heading and detail lines.

Printed reports may be on plain, lined, or unlined sheets as indicated in Figure 3.23, or on special, *preprinted forms*. Bank statements, commonly printed by a computer as output, are individual, preprinted forms with COMPANY NAME and other identifying information printed on each one. (See Figure 3.26.) Similarly, Accounts Receivable statements may be prepared by the computer as preprinted forms. (See Figure 3.27.) Note, however, that the heading and the

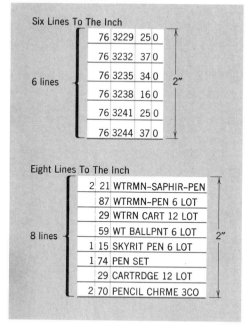

DOUBLE-SPACED

Six Lines To The Inch

76	3229	25 0
76	3232	37 0
76	3235	34 0
76	3238	16 0
76	3241	25 0
76	3244	37 0

6 lines — 2″

Eight Lines To The Inch

2	21	WTRMN–SAPHIR–PEN
	87	WTRMN–PEN 6 LOT
	29	WTRN CART 12 LOT
	59	WT BALLPNT 6 LOT
1	15	SKYRIT PEN 6 LOT
1	74	PEN SET
	29	CARTRDGE 12 LOT
2	70	PENCIL CHRME 3CO

8 lines — 2″

Figure 3.25
Examples of 6 lines per inch double
spaced (that is, 6 lines every two inches)
and 8 lines per inch double spaced.

vertical and horizontal lines are preprinted on the continuous form, *prior* to entering the printer. They are *not* prepared by the computer. Keep in mind that these preprinted forms must be ordered from a company specializing in printed forms.

Thus printed reports may be produced on plain continuous forms or on preprinted continuous forms. Either may be utilized with carbons to provide additional copies. The plain 12-inch continuous forms usually can be obtained in 1, 2, 3, 4, or 5 parts. Preprinted forms may be ordered with as many copies as are required.

The Printer (Figure 3.21) is used to transmit information from the computer to the printed report. It is a device that can print generally 600 to 1000 lines per minute, although the most modern printers can operate at more than 2000 lines per minute. It is not, however, considered a high-speed device since other devices produce data at far greater rates.

Figure 3.24 (at left)
(a) Decollator, model 620. Courtesy Monarch Co. Features—separates multiple part forms and refolds them in continuous stacks (on refolding trays . . . at the same time removing the carbon insert. Handles forms set up to 300 feet per minute in sizes 3 to 12 inches long and 3½ to 20 inches wide—ledger or card stock—as well as regular paper.) (b) Burster, model 610. Courtesy Monarch Co.

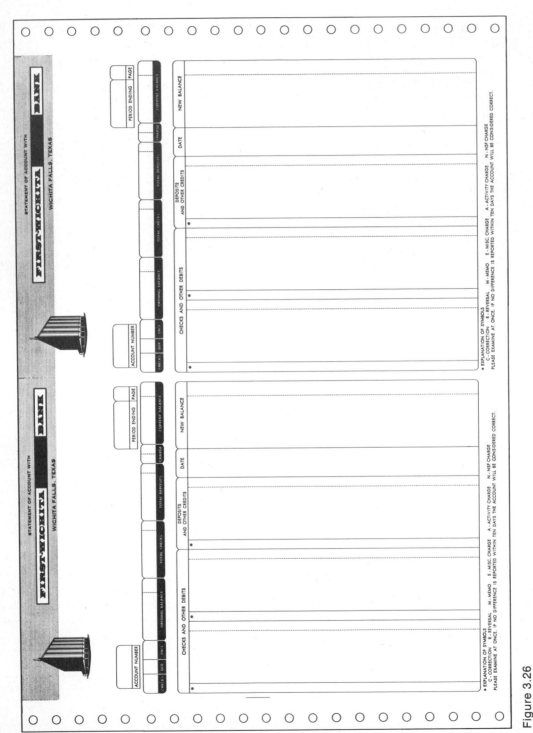

Figure 3.26

Example of preprinted bank statement. This statement is an example of a preprinted, side-by-side form that allows the computer to print two different bank statements at the same time by dividing the print area into two records—one for each statement. Courtesy International Business Forms, Inc.

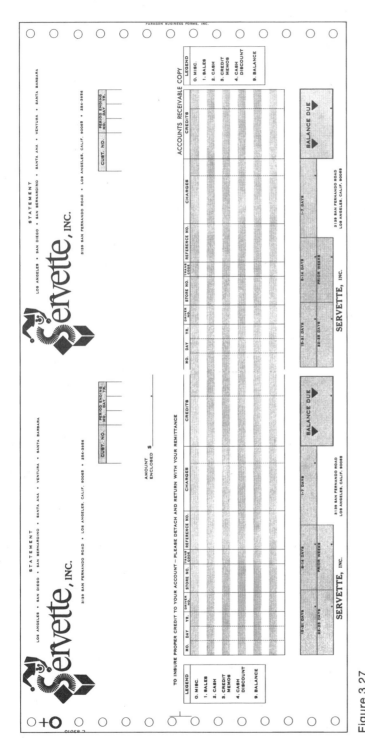

Figure 3.27
Example of a preprinted form. Courtesy International Business Forms, Inc.

83

Note that, unlike the typewriter, the printer does not print one character at a time. Instead, a typical computer, for example, transmits 132 characters to the printer, which then prints the data one *line* at a time. The computer transmits a *total* line with significant characters and blanks included for spacing. The blanks are transmitted as if they were significant characters. Thus, the printer prints a line at a *constant* speed, regardless of whether the line contains 100 blanks or 5 blanks.

The device that moves the continuous forms through the printer is called the *carriage*.

The continuous form may be easily programmed for *single, double,* or *triple* spacing. The programmer can also instruct the printer to *skip* to a specific line of the form. You will recall that there are generally 72 lines on a form. Any one of these lines may be accessed by the programmer for printing.

Thus, the printing of lines may be controlled by *skipping* to a specific line or by *spacing* the form 1, 2, or 3 lines.

In short, it is possible for the businessman to obtain computer-generated output records in almost any format desired, if he communicates his needs to the computer specialist.

SELF-EVALUATING QUIZ

1. (T or F) A printer prints data a single character at a time.
2. _____ are needed on printed documents to insure the proper identification of each page.
3. _____ is performed on printed data to insure its readability.
4. A typical printer can print _____ characters per line, but many of these are _____ for ease of reading.
5. A layout form called a _____ is used by programmers and analysts, and verified by businessmen, to insure that output data will be aligned properly.
6. The blank paper that is fed into a Printer is an example of a _____ .
7. Most standard stock paper is _____ inches long, and usually _____ lines may be printed per inch.
8. (T or F) Reports generally contain less than 72 lines per page because of margins.
9. In addition to standard stock continuous forms, _____ forms for special purposes may be used for printing particular reports.
10. _____, _____, or _____ spacing may be programmed, but the programmer can also instruct the printer to _____ to a specific line.

SOLUTIONS

1. F
2. Headings
3. Editing
4. 132; left blank
5. Printer Spacing Chart

6. continuous form
7. 12; 6
8. T
9. preprinted
10. single; double; triple; skip

Chapter 4 *The Processing of Data by Computer*

I. Basic Concepts

Thus far, we have seen that a computer, commonly regarded as a "thinking machine," is really a programmed unit that performs only the operations it is instructed to do. *For repetitive type operations,* a computer is faster, more economical, and more reliable than manual techniques. Let us now consider *how* the computer performs its various tasks. This will provide an understanding of how and why *any* business operation can be computerized, if the businessman is willing to pay the associated price.

We have considered, thus far, the punched card as both an input and output form and the printed report as an output medium. In this chapter, we will discuss how the computer can read in the punched card, as input, process the data, and convert it to output, as either another punched card or a printed report. Notice that we are using the punched card and the printed report as *examples* of input/output (I/O) media because of their relative simplicity. The objective of this chapter is to familiarize the student with the way in which a computer processes input data and converts it to output. Later we shall see that processing remains very similar, regardless of the form that the input or output takes.

A. HARDWARE

The objective of computer processing is to convert input data to output data by operating on it. The computer processing is performed by a *program,* written by a computer programmer, which indicates all the instructions necessary to operate on the input so that meaningful output is realized.

Hardware is the term used to indicate all physical components associated with a computer system. An *input device* is the actual machine or physical device that reads data. An *output device* is the actual machine or physical device that writes or produces output. The *Central Processing Unit* (CPU) is the physical device that controls the computer operations. It is the ''brains'' of the computer system; it is instructed by each program as to the functions required for a particular problem.

Thus a computer system consists of independent machines that function, in an integrated manner, to produce desired output. Keep in mind that typical computer systems have many input/output devices with varying degrees of sophistication. All operations performed by the computer system are controlled by the Central Processing Unit. The CPU is connected by cable to each of the input/output devices and can control the processing of each. As mentioned above, the CPU itself is under the control of a computer program, which indicates what operations are to be performed. Figure 4.1 illustrates a typical computer system with numerous input/output units linked to a Central

Figure 4.1
IBM System/370. Courtesy IBM.

Figure 4.2
The console typewriter can be used to write instructions directly into the main, control, or scratchpad memory areas of the computer and can also operate as a logging typewriter. The compact keyboard-and-control panel design of Honeywell's Model 2200 computer console permits simplified operator control. Courtesy Honeywell.

Processing Unit. Note that typical computer systems utilize many and varied devices for all types of business applications. The use of each input/output device is under the control of the CPU. The next chapter discusses the various devices that may be linked in a computer system.

A computer system generally consists of *three* main components:

1. Input/output devices
2. Central Processing Unit (CPU)
3. Console typewriter (Figure 4.2)

Most third-generation computer systems utilize a console typewriter as the primary means of communication with the computer system by the operator. It is used, by the CPU to produce messages to the operator (mount tape No. 583, error in program, and so on) and, by the operator, to key in messages to the computer (cancel the job, ignore the error, and so on).

Fundamental Concepts of Data Processing

B. OPERATIONS PERFORMED BY A COMPUTER

The operations that the CPU can perform are classified into five major categories:

1. Input
2. Data transfer
3. Arithmetic
4. Logic
5. Output

These operations are performed as called for by the programmer's instructions.

An *input operation* is one that signals an input device to read data and then automatically transmits that data to the Central Processing Unit. That is, each program provides an area of computer storage within the CPU to hold an input record. Thus input operations perform two functions:

1. Cause an input device to physically *read* data.
2. *Transmit* the data from the input device to an input area of the CPU.

Data transfer, arithmetic, and logic operations (categories 2 to 4 above) are *processing* functions that operate on the input data.

In order for data to be written, it must appear in an output area within the CPU that is set up by each program. The *data transfer* operation *moves* data from the input area to the output area. The *arithmetic* operations can cause the adding, multiplying, subtracting, and dividing of fields by the CPU. The *logic operations* can test or perform simple decisions such as: Is one field less than, equal to, or greater than another?

An *output operation* (category 5) causes data to be transmitted from the output area, provided for by each program, to an output device where the data is then written out or recorded.

In short, each program that is read into the CPU provides for the following.

1. Instructions that will operate on input data to convert it to output.
2. An input area into which data read by an input device is transmitted.
3. An output area, from which data is transmitted when an output instruction is issued.

C. THE CENTRAL PROCESSING UNIT

The schematic in Figure 4.3 illustrates the integration of the basic elements in a computer system.

The Central Processing Unit is composed of three sections:

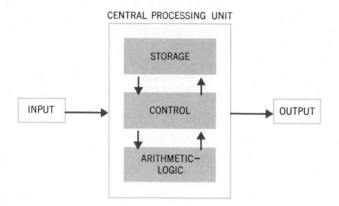

CENTRAL PROCESSING UNIT

INPUT

STORAGE

CONTROL

ARITHMETIC–
LOGIC

OUTPUT

Figure 4.3
Schematic of a Central Processing Unit.

1. Storage
2. Control
3. Arithmetic-logic

1. Storage

The *STORAGE* section within the CPU contains the stored program. The program, you will recall, consists of the set of instructions necessary to read input data and convert it to output. We will expand this definition slightly. The stored program consists of the set of instructions *and* the necessary input/output areas. Thus, if a program reads card data and converts it to printed output, storage areas would be required for the instructions, plus a minimum of 80 positions for card data and, typically, 132 positions for printed data.

Storage is composed of locations or addressable positions. On many computers, each position is composed of tiny ferrite rings or *cores* that are magnetized to reflect computer codes. (See Figure 4.4.) Thus the term *core storage* is used to denote this type of storage.

Instructions, as well as input/output areas, occupy storage positions. Each element of an instruction is placed in a storage position or storage location, called a *byte* on many computers. The number of storage positions available on a given computer is called its *memory size*. The memory size of a typical third-generation business computer ranges from approximately 32,000 positions to 128,000 positions, with large-scale computers possessing a memory size in excess of one million positions. Thus, on average- or medium-sized computers, we can have programs with thousands of instructions, in addition to many input/output areas. The notation K is often used as an abbreviation for approximately one thousand storage positions. Thus, average-sized business computers possess memory sizes of from 32K to 128K.

Most business computers also have a special program, usually supplied by the computer manufacturer, which resides in storage. This program, commonly called a *SUPERVISOR* or *MONITOR,* is

Fundamental Concepts of Data Processing

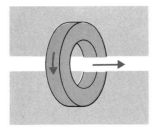

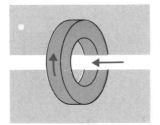

Core is magnetized.
Represents a 1,
or the presence
of a bit.

Current is reversed; the core
reverses its magnetic state.
Represents a 0,
or the absence of a bit.

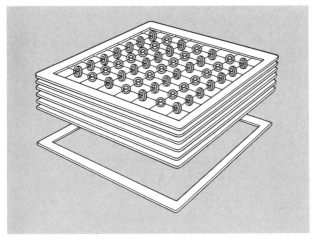

Cores in a plane.

Figure 4.4
Representation of Core
Storage

responsible for controlling the operations of the totally integrated
computer system. A detailed discussion of the various functions of the
SUPERVISOR will be found in Chapter 14, after the business and data
processing students have attained an appreciation of exactly how
programs operate in a computer system.

A useful and simplified way of visualizing the functions of the CPU
just discussed is to consider the diagram in Figure 4.5.

This diagram will serve as the means of illustrating the basic
concepts of how programs operate.

2. Control

The *CONTROL* section of the CPU is where the instructions of a
program are located in order for the computer to act on them. Since
the instructions of a program are initially in the storage section, they
must be transferred to the control section, one at a time, to be

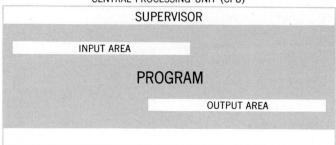

CENTRAL PROCESSING UNIT (CPU)

SUPERVISOR

INPUT AREA

PROGRAM

OUTPUT AREA

Figure 4.5
The supervisor within the CPU.

executed. In the control section, each instruction is broken down into parts that basically indicate to the computer what operation to perform and what device or data is affected by the particular operation. Thus, the control section is where the instructions of the stored program are actually interpreted by the computer and the appropriate actions taken.

3. Arithmetic-Logic

The *ARITHMETIC-LOGIC* section of the CPU is under the control of the particular program that is being executed. It is in this section where calculations and decisions are made. As mentioned previously, the computer essentially performs all arithmetic operations by the process of addition. The appendix to this book includes a discussion of computer arithmetic and numbering systems that are typically utilized in business computers. That discussion is actually a presentation of some of the concepts of mathematics currently being taught in many schools under the title of "Modern Mathematics."

In essence, whenever the computer performs arithmetic operations or makes a comparison, the arithmetic-logic section is being utilized. Special accumulators, or *registers,* necessary for performing the required operations are located in this unit. These registers are internal areas used to temporarily hold data that is being processed. When an instruction, while in the control section, is to be executed, it often requires the arithmetic-logic section to perform necessary functions.

The Central Processing Unit, which is composed of the three sections (Storage, Control, Arithmetic-logic) is housed in an independent device. The Storage section, which can consist of hundreds of thousands of addressable locations, is the major portion of the CPU. Often, the storage section is too large to be housed in a CPU. In such a case, an *Auxiliary Storage* Device, linked by cables to the CPU, is used to store the excess areas that cannot be adequately maintained by the CPU.

When an auxiliary storage device is linked to the CPU to contain

Fundamental Concepts of Data Processing

additional storage the CPU itself maintains control. That is, the programmer need not concern himself with distinguishing which instructions are in the CPU and which are in the Auxiliary Storage device.

D. ILLUSTRATIVE COMPUTER PROCEDURES

Now, that we have presented the basic structure of a computer system, we will illustrate essentially what happens when we want the computer to process a program. The details illustrating precisely how a program appears and how it gets into the storage unit of the CPU will be discussed in Chapter 14. The purpose of this chapter is to provide business and data processing students with a fundamental understanding of how the computer operates. In this way they can begin to conceptualize what can realistically be expected from a computerized system.

EXAMPLE 1

Suppose that in an Accounts Payable system, there is one card keypunched for each vendor from whom the company buys, as shown in Figure 4.6.

Thus the deck of all such cards represents a *VENDOR FILE*. The illustrated cards must be sorted into vendor number sequence. A program has been written that will take these cards, after they have been sorted, and produce the type of report shown in Figure 4.7. That

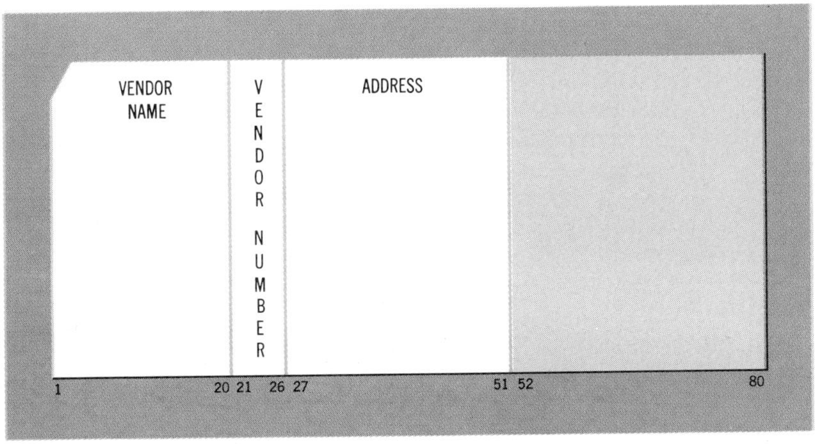

Figure 4.6
Data card illustration.

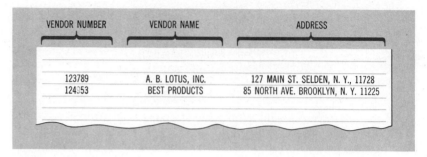

VENDOR NUMBER	VENDOR NAME	ADDRESS
123789	A. B. LOTUS, INC.	127 MAIN ST. SELDEN, N. Y., 11728
124953	BEST PRODUCTS	85 NORTH AVE. BROOKLYN, N. Y. 11225

Figure 4.7
Report illustration.

is, every time the program reads in a card, it prints out the information with the fields arranged in a different order; thus, vendor number is printed *first* and then the corresponding vendor name and address.

We know that in order for the program to be executed, it must initially be placed in the *storage unit* of the CPU. As was discussed previously, when the program is located in the CPU it will include the required input and output areas. Therefore, we know that for this program there will be *two* I/O (Input/Output) areas established as follows.

1. *An input area* large enough to store information read from one card; that is, an 80-position area.
2. *An output area* to which information can be transferred when we want the computer to print one line. A typical printer allows 132 characters to be printed per line. Therefore, in our illustrations we will have an output area for the printer that is 132 positions long.

The basic format of the instructions in this program is indicated below. Note that these are not the *actual* instructions, but merely the fundamental form, since we are not teaching the student to program at this point but just to understand some basic concepts about computer operations.

1. READ a card.
2. MOVE the fields from the input area to the output area.
3. WRITE the information from the output area onto the printer.
4. Repeat steps 1 to 3 for each card and then stop the program when there are no more cards.

Note that we will process one card record at a time. Actual instructions can be written corresponding to each of the above steps to form a program.

Fundamental Concepts of Data Processing

The READ instruction causes the CPU to signal the card reader to read *one* card. The reader physically reads the card and automatically transmits the data from the card to the card input area of the CPU, as shown in Figure 4.8.

After a card has been read, we want the computer to transfer the information to the output area. Since we want the fields arranged in a different order than on the input, and we also want some space or blank areas between the fields to make the printed report easier to read, the program will probably consist of several MOVE (or data transfer) operations. The MOVE instruction actually causes information at the input area to be duplicated at the output area. For example, the MOVE operations might be as follows.

a. Move VENDOR NAME to positions 47 to 66 in the output area.
b. Move VENDOR NUMBER to positions 21 to 26 in the output area.
c. Move ADDRESS to positions 87 to 111 in the output area.

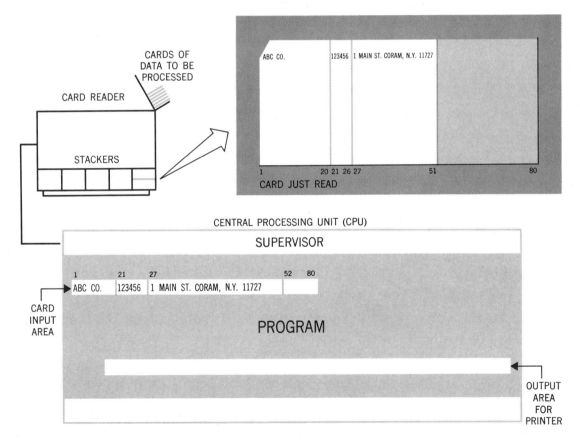

Figure 4.8
Schematic of a READ operation

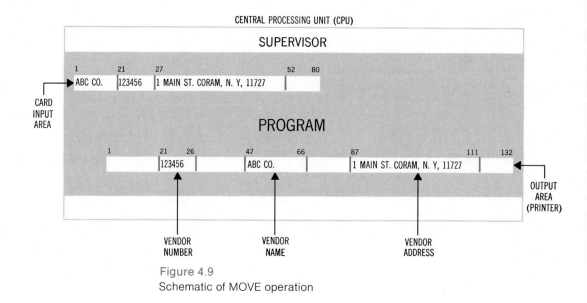

Figure 4.9
Schematic of MOVE operation

After these instructions have been completed, the contents of the CPU will be as shown in Figure 4.9.

The WRITE instruction causes all the data in the output print area, including the blanks, to be transmitted to the printer where one line is printed.

As the instructions are repeated, a new card is read and that information is transmitted to the card input area where it replaces the old data. Because each READ destroys previous input data, we will usually process a card immediately after reading it, so as not to lose the data when another card is read. When there are no more cards to be processed, there is an instruction which indicates that the computer is to STOP so that another program can be run. Note that a STOP instruction, on modern computers, does not physically cause the computer to halt, but returns control to the SUPERVISOR so that the next program may be read and processed.

EXAMPLE 2

Using the problem just discussed we will now show what changes occur in processing a program when we want headings in addition to normal print lines to be printed out, as shown in Figure 4.10.

One way of obtaining a heading is to MOVE the characters that comprise the heading into the output print area. In this program, we would include this MOVE as one of the first instructions. However, it is usually necessary to have a special instruction preceding this MOVE.

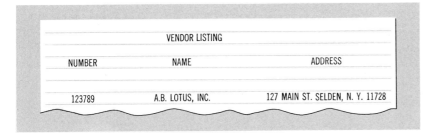

Figure 4.10 Report illustration

The purpose of that special instruction is to "erase," the output area, so that there is no information left from the previous program. Third-generation computers are *not* automatically cleared at the onset of a new program. Thus if a "clear" instruction were not issued on third-generation computers, we might obtain extraneous information on the report, which would undoubtedly detract from its appearance.

For this program, we would begin as follows.

1. Clear the output print area to eliminate information that may still be there from the previous program.
2. MOVE the heading "VENDOR LISTING" to positions 60 to 73 in the output area. The contents of the CPU will be as shown in Figure 4.11.
3. WRITE the heading. This causes the first line to be printed with the heading aligned in the center, and blanks on either

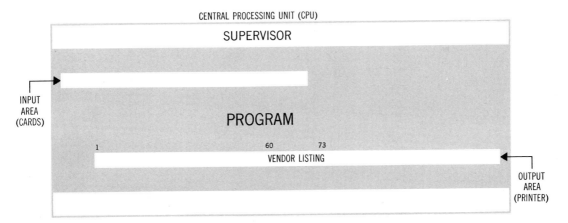

Figure 4.11 CPU containing header information

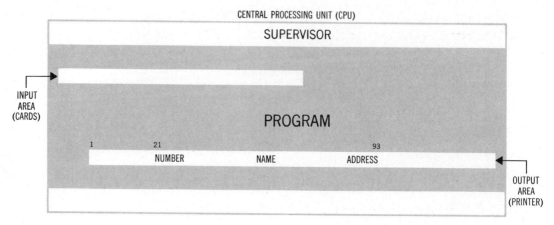

Figure 4.12 CPU containing field headings

side. Note that we insure that *blanks* are on either side by initially clearing the area.

4. Clear the output area, so that the next heading can be moved in without causing any possible overlap.

5. MOVE the heading "NUMBER   NAME   ADDRESS" to positions 21 to 93 in the output area. At this point, the CPU, as shown in Figure 4.12, contains the appropriate field headings.

6. WRITE the column headings after double spacing. (It is very easy to instruct the computer to *double space* or to write this information on the third line thus skipping a line between the first heading and the column headings.)

7. Clear the output area, so that we can now read the first card and move the information to the output area without any possible printer overlap resulting.

The program can now continue with the instructions presented in Example 1, that is,

8. READ a card.

9. MOVE the fields from the input area to the output area.

10. WRITE the information out onto the printer.

11. Repeat steps 8 to 10 for each card and then stop when there are no more cards.

Note that we can fundamentally utilize the same set of instructions to read from a magnetic tape instead of a card. We merely state READ

Fundamental Concepts of Data Processing

a tape rather than *READ a card*. To read from media other than cards or to write on media other than printed documents requires *only minor programming* changes. Chapter 5 includes a discussion of other major media used.

EXAMPLE 3

Thus far, we have discussed simple computer concepts, where one input card is used to create one output line. Now we will illustrate that, just as simply, more than one input card can be used to create a single output line.

We will use as an example a Personnel system, where the input consists of a set of *two* punched cards for each employee who works in the company, as shown in Figure 4.13.

A program has been written that will produce the report, shown in Figure 4.14, which lists the information from each set of two cards, on a single line. That is, *two* cards will produce *one* output line. Headings have been eliminated in order to clarify the point being illustrated in this example.

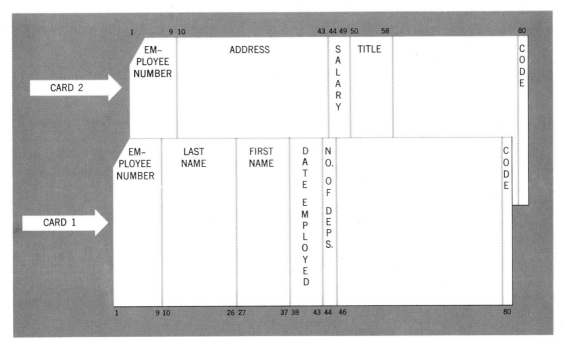

Figure 4.13
Card formats for Example 3

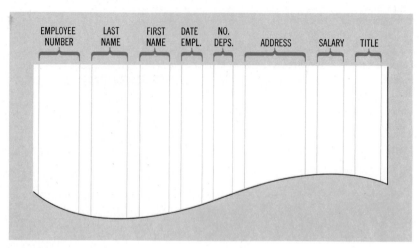

Figure 4.14
Print format for Example 3

We know that this program establishes two areas in the CPU—*one* for card input, and one for output on the printer, as shown in Figure 4.15.

Notice that even though we have two input card formats, we use a *single* input area to store both cards. That is, we process the first card of each record before reading the second card into the same input area.

The program will process information as follows:

> **1.** Clear the print area to "erase" data remaining from the previous program.
> **2.** READ the first card of a set of cards.
> **3.** MOVE the fields from the first card to the print area as follows.

MOVE	*TO PRINT AREA POSITIONS*
EMPLOYEE NUMBER (1–9)	5–13
LAST NAME (10–26)	18–34
FIRST NAME (27–37)	39–49
DATE EMPLOYED (38–43)	54–59
NUMBER OF DEPENDENTS (44–45)	64–65

The CPU, at this point, is as shown in Figure 4.16.

We will now instruct the computer to read the next card so that the information can be transferred to the print area. Note that we do *not* write a line until the second card's data has been accumulated at the output area.

Fundamental Concepts of Data Processing

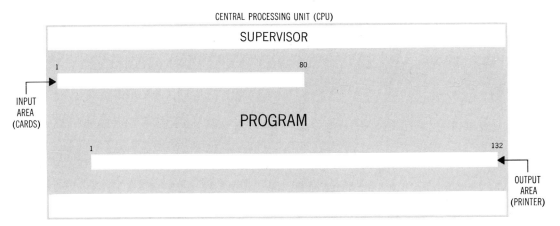

Figure 4.15
Input and Output areas within the CPU

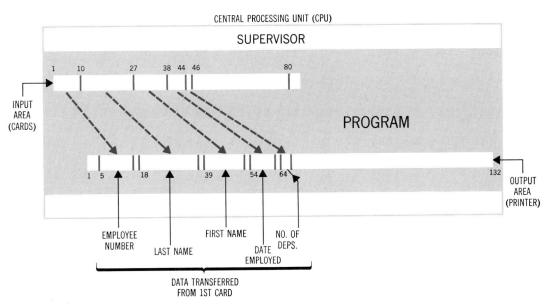

Figure 4.16
The transfer of data in the CPU for Card 1

4. READ the second card pertaining to the same employee.
5. MOVE the fields from the second card to the print area as follows.

MOVE	TO PRINT AREA POSITIONS
ADDRESS (10–43)	70–103
SALARY (44–49)	108–113
TITLE (50–58)	118–126

At this point, the status of the CPU is as shown in Figure 4.17.

6. WRITE the information onto the printer. Since a WRITE instruction causes all 132 positions in the print area to be transmitted to the printer, we will achieve the desired results.
7. Repeat steps 2 to 6 until there are no more cards left to be processed. At that time, STOP.

EXAMPLE 4

In this example, we will illustrate the simple manner in which we can have the computer read punched cards and then create *two* output

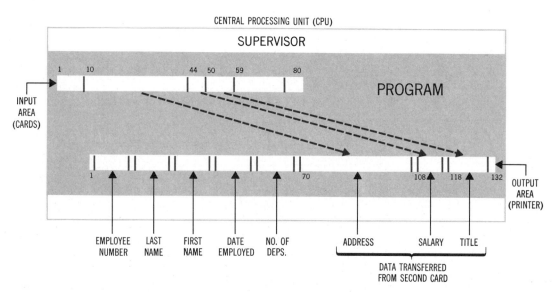

Figure 4.17
The Transfer of Data in the CPU for Card 2

Fundamental Concepts of Data Processing

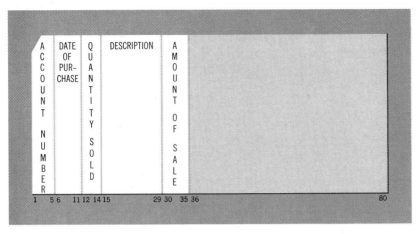

Figure 4.18
Card Format for Example 4

cards for each input card. That is, one input card will be used to create *two* output cards.

Consider the card input representing charge sales in a particular Accounts Receivable system, as shown in Figure 4.18.

For each input card, we want the computer to punch two cards from the information, as shown in Figure 4.19.

That is, the first output card will contain only two of the input fields—QUANTITY SOLD and DESCRIPTION, since this card will be sent to the Inventory Department where the other fields are not required. The second output card will be an exact duplicate of the input card, containing the same fields in the same sequence, to be sent to the customer. (The original card is kept in the Data Processing Department for additional processing at a later date.)

For this program, two areas will be set up in the CPU—*one* for card input, and *one* for card output, as shown in Figure 4.20.

Notice that only *one* output area need be established, even though it will contain two separate formats.

The essence of the program is as follows.

---

1. Clear the punch area to "erase" data remaining there from either the previous program or the previous card that was punched.
2. READ a card.
3. MOVE the information to the output card area as follows.

MOVE	TO POSITIONS IN CARD PUNCH AREA
QUANTITY SOLD (12–14)	1–3
DESCRIPTION (15–29)	4–18

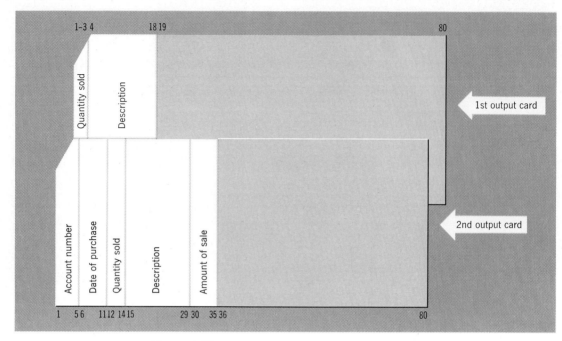

Figure 4.19
The Two Output Card Formats for Example 4

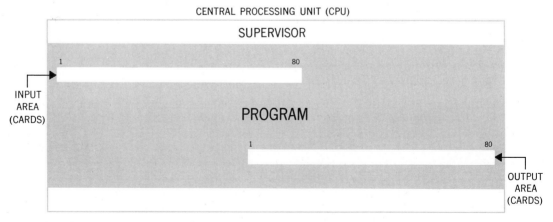

Figure 4.20
Input and Output Areas in the CPU for Example 4

Fundamental Concepts of Data Processing

At this point, the status of the CPU is as shown in Figure 4.21.

---

4. PUNCH a card with the information that is in the output punch area.

5. MOVE positions 1 to 35 from the card read to positions 1 to 35 in the output punch area.

6. PUNCH an output card with the information in the output area, creating a duplicate card, in this case.

7. Repeat steps 1 to 6 until all input cards have been processed, and then STOP.

Note that we wish to punch two output cards for every card that is read as input. Thus we have one READ command for every two PUNCH commands. Notice also that it is necessary to repeat step 1 (clearing the output area) after each set of cards is punched.

After the computer punches the *first* card of the set in step No. 4, it is instructed in step No. 5 to move positions 1 to 35 into the output area, thus obviating the need to clear the output area. This is the case since positions 1 to 18 in the output area, which previously contained QUANTITY SOLD and DESCRIPTION, have now been replaced with position 1 to 18 from the input card.

Thus when an output area will be *completely* overlayed with new information, it is not necessary to clear out old information.

After the computer punches out a duplicate card in step No. 6,

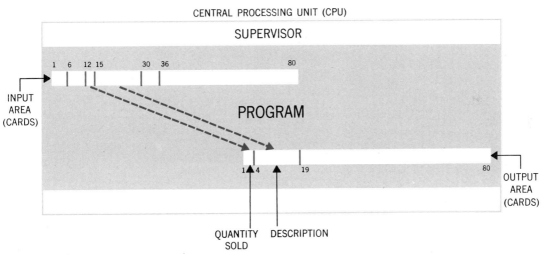

Figure 4.21
Data Transfer Operation for Example 4

however, the output area must be cleared. Now, when the next card is read, and the fields QUANTITY SOLD and DESCRIPTION are moved in step No. 3 to the output area, this is the only information that will be in the output area. That is, we will not have extraneous information remaining from the previous card that was duplicated.

With the examples presented above, we have attempted to show the business and data processing students that the basic concepts of a computer system are rather simple to understand. With an understanding of the above, one can begin to conceptualize the manner in which a computer processes data.

Similarly, with an appreciation of these concepts the business and data processing students can now proceed through the remainder of the text conceptualizing, with more insight, what is required for the computerization of business systems.

II. An Overview of Computer Elements

Thus far, we have seen how a computer basically processes data. Input and output units are linked by cables to a Central Processing Unit. The integrated activity of these devices compose a computer system.

You will note that there are numerous commercial computer systems in use today. Among the major manufacturers of average or medium-sized computers are IBM, Honeywell, Control Data, Burroughs, NCR, and Univac, each one of which makes many systems designed to fit the needs of any business organization.

In addition, there are hundreds of data processing companies that manufacture hardware devices designed to meet specific business needs and that are compatible or ''usable'' with these major computer systems. In this section, we shall discuss the various elements that distinguish one computer system from another. The businessman with knowledge of these elements can participate in the selection of new computer equipment for his company or in the evaluation of current computer systems. Data processing personnel are required to be familiar with new developments in equipment. You will recall that it is the businessman (or the manager or the top-level executive) in conjunction with the computer specialist who shares the responsibility for organizing an efficient and appropriate data processing installation. Thus these business leaders must be properly informed of the various elements that are used to distinguish one computer system from another.

A. MEMORY SIZE

You will recall that a computer system can have varying memory sizes. The medium-sized business computer has a storage capacity ranging from 32K to 128K, but large-scale computers can have a memory size

Fundamental Concepts of Data Processing

in excess of one million characters. In general, most computer systems can be acquired with memory sizes that are designed to fit the customer's needs.

B. SPEED

Early computers were measured in speeds of *milliseconds* or thousandths of a second. Second-generation computers were measured in speeds of *microseconds* or millionths of a second. Third-generation computers are measured in speeds of *nanoseconds*, or billionths of a second. Thus, we can see that each new generation of computers is designed with greatly increased speeds. Present computers perform each operation in billionths of a second, or faster. Yet a large volume input/output job, such as the processing of millions of records, where hundreds of operations are needed for each, can require several computer hours. Thus the faster computers, even though they cost more, may result in a savings, since they result in decreased processing time.

C. COST

The cost of computer operations is a determining factor in evaluating *any* computer system. Large-scale computers obviously cost much more than small-scale ones. Yet a user may require specific operations that can only be performed on large-scale computers. Thus cost, although an important factor, cannot be the primary one in selecting a computer system.

D. SOFTWARE DEVELOPMENT

Software is the term used to describe the programming support supplied by the manufacturer that is designed to maximize computer efficiency. Honeywell, as an example, has various prepackaged programs that are available with Honeywell Computer Systems. These software packages are different from those available with NCR equipment, for example. The software support available with each computer system must be evaluated before a valid selection can be made. (Chapter 14 discusses SOFTWARE in more depth.)

E. COMPATIBILITY

If programs and software prepared for one computer can be utilized, without rigorous conversion, by another computer, then the two machines are compatible. Third-generation computers have been designed with this facility. The IBM S/360 line, for example, consists of many models of computers; yet the 360 line is said to have upward compatibility. That is, a company that acquires an IBM S/360 model 30 can "trade it in" for a more sophisticated model, such as the S/360 model 50, and still maintain the same programs that were run on the model 30. This is a recent development. To acquire a more sophisticated computer in the past meant a huge reprogramming effort. The computer specialist and businessman should ascertain that the computer system acquired by their company has compatibility with other makes and models.

F. HARDWARE DEVELOPMENT

Hardware, you will recall, is the term used to designate the devices associated with a particular computer system. Each business organization will have specific needs that can be met by utilizing the appropriate hardware with a computer system. One business, for example, may find that a device called an *optical scanner,* which can read printed documents and convert data directly into machine-readable codes, is best suited for its needs. Although costly, this device may save the company money, since keypunching of data is thereby eliminated.

Each computer system can be linked to specific hardware. That is, a device manufactured by Bunker-Ramo, for example, may be compatible with an IBM computer system. Thus, the businessman must be cognizant of the various hardware available within the data processing environment and those that are compatible with his system. The next two chapters discuss, in depth, various types of hardware that may be used in conjunction with a computer system.

G. TYPE OF PROCESSING

Computer systems are designed to handle data and produce information in different ways, depending on hardware and software limitations. The following represents methods that may be used to process data.

Batch Processing

Data is entered into the information flow in large volumes, or batches. That is, the processing by computer is performed in some time interval (weekly, monthly, etc.) when large volumes are accumulated. Daily Accounts Receivable tickets, for example, may be *batch processed.* Instead of processing the tickets as they are received, they are processed weekly, when a sufficient volume has been accumulated.

There are several inherent disadvantages to batch processing. The system that utilizes batch processing is not very timely, since it takes a fixed time interval before current information is added. That is, the main or master Accounts Receivable File, in our example, does not contain the current Accounts Receivable data for a full week. For this reason, a system that utilizes batch processing cannot effectively answer inquiries *between* processing intervals. The Accounts Receivable File in our example is only current on the day of the processing cycle; after

Fundamental Concepts of Data Processing

that, current information will not be processed until the following
week's run.

Online Processing
Data is entered into the information flow immediately, without waiting
for a fixed time interval. Similarly, inquiries may be answered by the
computer system in relatively short intervals,

A bank, for example, may utilize online processing to maintain a
transaction file. Each time a customer makes a deposit or withdrawal, it
is entered into the computer flow, via an online device called a
terminal.

Online processing will be discussed in depth in Chapter 6.

Real-Time Processing
Real-time processing utilizes online operations in an environment that
is so responsive that it produces output quickly enough to affect
decision making or to serve customer's needs.

The bank, in our previous example, which utilizes online processing
and which operates on the deposits and withdrawals quickly enough to
give the customer a current status of his account, at any given time, is
said to function in a real-time environment. Chapter 6 also discusses
this in depth.

Offline Processing
Computer processing is, without question, expensive. Thus, any
operation that can avoid direct utilization of computer equipment can
save a company much money. Offline processing is the processing of
information that is *not* directly under the control of the CPU.

A card-to-print offline hardware device, for example, is one that can
take data from a card and print it according to a specified format,
without the use of a central processing unit of a computer. There are
numerous offline devices that are compatible with most computer
systems. These are discussed in Chapter 5.

Thus the businessman can see that the type of processing utilized
can directly affect the efficiency of a computer system. Each of the
above processing techniques will be discussed, in depth, in the next
two chapters.

H. CATEGORIES OF COMPUTERS

We have thus far discussed computer systems, in general. The reader
is now aware that computer systems can consist of many diversified
devices and complex CPUs. The extent of diversification in I/O devices
will be realized in the next chapter. We have also seen that computer
systems vary broadly in capability and cost. Figure 5.23 gives a
broad cost and specification breakdown of most medium- and
large-scale computer systems. Let us now discuss the various classes
of computers.

1. Mini-Computers

These are relatively new computers (1968) that are designed to handle simple data-processing functions. While medium- and large-scale computers are used to process the information flow of relatively complex systems that are then broken down into smaller aspects, mini-computers are capable of performing these independent tasks and do not lend themselves to integrated networks of systems.

Mini-computers are manufactured by Digital Equipment Co., which has a major share of the market, Varian Data Machines, and Wang Laboratories, just to name some of the larger manufacturers. These machines are generally small and often fit on a desk top. Some are punched-card systems capable of reading and/or producing punched

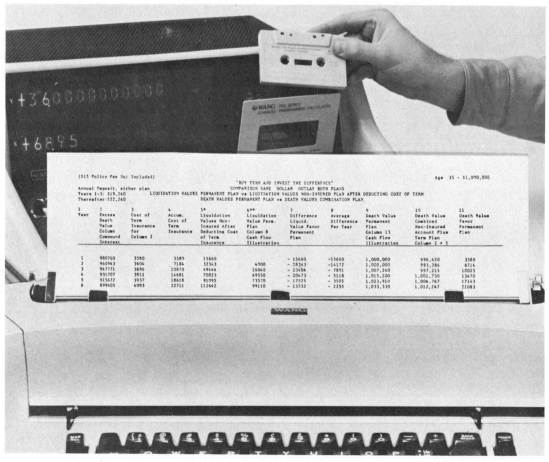

Figure 4.22
Example of a mini-computer. Courtesy Wang Laboratories, Inc.

Fundamental Concepts of Data Processing

cards. Most mini-computers have the ability to print data. Some just contain a keyboard, for input entries, where data is keyed in by an operator or programmer. Others can contain far more sophisticated input/output forms, but these are more costly. They are designed to be stand-alone computers, which means that they operate independently, or they can be part of a vast network or system. Many mini-computers, for example, at different locations can amass data, edit and verify it, perform simple calculations and then transmit it to a large-scale computer for manipulation of all the elements. Mini-computers are capable of handling typical I/O forms such as those used with much larger machines. There are, however, limitations in core capacity, speed, and functions that can be performed. They have the major advantage of being relatively inexpensive—selling for between $10,000 to $20,000.

Figure 4.22 illustrates a mini-computer manufactured by Wang Laboratories, Inc. This is a device to be used by insurance agents that will enable them to develop a personalized statement for each client, quickly and accurately, that explains financial benefits.

This mini-computer consists of an electronic calculator and an output writer. It comes equipped with preprogrammed tape cassettes, on which the manufacturer-supplied programs are written.

Utilizing the system, an agent can custom design each client's exact insurance needs. Increased insurance sales result from this system, indirectly, because clients are impressed by an agent who can design an insurance investment portfolio on his own computer.

Cost of the system is under $10,000. With the use of this mini-computer, agents need not submit requests for the preparation of such personalized benefit statements for each client, which would then require massive clerical assistance and/or use of a large-scale computer.

Figure 4.23 illustrates a typical mini-computer manufactured by Varian Data Machines, Inc. Such a computer is used in online and real-time systems for the following applications.

a. Baggage-handling systems, by maintaining data on the destination of as many as 12,000 suitcases per hour in order to make sure that passengers and their luggage depart on the same flight.
b. Teaching-machine systems, by providing computer-aided instruction *and* pupil profiles for teachers.
c. Tracking systems, by supplying real-time display of information relative to airplane flights.

These systems are utilizing a relatively inexpensive mini-computer to perform operations that were heretofore performed by large-scale expensive computer systems. These are but a few of the newer systems currently employing mini-computers. In short, this relatively new advance of mini-computers will undoubtedly become a very important and substantial element in the succeeding years.

Figure 4.23
Varian 620/i mini-computer. Courtesy Varian Data Machines, Inc.

Fundamental Concepts of Data Processing

2. Small-Scale Computers

These include computers designed to perform unit-record functions in far less time and with greater accuracy than EAM equipment. IBM system 360/20, the IBM System/3, (Figure 4.24) NCR 50 and 100, Univac 9400, as examples, fall into this category. They utilize predominantly punched-card input and, although they have the capability of producing high-level output, they are basically used to produce printed output. The IBM System/3 uses a new 96-column card designed with 20% more capacity than the 80-column card. The disadvantage of this card used in conjunction with the System/3 is that it cannot be used with other data-processing equipment. Thus a company that rents such equipment and uses this card cannot use it with EAM devices or other computers that employ the standard 80-column card.

Figure 4.24
IBM System/3. Courtesy IBM.

3. Medium-Scale Computers

The medium-scale computers are the more widely used and more capable machines. These include the IBM S/360 models 30 and 40, Burroughs 3500, 4500, and 5500 series, Xerox Sigma 5, and so on. These devices are most often employed at typical business organizations throughout the country. Their average rental is approximately $5,000 to $20,000 per month and they are capable of high speed and complex operations. They can also use the high-level I/O devices indicated in the next chapters. They do, however, require some operator intervention, even though they utilize supervisors to handle many typical control procedures.

4. Large-Scale Computers

These are the really high-level machines that have storage capacities in the million-byte range and rent for about $100,000 per month. These usually contain full control systems with minimal operator intervention. They are capable of linking up with dozens of high-level I/O devices and performing operations at phenomenal rates. Such large-scale computers include the IBM S/360 models 85, 95, 195, the new IBM S/370 (Figure 4.1), Burroughs 700, and others.

A word, now, is necessary about the IBM S/360 series. You will note that model numbers range from model 20 to model 195, where higher model numbers mean greater capability and greater cost. Most options on these machines have *upward compatibility,* which means that whatever can be performed on a lower model machine can also be performed on a higher model. That is, any programs that are designed for the IBM S/360 model 30 can also be used on the 40 and all higher models. With this facility, IBM hopes to enable its users to acquire higher level computers (higher models) without requiring a complex conversion process.

You will note that mini-computers or even medium-sized computers often work in conjunction with large-scale computers to alleviate the load of the latter. A Varian 620/i mini-computer, for example, is used in conjunction with an IBM 360/95 to provide world-wide weather information. The job of the Varian unit is to *edit* the stream of data being transmitted via satellite. Rather than expend unnecessary time of the big IBM computer, the data is fed into the Varian, which produces a magnetic tape containing only significant data. For a discussion of the diversified and rather interesting applications of computers see the workbook.

Most business organizations use medium-sized commercial computers to perform daily processing. Our discussions of programming languages and devices will assume that the typical user employs this type of machine.

Fundamental Concepts of Data Processing

SELF-EVALUATING QUIZ

1. A computer is generally faster, more economical, and more reliable than manual techniques for _____ type operations.
2. The objective of computers is to convert _____ into _____ by _____ on it.
3. A program is a _____ .
4. A computer system consists of a _____ , and one or more _____ devices.
5. A(n) _____ is the actual machine that reads data.
6. A(n) _____ is the actual machine that produces data.
7. CPU is an abbreviation for _____ _____ .
8. The 5 categories of operations that the CPU can perform consist of _____ , _____ , _____ , _____ , and _____ .
9. Fill in the basic elements of a computer system:

10. The _____ unit of the CPU contains the entire program.
11. Storage is composed of _____ .
12. The memory size of a given computer is _____ .
13. The abbreviation for a thousand storage positions is _____ .
14. The supervisor is the _____ .
15. The _____ unit of the CPU is where the instructions of a program are executed, one at a time.
16. Calculations and decisions for each specific program are performed in the _____ unit.
17. Before moving information to an output area, we should generally _____ that area to insure that _____ .
18. (T or F) A STOP instruction causes the computer to come to a full stop.
19. (T or F) A program must provide for both an input and an output area.
20. (T or F) A READ command overlays previous information in the input area with a new record's information.

Consider the following requirement for questions 21 to 23:

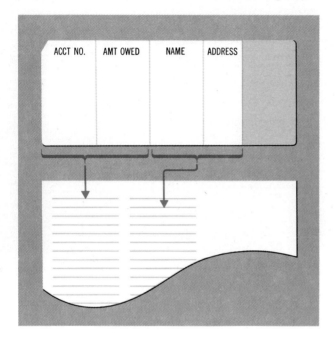

21. For _____(no.)_____ READ command(s), we will have _____(no.)_____ WRITE command(s).
22. After a card is read, we must _____ the data to the _____ area.
23. The basic instruction format is as follows:
24. (T or F) Mini-computers are small devices, often desk size, which operate in a manner similar to calculators and which often cost under $10,000.
25. The term compatibility means _____ .
26. (T or F) The core storage capacity of large-scale computers is approximately 10,000 characters.
27. (T or F) Small-scale computers were developed essentially to take over unit-record functions.
28. The card used by the new IBM System/3 is ____(no.)____ columns.

SOLUTIONS

1. repetitive
2. input data; output data; operating
3. set of instructions that will convert input data to output.
4. Central Processing Unit; input/output
5. input device
6. output device
7. Central Processing Unit

8. input; data transfer; arithmetic; logic; output
9. (a) Input
   (b) Storage
   (c) Control
   (d) Arithmetic-Logic
   (e) Output
10. storage
11. addressable locations
12. the storage capacity or number of addressable locations
13. K
14. control program supplied by the computer manufacturer that monitors or controls the activities of the computer system.
15. control
16. arithmetic-logic
17. clear; data is not remaining from previous programs
18. F
19. T
20. T
21. one; two
22. move; output
23. READ; MOVE; MOVE; WRITE; MOVE; MOVE; WRITE; REPEAT
24. T
25. the ability of a computer to operate effectively on programs designed for another computer system.
26. F
27. T
28. 96

Chapter 5 *Input/Output Devices*

As we have seen, computer systems consist of the following.

1. A series of input devices that accept data and transmit it to the CPU.
2. A Central Processing Unit (CPU) that processes incoming data by performing arithmetic operations, logic functions, and by otherwise manipulating data to produce output.
3. A series of output devices that transmit resultant data from the CPU to an output medium, by converting it from the computer code to an acceptable output format.

A very simplified computer system could function with a Card Reader, a Central Processing Unit, and a Printer. That is, the system utilizes card input only and produces printed reports as the sole form of output. Most computer centers, however, require more diversified equipment to handle files of data for a varied list of business applications.

Each device can handle a *form* of computer input or output. Some devices are input/output machines that can function by reading a specific form or by writing output using the same form. A Card Read/Punch, for example can read card input and produce card output.

Each input or output device is linked to the Central Processing Unit by cables which operate by electronic transmission.

The medium on which data is recorded (such as cards and printed reports) is determined by computer specialists, usually the systems analysts, and is a direct function of each business application. The media used must be compatible with the equipment or computer devices available at the installation. That is, cards are a feasible medium only if the company has acquired, or plans to acquire, a Card Reader.

The businessman and the computer specialist must work together to decide on file types for input and output that will best suit the department's needs without being excessively costly for the company. As was previously mentioned, the businessman must take part in preparing a meaningful output report, for example. In addition, however, he may help to determine whether the source documents should be converted to punched cards or magnetic tape in an effort to produce the output as efficiently as possible. He must also be aware of the advantages and the limitations of the file type and its respective hardware devices so that he can be cognizant of reasonable expectations and costs for the automated procedure.

The file types selected for each application, and thus the computer devices or *hardware* utilized, will be discussed with respect to the following elements.

1. Speed
Some devices are much slower than others, thereby causing increased processing time and longer delay time.

2. Cost
Slower, more cumbersome devices can process data at a more reasonable cost than high-speed, specialized equipment.

3. Volume
Note that the *volume* of data to be processed for a given application will directly relate to both speed and cost. Specific file types handle large volumes of data more efficiently than others. Thus, the number of input and output records within the corresponding files will be a decisive factor in determining file type. High volume files require devices that:

1. process data very quickly;
2. store data in a neat, compact form; and
3. process data cheaply.

4. Frequency of Processing
Files that are accessed or processed daily, for example, will require different consideration than those that are processed monthly. Frequent handling necessitates files that are very durable and that are processed quickly and cheaply.

5. Nature of Source Document

Sometimes the form of the source document predetermines the input file type. A utility company bill (for example, gas bill) that is really a punched card, and a punched paper tape registering cash receipts are examples of source documents already in machine-readable form. To convert to another input form, even one that is more suitable, might be too costly. Similarly, if the source document is a printed report that must be entered into the computer flow in voluminous quantity, it might be cheaper in the end to use a device that can read printed reports, such as an optical scanner, even though this device is costly.

6. Record Size

As we have indicated, most card records are restricted to 80 characters or multiples of 80 characters, when more than one card record is used. Most other file types, as we will see, do not have this limitation. Thus, while cards, for example, are cheap, they may not be suitable for applications that have relatively large record sizes.

7. Type of Processing

Records can be processed *sequentially,* one at a time in sequence, or *randomly,* in no specific sequence. Some devices are equipped to process records randomly while others can only process them in sequence. When files must be processed sequentially, they must be *sorted* prior to entering the data flow.

Similarly, some files may be *batch processed,* or used in a computer run in periodic intervals, a group or batch at a time. Other files require immediate or *online*[1] computer processing because on-the-spot changes are crucial to the system. The type of processing will affect the file type and device selected for a specific application.

8. Equipment Available at the Installation

Usually, computer specialists will attempt to satisfy a businessman's needs with the hardware or computer devices currently available at the center. To order new equipment because of a specific application is not a usual procedure unless the device can be justified from a cost standpoint. That is, if a very costly procedure is computerized and a specific device, not on hand, is ideally suited to it, the acquisition of the equipment might result in an eventual savings to the company. If not, the computer specialist will utilize the equipment on hand.

9. Accuracy of Records

Some devices read or write with more reliability than others. Where large numbers of records are processed and errors occur infrequently and are easily correctable, the more reliable devices may not be required.

Let us consider the file types and corresponding devices that are available for computer processing. Each will be considered with regard

---

[1] *To be discussed in more depth in Chapter 6.*

to the nine elements above. Such devices will be discussed as they relate to medium-sized computers. We will segment our discussion into:

    I. The most frequently used devices.

    II. Specialized equipment.

I. The Most Frequently Used Devices

A. CARD READ/PUNCH (Figure 5.1a)

We have already discussed the punched card as a file medium in Chapter 3.

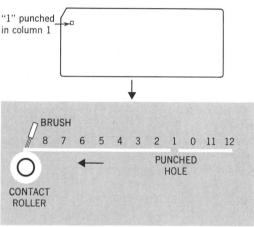

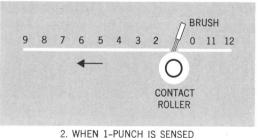

(a)

(b)

Figure 5.1
(a) Card Read/Punch. (Courtesy IBM.)

(b) How punched holes are mechanically sensed.

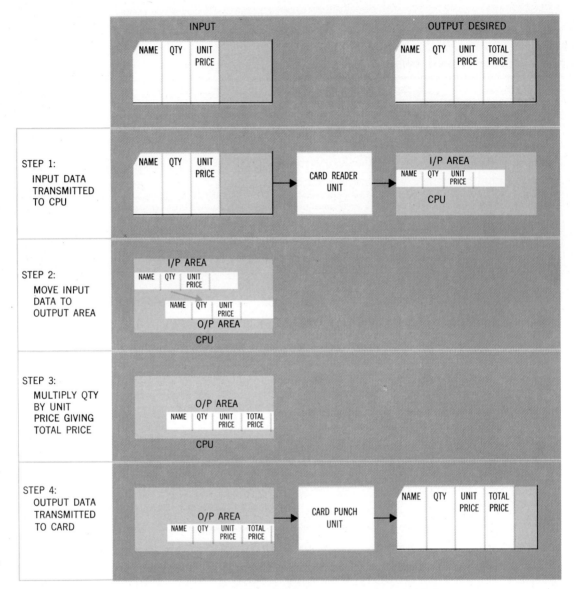

Figure 5.2
Illustration of card processing.

The Card Read/Punch is a single device that houses two separate units: a Card Reader and a Card Punch. The Card Reader section reads input punched card data by mechanically sensing the holes and transmitting the data to the Central Processing Unit. See Figure 5.1*b*.

Fundamental Concepts of Data Processing

The Card Punch section punches output cards from data that has been transmitted to it by the CPU. The Card Punch converts the computer's character codes to the appropriate Hollerith code.

Note that some manufacturers market *independent* Card Reader devices and Card Punch devices. The Card Read/Punch device is, however, more common. Keep in mind that it houses two *separate* units. Thus an input card read by the Card Reader cannot generally be punched with additional information by the Card Punch, although there are some Card Read/Punch machines with this capability. Figure 5.2 shows what is required for the typical Card Read/Punch. Note that the TOTAL PRICE cannot be computed and then added to the input card. A new output card must be created to contain the resultant field.

Step 1 requires the Card Reader section of the Card Read/Punch to read data and transmit it to the CPU. Step 4 requires the Card Punch section of the Card Read/Punch to transmit data from the output area of the CPU to a *new* output card.

Cards can be *read* at an average rate of 800 to 1200 cards per minute. Output Cards are punched at a much slower rate, approximately 300 to 600 cards per minute.

Note that computer-produced output cards do not usually contain the imprinting of the data on the face of the card. Keypunching of

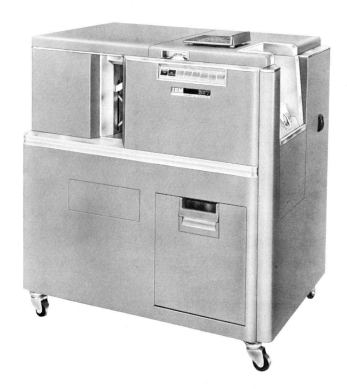

Figure 5.3
Interpreter. Courtesy IBM.

cards generally produces such printing, but computer-produced output cards do not. Although Card Read/Punch devices can be equipped with special print features, such features are very costly and rarely acquired. Where the printing of the data that is punched into a card is required on the face of a card, an EAM machine called an Interpreter (Figure 5.3) may be used.

Data, then, can be recorded onto a punched card by:

1. a Card Punch of a computer system; or,
2. a Keypunch Machine, requiring manual operation.

The basic advantages of card processing are:

1. low cost,
2. manual readability as well as computer readability, where the data is imprinted on the face of the card.

The disadvantages of cards are:

Figure 5.4
Line printer. Courtesy Honeywell.

Fundamental Concepts of Data Processing

1. low durability: cards bend, warp, rip, and so on,

2. Card Read/Punch devices are *mechanical* and thus are subject to frequent jams,

3. difficulty in storing large numbers of cards conveniently.

B. LINE PRINTER (Figure 5.4)

The line printer is a computer output device that converts data transmitted from the CPU into a printed report. Most line printers for medium-sized computers can print data at the approximate rate of 600 to 1500 lines per minute, while high-speed printers for large-scale computers can print at the rate of 3000 lines per minute. Each line can typically contain a maximum of 100 or 132 characters, including the blank spaces left for readability.

The printed report, as an output medium has already been discussed in depth in Chapter 3.

C. MAGNETIC TAPE DRIVE (Figure 5.5)

A magnetic tape is a *high-speed* medium that can serve as input to, or output from, a computer. It is the most common file type for medium- or large-scale processing.

A magnetic tape drive is the device that can either read a tape or write onto a tape. It has a READ/WRITE HEAD that is accessed by the computer for either reading or writing.

Magnetic tape drives function like home tape recorders. Data can be recorded, or written, onto a tape and ''played back,'' or read, from the same tape at a later date. If data is written on a tape, previous data in that area is written over or destroyed. For this reason, computer centers must take precautions to protect important tapes that should not inadvertently be ''written over.''

A typical magnetic tape is generally 2400 to 3600 feet long and $\frac{1}{2}$ inch wide. The tape is made of plastic with an iron oxide coating that can be magnetized to represent data. Since the magnetized spots or *bits* are extremely small and not visible to the human eye, large volumes of data can be condensed into a relatively small area of tape. Information from an entire 80-column card, for example, can typically be stored in one tenth of an inch of magnetic tape, or less. The average tape, which costs approximately $25, can store approximately 20 million characters.[2] After a tape file has been processed and is no longer needed, the same tape may be reused repeatedly to store other information.

Because tape drives read data *electronically* by sensing magnetized areas, and write data electronically by magnetizing areas, tapes may

---

[2] *The more technical aspects of magnetic tape are presented in the Appendix to this chapter.*

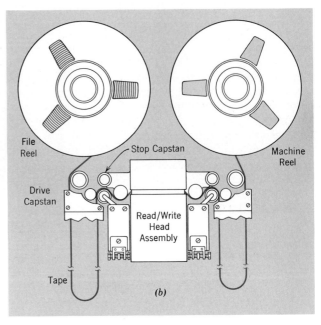

(b)

Figure 5.5
(a) Magnetic tape drive. Courtesy Burroughs Corp. (b) Read/write head for tape. Courtesy IBM.

be processed at very high speeds. Data can be read or written at speeds of from 100,000 to 300,000 characters *per second*.

Thus tape files are frequently used for large volumes of data. One tape can store hundreds of thousands of records, transmit and receive data at very high speeds, and store the data in a compact form. In many medium- or large-scale companies, *master files* for Payroll, Accounts Receivable, Accounts Payable, Inventory, and so on are stored on tape. A master file is the main data file that holds all current information for a specific department or system.

A record on a tape may be any size, as long as it is physically consistent with the size of core storage. That is, it is not feasible to create 5000 position records using a 4000 position computer, since the output area (5000 positions) must be located in storage. Aside from this limitation, tape records may usually be any size. Keep in mind, however, that extremely large records sizes are more difficult to process.

Fundamental Concepts of Data Processing

Because of a tape's capacity to handle large volumes of data in a relatively short time, it is ideally suited for *batch processing,* or processing in cumulative groups.

The tape files may be created by:

1. A tape drive of a computer system: In such a case, the tape serves as output, when it is the product of a computer run. The data is initially entered from some other device, such as a Card Reader, and then converted, by the computer, to magnetic tape.
2. A key-to-tape encoder or converter (Figure 5.6): This device is similar to a keypunch machine. It requires an operator to code data from a source document to a magnetic tape via a typewriter-like keyboard. The operator depresses a specific character key and the device converts it to the appropriate magnetized coding. Tapes encoded in this manner may be verified by the same device to insure their accuracy. We shall see in the next chapter, that key-to-tape encoders are also used for creating tape cassettes, ''mini''-tapes, or cartridges for eventual use in a data communications environment.

The key-to-tape equipment in use today can be divided into two basic categories:

1. Stand-alone encoders, which, as indicated above, are used to convert source documents to a magnetic tape.
2. Key-to-tape preparation systems, which include a small computer with a core capacity of 8K (8000) to 16K, a tape drive, and from 6 to 64 key entry stations. With the use of this processor, data keyed in by an operator may be formatted, verified, edited, and then placed on a tape for use by the standard computer at the installation.

In short, tape is a very common file medium for high-speed, voluminous processing. It does, however, have several inherent disadvantages, as discussed below.

Data recorded on a tape may only be processed *sequentially.* That is, to access a record with TRANSACTION NUMBER 254 from a tape file that is maintained in TRANSACTION NUMBER sequence, we must read past the first 253 records. We instruct the computer to read a record; test if it contains TRANSACTION NUMBER 254; and, if it does not, to read the next record. Thus, 254 records are read. There is no convenient method to instruct the tape drive to skip the first few inches of tape or to go directly to the middle of the tape.

Thus, unless all or most records from a tape file are required for processing *most of the time,* this method could become inefficient and costly.

If an INVENTORY FILE is created on tape with 100,000 records and only a handful of these are required to print a report, then tapes may

Figure 5.6
Keytape encoder. Simple keyboard—operating ease is one of the many advantages of Honeywell's Keytape devices. The units bypass conventional punched card preparation by transcribing information directly onto magnetic tape from the keyboard. Typing and control functions are similar to those on a keypunch machine, easing the task of keypunch operators in learning to use the devices. Courtesy Honeywell.

not provide the best file type. Processing time and, thus cost, would be excessive, since most of the file must be read even to process only a small number of records. Sequential processing is beneficial only when *most* records on the file are required for normal processing in sequence. Again, Master Payroll, Accounts Receivable and Accounts Payable files are ideally suited to magnetic tape, since most records are required for processing during normal runs. We must read an entire Payroll file, for example, to print checks; thus, a tape file is suitable.

Another disadvantage of tape processing is that a given tape can usually be used *either* as input or output during a single run, but cannot serve as both an input/output medium. That is, an *updating* application, or the process of making a master file of data current, generally requires the master file as input and the creation of a *new* physical tape. Consider the update illustration in Figure 5.7.

A new tape must be created that, in effect, rewrites the information from the previous master tape and adds the current month's changes. The input master tape cannot be conveniently processed to add new records, delete some records, and make changes to existing records. A *new tape* must be created which incorporates master information along with the current changes.

This inability of the tape to be conveniently processed as *both* input and output during a single computer run results in several limitations.

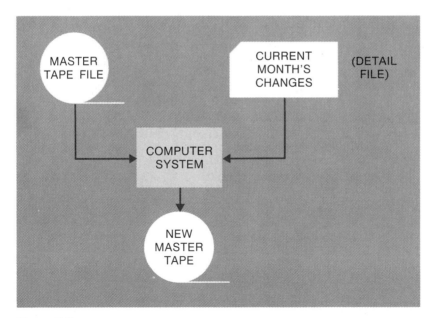

Figure 5.7
Illustration of an update procedure.

Since two tapes are required for such runs, *two* tape drives are necessary to process them. The necessity of having to read many master records, that have *not* changed during the present month, and to recreate them without alteration on an output tape drive, results in increased processing time. That is, if only 30 payroll changes, for example, are needed to amend a 1000 record Master Tape, then 970 master records that do not require revisions must be read and rewritten onto the new tape. Keep in mind that although this inability results in increased processing time, the increased time is not usually excessive, since tape records are written very quickly. We would require tapes with hundreds of thousands of inactive records in order to substantially affect the processing time.

A third disadvantage of tape processing is the identification problem. Most medium- and large-scale computer installations have hundreds or even thousands of magnetic tapes, each utilized for a specific application. Because data recorded on these tapes are not "readable" or visible to the naked eye, it is often difficult to maintain identification of them. If a Master Accounts Receivable Tape is inadvertently "written over," or used as *output* for some other job, for example, the result could be an expensive recreation process, since the writing of output would destroy the existing information. Several steps have been implemented at most installations to prevent such occurrences, or to reduce the extent of damage, should they occur:

1. Tape Labels

External gummed labels are placed on the face of each tape (See Figure 5.8), identifying it and indicating its *retention cycle,* or how long it should be maintained. These labels are clearly visible to anyone, so that chances for inadvertent misuse of a valuable tape are reduced. The problem with gummed labels, however, is that they sometimes become unglued. Their effectiveness is also directly related to the effort and training of the computer staff. If operators are negligent, then they will not be used properly.

To make the identification of tapes more reliable, most programs include a built-in routine which, for output tapes, creates a *tape label record* that is produced as any other tape record, with magnetized bits. The label is the first record on the tape. When the tape is used as input, at some later date, then this first label record, called a *HEADER LABEL,* is checked as part of the program, to ascertain that the correct tape is being used.

Thus header labels are created on output tapes and checked on input tapes. This label creation for output and label checking for input is a standard procedure in most programs. Since it uses the computer to verify that the correct tapes are being used, there is less danger of manual inefficiency.

2. Tape Librarian

Most medium- and large-scale companies have numerous tapes that must be filed or stored, handled properly, and released for reuse when

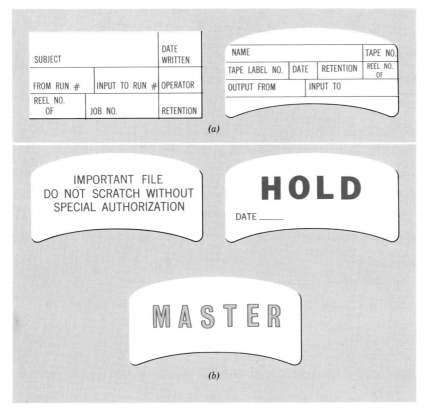

SUBJECT			DATE WRITTEN
FROM RUN #	INPUT TO RUN #	OPERATOR	
REEL NO. OF	JOB NO.		RETENTION

NAME			TAPE NO.
TAPE LABEL NO.	DATE	RETENTION	REEL NO. OF
OUTPUT FROM		INPUT TO	

(a)

IMPORTANT FILE
DO NOT SCRATCH WITHOUT
SPECIAL AUTHORIZATION

HOLD

DATE ____

MASTER

(b)

Figure 5.8
External tape labels: (a) Two commonly used external labels. (b) Three
commonly used special-purpose tape labels.

no longer required. Such companies employ a tape librarian to
maintain the proper usage of tape files. If he or she performs the job
properly, there will be less misuse or misplacing of tapes.

3. File Protection Ring (Figure 5.9)

Those available tapes that may be written on, or used as output, have a
file protection ring inserted in the back. The tape drive is electronically
sensitized so that it will *not* create an output record unless this ring is
in its proper place. For those tapes that are to be maintained and not
"written over" the ring has been removed. Thus if an operator
inadvertently uses such a tape for an output operation, the computer
prints a message that tells him, in effect "NO RING—NO WRITE." If the
operator is cautious, he will examine the external label and, hopefully,
he will realize that he is using the wrong tape. If he is persistent he will
merely place a ring on the tape (any file protection ring fits all tapes)

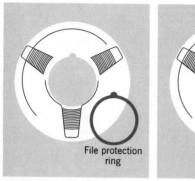

File protection
ring

File protection
ring in place

Figure 5.9
The file protection ring is a plastic ring that fits into the
groove in the tape reel. When the ring is in place, both
writing and reading of tape records can occur. When the
ring is removed, only reading can occur. In this way, the
file is protected from accidental erasure.

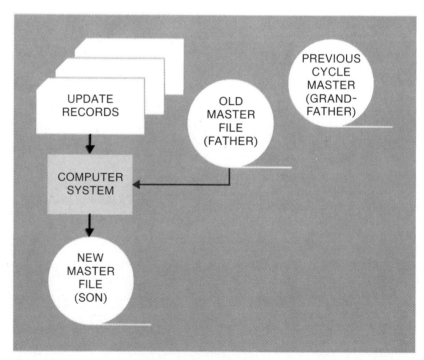

UPDATE
RECORDS

OLD
MASTER
FILE
(FATHER)

PREVIOUS
CYCLE
MASTER
(GRAND-
FATHER)

COMPUTER
SYSTEM

NEW
MASTER
FILE
(SON)

Figure 5.10
Grandfather-father-son method of file backup.

Fundamental Concepts of Data Processing

and restart the job. Thus this method, alone, deters the misuse of tapes but does not totally alleviate the problem.

4. Back-up Tapes

Since tapes can sometimes be written over or even become physically damaged, it is necessary to maintain backup tapes so that the recreation process, should it become necessary, does not become enormously costly and cumbersome.

Suppose the update procedure shown in Figure 5.7 is performed each month. After processing, it is best to store the old master tape and the detail records *along with* the new master tape. In this way, if some mishap should befall the new master tape, it is a simple task to recreate it from the two forms of input. Normally, we maintain *two* previous tapes as backup, in addition to the present one, in order to prevent any serious problem. Hence, the three *generations* of tapes maintained for important files are called the *grandfather-father-son* tapes. (See Figure 5.10.)

D. MAGNETIC DISK DRIVE (Figure 5.11a)

The magnetic disk is another high-speed medium that can serve as either input to, or output from a computer system. Like tape, it has an iron oxide coating that is used to store millions of characters of data,

(a)

(b)

Figure 5.11
(a) Disk drive. (b) Disk pack. Courtesy Burroughs.

typically 6 to 10 million, but not usually as many as a standard tape. The magnetic disk drive is used to record information onto the disk and to read information from it.

Figure 5.11*b* illustrates a typical disk pack. The pack resembles a series of concentric disks similar to phonograph records that rotate on a vertical shaft.

Each surface of the disk consists of numbered concentric tracks. Each track is used to store information. A READ-WRITE HEAD is used to read information from, and record information onto, any of the tracks.[3]

Disk processing has many of the same advantages as tape processing. It can store large numbers of records in a condensed area. The disk drive, like the tape drive, reads and records information electronically and thus is a high-speed device. Records on a disk can essentially be any length. They are not fixed, as is the case with 80-column cards, for example.

Disk processing, however, has some additional features that are not available with tape processing. A disk may be used for either *random or sequential* processing.

In addition to handling records in sequence, a disk has the facility to access records in some order other than the one in which they were originally recorded. The processing of records on disk is similar to the accessing of phonograph records from a juke box. By indicating that phonograph record 106 is required, for example, the mechanism is capable of accessing 106 *directly* without first reading records 1 to 105, as is required with tape processing.

The most common method for accessing magnetic disk records randomly is with the use of an *index*.[4] During the creation of records, the computer establishes an index on the disk itself. The index essentially indicates where each record is located. This is similar in concept to the index found at the end of a textbook, which indicates the page where each item of information can be located.

The disk index indicates the "address" or location of records that are stored on the disk. The address, in basic terms, refers to the surface number and track where a particular record can be found. A *key data field* in each record, as indicated by the programmer, is used by the computer as the basis for establishing address information in the index. As an example, if a Payroll file is stored on disk, a key field would probably be SOCIAL SECURITY NUMBER or EMPLOYEE NUMBER, if this is to be used as a means of identification.

To access any disk record, then, the user need only supply a particular key data field, such as EMPLOYEE NUMBER 17537. The

[3] *For a more thorough description of the physical characteristics of a disk, see the Appendix to this chapter.*

[4] *For the other method for accessing magnetic disk records, see the Appendix to this chapter.*

Fundamental Concepts of Data Processing

computer then "looks up" the corresponding disk address for this record from the index and seeks that record directly.

In addition, disks have the added advantage of permitting updates or changes to existing records *on the same disk*. In this way, a new disk need not be created to incorporate the current changes, as is required with tape processing. That is, the same disk may be used for *both* input and output. We can read a record from a disk and make changes to that record on the same disk; we can add records to the disk; we can delete records from the disk.

This type of processing is extremely advantageous for specific applications. Suppose, for example, a police department wishes to obtain information on three known criminals, immediately. Suppose, too, that the department maintains a 100,000 record criminal file. If the criminal file were on tape (a sequential medium) each tape record would be read, in sequence, until the appropriate ones were found.

To read 100,000 data records would require some time. If, however, the file were on a disk pack, then each of the three records could be accessed directly, in a much shorter time period. We merely supply the key data field, which may be MAN NUMBER or PRISON RECORD NUMBER. Where time is critical and random processing is frequently required, disks are far more suitable than tapes. For *online* processing, or immediate processing of data, a disk file is usually used, since individual detail records can be used to update the disk file quickly and easily.

Businesses find innumerable uses for random processing. Large Accounts Receivable Systems that may have master files with 50,000 customers may utilize a disk so that daily changes to a small number of these customer records can be performed quickly in an online environment, (or even in a batch-processing environment). The detail records, with the changes, need not be sorted. They can be used to look up the disk record, by providing the key field such as CUSTOMER NUMBER. Changes can then be made to existing accounts; new accounts can be added and accounts with no balance or no activity in recent months can be deleted. All this can be performed on a single master disk; no recreation is necessary.

Notice that this type of random processing is timesaving only if a relatively small number of records need be altered on a relatively large file. If most of the records have some activity, then it is just as efficient to sort the detail cards and use a magnetic tape for the master file in a batch-processing environment. In this way, the reading of the tape file will result in most of the records being processed. Thus excessive read commands for bypassing records would not be a factor. Note, however, that tape processing would require a *new* output tape for each run.

It should be noted that a sequential file can also be established on disk, *without* the index, similar to a tape file. In such a case, the disk is essentially being used as a high-speed tape. In addition, there are other methods of file organization besides the one described above, which utilizes an index. For a more thorough presentation, of these methods see the Appendix to this chapter.

In short, a disk is extremely advantageous for processing records randomly (or directly), as well as sequentially. Disks do, however, possess some inherent limitations: (a) The disk drives are relatively expensive devices compared to others, such as tape drives. (b) Because of the sophisticated procedures required to process disks, a relatively small number of disk drives can be used at a given installation. Although eight or ten tape drives may be available with medium-sized computers only two or four disk drives are usually permitted. (c) The identification of disk files, just as with tapes, often results in some problems. Since disk files, like tape files, cannot be visibly read, labels, both external (physically glued to the pack) or internal (programmed data labels) are required. (d) Tape update procedures usually result in a new master file that is created from the previous master file and a series of change records; the previous master can always be used as backup, should the new master be defective and a re-creation process deemed necessary. Since update procedures on a master disk file add to or delete from the one master, re-creation, if it becomes necessary, is very difficult.

Most disk files are created by computer output, although key-to-disk recorders are available. As of this writing, key-to-disk recorders or encoders have only recently been manufactured. They are first beginning to serve the needs of many businesses, which welcome this innovation. But because they are relatively new, they are extremely costly. Like key-to-tape encoders, there are two types of key-to-disk encoders: stand-alone and key-to-disk preparation systems. The latter type, with the use of a small processor, formats, edits, and verifies disk data in addition to recording it. The key-to-disk preparation system is far more prevalent in business today.

Because of the cost of these devices, most businesses still utilize other input media and then rerecord data onto a disk via a normal updating procedure. Master disk files, then, are usually converted from another input medium; they are still not created, generally, from a source document directly.

E. COMPARING CARDS, TAPE, AND DISK AS FILE TYPES

The businessman, along with the computer specialist, plays an integral role in determining the most efficient files to be used for his systems. Selecting an inefficient medium would be extremely costly in the end. Thus every attempt must be made to find the appropriate file types. Table 5.1 is a summary of the major characteristics of card, tape, and disk files. This table should serve as a review of the previous sections.

Let us use the following examples to illustrate how file types are selected.

Fundamental Concepts of Data Processing

Table 5.1

Characteristics of the Three Major File Types

File Type	Characteristics	Advantages	Disadvantages
Punched Card	80 columns; data recorded by keypunch machine or card punch of computer.	Utilized by electronic accounting machines to supplement computer use; relatively inexpensive in small volume jobs; can be maintained by operator because data is visual.	Warps easily; easily mishandled; very inefficient for large volume jobs because of relatively slow I/O capability.
Magnetic Tape	Data represented as magnetized bits on an iron-oxide coating; data recorded by computer via tape drive or a keytape converter.	Efficient for large volume jobs; any size record can be stored, stores millions of characters on a single tape.	Information not visible with the naked eye; strictly sequential processing; cannot easily read and write from same tape during a single operation.
Direct Access Files	Includes magnetic disk, drum, and data cell; addresses of disk records may be "looked up" on an index—data recorded by computer via disk drive or key to disk recorders.	Efficient for large-volume jobs; any size record can be stored; stores millions of characters on a single disk; random and sequential processing; can read and write from one disk during a single operation.	Data usually recorded by computer only—keying devices relatively expensive; disk drives expensive; requires much software; restrictions must often be placed on number of drives in an installation.

EXAMPLE 1

A Payroll System, servicing 75,000 employees, produces weekly payroll checks in social security number sequence. Two reports are also produced, both in social security number sequence.

Since the volume is relatively large and the output must be produced as efficiently and timely as possible, card processing would not be adequate. Since records in a Payroll File would generally be processed in a fixed sequence (social security number, usually), the direct access feature of disk would not be applicable. Thus tape is the best medium for a Payroll File, such as the one above.

EXAMPLE 2

A small-scale company has 500 customers and wishes to maintain a single Accounts Receivable File that can be used by the computer to produce monthly bills and that can be used by the clerks to answer inquiries.

Since the volume is relatively small, cards would be a suitable medium. They can be entered as input to the computer and also manually read to answer inquiries.

EXAMPLE 3

A large department store has 200,000 charge customers and wishes to maintain a computerized Accounts Receivable file. The file is used once a month to prepare customer bills. In addition, a program has been written that would utilize inquiry cards as input, search the file, and print answers to the inquiry. Inquiries are made at the volume of 15,000 daily and are fed into the computer on cards that are entered in no specified sequence.

A direct access file is the only viable alternative for this system. The volume of the file necessitates a high-speed device. The inquiry cards necessitate a file search in random sequence. Thus, a direct access file would be required.

EXAMPLE 4

A medium-sized company now maintains an inventory on 2000 stock parts. The company plans to merge with another organization in the near future and maintain an inventory on all parts currently held by both companies.

Ordinarily, if only 2000 records on parts are to be stored on a file, a card file could be least costly. But since the company expects a rapid growth shortly, a tape file would probably be a better alternative.

SELF-EVALUATING QUIZ

1. Three physical components that are generally required for any computer application are _____, _____, and _____.
2. The CPU is a machine that _____.
3. An input device _____.
4. An output device _____.
5. Each input or output device is linked to the Central Processing Unit by _____.
6. Batch processing is _____.
7. The term _____ is used to denote computer input/output devices.
8. The Card Read/Punch is a single device that houses ___(no.)___ separate units.

Fundamental Concepts of Data Processing

9. (T or F) Most Card Read/Punch devices can read card data and punch additional data into the same card.
10. (T or F) Cards are generally punched at a much slower rate than they are read.
11. (T or F) Computer-produced punched cards generally contain the imprinting of data on the face of the card.
12. (T or F) Keypunched cards generally contain the imprinting of data on the face of the card.
13. An EAM device called an _____ imprints data punched into a card on the face of the card.
14. The basic advantages of card processing are _____ and _____ .
15. Two disadvantages of card processing are _____ and _____ .
16. Each line of a computer printed output generally contains a maximum of _____ or _____ characters per line.
17. A _____ is the device most often used to produce computer printouts.
18. The most common master file type in medium- or large-scale computer centers is _____ .
19. (T or F) A magnetic tape can serve as either input to or output from a computer system.
20. A magnetic tape drive resembles a home _____ .
21. (T or F) After a tape has been processed and is no longer needed, the same tape may be reused to store other data.
22. The three major advantages of tape processing as compared to card processing are: _____ , _____ , and _____ .
23. Two methods of recording data onto a magnetic tape are with the use of a _____ and a _____ .
24. Because of a tape's capacity to handle large volumes of data in a relatively short time, it is ideally suited to _____ processing.
25. A disadvantage of tapes is that they can only be processed _____ .
26. This method of processing creates no time problem when _____ .
27. An update is the _____ .
28. With tape processing, update applications generally require _____(no.)_____ files.
29. Because of the vast numbers of magnetic tapes in many installations, _____ often becomes a problem.
30. The creation of _____ on output tapes in a program is used for checking purposes when the tapes are used as input.
31. Most computer installations hire _____ to insure proper handling of tapes.
32. Three advantages of disk processing that are common to tape processing are _____ , _____ and, _____ .

33. An advantage of disk processing that makes it more suitable for some applications than tape processing is the _____ .
34. The most common method for accessing magnetic disk records randomly is with the use of an _____ .
35. Random processing is advantageous where _____ .
36. A major disadvantage of disk processing is _____ .
37. With disk processing, update applications require ____(no.)____ files.

SOLUTIONS

1. Central Processing Unit (CPU); input device; output device
2. processes data by performing arithmetic operations, logic functions, and manipulating data to produce output.
3. accepts data and transmits it to the CPU.
4. transmits resultant data from the CPU to an output medium.
5. electronic cables
6. the collection of groups or batches of records to be processed, collectively, in a computer run at periodic intervals.
7. hardware
8. two
9. F
10. T
11. F
12. T
13. Interpreter
14. its relatively low cost; its ability to be read both manually and electronically
15. its relative lack of durability; its relatively slow speed
16. 100; 132
17. line printer
18. tape

19. T
20. tape recorder
21. T
22. speed; storage space is saved; records can be any size
23. tape drive of a computer system; key-to-tape encoder
24. batch
25. sequentially
26. all or most of the records on a tape must be processed in sequence
27. process of making a file of data current
28. three: Input Master, Input Detail, Output Master
29. identification
30. labels
31. tape librarians
32. speed; storage space is saved; records can be any size
33. random processing capability
34. index
35. small numbers of records from a large file are required for processing in a random sequence.
36. its cost
37. two: Master (I/O), Input Detail

II. *Specialized Equipment*

A. DEVICES THAT CAN READ SOURCE DOCUMENTS

The computer hardware thus far mentioned represents the devices that are most commonly integrated in a computer system.

Notice, however, that cards, tapes, and disks, the media most often used as input, require *conversion from a source document*. This conversion process, using keypunch machines or key-to-tape encoders with operators, can be extremely costly and time-consuming. In addition, it requires a major control procedure. Source documents must be counted and the total number compared against the number of input records (created by the conversion) to insure that records have not been misplaced. Manual procedures must be employed to physically transport source documents to an Operations or Control Staff, and then to transport the machine-readable input records to the computer room.

As computer equipment becomes even faster and more sophisticated, this conversion process consumes a greater percentage of total data processing time. In many companies, where inputs are voluminous, this conversion process can require up to 35% of the total operation time.

In an effort to alleviate the increased cost and time alloted to conversion, manufacturers have sought to produce equipment that will accept source input without requiring extensive conversion. The major devices thus far in use today include:

1. Magnetic Ink Character Recognition (MICR) Equipment
2. Optical Character Recognition (OCR) Equipment
3. Punched Paper Tape Read/Punch
4. Terminal Devices. Terminal equipment requires special consideration because it functions in an online environment. Thus, it will be discussed in depth in Chapter 6. Table 5.2 provides a synopsis of file types discussed in this section.

Let us now discuss the first three devices (1 to 3 above). These usually employ *batch-processing* procedures. That is, they are best suited for applications that utilize large volumes of data, processed in a group, where conversion from a source document is relatively costly. The above devices perform the conversion from a source document to a machine-readable form directly, as discussed below.

1. Magnetic Ink Character Recognition (MICR) Equipment

The banking industry is a specific area where the conversion of source documents, or checks, requires a massive operation. Thus, about a decade ago, the Federal Reserve System adopted a new technique whereby checks have account numbers and check amounts recorded in special type characters (Figure 5.12) that are printed on the bottom of the check. These special characters are treated with a magnetic ink that can be sensed by MICR equipment. Magnetic Ink Character Reader-Sorter units interpret checks, sort them by account or bank number into pockets, and transfer the data to the CPU.

Thus blank checks are prepared by special machines that imprint account number, bank number, and other identifying data. These

Table 5.2

Major Characteristics of Specialized File Types

File Type	Characteristics	Advantages	Disadvantages	Major Users
MAGNETIC INK CHARACTER RECOGNITION (MICR) FILES	Data is recorded in special type characters of magnetic ink. Such data may be read and sorted by MICR devices used in conjunction with computer systems.	This file type enables the computer to read source documents imprinted with magnetic numbers without requiring a conversion process; the devices used with this file type are highly accurate even if an input document is bent or slightly mutilated; such devices can handle any size document.	MICR devices can only detect numbers.	Banking Systems utilize checks with MICR numbers imprinted on bottom as ACCOUNT NUMBER and AMOUNT (after check has been processed).
PRINTED DOCUMENTS READ BY OPTICAL CHARACTER RECOGNITION (OCR) EQUIPMENT	Data is recorded in regular type or even handwritten form; such data may be read by OCR equipment and transmitted to a computer, without requiring the conversion process from a source document to a machine-readable form; characters must be printed or typed in designated positions.	Saves considerable time and expense by eliminating the conversion process.	Rigid conformance to standard type fonts is required by devices; erasures and slight overlapping of positions cause enumerable errors in transmission; OCR devices are extremely expensive compared to other input/output devices and cannot be justified unless input to the system is considerable (e.g., 20,000 documents or more per day).	Department stores utilize OCR devices to read handwritten sales slips for charge customers. The sales slips are meticulously prepared by trained sales personnel; they are then read by OCR equipment which transmits the data to the computer which then updates the Accounts Receivable file.
PUNCHED PAPER TAPE	Tape is punched by machine (computer device, cash registers,	File can be represented on a continuous tape without record	Paper Tape files are not as durable as card files; the punched	Punched Paper tape in the form of cash register receipts, adding

Table 5.2 (*cont.*)

Major Characteristics of Specialized File Types

File Type	Characteristics	Advantages	Disadvantages	Major Users
PUNCHED PAPER TAPE	adding machines) with holes in specified rows and columns; it then is read by a PAPER TAPE READ/PUNCH of a computer system.	length restrictions; it is easier to transport and store paper tape than cards; there is no sequencing problem with a continuous tape.	paper tape read/punches are slower than card devices.	machine tapes are read by computer. Communications companies can maintain records of all telephone calls for example from a given area on paper tape.
MICROFILM	A microfilm is a photographed record in miniature—$\frac{1}{24}$ to $\frac{1}{42}$ of its original size; there are computer devices that create microfilm records as a result of a computer run—this is called Computer Output Microfilm (COM) equipment; there are special viewers that may then be used to read the microfilm records and/or convert them to a printed report; there are computer devices that can read microfilm called Computer Input Microfilm (CIM) equipment.	The two major advantages of microfilm is the greatly reduced storage area required to maintain computer output (as opposed to the printed report which is the most common output form) and the ability of high speed microfilm readers to access this computer output speedily.	The use of microfilm as a file type requires additional computer hardware and viewers that are relatively costly.	Any firm which must store large amounts of printed information and which must be able to retrieve it speedily can benefit from the use of microfilm. Motor Vehicle Bureaus which must maintain millions of records and which also must be able to access these records fast in case of accidents, stolen cars, etc., are sometimes dependent on microfilm. Similarly, personnel records, accounting ledgers, etc., at large companies are stored on microfilm.

checks are then used by the customer for transactions. When the checks that have been transacted and signed are returned to the bank, an operator uses a machine to encode the amount of the check in magnetic ink at the bottom. Thus an MICR device may be used to sort the checks into account number or bank number sequence. Similarly,

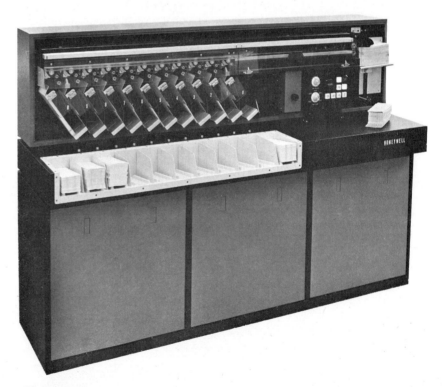

Figure 5.12
MICR Reader-Sorter. Especially for bankers—This low-cost document reader-sorter for banks is marketed by Honeywell Information Systems. This unit reads magnetic ink-encoded documents at speeds up to 600 documents per minute and sorts them into 11 different pockets (10 accept and one reject). Called the Type 232 MICR Reader-Sorter, the device can be operated as a free-standing unit or on-line to any Series 200 computer, including Honeywell's small scale, low-cost 110 system. Courtesy Honeywell.

148

an MICR device may be used to transmit the information on the check to the CPU. In this way, the checks themselves can serve as input to a data-processing installation. They need not be converted to cards or tape or disk. Deposit slips in commercial banks are also encoded in this manner.

The average speed of MICR equipment ranges from approximately 600 to 1600 checks per minute or from 100 to 500 characters per second. The main purpose of the device is to enable the computer to read source documents that are also manually readable without requiring a conversion process. MICR equipment can handle almost any size check or deposit slip so that an industry-wide standard check size is not required. These devices are also highly accurate; they do not missort or transmit incorrectly, even if the condition of the check is poor.

The one main disadvantage is that currently only *numbers* have been used as MICR characters, to be read by MICR equipment. Thus any application requiring the encoding of letters or special characters cannot utilize this equipment.

As indicated, MICR equipment is used as a standard in the banking industry. Any industry, however, that performs voluminous source document conversion and that uses exclusively digits as identifying characters, may employ this equipment.

2. Optical Character Recognition (OCR) Equipment (Figure 5.13) and Other Optical Readers

An OCR device, commonly referred to as an *Optical Scanner,* reads characters from printed documents. No special ink (as with MICR devices) or typing is required.

The optical scanner senses typed data with the use of a photoelectric device. The printed data is read by an ultrabright light source, which converts these characters into electrical impulses. On many devices, the printed input document must have characters or marks in designated positions in order to be properly sensed. The computer, then, must be instructed as to which positions will contain the data.

A major use of optical scanners is in conjunction with gasoline company credit card receipts. Credit card identification from a plastic plate is imprinted on the receipt along with the amount of purchase. These receipts are then read into a computer with the use of an optical scanner that senses the amount and customer account number. Another major user of optical scanners is the Accounting Department of numerous businesses which use adding machine tapes and cash register tapes that contain typed data, as direct input. That is, the optical scanner can read these tapes directly.

The optical character recognition device is unquestionably a major breakthrough in computer technology. Source documents that contain regular typed printing can be read as input, directly into a computer system. (See Figure 5.14.) With some sophisticated optical scanners, handwritten material can be accepted if the characters are printed in a standard form. Many department stores train their clerks to print a sales slip total in a standard manner. These sales slips are then entered as input to a computer system with the use of an optical scanner. No manual conversion is required. Consider the tremendous advantage of reducing the need for a large and costly operations staff by using the source document as machine-readable input.

OCR equipment varies in speed from approximately 50 characters per second, for devices that can read handwritten letters, to 2400

(a)

Figure 5.13
(a) Optical character reader. Courtesy IBM.

IMPORTANT: THE NUMBERS WRITTEN IN THE GREEN BOXES MUST

BE HANDWRITTEN IN THIS STYLE ➡ |1|2|3|4|5|6|7|8|9|0|

FORMOST FORM-PRINT, NEW YORK, N.Y. 10001

CLIENT DISBURSEMENT CHARGE FORM
PAUL, WEISS, GOLDBERG, RIFKIND, WHARTON & GARRISON

HAND
ENTRY

L   X   013

CASE NUMBER	DISBURSEMENT	DATE	AMOUNT
CLIENT	MATTER	CODE	MONTH	DAY	YEAR	DOLLARS	CENTS

023

CASE NUMBER	DISBURSEMENT	DATE	AMOUNT

CLIENT

MATTER

LAWYERS NAME   DELIVER BY ☐   AM   PM

PICK UP BY ☐

SPECIAL INSTRUCTIONS

DO NOT CHARGE CLIENT	TRANSPORT COST	TOT. TIME FOR DEL.		DELIVERED BY	SIGNATURE OF MAILROOM PERSONNEL
		HOURS	MINUTES		
☐	$				

ACCOUNTING DEPT. COPY

HAND DELIVERY

PAUL, WEISS, GOLDBERG, RIFKIND, WHARTON & GARRISON

(b)

(b) Sample input. Courtesy International Business Forms.

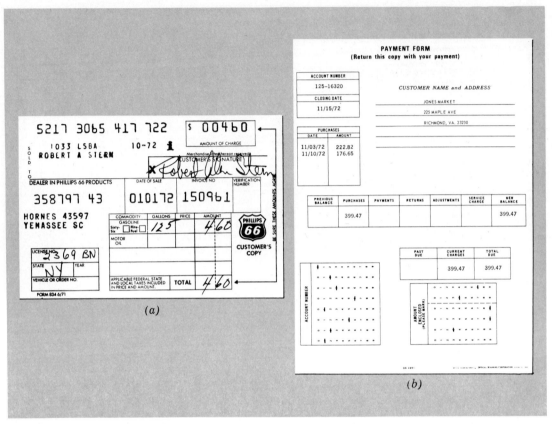

Figure 5.14
Sample input to optical reader. (a) On gasoline credit slip only imprinted data
is read by the optical reader. (b) Payment form serves as a statement to the
customer and, when returned, the Account Number and Amount Enclosed
(marked at the bottom of the form) serve as input to an optical scanner.
Courtesy Optical Scanning Corporation.

characters per second, and from 200 to 1200 documents per minute.
Most page readers are very costly, however, ranging in price from
$160,000 to $400,000 on the average, with monthly rentals from
$2500 to $6000. Considering the savings of keying machines with
operators for the typical conversion process, the expense can often be
justified in a cost analysis. In one company, a systems analyst
performed a cost study to determine the feasibility of acquiring an OCR
device for a billing system. It was determined that an OCR device could
only be monetarily justified where the system processed 20,000
documents per day. With fewer documents, the standard conversion
process would be more economical. Thus we can see that such a

device is relatively costly and is justifiable only when processing a voluminous quantity of input.

Thus far, we have discussed the optical scanner as the major type of optical reader. This optical scanner may be one of the following.

1. Hand-print reader—where the printing must conform to a specified pattern.
2. Single-font reader—where the typed printing may be in only one type font or style.
3. Multi-font reader—where two or more different type styles may be used.

In addition to the optical scanner, the *mark reader* is considered an optical reader. Mark-sensed cards, which have been discussed in Chapter 3, may be read by a mark reader. In addition to mark-sensed cards, there are other documents that may be read by mark readers.

Optical mark reading and bar-code reading devices are optical readers, far simpler in principle than optical scanners, which may also be used for converting data from a source document into a machine-readable form. A bar code reader can read preprinted codes on documents by detecting spots at various predetermined sections across the reading path. Bar-code readers are often employed to read amount figures on payment cards or stubs. After reading the data, it then transforms the information into punched cards, magnetic tape, or some other medium.

A mark-sense reader detects the presence of pencil marks on predetermined grids. The typical documents to be mark-sensed are the computer-scored test papers, where students are required to indicate the correct answer by pencilling in grid A, B, C, D, or E. Note that the mark-sensed cards discussed in Chapter 3 are examples of input documents that can be read by mark-sense readers. Here again, the data can be transformed into an input medium. Note that while these are optical readers, they have limited facility and therefore limited use. Their capability is much less than optical scanners, where actual handwritten or typed data can be read.

Optical readers, although a real asset to many computer installations, have several inherent disadvantages. Characters that are sensed by this device often must *rigidly* conform to the standard. Typing erasures, overlapping of positions, and so on can cause the erroneous transmission of data. In some applications, as much as 10% of the input data is unreadable because of such errors. In addition, optical scanners are very costly devices. In short, the promise of increased reliability and decreased cost in future years will make OCR equipment more widespread than it is today.

3. Punched Paper Tape Read/Punch (Figure 5.15)

A punched paper tape (Figure 5.16) is a paper tape that, like a card, is punched with holes in specified rows and columns. A paper tape

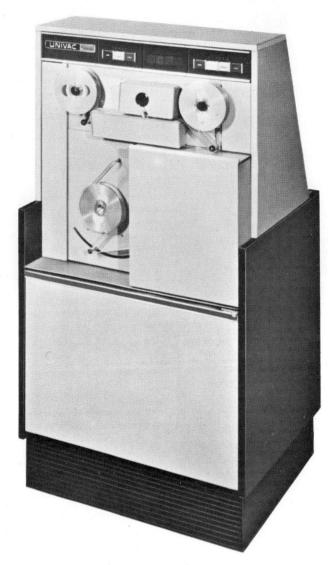

Figure 5.15
Punched paper tape read/punch.
Courtesy Sperry Rand.

read/punch is, like a card read/punch, two separate units that can read from a paper tape or punch data into one.

Punched paper tapes may be produced by special adding machines, accounting machines, and cash registers. With the use of the read/punch it can then be used, as a source document, by the computer system.

The punched paper tape has several advantages that make it more suitable for some applications than card processing. A file can be

Fundamental Concepts of Data Processing

Figure 5.16
Punched paper tape.

represented on a continuous tape; thus there is no limitation on record size as with punched cards. Punched paper tape equipment is less expensive than card equipment. It is easier to store and transport paper tapes than large volumes of cards. There is no problem with sequencing the tape records, since the file can be represented on one contiguous tape.

There are, however, several limitations to paper tape processing. Paper tape is not as durable as cards. Paper tape devices are slower than card equipment. Typical paper tape read/punch devices can read 300 characters per second and punch 110 characters per second. In general, only applications that use cash register or adding machine tapes or other specialized systems employ paper tape devices.

In short, there are several computer devices available that can read source documents directly without requiring a conversion to some other medium, such as cards, tape, or disk. Terminal devices are also included in this category, but because they are utilized in an online environment, they require special consideration, which will be noted in the next chapter.

B. COMPUTER OUTPUT MICROFILM (COM) DEVICES

Microfilm, as a noncomputerized storage medium, has been in existence for many years. It is a photographed record or document in miniature. Devices are required to *create* the microfilm. Because of its miniature size, devices are also required to *read* the microfilm. Many newspapers use microfilm for storing reproductions of the paper, in miniature, for a fixed number of years. An individual can locate and read a given newspaper article by accessing the film and utilizing a microfilm reader to view it.

In recent years, the computer industry has recognized the distinctive assets of microfilm. Since storage of large numbers of cards or even printed reports has proved cumbersome, microfilm devices can be used to reproduce such records in miniature. Computer Output Microfilm (COM) devices (Figure 5.17) have been developed to produce human readable microfilmed output from a computer system at relatively high speeds. Most often, magnetic tape information to be

Figure 5.17
Computer Output Microfilm (COM) Recorder. Courtesy Stromberg
Datagraphix.

printed as a report is recorded on microfilm instead, using a computer
system. In addition to high-speed output, microfilm can save about
98% of the storage space that is required for cards or reports. Typically
microimage forms are from $\frac{1}{24}$ to $\frac{1}{42}$ of their original size. Most often, the
magnetic tape drives convert data to microfilm using special devices
not under the control of a computer, since such a conversion requires
much time, when many records are to be created on microfilm.

Forms of this Computer Output Microfilm include:

1. Rolled film represented on reels.
2. Cards containing individual microfilm records.

Fundamental Concepts of Data Processing

Microfiche Card   Aperture Card

Figure 5.18
Microfiche and aperture cards.

(a)

Each microfiche card
contains dozens of
microfilm images. To
access an individual
record, a microfiche
viewer must be
used.

(b)

Each aperture
card contains punched card
data with an individual
microfilm image.

The film used to produce microfilm can be 16mm, 35mm, or 105mm.

Microfilm output can be created at computer speeds up to 120,000 characters per second or 21,800 lines per minute.

Thus rolled film and cards are the two forms of microfilm. There are 2 types of microfilm cards: (1) microfiche cards—with rectangular holes that can store frames of microfilm. One card can typically store *many* records. (2) Aperture cards—unit-records of film. Typically these are punched cards that provide an area for individual frames of microfilm—one card contains *one* record. There are microfiche viewers and hard copy printers that can produce reports from these cards. Figure 5.18 illustrates these cards. The microfiche viewer, for example, can hold typically 750 microfiche cards and access any one of them in approximately 3 seconds (see Figure 5.19).

Aperture cards contain punched data, which serves as identification, in addition to the film. In this way, standard card devices can be used to process the punched-card information, while microfilm readers can be used to read the filmed portion.

Similarly, there are microfilm card reader-printers that can access an aperture or microfiche card or rolled film in seconds and print the corresponding photographed image. In this way, computer printouts can be stored on microfilm, accessed immediately when they are needed, and reproduced without the use of a computer.

Computer devices, can also be used to *read* microfilm. CIM (Computer Input Microfilm) is then used when data is *read* from a high-speed microfilm device and is *transmitted* to the computer. To date, there are far less applications for CIM than for COM. This is because microfilm is generally used to store *output* documents that are not intended to reenter the data flow as input.

Thus the two major advantages of microfilm are in the compact

Figure 5.19
Remkard display unit. Microfiche viewer. This system can store 75,000 microfilmed pages of information on 750 microfiche cards each with an individual index that permits fast random push button selection. Courtesy Remington Rand.

storage of records and in the speedy retrieval of data. Microfilm is most often used to store the following types of data:

Engineering drawings (maps, blueprints, and so on)
Customer records
Accounting ledgers
Personnel records
Assorted computer printouts
Toll billing

Figure 5.20 illustrates a comparison between normal printing and microfilm operations.

Fundamental Concepts of Data Processing

C. OFFLINE DEVICES

As we have seen, utilization of computer equipment, in conjunction with a CPU, is very costly. There are devices available that can operate on computer files or media, *without requiring the CPU*. These are called *offline* devices.

Thus far, we have been exposed to keypunch machines, key-to-tape encoders, and key-to-disk recorders, which are characterized as *offline* equipment, since they do not require the Central Processing Unit for their conversion processes. A keypunch machine is an offline device that creates card output. Similarly, a key-to-tape encoder is an offline device that creates tape records from source documents.

There are, however, numerous other offline devices which, if utilized properly, result in substantial savings to a company. That is, rather than using hardware devices under the control of the CPU, the following may be employed offline:

1. Pencil-marked Document-to-Tape Devices (see Figure 5.21)
2. Tape-to-Print Offline Devices
3. Card-to-Tape Offline Devices
4. Card-to-Print Offline Devices.
5. Punched-Paper-Tape-to-Magnetic-Tape Offline Devices.
6. Tape-to-Microfilm Offline Devices

Note that offline operations often utilize auxiliary *mini-computers* to perform required conversions. Although a computer is employed, this conversion is considered offline since processing is not under the control of the *main* computer. Figure 5.22 illustrates an optical page reader used in conjunction with a mini-computer to produce a tape or disk file offline. This utilization of mini-computers for offline operations to relieve the load of full-size computers is becoming increasingly popular because of the monetary savings.

There are many, many more offline devices. The essential concept of these is to take information, usually entered at different points and usually requiring a relatively slow conversion process, and produce a machine-readable form. The output then is usually some high-speed medium that can be entered as input to a CPU much faster.

We shall see that data communications systems, as discussed in the next chapter, rely heavily on offline operations.

In summary, we have presented the major forms of hardware (with the exception of terminal devices to be discussed in the next chapter) that are used in most companies.

Figure 5.23 is a chart illustrating price specifications for selected computer systems. Note that these figures cannot be taken as *exact,* since speed and cost lists become obsolete almost as soon as they are published. Such a chart can, however, be extremely significant when comparing devices and systems for *relative* speed and cost.

This equipment will serve the needs of most business applications today. Typical applications of these devices are discussed in detail in

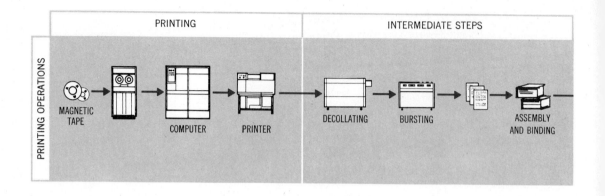

PRINTING | INTERMEDIATE STEPS

PRINTING OPERATIONS

MAGNETIC TAPE → COMPUTER → PRINTER → DECOLLATING → BURSTING → ASSEMBLY AND BINDING

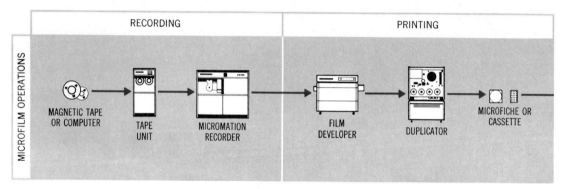

RECORDING | PRINTING

MICROFILM OPERATIONS

MAGNETIC TAPE OR COMPUTER → TAPE UNIT → MICROMATION RECORDER → FILM DEVELOPER → DUPLICATOR → MICROFICHE OR CASSETTE

Figure 5.20 (above—continued at right)
Comparison of printing operations and microfilm operations. Courtesy Stromberg Datagraphix Inc.
Where volume is very great, microfilm can result in savings of computer time, paper bursting, binding, retrieval, and distribution of information.
Computer output is converted into readable text at speeds up to 342 completely filled, standard-sized computer pages a minute. The output is printed on film which may be viewed at a Micromation Inquiry Station or used to produce hard copies (printed reports).

Figure 5.21 (at right)
Offline Optical Scanner. Pencil-marked information is optically scanned and transferred to tape at speeds up to 2400 sheets per hour. Courtesy Optical Scanning Corp.

160   *Fundamental Concepts of Data Processing*

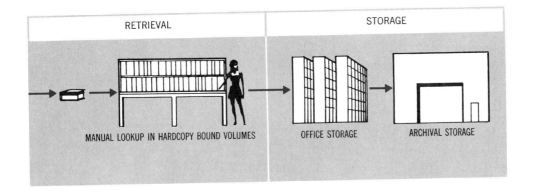

RETRIEVAL | STORAGE

MANUAL LOOKUP IN HARDCOPY BOUND VOLUMES | OFFICE STORAGE | ARCHIVAL STORAGE

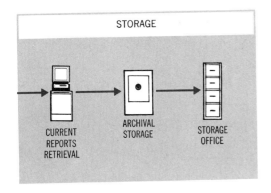

STORAGE

CURRENT REPORTS RETRIEVAL | ARCHIVAL STORAGE | STORAGE OFFICE

Figure 5.22
A page reader used in conjunction with minicomputers, offline. An office worker feeds printed information to the Farrington 3030 Page Reader. In background is the Varian 620/i mini-computer, which lets the office worker perform the task without having to access a central processing mainframe unit. Courtesy Varian Data Machines.

the workbook. In this ever-changing age of automation, however, it is quite possible that new equipment will be manufactured in the near future that will serve specific applications even better.

It is the responsibility of businessmen, as well as computer specialists, to keep abreast of new advances in technology. Businessmen often are responsible for initiating feasibility studies to determine if newer, more sophisticated, or more suitable computer equipment should be acquired. Note, too, that the businessman or computer-specialist of today is quite possibly the top-level executive of tomorrow. And top-level management is ultimately responsible for major decisions on all aspects of computer acquisition. Thus, we cannot overestimate the importance of familiarity with recent advances in hardware devices for the businessman and the computer specialist.

Fundamental Concepts of Data Processing

SELF-EVALUATING QUIZ

1. The process of _____ , although mainly a manual operation, utilizes much time in data processing installations.
2. The banking industry uses _____ devices to minimize the conversion process.
3. Computer-processed checks and deposits slips have special _____ on the bottom that can be read by MICR devices.
4. (T or F) MICR equipment can handle almost any size check or deposit slip so that an industry-wide standard size is not required.
5. (T or F) Letters and numbers can be read by MICR devices.
6. The device that can read printed characters typed in regular ink is called a(n) _____ or a(n) _____ .
7. The OCR device is used to eliminate the manual _____ process from source documents to a computer medium.
8. (T or F) With some OCR devices, handwritten material can be read.
9. OCR equipment is monetarily justifiable when _____ .
10. (T or F) OCR equipment is slow compared to devices such as tape and disk drives.
11. Major disadvantages of OCR equipment include _____ .
12. Punched paper tapes commonly produced by special _____ and _____ can be used as input to a computer.
13. (T or F) Paper Tape Read/Punch devices are slower than Card Read/Punch devices.
14. Microfilm is a _____ .
15. The two major computer advantages of microfilm are in the areas of _____ and _____ .
16. The two forms of computer output microfilm are _____ and _____ .

SOLUTIONS

1. conversion
2. Magnetic Ink Character Recognition (MICR)
3. magnetic ink digits
4. T
5. F—only numbers
6. optical character recognition (OCR) device; optical scanner
7. conversion
8. T
9. voluminous input records need to be processed frequently
10. T
11. its lack of reliability because of typing erasures; overlapping of characters; its expense
12. adding machines; cash registers; accounting machines
13. T
14. photographed document or record in miniature
15. conserving storage; automated retrieval of data
16. rolled film; aperture or microfiche cards

Figure 5.23

Computer Characteristics

Manufacturer/ Model Number	Average Purchase Price ($1000)	Average Rental Price ($ per month)	Central Processor					Typewrite Console	Number CPU I/O Channels	Data Word Length[c]	Buffering
			Speed (nanoseconds)		Storage						
			CPU Cycle Time	Add Time[a]	Medium[b]	Maximum Capacity (in characters)	Access Time (in nanoseconds)				
Burroughs Corporation											
B3500	600	12.5 K	2 mc	35	C DI	500 K 4b	0.5 23	X	20	2B	X
B4500	1500	30 K	4 mc	14	C DI	500 K 4b	.25 20	X	20	2B	X
B5500	800	15 K	1 mc	9	C DR DI	32 K 262 K 960 b	4 8.5 23	X	4	B	
Control Data Corporation											
3300	700	15 K	1.2	2.75	C DR DI	262 Kw 4 m 838 m	0.8 17 ms 80 ms	X	8	B D	X
Honeywell Information Services											
115	138.5	2775	2.75	66	C DI	32 K 36.8 ms	1.375 62.5 ms	X	3		

Source: Selected computer systems—specification, rental and purchase price. (Business Automation, December 1971, pages 166–177.)
[a] *this speed is the complete add time for two six digit numbers from memory to memory;* [b] *= core, DR = drum, DI = disc, TF = thin film;* [c] *= binary, D = decimal;* [d] *ips = increments per second, sps = steps per second, ppm = points per minute; spm = steps per minute; K = thousand; m = million; b = billion; usec = microseconds; ms = milliseconds; ns = nanosecond; w = words; x = yes; mc = megacycle; cps = characters per second.*

Readers			Input/Output									Software								
			Printers		Magnetic Tape		Punched Cards		Punched Paper		Data Communications										
Data Collection	MICR	OCR	Lines per Minute	Plotter[d]	7-Channel K/Characters per Second	9-Channel K/Characters per Second	Cards per Minute Input	Cards per Minute Output	Characters Per Second Input	Characters Per Second Output	Number of Transmission Lines	Visual Display	Operating System	Time Share Capability	Multiprogram	Cobol	Fortran II, IV, or VI	Utilities	Communications	Other
X	X	X	1100		96	240	1400	300	1000	100	1300	X	X	X	X	X	X	X	X	X
X	X	X	1100		96	240	1400	300	1000	100	240	X	X	X	X	X	X	X	X	X
X	X	X	1040		96		1400	300	1000	100	240	X	X	X	X	X	X	X	X	X
X		X	1200	X	120	30	1200	250	1000	120	512	X	X	X	X	X	X	X	X	X
	X	X	300–1100		4.8–144	37.3–149.3	1050	600	600	120	63	X	X	X	X	X	X	X	X	X

Figure 5.23
Computer characteristics.

Figure 5.23 (*cont.*)

Computer Characteristics

Manufacturer/ Model Number	Average Purchase Price ($1000)	Average Rental Price ($ per month)	Central Processor						Typewrite Console	Number CPU I/O Channels	Data Word Length[c]	Buffering
			Speed (nano-seconds)		Storage							
			CPU Cycle Time	Add Time[a]	Medium[b]	Maximum Capacity (in characters)	Access Time (in nanoseconds)					
120	165	3200	3	69	C DR DI	32 K 2.6 m 300 m	1.5 27 ms 15 ms		X	3		

International Business Machines Corporation

Manufacturer/ Model Number	Average Purchase Price ($1000)	Average Rental Price ($ per month)	CPU Cycle Time	Add Time[a]	Medium[b]	Maximum Capacity (in characters)	Access Time (in nanoseconds)	Typewrite Console	Number CPU I/O Channels	Data Word Length[c]	Buffering
System 3 Mod 6	48 (typical)		1.52	35	C	16 K	1.52	X	1	B	X
System 3 Mod 10	57 189		1.52	35	C DI	48 K 9.80 ms	1.52 153 ms	X	1	B	X
System/360 Mod 20	99	2.2 K	3.6	572	C DI	16 K 10.8 m	3.6 75 ms	X	1	B	X
System/360 Mod 20 (submodel 5)	157	3.5 K	2	150	C DI	32 K 21.6 K	2 75 ms	X	1	B	X
System/360 Mod 25	300	6 K	1.8	110	C DI	49 K 29 m	0.9 75 ms	X	1	B	X
System/360 Mod 30	420	8.5 K	1.5	61	C DI	65 K 233 m	1.5 60 ms	X	3	B	X
System/360 Mod 40	900	19.5 K	2.5	35	C DR DI	262 K 7.8 m 233 m	2.5 8.6 ms 60 ms	X	3	B	X
System/360 Mod 44	510	12 K	1	2.25	C DI	262 K 58 m	1 75 ms	X	3	B	X

Fundamental Concepts of Data Processing

Readers			Input/Output — Printers		Magnetic Tape		Punched Cards		Punched Paper		Data Communications			Software							
Data Collection	MICR	OCR	Lines per Minute	Plotter[d]	7-Channel K/Characters per Second	9-Channel K/Characters per Second	Cards per Minute Input	Cards per Minute Output	Characters Per Second Input	Characters Per Second Output	Number of Transmission Lines	Visual Display	Operating System	Time Share Capability	Multiprogram	Cobol	Fortran II, IV, or VI	Utilities	Communications	Other	
	X	X	300–1100		4.8–144	37.3–149.3	1050	100–400	600	120	1–63	X	X	X	X	X	X	X	X	X	
X	X						22	22			V	X	X		X	X	X	X	X	X	
X	X		1100			80	250–500	60–120			V	X	X		X	X	X	X	X	X	
X	X	X	300–1100		15	30	1000	500	1000	150	1							X	X	X	
X	X	X	300–1100		15	30	1000	500	1000		1							X	X	X	
X	X	X	240–1400		30	30	1000	500	1000	120	26	X	X		X	X	X	X	X	X	
X	X	X	240–1400		90	180	1000	500	1000	120	224	X	X		X	X	X	X	X	X	
X	X	X	240–1400		90	180	1000	500	1000	120	128	X	X		X	X	X	X	X	X	
X			240–1400		90	180	1000	500	1000		64	X	X	X	X	X	X	X	X	X	

Figure 5.23 (*cont.*)

Computer Characteristics

Manufacturer/ Model Number	Average Purchase Price ($1000)	Average Rental Price ($ per month)	Central Processor					Typewrite Console	Number CPU I/O Channels	Data Word Length[c]	Buffering
			Speed (nano-seconds)			Storage					
			CPU Cycle Time	Add Time[a]	Medium[b]	Maximum Capacity (in characters)	Access Time (in nanoseconds)				
System/360 Mod 50	1400	32 K	2	23	C DR DI	524 K 7.8 m 699 m	2 8.6 ms 60 ms	X	4	B	X
System/360 Mod 65	2400	56 K	0.75	3.9	C DR DI	1048 K 16.4 m 699 m	0.75 8.6 ms 60 ms	X	7	B	X
System/360 Mod 195	10,500	232 K	.054	.154	C DR DI	1240 K 4 m 233 m	810 8.6 ms 60 ms	X	7	B	X
System/370 Mod 135	472– 1020		.75		Mono lithic	245	0.77	X	3	B	X
System/370 Mod 165	3505– 6719	71 K 143 K	m 2 ms		C DI	3 mb 800 mb	2 ms 300 ms	X		B	X
1130	71	1.6 K	2.2	4.88	C DI	32 Kw 5 m	3.4 520 ms	X	1	B	X
National Cash Register Company											
Century 100	135	2.6 K	0.8	58.4	TF DI	32 K 16.8 m	0.8 43.7 ms	X	2	8	X
Century 200	305	6.2 K	0.65	12.4	TF DI	524 K 1.5 b	0.8 43.7 m	X	4–8	16	X

Fundamental Concepts of Data Processing

| Readers | | | Input/Output | | | | | | | | | Software | | | | | | | | |
Data Collection	MICR	OCR	Printers Lines per Minute	Plotter[d]	Magnetic Tape 7-Channel K/Characters per Second	Magnetic Tape 9-Channel K/Characters per Second	Punched Cards Cards per Minute Input	Punched Cards Cards per Minute Output	Punched Paper Characters Per Second Input	Punched Paper Characters Per Second Output	Data Communications Number of Transmission Lines	Visual Display	Operating System	Time Share Capability	Multiprogram	Cobol	Fortran II, IV, or VI	Utilities	Communications	Other
X	X	X	240–1400		90	320	1000	500	1000	120	256	X	X		X	X	X	X	X	X
	X		240–1400		90	320	1000	500			256	X	X		X	X	X	X	X	X
X			1100		90	300	1000	500			196	X	X		X	X	X	X	X	X
X	X	X	2000	X	90	320	1200	300	120	120	V	X	X	X	X	X	X	X	X	X
X			2000		90	320	1000	500				X	X	X	X	X	X	X	X	X
X		X	80–110	X			1000	270	60	15	1	X	X			X	X	X	X	
	X	X	450–3000	X	10–40	40–80	300–1200	82–240	1000–1500	200	1–256	X	X	X		X	X	X	X	
	X	X	450–3000	X	10–40	40–80	300–1200	82–240	1000–1500	200	1–256	X	X	X	X	X	X	X	X	X

Figure 5.23 (*cont.*)

Computer Characteristics

Manufacturer/ Model Number	Average Purchase Price ($1000)	Average Rental Price ($ per month)	Central Processor								
			Speed (nanoseconds)		Storage						
			CPU Cycle Time	Add Time[a]	Medium[b]	Maximum Capacity (in characters)	Access Time (in nanoseconds)	Typewrite Console	Number CPU I/O Channels	Data Word Length[c]	Buffering
Univac Division											
9300	140	3.7 K	0.6	60	TF DI	32 K 128 m	0.6 135 ms		4	D	X
9300II	151	4090	0.6	60	C DI	32 K 58 m	.6 75 ms		19	B	X
9400	380	10 K	0.6	22.2	TF DI	131 K 58 m	0.6 87.5 ms	X	3	B D	X
Xerox Data Systems											
Sigma 5	400	10 K	0.42	5.3	C DI	512 K 3b	0.85 17 ms	X	32	B	X
Sigma 6	600	12K–18K	0.36		C DI	512 K 3b	1.2 17 ms	X	256	B	X

Readers			Input/Output									Software								
			Printers		Magnetic Tape		Punched Cards		Punched Paper		Data Communications									
Data Collection	MICR	OCR	Lines per Minute	Plotter[d]	7-Channel K/Characters per Second	9-Channel K/Characters per Second	Cards per Minute Input	Cards per Minute Output	Characters Per Second Input	Characters Per Second Output	Number of Transmission Lines	Visual Display	Operating System	Time Share Capability	Multiprogram	Cobol	Fortran II, IV, or VI	Utilities	Communications	Other
			1200		34	34	2000	250			8		X		X	X	X	X	X	X
			600		34	34	600	200	300	110	8	X	X		X	X	X	X	X	
			1600		34	192	600	250			128	X	X		X	X	X	X	X	X
			1000	X	60	120	1500	300	300	120	1024	X	X	X	X	X	X	X	X	X
			1000	X	60	120	1500	300	300	120	1024	X	X	X	X	X	X	X	X	X

Appendix to Chapter 5 *Representation of Data on Magnetic Tape and Magnetic Disk*

I. REPRESENTATION OF DATA ON MAGNETIC TAPE

A. MAGNETIC TAPE CODE
B. DENSITY
C. BLOCKING
D. UTILITY PROGRAMS FOR TAPE PROCESSING

II. REPRESENTATION OF DATA ON MAGNETIC DISK

A. BASIC FEATURES OF THE MAGNETIC DISK PACK
B. ORGANIZATION OF FILES ON DISK
C. OTHER CONSIDERATIONS FOR EFFICIENT
   DISK UTILIZATION
D. CONCLUSION

Magnetic tape and magnetic disk are the two most frequently used high-speed storage media. Chapter 5 has outlined the utilization of these two as they relate to the businessman and to the computer specialist.

Although businessmen are not required to understand the exact representation of data on these media, familiarity with this topic often helps in establishing a proper perspective on how magnetic tape and magnetic disk are used. Thus, in this Appendix, we will attempt to familiarize business and data processing students with representation of tape and disk data.

A. MAGNETIC TAPE CODE

You will recall that data is recorded on magnetic tape on a thin film of iron-oxide coating. Many third-generation tapes have 9-tracks in which to record data (see Figure 5.24), although 7-track tapes designed for second-generation computers are still widely used.[1] We shall discuss 9-track tapes in detail.

Each of these tracks can be magnetized or demagnetized depending on the data represented. The coded representation of data on these 9 tracks, labeled P and 0 to 7, is the *same* code used by the computer for the internal representation known as EBCDIC, or Extended Binary Coded Decimal Interchange Code. The Hollerith code, on a punched card which uses a combination of a single zone and a single digit, can be converted to this *9-bit* machine code. The Appendix to the text outlines this representation in detail: here, we will merely present it briefly (See Figure 5.25.)

Disregarding the P-bit momentarily, we may represent any character using this combination of 4 zone and 4 digit bits.

The letter A, a combination of a 12-zone and a 1-digit in Hollerith, would be represented as indicated on tape in Figure 5.26.

A typical way to represent any *integer* on magnetic tape would be to use 1111, in the zone positions, in addition to the corresponding digit representation.[2] Thus the number 172 in a numeric field will be represented as indicated also in Figure 5.26.

Note that the illustrated code is the *same* one as the computer uses for internal representation of data. In essence, the 1's denote magnetized positions or current "on." The 0's denote demagnetized

---

[1] *The 7-track tape uses the BCD code, discussed in the Appendix to the text.*
[2] *See the Appendix to the text for other ways of representing numeric data.*

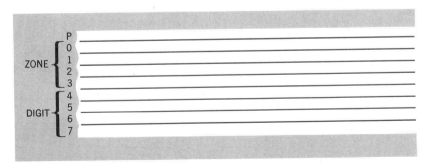

Figure 5.24
A 9-track tape.

<table>
<tr><th colspan="2">ZONE   BITS</th><th>0</th><th>1</th><th>2</th><th>3</th></tr>
</table>

ZONE BITS	0	1	2	3
12 (for letters A–I)	1	1	0	0
11 (for letters J–R)	1	1	0	1
0 (for letters S–Z)	1	1	1	0
DIGITS	1	1	1	1

ZONE PORTION

DIGIT BITS	4	5	6	7
0	0	0	0	0
1	0	0	0	1
2	0	0	1	0
3	0	0	1	1
4	0	0	0	0
5	0	1	0	1
6	0	1	1	0
7	0	1	1	1
8	1	1	0	0
9	1	0	0	1

DIGIT PORTION

Figure 5.25
Typical representation of data on a
9-track tape. Note: Digit Bits: 4 5 6 7
correspond to binary values 8 4 2 1.

positions or current "off." Magnetic tape can be processed quickly by computer because no code conversion is required. Data is represented on tape in 9-track form, with each track having current "on" or "off," in the same manner as is represented internally in the computer by

Fundamental Concepts of Data Processing

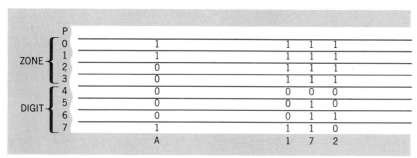

A:12 Zone:1100 Zone Bits 172:Zone Bits:1111

 1 Digit :0001 Digit Bits 8│4│2│1 Digit Bits : 8 4 2 1 │ 8 4 2 1 │ 8 4 2 1

         0│0│0│1   0 0 0 1 │ 0 1 1 1 │ 0 0 1 0

Figure 5.26

Representation of sample characters on a 9-track tape. (P-bit is subsequently to be discussed.)

9-core positions for each character, using current "on" or "off." Thus, for the computer to read from or write onto magnetic tape is a high-speed process.

 The P-bit corresponds to a *P*arity or check bit and is used to check the coded representation of data.

 When data is coded, both internally in the computer and on magnetic tape, there is a remote possibility that a single bit position can sometimes become demagnetized, or an "off" position can become magnetized. The Parity or P-bit is used to determine if this error has occurred.

 Odd Parity is the utilization of an odd number of on-bits to represent *any* character. Thus Figure 5.27 illustrates how the digit 5 is represented on tape.

 Note that there are *six* bits on, not counting the P-bit. Using the

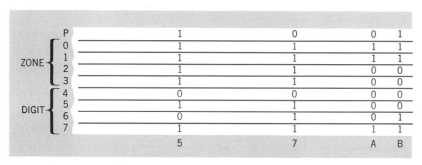

Figure 5.27

Representation of characters: 5,7, A, B on a 9-track tape.

concept of odd Parity, the machine would automatically magnetize or "turn on" the P-bit.

Thus, the complete codes for the number 7 and the letter A are denoted also in Figure 5.27.

The P-bit is used to insure that an odd number of bits is always on for the computer that uses odd-parity checking.

For *even*-parity computers, the P-bit is used to insure that an *even* number of bits is always on.

In short, the number of bits on must always be *odd* for odd-parity computers. Thus magnetic tapes typically utilize an odd number of bits for each character. During the reading of a magnetic tape, the number of bits on is checked to determine if, in fact, an odd number exists. If a single bit were inadvertently demagnetized or the current turned "off," or similarly an extra bit were magnetized, this would result in a parity error. The computer would not continue processing this tape until the problem was located.

Notice that this technique of parity checking only works when a *single* bit for a specific character is inadvertently misrepresented. If two bits are demagnetized, an odd number would still exist and no parity error would occur. Keep in mind, however, that the loss or gain of a single bit during processing is a remote possibility, but one that must nonetheless be properly handled; the loss of two bits, however, has almost no probability of occurring during processing and thus is simply not handled by most computers.

B. DENSITY

We have seen in Chapter 5 that millions of characters can be recorded on a single magnetic tape. Different tapes, however, have different storage capabilities. The *density* of a tape denotes the number of characters that can be represented in a given area of tape. Usually we indicate tape density as the *number of characters per inch*. The most frequently used densities are:

> 556 bpi
> 800 bpi
> 1600 bpi

Bpi is an abbreviation for *bits per inch*. In effect, this indicates the number of characters per inch. Thus the most frequently used tape densities are 556 to 1600 characters per inch.

Obviously, the larger tape densities enable the tape to store more characters. Some magnetic tapes have densities of up to 3000 or more characters per inch.

C. BLOCKING

We have seen that tapes, unlike cards, can utilize any record size. The size of tape records is only restricted by the physical limitations of the computer.

Thus we may have 100-position tape records or 500-position tape records. When all records on a single tape file are the same size, we say that the file employs *fixed-length* records. When records on a single tape file have different sizes depending on the format of each record, we say that the file employs *variable-length* records.

Programming effort is simplified by using fixed-length records on a tape. Variable-length tape records require far more sophisticated programming and thus are not usually employed unless processing is optimized by utilizing records of different sizes.

We will, therefore, restrict our discussion to fixed-length tape records, where each record is the same size. The specific size of each record, however, is determined for each application by the Systems and Programming Staff.

Many applications use, for example, 100 characters per record. We shall now see, however, that small records such as these can, if not handled properly, lead to inefficient processing.

Between tape records the computer automatically reserves a fraction of an inch of blank tape called an Interblock Gap (IBG). Thus when a tape is created as computer output, it is created as noted in Figure 5.28.

For some tape drives, this interblock gap between records is $\frac{3}{4}$ inch, for others it is $\frac{3}{5}$ inch. The smaller the IBG, the less wasted tape there is.

This blank area of tape called an IBG is a necessary part of tape processing. When a computer reads from a tape, it reads an entire record at the average rate of more than 100 inches per second. This is an extremely fast rate. Once a record has been read, and the computer senses its end, it requires a fraction of a second for the equipment to physically stop and cease reading because of the speed with which it functions. This concept is called *inertia*. It is similar to the automobile traveling 60 miles per hour which, after the brake has been applied, requires numerous feet before it actually comes to a full stop.

Thus a magnetic tape that is read or written at tremendous speeds needs a fraction of a second to physically stop after the end of a record has been reached. In this fraction of a second, a fraction of an

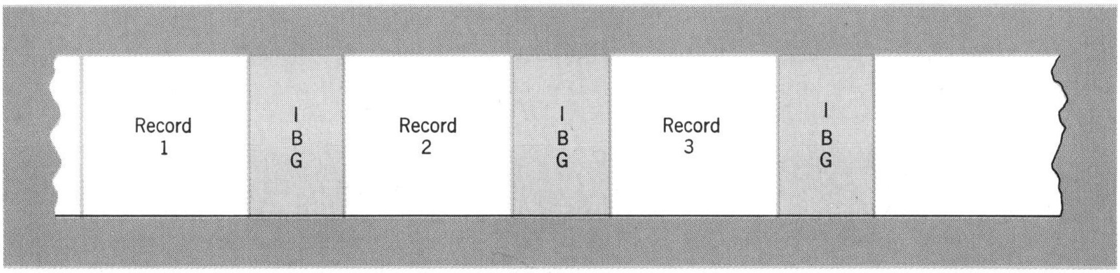

Figure 5.28
Physical records separated by interblock gaps on a tape.

inch of tape has been bypassed. That is, in the time it takes the read/write head of a tape drive to stop, an extra fraction of an inch of tape has been passed.

To accommodate for this inertia, each record, upon creation, is automatically written with a blank area of tape next to it. This blank area called an IBG is the exact size necessary to accommodate for inertia, so that when the fraction of an inch of tape has been bypassed, no significant data will be lost.

Thus each record has a blank area of tape called an IBG adjacent to it. Let us consider the size of the IBG to be 0.6 inches, which it is for some tape drives. If each tape record were 100 characters long, and the tape has a density of 800 bpi, we would have data represented on tape as indicated in Figure 5.29.

You will note that while each record occupies $\frac{1}{8}$ (0.125) of an inch, each IBG adjacent to it uses $\frac{3}{5}$ (0.6) inches. In effect, we would have more blank tape than recorded areas.

To alleviate this problem, the computer systems allow us to "*block*" or group tape records to make maximum use of the tape area. The Systems and Programming Staff determines the size of the block, or the blocking factor, as indicated in Figure 5.30.

In this way, the computer processes 8 records (as an example) as a group. If each record contained 100 characters, the physical record or block would contain 800 characters. At 800 bpi that would be 1 inch of tape. Thus we would have our 0.6 inch IBG between each inch of data. This is a distinct improvement over our previous example where we had substantially more blank area than recorded data.

The blocking of data on tape does *not* represent very much increase of programming effort. Most modern computers have advanced Input and Output Control Systems that facilitate programming effort using magnetic tape or disk processing. The programmer is merely required to supply the blocking factor and the record size and the computer itself will perform the specific input/output functions. When a computer is instructed to read from a

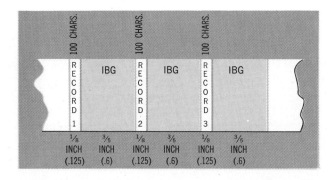

Figure 5.29
Physical representation of data on a tape—without blocking.

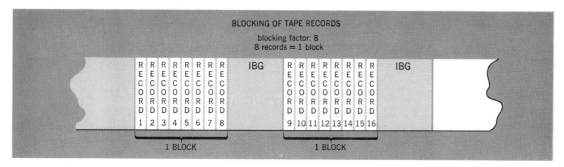

Figure 5.30
Blocking of tape records. Blocking factor: 8; 8 records = 1 block.

tape, for example, it reads a *physical record* or *block* into storage. (See Figure 5.31.)

It then makes the first *logical record,* Record 1, available for processing. When it is instructed to read a second record, it does *not* go to the tape again, but makes Record 2 *from storage* available for processing. Thus for the first 8 READ TAPE commands, the computer accesses the tape only *once.* It then makes each of the logical records available *from storage* as they are called on by a READ TAPE Command. On the ninth READ TAPE command, the computer must physically access the next block of 8 records, and place it in storage overlaying the previous 8 records.

The creation of output tape records operates similarly. If the blocking factor is again 8, the computer will accumulate 8 logical records in storage before it physically writes a block. Thus the first 8 WRITE TAPE commands merely result in the accumulation of 8 logical records *in storage.* The ninth WRITE TAPE command causes the previous block of 8 records to be created on tape and the ninth logical record placed in storage. Here, again, the computer accesses the tape only after every *8 records* have been processed.

In summary, tape records are blocked in an effort to make maximum use of the tape area. The blocking factor is determined by the Systems and Programming Staff and is subject again to the physical limitations of the computer. A record size of 1000 and a blocking factor of 50, for example, would simply be too cumbersome or too large to be effectively handled by most computers. In addition, the larger the physical block, the more chance there is for transmission errors.

The programming effort required for blocking records is not very great, since the computer's Input/Output Control System is capable of handling many of the details. The programmer is required to supply the record size and the blocking factor and the computer can perform much of the internal processing. The programmer need only

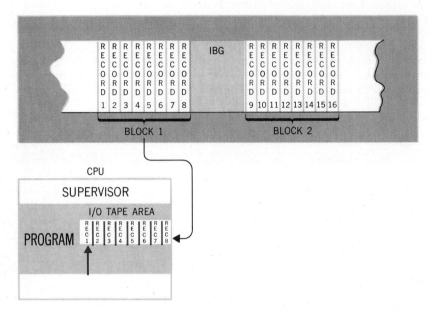

The first read tape command causes a physical block of records to be read in by the control system, with record 1, from storage, then available for processing. Each succeeding read command makes a record *from storage* available for processing, until the first block has been processed, at which point the next block is read from tape.

Figure 5.31
How blocked records are processed by a program.

supply READ and WRITE commands and the blocking and deblocking is automatically handled.

The complex coding of the following can usually be eliminated by utilizing the computer's control system:

1. Tape labels (header labels for identification, trailer labels for summary or total information)
2. Creation of IBGs
3. Blocking of records
4. End-of-file conditions
5. End-of-reel conditions (where a specific file requires more than one physical tape reel)

Fundamental Concepts of Data Processing

6. Wrong length record errors (where programming or transmission errors result in a record that is not of the specified length).

The programmer need only specify the length of a logical record, and the control system will incorporate in the program a wrong length record check. Similarly, the programmer need only specify blocking factor, and blocking techniques will also be included.

D. UTILITY PROGRAMS FOR TAPE PROCESSING

The computer manufacturers have available for the user *utility* or packaged *programs* to handle many types of tape processing. For example, the coding of a program to sort a magnetic tape into a specified sequence is a cumbersome and intricate task. Such sorts are often a necessity, since a tape may be initially created in one sequence, but another sequence is required for specified output reports. For example, a Payroll tape may be created in Social Security Number sequence, but for purposes of preparing payroll checks for distribution, it must be sorted into Department Number sequence.

Most computer manufacturers supply utility sort programs for tapes where the programmer need only supply specification cards denoting:

1. Sort field or fields
2. Ascending or descending sequence
3. Alphabetic or numeric sequence

Similarly, a utility program to merge tapes, called a MERGE utility, creates one tape from several individual tapes. To create a tape from card records a CARD-TO-TAPE utility can be utilized. To write a printed report from a tape can be accomplished using a TAPE-TO-PRINT utility. In all these utility or prewritten, manufacturer-supplied programs, the programmer need only supply specification cards.

Note that these utility programs are of great value at many installations. Consider the case of a Payroll Department that has 50,000 cards, one for each employee in the company. To sort these cards would require much EAM machine and operator time. A Card-to-Tape utility program can be used to create a tape *duplicating* the card records, and a Tape-Sort utility can be used to sort it, in far less time than if the original deck of cards were processed manually.

We have seen, in this Appendix, the intricacies of tape processing. It should provide a perspective on the specific ways in which tapes may be processed by the computer specialist. In addition, in an age where businessmen are often called on to assist in making decisions on computer equipment and computer staffing, a knowledge of magnetic tape processing, which is a significant area in most installations, is relevant and extremely important.

SELF-EVALUATING QUIZ

1. Data is recorded on magnetic tape on a thin film of _____ .
2. Most computer centers use _____(no.)_____ or _____(no.)_____ track tapes.
3. The tracks of a 9-track tape are labeled _____(no.)_____ to _____(no.)_____ and _____(letter)_____ .
4. Four bits are used to represent the _____ and four bits are used to represent the _____ .
5. To represent any integer on magnetic tape we typically use _____ in the zone positions.
6. The digit positions of bits 4 to 7 represent the integers _____ , _____ , _____ , and _____ , respectively.
7. The P-bit corresponds to a _____ or _____ bit.
8. _____ is the term used to represent the utilization of an odd number of on-bits for any character.
9. The number of characters per inch of tape is called _____ .
10. The most frequently used densities are _____ , _____ , and _____ , although some tapes have densities in excess of _____ .
11. When records on a single tape file have different sizes depending on the format of each record, then the file uses _____ records.
12. Between tape records the computer automatically reserves a fraction of an inch of blank tape called an _____ .
13. This fraction of an inch is necessary to provide for the physical concept of _____ .
14. To make maximum use of the tape area so that less tape is wasted, logical records are often grouped or _____ .
15. (T or F) Suppose an input file is blocked 8. The computer physically reads from the tape after every READ command.
16. (T or F) If an input file is blocked 8, after every eight READ commands a physical record is read into storage.
17. (T or F) The programmer is required to handle most of the sophisticated tape routines in his program.
18. Packaged programs to handle many types of tape processing are called _____ .
19. An example of a packaged tape program is a _____ .
20. A TAPE-TO-PRINT utility performs the operation of _____ .

Fundamental Concepts of Data Processing

SOLUTIONS

1. iron-oxide coating
2. 7 or 9
3. 0; 7; P
4. zone; digit
5. 1111
6. 8, 4, 2, 1
7. parity; check
8. Odd Parity
9. density
10. 556; 800; 1600; 3000

11. variable-length
12. interblock gap (IBG)
13. inertia
14. blocked
15. F
16. T
17. F
18. utility programs
19. SORT utility
20. printing the data that is written on a tape

II. Representation of Data on Magnetic Disk

A. BASIC FEATURES OF THE MAGNETIC DISK PACK

We have already discussed the primary feature of magnetic disk—the *random access* capability. We will now discuss, in greater depth, the distinguishing facets of a disk storage unit in order to present a comprehensive understanding of this important storage medium.

A typical disk storage unit consists of *six* platters, or *disks,* arranged in a vertical stack, called a *disk pack,* as shown in Figure 5.32.

Data may be recorded on both sides of the disks. There are, however, only *ten* recording surfaces, since the upper surface of the top disk and the under surface of the bottom disk cannot be utilized. Each of the ten recording surfaces is accessed by its own individual read/write head, which is capable of both retrieving and storing information.

Technically, the ten recording surfaces are numbered from 0 to 9. The corresponding read/write heads, which access each of these

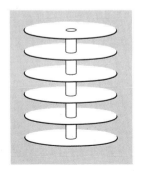

Figure 5.32
Typical disk pack.

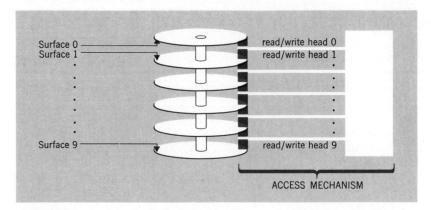

Figure 5.33
How data is accessed from a disk pack. Each read/write head accesses a specific surface. The read/write heads move in and out together as a function of the access mechanism.

surfaces, are similarly numbered. Figure 5.33 illustrates the relationship of the read/write heads to the disk pack.

Now that we have a general perspective of the composition of a disk unit, let us consider a typical recording surface. Each surface is composed of 203 concentric tracks numbered 000 to 202, as shown in Figure 5.34. Each track can store information in the form of magnetized spots. It may appear as if track No. 202 will contain far less data than track No. 000, but because of varying recording densities all

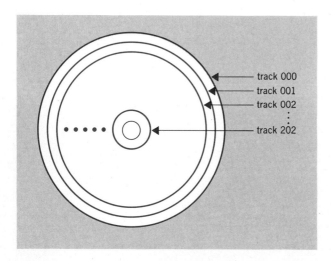

Figure 5.34
Tracks on a disk surface.

Fundamental Concepts of Data Processing

203 tracks store *exactly* the same amount of information. Typically, each track can hold a maximum of 3625 characters or bytes.

It should be noted that ordinarily only 200 of the 203 tracks are used for storing data, since the remaining three are held in reserve in case any other track becomes defective.

The disk pack can therefore store approximately 7.25 million characters of information (10 surfaces $\times$ 200 tracks $\times$ 3625 characters per track).

An important feature of the disk pack is the *cylinder* concept. One way of understanding this concept is to visualize, for example, all of the tracks numbered 050 *on the entire pack,* as shown in Figure 5.35.

The stack of vertical tracks can then be thought of as forming a hypothetical cylinder. There are, therefore, 203 cylinders on the pack, numbered 000 to 202.

It is important to understand the cylinder concept, since data is often stored by cylinder. That is, once a track on a particular surface has been filled, information will subsequently be stored on the same track number within the cylinder, but on the next surface. As an example, suppose track No. 001 has just been filled on surface 7. The next data element will typically be stored on track No. 001 but on surface 8, within the same cylinder. The advantage of storing data in this manner as opposed to other means (such as storing information

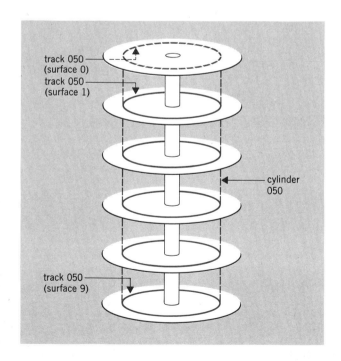

track 050
(surface 0)

track 050
(surface 1)

cylinder
050

track 050
(surface 9)

Figure 5.35
The cylinder concept on magnetic disk.

on an adjacent track on the same surface) is that time is saved in both storing and retrieving data. Since all read/write heads on the access mechanism move in and out *together,* rather than independently; after writing data on a particular track it would be easy to access the same track on the next surface. If a particular track has just been filled with data, there is no need to reposition the access mechanism in order to proceed with the recording of additional information within the same cylinder. All that is required is that a different read/write head, *which is already in position,* be activated to continue the processing on the next surface. No movement of the access arm is required, as would be the case if the adjacent track were used instead.

B. ORGANIZATION OF FILES ON DISK

As was indicated previously, the term *file* refers to a collection of related records. We speak of an Accounts Receivable file, for example, as being the collection of all records of customers who owe money to the company. We will now discuss the various ways in which files can be stored on a disk storage unit. With an understanding of how disk files can be organized, business and data processing students will be able to see the advantages of utilizing disk storage for meeting the requirements of information processing today.

There are generally three different ways in which information can be organized on a magnetic disk: *standard sequential, indexed sequential,* and *direct*. We will now discuss each of these types of file organizations in greater depth.

1. Standard Sequential File Organization

The simplest type of disk file organization is standard sequential. This type of file is identical in concept to the way in which information is stored on magnetic tape. Typically, the records to be stored on a standard sequential file are first sorted into some sequence such as Customer Number, Part Number, Employee Number, and so on. When this sorted file is stored on disk, it is then relatively easy to locate a given record. The record with employee number 00986, for example, would be physically located between records with employee numbers 00985 and 00987.

The main disadvantage with this type of processing, however, is that if we want to access *only* the 986th record in a standard sequential disk file, the read/write heads must first read past 985 records in order to be in the proper position. This process of reading past records can consume valuable time. Thus this type of file is identical to a sequential tape file as shown in Figure 5.36. Note that the part of the disk file which is illustrated appears in cylinder 000, the outermost cylinder.

In effect, then, a standard sequential disk file utilizes the disk as if it were a high-speed tape, with the added benefit that disk processing is many times faster than tape processing, since disk drives can access records more efficiently than tape drives.

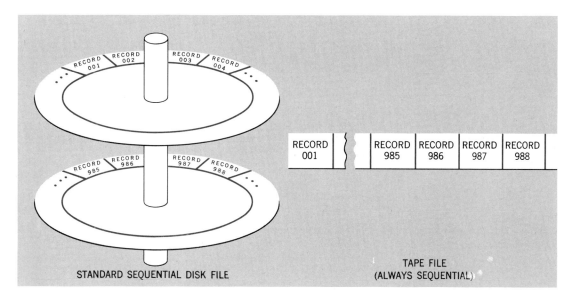

Figure 5.36
Comparison of sequential disk and tape files.

This type of file organization on disk is efficient only when there is a large number of records, such as in a major company's payroll file and when most or all of these would be required for processing. In that case, little time would be wasted in locating a particular record, since the read/write heads would be passing over the previous records anyway in order to process them. However, if all or most of the records in a file are *not* ordinarily required during processing for a given run, then the access time of sequential processing can sometimes be too excessive to make this method efficient. For example, suppose a company has an Inventory file with 10,000 records stored on a disk, with each record pertaining to a different part that is required by the Sales Department of the company. Suppose that most of the time the file is used to process only a small number of records. As an example, each day only those records pertaining to merchandise sold are updated to reflect the new stock status. If, on the average, only 1200 different items are sold daily, of the total 10,000 items, then much processing time would be wasted if a standard sequential file were used.

Standard sequential file organization, therefore, is not an efficient method when only small numbers of records are required for processing from a relatively large file. Standard sequential file organization is also not an efficient method when records required for processing must be accessed in some sequence other than the one in which the file is organized. That is, when input is entered randomly to update or make inquiries about a sequential disk file, then this access method is extremely inefficient. Suppose, for example, that inquiries about an Accounts Receivable disk file are made periodically throughout the day. If such inquiries represent a significant volume and if they are entered randomly, then access time could be excessive, unless another method of file organization were selected.

The two other commonly used methods of file organization for disk, indexed sequential and direct, offer alternatives to this processing problem. These methods of organization can utilize the disk pack's ability to access records in a random manner, providing the reference to disk storage as a random-access device.

2. Indexed Sequential File Organization

An indexed sequential file is a method of organization that facilitates random processing of disk files. An index, or reference table, is maintained as information is recorded on the disk. This index essentially references a *key field* within each record of the file and indicates the corresponding address of that record. The key field, such as Employee Number, Part Number, and so on, within the disk record must be designated by the programmer as a unique field within the record. Thereafter, when a specific record is required for processing, the computer can check the reference table or index to determine the address or location of that record once the key field is supplied. The address for a disk record consists of the cylinder and track numbers. It should be noted that the index is stored on the same disk pack as the file that it references.

Once the address has been obtained from the index, the access mechanism can move directly to the appropriate cylinder without requiring the read/write heads to read past all the previous records in the file until the desired one is found. This concept is analogous to the index in the back of a book that has unique subjects (keys) and their corresponding page numbers (addresses). Thus a specific topic can be accessed from the index without having to read the book from the beginning until that topic is found.

The programmer states, for example, that the Social Security Number of each record within the Employee File is to serve as a key field. This is appropriate, since all social security numbers are unique. The computer then establishes the index on the disk with references to the addresses of employee records, based on their Social Security Numbers. To access a specific record, the Social Security Number of the desired record is supplied, and the computer "looks up" its address on the index and then moves the access mechanism accordingly. Thus, when records must be accessed in a random manner, indexed sequential file organization can result in a substantial amount of time saved as compared to standard sequential organization. Suppose, for example, that the manager of a company wants to retrieve information pertaining to 1000 employees from a 75,000-employee file. The requested employee data is not sequenced. With an indexed sequential file, it is a relatively simple matter to read and extract these records randomly. Thus the term random-access implies that records are to be processed or accessed in some order other than the one in which they were written on the disk.

3. Direct File Organization

Another method of disk organization is called direct organization. In this type of file, records are accessed by a key field which, through some arithmetic calculations, reduces to the actual address (cylinder and track numbers) of the record, without the necessity to first seek the record and its address from an index. Suppose, for example, that the value of a specific key field, such as Part Number, can be multiplied by 859 and then divided by 87 to yield the cylinder number where the record is located. In addition, suppose that if that part number is divided by 63, the result is the track number. Thus, no table is required from which the actual address is searched; instead, some mathematical calculations are performed by the computer according to programmer-supplied formulas to yield the address.

Although direct organization can result in extremely fast access of specific records, in practice there are several factors that must be considered before this type of organization is adopted. More programming effort is required with direct files, since it is necessary for the programmer to supply the formula for converting the key fields into actual addresses. It should be noted that the example above used extremely simple formulas to determine the address. In reality, very complex formulas are often necessary. This is usually the case since the programmer can only use specified areas of the disk for his file; the remaining areas may be either filled with other data or "dedicated" for use later for a given function. As a consequence, the task of finding the appropriate formulas to refer to only certain available addresses can become very difficult. In addition to this difficulty, complex formulas may result in increased access time as compared to indexed sequential organization. It might require more time for the computer to perform the calculation to find the address than to look up the address in the index. Because of the aforementioned considerations, direct files are not as commonly used in business applications as indexed sequential files.

C. OTHER CONSIDERATIONS FOR EFFICIENT DISK UTILIZATION

When a programmer establishes a disk file, he must estimate how much of the physical area should be allotted for the file on the disk pack. This factor is based on the initial number of records that will be placed on the file plus an allowance for growth. Ordinarily, when the file is created all records will first be sorted into sequence by some key field such as Employee Number or Account Number.

You will recall that records cannot easily be added to a tape file. Since tape files are usually in an established sequence, a *new* tape file is required when additions or deletions are to be made to an existing tape. Because of the random-access ability of disks, it is not necessary to recreate a disk file each time additions must be inserted. These additions are merely placed in an *overflow* area, since they need not appear on the disk in a specified sequence. Thus, when *creating* a disk file, the file is generally established in two sections—the prime area to hold all the records necessary for establishing the file and an overflow area to hold new records that are subsequently added to the file.

The deletion of obsolete or unwanted disk records is also a relatively simple task. A special code is added to each record that is to be deleted. Periodically, the file is *rewritten*. All active records (those that are not to be deleted) from the prime and overflow areas are resorted into proper sequence, the newly organized file is temporarily stored on a work file and then rewritten onto the disk pack in the prime area, thus achieving a nonoverflow status. In this process of rewriting the file, all those records that were tagged for deletion have, in fact, been deleted, since they were bypassed when the file was reorganized.

In addition to deleting obsolete records, the rewrite process saves access time for future computer runs. It is less time-consuming for the computer to access data from the prime area only, than to be required to search the overflow area as well.

Note that disk files generally have header labels similar to those discussed for magnetic tape. In addition, records on a disk can also be blocked or unblocked, with fixed or variable lengths.

D. CONCLUSION

We have seen that one of the main advantages of disk storage as compared to magnetic tape is the random-access feature. We have also seen that there are basically three types of file organization for disk—standard sequential, indexed sequential, and direct.

Disk processing is most efficient when large numbers of data records are required for processing, in a random manner. Because of the random-access feature, disks are also commonly used to store *table* files. Table files are those items or records that are not part of data files but are an integral part of the processing function. Withholding tax rate tables, for example, are necessary in Payroll systems to compute each employee's withholding taxes (federal, state, and local) based on his salary. Such files are often stored on disk and accessed when required.

We will now illustrate the use of a withholding tax rate table that has been simplified for ease of discussion. Suppose, for example, that the tax bracket for each salary level is represented by 25 disk records. Each table record has a salary range and includes corresponding withholding tax percentages for federal and state taxes, as shown on the next page.

Salary Range	Federal Withholding Tax Percentage[a]	State Withholding Tax Percentage[a]
00001–01000	14.0	2.0
01000–02000	15.0	3.0
02000–03000	16.0	3.5
03000–04000	17.0	4.0
04000–08000	19.0	5.0
⋮	⋮	⋮

[a] *These figures are used for the purpose of illustration only.*

The salary for each employee must be taxed according to its appropriate bracket. That is, each employee record must be read and its corresponding tax percentage "looked up" on the salary table.

TABLE LOOK-UP PROCEDURE	Input Record	Salary Range	Federal W/H	State W/H
	Salary = 02226	00001–01000	14.0	2.0
		01000–02000	15.0	3.0
		⟶ 02000–03000	16.0	3.5

If this salary table file is put onto tape, sequential processing of salary levels is required. That is, each time a salary figure is read in on an employee record, the tape must be read from record 1, the lowest salary level, until the appropriate salary on the tax table is found. This can result in excessive processing time. If the first employee record contains a salary of $99,000, for example, much of the table would be read before the appropriate one is found.

If a disk is used to store the tax table with the salary as a *key* field, then each employee's salary can be looked up on the disk index, the appropriate record accessed directly and the corresponding tax percentages found quickly.

In addition to tax tables for payroll, we often find price tables for stock numbers (in order to process Purchasing Files), and so on.

Chapter 6 *A Guide to Terminals and Time-Sharing*

I. DATA COMMUNICATIONS CONCEPTS

A. REMOTE ACCUMULATION OF DATA
   1. Online Processing
   2. Offline Processing
B. INQUIRY
C. REAL-TIME SYSTEMS
D. TIME-SHARING

II. EQUIPMENT

A. TERMINAL DEVICES
   1. Input Terminal Units
      a. *Card Reader*
      b. *Magnetic Tape Drive*
      c. *Optical Character Reader or Optical Scanner*
      d. *Paper Tape Reader*
   2. Output Terminal Units
      a. *Line Printer*
      b. *Card Punch*
      c. *Paper Tape Punch*
   3. Sample Combination Input/Output Terminals
      a. *Terminal Typewriter or Keyboard*
      b. *Cathode Ray Tube with Keyboard or Light Pen*
      c. *Graph Plotter*
      d. *Audio Response Device*
      e. *Voice-Input to Control Station*
   4. Factors for Selecting Terminal Equipment
      a. *Computer and Communication Lines*
      b. *Functions To Be Performed by the Terminal*
      c. *Cost*
      d. *Speed*
      e. *Human Adaptability*
      f. *Size and Type of Display*
B. COMMUNICATION LINES
C. COMPUTER-REQUIREMENTS
   1. A Large Core Storage Capacity
   2. Complex Control
   3. Interrupt Ability

III. OTHER ELEMENTS OF DATA COMMUNICATIONS

A. ERRORS
B. SCHEDULING
C. SECURITY

We have seen that the major use of commercial computers is in the processing of vast amounts of data in relatively little time. Each new generation or model of computer has increased speed so that input data may be converted to output in even shorter time periods.

A major problem with the utilization of such equipment is not, however, the speed with which computers process data, but the time required to physically transport information into the computer room and to then transport the required output to the proper department or business area.

You will recall that there are several steps involved in obtaining required output from input. (See Figure 6.1.)

1. Incoming source documents must be transmitted from the user or requesting department to the Control Unit of a Data Processing Installation. The Control Unit must check these documents to determine if they are complete and proper. A count is maintained to insure that none are lost.
2. The source documents must generally be transmitted from the Control Unit to the Operations Staff for conversion to a machine-readable form such as cards, tape, or disk, unless the incoming documents are already in an appropriate form. If card processing is utilized, the deck often must be sorted, collated, reproduced, or in some other way operated upon by Electronic Accounting Machine (EAM) equipment.

Fundamental Concepts of Data Processing

Illustrative Terminal Equipment (Courtesy Data Pathing, Inc.)

3. The source documents and their converted counterparts must again be sent to the Control Unit for tally checks to insure that nothing has been lost.
4. The machine-readable input must then be sent to the computer room where it often must wait hours or even days, for processing because of unforeseen backlogs.
5. The output must be transmitted to the Control Unit for further checks.
6. The output must then be sent to the user or requesting department.

Each of the above procedures relies, in large part, on *manual* operations or operators. The result can thus be lengthy delays or other inefficiencies. Thus, while it may require 30 minutes to operate on input and convert it to output in a computer run, it may take three or four days in total, including the transmittal of the input to the Data Processing Center, conversion to a machine-acceptable form, and transmittal back again from the Data Processing Center. If such input

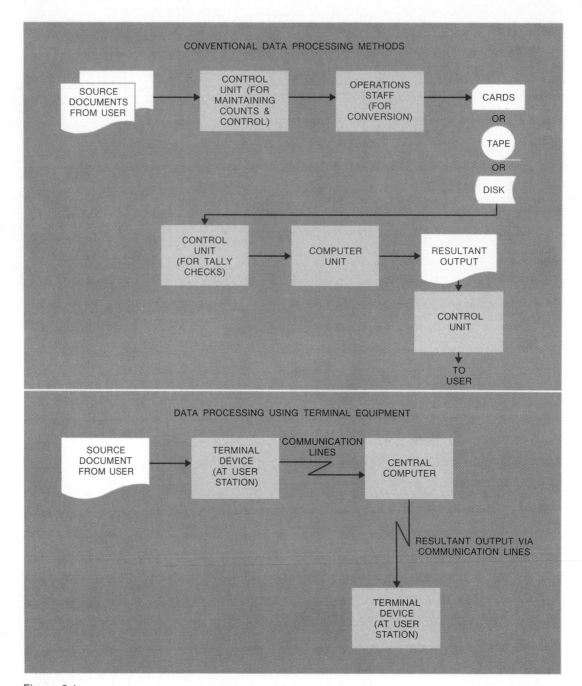

Figure 6.1
Comparison of conventional data processing methods with data processing
methods using terminal equipment.

Fundamental Concepts of Data Processing

and output is transmitted via interoffice mail instead of by a special messenger, the total elapsed time may even be longer. In either case, high-speed computer processing must wait for conventional distribution methods for transmittal. Thus any systematic procedure that could reduce this elapsed time would greatly enhance the total effectiveness of computer processing.

We have thus far discussed devices that can effectively eliminate step No. 2 above, the conversion of source documents to a machine-readable form. These include Magnetic Ink Character Recognition (MICR) and Optical Character Recognition (OCR) devices.

In this chapter we will discuss terminal equipment which:

1. effectively eliminates the conversion of source documents to a machine-readable form; and,
2. results in decreased manual intervention and thereby greatly enhances the speed with which output can be delivered to a requesting department or customer by employing online, or immediate, processing.

Data Communications sometimes called *Teleprocessing,* is a relatively new area of data processing that facilitates the flow of data both into and out from a computer center. Input devices, called *remote terminals* are placed strategically throughout a company, often within the requesting departments themselves. These devices, using leased or public telephone lines, are linked with a central computer in a Data Processing Center. They are called *remote* terminals since they do not appear in a data-processing center side-by-side with a computer. Operators key data into the terminal, where it is automatically transmitted to the central computer. These operators need only be familiar with a typewriter keyboard in order to key in required information. This system reduces the need for the following:

1. A Control Unit to maintain constant checks on incoming data. The incoming data is automatically transmitted to the central computer and thus information is not lost in transit. Similarly, data need not be manually checked for validity. The computer will automatically reject invalid information.
2. A Keypunch or Operations Staff to convert incoming source documents to a machine-readable form. The terminal operators "feed" the data directly to the computer, thus eliminating the conversion process. In this way, purchase orders, payroll changes, customer inquiries, and so on may be keyed directly into a computer via a terminal.
3. Backlogging of computer runs, since the computer can be programmed to operate on data as it is entered, or by some established priority.
4. Messengers to physically transport input data from the requesting department to the Data Processing Center and then to transport

output data from the Data Processing Center back to the department. The terminal is linked with the central computer thereby eliminating manual delivery. If the terminal can receive messages or accept output (some are strictly input devices), then again, manual intervention may be eliminated, since the computer can transmit the required output *directly* to the department via the terminal.

A central computer can have numerous terminals hooked up to it. These terminals may be utilized by separate *departments* employing a central computer, or by separate *companies* employing a central computer. These terminals may be located in the same building, to be used by various departments, or they may be spread out across the country if the user departments or businesses are not centrally located. (See Figure 6.2.)

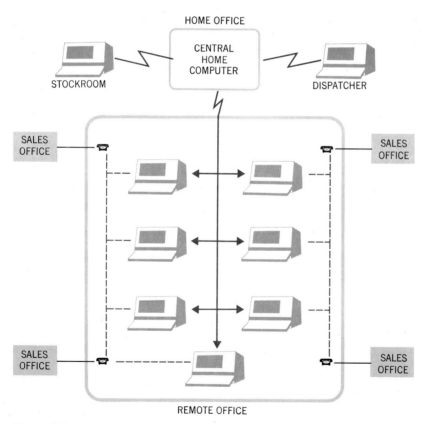

Figure 6.2
Illustration of terminals remotely linked to a central computer. Courtesy UNIVAC.

Fundamental Concepts of Data Processing

Source Data Automation (SDA) is the term now used for data processing systems where the conversion of data to machine-readable form is performed at the point where it originates instead of at some centralized location. High-level SDA systems today usually involve several departments; thus top management must be cognizant of the options available so that major company-wide decisions may be reached that will gain cooperation from all or most departments.

The recent rise of terminals in businesses today signals a major advance in computer technology. With the use of terminals in business areas throughout companies, the gap between data processing personnel and businessmen is greatly reduced. The *direct* transmittal of data from departments to the Data Processing Center minimizes inefficiencies and communication errors. Thus, it is imperative for business and data processing students to be cognizant of how these devices can enhance operations within specific business areas.

This chapter will attempt to enlighten these students as to the potential of terminals in business, and will indicate how to effectively utilize and understand terminal processing.

SELF-EVALUATING QUIZ

1. Computers can process data in a relatively short time. Timing problems in data processing do occur, however, in _____ .
2. Thus, while computer operations generally present no timing difficulties, _____ operations do.
3. _____ is the term applied to an area of data processing that facilitates the flow of information both into and out of a computer center with the utilization of terminal equipment.
4. Remote terminals are _____ .
5. (T or F) Remote Terminals are usually in the same physical room as the Central Processing Unit.
6. Remote Terminals sometimes use _____ to connect them to the CPU.
7. (T or F) Data entered into a terminal must be converted to a machine-readable form.
8. (T or F) The input unit of a terminal usually resembles a typewriter keyboard.
9. Terminal processing eliminates much of the _____ necessary in other forms of processing data.
10. (T or F) Some terminals are strictly input devices, but most are input/output devices.
11. (T or F) A central computer can have only one terminal hooked up to it.
12. The direct transmittal of data from departments to the Data Processing Center minimizes _____ .

SOLUTIONS

1. getting the data *to* the computer and transmitting the output *from* the computer to the business area
2. manual
3. Data Communications or Teleprocessing
4. devices that are hooked up to a central computer but are physically located in different areas or business departments so that these departments can have access to a computer.

5. F
6. leased or public telephone lines
7. F
8. T
9. manual intervention or control
10. T
11. F
12. manual inefficiencies or communication gaps

I. Data Communications Concepts

There are four major areas in which terminal technology is most often employed. Let us discuss each in detail.

A. THE REMOTE ACCUMULATION OF DATA

As we have noted, numerous terminals, spaced remotely in key locations, may have access to a central computer for the purpose of entering input. These terminals may be placed in different departments, such as Payroll, Accounts Receivable, Inventory, Accounts Payable, and so on. In this way, the Accounts Receivable Department, for example, can enter billing data into the computer via its terminal and the Payroll Department can similarly enter salary changes via its terminal. Both departments, then, have direct access to one central computer that is capable of processing all the data.

Several terminals may also be used within a *single* department. Suppose, for example, that the Inventory Department has several warehouses throughout the United States. To computerize inventory procedures *without* the use of Data Communications, these warehouses would be required to prepare inventory statements and send them to the Data Processing Center where they would be verified and then converted to a machine-acceptable form, prior to computer processing. The transmittal of this data would be performed manually and, therefore, could become very inefficient. With the use of Data Communications, however, remote terminals can be placed at each of these warehouses. The inventory data can then be transmitted speedily and *directly* to the computer via the terminal without conversion or rigid manual controls. The computer can then accumulate all warehouse data efficiently and effectively by minimizing manual intervention. (See Figure 6.3.)

Thus terminals may be used in many different business areas for the remote accumulation of data. Let us consider how the computer can operate on this data.

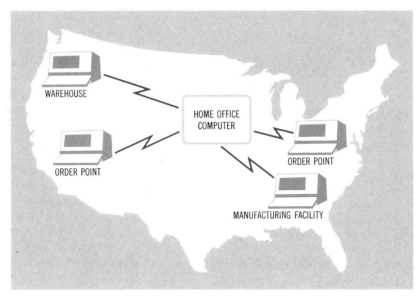

The above figure represents typical terminal usage for an Inventory System with branch offices throughout the country. There may be two Order Points, as shown, or many more. A request for an item is made at an Order Point. If the item is available, the Warehouse is notified, by computer, and the item is shipped. If the number of such items at the Warehouse reaches a prescribed minimum number, then the Manufacturing Facility is notified, by computer, to produce more.

Figure 6.3
The use of data communications for an inventory system. Courtesy UNIVAC.

1. Online Processing

When input data is entered from a terminal for the purpose of *immediately* altering the contents of records on a file, an *online* operation is required. That is, the computer processes the input data as it is entered and alters or *updates* the required files immediately. Terminals are utilized to enter data for online operations, since they provide immediate and direct input to the data processing flow, eliminating the need for manual transmittal. Magnetic disks are most often utilized for storing files when data is to be updated online, since they provide the ability to access records via terminals directly and, therefore, rapidly.

An Inventory Disk File, for example, may be altered or updated by an online operation at the precise time that changes in stock items are keyed into the computer via a terminal. In this way, all inventory data on the disk is current and may be used to answer inquiries or to produce printouts, with relative accuracy, at any time. Without the use of online processing, data files would only be current immediately after a periodic (weekly, semi-monthly, monthly) update procedure. At all other times, these files would not contain changes that have occurred during the current period or cycle.

In short, where terminals are used for online operations, *immediate* updating of files is considered a necessity.

2. Offline Processing

Terminals may also be used mainly to eliminate manual controls where online or immediate computer processing is *not* required. In this case, terminal data that is to be entered into the computer can be initially *stored* until other terminal data is received. That is, terminal data is first converted to a separate medium such as punched cards, punched paper tape, magnetic tape, magnetic disk, in an *offline* operation. When all such terminal data has been entered, the resultant medium (punched cards, punched paper tape, magnetic tape, or magnetic disk) is then used to transmit the data to the computer via communication lines in a *batch-processing* mode. In this way, the computer can process the data more efficiently. Thus the terminal serves a two-fold purpose:

1. It is used to enter source data, which is then converted to a medium that can be more quickly processed by the computer. This is performed *offline*.
2. It is used to then transmit the data from this converted form to the computer in a batch-processing mode, that is, when the data has been collected in a large quantity.

The terminal can contain a keyboard, for example, to enter the data, and a high-speed device, such as a punched paper tape drive or a magnetic tape drive, to store the data. The latter unit of the terminal is then used to transmit the data to the computer via telephone or teletype lines.

A Payroll System, for example, may utilize a terminal to:

1. Read payroll data from time cards and convert the information to a magnetic tape in an *offline* operation.
2. Transmit the grouped payroll data from magnetic tape to the computer in a batch-processing operation, from a remote location.

Figure 6.4 serves as a similar illustration of the utilization of terminals offline.

In summary, when a terminal is used for converting data to a more efficient medium using specialized equipment *not directly under the control of the computer,* we call this an offline operation. Offline conversions and then the batch processing of data from high-speed devices can result in substantial savings of computer time, where online processing is not required.

Fundamental Concepts of Data Processing

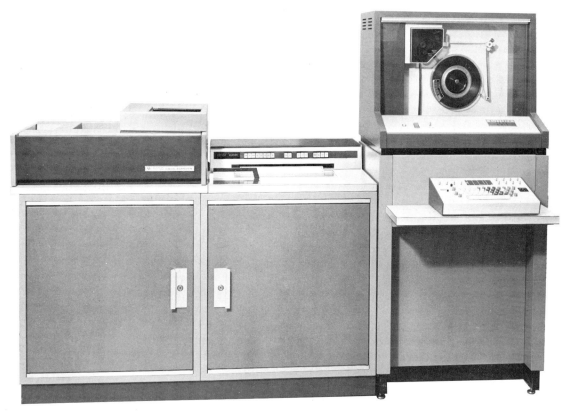

Figure 6.4
C.O.D.E. (Computer Oriented Data Entry) Scanner. This is a terminal device which reads data from embossed plastic cards utilizing an optical scanning unit and converts the data, offline, to either a punched paper tape or a magnetic tape. The paper tape or magnetic tape then serves as input, using communication lines, to a computer system. Courtesy Addressograph Multigraph Corp.

B. INQUIRY

A central computer with files of data stored on a medium such as a disk may be accessed by a terminal for the purpose of requesting information. That is, the terminal at a remote location is *not* used to update or alter a file, but to make inquiries concerning the data on that file.

Consider a terminal in the Accounts Receivable Department of a large company. Because of the large clientele, it may not be feasible for the department itself to maintain, within its manual records, billing information on each of its customers. This information can be stored, instead, at a computer center on a magnetic disk. When a customer requests information pertaining to a bill, a terminal device linked to a central computer can extract the appropriate information. The terminal must be capable of entering the request and also of receiving a reply. That is, the terminal must be an input/output device.

The terminal is a beneficial method of access or inquiry only when information must be extracted from a file *immediately*. When a request can be delayed, or answered at a later date, then the expense of utilizing terminals may be unjustified.

Usually *direct-access* files are used to store the data, since these increase access speed. In most cases the files themselves are updated *online,* since the inquiries require records with *current* information.

Various businesses find terminal devices for inquiry purposes a necessity. Brokerage firms, for example, rely on such devices for quoting stock prices to their customers. A direct-access file is maintained with stock prices. It is updated online as new prices become available.

This file is accessed by the stock broker via an input/output terminal at his desk. To obtain a price, he keys in the stock code; the computer receives this information immediately, accesses the price from the file and transmits the data back to the terminal. In this way, any stock price may be quoted within seconds. The computer itself must be preprogrammed to accept any inquiry, seek the appropriate information, and transmit it to the user.

Terminals are generally used for inquiry purposes where:

1. Customers need immediate replies to inquiries; and,
2. Business representatives or managers need information for decision-making purposes.

Figure 6.5 illustrates the use of terminals for *both* the remote accumulation of data and for inquiries. The stockroom, for example, has a terminal for accumulation of data, while the Executive Offices use a terminal for inquiry on stock levels about which company-wide decisions are made.

C. REAL-TIME SYSTEMS

A *real-time* system is one that has the capability of accessing and updating computer files using terminal equipment quickly enough to affect decision making. A typical example of such a system is an Airlines Reservation System. This is a real-time application, where customers can request airline information and receive responses quickly enough to make a decision concerning the reservation of an airplane seat.

Fundamental Concepts of Data Processing

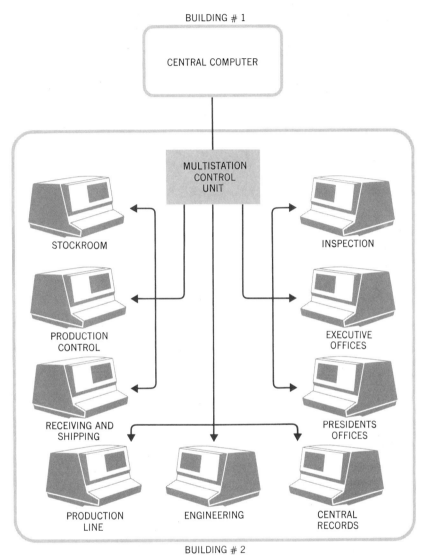

BUILDING # 1

CENTRAL COMPUTER

MULTISTATION CONTROL UNIT

STOCKROOM

PRODUCTION CONTROL

RECEIVING AND SHIPPING

PRODUCTION LINE

ENGINEERING

CENTRAL RECORDS

INSPECTION

EXECUTIVE OFFICES

PRESIDENTS OFFICES

BUILDING # 2

The above represents the usage of terminals for a typical Inventory and Sales system. Such a system gives immediate information to the various offices *which make inquiries* to prevent both overselling and underselling of space, time or material. It also provides for up-to-the-second inventory records which are modified by each transaction.

Figure 6.5
The use of terminals for inventory and sales systems. Courtesy UNIVAC.

A customer can inquire about a specific flight or about flights leaving for a specific location on a given day. The airline representative keys the inquiry into a terminal. The terminal is hooked up to a central computer, which immediately accesses the data and prints the requested information on the terminal (flight number, date of departure, time, destination, arrival time, number of seats available). If the customer wishes to make a reservation, the airline representative can enter the appropriate information into the terminal. The data will be used to immediately *update* the main file, which would then indicate one less space on the specific flight. Similarly, cancellations can be keyed into the terminal that would update the file so that it reflects one more space. These terminals may be placed in hundreds of airline offices throughout the country.

Thus real-time systems are *online* systems with the facility of *accessing and updating* files using terminal equipment, *quickly enough to affect decision making*. This type of processing is utilized by other reservation systems, such as hotels. Banks frequently use real-time systems to update accounts and to answer inquiries concerning specific transactions. Betting facilities use terminals in a real-time environment to key in betting statistics. The computer can then instantaneously print the existing odds.

Real-time systems may also be employed to process the internal operations of a company, in an integrated manner. In this way, management can make quick and effective decisions based on inquiries made to the computer via terminal equipment. That is, profits and losses, assets and liabilities, profit ratios, and so on may be maintained accurately and precisely through real-time processing, and may be accessed, at any time, by management for the purpose of making executive-level decisions.

Real-time systems utilize perhaps the most sophisticated programming and systems techniques in data processing today. They can generally be employed only in large-scale companies that can afford the vast equipment required. Real-time systems require large expenditures for sophisticated equipment and for enormous programming effort. Although they do not initially result in savings to a company because of their great expense, the intangible benefits (to the customers served, or to management, which can employ real-time systems for its decision-making) can produce huge profits.

D. TIME-SHARING

Small-scale companies often need data processing equipment, but find the cost of acquisition and maintenance prohibitive. Such companies can rent or lease computer time from leasing firms that profit from buying a large-scale computer and then renting time on it. The small-scale organizations, in effect, *share* the computer's use. This concept is called *TIME-SHARING*. Most often, time-sharing is achieved by the establishment of terminals at a specific location in each

Fundamental Concepts of Data Processing

company that wants to share a computer's use. These terminals are often employed by the user to transmit a program, or set of instructions, followed by the corresponding input to be processed. Similarly, the user can transmit input data to be processed by a program that has already been stored in the computer.

Terminals may also be used for time-sharing where a large company has one central computer and permits user departments or branch offices to access it via terminals for the purpose of entering programs and/or data to be processed.

Note that in the previous three applications of terminal equipment, the terminal devices were used for input or input/output. The program to accept and transmit this data must be previously stored in the computer. That is, an airlines reservation clerk who keys an inquiry into the computer will not receive a reply unless the computer has been programmed to accept the input. Similarly, the terminals at warehouses throughout the country may not be used to key in inventory information in an online environment unless the centralized computer has a stored program that instructs it to *accept* the data. With terminals used for time-sharing, however, these devices can be used to key in *programs* first. These programs are generally simplified, since the terminal, as a manual device, is not a very efficient method for entering large-scale programs. Most often, these programs are coded in BASIC, a programming language specifically suited for condensed or efficient coding. Once the program has been transmitted to the CPU via the terminal, any required data can then be entered.

An engineering company would find great benefit in using a central computer with terminals in various engineering offices for time-sharing. In this way, engineers with equations to solve can utilize a terminal in conjunction with a computer to obtain a solution. They are spared tedious hours solving mathematical problems that the computer can do accurately and efficiently in seconds. The engineers might, for example, write the equations in the BASIC language and obtain their answers, usually within seconds.

Time-sharing, using terminals linked to a central computer, has recently become highly effective in educational institutions for teaching programming. Some schools often cannot justify the cost of a computer system. Many of these collectively lease centralized equipment, with terminals at each campus. The students then learn the BASIC language and can write simplified programs. They can then use the computer to solve required problems. Similarly, large schools with numerous campuses can employ a central computer with terminals at each campus hooked up to it, in a time-sharing environment. In this way, there is only one expense for the central computer.

From the above, we can see that Data Communications holds a key position in the present and future of computer technology. Its concepts may be used in high-level, expensive Real-Time Systems or in small companies requiring minimum access to a computer. In short, where

Order Processing and Inventory Control

A company may have a number of warehouse and distribution points. By tying each of these locations to a computer through a terminal, one can transmit orders daily to the computer for processing. Almost immediately, the computer will determine which items are to be shipped from each location, and transmit shipping data to the appropriate terminal. The terminal, in turn, will print bills-of-lading, invoices and up-dated inventory listings, and also punch summary cards.

Now one can recognize and correct problem areas much sooner than by any previous method; warehouse space and shipping expenses are significantly reduced; and one can quickly revise and more accurately forecast sales and market trends.

Payroll and Accounting

With a terminal, at all or selected key locations, daily transmission of local data on payroll, purchasing, billing, etc. can be processed at a central computer site the same day it is generated—no more misunderstandings or delays due to mailing, loss or damage. Weekly financial reports are now ready on Monday morning instead of Wednesday afternoon—in fact, daily reports are possible now.

Optimum Scheduling of production, manpower, equipment and maintenance, as well as the routing and delivery of products to and from many widely separated points.

Information Retrieval of personnel or student records, medical data on patients, high-volume statistical data, etc., in industrial organizations, school systems, hospitals, and other large or decentralized operations.

Programming from a location other than a computer site. Programs in Basic or other source languages can be written locally and quickly transmitted by a terminal to the central computer. Almost immediately the results are returned to the terminal, saving valuable time between need and the reponse.

Management Reports summarizing current status of both headquarter and outlying operations, including trend analysis and product trade information.

Plus . . .
Accounts receivable, accounts payable, credit ratings, market research, operations research, customer inquiries . . . or any application in which one would normally use a computer.

Figure 6.6
The above figure illustrates how terminal equipment may typically be used. Courtesy UNIVAC.

immediate communication with a computer is needed for (1) inquiry or (2) updating of files or where (3) remote terminals can efficiently save manual intervention and extensive control of documents, or where a (4) central computer may be shared by several offices, Data Communications equipment is employed. (See Figure 6.6.)

SELF-EVALUATING QUIZ

1. The four major areas in which terminal technology is most often employed are _____, _____, _____, and _____ .

Fundamental Concepts of Data Processing

2. A(n) _____ operation is the entering of data from terminals so that it may be transcribed or converted to another medium for future batch processing.
3. (T or F) Offline operations result only in computer transmittal of data from the terminal to another device, such as a tape or disk drive, for future processing.
4. (T or F) Offline operations are performed when immediate processing by the computer is not required.
5. (T or F) A stock exchange would be likely to store incoming stock quotations on an offline device for future processing rather than immediately updating the master file.
6. (T or F) A bank that performs its updating once a day would be likely to store incoming transactions on an offline device for future processing rather than immediately updating the master file.
7. When input data is entered from a terminal for the purpose of immediately altering the contents of a file, a(n) _____ operation is required.
8. An area where online operations are required is a(n) _____ .
9. Data Communications Systems for inquiry purposes most often utilize _____ files, since they have the advantage of random access, which increases _____ .
10. Terminals are most often used for inquiry purposes for _____ and _____ .
11. A(n) _____ System is one that has the capability of accessing and updating computer files in an online environment using terminal equipment, for decision-making purposes.
12. (T or F) Real-Time Systems utilize offline operations to immediately update files.
13. (T or F) Real-Time Systems are generally used by large companies since they are very costly.
14. To rent or share time on a computer is called _____ .
15. _____ and _____ frequently utilize computers on a time-sharing basis.

SOLUTIONS

1. remote accumulation of data; inquiry; Real-Time Systems; time-sharing
2. offline
3. T
4. T
5. F-Stock exchanges require the data immediately.
6. T
7. online
8. reservation system
9. direct-access or disk; speed of access
10. customers requiring information; managers requiring company data
11. real-time
12. F-online
13. T
14. time-sharing
15. Educational institutions; engineering firms

II. Equipment

There are three major facets of a Data Communications system:

A. Terminal Devices
B. Communication Lines
C. Computer System

A. TERMINAL DEVICES

As we have indicated, terminal devices are located wherever large amounts of input data are anticipated. That is, it is important to space remote terminals at strategic points where the information flow is the greatest.

Terminals that we will be considering may be classified as:

1. Input to the computer (transmit only).
2. Output from the computer (receive only).
3. Sample combination input/output (transmit-only and receive-only units)

The vast majority of terminals in use today include both a receive-only unit (output terminal) and a transmit-only unit (input terminal). Terminals that can transmit only are rarely in use, since the computer needs some way usually to communicate with the terminal, even if only to provide error signals or wait impulses. The input or transmit-only terminals discussed below in Section 1, then, are generally part of input/output terminals. The receive-only or output terminals, however, can be used independently. These are discussed in Section 2. Section 3 includes the most frequently used receive-only terminals that are used in conjunction with transmit-only units.

1. Input Terminal Units

Transmit-only terminals are used to enter data from remote locations directly into a computer system. If a terminal were needed to enter data for an online or an offline operation and no inquiries were necessary, then an input or transmit-only terminal could be used independently, although it rarely is employed as a stand-alone device. As indicated above, input units are used almost exclusively in conjunction with output (transmit-only) units as combination input/output terminals. The typical input units include:

a. Card reader (where input is a punched card)

Many payroll systems utilize card readers at remote locations where employees are given time cards with which to check in and out. These readers read the data punched into each employee's time card.

b. Magnetic tape drive

When a magnetic tape drive serves as an input unit of a terminal, the data recorded on the tape has usually been entered in some offline

Fundamental Concepts of Data Processing

operation. Such tape data may be on typical reels of tape, or cassettes or cartridges.

c. *Optical character reader or optical scanner*

Where documents such as invoices, purchase orders, and bills are entered as input in large volume, from various locations, optical scanners can serve as remote input terminals.

Optical scanners may be located, for example, at various points on each sales floor of a large department store for the purpose of transmitting sales information directly into the computer. In this way, the Accounts Receivable File can be maintained with greater accuracy and precision, so that customer inquiries may be answered based on the most current information. Similarly, management can make inquiries on sales patterns, at any given time, for decision-making purposes.

d. *Paper tape reader*

These are often used to enter cash register tapes or accounting machine tapes from remote locations.

Note that there are numerous other input terminals, but the above represent the most frequently used. Note also that these input terminals are sometimes used in offline processing prior to entering the computer flow. That is, a card reader at a remote location may be linked, offline, to a magnetic tape drive. In this way, card data is read by the reader and immediately placed on tape. The tape is then used, at a later date, as input to the computer, remotely, in a batch-processing mode. Thus we may have terminal systems at remote locations with several devices that are integrated for offline processing prior to transmitting data to a central computer.

2. Output Terminal Units

When remote locations require output from a computer with minimum delay and maximum efficiency, then an output terminal is most appropriate. Note, however, that strict output terminals may *not* be used at remote locations when operator communication with the CPU is required. That is, a receive-only, or output terminal, displays information and cannot transmit requests back to the CPU. There is often a need for receive-only terminals but most receive-only units are used in conjunction with an input unit.

Frequently used output units include:

a. *Line printer*

Suppose, for example, a large company has numerous branch offices throughout the United States. Payroll checks may be printed directly at these branch offices utilizing one central computer and a line printer at each branch office. In this way, duplicate files need not be maintained at the various locations and only minimum control is required to see that checks are properly received.

b. *Card punch*

Devices that punch output cards may also be used to transmit central information to various locations. See Figure 6.7 for an illustration of several of these devices in an integrated network.

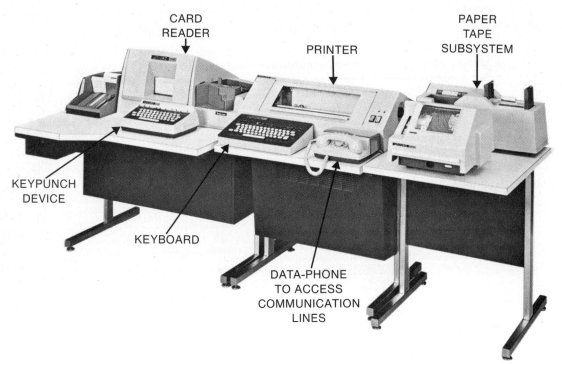

CARD
READER

PRINTER

PAPER
TAPE
SUBSYSTEM

KEYPUNCH
DEVICE

KEYBOARD

DATA-PHONE
TO ACCESS
COMMUNICATION
LINES

Figure 6.7
The above represents an integrated Data Communications terminal set-up. It
can be used to operate online or to batch process offline prior to
communications with the computer. That is, card data may be read by the
card reader and converted, offline, to a punched paper tape, or transmitted
directly to the computer. Courtesy UNIVAC.

c. Paper tape punch
   The above three output units can operate as transmit-only output
units if desired. The following devices (cathode-ray tube, audio
response unit, graph plotter) in the next section must be used in
conjunction with an input device, and thus will not be discussed here.

3. Sample Combination Input/Output Terminals
For most online teleprocessing applications, where requests are keyed
in at remote locations and the central computer transmits responses,
input/output terminals are used. That is, most terminals have the
capability of both transmitting to and receiving messages from a
computer. Any combination input/output keyboard is available but the
most commonly used I/O terminals include:

*a. **Terminal typewriter or keyboard*** (Figure 6.8).

This is the most widely used input/output terminal. The device is not unlike a typewriter. When input is entered, an operator keys the data by depressing the various keys in much the same way as data is typed on a typewriter. Depending on the data to be processed at the specific terminal, the keyboard may be strictly numeric, strictly alphabetic, or standard alphanumeric, where all characters are included. There is a typed *hard-copy* printout of all data entered. A *hard-copy* printout is one that may be maintained for future reference, as opposed to data displayed on a screen, for example, which is not available after it is viewed. When the computer communicates with the operator, the typewriter is activated by the CPU, and the required information is printed on the typed sheet.

As indicated, this is the most widely used I/O terminal. Operators may key in as input, stock receipts, purchase orders, payroll changes, and so on. In addition, these operators can make requests of the

Figure 6.8
Keyboard terminal. Courtesy IBM.

Figure 6.9
Computer terminal on wheels: a four-wheeled cart keeps up with quality at
American Motors. A computer terminal on wheels is helping American
Motors' production specialists assure the performance and safety of its cars.
This IBM communications terminal, mounted on a four-wheeled cart and
connected to an IBM computer by cable, lets an industrial engineer quickly
spot any recurring problems on the AM assembly line. After singling out a car
for computer review, the engineer uses his traveling computer terminal to tell
a centrally located IBM computer everything that has been listed on the car's
inspection log as it is indexed along the assembly line. Any recurring
problems are quickly spotted, and immediate action is taken to alleviate the
condition. Courtesy IBM.

computer via the terminal and receive immediate responses. See
Figure 6.9.

b. Cathode ray tube with keyboard or light pen (See Figure 6.10)

The keyboard is the standard input medium. An operator keys in
data or makes inquiries using this typewriter-like unit.

The Cathode Ray Tube (CRT) is a visual display device similar to a
television screen. This output unit instantaneously displays data from
the computer on the screen. This is a high-speed device, since data is
not transmitted to a typed page using a relatively slow print device.
Instead, large amounts of information can be displayed instantly.

As indicated, the keyboard is a standard *input* unit for the CRT. A
light pen can also serve as an input tool, to be used for making graphic

Fundamental Concepts of Data Processing

Figure 6.10
Cathode ray tube (CRT) with keyboard.
Courtesy Burroughs Corporation.

corrections or additions to the visual display on the cathode ray tube.
An operator simply uses the pen to modify data on the screen. These
modifications are then transmitted to the CPU. (See Figure 6.11)

CRT devices are extremely beneficial where output from a
computer is desired at remote locations very quickly. Airline

Figure 6.11
The above represents a Cathode Ray Tube terminal with keyboard. In addition, the operator can make modifications to the displayed data using a light pen. Drawings, diagrams, charts, words, and numbers displayed on the screen can be modified by the user with an electronic light pen. When the "copy" button is pushed on the display copier, shown at left, a photocopy is produced in 15 to 38 seconds, depending upon the complexity of the image. That is, the display copier produces a hard copy version of the visual display on the CRT. Courtesy IBM.

terminals, for example, use cathode ray tubes to display flight information. Changes to the data displayed on the screen are instantaneously added. Similarly, stock brokerage firms use CRTs in conjunction with a keyboard for requesting the latest stock quotations. The computer responses are displayed on the screen. (See Figure 6.12). Such CRT output provides *soft copy,* a visual display with no permanent record.

For high-speed output, CRT devices are extremely beneficial. They are, however, more costly than other terminals. If hard-copy versions of the output are necessary, then CRT devices must be equipped with additional features. (See Figure 6.11). Cost of these CRTs range from a purchase price of approximately $1000 or a rental of $50 per month to a purchase price of $200,000 with no rental available.

Fundamental Concepts of Data Processing

c. Graph plotter

A graph plotter is often used with a keyboard for input/output teleprocessing. The keyboard is used for making inquiries. The plotter produces an output graph that is transmitted from the CPU. This is a very useful terminal for management, to be used for decision making, and for engineers and mathematicians, who require charts and graphs that display specific activities.

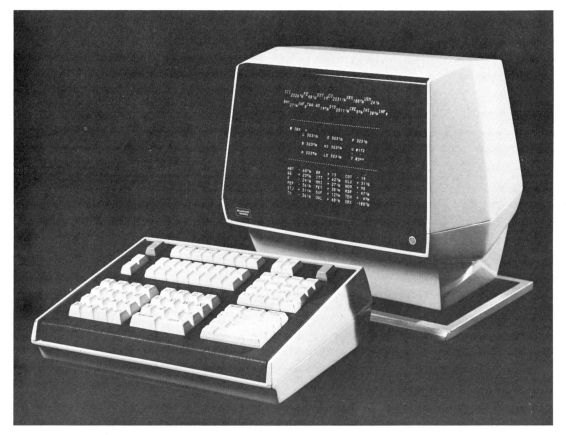

Figure 6.12
Bunker Ramo Market Decision System 7 provides brokers with simultaneous displays of data from three different sources, including tickers, newswires, computer and stock market data bases containing a variety of information on stocks, commodities and averages. In addition, these units perform all the functions of a programmable computer terminal enabling the user to perform trading computations, to transmit buy and sell orders, and to switch circuits at will to any of the many services to which the unit may be connected.
Courtesy Bunker Ramo Corporation.

d. Audio response device

The input unit may be a keyboard, where requests are typed. Or, the input unit may be telephone equipment, where the dialing of appropriate digits or codes or the depressing of keys with touchtone equipment, results in a computer inquiry. The computer-generated output or response is a verbal one instead of a printed one. The computer can be equipped with various prerecorded key phrases or words that are extracted, as required, for the purpose of answering a specific request, and are transmitted via an audio response unit.

Many banking establishments use telephone equipment as audio response units. A customer wishes to cash a check at a branch office. The touchtone digits are used to key in the customer's account number and the amount of his check. The computer then determines if the account has sufficient funds on hand. The appropriate response is then transmitted to the teller via the telephone (an audio response

(a)

(b)

Figure 6.13 Audio Response Unit

(a) In addition to its primary use as a telephone, the Touch-Tone® telephone can also function as an efficient data input device. Today, business and professional people use Touch-Tone telephones to transmit billing information to a central billing and service organization to control inventories, purchasing, and shipping, and for a variety of other business activities. (b) Here, a bank teller uses a Touch-Tone telephone to call a distant computer and request the status of an account. After tapping out the account number and a code for the information she wants, the teller receives a voice response. Courtesy Bell System Data Communications Service.

Fundamental Concepts of Data Processing

unit). The teller will then either cash the check or politely refuse, depending on the computer's response. (See Figure 6.13)

e. Voice-input to control station (Figure 6.14)

A recent advance in data communications is a Speaker Recognition System which currently utilizes a Varian *mini-computer*. The computer stores distinctive accoustical features of a person speaking his own name in its core memory. Companies or agencies requiring strict security systems or otherwise tightly selected admittance can use the mini-computer's memory to screen personnel or visitors. The comparison of the speaker's voice, transmitted via a telephone, as an input terminal, takes only milliseconds after the person speaks. This data communications technique will eventually be used for credit card holder verification.

4. Factors for Selecting Terminal Equipment

There are several factors that must be considered in determining the most suitable terminal equipment for a given application. The following represents a partial list:

a. Computer and communication lines (to be discussed in the next section)

The computer and the communication lines must be compatible with the terminals under consideration. You will see that some terminals require high-speed lines and highly complex computer equipment.

b. Functions to be performed by the terminal

It is obviously inefficient to select an input/output terminal if a strict output one would serve the purpose. That is, an input/output device should only be selected if computer response to the remote station is a requirement or if the businessman and computer specialist think that it may be a requirement in the future.

c. Cost

d. Speed

The speed of transmission will normally vary directly with the cost of the device. Slow-speed terminals transmit approximately 20 characters per second, while high-speed devices can transmit as many as several thousand characters per second. There are numerous speeds available between these limits. A device must be selected that is fast enough to serve the needs of the company within budgetary limitations.

e. Human adaptability

In most cases, input to the terminal is provided by an operator who keys in the appropriate data. Unless the device selected is easy to operate, training time may prove to be excessive. One reason for the popularity of the keyboard device is that it is very similar to a typewriter, and special training is therefore unnecessary. When establishing the type of data to be entered as input to the terminal, human adaptability must be considered. A *conversational code,* for example, is generally easier for an operator to transmit than, perhaps,

(a)

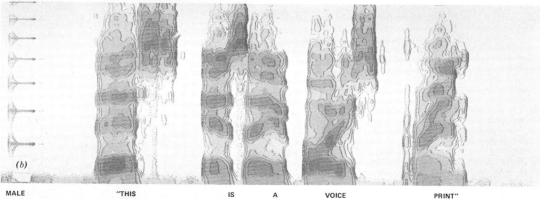

(b)

MALE   "THIS   IS   A   VOICE   PRINT"

(c)

Figure 6.14
Voice input in a data communications environment.
(a) In this three-photo sequence, a person
requesting entrance into a secured area uses
telephone portion of the Speaker Recognition
System for voice input to control station. This
could be the person's name or other code work or
number. (b) A technician calls up the voiceprint"
from a Varian 620/i mini-computer's core memory,
using teletype for verification of the matched
voiceprints. (c) A hard-copy version of a typical
male print showing the acoustical energy
concentrations called "formants." Courtesy Varian
Data Machines, Inc.

a digital code. The former consists of words and phrases that are more meaningful to an operator than a series of digits. In most cases, there is less error when transmitting conversational codes.

f. Sizes and type of display

If large amounts of data are required as output on a single printed line, then the size of the output display must be considered. That is, if 100 characters must be displayed on a single line, then the typewriter terminal is not appropriate, since generally a maximum of 72 characters can be displayed on that device. Since the various output units differ widely in their characteristics, we will not list them all. Notice, however, that size is a key factor when determining the terminal device to employ.

The type of output is generally classified as soft copy or hard copy. A hard copy is one that can be stored for future reference. A punched card and a printed sheet of paper are hard-copy items. Soft copy is output that can be seen or heard but that is not retained. Visual display units and audio response devices can produce soft copy, since the output can be indicated, with no written copy maintained for reference. Soft copy is used when an operator is required to receive responses that are needed at very frequent intervals and for which no document need be kept. Stockbrokers, for example, who are required to quote prices very often need output that can be displayed or heard quickly and for which no future reference is needed. When a permanent document must be maintained, such as an airline or hotel reservation, then hard copy may be necessary instead of, or in addition to, soft copy.

Keep in mind that for most operations, several terminals are linked to the same central computer. Where many terminals make requests or inquiries during a single time interval, it is not always feasible for the computer to handle them all within a matter of seconds. That is, some terminals may be required to wait for the computer to complete other operations.

For some systems, a priority arrangement should be established. That is, if one terminal's requests or input messages are more important to the system than another, this terminal must have priority.

If no schedule or priority is deemed necessary, each terminal message is processed in the order in which it is received. In this case, all terminal operations are considered independent, with none being more important than any other, and thus they are processed in a "first come, first served" manner.

Note that large third-generation computer systems have the ability to process several problems at one time. This is called MULTIPROGRAMMING and is discussed in depth in Chapter 14. Thus, a computer can handle several terminal requests at the same time.

When too many terminals require the use of the computer at the same time, a queue or "waiting line" may develop. This is the case where the computer has reached its capacity and the succeeding messages must wait in line. If, after a system has been implemented, queues are frequent and extend over long intervals, systems work is often required to enhance the flow of data. The use of additional terminals, for example, may be a method for alleviating the problem, or more offline processing may be required, or a greater capacity and faster central computer may be necessary.

Some terminals, however, require scheduling, or the establishment of priorities. Suppose, for example, that data from Terminal A is required before data from Terminal B can be processed. This requires a master station to control the transmission of messages. This master station must *invite* appropriate remote terminals to send messages according to an established sequence. This operation is called POLLING. Where an inventory system, for example, requires data to be *transmitted* from various locations according to a specified sequence then polling is required. This can be handled by sophisticated programming techniques.

Where messages must be transmitted from the computer to a terminal according to a given schedule, a master station must again be utilized to invite a remote terminal to *receive* a message. This operation is called ADDRESSING. Where Payroll Offices, for example, are required to *receive* output checks from terminal devices according to a specified sequence, then ADDRESSING is required. Keep in mind that both polling and addressing are utilized only when terminals are required to either transmit or to receive according to an established priority.

Notice, that there is additional programming effort required when terminals are employed. Programming packages or *software* support, may be obtained from the major computer manufacturers or *software* houses. These packages can greatly facilitate the programmer's task. They can, for example, establish priorities and, also, provide for polling and addressing. Extensive programming effort can be saved with the use of this software.

B. COMMUNICATION LINES

Most Data Communications systems utilize telephone or teletype lines for the transmission of data. Teletype lines are the least costly and the slowest. Voice grade telephone lines may be used with high-speed terminal equipment, but they were not designed for the degree of noise-free transmission and reliability required. Thus, although these lines provide fast transmission, the error rate is frequently unacceptable. Leased private telephone lines, while generally expensive, eliminate noise and interference. These are, however, slower than voice-grade lines. All three facilities are in frequent use today.

Note that two or more terminals may be hooked up to a central computer by a single communication line, not unlike the old telephone party line. This is often done to save expense. This operation is called a MULTIDROP FACILITY. Its major advantage is monetary savings, and its major disadvantage is increased contention for the line. One terminal hooked up to a multidrop facility may, for example, tie up the line for an extended transmission. In such a case, the other terminals must wait in line.

In general, when selecting either teletype lines, voice grade telephone lines, or leased private telephone lines, the major considerations are cost, speed, and the degree of noisefree transmission that is deemed acceptable.

In addition to communication lines, *modems* are required for data communication systems. Since terminals transmit data in digital form and telephone lines transmit in another form (analog), a converter called a modem (*mo*dulator-*dem*odulator) is required. (See Figure 6.15.) The modulator is that part of a modem that converts terminal data into a pattern that will be transmitted across the telephone lines, while the demodulator is that part of the modem that converts the telephone line's analog form back into digital form for transmission to a computer device.

C. COMPUTER REQUIREMENTS

A computer used in conjunction with teleprocessing equipment generally requires the following:

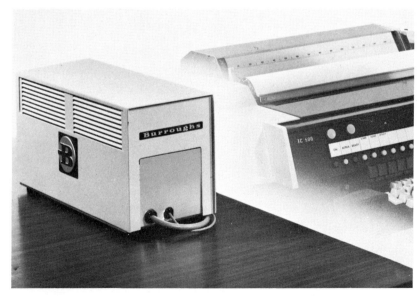

Figure 6.15
A Modem. Courtesy Burroughs Corporation.

1. A large core storage capacity. This is necessary so that it can hold incoming and outgoing messages in case of busy lines. That is, when queues occur, the computer must possess enough *buffer* areas to store messages.
2. Complex control. A highly sophisticated control system is required to effectively process data with numerous entry points.
3. Interrupt ability. Because of priority schedules, the computer is often required to interrupt a given task so that it may execute a more urgent one. It must possess the ability to then complete the previous one. This condition is often compounded by several operations that may require the use of a given device at the same time. In such cases, the interrupts must proceed from job to job.
4. Multiprogramming facility. That is, the ability to partition core storage so that several programs may be executed at the same time is called multiprogramming.

III. *Other Elements of Data Communications*

A. ERRORS

The three common types of teleprocessing errors result from operator mistakes, malfunction of communication lines (noisy lines, external disturbances such as lightning, etc.) and malfunction of the terminal equipment itself. These three factors generally result in a fairly high error rate. It has been estimated that an average of one error in 10,000 characters can result from equipment malfunctions alone. This is a much higher error ratio than when other hardware devices are integrated in a computer system.

The most effective method for determining if an error has occurred is to have the computer read back or retransmit all messages that it receives. This, however, is time consuming and, therefore, very expensive. For these reasons, it is often not done. Most errors can be prevented or checked by:

1. Using a start-of-message indicator and an end-of-message indicator. These indicators will be garbled if equipment failure has occurred. Thus they are effective to check against terminal and line malfunctions. In such cases, the computer would request retransmission.
2. Properly trained operators and the use of a conversational keying mode.
3. Automatic checking of data. This includes a *redundancy* check, similar to a parity or validity check, which is performed by the program to determine if the proper coding of data has been achieved.

B. SCHEDULING

The analyst who designs a Data Communications system must often establish priorities and must provide techniques for handling queues when the computer is tied up, and for handling busy signals when the lines are functioning at capacity. Keep in mind that a company ultimately loses business if customers are made to wait for a response to an inquiry. Proper systems analysis eliminates extensive queues by providing an adequate number of terminals at appropriate locations.

C. SECURITY

It is necessary to protect a Data Communications system from unauthorized use. It is important, for example, to classify a payroll system that utilizes terminals, so that only key personnel can access the files. Most employees would consider it a serious invasion of their privacy if any colleague could inquire about their salary history. If proper steps are not taken to prevent this occurrence, a company may find itself with an employee morale problem.

Passwords known only by a select few are sometimes required before a master file may be accessed. Where the terminals themselves are to be used by a select few, codes are sometimes required before the terminals can be employed.

Thus, we have seen that Data Communications systems, utilizing terminal equipment, can be of great service to the businessman. Such systems can result in increased productivity, efficiency, and ultimately, increased profits, by satisfying customer needs in very short time intervals. This chapter has provided business and data processing students with enough specifics on terminal equipment so that they can:

1. Understand how these devices can be employed to serve individual business needs; and,
2. Assist in evaluating or determining how these devices should be utilized.

SELF-EVALUATING QUIZ

1. The three major facets to a Data Communications system are
   _____ , _____ , and _____ .
2. Terminal devices may be classified as _____ ,
   _____ , or _____ .
3. Four frequently used transmit-only terminals are _____ ,
   _____ , _____ , and _____ .
4. Three commonly used receive-only or output terminals are
   _____ , _____ , and _____ .
5. Most online teleprocessing applications utilize _____
   terminals.
6. The most widely used input/output terminal uses a(n)
   _____ .
7. A hard-copy printout is one that _____ .
8. CRT is an abbreviation for _____ which displays data on
   a(n) _____ -like screen.
9. (T or F) A CRT is considered a high-speed device.
10. A device called a _____ may be used with a CRT as an
    input tool for making graphic corrections or additions to the visual
    display.
11. A common use of CRTs is by _____ .
12. An input/output terminal that has an output unit which gives
    verbal answers to inquiries is called a(n) _____ .
13. The above device is usually used in conjunction with a(n)
    _____ .
14. The factors that must be considered when determining the most
    suitable terminal equipment to employ at a given installation
    include _____ , _____ , _____ ,
    _____ , _____ , and _____ .
15. (T or F) It is sometimes necessary to include a priority system for
    terminal processing where a message from one remote location is
    deemed more important than from another.
16. The term _____ is used to describe the operation where a
    master station invites appropriate remote terminals to *transmit*
    messages according to an established sequence.
17. The term _____ is used to describe the operation where a
    master station is utilized to invite remote terminals to *receive*
    messages according to an established priority.
18. Most data communications systems utilize _____ or
    _____ lines for the transmission of data.
19. Voice-grade telephone lines provide fast transmission but the error
    rate due to _____ is frequently unacceptable.
20. _____ telephone lines, while expensive, eliminate noise
    and interference.
21. A computer utilized with teleprocessing equipment generally
    requires a large _____ and a highly sophisticated
    _____ system.

Fundamental Concepts of Data Processing

22. _____ is the term used to describe the execution of several programs simultaneously in a single computer.
23. Three common types of teleprocessing errors result from _____ , _____ , and _____ .

SOLUTIONS

1. terminal devices; communication lines; computer system
2. input (transmit-only); output (receive-only); input/output
3. Card Reader; Magnetic Tape Drive; Optical Scanner; Punched Paper Tape Reader
4. Line Printer; Card Punch; Paper Tape Punch
5. input/output
6. typewriter-like keyboard
7. can be maintained for future reference
8. cathode ray tube; television
9. T
10. light pen
11. airline reservation systems; brokerage houses

12. audio response unit
13. telephone
14. cost; speed; human adaptability; computer and communication lines; functions to be performed by the terminal; size and type of display
15. T
16. polling
17. addressing
18. telephone; teletype
19. noise on the line
20. Leased private
21. core storage capacity; control
22. Multiprogramming
23. operator mistakes; malfunction of the communication lines; malfunction of the terminal equipment

Section Two *Concepts of Computer Programming*

Chapter 7 *Steps Involved in Programming a Computer*

Thus far, we have introduced the business and data processing students to the general facets of a Data Processing System. This chapter will concern itself with the detailed steps involved in instructing a computer to produce desired output.

It is imperative that the student understand and appreciate all the operations that must be performed by the programming staff before a job is completed. The programmer is required to learn from the businessman and the systems analyst the details of a job so that he can effectively program it. Businessmen in industry are often required to work closely with all data processing personnel to achieve desired results. The businessman with an understanding of programming can:

1. Better pinpoint for the programmer the specific output required.
2. Make more efficient use of computer equipment by circumventing problem areas.
3. In general, better communicate with data processing personnel to increase productivity and efficiency.

A businessman with an appreciation of programming problems can determine what outputs can be combined, condensed, or even eliminated to make more efficient use of computers. He also understands which specific details he must impart to the data processing staff in order to facilitate their complete understanding of

Concepts of Computer Programming

the output required. In this way, the programmer is not burdened with extraneous information. Similarly, the businessman must insure that meaningful data is not inadvertently eliminated when he is communicating his needs to the programmer.

In discussing all the steps involved in instructing a computer to produce desired output, it is hoped that the business and data processing students will obtain a greater understanding of why procedures require weeks and even months to automate. It is also hoped that they will realize how errors can easily manifest themselves in some phase or aspect of the programming cycle.

In short, a businessman with a keen awareness of the programmer's responsibilities will have realistic expectations from automated procedures. That is, he can understand the steps involved in computerizing an application. In this way, he will not be as likely to face disappointment and annoyance, should a problem arise. Similarly, the computer specialist who can communicate effectively with the businessman is in a better position to understand the problems which he later faces.

I. Systems Preparation—Prior to Programming

As indicated in Chapter 2, the first step involved in realizing a department's needs is the systems study. This all-encompassing element is prepared by the systems analyst. The analyst studies company procedures, reorganizes them into more efficient operations, and then recommends utilization of computer equipment, where feasible.[1] Each application, or set of procedures within a system, may employ a computer to perform specific tasks so that desired output can be realized. The individual job is then assigned to a programmer.

The analyst supplies the programmer with specific job requirements and data layouts. The data layouts are pictorial representations of how input will appear and how output data must look (Figure 7.1). The job requirements are usually in the form of a narrative and indicate what operations must be performed to achieve desired output.

II. Program Preparation

Once the programmer understands the basic requirements of the job and how it will be integrated into the system as a whole, he often reinforces his understanding by communicating with the businessman. He must make certain that he understands every facet of the job. He must be fully cognizant of the following.

1. Each field of input data.

[1] *A system, in its entirety, is discussed, in Chapters 16 and 17.*

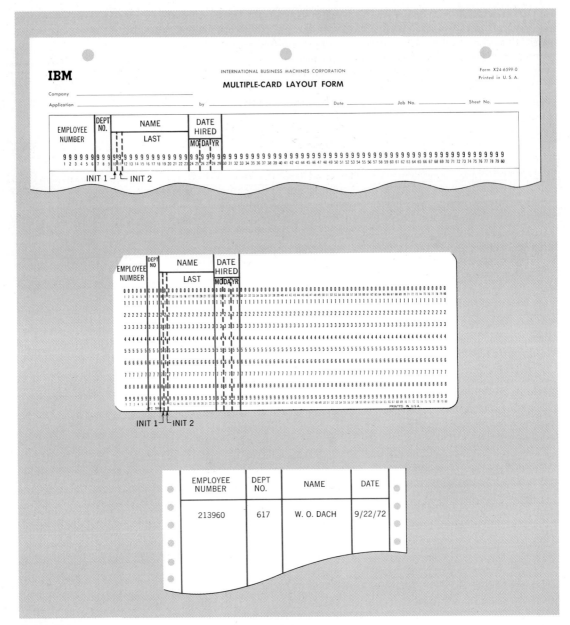

Figure 7.1
Sample data layouts.

Concepts of Computer Programming

2. The frequency of input data, the control of the data, and in what form the information will enter the data processing facility.
3. Every operation required.
4. Edit procedures.
5. Error procedures.
6. Each field of output data.
7. The frequency of output and its control.

Any element overlooked or misunderstood can mean significant reprogramming effort later on. To insert changes in a program is never as efficient, productive, or satisfactory as programming these elements from the beginning.

Figure 7.2 illustrates in pictorial form all the steps that will be discussed in Program Preparation.

A. DEFINING THE PROBLEM

Once the programmer understands every phase of the application or job he must perform, he is ready to define the steps involved in achieving the desired result. He must prepare a formalized document called a PROBLEM DEFINITION that describes, in detail, his understanding of the operations to be performed for the job. The businessman should, if possible, approve this PROBLEM DEFINITION, indicating that he concurs with the job description.

During this phase, the programmer and the businessman work closely to insure effective communication. These two, when working together, can often spot flaws in a job or pinpoint inefficiencies in output. In this way, they can sometimes produce job requirements that are more productive and effective. The programmer can sometimes suggest alternative or supplemental output that is more meaningful and desirable than originally outlined.

The result of this step, then, is a formal document, written by the programmer and approved, where possible, by the businessman, which specifies, in detail, what the program will achieve.

B. FLOWCHARTING

Once the programmer has outlined *what* his program will achieve, he must decide *how* to achieve it.

Often the steps involved in achieving a job's requirements are intricate and detailed. *Prior* to writing the set of instructions, it is imperative that the programmer outline the logic he will employ. In this way, he will avoid the omission of instructions or the inclusion of illogical functions.

A *standardized* method for outlining the logic to be utilized in a program has been employed for many years in the data processing industry. This is a pictorial representation called a *PROGRAM FLOWCHART*. It indicates, in pictorial or diagram form, the program

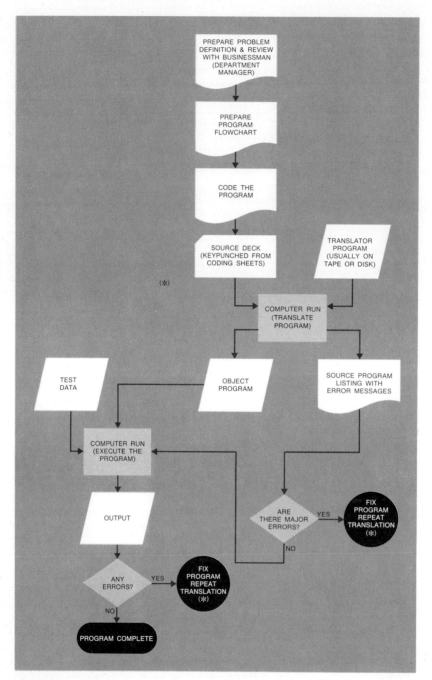

Figure 7.2
Steps involved in producing a computer program.

Concepts of Computer Programming

elements and how they will logically integrate. This FLOWCHART contains symbols, denoting specific functions, with explanatory notes inside. Each symbol is connected by flowlines indicating the flow of logic. Figure 7.3 illustrates a sample flowchart. Chapter 8 describes, in detail, the steps involved in flowcharting.

Keep in mind that the objective of the PROGRAM FLOWCHART is to map out all the logical steps to be programmed *prior* to the actual writing of the set of instructions. The process is analogous to the formulation of a blueprint prior to the construction of a building. The latter, like the flowchart, insures that all elements will logically integrate.

More and more businessmen today are becoming familiar with flowcharting. The flowchart provides another vehicle of communication between business areas and data processing. The specific steps to be utilized in a program and their logical integration are clearly detailed and easily seen. Thus a businessman who has the expertise to scrutinize a flowchart is in a far better position to understand the programmer's concept of the procedures involved. Any omissions or flaws in the programmer's logic can be easily seen by a businessman who understands flowcharting concepts.

C. CODING THE PROGRAM

Once the steps of a program have been outlined by the programmer in a flowchart and he is satisfied that they integrate logically, he can begin to write the set of instructions. The writing of these instructions is called *CODING THE PROGRAM*.

Programs are coded on sheets of paper called CODING or PROGRAM SHEETS. See Figure 7.4 for a sample coding sheet.

When the program has been completely coded on coding sheets, it must be converted to a form that can be accepted by the computer; typically, keypunching onto cards is performed. Each line of a coding sheet is keypunched into a single punched card. The entire deck of program cards is then read by the computer.

Here again, businessmen with an appreciation for and an understanding of program coding can communicate on a more detailed level with the programmer. Notice that the intention of this text is *not* to teach students how to program, but how to effectively read a program and discern its elements.[2]

Computers can operate on or *execute* programs only if they are coded, in *actual* or *absolute machine language*. This language requires:

1. Complex operation codes. An ADD instruction, for example, may be a 58 code in absolute machine language; a MULTIPLY may be a

[2] *There are four primers available (COBOL, FORTRAN, RPG, BASIC) which are to be used in conjunction with this text that will teach the various programming languages.*

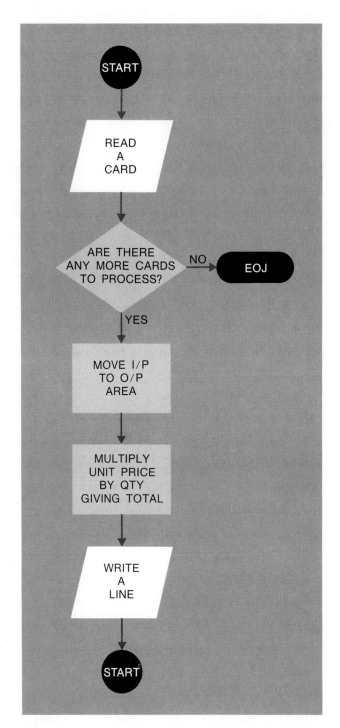

Figure 7.3
A sample flowchart.

Concepts of Computer Programming

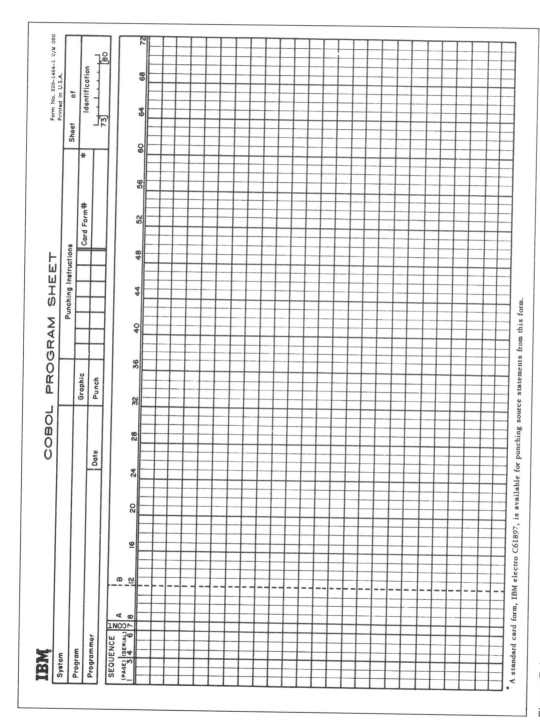

Figure 7.4
Sample coding sheet.

4J. For the programmer to code his program in actual machine language, he must remember such complex codes.

2. Actual machine addresses. An ADD instruction, for example, which adds two input fields, must place the result or sum in a third field. In absolute machine language, this third field must be an actual machine location. To program, then, in this language, requires the programmer to keep track of actual machine locations, a cumbersome and difficult task.

It is obvious, then, that programming in the actual machine language is complex and cumbersome. Few programmers code in the machine's own language. An alternative to absolute machine language coding is *symbolic programming language coding*.

A symbolic programming language is one that is far easier for the programmer to code. It uses *symbolic* operation codes, such as ADD or +, and *symbolic* addresses such as HOLD, RESULT, SUM. Thus we can say ADD TAX TO TOTAL rather than: 2R 406803. The overwhelming majority of programs are coded in a symbolic language as opposed to machine language.

Note that a symbolic program, although easier for the programmer to code, is *not* executable. It cannot be run or executed by the computer. It must first be *converted* to absolute machine language.

Thus a program in symbolic language requires two phases:

1. Translation phase—the program is translated to machine language.
2. Execution phase—once translated, the program is run, or executed.

As indicated, most programs are coded in a symbolic language. This symbolic program, written on coding sheets, must be converted to a form that can be accepted by the computer, such as cards or tape. This program written by the programmer is called a *SOURCE PROGRAM*. A SOURCE PROGRAM keypunched onto cards is called a *SOURCE DECK*. Source programs are nonexecutable—they must first be translated into machine language before they can be run.

Note that there are numerous symbolic languages, each serving a specific purpose.

Characteristics	Languages
High-level languages: Easier to program; more difficult to translate.	COBOL FORTRAN PL/1 RPG BASIC
Low-level languages: More difficult to program; easier to translate.	Assembler languages

Concepts of Computer Programming

We will discuss the advantages of each language later on in the chapter.

D. TRANSLATION OF SOURCE PROGRAM

All symbolic languages must be translated into machine language before they can be run or executed. The computer itself performs this translation. That is, the machine reads the source program as input, and converts it to output, which is the machine-language program.

High-level symbolic languages are those that are very simple to code but very difficult for the machine to translate. High-level languages require complex translations while low-level ones require simple translations. With high-level languages, such as COBOL, FORTRAN, RPG, PL/1, and BASIC, this translation process is called a *COMPILATION*.

A special program, supplied by the computer manufacturer, called a *compiler,* reads the source program, which is written in a symbolic language and produces, as output, a machine-language equivalence called the *OBJECT PROGRAM*.

Thus the compiler is merely a program that reads input, *the source program,* and translates it to output, which is a machine-language program.

FORTRAN, COBOL and, indeed, all high-level languages require individual compilations. That is, a FORTRAN compiler must be used to translate FORTRAN programs; a COBOL compiler must be used to translate COBOL programs, and so on.

Each computer requires a compiler program that can read the specific symbolic program and convert it to its *own* machine language. Since individual computers have their own unique machine language, each compiler for each machine will be different.

In every case, however, the result is the same: a machine-language or *Object* Program.

Low-level programming languages (Assembler Languages), similar to machine language, do *not* require complex translations. They require a simplified translation called an *ASSEMBLY*. A special program called the ASSEMBLER translates an assembler-language program into machine language. Keep in mind that an ASSEMBLER LANGUAGE, the language requiring the simplest translation, requires the *most* programming effort. The programming effort required by high-level languages is less, but the conversion process is more complex.

Since each computer has its own independent machine language, the translation or compilation will produce unique programs for each computer. Thus, a COBOL compiler for IBM S/360 would be different from a COBOL compiler for a Honeywell 200.

The translator (assembler or compiler) is a program that is usually on a tape or disk *file of programs,* ready to be accessed by the computer. The control system of the computer calls for these programs, as required. When a translator is read into core storage, it then calls for the source program as input and begins the translation.

Once a program is translated (either compiled or assembled) three forms of output usually result (see Figure 7.5).

1. Object Program—the machine-language equivalent of the source program.
2. A source program listing, which is far easier to follow than coding sheets or the source deck. The programmer uses the program listing to flag errors and check the logic.
3. A listing of diagnostics, or violation of rules. Any rules that have been disobeyed by the programmer will cause the computer to print an error message. If the add operation is spelled AD instead of ADD, for example, an error message will print. Any major error will result in an incomplete or erroneous object program. In such cases, the source program must be corrected and the translation process repeated. The object program originally created cannot be used, since it contains errors generated in the source program. Note that most programmers must translate their programs several times before they are "debugged," or free from rule violations. Thus businessmen should expect programmers to require numerous translations of their source programs. The detail and precision required in programming makes errors a commonplace occurrence.

Notice, also, that the list of diagnostics will indicate violations of rules but will *not* tag an error in logic. Logic errors can only be found by running or testing the program with sample data.

E. EXECUTION PHASE—TESTING THE PROGRAM

After a machine-language program has been produced that contains no rule violations, the execution phase can begin. In this phase, we test the program to determine if it performs all required operations and if it produces the desired output. Although the program contains no violation of rules, it may contain logic errors. The Execution Phase is used to "debug" a program or to eliminate all such errors.

We run or execute the program with *test* or *sample data*. The output produced is then compared against the output that has been manually prepared from the same data. If everything checks, then the program is considered debugged, or free from errors. It is then ready to be run on a scheduled basis.

Note that test data must be carefully prepared to incorporate *all possible conditions*. Any condition that is feasible must be included. In this way, the program tests for all possibilities and it is then unlikely that future scheduled runs of the program will result in errors.

Any condition that is inadvertently omitted can produce major errors later on. Suppose, for example, a program allows for from 1 to 10 transaction cards for each account within an Accounts Receivable File. The programmer should include test data that has accounts with 1 card, 2 cards, and so on up to 10 cards. In this way, every condition

Concepts of Computer Programming

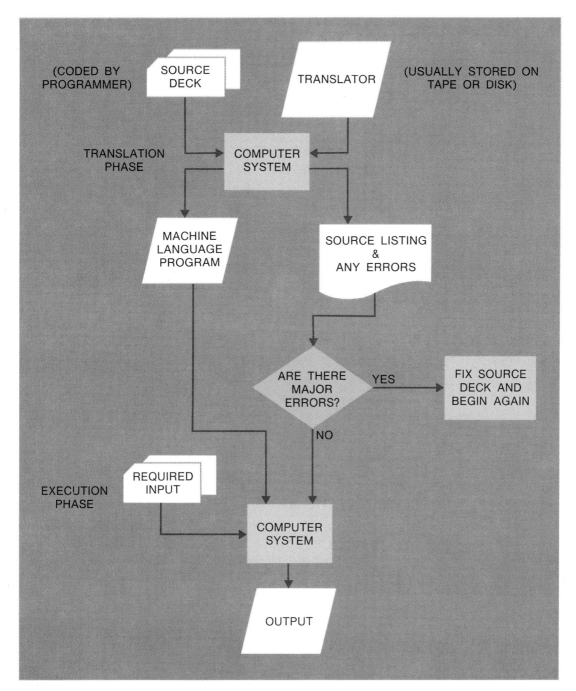

Figure 7.5
Pictorial representation of translation and execution of a program.

possible would be included within the test data. To assume that if the program works properly for 2 cards in an account that it will therefore work for 10 cards in an account, may be fallacious.

Suppose, for example, that the program provides only 1 position for the NUMBER OF CARDS field. Then when there are *10* (2 digits) cards for an account, erroneous processing would occur. Unless the test data includes an account with 10 cards, this erroneous condition will not be discovered until the program is run on a scheduled basis. At this time the necessity for corrections would result in a disruption of the normal computer processing and would waste valuable computer time.

It is also imperative that the programmer insure that erroneous input is handled properly in his program. His program should contain error procedures for invalid cards and his test data should contain invalid cards to insure their proper treatment. There is an adage in data processing that because of the large volume, anything that could *possibly* go wrong with input data *will* eventually go wrong. Thus, error conditions must be built into the program.

When errors in logic manifest themselves during the test run, then the programmer must find the errors in the source program, correct them, and begin again with the translation process.

F. PROGRAM DOCUMENTATION

Once the program is finalized and running properly, it must be prepared for the operations staff to be run on a regularly scheduled basis. That is, the programmer must provide the operations staff with enough detail and information about the program so that it can be run at required intervals. The PROGRAM DOCUMENTATION is a series of written documents that insures a smooth transition from the programming staff to the operations staff. If it is thorough and precise, it will eliminate the need for a computer operator to constantly question aspects of the run. Many programmers have been plagued by numerous phone calls from the operations staff requiring explanations of the run and the output, when documentation has not been properly provided.

Documentation should include:

1. PROBLEM DEFINITION—indicating a narrative on what the program accomplishes.
2. PROGRAM FLOWCHART—indicating the logic flow of the program.
3. DATA LAYOUT SHEETS OF REQUIRED INPUT AND OUTPUT—denoting precisely what the input and output looks like.
4. CONTROL PROCEDURES—indicating from whom input data is received and to whom output data should be sent, how totals should be specified for control of documents, and so on.
5. SCHEDULING PROCEDURES—indicating when runs are to be performed.
6. FORMAT FOR CONTROL CARDS—indicating date, or type of run (such as monthly or weekly) if required.

244

7. OPERATION PROCEDURES—indicating precisely what the operator must do for each phase of the run, for example, mount tape on Tape Drive 1, use 5-part paper on Printer, and so on.

8. SPECIFICATIONS REQUIRED FOR TAPE AND DISK—indicating formats for any external labels or header labels required.

9. ERROR SHEET—indicating what the operator should do in case specific errors occur.

10. HALT SHEET—indicating what the operator should do in case specified programmed halts occur.

In short, every detail should be included so that, once the job is "turned over" to the operations staff, the programmer is not constantly besieged with numerous questions. Too often, a programmer supplies a program with minimum documentation only to be called at 2:00 A.M. by an irate computer operator who does not know what to do because a specific error has occurred.

G. CONVERSION or CUT-OVER

Conversion or *cut-over* is the process of running a program, for the *first* time, with real or "live" data after it has been tested. Sometimes programming errors occur during conversion that were not found during testing. This is often embarrassing to the programmer, since the conversion process is undertaken only after he has rendered his program complete and adequate. For this reason, the necessity for including detailed test data prior to the conversion process cannot be overstated.

During the conversion process, the programmer works closely with the operations staff to insure that (1) the program works smoothly and that (2) the operators understand the requirements and specifications of the program.

Usually the program is run during conversion at the same time that the manual procedure is performed to produce the same result. This is called a *parallel run*. The computer-prepared output is compared with the manually prepared output and, barring minor discrepancies, they should be consistent. If not, the program must be rechecked to determine why errors have occurred.

Once the conversion process is complete, the manual method for preparing output is terminated. The operations staff is then responsible for the periodic computer run and the programmer's job is considered to be completed.

III. Major Programming Languages

You will recall that source programs, written by the programmer, must be translated into machine language before they can be executed. There are many programming languages that can be used on many different computers that serve varied business needs. The following represents the major languages in use today.

A. COBOL

COBOL, an acronym for *Common Business Oriented Language* is, as the name implies, a business language. It has been created to fill normal business needs, utilizing business terminology.

Since most business-oriented problems operate on vast amounts of data, requiring high-speed processing, a business language must be capable of easily and effectively handling high-speed storage media such as magnetic tape and disk. COBOL has appropriate subroutines that make programming for these high-level devices a simple task. That is, we can perform header label routines, blocking functions, indexing of disk records,[3] and so on with relative ease, in COBOL. Since most business problems do not require complex mathematical routines, a business language is not required to handle complex mathematics. Simple arithmetic operations are easily performed in COBOL, whereas mathematical functions such as square-root and trigonometric routines are not easily coded.

Thus, business-oriented problems are generally those that require large amounts of input/output with relatively simple arithmetic functions. Payroll jobs, for example, are typical business problems; they utilize great numbers of records with simple arithmetic routines. COBOL is a symbolic language ideally suited to such business problems.

COBOL is considered a *universal* or standard language. That is, it can be run on many computer makes and models. It is a *common* language, as its name implies. The same COBOL program, with little modification, can be run as effectively on an IBM S/360 as on a Honeywell 200. Similarly, both the IBM S/360 model 30 and the IBM S/360 model 50 can operate on the same COBOL program with little change.

COBOL is an English-like language. The similarity to English makes it easy to train programmers. To add two fields, we say ADD; to read a card, we say READ, and so forth. Since instructions read like English statements, it is easy to both understand and code COBOL programs.

B. FORTRAN

The symbolic programming language FORTRAN is an abbreviation for *Formula Translator*. FORTRAN is a mathematical language that is particularly conducive to setting down formulas. To add two fields, *A* and *B,* for example, and to place the answer in a field called *C,* we use the FORTRAN expression:

$$C = A + B$$

Note that this is equivalent to a mathematical formula.

FORTRAN is most often used for scientific or engineering applications because of its mathematical nature. It includes

[3] *See Chapter 5 for a discussion of these terms.*

subroutines for determining logarithms, trigonometric functions, and so on. It, like COBOL, is a standard language that can be used on many different computers.

Although FORTRAN can easily handle complex mathematical problems, it is not as well suited for high-level input/output operations as are some other languages.

Most scientific applications utilize numerous high-level mathematical problems with little input/output. That is, several numbers fed into a computer, pinpointing a moon trajectory, can result in hours of computer calculations.

For mathematical problems, we generally use much calculation and comparatively little input/output. FORTRAN, as a mathematical language, has much facility for handling complex calculations but sacrifices some of the ease with which high-level input/output, such as disk, can be handled.

Note that FORTRAN is used predominantly in business applications where mathematics is required. Sales Forecasting and Inventory Control are operations that most often use FORTRAN. In short, COBOL is a more effective language when dealing with business-oriented problems that include large amounts of input/output with relatively simple calculating. FORTRAN is a more effective language when dealing with scientific or business-oriented problems that include complex calculating routines with relatively simplified input/output.

C. PL/1

PL/1, an abbreviation for Programming Language/1, is a symbolic language that is designed to meet the needs of both scientific and commercial computer users. That is, it is designed to combine essentially the major advantages and features of COBOL and FORTRAN so that a user can employ it for both scientific and commercial problems.

PL/1 is a most effective and necessary tool in companies that utilize both scientific and commercial applications. An engineering firm, for example, that has one large computer that executes engineering and business (Payroll, Accounts Receivable, and Accounts Payable) applications might best utilize PL/1 for its prime programming language. In this way, the company need not hire two types of programmers, those with knowledge of FORTRAN and those with knowledge of COBOL. Similarly, transfers between the scientific programming staff and the commercial programming staff can easily be made.

There are, then, many advantages to adopting a single programming language for companies that possess both scientific and commercial applications. In this way, *both* high-level mathematics and high-level input/output can be effectively handled using one language and even one program. Originally an IBM language only, PL/1 is now used by other manufacturers as well.

D. RPG

Many business organizations, particularly small-scale ones, do not need the extensive options available with COBOL or PL/1. Their needs could be satisfied with a simplified language that is generally used to print output from cards or tape or disk. There is usually very little high-level programming involved to produce printed output.

RPG, an abbreviation for *Report Program Generator*, is a symbolic language ideally suited to creating printed reports from input media. There is a minimum of programming effort required with RPG. That is, it is a very simple language. Page numbers, page headings, field names on primary page breaks, editing, and printing final totals are performed in RPG with minimum programming effort.

Thus, it is relatively easy to train RPG programmers, since the various options of COBOL, FORTRAN, or PL/1 need not be learned. Since the prime purpose of this language is to create printed reports, few logic problems are encountered. Thus, RPG is an ideal language for individuals with little or no programming expertise.

Keep in mind, however, that RPG has only one primary function and that is to create printed output with minimum effort. It cannot perform complex decision or logic functions. It is a semistandard language in that it may be used on *some* computers, but not all.

E. BASIC

BASIC is a symbolic language that is most often used to program from terminals. It is essentially a simplified version of FORTRAN. Because of its simplicity, it is called a conversational language. This language can be learned in a matter of hours by people familiar with computers.

F. ASSEMBLER LANGUAGE

Assembler Language is a very complicated programming language that is similar to machine-language programming, with only minor variations to simplify programming effort. It is used usually when great programming efficiency is required to save core storage or to perform complex functions. Each machine has its own *individual* Assembler Language. That is, although the above five languages are relatively standard regardless of the computer on which they are run, each computer has its own independent Assembler Language that is very different from that of *another computer*. ALP (Assembler Language Programming) and BAL (Basic Assembler Language) are the IBM S/360 versions of this type of language.

Most companies would not have an Assembler Language as its main programming language because of its complexity and, for this reason, it is not discussed in detail in this text.

Concepts of Computer Programming

The symbolic language utilized at a data processing installation will depend on the type of applications or jobs generally required. That is, an organization that usually requires business-oriented programs and that has several different computers would probably utilize COBOL as a main language. A company that utilizes scientific applications or business functions with high-level mathematics to be included would probably use FORTRAN.

In summary, the programming cycle includes:

1. PREPARATION OF PROBLEM DEFINITION—to insure complete understanding of the job requirements.
2. PREPARATION OF PROGRAM FLOWCHART—to formalize the logical integration of elements to be written in the program.
3. CODING THE SOURCE PROGRAM.
4. TRANSLATING THE SOURCE PROGRAM INTO MACHINE LANGUAGE—to permit execution, the program must be translated; this phase also produces a listing of rule violations (diagnostics) that must be corrected before execution can begin.
5. TESTING THE PROGRAM—to insure that there are no errors in logic; any such errors that occur must be corrected and the program then translated again.
6. PREPARATION OF PROGRAM DOCUMENTATION.
7. CONVERSION OR CUT-OVER OF PROGRAM.

The businessman should note that each of these steps involves detail and precision. Every facet is subject to errors which, because of the nature of the tasks involved, frequently occur. Programmers often require weeks or even months to complete applications. In addition to the expected programming errors that must be anticipated, revisions to the problem definition or unexpected computer ''down'' time (when the computer is being repaired or checked) cause further delays. The student should note that a definition of the problem should be complete and precise *prior* to the undertaking of any programming effort. Changes to aspects of the job *after* programming has begun often cause extensive delays. Thus businessmen and programmers must work closely to insure that they both have a total picture of the job requirements.

SELF-EVALUATING QUIZ

1. Programs are rarely written in _____ language because of its _____ .
2. Programs are generally written in a _____ language that must be converted or translated into machine language.
3. COBOL is an acronym for _____ .
4. COBOL is a common language in the sense that _____ .
5. COBOL is a business language in the sense that _____ .
6. Business problems have need for _____ but usually do not involve complex _____ .
7. (T or F) Logarithmic functions and other complex mathematical routines can easily be handled in COBOL.
8. COBOL is a(n) _____ -like language, which makes it easy to train programmers.
9. FORTRAN is an abbreviation for _____ .
10. Complex _____ routines can easily be performed in FORTRAN while large amounts of _____ can best be handled in COBOL.
11. An Inventory program for a department store would probably be written in the _____ language.
12. (T or F) Because of all the steps involved, a programmer may require many weeks to complete a program.
13. (T or F) The systems analyst provides the programmer with job requirements from which the programmer must create his program.
14. (T or F) Any aspect of an application that the programmer finds confusing he should question after he has completed his basic program.
15. A formalized document called a _____ describes, in detail, the programmer's understanding of the operations to be performed.
16. This document should be approved by _____ to insure _____ .
17. The PROGRAM FLOWCHART indicates _____ .
18. The process of writing the actual computer instructions is called _____ .
19. Each line of a coding sheet converts to _____ in the _____ .
20. In order for programs to be executed, they must be in _____ or _____ .
21. Programmers rarely code in actual machine language because of its _____ .
22. Most programmers code in a _____ _____ _____ .
23. Symbolic programs must be _____ before they can be _____ .
24. A source program is _____ .

250   *Concepts of Computer Programming*

25. Four examples of symbolic programming languages are
_____ , _____ , _____ , and _____ .
26. RPG is an abbreviation for _____ .
27. PL/1 combines the advantages of _____ and

_____ .
28. _____ is a language most often used with terminals.
29. _____ is a language that is similar to machine language
with only minor variations to simplify programming effort.
30. A business function usually requires _____ input/output
with relatively _____ mathematical operations.
31. A scientific function usually requires _____ input/output
with _____ mathematical operations.
32. _____ is a programming language ideally suited to
business applications, while _____ handles complex
mathematical functions with relative ease.
33. A compiler is a _____ .
34. An object program is _____ .
35. The output from a compilation is _____ , _____ ,
and _____ .
36. After a program has been compiled successfully, with no errors,
then the _____ phase is undertaken.
37. The execution phase will determine if there are _____ in
the program.
38. The _____ is a series of written documents that insures a
smooth transition from the programming staff to the operations
staff.
39. The _____ process is the running of a program for the first
time with "live" data.

SOLUTIONS

1. actual (or absolute) machine; complexity
2. symbolic
3. *Common Business Oriented Language*
4. it can be run on many different makes
and models of computers.
5. it is especially conducive to handling
business-type problems such as Payroll
and Accounts Receivable.
6. large volumes of input/output;
mathematical functions
7. F
8. English
9. *For*mula *Trans*lator
10. mathematical; input/output
11. COBOL

12. T
13. T
14. F—*before* completion
15. PROBLEM DEFINITION
16. businessmen; that the programmer's
understanding of every facet and detail of
the procedure is correct.
17. the logical integration of the flow of data
in a program.
18. CODING THE PROGRAM
19. a single punched card; source deck
20. absolute; actual machine language
21. complexity
22. symbolic programming language
23. translated; run or executed

24. a program written in a symbolic language.
25. RPG; FORTRAN; BASIC; COBOL; PL/1; ASSEMBLER LANGUAGE
26. *Report Program Generator*
27. FORTRAN; COBOL
28. BASIC
29. Assembler Language
30. large volume *or* high-level; simple or low-level
31. low volume or low-level; high-level
32. COBOL; FORTRAN
33. translator program that converts an input source deck in a symbolic language to an output object program in machine language.
34. the machine language equivalent of the source deck.
35. an object program; a listing of violations in rules; a program listing
36. execution
37. logic errors
38. PROGRAM DOCUMENTATION
39. conversion

Chapter 8 *Program Flowcharting*

253

I. Introduction

As we have seen, a businessman must understand the organizational structure within a computer installation and the specific tasks of each computer specialist. This understanding will enhance communications during the task of investigation and then computerization of his specific business function.

From the brief exposure to the tasks of the analyst and the programmer, the student should have discerned that the element of *logic* is crucial to both. A logical representation of how data will first flow through a *system* and, more specifically, how it will flow through a *program* is the crux of data processing. Experienced data processing personnel are those who can systematically create a more logical approach to the flow of data.

A businessman with understanding of the logic necessary to create a more meaningful flow of data is an asset to any organization. Even without data processing expertise, he can make many manual operations more efficient and systematic. Indeed, most executive positions in companies require businessmen with the ability to enhance the logical integration of company procedures and operations.

This chapter will expose the student to the method used by programmers and analysts to represent the logical flow of data, in a data processing context. That is, the chapter will introduce the student

Concepts of Computer Programming

to *program flowcharting,* a programming technique used to pictorially represent the logic of a program.

The purpose of the chapter is fourfold:

1. It is hoped that the technique of flowcharting will assist the student in understanding logical relationships between elements, in a data processing sense. This understanding can apply to manual operations and thus increase the student's ability to systematize elements within his realm.

2. The chapter will show the business student why it is so essential to describe to data processing personnel, *in the utmost detail,* all facets of his operations.

3. It will enable the business student to review flowcharts prepared by data processing personnel to insure that the logic is correct, prior to the undertaking of any extensive programming.

4. It will provide the data processing student with sufficient tools to be able to draw program flowcharts on his own.

II. Elements of a Flowchart

A program flowchart is a diagram, or pictorial representation, of the logical flow of data in a particular program.[1] Its relative position in the programmer's sequence of activities is indicated in Figure 8.1.

The flowchart is drawn *before* the program is written to insure that the instructional steps will be logically integrated. The concept is not unlike that used by architects who prepare pictorial representations, called blueprints, prior to the actual design of a building. Blueprints verify and integrate elements of a building before construction. Similarly, flowcharts verify and integrate elements of a program prior to coding.

The flowchart is drawn by the programmer to insure that his interpretation of the logic required in the program is accurate. Notice that the writing of the instructions is only part of a program; the sequence in which these instructions are executed represents the logic of the program. In most cases, the logic is far more important in determining the level of sophistication of the programmer. Coding errors are easily detected by the computer during program translation; errors in logic require more intricate and rigorous revamping. These logic errors can often be avoided when precise program flowcharts are drawn.

The analyst and the programmer often work closely in refining the flowchart. The collection of data on a system and thus on the individual programs is integrated in the formulation of the necessary program flowcharts. Any discrepancies, misconceptions, or lack of detail, will

[1] *The Systems Flowchart, a more general representation of data flow in a system, as a whole, will be discussed in Chapter 17.*

DETAILED BREAKDOWN OF OPERATIONS	VEHICLE
ANALYST FORMULATES PROBLEM FOR PROGRAMMER	SYSTEMS DESIGN PACKAGE
PROGRAMMER FORMULATES HIS CONCEPTION OF THE PROBLEM	PROGRAMMER'S PROBLEM DEFINITION
PROGRAMMER PREPARES PROGRAM FLOWCHART TO DEPICT LOGIC	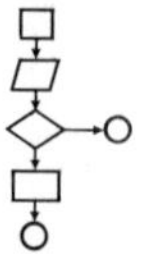
PROGRAMMER REVIEWS FLOWCHART WITH ANALYST & BUSINESSMEN	INTERVIEW
PROGRAMMER CODES THE PROBLEM	CODING SHEET 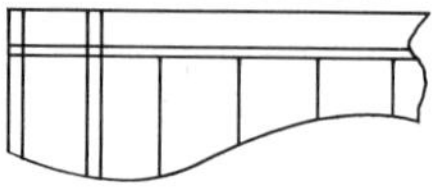

Figure 8.1

The programmer's sequence of activities.

manifest themselves when the logic is represented in flowchart form. The flowchart, then, provides a common foundation with which computer specialists can bridge communication gaps. In the end, the flowchart must be approved by analysts and programmers before detailed coding is undertaken.

Communication between data processing personnel and the businessman, however, has no such common ground. Thus, misconceptions do not manifest themselves until the detailed workings of a new design have been completed. However, if businessmen could understand the nature of a flowchart, they, too, could participate in its ultimate approval, thereby eliminating misconceptions and inconsistencies well before detailed programming effort has been undertaken.

Let us first illustrate a flowchart, sometimes called a *block diagram,* to note the logical integration of elements in a *manual* business system. Suppose, for example, we wish to pictorially represent the manual preparation of payroll checks from time cards.

If the diagram is a logical and thorough one, *any* individual should be able to perform the manual preparation of such checks after

Concepts of Computer Programming

studying the flowchart. The time cards will contain HOURS WORKED and RATE. For regular hours worked, the WAGES are computed as HOURS WORKED × RATE. If the HOURS WORKED exceed 40, then the number in excess of 40 (OVERTIME-HRS) is multiplied by 1.5 × RATE (time-and-a-half for overtime).

Examine the flowchart in Figure 8.2. Notice that we read the chart from *top* to *bottom,* as indicated by the arrows. The purpose of each symbol will be described in depth later. Observe, however, that an explanatory note is provided within each symbol. We begin with the major sequence. The two sequences beginning with OVERTIME and END OF JOB are just "offshoots" of the major sequence.

The first step is to obtain the cards. The next step is to read *one* card, since data is processed a single record at a time. (The A between the first and second steps is an entry point that will be discussed later). If, in attempting to read a card, we find that there are no more cards, we leave the normal flow and proceed with the step labeled END OF JOB, to be discussed later. If, however, there are cards remaining to be processed, we continue with the next sequential step.

If HOURS WORKED is in excess of 40, we proceed to the step labeled OVERTIME, where we multiply 40 by RATE, subtract 40 from HOURS WORKED to obtain the OVERTIME-HRS, and then multiply OVERTIME-HRS by 1.5 times the RATE. We then add the amounts and continue with the check processing functions. If the HOURS WORKED is not in excess of 40, then we simply multiply HOURS WORKED by RATE to obtain the TOTAL AMOUNT. After the TOTAL AMOUNT is calculated, we prepare the check. For the sake of simplicity, the process of computing payroll deductions for tax purposes has not been included.

This terminates the processing of a single card. Since there are many cards to process, we continue by reading the next card, by proceeding back to entry point A, and repeating the sequence of steps.

The flowchart indicates that processing continues in this way, until there are no more cards, in which case we proceed to END OF JOB. At END OF JOB, we bring all the checks to the Payroll Manager for his signature, and the procedure or *routine* is then terminated.

Note that the overall purpose and structure of a procedure, even a manual one, is readily seen by examining the flowchart. In many ways it is far easier to explain such a procedure by illustrating it, pictorially, rather than simply describing it in a narrative. In addition, it is relatively easy to review for errors in procedures by examining a block diagram. A businessman, then, with little or no understanding of data processing can utilize a flowchart to depict a manual procedure.

Notice, however, that the above flowchart is not totally complete. There are conditions that may occur and that are not provided for in the above. That is, there may be some conditions that occur and that the individual performing the procedures cannot handle because he was not given enough information. For example, suppose the time cards are not in their proper place when the employee goes to obtain

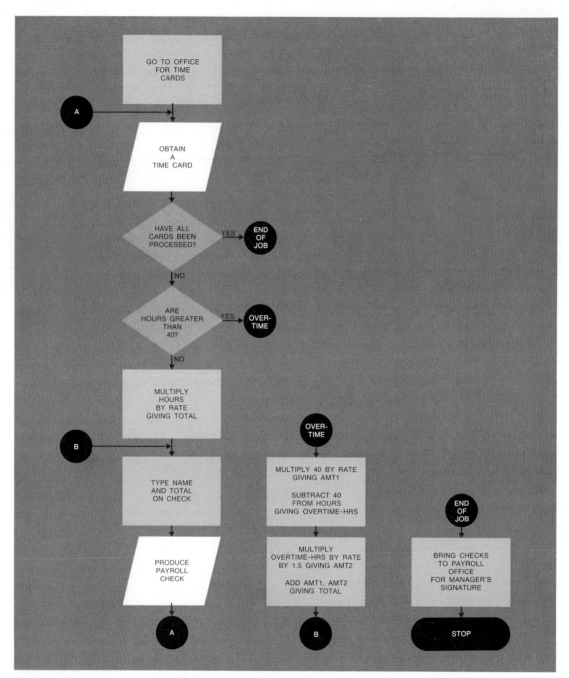

Figure 8.2
Flowchart for manual procedure for preparing payroll checks-rough draft.

258   *Concepts of Computer Programming*

them. What should he do? Suppose, also, that specific time cards do not have name fields, or that HOURS WORKED or RATE is erroneously blank. What should be done? Suppose there are no more blank checks available. What should be done?

To adequately describe a set of procedures, a flowchart must be thorough and include *every possible detail* by testing for every possible contingency. The businessman who outlines the manual procedures so that every possible condition and associated action is accounted for, will not be plagued later by numerous questions from the employee. If unanswered questions arise during the preparation of the checks, much time and efficiency will be lost, since the individual must stop and seek a solution. Thus the system must be described in every facet. The revised flowchart in Figure 8.3 is more efficient than the preceding because it provides for all possibilities.

In short, a flowchart is a pictorial representation of the logical integration of elements in a procedure. We have seen how it can be used to illustrate the flow of data in a manual system. We have also seen that in order to be meaningful, it must be thorough and include every possible condition. A program flowchart that maps out the logical flow of data in a program also requires the utmost precision. Any condition not tested will, in the subsequent execution of the program, create problems that will require major revision. Thus, in analyzing and designing procedures, we use flowcharts that must be thorough, detailed, and precise.

Because of the blocks in a flowchart, the diagram is often referred to as a *block diagram*. Note that the flowchart depicts the logic of the program. It performs this by illustrating the steps involved and the order of steps with the use of standardized symbols.

A. THE STEPS INVOLVED

Each function is indicated by a symbol. You will note, for example, that reading a card and writing a check are notes within the *same* symbol type, an input/output symbol, in the flowcharts above. The specific operation to be performed is indicated by a note inside the symbol.

B. THE SEQUENCE OR ORDER OF THESE STEPS

The symbols are connected by *flowlines* that indicate the *sequence* of these steps. The flowchart usually reads from top to bottom unless a decision changes the flow. If a card were read with HOURS WORKED in excess of 40, for example, the normal path would be altered, and a *branch* to the routine called OVERTIME would occur.

Each of the operations indicated above converts to a program step during coding. Thus it is a relatively simple task to code a program from a flowchart, where the logic is clearly indicated. Those programmers who do not write flowcharts prior to coding complex programs often find that their logic is incorrect or that they did not

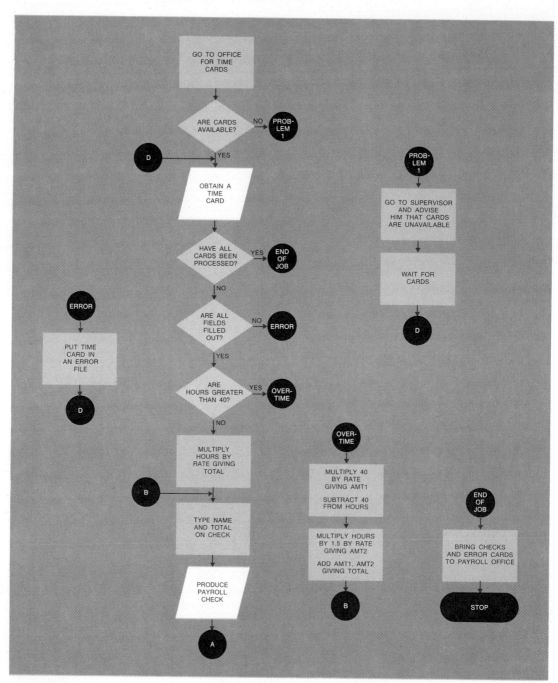

Figure 8.3
Manual procedure for preparing payroll checks-revised copy.

Concepts of Computer Programming

provide for all possible conditions. Flowcharts provide a means of illustrating the sequence of instructions prior to writing the program.

Thus flowcharts show the sequence or order of instructions that will appear in a program.

A Flowcharting Template (Figure 8.4) is used to draw the symbols representing specified functions. This template illustrates the established standard for flowcharting symbols. Thus *all* flowcharts written by programmers conform to a specified standard.

C. SYMBOLS

The major Symbols utilized are indicated in Table 8.1. Study them carefully before proceeding to the next paragraph.

Most flowcharts can be effectively written using these five basic symbols. Note that these symbols conform to a data processing standard. Thus data processing personnel in diversified areas can still understand the symbols and the logic used in any flowchart.

Let us consider the flowchart *excerpt* in Figure 8.5 (DRAFT VERSION). The flowchart indicates that we wish to print data from input cards.

The last symbol (BEGIN) indicates that after a card has been read, the data moved to the output area, and a line written, the flow should unconditionally branch, or proceed to, the instruction labeled as, or corresponding to, BEGIN.

The flowchart is not correct unless there is an entry connector indicating where BEGIN is. See Figure 8.6 (REVISED VERSION).

This flowchart depicts a set of instructions that will read cards and write a line for each. We will see later that for the flowchart to be complete there must be an exit point where the program is terminated.

When the point of entry is at the beginning of a flow then the entry

connector appears as . When the point of entry is within a

sequence, then the entry connector must appear as

Consider the program flowchart excerpt in Figure 8.7, which utilizes exactly the same symbols as above, but which *significantly* changes the sequence and thus the logic.

The entry connector BEGIN is coded as (BEGIN)➤ because it is a

point of entry *within* a sequence. While in the former case, we read as many cards as are required and write a line for each, in the above we

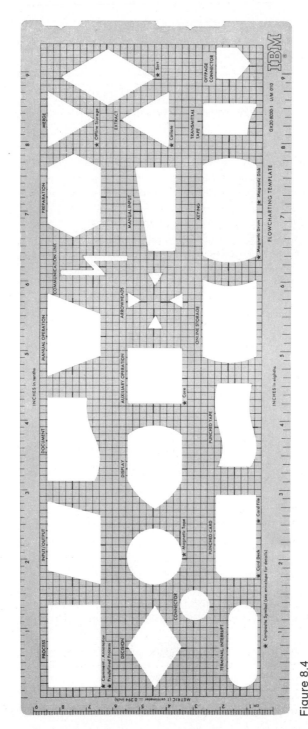

Figure 8.4
Flowcharting template.

Table 8.1   *Major Flowcharting Symbols*

	Symbol	Explanation
1.		**INPUT/OUTPUT (I/O) SYMBOL** This symbol represents any input or output operation such as READ A CARD, READ A TAPE, WRITE A LINE, etc. The specific operation at a particular point is indicated by a note inside the symbol.
2.		**PROCESSING** This symbol indicates any internal computer processing, that is, any series of data transfer or arithmetic operations. We may have, for example, ADD AMOUNT TO TOTAL or COMPUTE TAX = .05 × SALES or AVERAGE = X + Y + Z or MOVE INPUT TO OUTPUT
3.		**DECISION** This symbol is used to test for a logical comparison. Basically, it is used when we want the computer to ask a question. Examples of decision tests include: (a) IS AMOUNT OF SALES GREATER THAN 100.00? (b) IS AMOUNT OF SALES LESS THAN AMOUNT OF CREDIT? (c) DOES SEX FIELD = 'M'? (d) IS TOTAL = ZEROS?
4.		**CONNECTORS** This symbol denotes a cross reference point indicating where the flowchart should continue. It is used to indicate a change in the normal flow of data. There are three types of connectors:
4a.		**UNCONDITIONAL BRANCH CONNECTOR** This symbol is used to unconditionally alter the flow within a block diagram or flowchart. The note inside will indicate where the flow shall proceed or continue. Thus **EDIT** represents an unconditional sequence which indicates that the logic flow is to continue at the operation designated as EDIT. There must be a corresponding *ENTRY CONNECTOR* that is labeled as EDIT somewhere in the flowchart.
4b.		**ENTRY CONNECTOR** For every unconditional branch connector indicating a sequence change to a specified place (EDIT above) there must be an entry connector at that desired point (at EDIT): **A**
4c.		**CONDITIONAL BRANCH CONNECTOR** This symbol is associated with a decision and denotes that a branch is to occur only if a condition is met. To each conditional branch connector, for example, ◇ → **A** there must be a corresponding entry connector **A** or **A** .
5.		**TERMINAL** This symbol is used to denote the end point of a program.

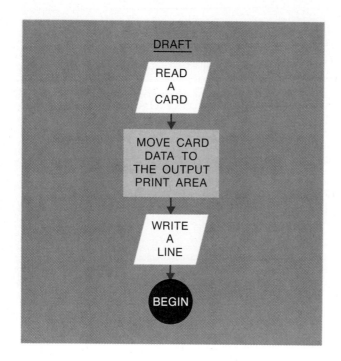

Figure 8.5
Flowchart illustrating the reading of input cards and printing of output lines.

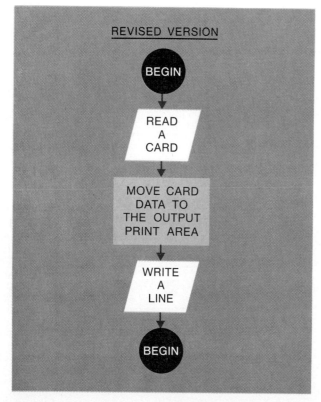

Figure 8.6
Revision.

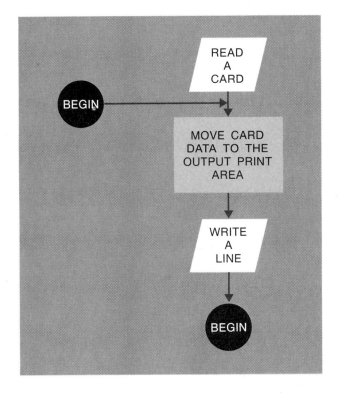

Figure 8.7
Flowchart illustrating the reading of a
single card and indefinitely printing it.

read only one card and write numerous lines from it. The sequence
indicated here is:

1. READ
2. MOVE
3. WRITE
4. MOVE (same data as step 2)
5. WRITE (same data as step 3)
6. MOVE (same data as step 2)
7. WRITE (same data as step 3)
   etc.

We are moving the *same* data from the input area to the output area
and writing the same data line. Each print line would be identical.
Usually this type of processing is considered illogical. Why print the
same line of data indefinitely?

Note, then, that although two flowcharts use the same symbols, the
order or logical integration of these can produce dramatic differences.
In the former case, a logical and meaningful program can be created;
in the latter, illogical output results.

Note that connector symbols may be identified by any notational insert. Some programmers prefer to use notes 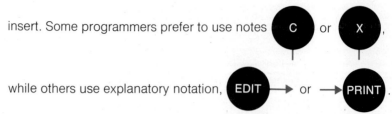 C or X ,

while others use explanatory notation, EDIT ➔ or ➔ PRINT .

Notice, too, that the unconditional branch connector is always the *last* element in a sequence. Once we issue an instruction that causes the flow to proceed elsewhere, there is no need for further instruction at that point. The following is *invalid* and meaningless.

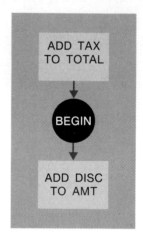

Once an unconditional branch to BEGIN is executed, the instruction following the connector cannot be completed.

Keep in mind that the decision symbol and the conditional branch connector are always coded together.

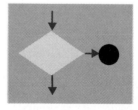

This indicates that *if* a condition is met, then a branch to the entry point indicated should occur. Otherwise, the flow continues with the next sequential step. Every conditional branch connector must have an entry connector associated with it. Figure 8.8 helps to illustrate this point.

A card is read. If there is a C in card column 1 (denoting a credit), a conditional branch to CREDIT occurs. At CREDIT, which is executed

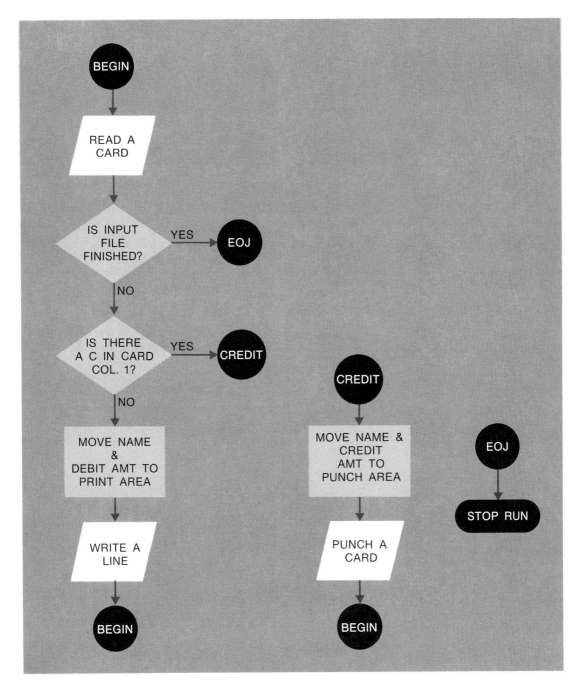

Figure 8.8
Sample Flowchart

only if there is a C in card column 1 of the card read, a new card is punched with the NAME and CREDIT AMOUNT, and an unconditional branch to BEGIN (READ A CARD) occurs. If there is no C in card column 1, then execution continues with the next sequential step, where a line is printed with the NAME and DEBIT AMOUNT and a new card is read.

Notice that in the above there are two unconditional branches to BEGIN, from *different* points. There must, however, be only *one* entry point labeled BEGIN. That is, we may branch to the *same* entry point in a flowchart from many different conditional or unconditional branch points.

You will recall that flowcharts must indicate a terminating or final end point in order to be complete. Thus each of the above flowcharts is only partially correct. Every set of instructions, and thus every program, must have a stopping point. Usually this point is reached only when input data has been completely processed.

Prior to processing each card, we test to determine if, in fact, there are no more cards. That is, a card is read; if that card contains an end of file code (usually a blank card with a /* in the first two columns), we proceed to an end of job sequence. Thus all flowcharts that utilize input cards follow each read-a-card instruction with an end-of-file test. If the computer reads in an end-of-file card, then a branch is taken. Similarly, read tape instructions must be followed by end-of-file tests. If an end-of-file tape record is reached, a conditional branch to an end-of-job procedure should be taken. Thus, when all input has been processed a conditional branch to EOJ (a common label for *End Of Job*) occurs, where the program is terminated. If there were end of job totals required, for example, they would be printed at the *routine,* or sequence, labeled EOJ.

Let us now employ the symbols learned to create more complex flowcharts.

Suppose we wish to punch five output cards for every input card read. That is, we wish to perform a punch *routine,* or *sequence,* five times. A sequence of steps to be executed a fixed number of times is referred to as a *loop*. Generally, for looping operations, we:

1. Establish a counter with zero contents.
2. Perform the required operation (punching of a card).
3. Add 1 to the counter. (Every time we perform the required operation, 1 is added to the counter. Thus the counter reflects the number of times the operation has been performed.
4. Test the counter for the required number of operations (5 punched cards).
5. If the counter is not equal to the required number of operations, the sequence is repeated; otherwise a branch occurs.

Note that we cannot merely tell the computer to punch a card five times. The looping routine is required to perform an operation a fixed number of times.

Thus the flowchart reads as indicated in Figure 8.9.

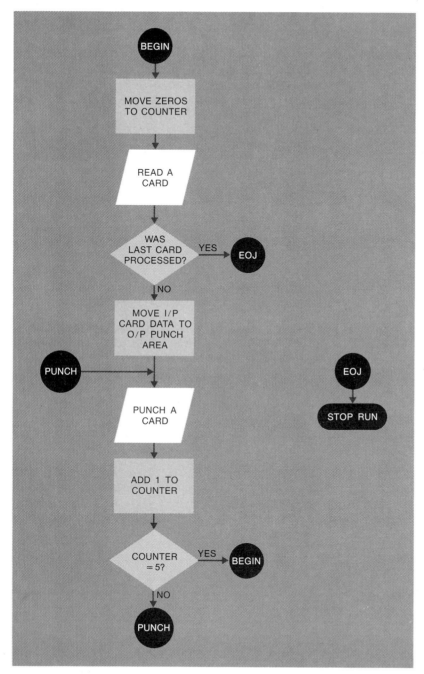

Figure 8.9
Flowchart of a looping routine—5 output cards punched for every input card read.

You will recall that a program residing in core storage includes the set of instructions and the necessary input/output areas. In addition a program must provide for constants and work areas that may be required. COUNTER, for example, in the above flowchart, would have to be defined as a work area in the corresponding program, while 1 would be a constant that would also require a core storage area.

SELF-EVALUATING QUIZ

1. A flowchart is a diagram that illustrates the _____ of _____ in a _____ .
2. A sequence of steps in a flowchart consists of _____ connected by _____ .
3. The direction of flow in a flowchart is usually from _____ to _____ .
4. A symbol represents _____ .
5. All symbols must be connected by _____ ; each symbol contains a _____ inside it.
6. A flowcharting _____ contains all the standard symbols used to draw flowcharts.
   Identify each of the symbols in Questions 7 to 14:

7.

8.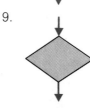

9.

10.

11.

12.

13.

15. Arithmetic operations are coded in _____ symbols.
16. Each symbol can generally be used to code a program

_____ .

17. If a decision is *met,* then the _____ indicates where the flow is to continue; otherwise the program proceeds with the

_____ .

18. When the flow of a sequence is interrupted and is to continue at some step other than the next sequential step, a(n) _____ is said to occur.
19. No decision is involved in a(n) _____ branch.
20. Consider the following:

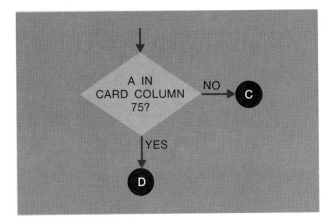

If there is *not* an A in card column 75, a _____ to _____ will occur.

21. The unconditional branch connector must be the _____ step in a sequence.
22. To every branch connector, there must correspond a(n) _____ .
23. (T or F) A branch to one entry point may occur from several different points in a flowchart.
24. A _____ is a group of integrated steps connected by flowlines.
25. Consider the flowchart in Figure 8.10. The flowchart depicts the logic in an automobile insurance company procedure. Column 18 denotes marital status (M = married, S = single, O = other, such as widowed, divorced, separated). Column 19 denotes sex (M = male, F = female, blank denotes that sex is unknown). The procedure or *routine* determines the total number of individuals who will receive discounts because they are either:

    (1) female, or
    (2) married and male

It has been determined by several studies that female drivers and married, male drivers have fewer accidents than other people. Because of this fact, this insurance company will issue discounts to those categories of people. With the following input cards, what will be the contents of TOTAL at the end of all operations?

Card No.	Contents of Column 18	Contents of Column 19
1	M	M
2	M	F
3	S	M
4	M	F
5	O	F
6	M	-
7	S	F
8	M	M

Consider the flowchart in Figure 8.11 for questions 26 to 33.

26. For every ____(no.)____ cards read, 1 line is printed.
27. The MOVE ZEROS instruction insures that the fields indicated will not be _____ at the onset of execution.
28. When there are no more cards, a(n) _____ to _____ occurs.
29. At EOJ _____ is printed which is obtained from the total of all _____ .
30. INDEX is a field used as a _____ for _____ .
31. After 10 cards have been read and added, a branch to _____ occurs.

Concepts of Computer Programming

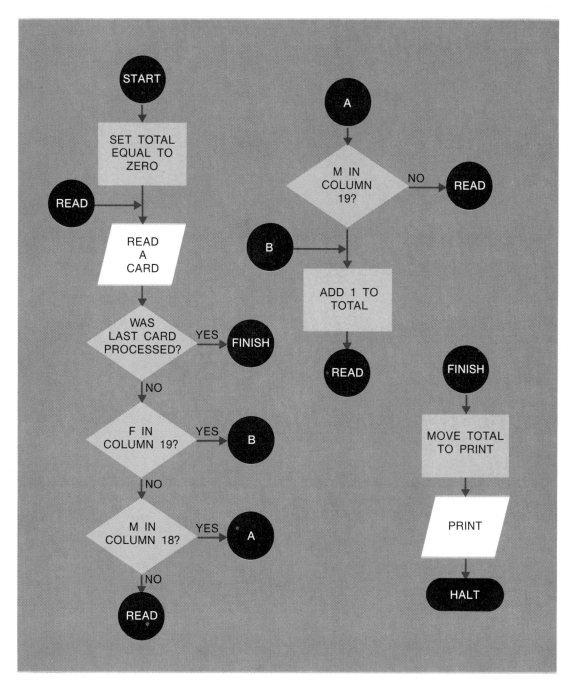

Figure 8.10
Problem flowchart I.

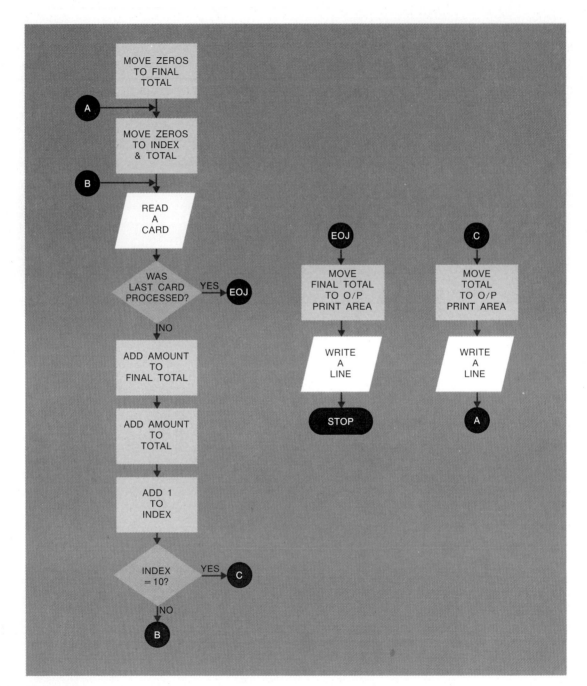

Figure 8.11
Problem flowchart II.

Concepts of Computer Programming

32. After the data has been printed for each group of 10 cards, _____ and _____ must be initialized, or restarted at zero.

33. Each time a card is read and an amount is added to TOTAL, ____(no.)____ is added to INDEX.

SOLUTIONS

1. order (logic); functions; program
2. symbols; flowlines
3. top; bottom
4. a function
5. flowlines; note
6. template
7. processing
8. input/output (I/O)
9. decision
10. unconditional branch connector
11. entry connector
12. entry connector
13. conditional branch connector
14. terminal
15. processing
16. instruction
17. conditional branch connector; next sequential step
18. branch
19. unconditional
20. branch; C
21. last
22. entry connector
23. T
24. sequence
25. 6
26. 10
27. filled with irrelevant data
28. branch; EOJ
29. a final total; amount fields
30. counter; looping
31. C
32. index; total
33. 1

III. Illustrative Flowcharting Procedures

Now that we have noted the basic flowcharting symbols and how they are used to create simple block diagrams, let us study illustrative business applications.

A. EXAMPLE 1: INVENTORY SYSTEM

An inventory program is to be created that utilizes inventory cards to produce a monthly inventory reorder report.

The cards have the following format:

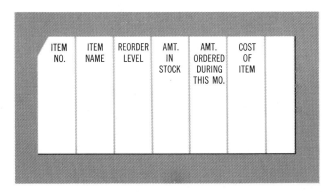

ITEM NO.	ITEM NAME	REORDER LEVEL	AMT. IN STOCK	AMT. ORDERED DURING THIS MO.	COST OF ITEM	

The printed report has the following format:

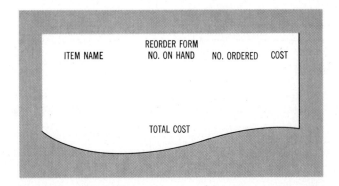

NO. ON HAND = AMT. IN STOCK + AMT. ORDERED DURING THIS
MONTH

NO. ORDERED = REORDER LEVEL — NO. ON HAND (if reorder level
is greater than no. on hand)
= 00 (if reorder level is less than or equal to no. on
hand)

COST = COST OF ITEM × NO. ORDERED

TOTAL COST = SUM OF ALL COST FIELDS

The flowchart is indicated in Figure 8.12. *TOTAL* is a field that must
be initialized at zero, since we wish to accumulate amount fields in it.

The print area is cleared by moving blanks or spaces to it, since
most modern computers do *not* automatically clear storage with *each*
new program that is read.

Each card is then processed according to the formulas above.
When all data has been accumulated in the print area, a line is written.

Processing continues in this way until all cards have been read.
Then a branch to EOJ occurs. At EOJ, we print the TOTAL field and
then terminate the job.

In order to be considered complete, this inventory flowchart must
include a heading routine. All reports that are produced should have
headings on the top of each page. This involves printing a heading
initially and then, after each normal line is written, we should determine
if the end of the page has been reached. If it has, we write headings on
a new page. If not, we continue with the normal flow.

B. EXAMPLE 2: A BANKING OPERATION

A banking organization uses punched cards to store all transaction
data for the week. The card format is as follows:

Concepts of Computer Programming

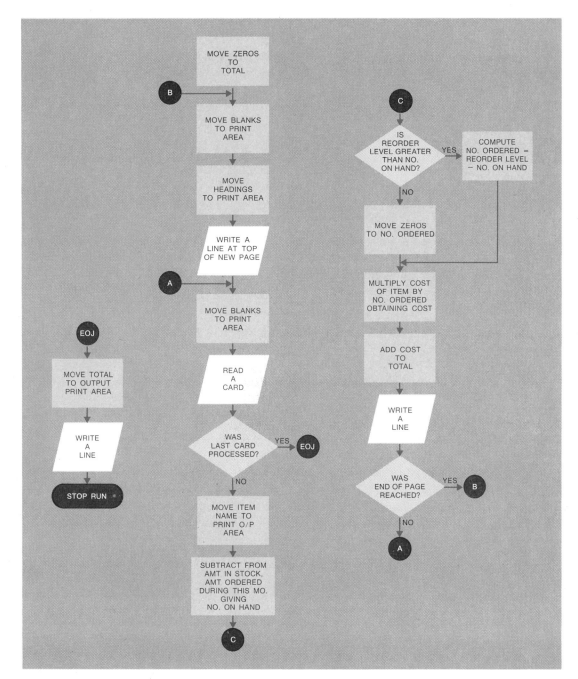

Figure 8.12
Program flowchart of inventory problem.

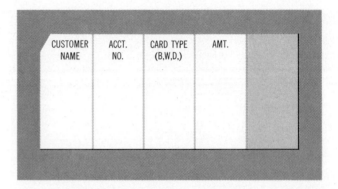

Cards are in sequence by ACCOUNT NUMBER. Each customer has one type "B" card (balance on hand at beginning of week). This will be the *first* card for each account or customer. In addition, there *may* be several "D" (deposit) or "W" (withdrawal) cards following a "B" card for a customer, depending on the number of transactions during the week. Thus, all cards for a single account will appear together, with the "B" card being the first for the group.

The output of the program will be a printed report with the following information:

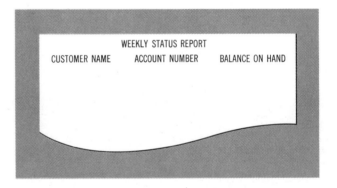

BALANCE ON HAND = BALANCE (from "B" card) + DEPOSITS (from "D" cards) − WITHDRAWALS (from "W" cards)

The flowchart is illustrated in Figure 8.13. Note that the headings are printed first, prior to any card processing. Since the first card read is a "B" card, a branch to NEW-ACCT occurs, where a line is printed. For normal processing this line contains the data for the previous account. That is, a "B" card signals the start of a new account and thus the previous one must be printed. For the first card, however, there is no previous account. Since no data was moved to the print area, a blank line is in effect printed. The total area is cleared and

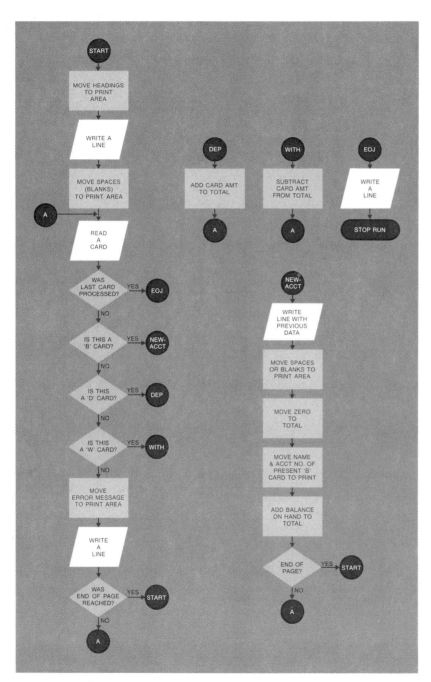

Figure 8.13
Program flowchart of a banking problem.

information from this new balance card is moved to the print area. More cards are read. Deposits, denoted by "D" cards are added to the TOTAL, and withdrawals, denoted by "W" cards, are subtracted. There may be many "D" and "W" cards for a specific account, depending on the number of transactions for the week. When a "B" card is read, the previous data (NAME, ACCOUNT NUMBER, and BALANCE ON HAND) is printed, the print area is cleared, and the new data is read.

Each card read is tested for a "B," "D," or "W." If it is a "B" card, it signals a new account, since the first card of an account must be a "B" card. If it is a "D" or "W" card, the amount is added or subtracted, correspondingly. If it is not a "B," "D," or "W" card, then an error message is printed. It is always good practice to test for validity in a card program, since keypunching errors are relatively frequent.

When there are no more cards to be read, a branch to EOJ occurs. At EOJ, we must print the *last* account group. Since accounts are only printed when a *new* account number (a "B" card) is read, the last account must be "forced." That is, the last account group does not have a "B" card following it to signal a print routine. Thus at EOJ, a print routine must be performed.

Note, too, that print programs test for the end of the page. When the end of a page has been reached, we generally wish to print headings on top of the next page.

C. EXAMPLE 3: SIMPLIFIED ACCOUNTS RECEIVABLE BILLING PROGRAM

This program will utilize, as input, a master file with information on all charge accounts for a particular department store. The input is on tape:

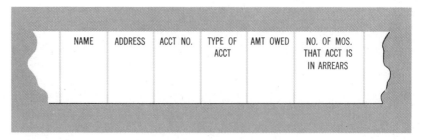

NAME	ADDRESS	ACCT NO.	TYPE OF ACCT	AMT OWED	NO. OF MOS. THAT ACCT IS IN ARREARS

The output is a monthly statement or bill submitted to the customer:

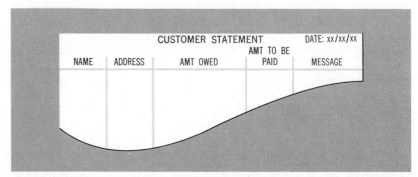

| | | CUSTOMER STATEMENT | | DATE: xx/xx/xx | |
| NAME | ADDRESS | AMT OWED | AMT TO BE PAID | MESSAGE | |

Note that the bills are produced on a series of preprinted continuous forms that contain the headings. The programmer must merely insert the date and required data.

The operations to be performed are as follows.

1. Compilation of Billing Data

If TYPE OF ACCOUNT contains a 1 (regular charge), the *entire* bill is to be paid each month. In this case, AMT OWED is transmitted to the output field, AMT TO BE PAID, with no interest computed.

If TYPE OF ACCOUNT is a 2 (budget charge) then $\frac{1}{12}$ of AMT OWED + INTEREST CHARGE (1% of entire AMT OWED) is recorded on the bill as AMT TO BE PAID.

In each case, NAME, ADDRESS, and AMT OWED are placed directly on the customer statement from the master tape. DATE is obtained from a control card, which is the only card read. The information from this control card is placed in the computer in a field called DATE-IN. Thus DATE-IN is used to transmit the month and year to the Customer Statement.

2. Determination of Charge Status

The field called NO. OF MOS. THAT ACCT. IS IN ARREARS denotes the number of months since a payment has been made to an account that has a balance. If 2 months have elapsed (a 2 is in the field) then a message: REMINDER—YOUR ACCOUNT IS IN ARREARS is to print on the statement. If 3 months have elapsed (a 3 is in the field) then a message: WARNING—YOUR CHARGE PRIVILEGES HAVE BEEN SUSPENDED is to print. A separate monthly run provides a listing of all customers that have not made payments in three months. This list is then distributed to sales personnel who are told not to honor the customers' charge cards.

The flowchart is indicated in Figure 8.14.

D. EXAMPLE 4: UPDATE PROGRAM—ILLUSTRATING MORE COMPLEX LOGIC

An updating procedure is the process of making a file of data current. The updating of files is an essential and widely used application of computers. A Payroll File, for example, must be updated weekly or monthly with new hires, separations from the company, promotions, salary increases, and so on. A Purchasing File must be updated with, for example, new orders and filled orders.

Before flowcharting an update procedure, let us outline the major facets of a typical procedure for updating a *sequential* file. This update procedure generally consists of *three* files.

1. Input Master File. The input *master* file has all the data except that which is most current. That is, it contains master information that is current only up to the previous updating cycle. We will call this file OLD-MASTER.

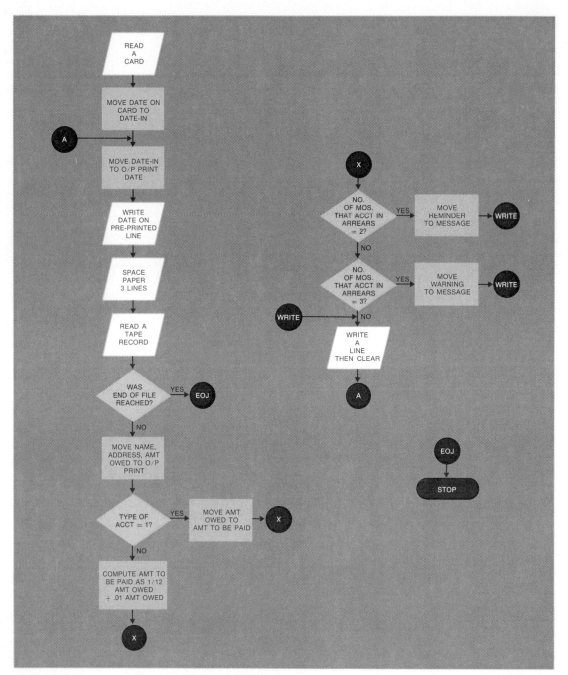

Figure 8.14
Program flowchart of accounts receivable problem.

Concepts of Computer Programming

2. Input Detail File. The input *detail* or *transaction file* contains data for the present updating cycle only. If updates are performed weekly, for example, then the Detail File will contain only the present week's activity. We will call this file DETAIL.

3. Output Master File. The output master file incorporates the current detail data and the previous master information. That is, the output master file will combine data from OLD-MASTER and DETAIL. We will call this file NEW-MASTER.

To update files, data must be read into the computer in a specific sequence. Since we wish to update particular master records with corresponding detail records, we must insure that each file is in the same sequence.

Let us assume that we are performing an Accounts Receivable operation, updating a master transaction file with detail transaction records. That is, OLD-MASTER contains all transaction data current through the previous updating cycle; DETAIL contains transactions of the current period, and NEW-MASTER will incorporate both files of information. A *systems* or general flowchart of the operation appears as follows.

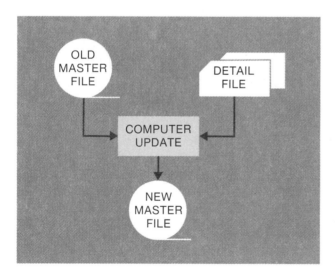

The OLD-MASTER is a tape file, the DETAIL is a card file, and the NEW-MASTER, which incorporates both, is also a tape file. Consider the new and old master files to have the following format:

Positions 1 to 5 = ACCOUNT NUMBER
Positions 6 to 10 = AMOUNT DUE

The DETAIL file has the following format:

Positions 1 to 5 = ACCOUNT NUMBER
Positions 6 to 10 = AMOUNT OF CURRENT TRANSACTION

Note that AMOUNT OF CURRENT TRANSACTION can be negative (to reflect a Credit or payment) as well as positive (to indicate a purchase).

The update program will read data from cards and tape, both of which are in ACCOUNT NUMBER sequence. For each ACCOUNT NUMBER that is on both the DETAIL and OLD-MASTER files, AMOUNT OF CURRENT TRANSACTION will be added to the AMOUNT DUE to obtain a resultant AMOUNT DUE. If an ACCOUNT NUMBER is on the OLD-MASTER file but not on the DETAIL FILE, then no business was transacted for that specific account, and the NEW-MASTER will merely contain the OLD-MASTER data. In such a case, we say that no updating of the master record is necessary.

If an ACCOUNT NUMBER appears on the DETAIL FILE but not on the OLD-MASTER file, then a new account has been added during the present updating cycle. The NEW-MASTER will then contain only data from the DETAIL file.

Thus the sequence control field on all files is ACCOUNT NUMBER. The detail cards and the input master tape will both be in sequence by ACCOUNT NUMBER. After reading a single card and tape record, we will test for three possible conditions.

1. ACCOUNT NUMBER OF DETAIL = ACCOUNT NUMBER OF OLD-MASTER.

When the account numbers are equal, the input master record is to be updated; that is, the card amount is added to the OLD-MASTER amount to obtain a NEW-MASTER amount. A NEW-MASTER record is then created and another DETAIL card and OLD-MASTER tape record is read.

2. ACCOUNT NUMBER OF DETAIL IS GREATER THAN ACCOUNT NUMBER OF OLD-MASTER.

In this case, there is an OLD-MASTER record with no corresponding DETAIL record. As an example, suppose the first two records read are ACCOUNT NUMBER 00805 on the DETAIL file and ACCOUNT NUMBER 00800 on the OLD-MASTER file. Since both files are in sequence by ACCOUNT NUMBER, this indicates that there is no ACCOUNT NUMBER 00800 on the Detail File (00805 is greater than 00800). Thus there were no transactions for ACCOUNT NUMBER 00800 during the updating cycle.

In this case, the NEW-MASTER record is created directly from OLD-MASTER. Notice that we then read *only* an OLD-MASTER record; we do *not* read another card. In the above example, after we put record 00800 on the new file, we still have not processed detail record 00805; thus, we read another OLD-MASTER record only.

3. ACCOUNT NUMBER OF DETAIL IS LESS THAN ACCOUNT NUMBER OF OLD-MASTER.

In this case, a DETAIL card record exists for which there is no corresponding master record. We will consider this to be a new account. The NEW-MASTER tape record, then, will be created directly from the DETAIL card. Note that we read only another DETAIL record at this point; we do *not* read an OLD-MASTER record, since the previous tape record has not been processed.

The flowchart for this update procedure is illustrated in Figure 8.15.

Examine the flowchart carefully. Note that all operations indicated in the narrative are followed in the flowchart. Let us discuss the end-of-file routines.

When there are no more cards to process, there may still be OLD-MASTER tape records that must be rewritten onto the NEW-MASTER tape. This is performed until there are no more tape records, when an end-of-job condition is met. Note that when we reach EOJ2, we have *already* read a tape record which must be processed before reading another one.

When there are no more OLD-MASTER tape records to process there may still be DETAIL cards to process. That is, there may still be new accounts that must be added to the NEW-MASTER file. Thus the DETAIL file is read and processed until there are no more cards. Then an end-of-job condition is reached.

An update procedure, such as the one discussed above, is a common task performed for business systems. It includes complex logic that is best illustrated by a flowchart. Generally, most update procedures on any business system conform to the above.

Note, however, that if master information is on disk rather than tape, the procedure is simplified considerably. It is not necessary to create a new disk file. The detail records can simply be added to an existing master disk file.

Although we cannot easily read from a tape and then write new data back onto it, the disk is readily adapted to input/output functions. Thus, update procedures are generally easier to perform using disk processing.

Chapter 15 discusses in more depth the updating of files as an example of a commonly used programming technique.

This chapter has attempted to show how the logical integration of programming steps is illustrated with the use of a program flowchart. Businessmen with an understanding of, and an appreciation for, this technique can communicate far more effectively with computer specialists. In this way, the two organization groups can understand each other's requirements and thus bridge the communications gap that has been for many years, a major stumbling block to efficient computer systems.

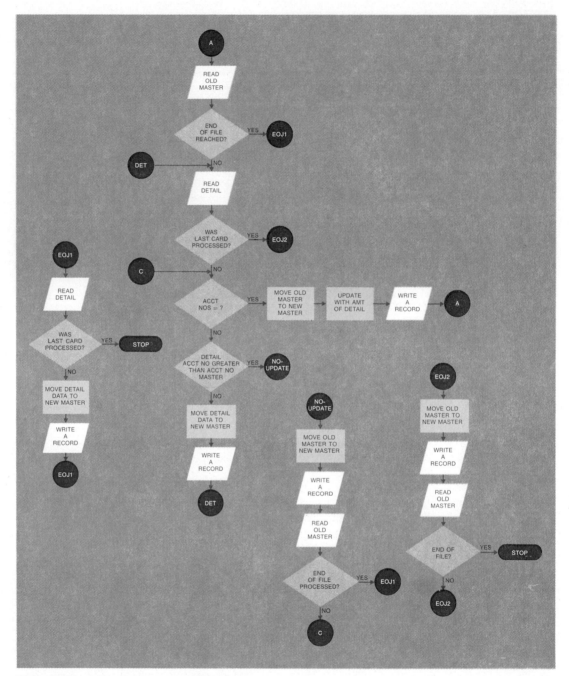

Figure 8.15
Program flowchart of update procedure.

Concepts of Computer Programming

SELF-EVALUATING QUIZ

The questions will relate to the flowchart in Figure 8.16. This flowchart illustrates a *merging* procedure where two tape files, each in ACCOUNT NUMBER sequence, are merged into a single sequential tape file. Each input file in this particular case contains unique account numbers. That is, if a record on Tape File 1 has an ACCOUNT NUMBER that matches Tape File 2, then we will consider this to be an error condition. ACCT NO. 1 is the Account Number for Tape 1; ACCT NO. 2 is the Account Number for Tape 2.

1. If ACCOUNT NO. of Tape 1 is less than ACCOUNT NO. of Tape 2, then a record from Tape ____(no.)____ is written. This is noted by the branch taken to _____ .
2. If ACCOUNT NO. of Tape 1 is Greater than ACCOUNT NO. of Tape 2, then a Record from Tape ____(no.)____ is written. This is noted by the branch taken to _____ .
3. If neither of the above conditions are met, then this indicates that the ACCOUNT NO. from Tape 1 and the ACCOUNT NO. from Tape 2 are _____ .
4. If the condition in question 3 is met then _____ is printed.
5. When a record from Tape 1 is written, _____ is read and a branch to _____ occurs.
6. When a record from Tape 2 is written, a branch to _____ occurs where _____ is read.
7. When we branch to EOJ1, there are no more records from _____ to process, but there may still be records from _____ to process.
8. Thus at EOJ1, we add _____ records to the output file until _____ .
9. When we branch to EOJ2, there are no more records from _____ to process, but there may still be records from _____ to process.
10. At EOJ2, we add _____ records to the output file until _____ , at which time we _____ .
11. The job is terminated when _____ .
12. A merge program creates an output file from ____(no.)____ input files. The input files must be _____ .

SOLUTIONS

1. 1; TAPE 1
2. 2; TAPE 2
3. equal
4. an error message
5. Tape File 1; C
6. B; Tape File 2
7. Tape File 1; Tape File 2

8. Tape File 2; there are no more records from Tape File 2
9. Tape File 2; Tape File 1
10. Tape File 1; there are no more records from Tape File 1; STOP
11. there are no more records from either file.
12. 2; in sequence

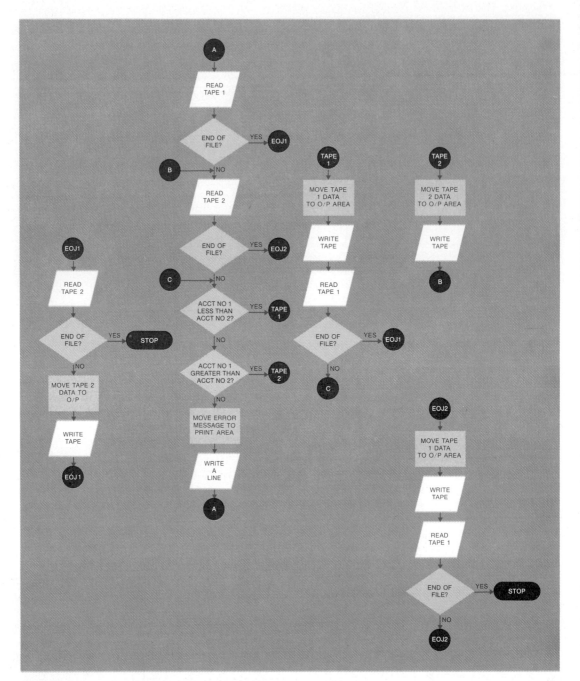

Figure 8.16
Flowchart for sample merge problem.

Concepts of Computer Programming

Appendix to Chapter 8 *Decision Tables*

We have thus far seen how flowcharts can be an extremely useful tool in determining the logic necessary for a program. Keep in mind that a program is a set of instructions to the computer to enable it to perform a procedure that is most often performed manually. Such procedures sometimes involve numerous conditions with corresponding actions.

When the logic of such possible alternatives becomes complex, the need for a thorough and detailed flowchart increases. When conditions become so involved and intricate, sometimes even a flowchart is as cumbersome as a pictorial representation. Because of all the flowlines required for vast and complex processing of conditions, this method of representation is sometimes unsuitable. In such a case, DECISION TABLES are often a more appropriate alternative. Note that DECISION TABLES are not universally accepted as a standard the way flowcharts are and, for this reason, this discussion has been included as an appendix.

Decision tables, then, are most often utilized for describing a set of procedures usually within a program where numerous and complex conditions affect the logic flow. That is, if operations and procedures within a program are greatly affected by specific conditions, then a decision table is an extremely useful tool for describing that program.

Note that the decision table does not replace a flowchart, but generally supplements it where complex conditions make a flowchart

Schematic

CONDITIONS	CONDITION ENTRIES
ACTIONS	ACTION ENTRIES

Illustration: Airline Reservation System

		RULE 1	RULE 2	RULE 3	RULE 4
CONDITIONS	Request is for	1st Class	1st Class	Tourist	Tourist
	1st Class Available	Y	N		
	Tourist Class Available			Y	N
ACTIONS	Issue	1st Class		Tourist	
	Place on Waiting List		X		X

Figure 8.17
Basic entries within a decision table.

cumbersome. The decision table, like the flowchart, is a graphic representation of procedures and operations.

Figure 8-17 illustrates the four basic entries within a decision table.

Notice that Y denotes yes, that the condition exists; N denotes no, that the condition does not exist; and X denotes that the corresponding action is taken. Reading from top to bottom and beginning with the first rule, we have

CONDITIONS	1st Class Available	Y
	Tourist Class Available	
ACTIONS	Issue	1st Class
	Place on Waiting List	

If 1st class is available (Y in condition *1st class*) then ISSUE 1st class ticket (Action taken).

With Rule 2, we have

CONDITIONS	1st Class Available	N
	Tourist Class Available	
ACTIONS	Issue	
	Place on Waiting List	X

Use the following in determining the meaning of decision table entries:

If (condition), then (action):

If 1st class is *not* available (N for not), then place on waiting list. With Rule 3, we have

CONDITIONS		
	1st Class Available	
	Tourist Class Available	Y
ACTIONS		
	Issue	Tourist
	Place on Waiting List	

If (condition), then (action); that is, *if* tourist class is available, then issue tourist ticket.
With Rule 4, we have

CONDITIONS		
	1st Class Available	
	Tourist Class Available	N
ACTIONS		
	Issue	
	Place on Waiting List	X

If tourist class is *not* available, then place on waiting list.

Notice that the above can also be presented in a flowchart (see Figure 8.18).

Note also that this is not the only method for preparing a decision table of this series of conditions. The decision table in Figure 8.19 provides for *exactly* the same conditions as above.

Let us now examine a more sophisticated airline reservation system. This system will also grant first class tickets, if available, to those who request them and, similarly, it will grant tourist tickets, if available, to those who request these. If however, a particular class ticket is not available on request, then the reservations clerk will determine if the other class ticket is acceptable by the individual and is also available. If both these conditions are met, then the clerk will make out the appropriate ticket; if not, then the individual's name must be placed on the corresponding waiting list.

The above may be expressed in terms of the following criteria:

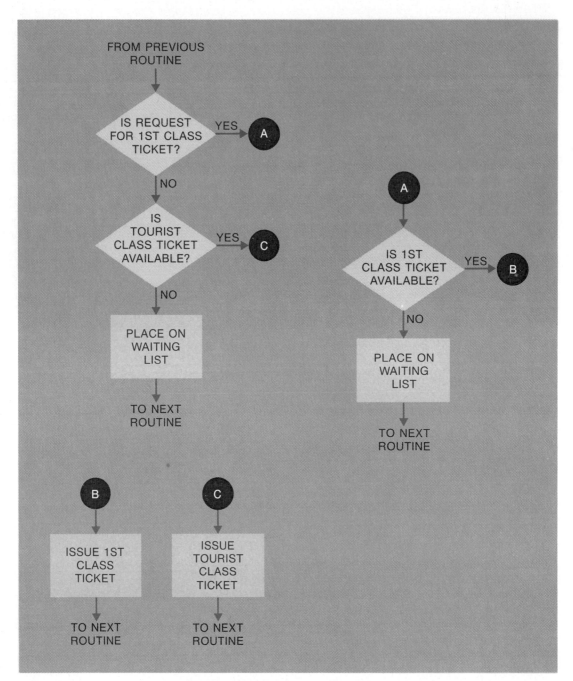

Figure 8.18
Program flowchart excerpt.

Concepts of Computer Programming

	RULE 1	RULE 2	RULE 3	RULE 4
CONDITIONS				
Request is 1st Class	Y	Y		
Request is Tourist			Y	Y
1st Class Available	Y	N		
Tourist Available			Y	N
ACTIONS				
Issue 1st Class Ticket	X			
Issue Tourist Ticket			X	
Place on Waiting List		X		X

Figure 8.19

1. If first class ticket is requested and available, then first class ticket is issued.
2. If tourist class ticket is requested and available, then tourist class ticket is issued.
3. If first class ticket is requested but not available, determine if tourist class is acceptable and available. If tourist class is acceptable and available, issue tourist class ticket; if not, place individual's name on first class waiting list.
4. If tourist class ticket is requested and not available, determine if first class ticket is acceptable and available; if first class ticket is acceptable and available, issue first class ticket; if not, place individual's name on a tourist waiting list.

The decision table in Figure 8.20 represents a schematic for the above.

	RULE 1	RULE 2	RULE 3	RULE 4	RULE 5	RULE 6	RULE 7	RULE 8
CONDITIONS								
1st Class Request	Y	Y	Y	Y				
Tourist Request					Y	Y	Y	Y
1st Class Open	Y	N	N	N		Y	N	
Tourist Open		Y	N		Y	N	N	N
Alternate Class Acceptable		Y	Y	N		Y	Y	N
ACTIONS								
Issue 1st Class Ticket	X					X		
Issue Tourist Ticket		X			X			
Place on Tourist Wait List			X				X	X
Place on 1st Class Wait List			X	X		X	X	

Figure 8.20

Chapter 9 *Introduction to COBOL Programming*

I. The Nature of COBOL

COBOL is the most widespread commercial programming language in use today. Students with any knowledge of data processing should therefore be familiar with COBOL. You will recall that COBOL is an abbreviation for *CO*mmon *Business* Oriented *L*anguage. It is a business-oriented language designed specifically for commercial applications. It is also a computer language that is universal, or common to many computers. The universality of COBOL allows computer users greater flexibility. A company is free to use computers of different manufacturers while retaining a single programming language. Similarly, conversion from one model computer to a more advanced or newer one presents no great problem. Computers of a future generation will also be equipped to use COBOL.

Thus the meaning of the word COBOL suggests two of its basic advantages. It is common to most computers and it is commercially oriented. There are, however, additional reasons for its being such a popular language.

COBOL is an English-like language. All instructions are coded using English words rather than complex codes. To add two numbers together, for example, we use the word ADD. Similarly, the rules for programming in COBOL conform to many of the rules for writing in English, making it a relatively simple language to learn. It therefore becomes significantly easier to train programmers. In addition, COBOL

Concepts of Computer Programming

programs are generally written and tested in far less time than programs written in most other computer languages.

Thus the English-like quality of COBOL makes it easy to *write* programs. Similarly, this quality makes COBOL programs easier to *read*. Such programs can generally be understood by nondata processing personnel. The businessman who is not an expert on computers can better understand the nature of a programming job simply by reading a COBOL program.

With a brief introduction to the language, a student can effectively read a program and understand its nature. This significantly reduces the communications gap between the programmer and the businessman. Both can work jointly to correct or improve the logic of a COBOL program.

II. Basic Structure of a COBOL Program

A. THE CODING SHEET

COBOL programs are written on coding or program sheets (Figure 9.1). The coding sheet has space for 80 columns of information. Each line of a program sheet will be keypunched into *one* punched card. Usually the standard COBOL card (Figure 9.2) is used for this purpose.

Thus, for every *line* written on the coding sheet, we will obtain *one punched card*. The entire deck of cards keypunched from the coding sheets is called the *COBOL SOURCE PROGRAM*. Note that *all* programming languages utilize specially designed coding sheets, except PL/1—a free-form language that does not require characters to be in any specific positions. Similarly, all source decks consist of cards keypunched from coding sheets, where one line is punched into one card.

Let us examine the COBOL program sheet more closely. The body of the form is subdivided into 72 positions or columns. These positions, when coded, will be keypunched into card columns 1 to 72, respectively. In the upper righthand corner, there is provision for the program identification, labeled positions 73 to 80. The identification, usually a number, will be entered into columns 73 to 80 of all cards keypunched from this form. This number is usually supplied by the systems analyst and represents the number by which the program will be known to systems and operations personnel. The other data recorded on the top of the form is *not* keypunched into cards. It supplies identifying information only, should the sheets themselves be lost or misplaced.

The identification number, positions 73 to 80, and the page and serial number, positions 1 to 6, are optional entries in a COBOL program, and in *all* other programming languages. Both fields, however, can be extremely useful, should cards in the source deck be misplaced or lost.

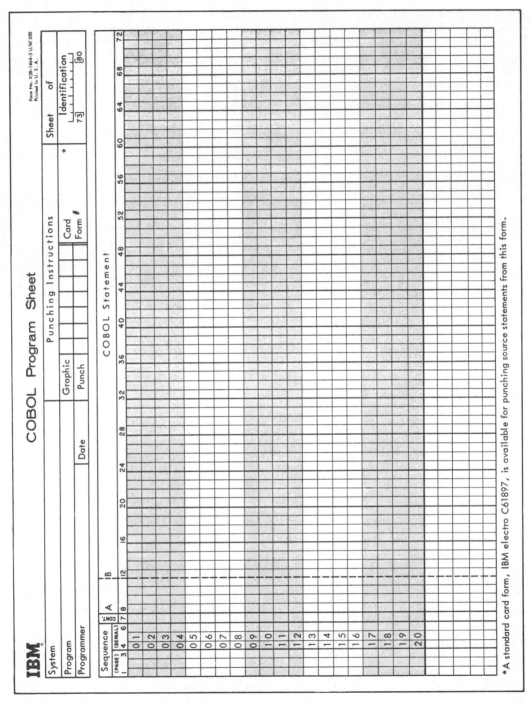

Figure 9.1
COBOL coding sheet.

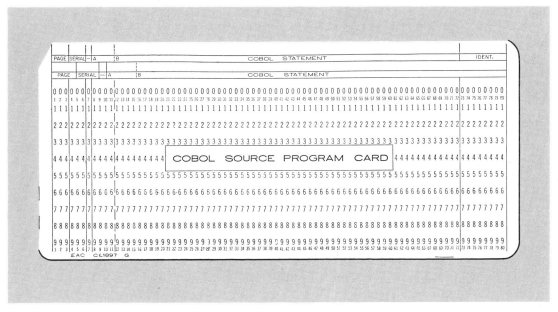

Figure 9.2
COBOL source program card.

Page and serial (line) numbers on each line, and therefore, on each punched card are advisable, since cards are sometimes inadvertently dropped. In such cases, resequencing of the deck is necessary.

If page and serial numbers are supplied, it is also an easy task to insert cards in their proper place. Note that some coding sheets preprint the serial numbers to assist the programmer.

B. THE FOUR DIVISIONS

Every COBOL program consists of four separate *divisions*. Each division is written in an English-like manner designed to decrease programming effort and to facilitate the understanding of a program by nondata processing or business personnel. Each of the four divisions has a specific function.

1. The IDENTIFICATION DIVISION serves to identify the program to the computer. It also provides pertinent documentary information that assists the businessman in understanding the nature of the program and the techniques that it will employ.

2. The ENVIRONMENT DIVISION describes the computer equipment that will be utilized in the program.

3. The DATA DIVISION describes the input and output formats to be processed by the program. It also defines any constants or work areas necessary for the processing of data.

4. The PROCEDURE DIVISION contains the instructions and the logic flow necessary to create output data from input. The PROCEDURE DIVISION is coded directly from the flowchart.

The structure and organization of a COBOL program can best be explained by an illustration.

III. *Illustrative COBOL Programs*

A. SAMPLE PROGRAM 1

1. Definition of the Problem

A computer center of a large company is assigned the task of calculating WEEKLY-WAGES for all nonsalaried personnel. The HOURLY-RATE and the number of HOURS-WORKED are supplied for each employee, and the WEEKLY-WAGES figure is computed as follows:

$$\text{WEEKLY-WAGES} = \text{HOURS-WORKED} \times \text{HOURLY-RATE}$$

You will recall that to process data, the incoming information or input must be in a form that is acceptable or understandable to the computer. Punched cards, magnetic tape, and magnetic disk are common forms of input to a computer system.

Thus the employee data will be received from the Payroll Department in the form of time cards. These time cards will contain EMPLOYEE-NAME, HOURS-WORKED, and HOURLY-RATE. The three fields of data will be transcribed or keypunched onto a punched card so that it may be accepted as input to the data processing system. These data items, you will recall, are called *fields* of information. Specific columns of the card must be set aside to accept each field. The data will be entered on the card as is shown in Figure 9.3.

Card columns 1 to 20 are reserved for each EMPLOYEE-NAME. If any name contains less than 20 characters, the low-order, or rightmost, positions are left blank. Similarly, HOURS-WORKED will be placed in Columns 21 to 22 and HOURLY-RATE in Columns 23 to 25. The HOURLY-RATE figure, as a dollars and cents amount, is to be interpreted as a two-decimal field. That is, 125 in columns 23 to 25 is to be interpreted by the computer as 1.25. The decimal point is not generally punched into a card used for commercial applications, since it would waste a column. We will see that this method of implying or assuming decimal points is easily handled in COBOL.

A deck of employee cards, with the above format, will be keypunched and then read as input to the computer. WEEKLY-WAGES will be calculated by the computer, as HOURS-WORKED multiplied by

Figure 9.3
Input card format for sample program 1.

HOURLY-RATE. The computed figure, however, *cannot* generally be added directly to the input record unless disk processing is utilized. That is, with card or tape processing we cannot easily create output data on an input record. Input and output for tapes and cards must ordinarily utilize separate devices.

We will create, in this way, an output file that contains all input data in addition to the computed wage figure. The output PAYROLL-FILE will be placed on a magnetic tape with the record format shown in Figure 9.4. At a later date, the tape will be used to create Payroll checks.

Thus the input to the system will be called EMPLOYEE-CARDS. The computer will calculate WEEKLY-WAGES from the two input fields HOURS-WORKED and HOURLY-RATE. The input data along with the computed figure will be used to create the output tape called PAYROLL-FILE. Figure 9.5 represents the flowchart for the problem.

2. The Program

Once the input and output record formats have been clearly and precisely defined as in Figures 9.3 and 9.4, and the logic has been determined and represented by a flowchart, as in Figure 9.5, the program may be written. You will recall that a program is a set of instructions and specifications that operate on input to produce output. Figure 9.6 is a simplified COBOL program that will operate on employee cards to create a payroll tape file with the computed wages.

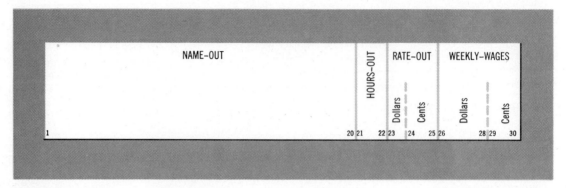

Figure 9.4
Output tape format for sample program 1.

Notice that the program is written in an English-like language. Note also that the program is divided into *four major divisions*. The IDENTIFICATION, ENVIRONMENT, DATA, and PROCEDURE DIVISIONS are coded on lines 01, 03, and 07 of page 1, and line 01 of page 2, respectively. Every COBOL program must contain these four divisions in the above order. Each must appear on a line by itself, with no other entries, and must be followed by a period. Punctuation in COBOL is just as important as it is in English.

In this program, the IDENTIFICATION DIVISION has, as its only entry, the PROGRAM-ID. That is, the IDENTIFICATION DIVISION of this program merely serves to identify the program.

The ENVIRONMENT DIVISION assigns the input and output files to specific devices in the INPUT-OUTPUT SECTION. EMPLOYEE-CARDS, the name assigned to the input file, will be processed by a card reader. Similarly, PAYROLL-FILE is the output file assigned to a specific tape drive.

The DATA DIVISION describes, in detail, the type of files and the field designations within each record. The input and output areas in core storage are fully described in the DATA DIVISION in the FILE SECTION. The File Description, or FD, for EMPLOYEE-CARDS indicates that labels[1] are not needed, that the record mode is F for fixed, and that the card format will be called EMPLOYEE-RECORD. This record includes three input fields called EMPLOYEE-NAME, HOURS-WORKED, and HOURLY-RATE. The fourth field called FILLER is just the blank area at the end of the card. FILLER (a COBOL RESERVED WORD) denotes that the field has no significance in the program. Each field has a corresponding PICTURE clause denoting the size and type of data that will appear in the field.

The EMPLOYEE-NAME field is an alphabetic data field containing 20 characters. PICTURE A(20) indicates the *size* of the field (20

[1] *For a complete discussion of label use, see Chapter 5.*

302   *Concepts of Computer Programming*

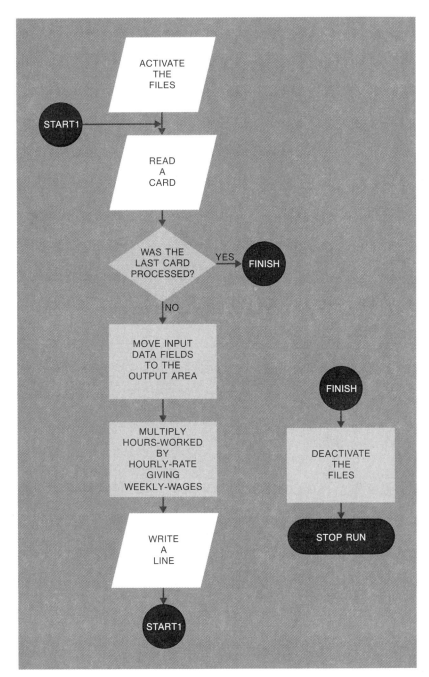

Figure 9.5
Program flowchart for sample program 1.

Form No. X28-1464-1 U/M 050
Printed in U.S.A.

System
Program SAMPLE
Programmer N. STERN

Sheet 1 of 2
Identification 73 ... 80

Punching Instructions — Graphic / Punch — Card Form #

SEQUENCE		A / B		
001 01		IDENTIFICATION DIVISION.
02		PROGRAM-ID. 'SAMPLE'.
03		ENVIRONMENT DIVISION.
04		INPUT-OUTPUT SECTION.
05		FILE-CONTROL. SELECT EMPLOYEE-CARDS ASSIGN TO READER.
06		SELECT PAYROLL-FILE ASSIGN TO TAPE-1.
07		DATA DIVISION.
08		FILE SECTION.
09		FD EMPLOYEE-CARDS
10		LABEL RECORDS ARE OMITTED, RECORDING MODE IS F,
11		DATA RECORD IS EMPLOYEE-RECORD.
12		01 EMPLOYEE-RECORD.
13		02 EMPLOYEE-NAME PICTURE A(20).
14		02 HOURS-WORKED PICTURE 99.
15		02 HOURLY-RATE PICTURE 9V99.
16		02 FILLER PICTURE X(55).
17		FD PAYROLL-FILE
18		LABEL RECORDS ARE STANDARD, RECORDING MODE IS F,
19		DATA RECORD IS PAYROLL-RECORD.
20		01 PAYROLL-RECORD.
21		02 NAME-OUT PICTURE A(20).
22		02 HOURS-OUT PICTURE 9(2).
23		02 RATE-OUT PICTURE 9V99.
24		02 WEEKLY-WAGES PICTURE 999V99.
001 25		

* A standard card form, IBM electro C61897, is available for punching source statements from this form.

304

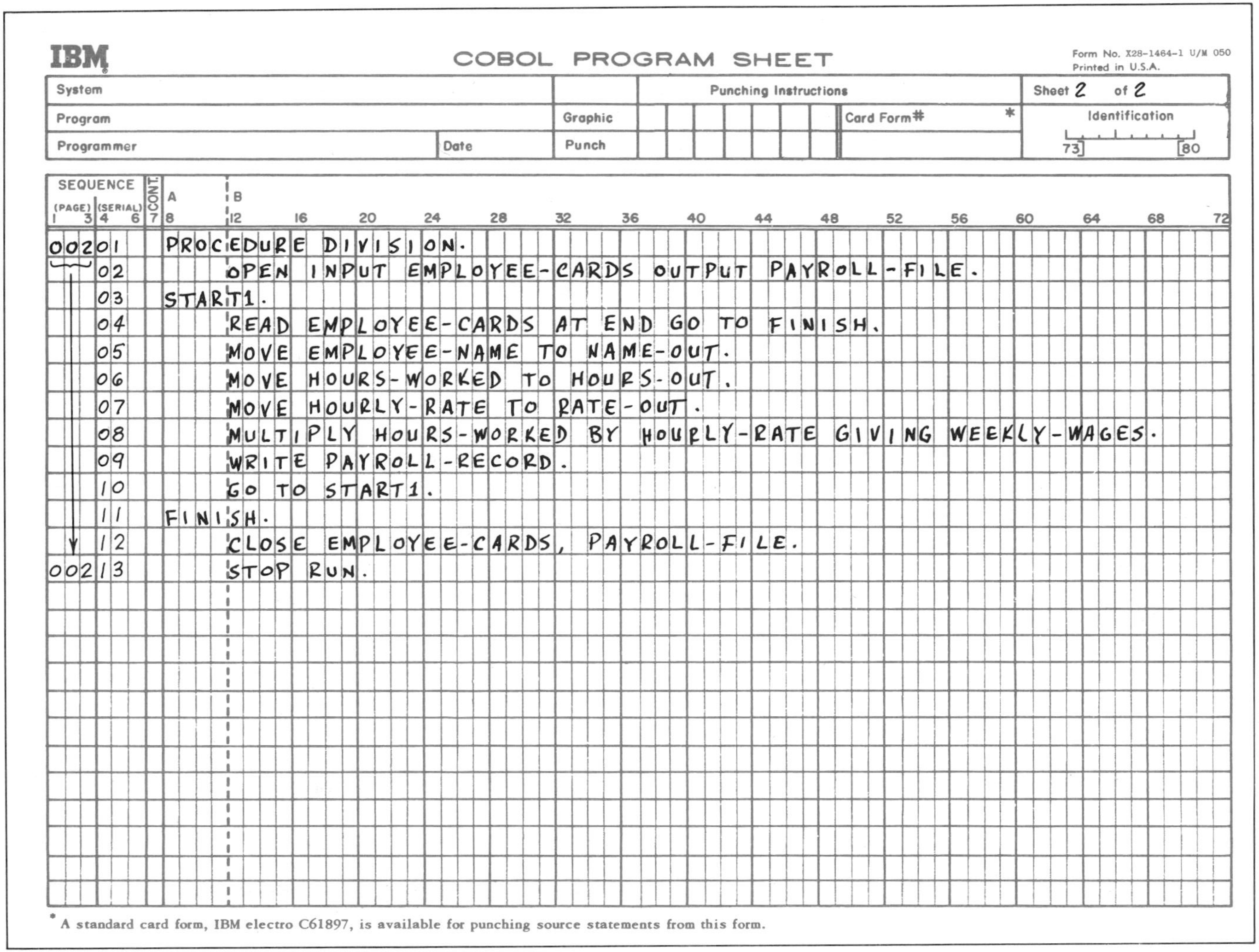

System
Program
Programmer   Date

Punching Instructions
Graphic   Card Form #   *
Punch

Identification
73 |_____| 80

```
SEQUENCE
(PAGE) (SERIAL)  A   B
  1 3  4  6 7 8 12  16

002010   PROCEDURE DIVISION.
    02       OPEN INPUT EMPLOYEE-CARDS OUTPUT PAYROLL-FILE.
    03   START1.
    04       READ EMPLOYEE-CARDS AT END GO TO FINISH.
    05       MOVE EMPLOYEE-NAME TO NAME-OUT.
    06       MOVE HOURS-WORKED TO HOURS-OUT.
    07       MOVE HOURLY-RATE TO RATE-OUT.
    08       MULTIPLY HOURS-WORKED BY HOURLY-RATE GIVING WEEKLY-WAGES.
    09       WRITE PAYROLL-RECORD.
    10       GO TO START1.
    11   FINISH.
    12       CLOSE EMPLOYEE-CARDS, PAYROLL-FILE.
002013       STOP RUN.
```

* A standard card form, IBM electro C61897, is available for punching source statements from this form.

Figure 9.6
Coding for sample program 1.

characters) and the *type* of data, <u>A</u> denoting alphabetic information. Similarly, HOURS-WORKED is a two-position numeric field. PICTURE 99 indicates the type of data, with each *9* denoting a position that contains numeric data. Note that PICTURE 99 is the same as 9(2). HOURLY-RATE is a three-position numeric field with an implied or assumed decimal point. PICTURE 9V99 indicates a *three*-position numeric field with an implied or assumed decimal point after the first position. Thus 125 in the field will be interpreted by the computer as 1.25. The decimal point does *not* appear on the input card but is nonetheless implied.

Similarly, the output file called PAYROLL-FILE has standard labels and has a fixed record format called PAYROLL-RECORD. PAYROLL-RECORD is subdivided into four fields, each with an appropriate PICTURE clause. The first three fields, NAME-OUT, HOURS-OUT, and RATE-OUT will be taken directly from each input record, using a MOVE statement. The last field, WEEKLY-WAGES, with 3 integer, or dollar, positions and 2 decimal, or cents, positions must be computed. Since HOURS-WORKED has two integer positions and HOURLY-RATE has one, *three* integer positions are needed for the product of these two fields.

If any constants or work areas were required in the program, they, too, would be described in the DATA DIVISION.

The PROCEDURE DIVISION contains the set of instructions or operations to be performed by the computer. Each instruction is executed in the order in which it appears, unless a GO TO statement, or branch, alters the sequence. You will note that the PROCEDURE DIVISION may be coded directly from the flowchart.

Notice, also that the PROCEDURE DIVISION in the above program is divided into two paragraphs, START1 and FINISH. Prior to START1, the files are OPENed, or prepared for processing.

The COBOL statement: READ EMPLOYEE-CARDS AT END GO TO FINISH will read card data from the card reader into core storage. If there are no more cards to be processed, a branch to FINISH is executed. Thus a card is read and the next instruction is processed unless there are no more cards, in which case a transfer to FINISH occurs.

The MOVE and MULTIPLY instructions on lines 05 to 08 of page 02 of the program are self-explanatory. The input data is moved to the output area.

Note, however, that although three MOVE instructions are coded in the program, a *single* flowcharting step is used to denote that input data fields are moved to the output area. Often, flowcharts utilize a single step to represent several program instructions. The WEEKLY-WAGES figure on the output file is then calculated by multiplying HOURS-WORKED by HOURLY-RATE.

After the data is accumulated in the output area, a WRITE command is executed. The WRITE operation takes the data in the output area and transmits it to the tape drive, which puts it on magnetic tape.

The above instructions will process *one* card and create *one* tape record. To be of any significance, the program must be able to process many cards. Thus the above series of instruction must be repeated. The GO TO START1 instruction permits the program to repeat the sequence of operations.

Execution continues in this manner until there are no more input cards to be processed. Then a branch to FINISH is performed and the program is terminated. Figure 9.6, then, represents a sample COBOL program in its entirety. Since the ENVIRONMENT DIVISION varies, depending on the equipment utilized, the program will run on *any* commercial computer, with only slight changes required, usually in the ENVIRONMENT DIVISION. Figure 9.7 is a sample program listing as prepared by a computer from the source deck during compilation or translation into machine-language.

An analysis of the program reveals several essential points. The English-like manner and the structural organization of a COBOL program make it comparatively easy to learn. Similarly, the ease with which a COBOL program may be read by businessmen with only minimal exposure to the language makes it a distinct asset to most data processing installations. Note, however, that COBOL, unlike the remaining languages we will consider, is very wordy, requiring much writing. Other languages are more compact, requiring fewer rules and words to be coded by the programmer.

SELF-EVALUATING QUIZ

1. The word COBOL is an abbreviation for _____ .
2. COBOL is a common language in the sense that _____ .
3. COBOL is a business-oriented language in the sense that

   _____ .
4. All COBOL programs are composed of _____ .
5. The names of these four divisions in the order in which they must be coded are _____ , _____ , _____ , and

   _____ .
6. The function of the IDENTIFICATION DIVISION is to _____ .
7. The function of the ENVIRONMENT DIVISION is to _____ .
8. The function of the DATA DIVISION is to _____ .
9. The function of the PROCEDURE DIVISION is to _____ .

SOLUTIONS

1. *CO*mmon *B*usiness *O*riented *L*anguage
2. it may be used on many different computers
3. it makes use of ordinary business terminology
4. four divisions

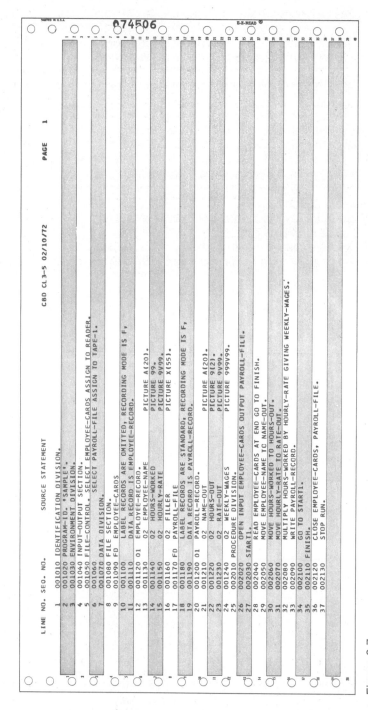

Figure 9.7
COBOL program listing.

5. IDENTIFICATION; ENVIRONMENT; DATA; PROCEDURE

6. identify the program

7. describe the equipment to be used in the program

8. describe the input, output, constants, and work areas used in the program

9. define the instructions and operations necessary to convert input data to output

B. SAMPLE PROGRAM 2

An Accounts Receivable Department wants to computerize the processing of customer tickets. The customer tickets will be keypunched into cards with the format indicated in Figure 9.8. The purpose of the program is to extend the ticket amounts from the card by multiplying UNIT-PRICE by QUANTITY. The DISCOUNT-AMOUNT from the card is then subtracted from the total. The CUSTOMER-NAME and the TOTAL are punched into an output card, with the format denoted in Figure 9.9.

The flowchart for this program is indicated in Figure 9.10. The first two divisions may be coded as follows:

```
IDENTIFICATION DIVISION.
PROGRAM-ID. 'SAMPLE2'.
ENVIRONMENT DIVISION.
INPUT-OUTPUT SECTION.
FILE-CONTROL. SELECT TICKET-FILE   ASSIGN TO READER.
              SELECT OUTPUT-FILE   ASSIGN TO PUNCH.
```

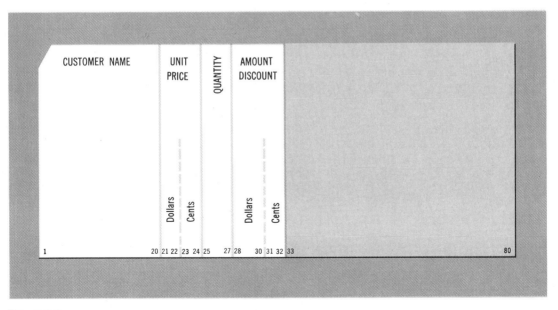

Figure 9.8
Input card format for sample program 2.

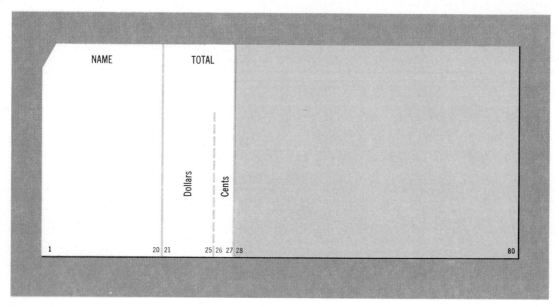

NAME   TOTAL

Dollars   Cents

1   20 21   25 26 27 28   80

Figure 9.9
Output card format for sample program 2.

The IDENTIFICATION DIVISION merely gives the name of the program. It may include other identifying data such as author and date of compilation as required.

The ENVIRONMENT DIVISION supplies information on the nature of the computer equipment utilized within the program. From the above ENVIRONMENT DIVISION, we learn that there are two files, the input file using the card reader and the output file using the card punch. You will note that the Card Read-Punch is considered *two* separate devices.

The ENVIRONMENT DIVISION also assigns file names to each of these devices. The input file is assigned the name TICKET-FILE in the ENVIRONMENT DIVISION. Throughout this program the input file will be called TICKET-FILE. Similarly, the output file is assigned the name OUTPUT-FILE in the ENVIRONMENT DIVISION.

The third division, the DATA DIVISION, is coded directly from the input and output formats. Both TICKET-FILE and OUTPUT-FILE, the two file names specified in the SELECT statements of the ENVIRONMENT DIVISION must be defined as FD entries (File Description) in the DATA DIVISION.

Concepts of Computer Programming

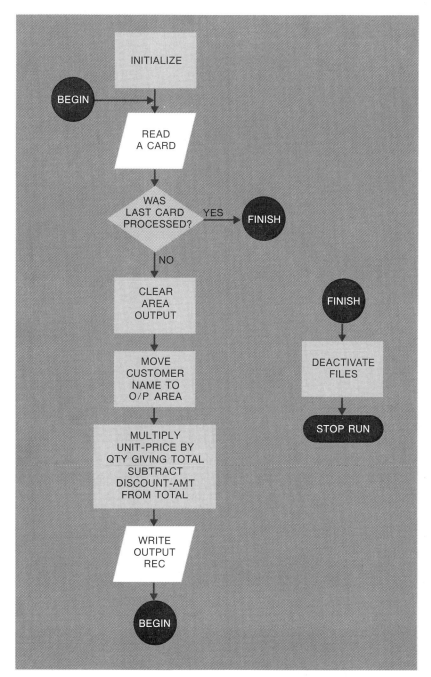

Figure 9.10
Flowchart of sample program 2.

The input file is a card file with no labels. Thus the File Description (FD) entries for this would appear as follows:

```
DATA DIVISION.
FILE SECTION.
FD   TICKET-FILE
     LABEL RECORDS ARE OMITTED,
     DATA RECORD IS TICKET-REC.
01   TICKET-REC.
     02 CUSTOMER-NAME              PICTURE A(20).
     02 UNIT-PRICE                 PICTURE 99V99.
     02 QTY                        PICTURE 999.
     02 DISCOUNT-AMT               PICTURE 999V99.
     02 FILLER                     PICTURE X(48).
```

CUSTOMER-NAME is the first field within the record. It is alphabetic and 20 characters in length as indicated by its PICTURE clause. That is, this field occupies card columns 1 to 20. The second field, UNIT-PRICE, is a four-position numeric field representing two integer positions (dollars) and two decimal positions (cents). You will recall that the V within the PICTURE clause denotes an implied or assumed decimal point. Thus 1387 in card columns 21 to 24 will be interpreted by the computer as 13.87.

QTY is a three-position numeric field. Its PICTURE clause could also be coded as PICTURE 9(3). DISCOUNT-AMT has three integer positions and two decimal positions. Since the card is 80 columns, the total of all PICTURE clauses must equal 80 positions. Thus the last field, FILLER, indicates that the remaining 48 positions of the card will not be used in the program.

The output file, a card file, also has no labels and its record format has just three fields.

```
FD   OUTPUT-FILE
     LABEL RECORDS ARE OMITTED,
     DATA RECORD IS OUT-REC.
01   OUT-REC.
     02 NAME-OUT                   PICTURE A(20).
     02 TOTAL                      PICTURE 99999V99.
     02 FILLER                     PICTURE X(53).
```

If any constants or work areas were required in the program, they, too, would be coded in the DATA DIVISION, in a separate section called the WORKING-STORAGE SECTION.

In summary, the first two divisions, the IDENTIFICATION DIVISION and the ENVIRONMENT DIVISION are relatively simple to code. The former merely serves to identify the program; the latter specifies the equipment utilized. The ENVIRONMENT DIVISION is *not* standard, as are the other divisions, and its format will depend on the computer on

Concepts of Computer Programming

which the program is run. The DATA DIVISION is taken directly from the input and output formats. The PROCEDURE DIVISION, containing all the instructions, is coded directly from the program flowchart.

```
        PROCEDURE DIVISION.
        OPEN INPUT TICKET-FILE, OUTPUT OUTPUT-FILE.
BEGIN.
        READ TICKET-FILE AT END GO TO FINISH.
        MOVES SPACES TO OUT-REC.
        MOVE CUSTOMER-NAME TO NAME-OUT.
        MULTIPLY UNIT-PRICE BY QTY GIVING TOTAL.
        SUBTRACT DISCOUNT-AMT FROM TOTAL.
        WRITE OUT-REC.
        GO TO BEGIN.
FINISH.
        CLOSE TICKET-FILE, OUTPUT-FILE.
        STOP RUN.
```

The OPEN statement accesses the devices required and designates which file is input and which is output. The READ statement causes a card to be read by the card reader and placed in core storage, according to the format specified in TICKET-REC. The next instruction, MOVE SPACES TO OUT-REC, clears the area called OUT-REC by moving SPACES, or blanks, to it. The instructions following perform the necessary operations. The WRITE statement, a standard output operation, causes a card to be punched. The branch, or GO TO BEGIN, instruction causes the steps to be repeated.

The FINISH paragraph is only executed when there are no more cards to be processed and the AT END GO TO FINISH clause of the READ statement is performed. The two devices are deactivated by the CLOSE statement and STOP RUN completes the program.

Figure 9.11 is the program on a coding sheet. Figure 9.12 represents the first cards of the source deck that must be keypunched from the coding sheet.

The source deck is then translated, or compiled, into machine language. If there are no errors, the program is ready to be tested. Sample or test data representing TICKET-REC cards are created by the programmer and entered into the computer as input. The output deck that will subsequently be punched by the computer must be manually checked for accuracy. If the output is correct, the programming staff can perform the conversion or implementation of the job and then give the program to the operations staff for weekly runs.

C. SAMPLE PROGRAM 3

The Sales Department of a large corporation wants to computerize the processing of salesmen's commissions. The commission is based on

Form No. X28-1464-1 U/M 050
Printed in U.S.A.

Sheet 1 of 2

System				
Program		Graphic		
Programmer	Date	Punch		

Punching Instructions — Card Form # — Identification (73-80)

SEQUENCE					
(PAGE)	(SERIAL)	A	B		
001	010	IDENTIFICATION DIVISION.
	020	PROGRAM-ID. 'SAMPLE2'.
	030	ENVIRONMENT DIVISION.
	040	INPUT-OUTPUT SECTION.
	050	FILE-CONTROL. SELECT TICKET-FILE ASSIGN TO READER.
	060	SELECT OUTPUT-FILE ASSIGN TO PUNCH.
	070	DATA DIVISION.
	080	FILE SECTION.
	090	FD TICKET-FILE
	100	LABEL RECORDS ARE OMITTED
	110	DATA RECORD IS TICKET-REC.
	120	01 TICKET-REC.
	130	02 CUSTOMER-NAME PICTURE A(20).
	140	02 UNIT-PRICE PICTURE 99V99.
	150	02 QTY PICTURE 999.
	160	02 DISCOUNT-AMT PICTURE 999V99.
	170	02 FILLER PICTURE X(48).
	180	FD OUTPUT-FILE
	190	LABEL RECORDS ARE OMITTED,
	200	DATA RECORD IS OUT-REC.
	210	01 OUT-REC.
	220	02 NAME-OUT PICTURE A(20).
	230	02 TOTAL PICTURE 99999V99.
	240	02 FILLER PICTURE X(53).
001	250	

*A standard card form, IBM electro C61897, is available for punching source statements from this form.

IBM COBOL PROGRAM SHEET

Form No. X28-1464-1 U/M 050
Printed in U.S.A.

System		Punching Instructions	Sheet 2 of 2
Program	Graphic	Card Form# *	Identification 73–80
Programmer / Date	Punch		

```
SEQUENCE    A   B
(PAGE)(SERIAL)
002010 PROCEDURE DIVISION.
   020     OPEN INPUT TICKET-FILE, OUTPUT OUTPUT-FILE
   030 BEGIN.
   040     READ TICKET-FILE AT END GO TO FINISH.
   050     MOVE SPACES TO OUT-REC.
   060     MOVE CUSTOMER-NAME TO NAME-OUT.
   070     MULTIPLY UNIT-PRICE BY QTY GIVING TOTAL.
   080     SUBTRACT DISCOUNT-AMT FROM TOTAL.
   090     WRITE OUT-REC.
   100     GO TO BEGIN .
   110 FINISH.
   120     CLOSE TICKET-FILE, OUTPUT-FILE
002130     STOP RUN.
```

* A standard card form, IBM electro C61897, is available for punching source statements from this form.

Figure 9.11
Coding for sample program 2.

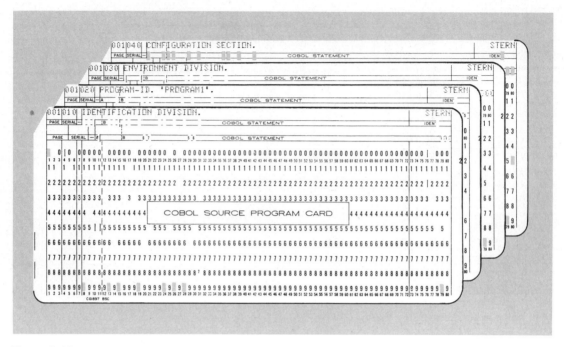

Figure 9.12
Sample source deck cards.

the amount of sales that each specific salesman has accumulated for the week.

A punched card will be created for each salesman, with the format indicated in Figure 9.13.

The output will be a printed report with the format denoted in Figure 9.14.

Thus we need *two* record formats for the output, one for the report heading and one for the data.

That is, we need a heading record with the following data printed in the corresponding columns.

Columns	Data
1 to 56	(blanks)
57 to 76	MONTHLY SALES REPORT
77 to 132	(blanks)

Concepts of Computer Programming

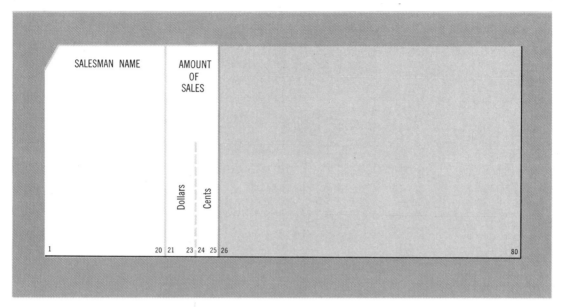

Figure 9.13
Input card format for sample program 3.

You will recall that printed output is to be read by individuals rather than machines, and therefore must contain headings neatly spaced across the page to identify each sheet.

The normal or *detail* print line will contain the following fields.

Columns	Fields
1 to 16	(blanks)
17 to 36	SALESMAN-NAME-OUT (Actual data)
37 to 56	(blanks)
57 to 63	COMMISSION ($999.99)
64 to 132	(blanks)

Note that while there is only one print *file* there must be two print *records*. That is, the FD for the print file called COMMISSION-PRINT must specify two records: DATA RECORDS ARE HEADING, DETAIL-LINE. Thus there must be two 01 levels within COMMISSION-PRINT, one for HEADING with its field specifications, and one for DETAIL-LINE with its field specifications.

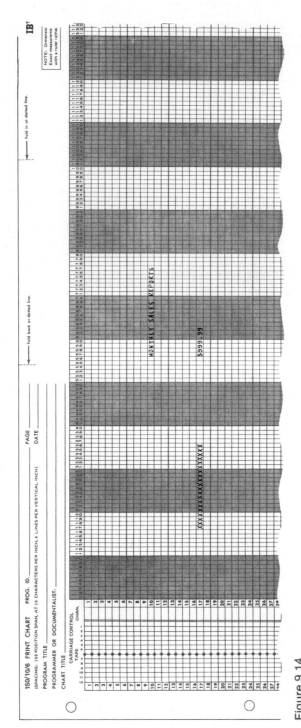

Figure 9.14
Output format for sample program 3.

The first three divisions are coded as follows:

```
                    IDENTIFICATION DIVISION.
                    PROGRAM-ID. 'SAMPLE3'.
                    ENVIRONMENT DIVISION.
                    INPUT-OUTPUT SECTION.
                    FILE-CONTROL.
                         SELECT SALES-CARD   ASSIGN TO READER.
                         SELECT COMMISSION-PRINT   ASSIGN TO PRINTER.
                    DATA DIVISION.
                    FILE SECTION.
                    FD   SALES-CARD
                         LABEL RECORDS ARE OMITTED,
                         DATA RECORD IS IN-REC.
                    01   IN-REC.
                         02 SALESMAN-NAME              PICTURE A(20).
                         02 AMT-OF-SALES               PICTURE 999V99.
                         02 FILLER                     PICTURE X(55).
                    FD   COMMISSION-PRINT
                         LABEL RECORDS ARE OMITTED,
                         DATA RECORDS ARE HEADING, DETAIL-LINE.
                    01   HEADING.
                         02 FILLER                     PICTURE X(56).
                         02 LITERAL1                   PICTURE A(20).
                         02 FILLER                     PICTURE X(56).
                    01   DETAIL-LINE.
                         02 FILLER                     PICTURE X(16).
                         02 SALESMAN-NAME-OUT          PICTURE A(20).
                         02 FILLER                     PICTURE X(20).
                         02 COMMISSION                 PICTURE $999.99.
                         02 FILLER                     PICTURE X(69).
```

The File Description (FD) for the input card is fairly straightforward. SALESMAN-NAME, the first field specified, is coded in card columns 1 to 20 and is alphabetic. AMT-OF-SALES is a 5-position numeric field in card columns 21 to 25, with an implied decimal point after the first three digits. The rest of the card is unused.

The output is a printed report consisting of two different record layouts. One is a heading record and the other is a normal or detail line. LITERAL1, the *name* of a field in the HEADING record, will be filled with the word or *literal* MONTHLY SALES REPORT. Note that the field name LITERAL1 merely *reserves space* in core storage; it does not indicate anything about the actual contents of the field. To obtain a specific word or group of words in the field, we must MOVE the desired data *into* the field name in the PROCEDURE DIVISION.

Thus the following represents the PROCEDURE DIVISION entries for the above program. Figure 9.15 illustrates a sample flowchart for the problem.

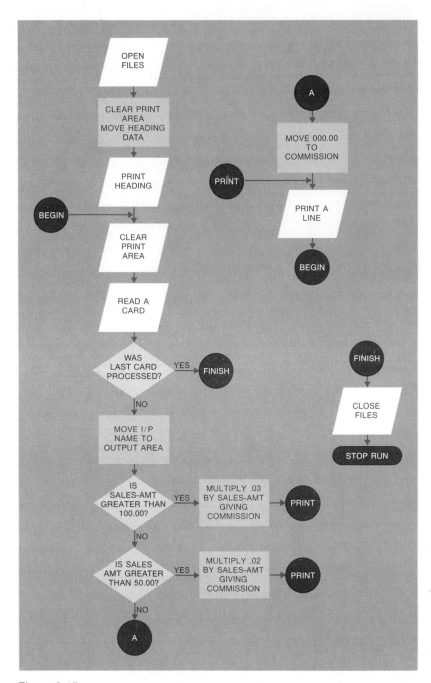

Figure 9.15
Flowchart for sample program 3.

Concepts of Computer Programming

PROCEDURE DIVISION.
        OPEN INPUT SALES-CARD OUTPUT COMMISSION-PRINT.
        MOVE SPACES TO HEADING.
        MOVE 'MONTHLY SALES REPORT' TO LITERAL1.
        WRITE HEADING.
BEGIN.
        MOVE SPACES TO DETAIL-LINE.
        READ SALES-CARD AT END GO TO FINISH.
        MOVE SALESMAN-NAME TO SALESMAN-NAME-OUT.
        IF AMT-OF-SALES IS GREATER THAN 100.00 MULTIPLY .03 BY AMT-OF-SALES GIVING
            COMMISSION, GO TO PRINT.
        IF AMT-OF-SALES IS GREATER THAN 50.00 MULTIPLY .02 BY AMT-OF-SALES GIVING
            COMMISSION, GO TO PRINT.
        MOVE 000.00 TO COMMISSION.
PRINT.
        WRITE DETAIL-LINE.
        GO TO BEGIN.
FINISH.
        CLOSE SALES-CARD, COMMISSION-PRINT. STOP RUN.

Let us take each instruction independently.

1. The OPEN statement indicates which files are input and which are output. It also makes certain that the input and output devices (in this case the reader and printer) are ready for processing.
2. HEADING is a 132-position record format with two FILLER or unused fields. On modern computer equipment, core storage fields are *not* automatically cleared with the initialization of each program. To insure, then, that these two FILLER or unused fields do not contain extraneous or irrelevant data, the record area should be cleared. The statement MOVE SPACES TO HEADING transmits 132 positions of blanks to this area.
3. LITERAL1 is a 20-position alphabetic field in the HEADING record. To place the required data or constant in the field, we write: MOVE 'MONTHLY SALES REPORT' TO LITERAL1. The quotation marks signal the computer that the constant therein contained should be transmitted to the field called LITERAL1.
4. With blanks insured in the positions on either side of MONTHLY SALES REPORT (MOVE SPACES TO HEADING prior to MOVE of the constant) we write the heading record.
5. DETAIL-LINE, the second record format for the printer, also contains FILLER or unused areas between fields. To insure that these fields are properly cleared, we code: MOVE SPACES TO DETAIL-LINE.
6. A card is read. The next statement, in sequence, is executed unless there are no more cards to be processed. In the latter case, a branch to FINISH is performed.

7. The input field SALESMAN-NAME is transmitted to, or duplicated at, the output field.

8.–10. These instructions test the contents of AMT-OF-SALES. If this field contains a number that exceeds 100.00 the commission is calculated as .03 or 3% of AMT-OF-SALES. A branch to the print routine is then performed. If, however, this field contains a number not in excess of 100.00 *but* more than 50.00 (between 50.00 and 100.00) then the commission is only 2% of AMT-OF-SALES. For AMT-OF-SALES not more than 50.00, that is, less than or equal to 50.00, *no* commission is credited for the salesman.

11., 12. The output record is printed and a branch to the beginning of the read cycle is again performed.

13. The CLOSE statement deactivates the files and devices.

14. The STOP RUN, when executed, signals the computer that the program is terminated and that another program may be run. Note that statements may appear on individual lines or that two or more statements, as these last two, can occupy a single line.

The labels or paragraph-names BEGIN, PRINT, and FINISH are coded as branch points. That is, a statement GO TO BEGIN or GO TO PRINT or GO TO FINISH appears somewhere in the program.

Keep in mind that the programs illustrated in this chapter are *not* excerpts but complete programs that will run on most commercial computers with only minor changes required, usually in the ENVIRONMENT DIVISION.

At this point it should be clear to the reader that COBOL, as a business-oriented language, is relatively simple to understand. A businessman with minimal understanding of computer terminology can generally follow the logic of a COBOL program. This facility enables him to better understand (1) the tasks required of the programmer and (2) the instructions utilized to produce desired output. The COBOL language, then, is a significant development in bridging the communication gap between businessmen and computer specialists.

SELF-EVALUATING QUIZ

The following represents a COBOL program used for determining
college course grades. Examine the program and then answer the
questions that follow.

```
                IDENTIFICATION DIVISION.
                PROGRAM-ID. 'EX1'.
                ENVIRONMENT DIVISION.
                INPUT-OUTPUT SECTION.
                FILE-CONTROL.
                        SELECT STUDENT-TEST-SCORES ASSIGN TO READER.
                        SELECT STUDENT-FINAL-GRADES ASSIGN TO PRINTER.
                DATA DIVISION.
                FILE SECTION.
                FD   STUDENT-TEST-SCORES
                        LABEL RECORDS ARE OMITTED,
                        DATA RECORD IS IN-REC.
                01   IN-REC.
                        02 STUDENT-NAME      PICTURE X(25).
                        02 TEST-SCORE-1      PICTURE 999.
                        02 TEST-SCORE-2      PICTURE 999.
                        02 TEST-SCORE-3      PICTURE 999.
                        02 FILLER            PICTURE X(46).
                FD   STUDENT-FINAL-GRADES
                        LABEL RECORDS ARE OMITTED,
                        DATA RECORDS ARE HEADING, STANDARD-LINE.
                01   HEADING.
                        02 FILLER            PICTURE X(59).
                        02 LITERAL1          PICTURE A(14).
                        02 FILLER            PICTURE X(59).
                01   STANDARD-LINE.
                        02 FILLER            PICTURE X(15).
                        02 NAME-OUT          PICTURE A(25).
                        02 FILLER            PICTURE X(15).
                        02 GRADE             PICTURE A.
                        02 FILLER            PICTURE X(76).
                WORKING-STORAGE SECTION.
                77   AVERAGE            PICTURE 999.
                PROCEDURE DIVISION.
                        OPEN INPUT STUDENT-TEST-SCORES, OUTPUT STUDENT-FINAL-GRADES.
                        MOVES SPACES TO HEADING.
                        MOVE 'STUDENT GRADES' TO LITERAL1.
                        WRITE HEADING.
                BEGIN.
                        MOVE SPACES TO STANDARD-LINE.
                        READ STUDENT-TEST-SCORES AT END GO TO FINISH.
                        MOVE STUDENT-NAME TO NAME-OUT.
```

COMPUTE AVERAGE = (TEST-SCORE-1 + TEST-SCORE-2 + TEST-SCORE-3)/3.
IF AVERAGE IS GREATER THAN 89 MOVE 'A' TO GRADE, GO TO PRINT.
IF AVERAGE IS GREATER THAN 79 MOVE 'B' TO GRADE GO TO PRINT.
IF AVERAGE IS GREATER THAN 69 MOVE 'C' TO GRADE GO TO PRINT.
IF AVERAGE IS GREATER THAN 59 MOVE 'D' TO GRADE GO TO PRINT.
MOVE 'F' TO GRADE.
PRINT.
WRITE STANDARD-LINE.
GO TO BEGIN.
FINISH.
CLOSE STUDENT-TEST-SCORES, STUDENT-FINAL-GRADES. STOP RUN.

1. The main purpose of the IDENTIFICATION DIVISION is to
   _____ .
2. The ENVIRONMENT DIVISION of this program indicates
   _____ .
3. The two files used in the program are called _____ and
   _____ .
4. The first file is a _____ file.
5. The second file is a _____ file.
6. The card file has _____ labels and its record format is
   called _____ .
7. The first field within the card file is called _____ .
8. The above field is _____ positions and is _____ in
   nature.
9. The next three fields of the card file represent _____ . Each
   is 3 positions in length to allow for a maximum of _____ .
10. The field FILLER indicates, by its name, _____ .
11. FILLER is the field assigned to card columns _____ .
12. The print file consists of ___(no.)___ record formats.
13. Indicate the appearance of the heading record.
14. The field LITERAL1 is to be filled with the data _____ .
15. Why are there FILLER positions between data fields in
    STANDARD-LINE?
16. State the purpose of the WORKING-STORAGE SECTION.
    (Although the WORKING-STORAGE SECTION has not been coded
    prior to this program, the student should be able to state its
    function.)
17. The purpose of the OPEN STATEMENT is to _____ .
18. The purpose of the statement MOVE SPACES TO HEADING is to
    _____ .
19. Although flowcharts are generally written *prior* to programs, write
    the flowchart indicating the logic used in the program.
20. The purpose of the CLOSE statement is to _____ .
21. The purpose of the STOP RUN statement is to _____ .

324   *Concepts of Computer Programming*

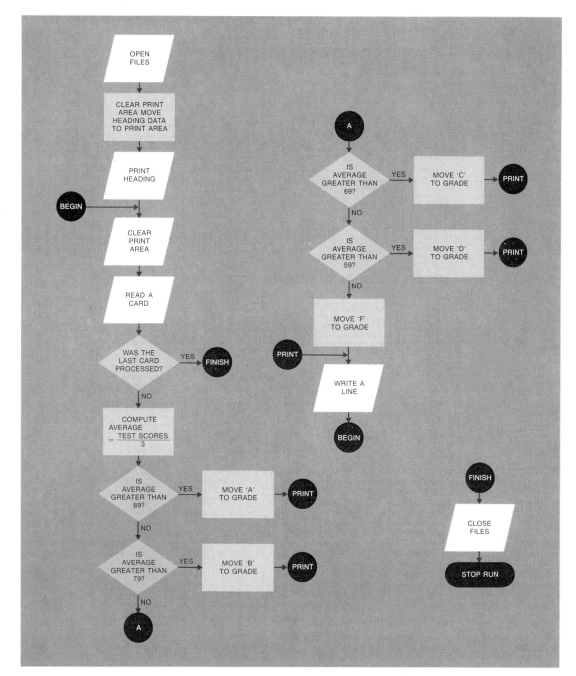

Figure 9.16
Flowchart of quiz program (solution to question 19).

22. The paragraph-names in the program are _____,
    _____, and _____.
23. The purpose of the paragraph-names is to _____.

SOLUTIONS

1. supply a name for the program
2. the devices to be used in the program
3. STUDENT-TEST-SCORES;
   STUDENT-FINAL-GRADES
4. card
5. print
6. no; IN-REC
7. STUDENT-NAME
8. 25; alphabetic
9. 3 test scores; 100
10. an unused area
11. 35 to 80
12. 2
13. print positions 1–59: blank; print positions 60–73: STUDENT GRADES; print positions 74–132: blank

14. STUDENT GRADES
15. Because there are to be blank fields between data fields to insure readability.
16. AVERAGE is a field, not part of input or output, that is needed as a work area. Thus the WORKING-STORAGE SECTION is used to define constants and work areas.
17. assign input and output files and to activate appropriate devices
18. clear the area in storage called HEADING
19. See Figure 9.16
20. deactivate the files
21. allow the next program to be read in
22. BEGIN; PRINT; FINISH
23. provide branch points

Concepts of Computer Programming

Chapter 10 *Introduction to RPG Programming*

I. The Nature of RPG

RPG is an abbreviation for *Report Program Generator*. It is a high-level language in which the programmer codes specifications for a problem and the computer generates a program. That is, coding in RPG does not result in a source program but in a set of specifications that will be used to generate a program.

Since RPG consists, basically, of a series of specifications, it is considered very easy to code and is generally regarded as the highest level or least machine-like language offered. Because of the relative ease with which RPG can be learned, it is used in many colleges and businesses.

Since RPG consists of only a set of specifications, it requires minimal core storage capacity. Thus small-scale computers, such as the IBM S/360 model 20, that do not have adequate core to run large COBOL or PL/1 programs, often utilize RPG.

RPG, as a program generator, is used to produce reports or report-type output. Although it may create tape or disk output, it is not as effective a language for handling complex input/output controls, such as creating nonstandard header labels or employing key fields for indexing, as are other high-level languages. In short, it is an excellent business tool for producing reports and report-type output.

Note, however, that RPG is usually used for simple applications.

Where complex logic is not required and report-type output is needed, RPG has considerable advantages. Whenever the logic becomes complicated, the programmer would probably code in a more powerful language such as PL/1, COBOL, or FORTRAN.

Keep in mind that coding in RPG does *not* result in a source program. The coded specifications must be used to *generate* a source program. Thus any logic errors made by the programmer are difficult to find and debug since they require evaluation of a new source program.

Note, too, that although RPG may be used on many computers such as IBM, HONEYWELL, and UNIVAC, it is less standardized than the other languages thus far discussed. That is, to run an RPG program written for a UNIVAC computer, on an IBM computer, would require many more changes than perhaps a FORTRAN program.

Let us consider a data processing installation that has a Personnel System which is computerized. Suppose the Personnel Department frequently requests special reports that require data from the computerized Personnel file. For example, a listing of all employees who are college graduates with degrees in Industrial Engineering may be required one day while a listing and tabulation of all employees who have a military status of 1-A may be necessary the next day. RPG is an appropriate language for coding the above types of problems to produce the desired output. It is a relatively simple language and since no complex computations are required, it is ideal in the above case. Programmers can code the problems in a matter of minutes and obtain the desired output very quickly. Similarly, businessmen with some exposure to data processing can learn the RPG specifications in a matter of hours and code such special programs themselves. This is often done in large companies where the programming staff is already overburdened.

In short, RPG has real advantages in small data processing installations where the computers are not large enough to run COBOL, PL/1, or FORTRAN programs, and in companies where report-type problems utilizing relatively simple logic is required.

A simple RPG program is coded on 4 specification forms (see Figure 10.1).

1. *FILE DESCRIPTION SPECIFICATIONS.* This form describes a listing of the files to be utilized and the devices that they will employ.
2. *INPUT SPECIFICATIONS.* This form describes the input fields.
3. *CALCULATION SPECIFICATIONS.* This form describes the arithmetic and logic operations to be performed.
4. *OUTPUT-FORMAT SPECIFICATIONS.* This form indicates the output format.

Notice that instructions, as we have seen them in COBOL, FORTRAN, and PL/1, are *not* coded in RPG. The compiler generates the set of instructions based on cards keypunched from the specification sheets indicated.

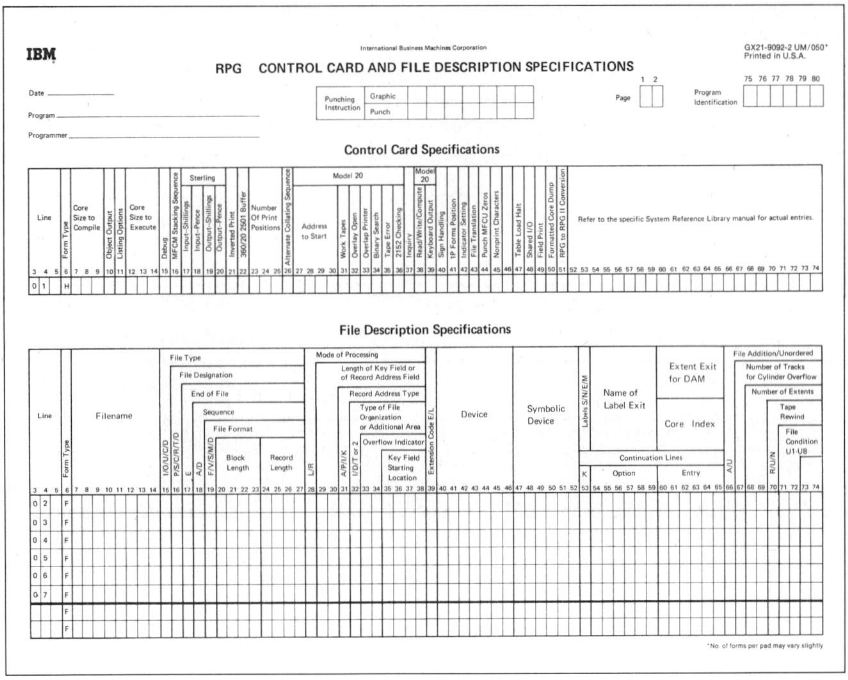

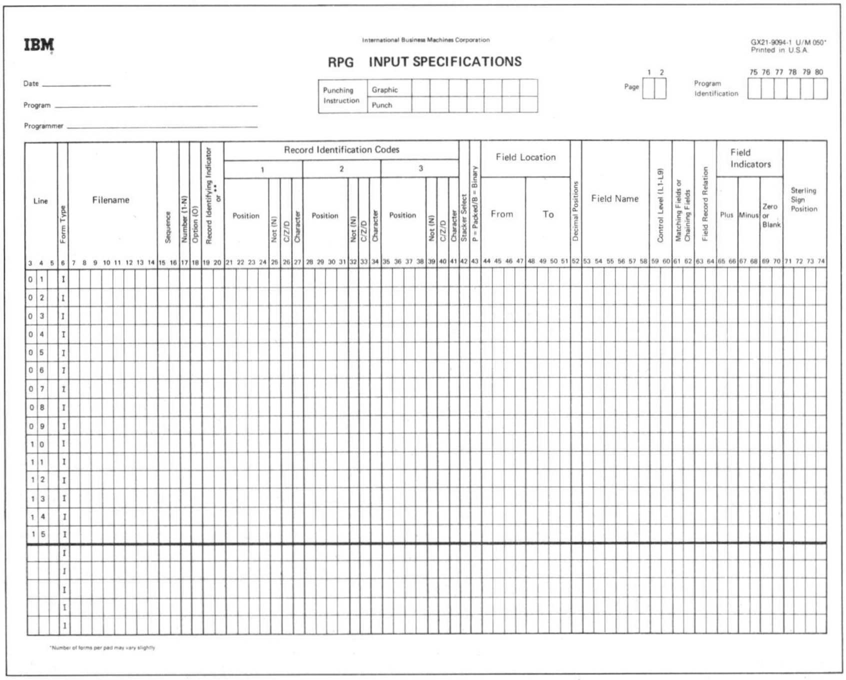

Figure 10.1
RPG specification sheets.

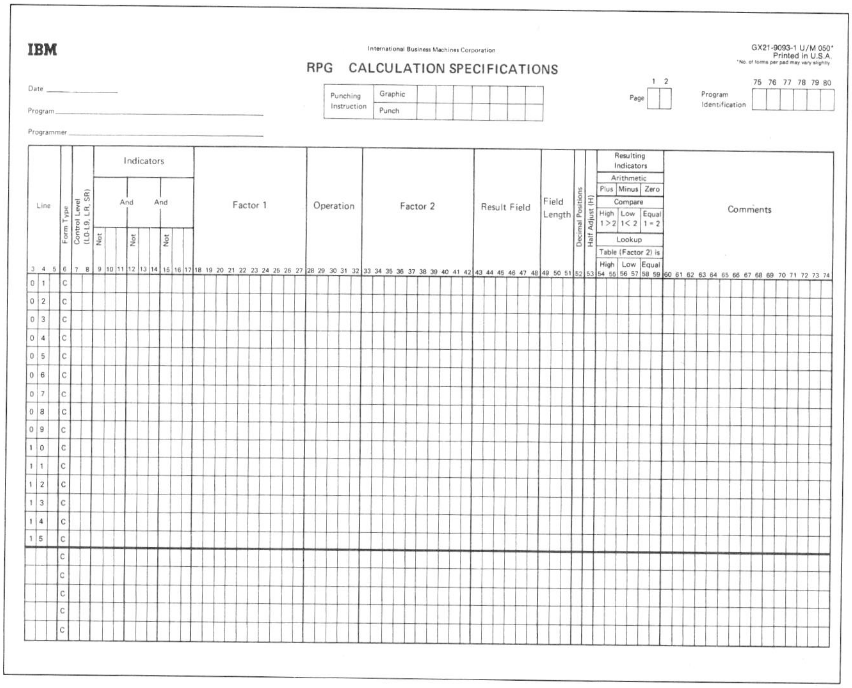

RPG CALCULATION SPECIFICATIONS

IBM

International Business Machines Corporation

GX21-9093-1 U/M 050*
Printed in U.S.A.
*No. of forms per pad may vary slightly

Date _____
Program _____
Programmer _____

Punching Instruction — Graphic / Punch

Page [ ][ ]

Program Identification [ ][ ][ ][ ][ ][ ]

Indicators — Line, Form Type, Control Level (L0-L9, LR, SR), And, Not, And, Not, Factor 1, Operation, Factor 2, Result Field, Field Length, Decimal Positions, Half Adjust (H), Resulting Indicators, Arithmetic, Plus, Minus, Zero, Compare, High 1>2, Low 1<2, Equal 1=2, Lookup, Table (Factor 2) is, High, Low, Equal, Comments

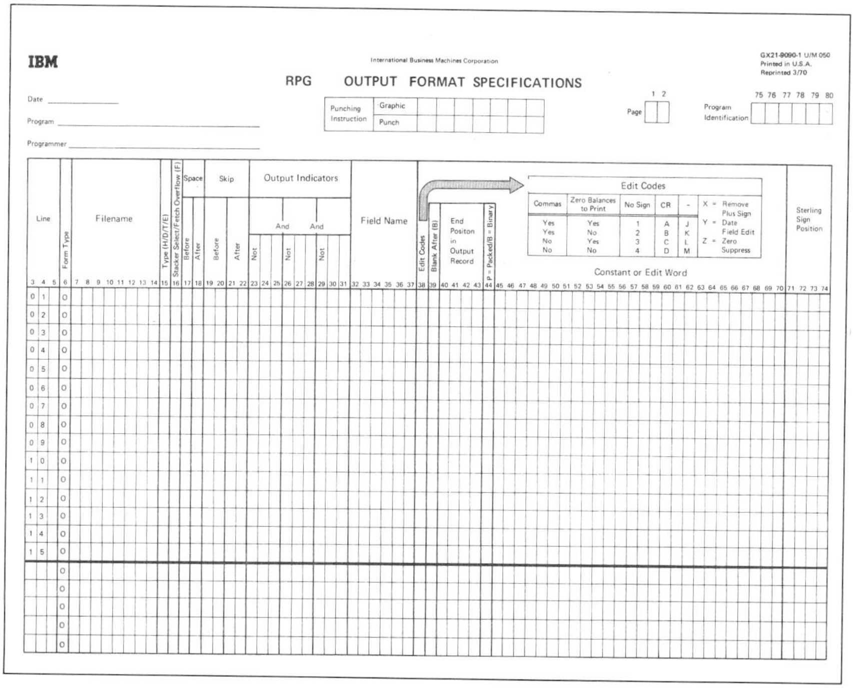

RPG OUTPUT FORMAT SPECIFICATIONS

IBM

International Business Machines Corporation

GX21-9090-1 U/M 050
Printed in U.S.A.
Reprinted 3/70

Date _____
Program _____
Programmer _____

Punching Instruction — Graphic / Punch

Page [ ][ ]

Program Identification [ ][ ][ ][ ][ ][ ]

Line, Form Type, Filename, Type (H/D/T/E), Stacker Select/Fetch Overflow (F), Space, Before, After, Skip, Before, After, Output Indicators, And, Not, And, Not, Field Name, Edit Codes, Blank After (B), End Position in Output Record, P = Packed/B = Binary

Edit Codes

Commas	Zero Balances to Print	No Sign	CR	−	X = Remove Plus Sign
Yes	Yes	1	A	J	Y = Date Field Edit
Yes	No	2	B	K	Z = Zero Suppress
No	Yes	3	C	L	
No	No	4	D	M	

Constant or Edit Word

Sterling Sign Position

Figure 10.1 (*Cont.*)
RPG specification sheets.

331

Each form is used to code as many lines as are required. If there is one input and one output file for a specific program, for example, then two lines only will be coded on the FILE DESCRIPTION SPECIFICATIONS sheet. Each *line* from a form is punched into a single card. The deck of cards created from all the forms comprise the *RPG program deck,* which must be compiled, or translated, into machine language before it can be run or executed.

II. Basic Structure of an RPG Program

RPG programs are generally written on the above four SPECIFICATION SHEETS, in the order indicated. There are additional sheets, which we will not discuss in the main text, that are required for specialized processing.

You will note that on the same sheet used for FILE DESCRIPTION SPECIFICATIONS, there is provision for CONTROL CARD SPECIFICATIONS. (See Figure 10.1.) RPG, for most computers, requires a special card, usually called a control card, as the first card for *all* RPG programs. Different versions of RPG have different requirements for this card. For most installations, all that is required is an H in column 6, denoting a Heading card. Thus control card specifications for all illustrations will merely have an H in column 6.

Each SPECIFICATION SHEET has space for 80 columns of information. As indicated, each *line* of a sheet is keypunched into one punched card.

Let us examine the RPG program more closely. The body of the form is subdivided into 72 positions, or columns, numbered 3 to 74. The small numbers 3 to 74 above the coding lines represent the corresponding card columns into which the specifications are punched.

In the upper right-hand corner, there is a provision for a program identification field, labeled as positions 75 to 80. The identification number provided here will be punched into columns 75 to 80 of *all* cards keypunched from this form.

Although this identification field is not required for processing, it should be used in case cards are misplaced or lost.

This identification field can be *alphanumeric,* consisting of any combination of characters, or *numeric,* consisting of digits only. Any field that can uniquely identify the program is used.

Columns 1 and 2, representing page number, are the same for an entire sheet, and thus are also coded only once at the top of the form. Page and line numbers, representing columns 1 to 5 of each card in the RPG deck, are not required for processing, but are highly recommended should the deck drop or be missorted. If a deck is out of sequence, the page and line number information is of great assistance for resorting the cards.

The remaining data recorded on the top of each form is *not* keypunched into cards. It supplies identifying information only, should the coding sheets be misplaced.

Note that position 6 on each sheet, which corresponds to card column 6 on each program card, represents the Form type. This entry is

F for File Description Specification
I for Input Specification
C for Calculation Specification
O for Output Specification

Thus, if an RPG card is misplaced, a quick glance at column 6 indicates the form from which it was punched. An asterisk (*) in column 7 of any form is used to designate the entire line as a comment, not to be compiled.

III. Illustrative RPG Programs

A. SAMPLE PROGRAM 1

Let us illustrate in RPG the simplified payroll program exhibited in the previous chapter. The card format is indicated in Figure 10.2.

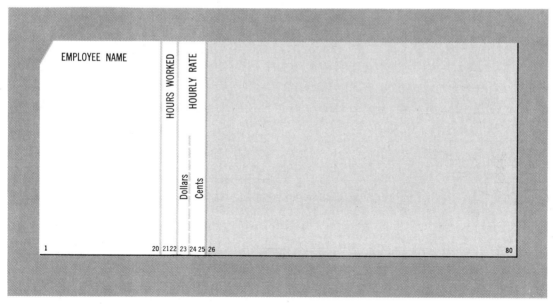

Figure 10.2
Input card format for sample program 1.

The output will be a printed report with the format illustrated in the Print Layout Sheet in Figure 10.3. The output, in this case, has been designated as a printed report since RPG is most often used to produce this form. The three input fields will be printed in addition to a WAGES field to be calculated as:

$$WAGES = HOURS \times RATE$$

Figure 10.4 illustrates the specifications sheets required to code the problem in RPG.

We will now discuss each of the specification sheets in detail.

1. File Description Specifications

This sheet supplies pertinent data on the input and output files utilized. Each file is indicated on a *single* line of this sheet. Since our program consists of two files, an input file and an output file, this FILE DESCRIPTION SPECIFICATIONS sheet will have *two* lines completed. Notice that there are, however, many programs with more than two files. A tape update program, for example, consists of *two* input files, a master input and a detail input, and an output file, an updated master. Thus *three* lines would be required for a tape update program.

Columns 7 to 14 of each line represent the name assigned by the programmer to each of the files. These same file names will be used on the INPUT and OUTPUT-FORMAT SPECIFICATIONS sheets. In our example, CARDS is the name assigned to the input card file and REPORT is the name assigned to the output print file. The file name field, as all alphanumeric fields in RPG, is left-justified. Names begin in the leftmost positions of the field and nonfilled low-order or rightmost positions remain blank.

Column 15 is simply indicated as an I, for input, or an O for output.

Input files require an entry in column 16; output files do not. For input files, the File Designation in column 16 must be either P, for primary input form, or S, for secondary input. For single input files, this entry is always P. For multiple input files, one must be designated as P for primary and the other as S, for secondary. An update program, for example, uses a *primary* master input file and a *secondary* detail input file. Output files do *not* have a File Designation.

Column 17, End of File Indicator, contains an E for the input file. This indicates that we want an end-of-file condition to exist when this file has been completely processed; that is, when there are no more cards in our input file, we want this to denote an end-of-file condition.

Column 18, Sequence, is an entry that is used for some tape and disk processing.

Column 19 is the File Format field and is always F, denoting Fixed format, for card files. This indicates that all records within the file are the same size. V, for variable, is indicated in this field when record sizes are not the same within the file. Print files contain a V in Column 19 since print records, in essence, can be any length and require

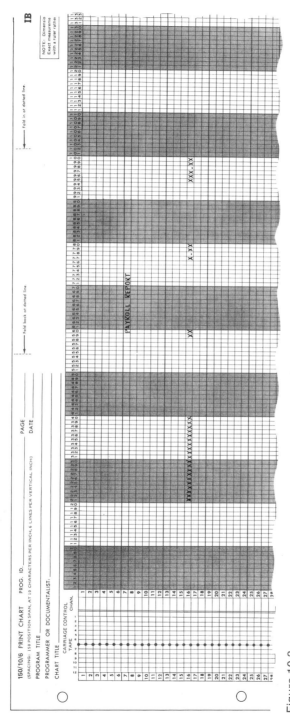

Figure 10.3
Output format for sample program 1.

RPG CONTROL CARD AND FILE DESCRIPTION SPECIFICATIONS

International Business Machines Corporation

IBM

GX21-9092-2 UM/050*
Printed in U.S.A.

Date _____
Program _____
Programmer _____

Punching Instruction: Graphic / Punch

Page [ ][ ] Program Identification [ ][ ][ ][ ][ ][ ]

75 76 77 78 79 80

Control Card Specifications

Refer to the specific System Reference Library manual for actual entries.

File Description Specifications

Line	Form Type	Filename	File Type	File Designation	End of File	Sequence	File Format	Block Length	Record Length	Mode of Processing	Length of Key Field or of Record Address Field	Record Address Type	Type of File Organization or Additional Area	Overflow Indicator	Key Field Starting Location	Extension Code E/L	Device	Symbolic Device	Labels S/N/E/M	Name of Label Exit	Continuation Lines	File Addition/Unordered	Number of Tracks for Cylinder Overflow	Number of Extents	Tape Rewind	File Condition U1-U8
02	F	CARDS	I	P	E		F	80	80								READ40	SYSRDR							
03	F	REPORT	O				V	132	132					OF			PRINTER	SYSLST							
04	F																								
05	F																								
06	F																								
07	F																								

*No. of forms per pad may vary slightly

(a)

Figure 10.4
Coded specification sheets for sample program 1—file description.

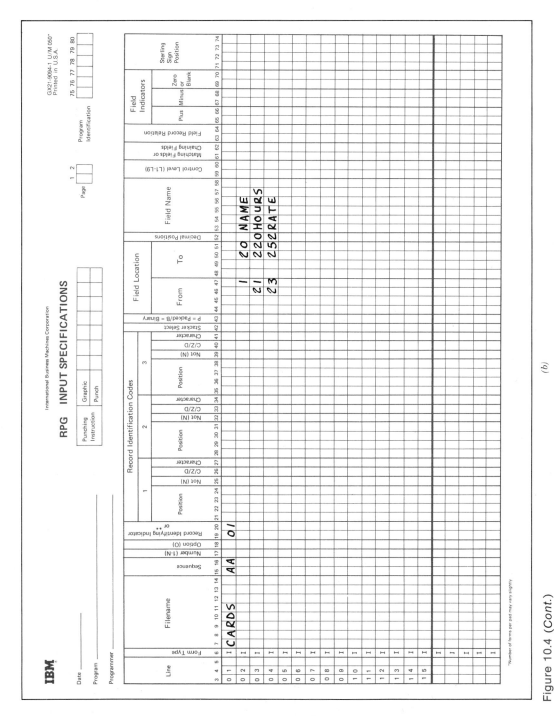

Figure 10.4 (Cont.)
Coded specification sheets for sample program 1—input specifications.

337

IBM

International Business Machines Corporation

RPG CALCULATION SPECIFICATIONS

GX21-9093-1 U/M 050*
Printed in U.S.A.
*No. of forms per pad may vary slightly

Date ______

Program ______

Programmer ______

Punching Instruction: Graphic / Punch

Page 1 2

Program Identification 75 76 77 78 79 80

Line (3–5)	Form Type (6)	Control Level (L0-L9, LR, SR) (7–8)	Indicators: Not (9)	Indicators (10–11)	And: Not (12)	And (13–14)	And: Not (15)	And (16–17)	Factor 1 (18–27)	Operation (28–32)	Factor 2 (33–42)	Result Field (43–48)	Field Length (49–51)	Decimal Positions (52)	Half Adjust (H) (53)	Resulting Indicators: Arithmetic Plus / Compare High 1>2 / Lookup Table (Factor 2) is High (54–55)	Arithmetic Minus / Compare Low 1<2 / Lookup Low (56–57)	Arithmetic Zero / Compare Equal 1=2 / Lookup Equal (58–59)	Comments (60–74)
01	C			01					HOURS	MULT	RATE	WAGES	5	2					
02	C																		
03	C																		
04	C																		
05	C																		
06	C																		
07	C																		
08	C																		
09	C																		
10	C																		
11	C																		
12	C																		
13	C																		
14	C																		
15	C																		
	C																		
	C																		
	C																		
	C																		
	C																		

(c)

Figure 10.4 (*Cont.*)
Coded•specification sheets for sample program 1—calculation specifications.

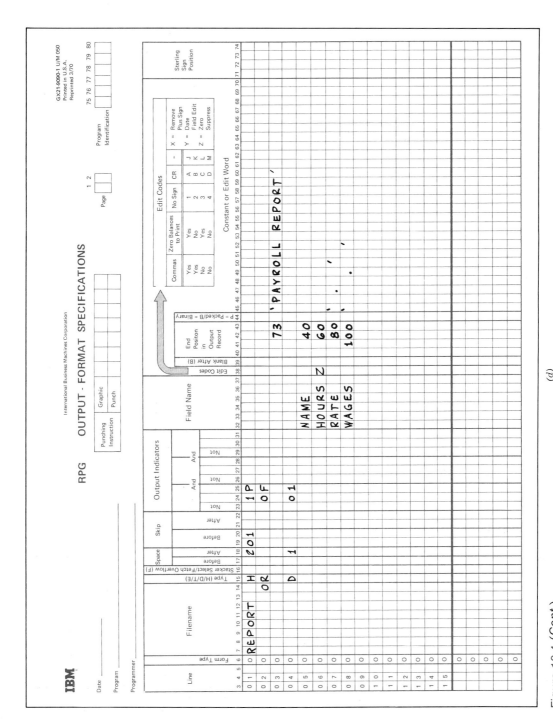

Figure 10.4 (Cont.)
Coded specification sheets for sample program 1—output-format specifications.

(d)

339

carriage control characters. We may have 80 position headings and 132 position detail records, for example. Thus card files are coded with an F in Column 19 to denote fixed length, while print files are coded with a V in that column to denote variable length.

Block length, columns 20 to 23, and Record length, columns 24 to 27, are typically 80 for cards and 132 for printed reports. Note that these fields, as all numeric fields in RPG, are right-justified; that is, high-order or leftmost nonfilled positions are left blank.

Positions 28 to 32, representing several fields, are used predominantly for tape and disk processing and will not be discussed here.

Columns 33 and 34 are required for print files to denote that a page overflow indicator is to be used. That is, if we desire the report to proceed from page to page with the desired headings, we must use an overflow indicator to sense the end of a specified form. Thus print files should have an OF, for overflow, in Columns 33 and 34.

Columns 35 to 39 are not used for simple RPG programs and thus will not be discussed.

The Device and the Symbolic Device names, columns 40 to 46 and 47 to 52, respectively, are assigned specifically at each data processing installation and thus will vary from one computer center to another. In the above illustration, the input device is the READ40 with symbolic name SYSRDR (system reader) and the output device is PRINTER with symbolic name SYSLST (system list device). The programmer must obtain the appropriate entries for these fields from the operations staff at his computer center.

The remainder of the FILE DESCRIPTION SPECIFICATIONS sheet is not used unless tape or disk processing is required.

2. Input Specifications Sheet

Each input file is described on the INPUT SPECIFICATIONS sheet. Since our sample RPG program has only one input file, called CARDS, then CARDS is described on this sheet.

The sequence AA describes the first card record format within the file. If additional types of records existed within the file they would be coded as AB, AC, and so on.

Columns 17 and 18 are not used. Columns 19 and 20 represent the Resulting Indicator. In our example, indicator 01 is turned on every time a card record is read. This indicator will then be used to determine, for output specifications, when a line is to be printed. If 01 is used in the OUTPUT-FORMAT SPECIFICATIONS SHEET, then a line will print each time indicator 01 is "turned on," that is, for every card read.

Record Identification Codes (21 to 41) are used to test input positions for specific contents. It will be used in our next illustration, but is not required in this sample program.

Columns 42 and 43 have specialized use and will not be discussed here.

Concepts of Computer Programming

Field indicators located in the group of columns from 44 to 58 are used to denote fields within the input record. "Field Location From," columns 44 to 47, denotes the high-order or leftmost position of a field and "Field Location To" denotes the low-order or rightmost position of a field. For numeric fields, column 52 must be completed to denote the number of decimal or fractional positions. For alphanumeric fields, it is left blank.

Thus we have for CARDS:

Card Columns
Columns 1 to 20—alphanumeric (no entry in 52) and called NAME
Columns 21 and 22—numeric-integer with no decimal positions (0 in 52) and called HOURS
Columns 23 to 25—numeric with 2 decimal positions (2 in 52) and called RATE
(Thus 428 in columns 23 to 25 of a data card would be called RATE and treated as 4.28 by the computer)

Positions 59 to 74 of this sheet have specialized use and will not be discussed here.

3. Calculation Specifications Sheet
Any arithmetic or logic operation is defined on this sheet.

Since we wish to perform a multiplication operation (HOURS × RATE) for *all* input cards, we use indicator 01, which is "turned on" for all input cards. This is the only indicator required.

Since no control levels are used here, columns 7 and 8 are blank.

Factor 1, HOURS, is multiplied (MULT) by Factor 2, RATE, to produce a resultant field called WAGES. For other operators we may use:

ADD
SUB
DIV
COMP   (compare)
etc.

The field length for the resultant numeric field, WAGES, is 5 (column 51) including 2 decimal positions (2 in column 52). Column 53, HALF ADJUST, is used for rounding. That is, when we wish the computer to round the results to the nearest position, we use this field. The Resulting Indicators in Columns 54 to 59 are turned on only for compare (COMP) operations.

Any comments in columns 60 to 74 may be included. These are printed on the listing, but do not affect processing. We may also include entire lines as comments by utilizing an asterisk (*) in column 7 of *any* sheet.

4. Output-Format Specifications (O in Form Type) Sheet

The output file REPORT is described here. Three types of records may be included:

HEADING (H)
DETAIL   (D)
TOTAL   (T)

Since we only have Heading and Detail records, only H and D types (column 15) have been included.

Column 16 is a STACKER SELECT field, which is appropriate only for punched output, where output data cards can fall into several pockets or stackers.

Columns 17 to 22 represent the SPACE and SKIP options that are appropriate only for printed output. You will recall that a printer can be made to space 1, 2, or 3 lines either *before* or *after* it writes a line. The 2 in SPACE-AFTER of our illustration indicates that *after* the Heading line is printed, we wish to space the form two lines. Only the digits 1, 2, or 3 may be used in *either* column 17 or 18.

The SKIP option for printed output is used to position the form at a specific line. A 01 in either SKIP field is a code for skipping to the beginning of a new page. In our illustration, we skip to a new page *before* printing.

Thus the output file REPORT has a heading record (H), which requires the skipping to a new page *before* printing, and the spacing of the form two lines *after* printing.

The OUTPUT INDICATOR 1P implies that we wish to print the H record (Heading) on the first page (1P). If any other conditions also require the printing of this record, then we code OR on the next line in columns 14 and 15 and the corresponding condition. OF in columns 24 and 25 indicates that we also wish to print a heading on an overflow, or end-of-page condition.

In short, we are indicating that we wish the H or heading type record to print on the first page *or* when the end of a page is reached. In either case, we skip the paper to a new page, print the heading, and then advance the paper two lines.

In most print applications, we want headings to print on the first printed page. Also, when we have reached the end of a page, we want the program to skip to a new page and print new headings. In this way, each individual page of the continuous form has a heading so that when the report is "burst" into individual sheets, each can be identified.

The heading PAYROLL REPORT is to print with the last character in position 73 (Print Layout Sheet, Figure 10.3).

The Detail line, D, prints when indicator 01 is on, which is for all cards. Each time a detail line prints, the form is spaced 1 line (after printing). Since each input card turns on indicator 01, a detail line will print for each input card.

342

Four output fields print:

NAME ending in print position 40
HOURS ending in print position 60
RATE ending in print position 80
WAGES ending in print position 100

The first three fields are directly transmitted from the card record. Note that these input and output fields have the same name. NAME requires no editing. HOURS requires zero suppression (Z in column 38) to eliminate leading zeros and also the standard plus sign generated by the computer. RATE requires a decimal point to print after the first integer position. You will recall that to save space on a card, decimal points are often not coded. They are *implied* or *assumed* in input records. The output document, however, must have these decimal points for readability. Hence the Edit Word, columns 45 to 70, is used. WAGES, obtained from the calculations, requires the printing of a decimal point, after the first three integer positions. Thus,
'   .   ' is the Edit Word.

If, in addition we wish to suppress leading or nonsignificant zeros, we include a zero in the low-order integer position. Thus if WAGES contained an Edit Word of '   0. ' then $003_\wedge 42$ would print as 3.42 instead of 003.42. If we also desire a dollar sign to print out, we would include the following Edit, Word: '$ 0. '.

The above four specification sheets will result in a complete RPG program that performs the required operations. Notice that there is no visible step-by-step logic displayed in the specifications. When the sheets are coded so that they conform to the RPG rules, however, then a program is compiled which contains the step-by-step logic. Thus flowcharting is not a required programming tool when RPG coding is employed unless complex calculations are necessary.

Let us now revise the above program to make more appropriate use of RPG special features. Suppose, now, that we wish to have *two* headings, a report heading, as before, and a field delineating heading. (See Revised Print Layout Sheet, Figure 10.5). Suppose, also, that all payroll cards should have a P in column 80. If a card does not have a P in column 80, then we do not want to process it.

Let us also modify the calculation routine as follows:

WAGES = HOURS × RATE when HOURS are less than or equal
            to 40
WAGES = 40 × RATE + (HOURS − 40) × 1.5 × RATE for
            HOURS in excess of 40

That is, if an employee works more than 40 hours, he is paid time-and-a-half for overtime. He is given the normal rate based on 40 hours and 1.5 × RATE for all hours in excess of 40.

Let us now consider the revised RPG specification sheets. (Figure 10.6).

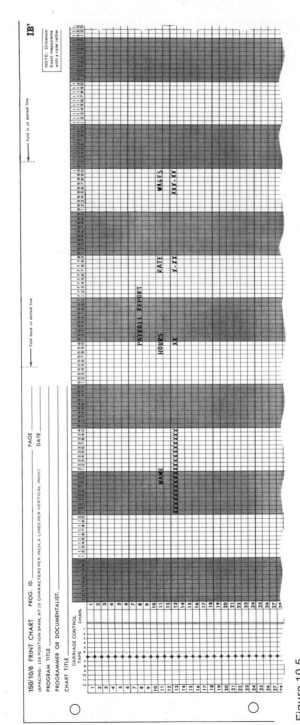

Figure 10.5
Revised output format for sample program 1.

344

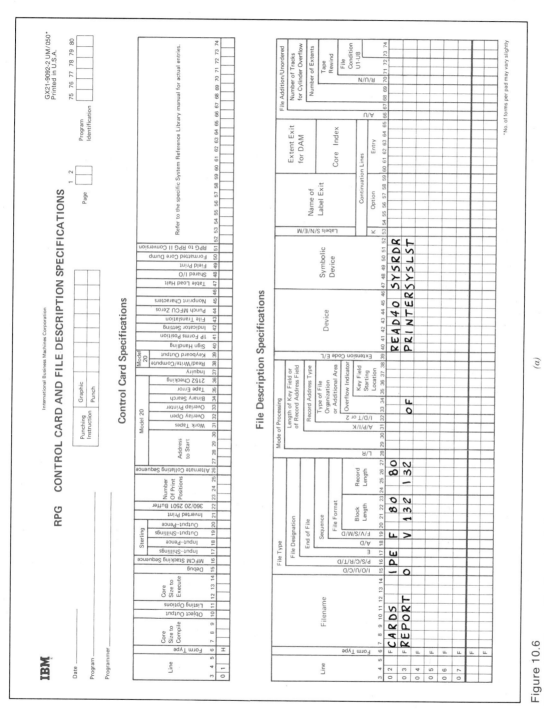

Figure 10.6
Revised RPG specification sheets for sample program 1—file description.

(a)

345

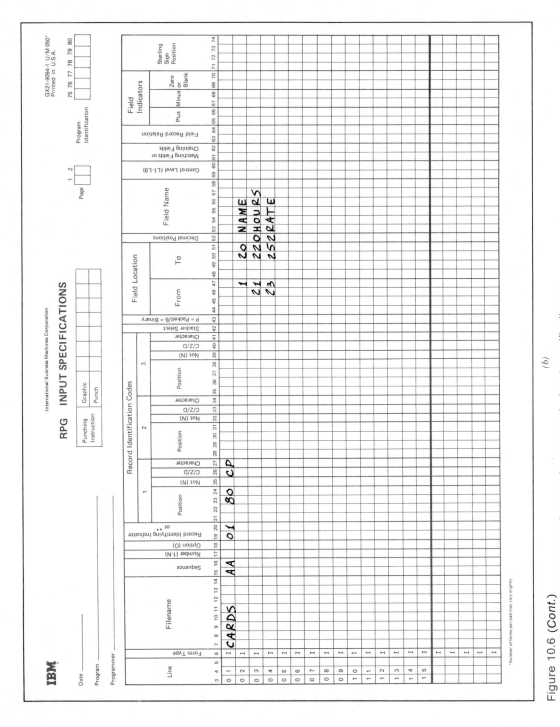

(b)

Figure 10.6 (Cont.)
Revised RPG specification sheets for sample program 1—input specifications.

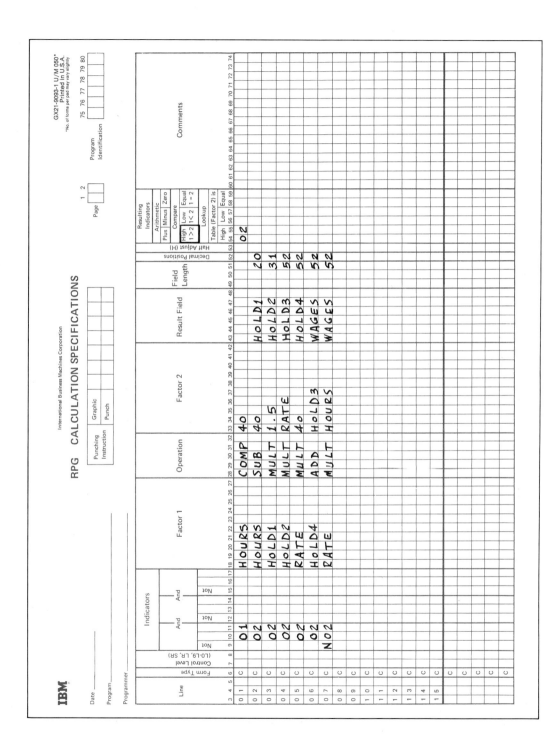

Figure 10.6 (Cont.)
Revised RPG specification sheets for sample program 1—calculation specifications.

(c)

347

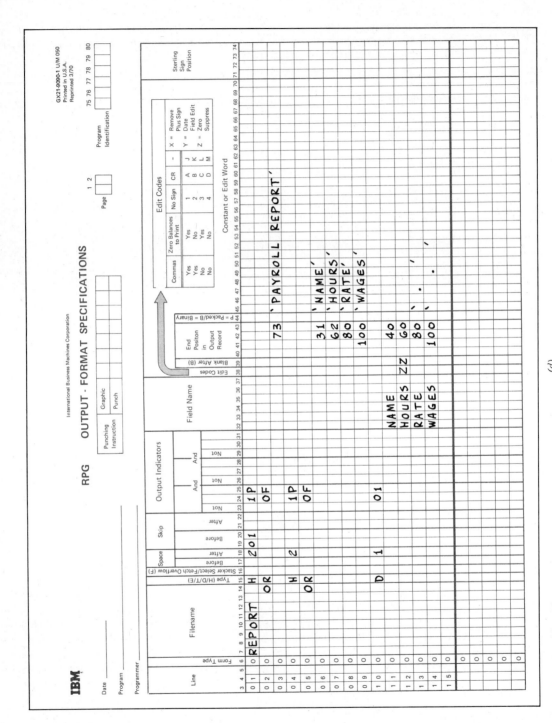

Figure 10.6 (*Cont.*)
Revised RPG specification sheets for sample program 1—output-format.

(*d*)

Note that the FILE DESCRIPTION sheet has not been changed. There are still two files with the same relative format.

The INPUT SPECIFICATIONS sheet has one major revision on the first line. The RECORD IDENTIFICATION CODES are now used to "turn on" indicator 01. If card column (POSITION) 80 in a data card has the Character (C) of "P," then indicator 01 is turned on. That is, C in column 26 denotes that a character test will be performed and the P in column 27 denotes that the test performed examines card column 80 for a *P*. Since calculations and detail line printings are only performed when indicator 01 is turned on, then the absence of a P in column 80 will result in no processing. The POSITION field within the RECORD IDENTIFICATION CODE is coded with the card column that contains the character. The NOT field in this RECORD IDENTIFICATION codes is only used when we wish an indicator turned on for the *absence* of a condition. C/Z/D in column 27 denotes either Character, Zone, or Digit test. C is most often used. The term Character denotes the specific character to be tested. Thus "*80 CP*" in positions 23 to 27 denotes that we wish indicator 01 turned on when card column 80 of the input has the character P.

Notice that the repetition of these fields within the RECORD IDENTIFICATION CODES implies that the existence of *several* conditions may be used to turn on a single indicator.

Thus, if we wish to test for

      N in column 7
   and O in column 8
   and V in column 9
         (the code NOV in columns 7 to 9)

we may use the input specification line in Figure 10.7.

Note that while line 01 of the INPUT SPECIFICATIONS SHEET in our revision of SAMPLE PROGRAM 1 contains the test for a P in card column 80, the remaining three lines contain the same field designations as in the original program.

The CALCULATION SPECIFICATIONS sheet of the revised program outlined above includes some major revisions.

First, when indicator 01 is on (for all Payroll cards with P in column 80) we wish to compare (COMP) HOURS to 40. If Factor 1 (HOURS) is greater than Factor 2 (a constant of 40) then indicator 02 is "turned on."

If indicator 02 is on (when HOURS is greater than 40) we:

1. Subtract 40 from HOURS giving HOLD1, a 2-position field with no decimal positions. Note that field to be subtracted appears as Factor 2.
2. Multiply 1.5 by HOLD1 (HOURS — 40) giving HOLD2, a 3-position field with 1 decimal position.
3. Multiply RATE by HOLD2 giving HOLD3, a 5-position field with 2 decimal positions.

Introduction to RPG Programming

349

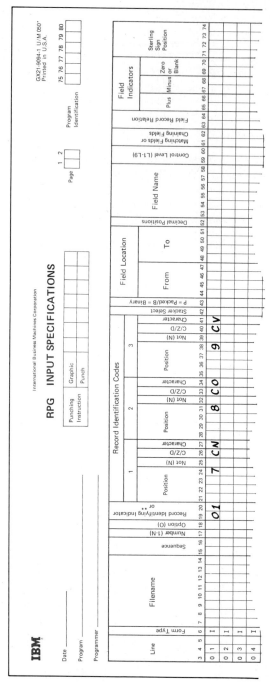

Figure 10.7

350

Thus in HOLD3 we have:

RATE $\times$ 1.5 $\times$ (HOURS $-$ 40)

4. Multiply RATE by 40 giving HOLD4 a 5-position field with 2 decimal positions.

5. Add HOLD4 to HOLD3 giving WAGES.

Thus, WAGES = 40 $\times$ RATE + (HOURS $-$ 40) $\times$ RATE $\times$ 1.5

Notice that all 5 calculations are performed only when indicator 02 is turned on.

That is, the above formula is the one required when the HOURS field is in excess of 40. For HOURS not in excess of 40 (when indicator 02 is not turned on as a result of the original comparison), we merely multiply RATE by HOURS to obtain WAGES. "N02" in columns 9 to 11 of the coding sheet indicate that the operation on that line (multiplication of RATE by HOURS) is performed only when indicator

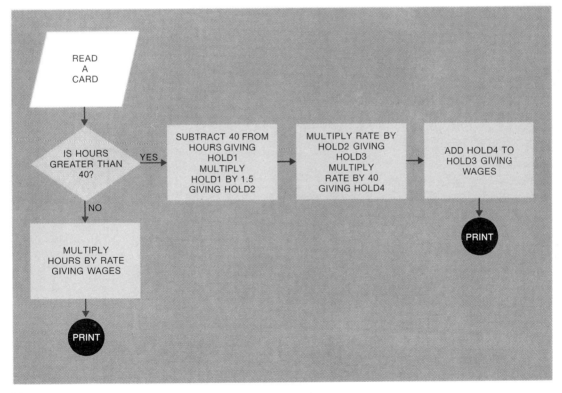

Figure 10.8
Program flowchart excerpt for revised sample program 1.

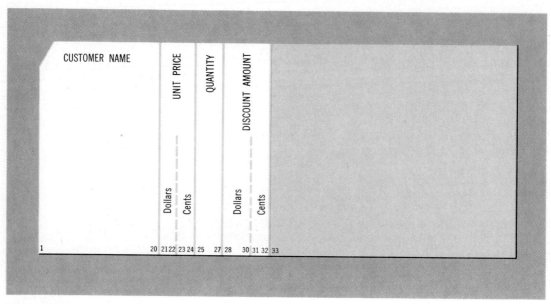

Figure 10.9
Input card format for sample program 2.

02 is *not* turned on (when HOURS is not in excess of 40). Thus WAGES is either a simple product field, when there is no overtime, or it reflects the more complicated formula for wages that are calculated to include the overtime amount. The flowchart excerpt in Figure 10.8 may help in explaining the above logic.

From the above, we can see that numerous logic and arithmetic operations can be performed in an RPG program.

The revised OUTPUT-FORMAT SPECIFICATIONS sheet is basically the same as the previous one, but a second heading is printed. The headings are printed in the order in which they appear on the coding sheet. Thus 'PAYROLL REPORT' prints first, followed, 2 lines later, by 'NAME HOURS RATE WAGES'. The output then should appear as in Figure 10.5.

B. SAMPLE PROGRAM 2

An Accounts Receivable Department wishes to computerize the processing of customer tickets. The customer tickets will be keypunched into cards with the format indicated in Figure 10.9.

The purpose of the program is to extend the ticket amounts by multiplying UNIT-PRICE by QUANTITY. The DISCOUNT-AMOUNT on the card is then to be subtracted from the total. The CUSTOMER NAME and TOTAL are then punched onto an output report with the format denoted in the Print Layout Sheet in Figure 10.10. Here again

Concepts of Computer Programming

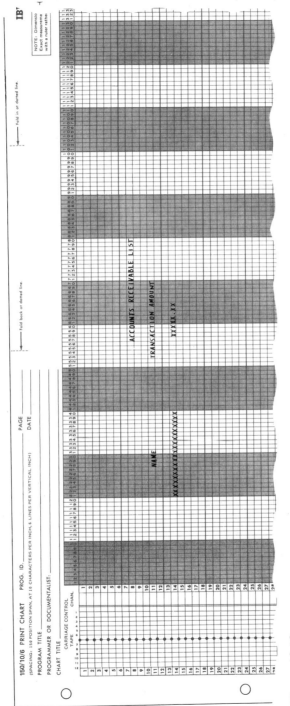

Figure 10.10
Output format for sample program 2.

353

we have altered this second illustration so that the output is a printed report. RPG, as the name implies, is ideally suited to *report* programming and thus most illustrations should indicate this.

Figure 10.11 illustrates the four required coding sheets.

We have, as before, two files, card input and printed output. You will note that except for the File names, the FILE DESCRIPTION SPECIFICATIONS are exactly the same as in SAMPLE PROBLEM 1.

The card file is an input file; thus an I is coded in column 15. Since there is only one input file, it is the primary one; thus a P is coded in column 16. Column 17 contains an E to denote that the end of file condition is to occur when this file is depleted. F for File Format denotes fixed length records. An 80 in the Block and Record Length fields indicates that there are 80 positions per record. READ40 is the Device Name for this file in a specific computer center. This entry will vary among computer installations. The rest of the fields are not used for simple card files.

The print file is an output file; thus O is coded as file type. There is no Primary or Secondary indicator for output files; thus File Designation is blank. V is for variable length records and 132 is the maximum size of a record. OF in columns 33 and 34 denote that we will use the overflow indicator for this file. PRINTER is the Device Name at this specific installation.

The INPUT SPECIFICATIONS sheet indicates the record description entries of the input file, IN. AA is the initiating sequence or first record format. Succeeding record formats, if they existed, would be indicated by AB, AC, and so on. Indicator 01 is turned on for *all* input cards since the Record Identification Codes are blank. If specific conditions were required to turn on the indicator, these would be denoted in the Record Identification fields.

Field Locations are then indicated for each field within the input record. Notice that the decimal position field is left blank for alphanumeric fields. For numeric fields, this decimal field indicates the number of positions to the *right* of the decimal point. Note, too, that alphanumeric fields are left-justified (begin in the leftmost column), while numeric fields are right-justified.

The CALCULATION SPECIFICATIONS sheet indicates the required multiplication operation to be performed whenever indicator 01 is turned on. You will recall that indicator 01 is turned on for *all* input cards. Factor 2, the DISCOUNT-AMOUNT, is then subtracted from the product.

The OUTPUT-FORMAT SPECIFICATIONS SHEET indicates two headings (H in Type field, column 15). The first Heading is printed on the first page (output indicator 1P) or on an overflow condition (OR output indicator OF), when the end of a page is indicated. It prints 'ACCOUNTS RECEIVABLE LIST', *then* it advances the paper 2 lines (space 2 after print). The second header is a field delineator indicating the names of the various fields. It, too, prints on the first page or on an

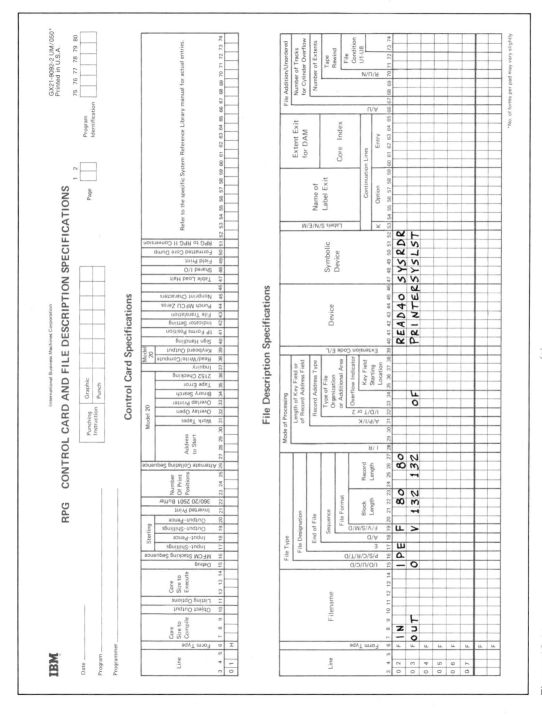

Figure 10.11
Coded specification sheets for sample program 2—file description.

(a)

355

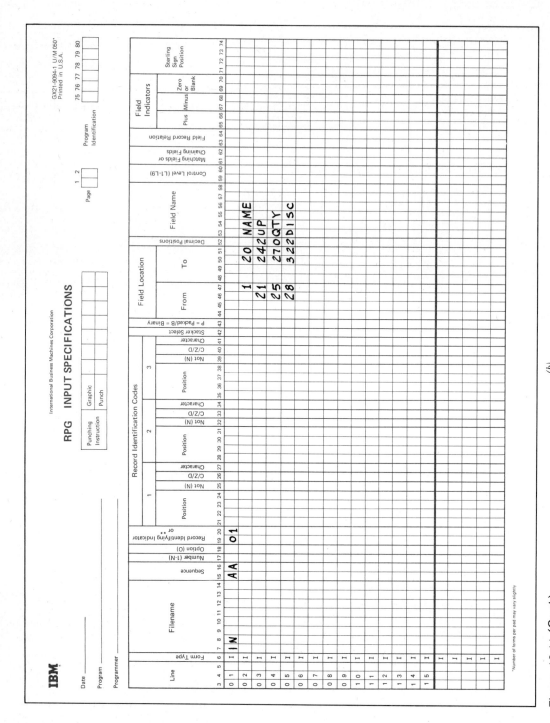

Figure 10.11 (*Cont.*)
Coded specification sheets for sample program 2—input specifications.

(b)

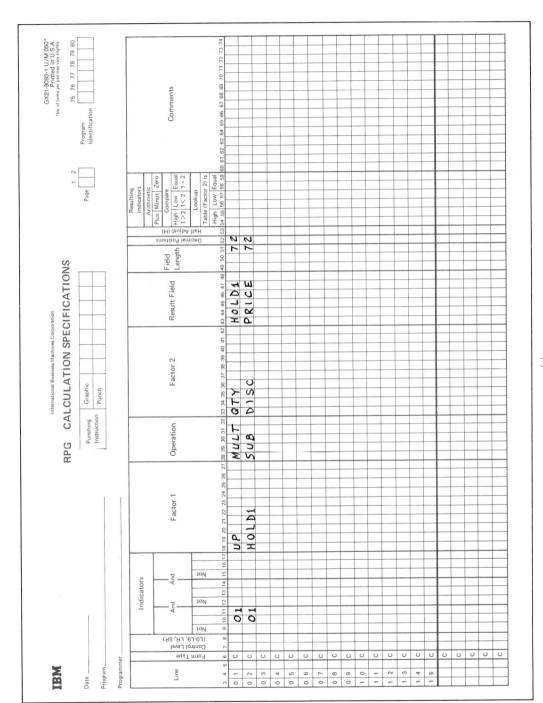

Figure 10.11 (Cont.)
Coded specification sheets for sample program 2—calculation specifications.

(c)

357

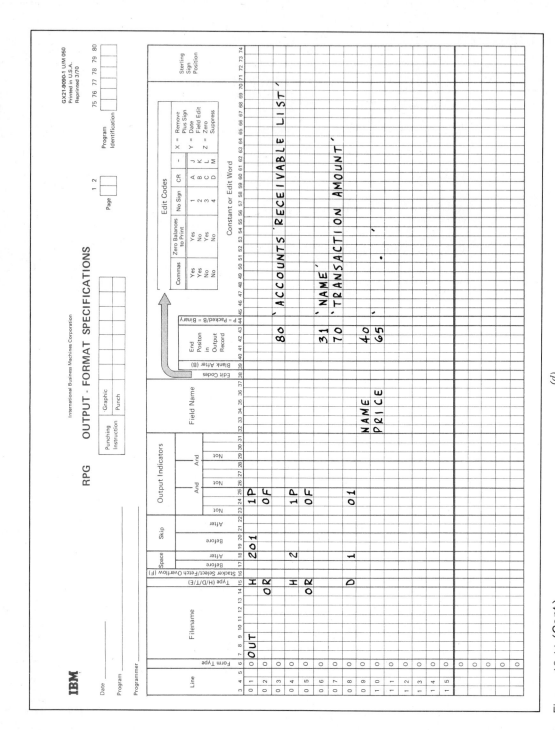

Figure 10.11 (Cont.)
Coded specification sheets for sample program 2—output-format specifications.

(d)

overflow. It will follow the first heading since it appears directly after it on the OUTPUT-FORMAT SPECIFICATIONS sheet.

The detail line (D in Type field) prints whenever indicator 01 is on, or each time a card is read. The input fields will print with minimum editing. That is, decimal points will be included where appropriate. In addition, the calculated field PRICE is printed on each line with a decimal point.

Let us revise SAMPLE PROGRAM 2, slightly, so that in addition to printing detail lines for each input card, we print a final total, at the very end, when all records have been processed.

The FILE DESCRIPTION and INPUT SPECIFICATIONS are the same as in Figure 10.11.

We must now calculate a final total. For each input card, we perform the extension or multiplication to obtain PRICE. In addition we should add the PRICE figure to a final total (FINTOT). See Figure 10.12 for a revision to the CALCULATION SPECIFICATIONS sheet.

The OUTPUT-FORMAT SPECIFICATIONS must now include, at the end, a total line (T in Type—column 15) when the last record has been processed (LR in output indicator—columns 24 and 25). See OUTPUT-FORMAT SPECIFICATIONS in Figure 10.13. You will recall that the zero (0) in the Edit Word of FINTOT causes suppression of leading or high-order zeros.

Note, also that the literal '**TOTALS**' will print on the same line as the Final Total.

From this brief exposure to total lines, the reader should observe that totals can print, for specific control breaks, as well as for end of job routines.

C. SAMPLE PROGRAM 3

This is the Sales Commission Problem coded in the COBOL language thus far. The input and output formats are noted in Figure 10.14. The RPG coding is illustrated in Figure 10.15. You will note that the coding is very similar to that indicated in the previous examples.

Notice, however, how the compare operation is specified on the CALCULATION SPECIFICATIONS sheet. For example, for every record (01 indicator) a comparison is made of SALES to 100.00. If SALES is greater than 100.00, then the 02 indicator is turned on. This is coded in columns 54 and 55—High indicator. If SALES is less than 100.00, then the 03 indicator is turned on. This is coded in columns 56 and 57—Low indicator. If SALES is equal to 100.00, then we want the 03 indicator turned on. This is coded in columns 58 and 59—Equal indicator.

You will note that the three illustrated problems use card input and print output. The majority of RPG programs employ cards as input, and a report as output. Notice also that most of the entries are relatively standard. The FILE DESCRIPTION SPECIFICATIONS sheet, for

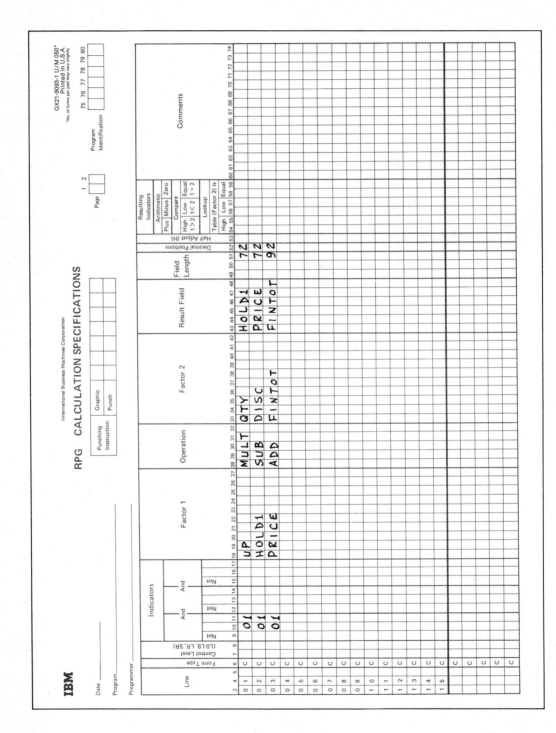

Figure 10.12
Revised calculation specifications for program 2.

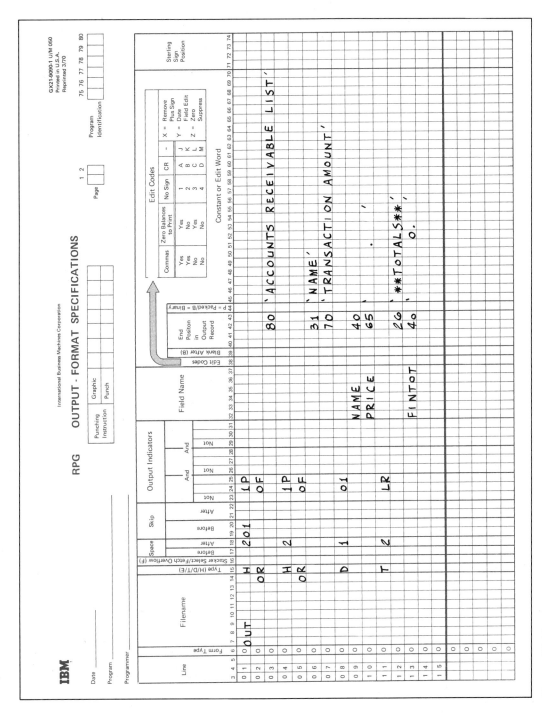

Figure 10.13
Revised output-format specifications for program 2.

361

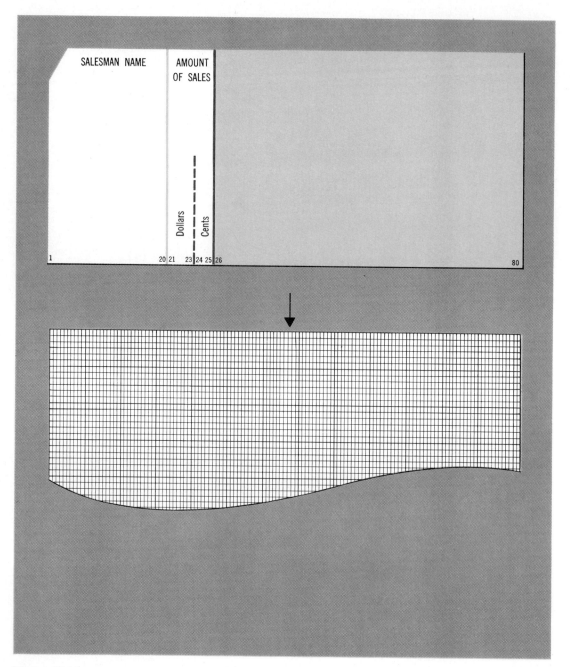

Figure 10.14
Input and output formats for sample program 3.

Concepts of Computer Programming

example, has uniform entries (with the exception of FILENAME) for a given installation.

With this brief exposure to RPG, the student should realize the numerous advantages of RPG for simple card-to-print programs. In a single lesson, a businessman or programmer can learn to program simple applications in RPG. Understanding the basic format of the language is enough to code elementary programs. Thus a businessman with little knowledge of computers and data processing can obtain a simple computer report in relatively little time.

RPG can be used with other forms of input and output as well. File specifications for a Punch file or a Tape file, for example, are also relatively simple.

Note that for tape records, block and record length on the FILE DESCRIPTION SPECIFICATIONS SHEET are not necessarily the same. Records are blocked on tape, to make maximum use of the tape areas.[1]

The *blocking factor,* or number of records in a block, is determined by the systems analyst or the programmer. The BLOCK LENGTH for tape processing is equal to the blocking factor times record length. If the blocking factor is 5, denoting 5 records per block, for example, and the record length is 50, then the BLOCK LENGTH is 250. The label notation on the FILE DESCRIPTION sheet indicates (column 53) S for *standard* tape labels. You will recall that header labels are generally indicated as the first record of a tape to insure proper identification.

A STANDARD LABEL is one created for output or checked for input, automatically by the computer, because it has a standard format.

For output files other than Print files, the heading records would usually not be required as part of OUTPUT-FORMAT SPECIFICATIONS. Otherwise, all data on the other sheets, are coded exactly the same way.

[1] *See Chapter 5 for a detailed discussion of blocking factors.*

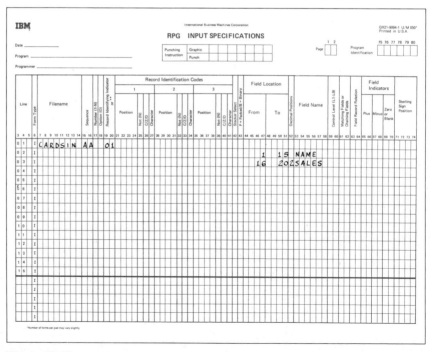

Figure 10.15
Coded specification sheets for sample program 3.

International Business Machines Corporation

RPG CALCULATION SPECIFICATIONS

GX21-9093-1 U/M 050*
Printed in U.S.A.

Date _____
Program _____
Programmer _____

Line	Form Type	Control Level (L0-L9, LR, SR)	Indicators Not	And	And Not	Factor 1	Operation	Factor 2	Result Field	Field Length	Decimal Positions	Half Adjust (H)	Resulting Indicators	Comments
0 1	C		01			SALES	COMP	100.00					020303	
0 2	C		02			SALES	MULT	.03	COMM	42				
0 3	C		03			SALES	COMP	50.00					040505	
0 4	C		04			SALES	MULT	.02	COMM	42				
0 5	C		05			SALES	MULT	00	COMM	42				
0 6	C													
0 7	C													
0 8	C													
0 9	C													
1 0	C													
1 1	C													
1 2	C													
1 3	C													
1 4	C													
1 5	C													

International Business Machines Corporation

RPG OUTPUT - FORMAT SPECIFICATIONS

GX21-9090-1 U/M 050
Printed in U.S.A.
Reprinted 3/70

Date _____
Program _____
Programmer _____

Line	Form Type	Filename	Type (H/D/T/E)	Stacker Select/Fetch Overflow (F)	Space Before	Space After	Skip Before	Skip After	Output Indicators Not	And Not	And Not	Field Name	Edit Codes	End Positon in Output Record	Constant or Edit Word
0 1	O	PRINTOUTH					201		1P						
0 2	O		OR						OF					76	'COMMISSION PRINTOUT'
0 3	O														
0 4	O		H	2					1P						
0 5	O		OR						OF						
0 6	O													35	'NAME'
0 7	O													70	'AMOUNT OF COMMISSION'
0 8	O		D	2					01						
0 9	O											NAME		40	
1 0	O											COMM		63	' . '
1 1	O														
1 2	O														
1 3	O														
1 4	O														
1 5	O														

Figure 10.15 (Cont.)
Coded specification sheets for sample program 3.

SELF-EVALUATING QUIZ

1. RPG is an abbreviation for _____ .
2. The coding sheets for an RPG program are called _____ sheets.
3. The usual form of input for an RPG program is _____ , and the usual form of output is a _____ .
4. (T or F) Small-scale computers that do not have adequate core to run large COBOL or PL/1 programs often utilize RPG.
5. (T or F) RPG is best suited for programs with complex logic.
6. The four specifications forms that may be used in an RPG program are _____ , _____ , _____ , and _____ .
7. Each line for every form is punched into a single _____ which is then part of the _____ .

SOLUTIONS

1. *Report Program Generator*
2. specifications
3. cards; printed report
4. T
5. F
6. FILE DESCRIPTION; INPUT; CALCULATION; OUTPUT-FORMAT
7. card; RPG program deck

Concepts of Computer Programming

Chapter 11 *Introduction to FORTRAN Programming*

FORTRAN is a computer language which, like COBOL, is universal, or common to many computers. The name FORTRAN is an acronym for *FOR*mula *TRAN*slator. This suggests that this language is particularly suited for writing programs that deal primarily with formulas. FORTRAN is widely used for scientific and engineering applications. Notwithstanding this fact, it is also true that FORTRAN is utilized to program many traditional business applications.

The purpose of this chapter is twofold:

1. To enable a business student to read and understand simple FORTRAN programs.
2. To explore typical business applications that are programmed in FORTRAN.

I. Understanding Simple FORTRAN Programs

The essence of the FORTRAN language is that most instructions are written in terms of mathematical formulas or expressions. Whereas, in COBOL we might say:

MULTIPLY HOURS-WORKED BY HOURLY-RATE GIVING WEEKLY-WAGES

Concepts of Computer Programming

in FORTRAN we would use the following instruction to accomplish the same result:

$$WAGES \quad = \quad HOURS \quad * \quad RATE$$

Notice that in COBOL the instruction reads like an English sentence, while in FORTRAN we have what appears to be an equation.

To demonstrate the nature of this language, we will present below a simplified FORTRAN program to calculate weekly wages for employees. This program is equivalent to the COBOL program presented at the beginning of Chapter 9. We want to create a Payroll File from Employee Time Cards, as shown in Figure 11.1.

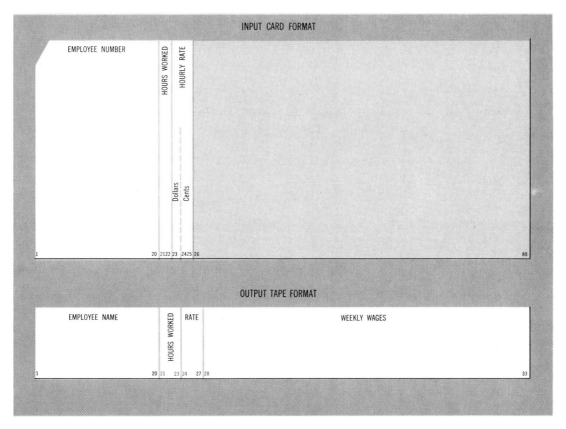

Figure 11.1
Input and output formats for sample program 1.

```
C     THIS FORTRAN PROGRAM ACCOMPLISHES THE SAME THING AS
C     THE COBOL PROGRAM PRESENTED AT THE BEGINNING OF CHAPTER 9
      DIMENSION NAME (5)
   1  READ (1, 100, END=99) NAME, HOURS, RATE
      WAGES = HOURS * RATE
      WRITE (6,110) NAME, HOURS, RATE, WAGES
      GO TO 1
  99  END FILE 6
      STOP
 100  FORMAT (5A4, F2.0, F3.2)
 110  FORMAT (5A4, F3.0, F4.2, F6.2)
      END
```

An explanation of this program is as follows:

Line	*Statement and Explanation*

1st and 2nd

```
C   THIS FORTRAN PROGRAM ACCOMPLISHES THE SAME THING AS
C   THE COBOL PROGRAM PRESENTED AT THE BEGINNING OF
    CHAPTER 9
```

The "C" in column 1 of each card indicates that these cards contain only Comments for the purpose of clarification for someone reading the program. These lines have no effect on the logic of the program itself.

3rd

```
DIMENSION NAME (5)
```

This instruction is technically necessary, since FORTRAN compilers generally do not allow an alphanumeric field as large as 20 positions to be read in and stored in one field. It is therefore necessary in this program to instruct the computer to set up several adjacent fields to hold all of the characters from the input field (NAME). We will use 5 adjacent fields, each 4 positions long.

4th

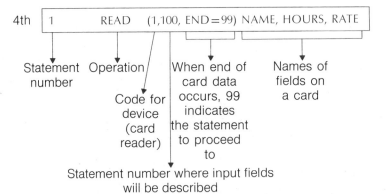

370

5th

| WAGES = HOURS * RATE |

Formula to perform desired calculation. Note the use of the asterisk in place of the multiplication sign.

6th

| WRITE   (6,110) NAME, HOURS, RATE, WAGES |

Instruction to tell computer to write on tape unit 6, the following fields: NAME, HOURS, RATE, and WAGES, which are further described as to field specifications in statement number 110.

7th

| GO TO 1 |

A branch back to statement number 1 to repeat the process if there are cards left.

8th

| 99   END FILE 6 |

This statement is the one to which a branch occurs after there are no more cards to be processed. That is, the END=99 in statement 1 causes a branch to statement number 99 after all cards have been processed. The END FILE command in this statement is an instruction which causes the computer to place an end of file indicator on the tape.

9th

| STOP |

We are now ready to stop the program, since all cards have been processed.

10th

| 100   FORMAT (5A4, F2.0, F3.2) |

The purpose of the FORMAT statement is to describe the specifications or format of the input or output, in detail. This FORMAT, numbered 100, is associated with the input cards (READ(1,100 . . .)). The first specification of 5A4 indicates that the first five adjacent groups of four positions each contain alphanumeric (A) data pertaining to NAME, the first field listed in the READ statement. That is, columns 1–20 in the card contain this data.

Since the FORTRAN compiler does not ordinarily allow for an alphanumeric specification larger than four positions, such as A20, we must accommodate large fields by grouping the data in some manner that will yield the desired size. A specification of 10A2, for example, would achieve the same result as the specification used above. However, a different statement (DIMENSION NAME (10)) would have to be put at the beginning of the program. The next specification is the F, or floating-point, specification which indicates the length of the field on the card and the number of decimal positions. In this case, the F2.0 indicates that the second field (HOURS) will be two positions long with no (0) decimal positions. The last specification, F3.2, indicates that the third field (RATE) will be 3 positions long, and should be stored with a decimal point and 2 digits to the right of the point.

11th

```
110   FORMAT (5A4, F3.0, F4.2, F6.2)
```

This FORMAT describes the output listed in the WRITE statement: WRITE (6,110) NAME, HOURS, RATE, WAGES. We are asking the computer to store NAME, HOURS, RATE, and WAGES on tape for the card just processed. The FORMAT statement describes each of these fields. The specification 5A4 has the same meaning as in the previous FORMAT. The second specification (F3.0) indicates that HOURS is to occupy three positions on the tape—two integers and the decimal point, with no (0) decimal digits after it. The next specification of F4.2 indicates that RATE is to occupy four positions on the tape, including the decimal point with two digits to the right. The last specification of F6.2 describes how WAGES is to be stored. It is to occupy six positions, including a decimal point with two digits to the right.
Note that in FORTRAN, unlike COBOL, there is no convenient way of storing a field on tape, for example, with an implied decimal point to separate dollars from cents. In FORTRAN, such a field is usually stored with the decimal point actually included.

12th

```
END
```

The END statement signifies to the computer that there are no more statements in this program.

Now that we have seen the structure of a FORTRAN program, we will discuss some programs that involve slightly more sophisticated logic in order to illustrate some of the common types of FORTRAN statements. As the next illustration, we will take Program 3, which was coded in COBOL in Chapter 9, and show the equivalent FORTRAN

372

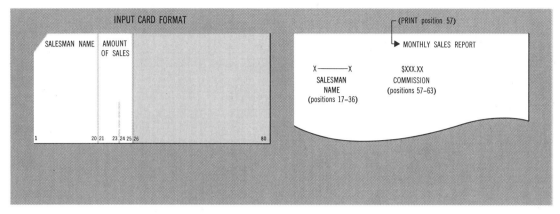

Figure 11.2
Input and output formats for sample program 2.

program. (The sales cards and the sales report have the formats as
shown in Figure 11.2. (Program 2, illustrated in the COBOL chapter,
has been left to the reader as an exercise.)

```
C     THIS PROGRAM TAKES CARDS WITH THE WEEKLY SALES
C     FIGURES FOR EACH SALESMAN, AND PRODUCES A REPORT
C     WHICH SHOWS COMMISSIONS THAT HAVE BEEN CALCULATED.
      DIMENSION NAME (5)
      WRITE (3,5)
   5  FORMAT ('1', 56X, 'MONTHLY SALES REPORT')
   7  READ (1,10, END = 100) NAME, SALES
  10  FORMAT (5A4, F5.2)
      IF (SALES .GT. 100.00) GO TO 20
      IF (SALES .GT. 50.00) GO TO 30
      COMMIS = 000.00
      GO TO 40
  20  COMMIS = SALES * .03
      GO TO 40
  30  COMMIS = SALES * .02
  40  WRITE (3,50) NAME, COMMIS
  50  FORMAT ('0', 16X, 5A4, 20X, '$', F6.2)
      GO  TO 7
 100  STOP
      END
```

This program points out some interesting features of FORTRAN not
encountered in the first illustration.

1. The first WRITE instruction tells the computer to print out a specified heading. Notice that there are no field names indicated next to the WRITE statement. However, the associated format, statement number 5, tells the computer what to do. The first specification, '1', is a code for carriage control purposes that tells the computer to begin the report on the first line of a new page. The next specification, 56X, tells the computer to skip 56 positions on the first line and then begin the heading (between quotation marks) in the 57th print position.

2. After the READ instruction and the associated FORMAT statement, we tell the computer that IF SALES is greater than (.GT.) 100.00, a branch to statement 20 should be executed. If it is not, the computer automatically goes to the next instruction, which, in this case, is another test.

3. Statement 40 instructs the computer to write out the values for NAME and COMMIS in accordance with the specifications in statement 50. This statement shown below, is explained as follows:

50   FORMAT ('0', 16X, 5A4, 20X, '$', F6.2)

The first specification, '0', is a code for carriage control purposes that tells the computer to double space before printing the line. The 16X tells the computer to skip the first 16 print positions on the line and then print the NAME field, which is a 20-position alphanumeric (A) field. After the NAME field, 20 positions are skipped (20X), a dollar sign is printed, and right next to the dollar sign, COMMIS will print out with three integers, a decimal point and two decimal positions.

II. Comparison of FORTRAN to COBOL

At this point, we can make several observations about FORTRAN as compared to COBOL.

1. COBOL is a more structured language than FORTRAN, in the sense that COBOL has four DIVISIONS (IDENTIFICATION, ENVIRONMENT, DATA, and PROCEDURE) that *must* be included in every program in the sequence specified. FORTRAN, on the other hand, is more flexible. There are no particular statements that must be included.

2. A program in FORTRAN, being generally more mathematical in nature, may not be as easy for a businessman to understand as one in COBOL, which is similar to English. The following comparison from PROBLEM 3 (which was coded in Chapter 9 in COBOL and in the previous illustration in FORTRAN) dramatizes this point.

COBOL	FORTRAN
IF SALES-AMT IS GREATER THAN 100.00 MULTIPLY .03 BY SALES-AMT GIVING COMMISSION, GO TO PRINT.	IF (SALES .GT. 100.00) GO TO 20 ⋮ 20 COMMIS=SALES * .03

Notice for example, that the code .GT. in FORTRAN is not as easy to read as the words GREATER THAN in COBOL. That is, it requires prior familiarity with a code rather than simple understanding of English.

3. In FORTRAN, the rules of the language limit to six the maximum number of characters used to identify a field, whereas in COBOL, the maximum is 30 characters. This often results in abbreviated field names in FORTRAN that may not be as self-explanatory for the businessman as corresponding names in COBOL. For example, in COBOL we might call a field YEAR-TO-DATE-GROSS-EARNINGS or perhaps Y-T-D-GROSS-EARN. In FORTRAN, the best we can do is something like YTDGRS.

4. From the examples presented in FORTRAN, you may have noticed the amount of effort required by the programmer to code FORMAT statements that precisely specify what the input or output looks like. In COBOL, with the aid of PICTURE clauses, it is usually easier to describe input or output specifications. However, although FORTRAN is considered to be cumbersome in the area of input/output specifications, it is much easier to code arithmetic operations. That is, arithmetic instructions are less verbose and easier to write in FORTRAN than in COBOL. In addition, FORTRAN enables the programmer to include complex mathematical functions that cannot be included in a COBOL program. In some business applications, such as sales forecasting, or inventory control, there is often the need to use mathematical concepts such as trigonometric functions; that is, a formula might require the computer to find the cosine of a particular angle. In FORTRAN, we can easily write an instruction such as:

$$Y = COS(X)$$

and the FORTRAN compiler, or translator, will recognize what is meant by the operation "COS." In COBOL, this cannot be done very easily, since the COBOL compiler is not equipped to recognize the code COS, or most other mathematical functions.

Although a programmer can write instructions that will allow the COBOL compiler to compute the cosine, it obviously takes more effort than in FORTRAN, where it can be performed with the use of a function. Note that it is possible to write part of a program in COBOL and part in FORTRAN assuming that the computer used has both compilers.

III. Understanding More Advanced FORTRAN Programs

In the following paragraphs, we will present some additional concepts of FORTRAN that will allow the business student to more easily understand and review FORTRAN programs for business applications.

A. MATHEMATICAL OPERATIONS

The following table lists the fundamental mathematical operations and the symbols utilized in FORTRAN:

Symbol	Operation
**	Exponentiation
*	Multiplication
/	Division
+	Addition
−	Subtraction

Exponentiation involves raising some number to a power, or multiplying a number by itself a specified number of times. That is, 2^3 is represented as 2 ** 3 in FORTRAN and is calculated as the number 2 multiplied by itself 3 times ($2^3 = 2 \times 2 \times 2 = 8$). For example, if a programmer wishes the computer to add A^2 and B^2 to obtain the result X, where A, B, and X are fields, the following instruction would be indicated in FORTRAN:

$$X = A ** 2 + B ** 2$$

Similarly, the FORTRAN expression:

$$ANSWER = (AMT1 + AMT2 + AMT3)/3.0$$

calculates the average of the three fields—AMT1, AMT2, AMT3. Suppose the parentheses were omitted from the above arithmetic expression. The question is whether this instruction would still calculate the average. That is, the expression:

$$ANSWER = AMT1 + AMT2 + AMT3/3.0$$

might reduce to either of the following two formulas

$$ANSWER = \frac{AMT1 + AMT2 + AMT3}{3.0}$$

Concepts of Computer Programming

or

$$\boxed{\text{ANSWER} = \text{AMT1} + \text{AMT2} + \frac{\text{AMT3}}{3.0}}$$

If the parentheses were not included, the average would *not* be calculated properly. ANSWER would, in fact, equal

$\text{AMT1} + \text{AMT2} + \dfrac{\text{AMT3}}{3.0}$.

The reason has to do with the *hierarchy of operations;* that is, the computer does not necessarily perform operations in the order in which the expression is read. The basic rules of hierarchy are as follows:

1. Any operations within parentheses, if included, are performed first, in accordance with the rules below.
2. In the absence of parentheses, operations are normally performed in the following order:
I. Exponentiation (**)
II and III. Multiplication (*) or Division (/), whichever appears first.
IV and V. Addition (+) or Subtraction (−), whichever appears first.

Exponentiation is ordinarily performed first. After that, the computer looks at the mathematical expression beginning at the equal sign and proceeds to the right. It finds the next highest operation in the formula according to the hierarchy rules, and then it performs that operation. Therefore, the following FORTRAN statement mentioned above is evaluated as follows:

$$\text{ANSWER} = \underbrace{\text{AMT1} + \text{AMT2}}_{\text{2nd operation}} \underbrace{+}_{\text{3rd operation}} \underbrace{\text{AMT3}/3.0}_{\text{1st operation}}$$

Thus, we have:

$$\frac{\text{AMT3}}{3.0} + \text{AMT1} + \text{AMT2}$$

This explains why parentheses are required to obtain the correct formula for the average. As indicated in the hierarchy table above, multiplication and division both have equal priority below exponentiation, while addition and subtraction both have equal priority below multiplication and division. It is sometimes best to include parentheses around complex calculations when there is some doubt as to how the computer will evaluate the operations.

Introduction to FORTRAN Programming   377

B. UNDERSTANDING WHY EQUATIONS ARE NOT EQUATIONS

A very common FORTRAN statement is of the following type:

N = N + 1

This is obviously not a valid equation in the mathematical sense. That is, N = N and N cannot be equal to 1 more than N. However, the above *is* a valid FORTRAN statement. That is, we set N equal to one more than the original N. Thus, if N = 5 and the FORTRAN statement N = N + 1 is executed, N is then set equal to 6. The FORTRAN statement does not make the two items (N) and (N+1) equal; it sets the field on the left side of the equal sign equal to the result calculated on the right side.

Thus, in FORTRAN, for an arithmetic statement, the computer:

1. Performs all computations that are indicated to the right of the equal sign.
2. Takes the final result and moves it to the field whose name is specified to the left of the equal sign. Therefore, the statement N = N + 1 has the following meaning to the computer:
   a. Add 1 to the current value of the field called N.
   b. Take this result and move it to N. In other words, add 1 to N. The statement N = 0 technically abides by the same rules. Since there are no computations involved, the computer simply takes the result indicated at the right of the equal sign (zero) and moves it to the field called N. In essence, N = (constant) is a data transfer operation that moves the constant to the field name. The above method is used to establish counters. If, in a FORTRAN program, the programmer wants the computer to count the number of cards processed, we might expect to find the following instructions:

N = 0
READ (1,3) NAME, SALES
N = N+1

After every card is read, 1 is added to the field N. Thus, at the end of the run N reflects the number of cards read.

C. THE CONCEPT OF INFORMATION TABLES[1]

Suppose a programmer has written the following program to find the salesman who earned the highest commission last year:

---

[1] *This section contains more advanced instructions, which are frequently found in FORTRAN applications. It is considered an optional topic.*

Concepts of Computer Programming

```
                        DIMENSION TABLE (500)
                        READ (1,10, END=15) TABLE
               10  FORMAT (F9.2)
               15  NUMBER = 0
                        HICOM = 0.0
                        DO 20 NO = 1,500
                        IF (TABLE (NO) .GT. HICOM) GO TO 50
                        GO TO 20
               50  HICOM = TABLE (NO)
                        NUMBER = NO
               20  CONTINUE
                        WRITE (3,60) NUMBER, HICOM
               60  FORMAT ('1', I3, 5X, '$', F9.2)
                        STOP
                        END
```

There are 500 salesmen in the company, where each salesman has
a number from 1 to 500. The program reads in, for each of the 500
salesman, a commission. The program then determines which of the
salesmen has the highest commission.

The following is, in essence, the sequence of operations, as shown
in the program:

1. Instruct the computer to set up a table in the computer to hold
   commission figures for the 500 salesmen.
2. Read in all the commission figures from 500 punched cards, one
   for each salesman, and store the information in the computer table.
   The cards are in sequence by salesman number.
3. Set up a field, NUMBER, to retain the employee number of the
   person with the highest commission.
4. Set up a field, HICOM, to retain the highest commission figure.
5. Search the table to find the employee with the greatest commission.
   (Assume for the sake of simplicity that only *one* employee earned
   the highest commission, and not two or more; that is, if 600.00 is
   the highest commission, only *one* salesman has earned that much.)
   The instruction DO 20 NO = 1,500 is interpreted as follows: repeat
   (or DO) the following instructions up to and including the one with
   statement number 20, changing the value of the field called NO
   from 1 (the first time) by 1 each time the instructions are repeated.
   The sequence is to be repeated 500 times. Thus, the DO statement
   consists of several parts:

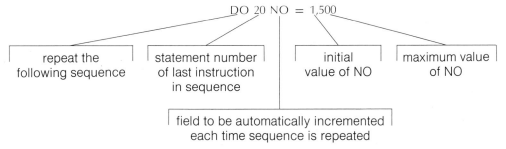

379

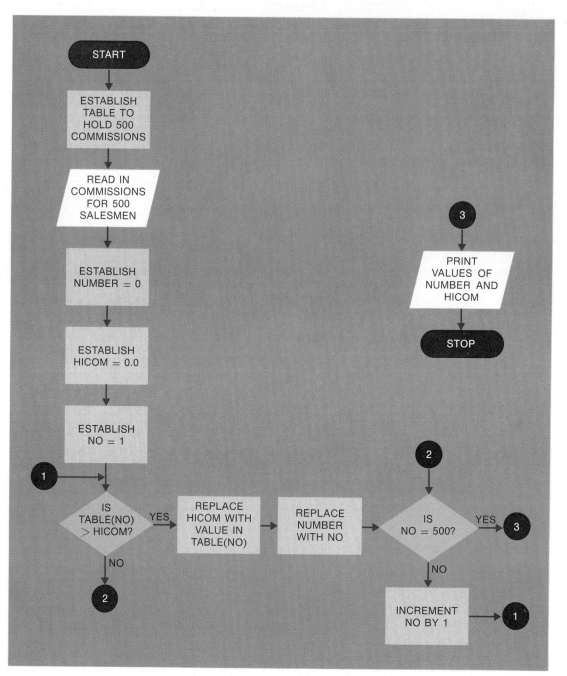

Figure 11.3
Flowchart for finding the salesman with the greatest commission.

Concepts of Computer Programming

6. TABLE (NO) refers to a specific item in the TABLE. For example, when NO is equal to 1, we are interested in the first value stored in the TABLE, which is the commission for employee number 1. When NO is equal to 10, TABLE (NO) refers to the 10th value in TABLE, or the commission for employee number 10. In our example, NO varies from 1 to 500. Thus we test each of the 500 values in the TABLE.

7. The statement IF (TABLE(NO) .GT. HICOM) GO TO 50 means that if the computer finds a value in the TABLE that is greater than the previous high commission, a branch should be made to statement 50. At statement 50, the new high value found for commission is stored along with the associated employee number. If the computer did not find the particular value in the TABLE to be higher than the value in HICOM, a branch to statement 20 would occur. At that point, the computer would CONTINUE with the next comparison.

8. After the whole TABLE is analyzed, the values of HICOM and NUMBER (the employee with this highest commission) are printed out. Note that the specification I3 indicates that NUMBER is to print out as a three-position integer (I).

The flowchart indicating the logic flow for this program is shown in Figure 11.3.

SELF-EVALUATING QUIZ

1. The name FORTRAN is an acronym for _____ .
2. FORTRAN is widely used for _____ problems.
3. While COBOL uses words such as ADD, MULTIPLY, SUBTRACT, DIVIDE to indicate mathematical expressions, FORTRAN uses
   _____ .
4. COBOL instructions read like sentences, while in FORTRAN instructions read like _____ .
5. In business areas such as _____ , where advanced mathematical concepts are employed, FORTRAN is most often used.
6. (T or F) The expression X = X + 1, although not a valid mathematical expression, is a valid FORTRAN expression.

SOLUTIONS

1. *FORMULA TRANSLATOR*
2. scientific or mathematical
3. mathematical symbols
4. mathematical equations
5. sales forecasting
6. T

Concepts of Computer Programming

Chapter 12 *Introduction to PL/1 Programming*

I. Basic Concepts

PL/1 is an abbreviation for PROGRAMMING LANGUAGE/ONE. Its basic structure combines the advantages of FORTRAN and COBOL, in addition to including some unique features. It is a programming language that is ideally suited to both scientific and business problems. That is, it may be used as an all-purpose programming language for companies that have both business and scientific applications.

Originally developed as an IBM language, PL/1 is now available for use on many different computers. Because of its dual purpose in handling both scientific and commercial applications, it has many advanced features and sophisticated techniques that the beginning programmer may have difficulty learning. That is, beginning programmers or business students learning PL/1 should concentrate on the general uses of PL/1 and leave the advanced concepts for the sophisticated programmer.

The PL/1 program is written in free form; that is, it has no specific structure. Unlike COBOL or even FORTRAN where specific elements must appear in specific columns on the coding form and thus on a source card, there are no such requirements for PL/1. Thus any all-purpose coding sheet may be used to code a PL/1 program (Figure 12.1). Similarly, any 80-column card may be used for keypunching a PL/1 source deck.

384

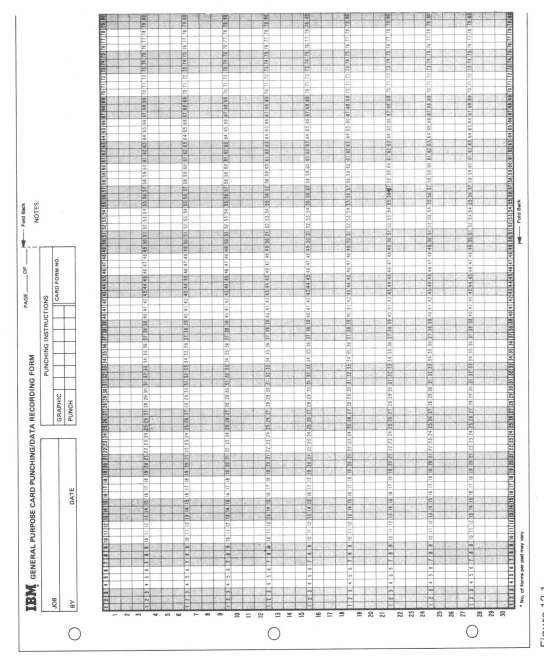

Figure 12.1
Sample all-purpose coding sheet.

385

Column 1, however, must *always* remain blank in PL/1 programs, since it is used by the computer's supervisory system. Columns 73 to 80 are not used for processing by the compiler. Thus they may be used either for sequencing or for program identification. The PL/1 program, then, is coded in positions, or columns, 2 to 72.

II. *Illustrative PL/1 Programs*

A. SAMPLE PROGRAM 1

Let us consider our sample program that uses the card format denoted in Figure 12.2.

We wish to produce an output tape with the information indicated in Figure 12.3.

The program would appear as follows:

```
PAY:      PROCEDURE OPTIONS (MAIN);
          DECLARE 1 INAREA,
                     2 NAME CHARACTER (20),
                     2 HOURS PICTURE '99',
                     2 RATE PICTURE '9V99',
                     2 UNUSED CHARACTER (55);
          DECLARE 1 OUTAREA,
                     2 NAME_OUT       CHARACTER (20),
                     2 HOURS_OUT      PICTURE '99',
                     2 RATE_OUT       PICTURE '9V99',
                     2 WEEKLY_WAGES   PICTURE '999V99';
          DECLARE CARDIN FILE INPUT RECORD ENVIRONMENT
             (CONSECUTIVE F(80) MEDIUM (SYS005,2540));
          DECLARE TAPE FILE RECORD OUTPUT ENVIRONMENT
             (CONSECUTIVE F(300,30) MEDIUM (SYS008,2400));
          OPEN FILE (CARDIN), FILE (TAPE);
          ON ENDFILE (CARDIN) GO TO ENDJOB;
BEGIN:    READ FILE (CARDIN) INTO (INAREA);
          NAME_OUT = NAME;
          HOURS_OUT = HOURS;
          RATE_OUT = RATE;
          WEEKLY_WAGES = RATE * HOURS;
          WRITE FILE (TAPE) FROM (OUTAREA);
          GO TO BEGIN;
ENDJOB:   CLOSE FILE (CARDIN), FILE (TAPE);
          END PAY;
```

Note that each statement in PL/1 ends with a semicolon. Since the first two DECLARE statements have several entries, only the *last* one in

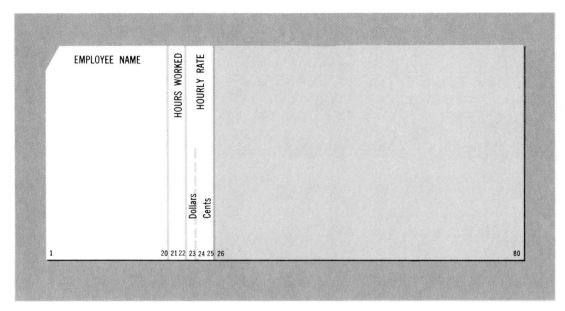

Figure 12.2
Input card format for sample program 1.

each group (UNUSED in INAREA and WEEKLY_WAGES in OUTAREA) is followed by a semicolon.

We have indicated that PL/1 is a free-form language. Thus each element may be written on a single line, as indicated above, or in the format shown below:

PAY: PROCEDURE OPTIONS (MAIN); DECLARE 1 INAREA, 2 NAME CHARACTER (20), 2 HOURS PICTURE '99', 2 RATE PICTURE '9V99', 2 UNUSED CHARACTER (55);

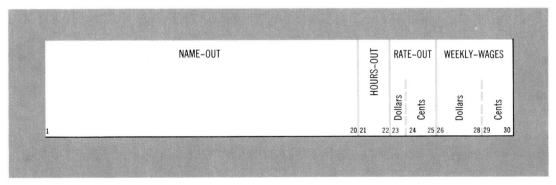

Figure 12.3
Output tape format for sample program 1.

Thus PL/1 is a totally free-form language. While COBOL and FORTRAN permit certain statements to be free form (such as PROCEDURE DIVISION entries in COBOL, and arithmetic statements in FORTRAN), PL/1 allows *all* statements to be unstructured. The only requirement is that each statement must end in a semicolon. While this unstructured format is permissible, we will use one statement per line to insure readability.

The first statement in a PL/1 program must always be a *PROCEDURE* statement and the last one must always be an *END* statement. Thus all PL/1 programs have the following format:

```
(label): PROCEDURE OPTIONS (    );
   ⋮
(source statements)
   ⋮
END (label);
```

The PROCEDURE statement essentially indicates the starting point of a procedure and associates a name (label) with it. The END statement terminates the named procedure.

PL/1 programs can consist of many procedures, which may be linked together to form an integrated program. In the above example, there is only one PROCEDURE.

Note that the DECLARE statements are very similar to DATA DIVISION entries in COBOL.

The first DECLARE in sample program 1 labels the record INAREA. This record consists of four fields:

NAME, a 20-position alphanumeric field;
HOURS, a 2-position numeric field (99's in a PICTURE clause denote numeric data);
RATE, a 3-position numeric field with an implied decimal point (V is an assumed or implied decimal position).
    (Thus 128 punched in these columns called RATE would be interpreted by the computer as 1.28, even though no decimal point has been punched into the card.)
UNUSED, a fill area at the end of the card record consisting of 55 positions.

The output record area has a similar format. OUTAREA, the name of the record format consists of:

```
NAME_OUT
HOURS_OUT
RATE_OUT
```

each with the same specifications as their input counterparts; and, WEEKLY WAGES, a 5-position numeric field that consists of 3 integer positions and 2 decimal positions.

Concepts of Computer Programming

The data names illustrated resemble COBOL data names. That is, they may contain a maximum of 31 characters in PL/1, similar to the 30 of COBOL, and much longer than the maximum of 6 in FORTRAN.

Note that the above two DECLARE statements are very similar to the record description entries in the DATA DIVISION of a COBOL program. Similarly, the two DECLARE statements that follow in the illustrated PL/1 program together with the OPEN statement serve to activate the necessary devices and to indicate the file types that serve as input or output.

The statement:

DECLARE CARDIN FILE INPUT RECORD ENVIRONMENT (CONSECUTIVE F(80) MEDIUM (SYS005,2540));

defines an input file called CARDIN that is composed of records[1] (as opposed to STREAM-oriented data, which is generally not structured—this will be discussed later). The file is specified as being a consecutive one, which means that the 51st record, for example, is located right after the 50th record. Each record in this file is fixed length (F) with 80 characters per record. The file is located on a card reader (device number 2540), whose system number is SYS005. The device number is the manufacturer's number for the reader; the system number is the number assigned at the specific computer center.

Similarly, the next DECLARE statement in the program on p. 386 defines an OUTPUT file called TAPE that is also composed of records. The F(300,30) in the statement means that the data will be stored on tape with 300 characters to a block, with each record containing 30 characters. The blocking factor is thus 10 (300 ÷ 30).[2]

Note that the DECLARE statement is not a difficult entry to code. For a given computer center, all entries except the file name are *standard* when the card reader is used as input:

DECLARE (file name) FILE INPUT RECORD ENVIRONMENT (CONSECUTIVE F(80) MEDIUM (SYS005, 2540)):

Thus the programmer need only supply the file name for this standard DECLARE statement for an input card file. Note, however, that the MEDIUM (SYS005, 2540) is standard only with respect to the given computer center. The entry SYS005 signifies the system number assigned to the card reader, and 2540 is the manufacturer's device number (in this case, IBM). At different locations, different systems and device numbers may be used, but for each location, these numbers will remain constant.

The OPEN statement serves to activate the card reader and the

---

[1] *Note that some PL/1 compilers restrict the length of a file name to a maximum of six characters.*

[2] *Tape processing sometimes requires additional entries that will not be discussed here.*

tape drive. The next statement performs the necessary test for end of input file:

ON ENDFILE (CARDIN) GO TO ENDJOB;

The above statement indicates that when there are no more records in the CARDIN file, the program should automatically proceed to the instruction labeled ENDJOB.

The READ statement reads a card record and places it in the storage area defined as INAREA, already described in the DECLARE statement above.

Thus far, the program is very similar to COBOL entries for describing records, opening files, reading records, and testing for the end of a file. That is PL/1 input/output entries resemble COBOL coding, with the same ability for handling complex I/O.

All programs must indicate to the computer the specifications of the input and output files and the equipment used. These specifications can appear in the program itself, as shown above with the ENVIRONMENT attribute which is similar to the ENVIRONMENT DIVISION entries of a COBOL program. For some PL/1 compilers, the specifications can appear in special messages to the control system of the computer. These messages are part of a *job control language* that accompanies a program and enables the programmer to communicate with the control system of a computer. The nature of the job control language will be discussed in Chapter 14.

The remaining processing instructions, however, are very similar to FORTRAN. That is, rather than verbose English-like sentences, we may use simplified expressions.

The first expression:

NAME_OUT = NAME;

has a similar format in FORTRAN. It moves the contents of NAME, which has been read in from a card, to the output area called NAME_OUT. Similarly, the succeeding statements move the contents of HOURS to the storage area called HOURS_OUT and the contents of RATE to RATE_OUT.

The arithmetic expression:

WEEKLY_WAGES = HOURS * RATE;

performs a multiplication operation. That is, the * denotes multiplication as it does in FORTRAN. Thus HOURS is multiplied by RATE and the result is placed in the WEEKLY_WAGES field.

The WRITE statement takes the record description defined as OUTAREA and writes the current contents of it on tape. The GO TO statement causes a branch to the instruction labeled BEGIN where a new card is read and processing continues.

Concepts of Computer Programming

The program proceeds in this way until there are no more cards, in which case a branch to ENDJOB occurs. At ENDJOB, the files are closed. That is, the CLOSE statement deactivates the input card reader and the output tape drive. The procedure, or program, is then terminated.

The reader should note that the PL/1 program illustrated combines the I/O (input/output) capabilities and options of COBOL with the simplified arithmetic processing format of FORTRAN. It represents an effort to create the best of all possibilities.

Suppose we wish to extend our problem and compute WEEKLY_WAGES as HOURS * RATE only if HOURS are not in excess of 40. For HOURS greater than 40, time-and-a-half is paid, and we compute WEEKLY_WAGES as:

$$WEEKLY\_WAGES = 40 * RATE + (HOURS - 40) * RATE * 1.50$$

In place of the processing step:

$$WEEKLY\_WAGES = HOURS * RATE;$$

we have the conditional statement:

(A) IF HOURS > 40 THEN
      WEEKLY_WAGES = (HOURS - 40) * 1.5 * RATE + 40 * RATE;
      ELSE WEEKLY_WAGES = HOURS * RATE;

or we may have:

(B) IF HOURS <= 40 THEN
        WEEKLY_WAGES = HOURS * RATE;
      ELSE WEEKLY_WAGES = (HOURS - 40) * 1.5 * RATE + 40 * RATE;

The symbols used indicate:

> greater than
< less than
= equal to

To indicate less than or equal to we have

IF HOURS < = 40 . . .

The THEN (statement) is executed if the condition is met; the ELSE (statement) is executed if the condition is not met. Thus in B, if HOURS worked is less than 40 or equal to 40, then WEEKLY_WAGES is computed as HOURS multiplied by RATE. If however, the condition is not met (HOURS are greater than 40), the extended multiplication, or ELSE clause, is performed.

The input and output data for the above illustration are in *record* format. We may also process data in *stream* format, as will be discussed below.

In the previous problem, the data was *record-oriented;* that is, when the instruction "READ" was executed, an *entire record* or card pertaining to *one* individual was read and made available for processing. Suppose, for example, that the data is *stream-oriented* and is keypunched as shown in Figure 12.4. The appropriate input instruction will now be "GET" instead of "READ."

We wish to process 25 characters per individual with no regard for physical card limitations. The fact that there are 80 columns per card is of no consequence. The first GET is to read 25 characters from card 1; the second GET reads the next 25; the third GET reads the next 25; the fourth GET reads 5 characters from card 1 and 20 from card 2, and so on.

By using the instruction "GET" rather than "READ," we are instructing the computer to treat the input data as being part of a continuous stream of characters. As illustrated in Figure 12.4, the fourth individual's data continues from the first card to the second without causing any processing problems. When the fourth "GET" instruction is executed, the computer will get the first 5 characters of the individual's name from the first card, and then automatically process the second card up to column 20, in accordance with the appropriate specifications. Thus each GET does not read a physical card, as each READ command would, but, rather, each GET reads an individual's data, or 25 columns.

The essence of a program to process stream-oriented data in accordance with the card format as just described is as follows:

```
PAY:    PROCEDURE OPTIONS (MAIN);
        DECLARE   NAME CHARACTER (20),
                  HOURS PICTURE '99',
                  RATE PICTURE '9V99',
                  WEEKLY_WAGES PICTURE '999V99';
BEGIN:  GET EDIT (NAME, HOURS, RATE) (A(20),F(2),F(3,2));
        IF HOURS > 40 THEN
           WEEKLY_WAGES = (HOURS − 40) *1.5 * RATE + 40 * RATE;
        ELSE WEEKLY_WAGES = HOURS * RATE;
          ⋮
        GO TO BEGIN;
          ⋮
        END PAY;
```

PL/1 is the *only* programming language that facilitates the processing of data in stream form with no regard to record size. In this way input card data can be keypunched without requiring rigid formats.

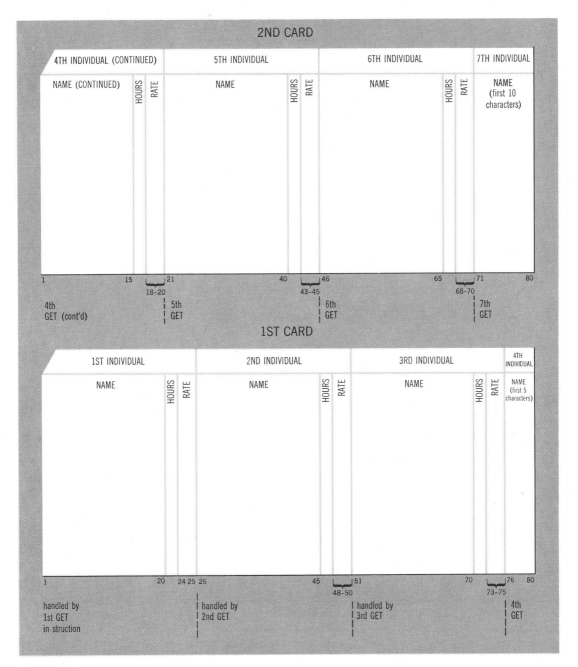

Figure 12.4
An example of stream-oriented punched card data.

The GET EDIT instruction lists the names of the fields that are to be transmitted from the stream of data, followed by the corresponding specifications, which show exactly how each field appears in the *stream*. The PL/1 compiler recognizes that the absence of a reference to a specific input device in this case implies the card reader. Notice that the DECLARE shows how each field should be stored once it has been read in or subsequently processed. NAME has a specification of A(20), which indicates that the field consists of 20 characters. The second specification of F(2), indicates that the next two positions in the stream consist of fixed-point data (data with integer and decimal or fractional components) which will be associated with the field HOURS. The specification of F(3,2) means that the next three positions contain fixed-point data for RATE, with two decimal positions (two digits to the right of an implied decimal point).

An output instruction with stream-oriented data uses the word "PUT," rather than "WRITE," which is used for record-oriented output. Without explicit reference to a specific output device, the printer is the device assumed by the PL/1 compiler. A typical output statement for a printed report would appear as follows:

```
PUT SKIP EDIT (NAME, HOURS, RATE, WEEKLY_WAGES) (A(20),
         X(5), F(3), X(5), F(4,2), X(5), F(6,2));
```

Note that the above specifications used to describe fields in input and output are very similar to those that appear in the FORMAT statements in FORTRAN. The use of the word SKIP indicates that the printer should proceed to a new line every time the instruction is executed.

PL/1 is a programming language designed to ease some of the cumbersome details of the programmer's task. The compiler, therefore, allows the programmer to *omit* specific entries, in which case the computer *assumes* their specifications. This is known as the *default* feature of PL/1. In the absence of some entries the computer assumes certain specifications *by default*. The programmer must be aware of the various defaults available in PL/1, since he may not find the specifications assumed by the computer to be suitable. In such cases, he must *explicitly* describe *all* the necessary entries and characteristics. Thus certain entries may be assumed by default or else they must be explicitly stated.

We have already considered certain defaults of PL/1. We indicated that in the absence of a reference to a specific input *device,* the computer assumes, by default, that the card reader is the one intended. Thus when the programmer wishes to use the card reader as input, he can omit the input device specification; if, however, he wishes to use another device, then he must explicitly state the specifications. Similarly, in the absence of a specific reference to an output device, the printer is assumed, by default.

Various specifications for fields are assumed by default unless their characteristics or *attributes* are explicitly stated. For example, the *first*

Concepts of Computer Programming

letter of each declared field is used by the computer to establish defaults. To specify a field such as

DECLARE HOURS;

establishes a field called HOURS with certain specifications. The letter H as the first letter of a field makes the field *decimal* (as opposed to binary), six characters in length, and representing a *floating-point* number or one utilizing a *scaled* value. To change the meaning of any of these defaults or assumed characteristics, the explicitly stated attributes must be included. For example, to establish HOURS as an 8-position fixed-point decimal number, we must use the following:

DECLARE HOURS FIXED DECIMAL (8);

The above statement *overrides* the default by establishing an 8-position fixed-decimal number.

Note that because of their complexity we will not discuss the many default features of PL/1, including the other attributes of field names that are assumed according to the first letter of the field. We are merely attempting, here, to familiarize the student with the concept of defaults.

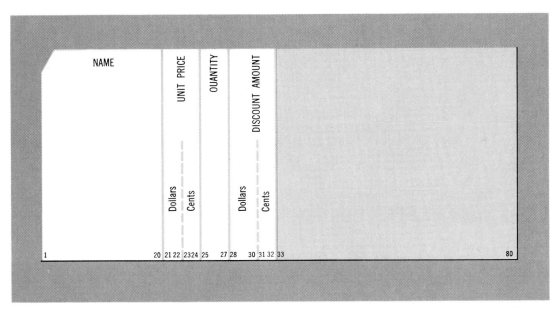

Figure 12.5
Input card format for sample program 2.

B. SAMPLE PROGRAM 2

Consider the Accounts Receivable problem of extending ticket amounts, which has been illustrated in both COBOL and FORTRAN. The input is indicated in Figure 12.5.

The output is a card file with the format shown in Figure 12.6, where TOTAL = UNIT_PRICE * QTY − DISC_AMT.

The PL/1 program that combines I/O features of COBOL with the processing features of FORTRAN results in an English-like, but less wordy, version of a commercial language.

```
TICKET:  PROCEDURE OPTIONS (MAIN);
         DECLARE 1 INAREA,
                    2 NAME          CHARACTER (20),
                    2 UNIT_PRICE    PICTURE '99V99',
                    2 QTY           PICTURE '999',
                    2 DISC_AMT      PICTURE '999V99',
                    2 UNUSED        CHARACTER (48);
         DECLARE 1 OUTAREA,
                    2 NAME          CHARACTER (20),
                    2 TOTAL         PICTURE '99999V99',
                    2 UNUSED        CHARACTER (53);
         DECLARE CARDIN FILE INPUT RECORD ENVIRONMENT
            (CONSECUTIVE F(80) MEDIUM (SYS005,2540));
         DECLARE CRDOUT FILE RECORD OUTPUT ENVIRONMENT
            (CONSECUTIVE F(80) MEDIUM (SYS006,2540));
         OPEN FILE (CARDIN), FILE (CRDOUT);
         ON ENDFILE (CARDIN) GO TO ENDJOB;
BEGIN:   READ FILE (CARDIN) INTO (INAREA);
         OUTAREA.NAME = INAREA.NAME
         TOTAL = UNIT_PRICE * QTY − DISC_AMT;
         WRITE FILE (CRDOUT) FROM (OUTAREA);
         GO TO BEGIN;
ENDJOB:  CLOSE FILE (CARDIN), FILE (CRDOUT);
         END TICKET;
```

You will recall that the first statement, the PROCEDURE statement, and the last one, the END statement, refer to the start and end of the named procedure (TICKET). Since a PL/1 program may have numerous procedures, each one must be identified. By denoting OPTIONS (MAIN) we are indicating that this procedure is the first of one or more to be executed in the program.

The DECLARE statement for INAREA is a record description to set up an area to hold information from the input card. Alphanumeric fields such as NAME and UNUSED (the blank area) are specified as

Concepts of Computer Programming

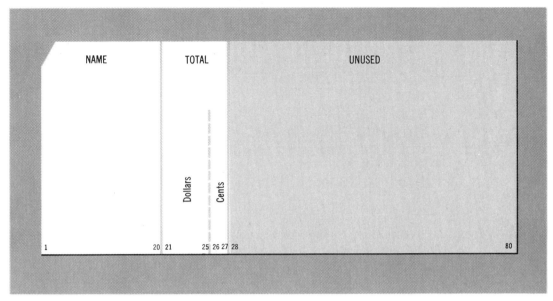

Figure 12.6
Output card format for sample program 2.

CHARACTER fields with their relative number of positions denoted in parentheses. The three numeric fields have PICTURE specifications as in COBOL. UNIT_PRICE consists of two integer and two decimal positions. QTY is a three-position integer field. DISC_AMT is a five-position numeric field with an implied or assumed decimal point after the first three positions.

Note that the 1 following the word DECLARE represents the record description level, comparable to 01 in COBOL. The fields that follow are on the 2 level, which indicates that they are contained within the record and that they are independent items. To denote a last name and first name contained with NAME, for example, the entries would be altered as follows:

```
DECLARE 1 INAREA,
        2 NAME,
        3 LAST_NAME CHARACTER (15),
        3 FIRST_NAME CHARACTER (5),
```

The output record description in SAMPLE PROGRAM 2 consists of a NAME and TOTAL field and of an UNUSED portion at the end of the card.

The DECLARE statements that follow essentially indicate the names of the input and output files, and the fact that they will appear in record rather than stream format. The OPEN statement activates the card reader and the card punch. The statement ON ENDFILE (CARDIN) GO TO ENDJOB is an end-of-file test. When there are no more input cards to process, the program will branch to ENDJOB.

The READ statement reads an input record into the input record area called INAREA.

Since there are two fields called NAME, one in the input area and one in the output area, the NAME field must be *qualified,* or further described when a reference is made to it. We say:

OUTAREA. NAME = INAREA. NAME

to make the move of NAME from the input area to the output area.

You will recall that this expression, as in FORTRAN, sets the first field (NAME of OUTAREA) equal to the contents of the second field (NAME of INAREA). That is, the contents of the input NAME field is moved to the output NAME field.

The arithmetic expression that follows is the formula given in the problem definition. Here, again, we can see the similarity to FORTRAN.

The WRITE statement takes the contents of OUTAREA and punches a card record from it. Then a branch to BEGIN occurs and the process is repeated.

ENDJOB is the label to which a branch occurs only on an end-of-file condition. The devices are then deactivated and the procedure is terminated.

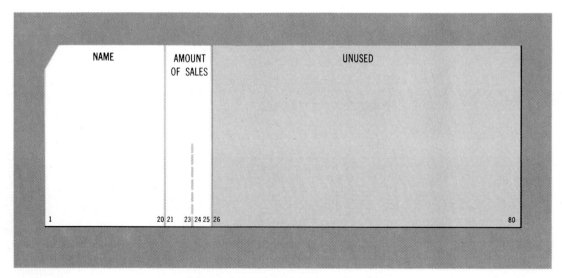

Figure 12.7
Input card format for sample program 3.

Concepts of Computer Programming

C. SAMPLE PROGRAM 3

This is a print program that utilizes heading and detail records. The input record is as indicated in Figure 12.7.

The output format is indicated in the print layout sheet in Figure 12.8.

To utilize various printer options in PL/1, we must use stream-oriented output. Thus the statement:

DECLARE OUTFIL FILE OUTPUT PRINT ENVIRONMENT (MEDIUM . . .);

implies the attribute of STREAM automatically by *default* since we have utilized the attribute PRINT.

1. DECLARE Statements
Thus we specify:

DECLARE 1 INAREA

with the corresponding record description entries as in previous examples. We do not, however, have to specify such entries for the output area. Since data is printed in STREAM format, our output is printed by merely indicating a PUT command in conjunction with the fields we wish to print. Since COMM (commission) is a storage field that we wish to print, we must give it a specification. To produce a field called COMM in storage in fixed-point format with five positions, including two decimal positions, we have:

DECLARE COMM FIXED (5,2);

Our first few entries, then, appear as follows:

```
EX3: PROCEDURE OPTIONS (MAIN);
DECLARE 1 INAREA,
           2 SALE_NAME CHARACTER (20),
           2 AMT_OF_SALES PICTURE '999V99',
           2 UNUSED CHARACTER (55);
DECLARE COMM FIXED (5,2);
DECLARE CARDIN FILE INPUT RECORD ENVIRONMENT
       (CONSECUTIVE F(80)MEDIUM (SYS005,2540)),
        OUTFIL FILE OUTPUT PRINT ENVIRONMENT
       (MEDIUM (SYS007,1403) F(133));
```

2. OPEN Statements
In conjunction with our OPEN statement for the print file, we may generally include the following options:[3]

[3] *Note that some PL/1 compilers do not allow the LINESIZE option.*

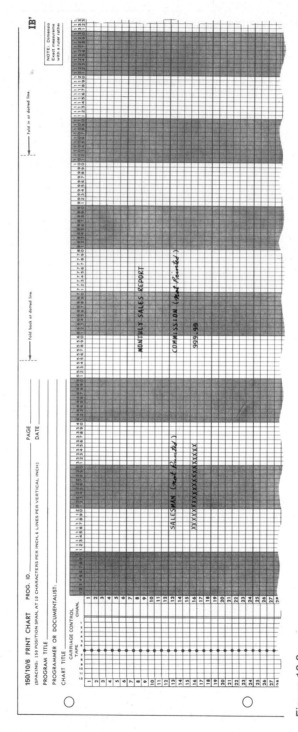

Figure 12.8
Output format for sample program 3.

a. PAGESIZE, denoting the number of lines we wish to print on a single page. PAGESIZE (50), for example, will cause the printing of 50 lines per page. You will recall that most forms allow a maximum of 70 lines per page. If PAGESIZE is *not* included as part of the OPEN statement, then by default, 60 lines will typically be printed on each page.

b. LINESIZE, denoting the number of characters we wish to print on a single line. LINESIZE (133), for example, will cause the printing of 132 characters, including spaces, per line, and allow one position (the first) for carriage control purposes. Printers range in their capability generally between 100 and 132 characters per line. If LINESIZE is not included as part of the OPEN statement, then, by default, 120 characters, including spaces, typically will print on each line.

Thus the following OPEN statement allows 40 lines per page and 132 characters per line (plus one for carriage control):

OPEN FILE (OUTFIL) PRINT LINESIZE (133) PAGESIZE (40);

3. PUT Statements

To print the data on each line we must use the STREAM format. Thus we do not have to establish a DECLARE statement for our output area. We use the PUT EDIT command in conjunction with the specific data to be printed. PUT EDIT commands specify data fields and literals to be printed, *together with* their corresponding formats.

a. Headings. To print a literal or a heading, we use the PUT EDIT command together with the literal and its specification, with the literal enclosed in quotes:

PUT FILE (OUTFIL) EDIT ('MONTHLY SALES REPORT') (A(20));

This indicates that we wish to write the literal MONTHLY SALES REPORT, a 20-position alphanumeric field. This command will result in the printing of MONTHLY SALES REPORT beginning in the *first* column of the print area, however, not in the 57th position as indicated in the Print Layout Sheet in Figure 12.8.

To properly space the data so that 56 blanks are inserted at the beginning of a line, we amend our specification to read:

PUT FILE (OUTFIL) EDIT ('MONTHLY SALES REPORT') (COLUMN (57), A(20));

The COLUMN (57) specifies that the data (MONTHLY SALES REPORT) must begin in column or print position 57 and the A(20) following it indicates that the data is 20 characters in length. Thus the COLUMN option is used to indicate in which print position we wish to start the data.

The following two options are also available with the printing of headings.

OPTION 1: PAGE to be used whenever we wish the data to print on a new page. Since headings usually are to print, beginning on a new page, we further amend our specification to read:

PUT FILE (OUTFIL) PAGE EDIT ('MONTHLY SALES REPORT') (COLUMN (57), A(20));

OPTION 2: LINE or SKIP, to be used whenever we wish to print on a specific line (LINE option) or whenever we wish to skip a specified number of lines prior to printing. LINE (3) indicates that we wish to print the data on the third printing line. SKIP without parentheses following it indicates that we wish to skip to the *next* line.

Thus the printing of our heading will be coded as follows:

PUT FILE (OUTFIL) PAGE LINE (8) EDIT ('MONTHLY SALES REPORT') (COLUMN (57), A(20));

The literal MONTHLY SALES REPORT is to print on a new page (PAGE option), on the eighth print line (LINE option) beginning in the 57th print position (COLUMN option) and it is an alphanumeric field of 20 characters (A(20)).

b. Detail lines. For printing out detail lines, the PUT EDIT command will appear as follows:

PUT FILE (OUTFIL) SKIP EDIT (SALE_NAME, COMM) (COLUMN (16), A(20), COLUMN(57), F(6,2));

The two fields SALE_NAME and COMM are to print on each line. SALE_NAME is to print beginning in print position 16 and is 20 characters in length. COMM is to print beginning in print position 57 and will occupy six positions, including a decimal point with two digits to the right.

Now that we have resolved the changes necessary for printed output, we are ready to code the entire PL/1 program.

```
EX3:     PROCEDURE OPTIONS (MAIN);
         DECLARE 1 INAREA,
                     2 SALE_NAME      CHARACTER (20),
                     2 AMT_OF_SALES   PICTURE '999V99',
                     2 UNUSED         CHARACTER (55);
         DECLARE COMM FIXED (5,2);
         DECLARE CARDIN FILE INPUT RECORD ENVIRONMENT
            (CONSECUTIVE F(80) MEDIUM (SYS005, 2540));
         DECLARE OUTFIL FILE OUTPUT PRINT ENVIRONMENT (MEDIUM
            (SYS007,1403) F(133));
         OPEN FILE (CARDIN);
         OPEN FILE (OUTFIL) PRINT LINESIZE (133) PAGESIZE (40);
         ON ENDFILE (CARDIN) GO TO LAST;
         PUT FILE (OUTFIL) PAGE LINE (8) EDIT
            ('MONTHLY SALES REPORT') (COLUMN (57), A(20));
BEGIN:   READ FILE (CARDIN) INTO (INAREA);
         IF AMT_OF_SALES <= 50.00 THEN COMM = 00.00;
         IF AMT_OF_SALES > 50.00 THEN IF AMT_OF_SALES <= 100.00
            THEN COMM = .02 * AMT_OF_SALES;
         IF AMT_OF_SALES > 100.00 THEN
            COMM = .03 * AMT_OF_SALES;
WRITE:   PUT FILE (OUTFIL) SKIP EDIT (SALE_NAME, COMM) (COLUMN (16),
            A(20), COLUMN (57), F(6,2);
         GO TO BEGIN;
LAST:    CLOSE FILE (CARDIN), FILE (OUTFIL);
         END EX3;
```

SELF-EVALUATING QUIZ

1. PL/1 is an abbreviation for _____ .
2. PL/1 basically combines the advantages of _____ .
3. PL/1 is an ideally suited language for companies that utilize a programming staff for both _____ and _____ applications.
4. (T or F) PL/1, unlike COBOL or even FORTRAN, is a free-form language.
5. (T or F) A specially designed PL/1 coding sheet is not necessary.
6. Every PL/1 program begins with a(n) _____ statement and ends with a(n) _____ statement.
7. The END statement indicates that _____ .
8. An OPEN statement _____ .
9. The statement: NAME_1 = NAME_2 performs a _____ .
10. The above statement has the same significance in the _____ language.
11. The purpose of a CLOSE statement is to _____ .
12. Printed output is always created using the _____ format.
13. Many I/O statements in PL/1 are coded in a manner similar to I/O statements in _____ , while calculations are performed in a manner similar to those in _____ .

SOLUTIONS

1. Programming Language One
2. FORTRAN and COBOL
3. commercial; scientific
4. T
5. T
6. PROCEDURE; END
7. there are no more steps to be executed in the procedure
8. activates the files
9. MOVE operation: NAME_2 is transmitted to NAME_1
10. FORTRAN
11. deactivate the files
12. STREAM
13. COBOL; FORTRAN

Concepts of Computer Programming

Chapter 13 *Introduction to BASIC Programming*

I. The Nature of BASIC

You will recall that data communications equipment, such as terminals, is often used by small companies and colleges for *time-sharing*. That is, several users share time on a computer by keying in simple programs and input on a terminal and receiving computer-produced results.

Such programs must be simple and easy to code, since most terminal keyboard devices are *not* ideally suited for high-speed interaction with the computer. Since terminals require manual operation, the programming language used must be simple in order to facilitate the coding.

BASIC is the programming language ideally suited for terminal processing in a time-sharing environment. It is a very simple programming language, as indicated by the name BASIC—an abbreviation for *Beginner's All-purpose Symbolic Instruction Code*. This language allows a user to communicate with the computer in a conversational mode. That is, a conversation or dialogue can be carried on between the terminal operator and the computer.

Time-sharing applications are ideally suited for:

1. Engineering applications, when individual engineers or mathematicians have access to terminals. In this way, they can

write simple programs to solve complex mathematical equations. The computer can perform the operations in seconds while the procedures performed manually would otherwise require hours of calculations.

BASIC is most often used by engineers or mathematicians in a time-sharing environment, since it contains simple mathematical notation, similar to that used in FORTRAN.

2. College campuses, where the cost of acquiring large-scale computers is sometimes prohibitive. Terminals are used as programming tools to train student programmers and business majors in the requirements of a program. That is, students can use the terminals for writing and executing simple programs.

BASIC is an ideally suited language for training programmers since it is relatively simple to learn and it is written in a conversational mode.

3. Businesses, where the business representatives or managers have access to terminals for the purpose of writing and/or running simple programs to extract data from computerized files. Where the programming staff is overburdened, there is a real advantage to training business leaders to write simple programs for extracting data, with the use of a terminal.

Here, again, BASIC, because of its simplicity, is often taught to business leaders. In this way, they can access central files with the use of a terminal and the BASIC language.

Terminals with keyboards require keying effort to communicate with the computer. Since such effort is relatively time-consuming for the professional, BASIC was designed to require minimum coding or keying. Instructions and data formats are simple and require less programming effort than in most other languages. Similarly, BASIC was not designed to handle sophisticated routines that are required in other languages. Thus, this language may be learned in a relatively short time.

BASIC can be regarded as a simplified version of FORTRAN, similar to the latter in format but without all of the intricate or sophisticated options. Both languages utilize mathematical notation and, as such, are generally regarded as scientific in nature. But, like FORTRAN, BASIC may be used effectively for simplified business applications. In addition, FORTRAN and BASIC are ideally suited for business applications where mathematical or scientific logic is appropriate, such as forecasting and graph plotting.

Note that the programmer communicates *directly* with the computer when coding on a terminal in BASIC. Since such programs are almost always short and simplified, they often contain *data* as well as *instructions*. That is, programs in most other languages are usually written so that they can be run by the operations staff in periodic intervals with voluminous input. A Payroll program written in COBOL, for example, will be implemented so that it may be run on a monthly basis with a large number of records. When a programmer, scientist, or businessman codes a BASIC program on a terminal, it is often a "one-shot" job. That is, a simple BASIC program is coded merely to obtain an output listing and *not* to be run periodically. It also requires minimal input since the keyboard device is far too slow to transmit a voluminous amount of data.

Note, however, that BASIC can be run on a computer *without* the use of a terminal. Thus a program in BASIC can be compiled and translated and utilized for periodic runs in the same manner as COBOL or FORTRAN programs, although it is not commonly used for this purpose.

Prior to coding the problems illustrated in the previous chapters, we shall first illustrate sample problems that are ideally suited to coding in BASIC.

II. *Illustrative BASIC Programs*

A. SAMPLE PROGRAM 1

Consider the problem of an engineer who wishes to compute the following:

$$(3.1416) \times (2.7)^{10}$$

Although he can easily compute the result himself, such calculations may be time-consuming. In addition to requiring valuable time of the engineer, such calculations lend themselves to errors. Manual methods for performing mathematical operations often produce erroneous results.

With the use of a terminal and the BASIC language, the engineer, in a fraction of a second, can write a two-line program to produce the result, with little chance of error:

```
10   PRINT (3.1416) * (2.7) ↑ 10
20   END
```

Fundamentally, the engineer is using the computer as a high-speed calculator. He keys in the two lines, waits approximately 0.5 seconds, and then receives the correct response from the computer.

Notice that the BASIC language is similar to FORTRAN. Mathematical operations are coded with symbols, as shown below.

↑ or **	Exponentiation (depending upon the computer)
*	Multiplication
/	Division
+	Addition
−	Subtraction

Note, also, that there was no input for the above problem. The input fields were part of the program itself.

Every instruction in a BASIC program must have a numeric line number, such as 10 for line 1, 20 for line 2, etc. as in the above. Every BASIC program must end with an END statement to signal the computer during the execution phase that there are no more instructions to execute.

B. SAMPLE PROGRAM 2

Suppose that an engineer or businessman wishes to compute a Centigrade temperature from a Fahrenheit temperature, for each of 10 Fahrenheit temperatures. The equation for this computation is as follows: $C = 5/9 \, (F-32)$. Here, again, the professional can perform the calculations himself, but often these are time-consuming and not always error-free.

Let us consider the BASIC program that can perform the calculations:

```
100   INPUT F
110   LET C = (F − 32) * 5/9
120   PRINT "CENTIGRADE:"; C
130   GO TO 100
140   END
```

The engineer or businessman who has programmed the above need only key in the quantities required.

An executed INPUT statement causes the computer to *request* the keying in of some input quantity. That is, an INPUT statement causes a question mark to *print,* in order to signal the programmer that he must key into the terminal some quantity. In response to the question mark, the programmer or user must key in a quantity which permits the program to continue, utilizing the quantity supplied.

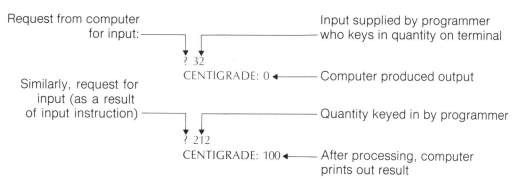

Request from computer for input:

Input supplied by programmer who keys in quantity on terminal

? 32
CENTIGRADE: 0 ◄——— Computer produced output

Similarly, request for input (as a result of input instruction)

Quantity keyed in by programmer

? 212
CENTIGRADE: 100 ◄——— After processing, computer prints out result

The engineer or businessman may continue, in this way, until he obtains all Centigrade temperatures required.

Note that all instructions in the above program have numeric line numbers. Let us discuss each instruction separately:

1. The first instruction, line 100, is basically a read command. When the program is executed, or run, the computer will request a quantity when the INPUT instruction is executed. The first quantity to be keyed into the terminal will be transmitted to the variable or field called F. Note that all variables in BASIC are represented by a single alphabetic character or an alphabetic character followed by a digit: A5, B7, for example. A field that contains alphanumeric data, such as a Name field, is represented by an alphabetic character followed by a dollar sign: A$, N$, for example. These field names are designed for simplicity and ease of keying.

2. LET is the BASIC word for the performance of an arithmetic operation. We merely use the given equation and the mathematical symbols to calculate a result. Thus C is made equal to the product of $(F-32)$ by $5/9$. The following would be equally correct:

110   LET C = 5/9 * (F−32)

There are no physical requirements for spacing or punctuation in BASIC, adding to the relative simplicity of the language. As many spaces as the programmer deems appropriate can be left between words, or even characters. The following:

110   L   ET   C=(F−32)   *   5   /9

is equally correct, although not as readable.

The second instruction performs the required operations, substituting for F the quantity that is entered as input, and then placing the result in the field called C.

3. The PRINT statement causes the literal *CENTIGRADE:* to print along with the contents of C. That is, to print any literal or *constant,* we enclose it in quotation marks. To print any *variable,* on the same line as a constant, we place the variable name within the same PRINT statement.

Thus 120 PRINT "CENTIGRADE:"; C results in the printing of:

CENTIGRADE: (the contents of C)

If we had, instead, coded:

120   PRINT "CENTIGRADE:"
125   PRINT C

We would have obtained:

CENTIGRADE:
(the contents of C)

That is, we would have obtained the word CENTIGRADE on one line and the contents of C on the next.

4. The GO TO 100 instruction is a branch that causes the program to be repeated, beginning with the instruction at line number 100.
5. An END statement must be the last one in a BASIC program to signal the compiler of the end of the source program.

Suppose we wish to skip a line after each Centigrade temperature, to facilitate reading. The following alteration will produce the printing of a *blank line* after each Centigrade temperature.

```
100   INPUT F
110   LET C=(F−32) * 5/9
120   PRINT "CENTIGRADE :"; C
130   PRINT
140   GO TO 100
150   END
```

Line 130, when executed, results in a blank line printing. Thus, the results may appear as follows:

```
?32
CENTIGRADE: 0

?212
CENTIGRADE: 100
```

Suppose, also, we wish to identify the Fahrenheit temperatures. That is, the printing of a question mark may not be enough to identify the input required. If the word FAHRENHEIT were to print in addition to the question mark, the data to be entered is more clearly defined. To achieve this we simply insert a print statement, prior to the input command:

```
100   PRINT "FAHRENHEIT"
110   INPUT F
120   LET C=(F−32) * 5 /9
130   PRINT "CENTIGRADE:"; C
140   PRINT
150   GO TO 100
160   END
```

The first two instructions will cause the following to print on the terminal:

```
FAHRENHEIT
?
```

You will recall that the question mark prints to signal the programmer that a quantity must be keyed in. Thus the resultant terminal data becomes more meaningful:

FAHRENHEIT
?32
CENTIGRADE: 0

FAHRENHEIT
?212
CENTIGRADE: 100

FAHRENHEIT
?98.6
CENTIGRADE: 37

Note that the above program has no end-of-job routine. Theoretically, the number of values that may be entered for F, Fahrenheit temperature, is infinite. We can, however, cancel the program at anytime by pressing the appropriate keys on the terminal according to the manufacturer's specifications.

We can also use a special input code to signal the end.

```
100    PRINT "FAHRENHEIT"
110    INPUT F
115    IF F=999 THEN 160
120    LET C=(F−32) * 5/9
130    PRINT "CENTIGRADE:"; C
140    PRINT
150    GO TO 100
160    END
```

Statement 115 is a *conditional* statement. If the variable or field called F is equal to 999, then a branch to the statement numbered 160 is executed.

To key in 999 for F is an end-of-job signal that causes the program to come to a *programmed halt*. Using a *coded number* for an end-of-file test, as above, is the established method for reaching an end-of-job condition in BASIC.

In place of the INPUT command, we may *READ* in the quantities as part of the program:

```
110    READ F
115    IF F=999 THEN 160
120    PRINT "CENTIGRADE:"; C
140    PRINT
150    GO TO 110
155    DATA 32, 121, 98.6, −40, 999
160    END
```

412   *Concepts of Computer Programming*

The READ statement, instead of the INPUT statement, allows the data to be entered as part of the program in a DATA statement; thus only the Centigrade figures will appear as output. That is, there will be no *requests* from the computer for INPUT; no question marks will print. The major advantage to the READ and DATA statements is that they can also be used in a nonteleprocessing environment. Keyboard terminals would not be required; the program may be punched into cards or some other medium. With the INPUT command, the programmer *must* utilize a terminal interface.

A distinct asset of BASIC programming in a time-sharing environment is that the program may be *corrected* from the keyboard anytime after it has been keyed. Thus the programmer is not required to wait for his source deck to be keypunched and then compiled in the traditional way before he obtains a listing of errors. Instead, he keys in the program, which is immediately compiled, and he receives a listing of errors, if any, in a matter of seconds.

If the programmer notices an error after a line has been keyed, or the computer prints a message during compilation that signals an erroneous line, the programmer need only retype that line, *using the same* line number. The new line, with the same number, will replace the previous one.

C. SAMPLE PROGRAM 3

In Chapter 9, we have seen a COBOL program that creates a tape from employee cards. The employee cards have the format indicated in Figure 13.1.

The tape has the format indicated in Figure 13.2 where WEEKLY-WAGES = HOURS-WORKED × HOURLY-RATE.

A simple BASIC program used in a data communications environment cannot usually accept card input nor can it create tape output unless the terminal system contains a card reader as input and a tape drive as output. Usually only a keyboard terminal serves as an input/output device. We will, then, examine a BASIC program that reads data as in Figure 13.1 from a *terminal,* determines WEEKLY-WAGES (W) and prints the result on the same terminal:

```
100   INPUT N$, H, R
105   IF H = 99 THEN 999
110   LET W = H * R
120   PRINT N$, H, R, W
130   GO TO 100
999   END
```

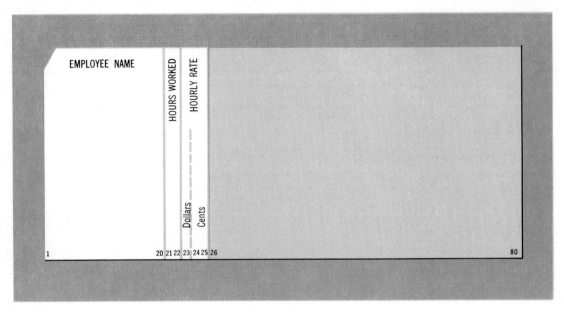

Figure 13.1
Input card format for sample program 3.

Notice that the BASIC program has significantly fewer steps than the COBOL program. However, although coding is simplified in BASIC, the form of input and output is severely limited.

In the above program, the terminal operator must key in Name (N$), Hours Worked (H) and Rate (R) for each employee. The results would then be printed again on the terminal device. Note that the rate, R, may be keyed in *with* the decimal point. For example, 1.25 is a valid entry for Rate; that is, the decimal point is coded rather than implied or assumed, as in COBOL or RPG.

A 99 keyed in as Hours Worked is used as an end-of-file signal. In the above program, we utilize the INPUT command rather than the

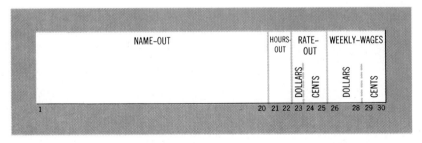

Figure 13.2
Output tape format for sample program 3.

Concepts of Computer Programming

READ statement, since we wish to enter data *after* the program has been entered and compiled. Usually the terminal operator will key such input from source documents. The READ statement, if used, would require that the data be entered as part of the program.

Note that this program would not be used in conjunction with a terminal device if large amounts of input were required. Fast I/O processing is not a characteristic of data communications.

D. SAMPLE PROGRAM 4

In chapter 9 we have seen a COBOL program that creates a tape with Customer Name and Transaction Amt from Sales Record Cards with the format indicated in Figure 13.3.

Transaction Amt on the output tape is equal to the Unit Price multiplied by the Quantity, minus the Discount Amt.

We will now consider a BASIC program that performs the same operations, but which utilizes the terminal to key in input and to print output:

```
100  INPUT N$, U, Q, D
110  IF Q = 999 THEN 150
120  LET T = U * Q - D
130  PRINT N$, T
140  GO TO 100
150  END
```

N$ is customer name, U is unit price, Q is quantity, D is discount amount.

The four fields are read in from the terminal as input. If Q = 999 this signals an end-of-file condition. Thus any quantity fields for normal

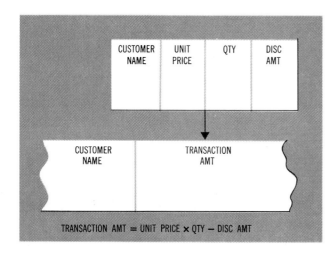

| CUSTOMER NAME | UNIT PRICE | QTY | DISC AMT |

| CUSTOMER NAME | TRANSACTION AMT |

TRANSACTION AMT = UNIT PRICE × QTY − DISC AMT

Figure 13.3
Input and output formats for sample program 4.

processing must not be equal to 999. T, the Total, is computed by multiplying unit price by quantity and subtracting the discount amount. Then Customer Name and the Total are printed and the steps are repeated. Thus processing will continue until a coded quantity field with 999 signals an end of job.

E. SAMPLE PROGRAM 5

In chapter 9, we have seen a COBOL program that prints Salesman Name and Amount of Commission from a card record with Salesman Name and Amount of Sales. Amount of Commission is: 3% of Sales Amount for Sales Amount in excess of $100; 2% of Sales Amount for Sales Amount between $50 and $100; and, zero for Sales Amount less than $50.

In this program, a print heading was also indicated.

Here, again, we will examine a BASIC program that performs the same operations but utilizes the terminal for the input and output operations.

```
100   PRINT "MONTHLY SALES REPORT"
110   INPUT N$, A
120   IF A = 999.99 THEN 220
130   IF A > 100.00 THEN 180
140   IF A > 50.00 THEN 200
150   LET C = 00.00
160   PRINT N$, C
170   GO TO 110
180   LET C = A * .03
190   GO TO 160
200   LET C = A * .02
210   GO TO 160
220   END
```

N$ is Salesman Name and A is Amount of Sales.

Note that the symbol > is used to represent "IS GREATER THAN." That is, in step 130, if A (AMOUNT OF SALES) is greater than 100.00, then a branch to statement 180 is executed, where Commission (C) is calculated as 3% of Sales. If A is not greater than 100.00 but is greater than $50.00 (between 50 and 100), then Commission is calculated as 2% of Sales. Otherwise Commission is zero. Name and Commission are the two output fields.

In short, BASIC is a simple programming language that may be used for scientific or business applications. Businessmen can learn BASIC in a relatively short time and can employ it to access data from centralized computer files, using terminals in a time-sharing environment. BASIC is considered such a simple language that it is employed by many colleges utilizing terminals that have access to a computer, for the purpose of teaching the concepts of programming.

416   *Concepts of Computer Programming*

SELF-EVALUATING QUIZ

1. BASIC is the programming language ideally suited for
   _____ processing in a _____ environment.
2. (T or F) BASIC may be regarded as a simplified version of
   FORTRAN.

Consider the following BASIC program for questions 3 to 15:

```
10   READ H,R,X
20   IF H=99 THEN 60
30   LET W= (H*R) +(X*1.5*R)
40   PRINT " WEEKLY WAGES IS $ "; W
45   GO TO 10
50   DATA 40, 4.86, 22
52   DATA 35, 3.25, 15
54   DATA 38, 6.35, 40
56   DATA 10, 4.36, 15
58   DATA 99, 99, 99
60   END
```

H represents regular hours worked
R represents hourly rate
X represents overtime hours

3. The number of hours worked for the first calculation is obtained
   from the _____ statement and is _____ .
4. The rate for the first calculation is obtained from the _____
   statement and is _____ .
5. The overtime hours for the first calculation is obtained from the
   _____ statement and is _____ .
6. (T or F) Every statement must have a line number.
7. The line number for the second instruction is _____ .
8. The DATA statement in conjunction with the READ command
   enables data to be entered _____ .
9. The IF statement is used as a(n) _____ .
10. The 1.5 in statement 30 is used to denote _____ .
11. The asterisk in statement 30 is used for the operation of
    _____ .
12. The formula represented in statement 30 is _____ .
13. The quotation marks in the PRINT statement are used for
    _____ .
14. The first line of printing will contain _____ .
15. (T or F) An END statement is required as the last statement in a
    BASIC program.

SOLUTIONS

1. terminal (data communications); time-sharing
2. T
3. DATA; 40
4. DATA; 4.86
5. DATA; 22
6. T
7. 20
8. as part of the program
9. end-of-file test
10. time-and-a-half for overtime
11. multiplication
12. (regular hours $\times$ rate) + ($1\frac{1}{2} \times$ rate $\times$ overtime hours)
13. literals or constants
14. WEEKLY WAGES IS $ 354.78
15. T

Chapter 14 *Software: Control and Optimization of Computer Capability*

Thus far, we have seen not only what constitutes a computer system but also how the computer can be instructed through the use of various programming languages. As was discussed previously, it is important that the businessman and, obviously, the computer specialist be cognizant of the current state of the art in data processing. This knowledge will allow the businessman to effectively communicate his information processing needs to data processing personnel. In companies without data processing facilities, it is often the business leaders in conjunction with key computer specialists who assume the responsibility for directing the acquisition of computer equipment and the hiring of computer personnel. It is therefore essential that both the businessman and the computer specialist possess a working knowledge of how the computer functions and of the various features that provide for the optimization of its capability.

We have seen that HARDWARE is the term used to denote those devices within a computer system that can be used to accept input or produce output. We discussed recent advances in HARDWARE in order to familiarize the student with the equipment available. In this chapter, we shall discuss SOFTWARE, or those programs usually supplied by the computer manufacturer that are designed to achieve maximum utilization of the computer. SOFTWARE includes those programs (such as compilers, assemblers, etc.) that are universally used and that facilitate the programmer's task. Although most software

Concepts of Computer Programming

is obtained from the computer manufacturer, there are *SOFTWARE houses* that develop packaged applications which are sold to computer users. *Facilities Management Companies* is the current term used to describe Software Houses.

With an appreciation of the nature of software, the student will thus be in a position to understand:

1. How computer operations are controlled so that programs can be processed at tremendous speeds without any loss of information.
2. The types of resources, in terms of software, that often go untapped in companies.
3. How the programmer can minimize his effort, when there are programs available that can perform the tasks he desires.

I. The Control System

We have already seen that a typical CPU (Central Processing Unit) can be portrayed, in its simplest state, as shown in Figure 14.1.

A. THE SUPERVISOR

The *supervisor,* sometimes called a *monitor,* is a special program usually supplied by the manufacturer, which is always stored within the CPU, in third-generation computers. That is, a supervisor resides in core storage for the purpose of controlling the operations of the computer. The supervisor is part of a larger control system that is typically stored on a high-speed input/output device such as a tape or disk. This control system is part of the software supplied by the manufacturer. The supervisor must be *loaded* into core storage each day prior to any processing. It, then, calls in each program and extracts items, as needed, from the control system. That is, if a program needs to be compiled, the supervisor calls in the corresponding compiler. If a complex input/output function is required

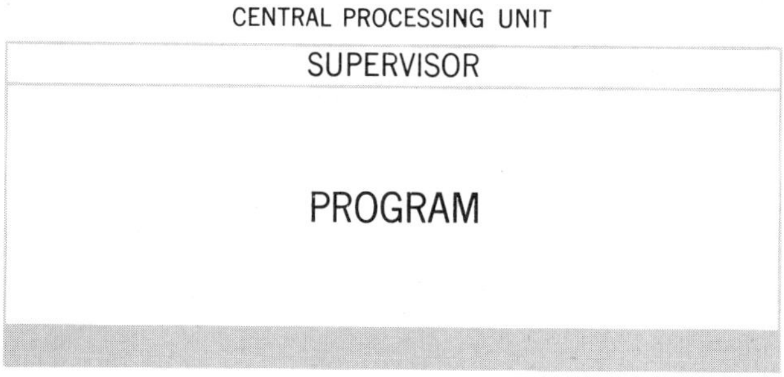

CENTRAL PROCESSING UNIT

SUPERVISOR
PROGRAM

Figure 14.1
The supervisor and the program within the CPU

Software: Control and Optimization of Computer Capability

for the program, the supervisor accesses the control system and calls the appropriate routines into core storage. Thus the supervisor controls the operations of the computer. When the end of a program is reached, for example, the supervisor calls in the next one.

B. THE OPERATING SYSTEM

The control system that is typically stored on a high-speed device such as tape or disk for accessibility, is sometimes referred to as an *operating system*. For many computer systems, where a modified operating system is stored on disk, it is referred to as DOS (*Disk Operating System*), and when it is stored on tape, as TOS (*Tape Operating System*).

The supervisor permits the computer to operate essentially without manual intervention in real-time applications as well as time-shared or multiprogrammed applications. A brief discussion of the major functions of the supervisor should help reassure the student that the computer is rigorously controlled and governed. It is thus an extremely remote possibility that the computer itself would malfunction and cause errors to go undetected. There are special circuits within the CPU which check to see if information put into the computer is inadvertently altered or destroyed by a machine malfunction. If information has been so destroyed, the supervisor will automatically interrupt operations. The manufacturer must then send its engineers to fix the equipment. When errors in final output do occur, they are usually traceable to data processing personnel and/or the businessman who have in some way misunderstood or improperly communicated all requirements of the particular problem that was programmed.

Up to this point, we have seen that the major steps involved in writing and running a program generally include keypunching the program, and then putting the source deck into the computer to be translated by a special program called a compiler or an assembler, depending on the language of the source program. Several points should be made here so that the student is fully aware of computer capabilities.

First, all third-generation commercial computers are capable of handling source programs written in several different languages. It is quite common, for example, to have a computer that can process source programs written in COBOL, FORTRAN, PL/1, ASSEMBLER Language, and RPG. Some of the smaller business computers can process only a few languages, often simply ASSEMBLER languages, RPG, and perhaps FORTRAN. Regardless of the specific combination of languages available, each machine must have available a translator, either a compiler or an assembler, for *each* language that it can translate into machine language.

The compilers and assemblers are typically located on a high-speed input/output medium such as a disk. When a source program is read into the computer, to be translated, the supervisor will

Concepts of Computer Programming

bring into the CPU the appropriate compiler or assembler to perform the translation. (The specific manner in which the supervisor recognizes which compiler or assembler is required will be discussed later in this chapter.) The diagram in Figure 14.2 will clarify the points just made for the case where a COBOL source program is entered into a system capable of handling many languages. The illustration shows what typically happens if the program is successfully translated.

C. STORING PROGRAMS ON A LIBRARY

Figure 14.2 shows the process involved if we take a source program, successfully translate it, and leave the object program in the CPU to be run immediately thereafter. There is one basic problem with this type of processing. Suppose a programmer has written a Payroll program in COBOL that will be run weekly. Once the source program has been debugged and can be successfully translated, it would be a waste of computer time to take the same source deck and have it translated each time the program is to be run. That is, once a working object program has been created, the translation process is no longer

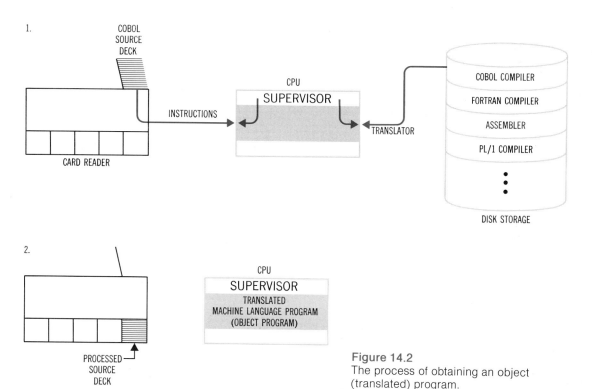

Figure 14.2
The process of obtaining an object (translated) program.

required. There are several methods for making the process more efficient. For example, once the program is successfully translated, the programmer could request the supervisor to have the object program punched onto cards by the computer. This object deck would then be fed into the computer each week and processed directly, thus eliminating the need for superfluous translation each time. This process is shown in Figure 14.3.

Although the technique just explained is more efficient than retranslating a working source program each time, there is an even better way of storing an object program that eliminates the need of having to physically take the object program in the form of an object deck and feed it into the CPU. That is, the supervisor can take a working object program and store it on a high-speed input/output device, such as disk, along with other object programs. Then, whenever a particular program is required, the supervisor can easily retrieve that specific program from the *library* of programs stored on this input/output device. The diagram in Figure 14.4, utilizing disk storage, illustrates this concept.

We have seen thus far that the supervisor plays an important role in the processing of programs by:

1. Bringing the appropriate translator into the CPU to translate a source program.
2. Typically, storing successfully translated programs in a library of programs on a high speed input/output medium such as a disk.

D. MULTIPROGRAMMING

The illustrations throughout this chapter have shown only the supervisor and *one* program in the CPU at any given time. A third-generation computer, however, usually has the control capability of allowing the simultaneous processing of more than one program at a given time in the same CPU. This is referred to as *multiprogramming*, which is an essential and integral feature necessary for time-sharing and data communications applications.

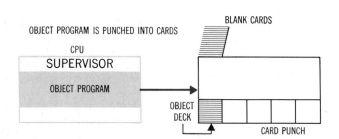

Figure 14.3
Obtaining and using an object deck.

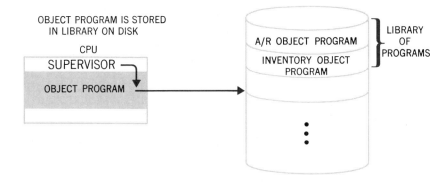

OBJECT PROGRAM IS STORED
IN LIBRARY ON DISK

SUPERVISOR RETRIEVES OBJECT PROGRAM FROM LIBRARY

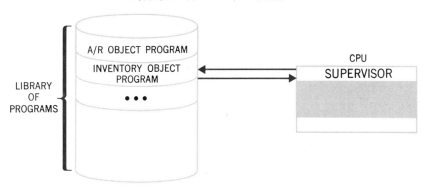

Figure 14.4
Storing an object program and then retrieving it.

Multiprogramming can be illustrated in the following manner. We will examine the situation where there are two programs in the CPU to be processed, as shown in Figure 14.5.

A computer traditionally performs input/output operations much slower than processing operations. Thus, in previous generation computers, much processing time is wasted while the CPU waits for read or write commands to be executed. Multiprogramming enables a computer with a sophisticated supervisor to interleave programs in

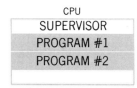

Figure 14.5
Two programs within the CPU

such a way that when an I/O operation is being performed for one program the CPU can perform the arithmetic or logic operations of another. Note, however, that the control process must be very complex and high level to permit the computer to effectively switch from one program to another.

Suppose at some particular point in program 1, there is an instruction to read in a punched card. Let us assume that the reader in this system can read at the rate of approximately 1000 cards per minute. This means that it will take at least 0.001 min (or 0.06 sec) to read one card. In this same time period required to perform *one* input/output (I/O) function, a typical commercial computer could, for example, perform more than 300 additions of six-digit numbers. Suppose, at the time program 1 is reading a card, arithmetic operations of program 2 can be performed. Then both programs can operate simultaneously without loss of time since, they will, in essence be utilizing different circuits within the CPU. After program 1 has finished its I/O operation, the next instruction might be an arithmetic one. It may be that, at this point, program 2 is ready to perform an I/O operation, such as read a tape. Assuming that the system has only one card reader, it might appear that an I/O operation in program 2 could not include the card reader as an input device, since this device is currently being used by program 1. However, this is not a problem, since card input data for program 2 might first be converted to another medium by the computer, thus enabling data to be processed in a multiprogramming environment.

The illustration in Figure 14.6 will help dramatize the major advantage of multiprogramming.

In essence, then, a program is not necessarily run continuously by itself from beginning to end in a computer capable of handling multiprogramming. If it were, then while a particular I/O operation were being performed, the rest of the computer would be idle. It is common to hear of computer systems being *I/O bound;* that is, the operations of the computer are hampered because of the extremely slow input/output processing that inhibits the rapid processing of non-I/O functions, such as arithmetic operations.

The student should be aware that many computer systems can operate in a multiprogramming environment. This results in the overall completion of programs in far less time then if they were stacked, where one program is executed completely, then another.

Thus there is great advantage to computers with a multiprogramming capability. Note, also that time-sharing and data communications systems, where programs and their corresponding input are entered from terminals at remote locations, *must* be used in conjunction with computers that have the ability to handle multiprogramming. In this way, several programs keyed in by terminals can be interleaved and processed quickly enough to provide each user with the required output in a relatively short time.

The illustration just discussed shows only two programs running

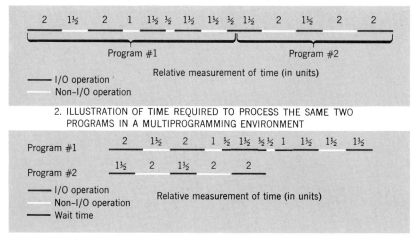

1. ILLUSTRATION OF TIME REQUIRED TO PROCESS TWO PROGRAMS IN A NON-MULTIPROGRAMMING ENVIRONMENT

2   1½   2   1   1½ ½ 1½ 1½ ½ 1½   2   1½   2   2

Program #1   Program #2

Relative measurement of time (in units)

—— I/O operation
—— Non-I/O operation

2. ILLUSTRATION OF TIME REQUIRED TO PROCESS THE SAME TWO PROGRAMS IN A MULTIPROGRAMMING ENVIRONMENT

Program #1   2   1½   2   1 ½ 1½ ½ ½ 1   1½   1½   1½

Program #2   1½   2   1½   2   2

—— I/O operation
—— Non-I/O operation   Relative measurement of time (in units)
—— Wait time

Figure 14.6
Illustration showing the major advantage of multiprogramming.

"simultaneously" in a multiprogramming environment. However, it is quite possible on many business computers to have *four* or more programs in the CPU being processed at essentially the same time.

It should be noted that the supervisor has an important function of scheduling programs that are run in a multiprogramming system. For example, suppose that there are two programs brought into the CPU at essentially the same time and both happen to have arithmetic instructions at the beginning. If one program is for Payroll, and the other is for Accounts Receivable, for example, which one should have priority? The supervisor can be directed to assign different priorities to different programs. In the above example, it might be that, based on the businessman's requirements, priority numbers have been assigned to programs, as follows: Payroll—9; Accounts Receivable—8; Sales Forecasting—7; and so on, where programs with the largest numbers have the highest priorities. Thus Payroll programs are of higher priority than Accounts Receivable programs. Therefore, whenever there is a situation in a multiprogramming environment where two or more programs require the same circuits in the CPU, the supervisor will process them in priority order, according to their preestablished priority ratings.

Priorities can also be assigned in some computer systems in such a manner that more important programs, when read by the computer, can interrupt other processing and thus receive the first order of preference. Thus an Inventory program with priority of 9 will be run before any programs with lower priority.

We have thus seen some of the major functions of a typical

supervisor which, as part of the software, can control and schedule the operations of programs within the computer. We will now proceed to discuss some of the other aspects of software that help to control and optimize the computer's capability.

II. Sort/Merge and Other Utility Programs

Thus far we have discussed compilers, assemblers and control systems as part of software. The student should also be aware of certain commonly used programs, called *utility programs,* that are usually supplied by the computer manufacturer to facilitate the efficient processing of operations. These operations include such things as the sorting of data and the transferring of data from one I/O device to another. Since the programs to perform these standard operations have already been supplied, they can be accessed immediately. In many cases, what may seem to a businessman to require complex programming effort is, in reality, a simple process because of the existence of the types of software mentioned above. The programmer need only supply a set of specifications indicating the type of processing required, and the utility program will then perform the operations.

A. THE SORT/MERGE PROGRAM

Typically, a sort/merge program is available that will, for example, take an input file of records and rearrange or sort them in a different sequence. This program also provides for the merging of two separate files into one file. The input files that can thus be processed can usually be on such devices as tape or disk.

The typical sort/merge program can accomplish more than just the sorting or merging of records. As an example, a Payroll file on tape could be sorted and the fields in the records rearranged, as shown in Figure 14.7.

The merging of files can easily be illustrated through the use of a specific type of update procedure in a Payroll system, where records for new employees are *added* and those for former employees are *deleted*. This is shown in the diagram in Figure 14.8, where we see the old Payroll file on tape, the new records along with those to be deleted on a separate tape (with appropriate codes for add or delete), and the resultant new Payroll file on tape.

The sort/merge program is typically stored in the library of programs that can be accessed by the supervisor and brought into the CPU. The supervisor must usually be supplied with certain specifications to inform the sort/merge program as to (a) the device on which the input is located; (b) the device where the resultant file should be placed; (c) the control field that will be used for sorting or merging of the records; (d) the type of sort involved (numeric,

Concepts of Computer Programming

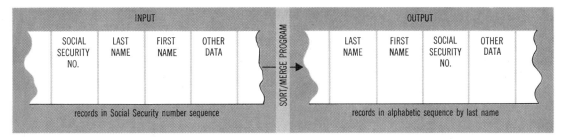

Figure 14.7
An application of the sort/merge program.

alphanumeric), as required; (e) any special modifications to records, such as the rearrangement of fields, the addition or deletion of records and so on.

B. OTHER UTILITY PROGRAMS

Frequently, data must be transferred from one I/O device to another. As an example, in many companies, data is first keypunched on cards and then fed into the computer where the information is stored on magnetic tape or a direct-access medium such as disk for future

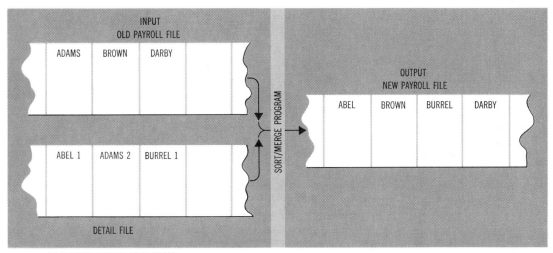

#1 DENOTES RECORDS TO BE ADDED
#2 DENOTES RECORDS TO BE DELETED

Figure 14.8
The use of the sort/merge program in a Payroll System.

high-speed processing. Likewise, it is often necessary to transfer a file for backup purposes. For example, an Accounts Receivable file on disk may be duplicated on tape, just in case the disk file should be inadvertently lost or damaged. Many times, a file will be transferred from a particular I/O device to the printer, so that a businessman can see what information is stored in that file. These types of operations are so common, that the manufacturer usually supplies programs, called utility programs, that will typically handle the operations indicated in Figure 14.9.

As with the sort/merge program, utility programs are usually stored in the library of programs and can thus be accessed by the supervisor and brought into the CPU.

The typical operating system, which includes a library of programs, is usually stored on a direct-access device such as disk, and thus can be pictured as indicated in Figure 14.10.

III. Communications Between the Control Program and Data Processing Personnel

As we have already seen, the supervisor controls the operations of the computer, allowing it to operate with minimal manual intervention. This is particularly important for real-time and time-sharing applications. We will illustrate below some of the common instances in which communications take place between the supervisor and the programmer or the operator.

A. THE PROGRAMMER AND THE SUPERVISOR

In our previous discussions, we have indicated that it is very common to have:

1. A source program read into the computer where it is translated (compiled or assembled).
2. The resultant object program then stored on a high-speed I/O medium, such as disk, or punched out onto cards.

For a source program processed in this manner, it is necessary for the programmer to give the supervisor such information as:

1. The language of the source program, so that the appropriate translator (compiler or assembler) for that language can be brought into the CPU by the supervisor from the library of programs.
2. Where the object program should be placed. That is, whether the object program should be stored in the library of programs or on a deck of cards, for example.
3. Identification of the program, so that if it is placed in the library it can be retrieved subsequently by that identification. In addition, if the computer system is operating in a multiprogramming

Concepts of Computer Programming

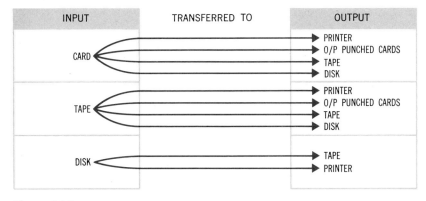

INPUT	TRANSFERRED TO	OUTPUT

Figure 14.9
Sample operations that can be performed by utility programs. (The term disk
is utilized here to represent any direct-access file.)

environment, the supervisor can thus maintain control of each
program by its specific identification.

One way that the programmer can inform the supervisor of the
above type of information is to use certain *job control cards* in
conjunction with the source deck, as shown in the diagram in Figure
14.11.

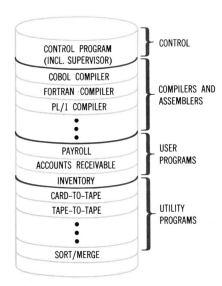

Figure 14.10
Example of typical programs stored on
magnetic disk.

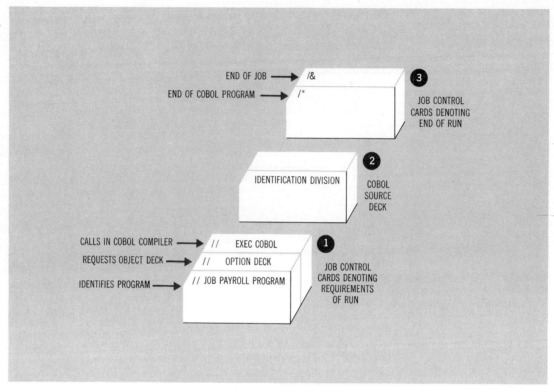

Figure 14.11
Example of job control cards used with a COBOL source deck to produce an object deck.

Note that the job control cards in Figure 14.11 indicate to the supervisor what operations the programmer wants the computer to perform on his COBOL source deck. The illustrated job control applies to a specific computer (IBM S/360). Note that although job control on all computers can accomplish similar tasks, the specifications may be slightly different.

The illustration in Figure 14.12 indicates how a programmer can direct the supervisor to:

1. Translate a COBOL Accounts Receivable program; and, if the translation is successfully achieved,
2. Execute the resultant object program in the CPU, running it with test data supplied by the programmer.

Similarly, if the programmer wants to direct the computer to use a sort/merge program, a card-to-tape utility program, or a user program

Concepts of Computer Programming

that is already in the library, the appropriate job control statements must be read into the computer to direct the supervisor. Thus, any operation that the programmer requires of the computer must be indicated by job control messages to the supervisor.

The various computer manufacturers have their own types of job control statements for communicating with the supervisor. Since there

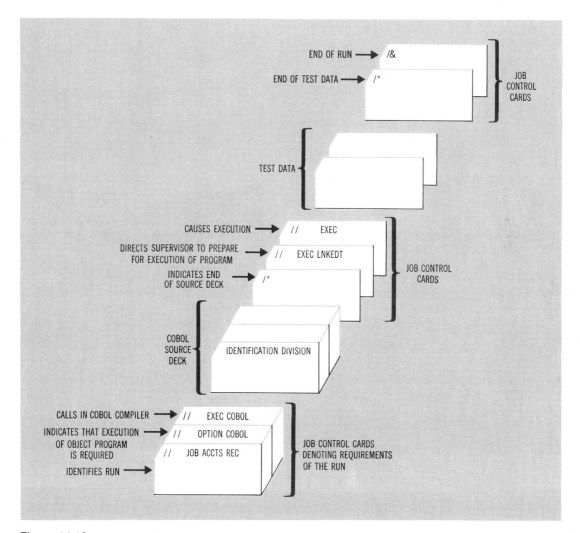

Figure 14.12
Example of job control cards used with a COBOL source deck to direct supervisor to translate and run program.

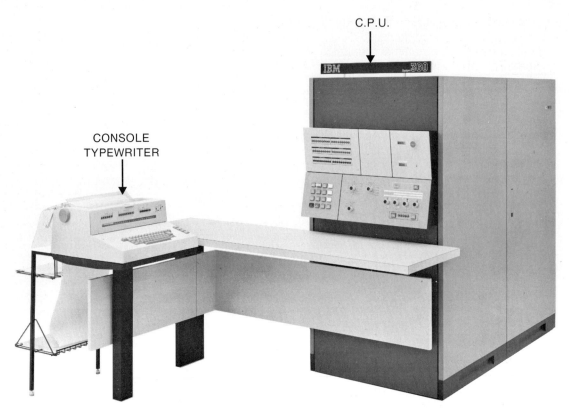

Figure 14.13
Console typewriter and CPU. Courtesy IBM.

are usually many job control statements to choose from, these statements are commonly thought of as comprising a job control *language* (JCL) by itself. JCL cards are an integral part of all computer runs.

B. THE COMPUTER OPERATOR AND THE SUPERVISOR

Although third-generation computers are designed to operate with minimal operator intervention, occasions do arise when the supervisor will request the operator to perform certain tasks. A common way for the supervisor to communicate with the operator is for it to print out its requests on a *console typewriter,* such as the one shown in Figure 14.13.

The supervisor may direct the operator to perform various tasks, such as typing in the current date on the console typewriter in the morning, so that the date of the run can appear on listings produced on the printer that day. Likewise, the operator may, for example, be requested to mount a specific tape file required for the processing of a specific program.

In addition, various errors may occur during the control or processing of a program which may require operator intervention. The supervisor will then request the operator to key in, on the console typewriter, what action should be taken. Suppose, for example, that a tape has labels which are not appropriate for the specific run; the operator can type in "ignore" if the error is not considered serious, or "cancel" if the job is to be aborted.

Frequently the operator will direct the supervisor to perform various jobs either through the use of job control instructions, as indicated previously, or through the use of messages typed on the console typewriter.

Additional Features to Optimize Computer Utilization

The student should also be aware of some special control features that are commonly found on third-generation computers and that are implemented by the supervisor.

A. THE TIMER

One of the features is the use of a *timer,* or clock, within the CPU that can be used to supply statistics on computer usage. With this timer, the control program can provide figures that will show, for example, the distribution of computer use by each department within the company. That is, each application and the time it takes to process it is logged for reference purposes. This can be of particular interest to the businessman, since, in many companies, computer usage is "charged" to each department that requires it for processing. In such an environment, the businessman might want to carefully review his data processing needs before he arbitrarily requests various outputs from the computer.

The timer is also of use to the programmer, since it provides him with an indication of the efficiency of each program. The programmer frequently analyzes the time it takes to run a program, and if such time is excessive, he can attempt to simplify the logic in order to reduce processing time.

It is thus possible to employ the results of the timer to achieve a more efficient utilization of the computer.

B. STORAGE PROTECTION

We have seen that it is common for more than one program to be in the computer at one time. The student might be concerned about the possibility that one program, if incorrectly coded, could inadvertently destroy or modify parts of another program and its corresponding data that are in the computer at the same time. This danger might arise especially when a new program is being tested.

To avoid this potential problem, a storage protection feature is generally available for third-generation computers which is managed by the control program. The businessman and computer specialist might therefore want to inquire as to whether such a feature has been incorporated in his company's computer to insure that files of data and programs are not inadvertently invalidated.

The primary purpose of this chapter has been to show the student how different types of software are employed to control the computer's operations and to help optimize its utilization. The student should now be able to understand and appreciate such data processing terminology as:

a. The Supervisor
b. Multiprogramming
c. The Library of Programs
d. The Sort/Merge Program
e. Utility Programs
f. Job Control Statements
g. The Timer
h. Storage Protection

Such features are an integral part of most computer systems but are frequently not used properly because of lack of knowledge on the part of the computer staff or because of malfunctions of the manufacturer-supplied equipment and/or the software.

The responsibility of selecting a new computer system or evaluating a current one often falls to the businessman and the computer specialist. They must, then, be cognizant of all the above features so that they can understand how computer systems can effectively employ them.

SELF-EVALUATING QUIZ

1. The term _____ denotes those programs usually supplied by the computer manufacturer that are designed to achieve maximum utilization of the computer.
2. _____ are those organizations that develop packaged applications which are sold to computer users.
3. The _____ is another name for the control program.
4. (T or F) The supervisor always resides in core storage for the purpose of controlling computer operations.
5. The control system is also referred to as a(n) _____ .
6. The purpose of a supervisor is to _____ .
7. The compilers and assemblers used with a computer are typically located on high-speed devices such as a _____ and are accessed by the _____ .
8. Working object programs are usually placed on a _____ for access by the supervisor.
9. The control program also enables more than one program to be run simultaneously within the computer, a concept referred to as _____ .
10. The Sort/Merge program is called a(n) _____ .
11. The typical operating system is usually stored on a _____ .
12. The programmer communicates with the supervisor with the use of _____ cards.
13. The computer operator communicates with the supervisor and accesses a program by using the _____ .
14. A(n) _____ within the CPU can be used to supply statistics on how long it takes to run programs.
15. Storage Protection is a term used to prevent _____ .

SOLUTIONS

1. software
2. Software Houses or Facilities Management Companies
3. supervisor
4. T
5. operating system
6. control the operations of the computer
7. direct-access device; supervisor
8. library
9. multiprogramming
10. utility program
11. direct-access device
12. job control
13. console typewriter
14. timer
15. accidental access by the programmer of a critical or reserved area of storage

Chapter 15 *Common Programming Techniques Used in Business Applications*

I. EDITS

    A. TYPES OF EDIT PROGRAMS
        1. Edits Prior to Master File Creation
        2. Edits Prior to Updates or File Maintenance
           Routines
    B. OUTPUTS FROM AN EDIT PROGRAM
        1. A Validated File
        2. An Error List
    C. TYPES OF EDIT TESTS
        1. Field Test
        2. Code Test
        3. Sequence Test
        4. Missing Data Test
        5. Check Digit Test
        6. Limit Test

II. UPDATES OR FILE MAINTENANCE ROUTINES

    A. TYPES OF UPDATES
        1. Online
        2. In a Batch-Processing Environment
    B. TYPES OF FILES UTILIZED IN FILE MAINTENANCE
        ROUTINES
        1. Master File
        2. Detail File
        3. History File
        4. Table File

III. FILE CLEANUPS
IV. UTILITY PROGRAMS

    A. SORTING OF FILES
    B. MERGING OF FILES
    C. CARD-TO-TAPE OR CARD-TO-DISK PROGRAMS

Thus far we have discussed the steps involved in obtaining computer output and the various programming languages that may be employed to produce that output.

Businessmen, as we have seen, must work closely with programmers to insure that the resultant program performs all required operations, tests for all possible conditions, and produces the necessary output.

There are several programming procedures that are common to many business applications. That is, the typical businessman and computer specialist will find that specific routines apply to many different business systems. Since these procedures are relatively common, they are frequently incorporated in most programming applications. In this chapter, we will discuss:

I. EDITS—The process of testing input data to determine if it is valid and, if it is not, to either reject it or substitute valid information.
II. UPDATES OR FILE MAINTENANCE ROUTINES—The process of adding information to a master data file to make it current.
III. FILE CLEANUPS—The process of deleting extraneous or unused records from a master file, while validating current information.
IV. UTILITY PROGRAMS—The process of employing packaged or prewritten programs to handle common procedures.

Concepts of Computer Programming

In most business applications, a *master* or primary data file must be created and maintained that contains all pertinent and necessary information. It is this file that is used to answer inquiries and supply output reports. Each record on the file must be accurately maintained and periodically *updated*, to insure that its content is current. Information used to update a master file must be valid or it will produce errors in master records that will result in inaccurate reports. Thus the information used to update a master file must be validated in an *EDIT* procedure.

Similarly, a master file must be "*cleaned up*" or purged periodically to insure that obsolete or unused data does not influence the output.

We will consider each of these procedures *independently* and in a general *context*. Note that a Payroll edit in a specific company may differ from an Accounts Receivable edit, but basically, some general rules apply. It is these rules that we shall discuss. Note, too, that an entire program may incorporate one *or more* of these procedures. A typical program may include both an edit and an update or it may be strictly an update program.

Figure 15.1 illustrates a sample system that incorporates the indicated procedures. It is a *systems* flowchart and thus contains some symbols that differ from those utilized in a program flowchart. Systems Flowcharts are discussed in Chapter 17.

Note that several computer runs, such as CREATION OF A MASTER FILE (step 2) and CREATION OF OUTPUT (step 5) are *not* included as typical routines in our discussion. Creation of a Master File (step 2) after editing is typically performed by a *utility* or packaged program. A card-to-tape utility, for example, will create a master tape file from card records in any format specified by the programmer on specification cards. This shall be discussed under UTILITY Programs. Step 5, Creation of Output, varies considerably from one system to another. One system produces lists of data in a report, while another creates only totals. There are few techniques, if any, that can be considered standard in this phase and thus we shall omit this step from our general discussion.

I. Edits

A. TYPES OF EDIT PROGRAMS

An edit procedure is the process of validating a file of data to insure that records do not contain obvious omissions, inconsistencies, or errors. Errors in files are relatively common because of (a) source document errors made by departmental employees; and, (b) conversion errors made by operations personnel in keypunching data onto cards, keying data onto tape, keying data into a terminal, and so on.

The common edit procedures are performed during the following phases.

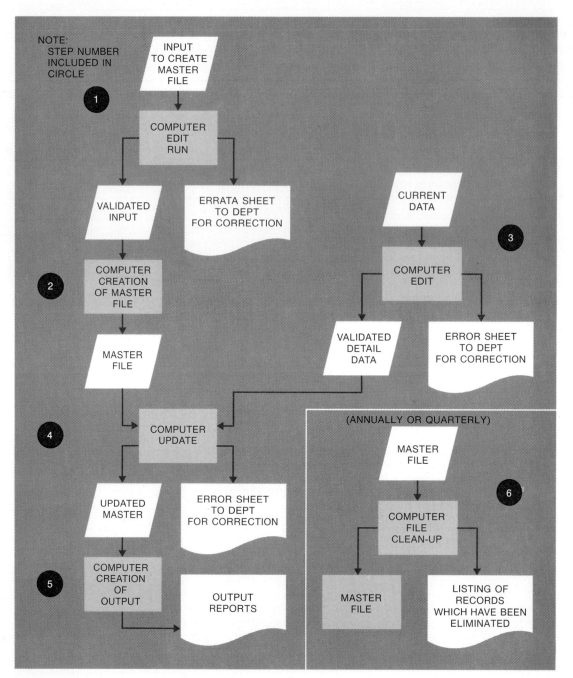

Figure 15.1
Systems flowchart of typical business procedures.

1. Edits Prior to Master File Creation
   (Step 1 in Figure 15.1)

When a new system is designed, a master file that will contain all pertinent data and will be used for all output operations, must be created. This is a "one-shot" program. That is, once the program successfully creates a master file it need not be used again. The master file is then maintained and updated using file maintenance routines. Such a master file creation is usually performed by a utility program (card-to-tape, card-to-disk, etc.).

   Since the master file is usually the most important file in a system, it must be created with as few errors as possible. Thus an edit operation is generally required prior to master file creation to insure relatively accurate recording.

2. Edits Prior to Updates or File Maintenance Routines
   (Step 3 in Figure 15.1)

We revise a master file with update or *file maintenance* routines. Before altering a master file, however, we must attempt to insure that the *change* or *detail records* contain as few errors as possible. Thus an edit operation is generally required prior to updating a master file, to insure that the data used to alter the master file is relatively accurate.

B. OUTPUTS FROM AN EDIT PROGRAM

Outputs to be discussed from an Edit program are: (1) a validated file and (2) an error listing.

1. A Validated File

This file will contain as few errors as possible. Any clearly erroneous data will either be rejected or corrected, if possible, depending on the system's requirements. Note that a validated file may simply be all input records minus the erroneous ones. This is the typical procedure with card data. For other types of files, a validated file may be a newly created one containing all valid input records and some erroneous records with incorrect fields zero-filled or blank-filled. Similarly, an edit procedure may utilize card input, for example, and create a validated tape as output.

   Note that it is not possible to validate *all* data. Without additional information, for example, it would not be possible to determine if an employee record with a birth date of 08/50 is valid or not. However, we can determine if such a date falls within proper limits. That is, the month is a valid number if it is between 01 and 12; and the year is valid if it is greater than 08 (there are no employees older than 65 and we are assuming a present year of 73: $73 - 08 = 65$) but less than 55 (there are no employees younger than 18).

   To validate a file, it is sometimes necessary to utilize another file, such as a table file, to compare against input data and to insure relative accuracy.

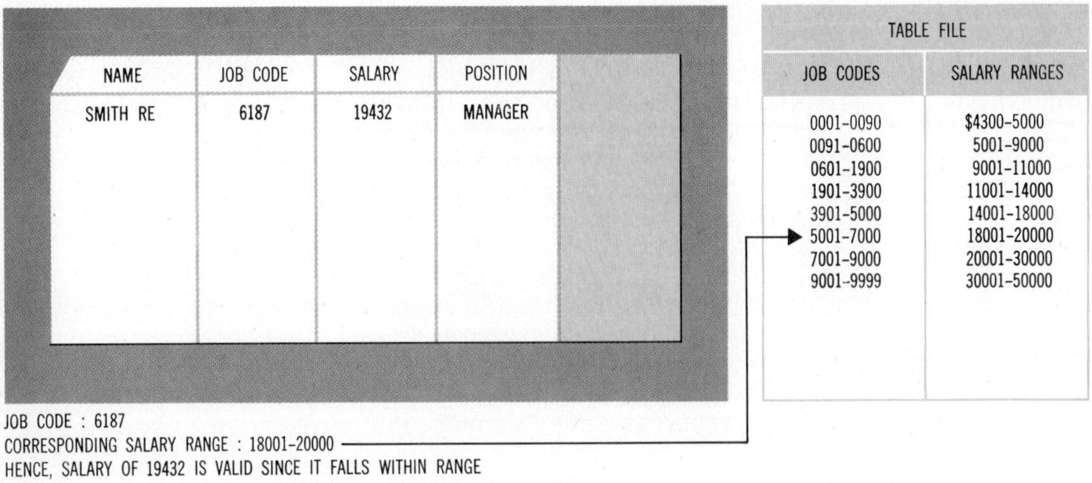

TABLE FILE	
JOB CODES	SALARY RANGES
0001-0090	$4300-5000
0091-0600	5001-9000
0601-1900	9001-11000
1901-3900	11001-14000
3901-5000	14001-18000
5001-7000	18001-20000
7001-9000	20001-30000
9001-9999	30001-50000

NAME	JOB CODE	SALARY	POSITION
SMITH RE	6187	19432	MANAGER

JOB CODE : 6187
CORRESPONDING SALARY RANGE : 18001-20000
HENCE, SALARY OF 19432 IS VALID SINCE IT FALLS WITHIN RANGE

Figure 15.2
Example of validating routine to determine if salary on card is consistent with job code.

For example, a Payroll Record may contain a job classification code together with an annual salary. It may be necessary to read a table file with job codes and their corresponding salary ranges. Thus, in the edit procedures, we can test to determine if the Payroll Record contains an annual salary that is within the established range for the given job code (see Figure 15.2).

Table files are often used in conjunction with edit programs to assist in validating input information.

2. An Error List

This is sent to the corresponding department so that errors may be subsequently corrected. This error list should clearly and concisely specify every error condition and the corresponding action taken. It should also indicate totals so that the percentage of errors or error rate can be determined.

C. TYPES OF EDIT TESTS

Keep in mind that the specific edit procedures required for an application are supplied by the programmer or analyst and are verified by the businessman. Typical edit procedures include the tests indicated in Figure 15.3.

1. Field Test

This is used to determine if specific data fields have valid formats, with regard to:
    (a) Class—numeric or alphabetic.
    (b) Sign (if numeric)—positive or negative.

Concepts of Computer Programming

An amount field, for example, on an input record must be numeric. If it is not, then an error on input has occurred, and unless the field is corrected or omitted, erroneous processing will occur. In some programming languages, an arithmetic operation performed on numeric fields that erroneously contain nonnumeric data will cause a program interrupt.

All numeric fields in an input record should be checked to determine if, in fact, they contain strictly numeric data. Erroneous coding of source documents or encoding (that is, keypunching) can produce errors. A blank for example, is *not* valid in a numeric field. Depending on the nature of the numeric field, we may *reject* an erroneously coded numeric field or we may simply fill it with zeros on the validated file (if the validated file is an output form from the edit procedure). If, for example, an ACCOUNT NUMBER field contains nonnumeric data and this is the key field on the master file, then we must reject the record.

Similarly, some fields such as NAME, DESCRIPTION, CITY should contain only alphabetic data. The edit routine should check to determine that they do, in fact, contain strictly alphabetic data. Here, again, we may reject records with erroneously coded alphabetic fields or we may simply fill the field with spaces. If the edit procedure does not create a new output file, then error records must be rejected.

Some numeric fields may contain a sign, while others require strictly unsigned data. This must also be tested.

You will recall that a sign is usually placed in the low-order or units position of a numeric field, together with the low-order digit, as indicated in Chapter 3. An AMOUNT field, for example, may contain a sign, but a QUANTITY field generally does not.

In short, the format of input records must be edited to insure accuracy. The programmer and the businessman work closely to determine what constitutes an error. Where an input record contains an erroneous format, the record may be rejected or, if possible, appropriate revisions may be made. For example, invalid numeric fields may be replaced with zeros, *when such fields are not absolutely critical for processing.* If a numeric field such as AMOUNT or QUANTITY or EMPLOYEE NUMBER is not coded with numeric data, then the entire record would generally be rejected since such fields are usually required for any significant processing.

2. Code Test

This test is used to determine if a coded field is valid; it can sometimes be performed with no other inputs required. Sometimes, however, it necessitates the use of a table file for comparison purposes.

EXAMPLE 1

Suppose we have a sales record with the format indicated in Figure 15.4.

Suppose, too, that there are currently 5 branch offices, coded 1 to 5. An edit program should incorporate a routine to determine if the field called BRANCH contains a number from 1 to 5. If it does not, an error

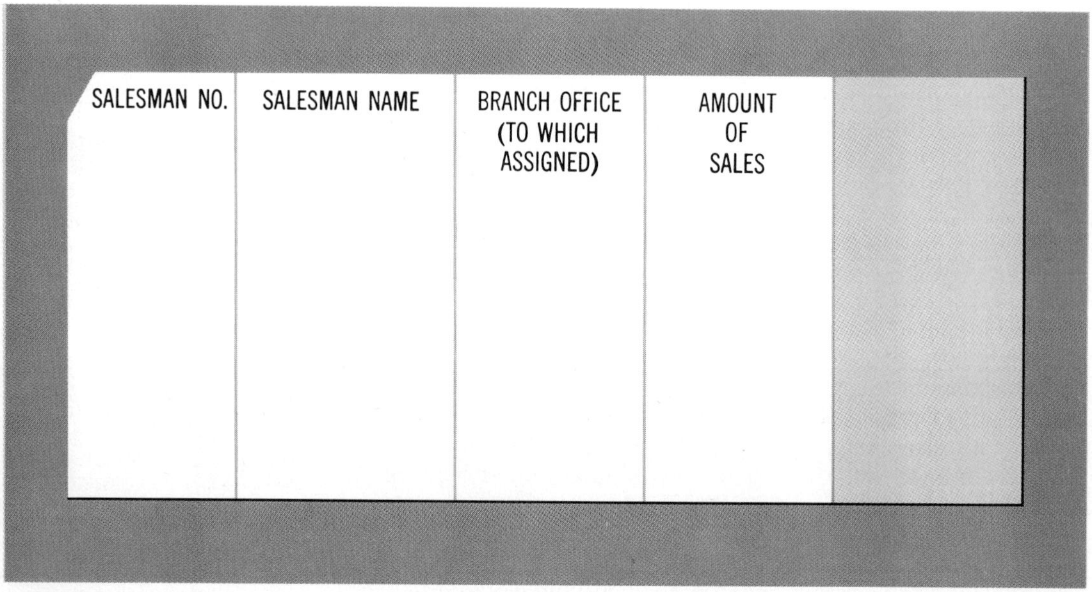

SALESMAN NO.	SALESMAN NAME	BRANCH OFFICE (TO WHICH ASSIGNED)	AMOUNT OF SALES	

Figure 15.4
Format of sales record.

446

condition must be noted. Either the record will be rejected because branch office is a key field, or the field will be flagged as erroneous, so that a future correction can be made.

EXAMPLE 2

Suppose we wish to validate ACCOUNT NUMBER on an Accounts Receivable File. Each customer is assigned an ACCOUNT NUMBER by the Accounts Receivable Department. There are currently 980 Accounts within the company, numbered 0001 to 0980.

We could write a procedure to insure that ACCOUNT NUMBER is between 0001 and 0980. This would require no additional input. However, it would not be a reliable or advisable test, since the program would require revision as soon as more accounts were added to the Accounts Receivable file.

Instead, a routine could be coded in the program to determine, for example, if the assigned ACCOUNT NUMBER is valid for a specific branch. Suppose the Accounts Receivable Department has assigned account numbers to branch offices according to Table 1.

Two possibilities exist here:

Table 1

Account Number	Branch
0001–0106	1
0107–0198	2
0199–0275	3
0276–0392	4
0393–0487	5
0488–0610	6
0611–0724	7
0725–0842	8
0843–	9

a. *The table remains constant*.

That is, the ranges of account numbers remain the same for each branch office. This is possible only if the Accounts Receivable Department periodically deactivates specific customers and assigns the corresponding ACCOUNT NUMBER to a new customer. If, for example, ACCOUNT NUMBER 0102 has not transacted any business in three years, this may be sufficient grounds for deactivating that account and reassigning the number to a new customer in branch office 2. In this way, the ranges of ACCOUNT NUMBERS and their corresponding branch offices remain constant.

If the table remains constant, then the corresponding figures may be used *within the program itself, as constants.*

Assume that ACCOUNT-NUMBER and BRANCH are input fields. This routine in COBOL may appear as below. Note that the symbol "<" means "less than" and ">" means "greater than".

```
IF ACCOUNT-NUMBER IS NOT NUMERIC OR NOT POSITIVE
        GO TO ERROR-1.
IF ACCOUNT-NUMBER < 0107 AND BRANCH = 1
        GO TO EDIT2.
IF ACCOUNT-NUMBER < 0199 AND BRANCH = 2
        GO TO EDIT2.
IF ACCOUNT-NUMBER < 0276 AND BRANCH = 3
        GO TO EDIT2.
            ⋮
IF ACCOUNT-NUMBER > 0842 AND BRANCH = 9
        GO TO EDIT2. GO TO ERROR-2.
```

We first test to insure that ACCOUNT-NUMBER is numeric and positive. If not, then it has been erroneously coded and an error condition must be indicated. Then we test the ACCOUNT-NUMBER for the proper ranges for each BRANCH. If the range is proper we proceed to the next Edit test, EDIT2, otherwise we go to ERROR-2.

b. *The table varies.*

When changes to a table occur frequently, it is better programming form to read in the table each time as part of the program and provide a routine to determine if the input ACCOUNT NUMBER and BRANCH are consistent, using the *variable entries* in the table as a comparison.

This routine would require a *table look-up,* a procedure whereby a table is read into storage and used for comparison to determine if a specific condition is met.

```
IF ACCOUNT-NUMBER IS NOT NUMERIC OR NOT POSITIVE
        GO TO ERROR-1.
IF ACCOUNT-NUMBER < TABLE-ENTRY-1 AND BRANCH = 1
        GO TO EDIT2.
IF ACCOUNT-NUMBER < TABLE-ENTRY-2 AND BRANCH = 2
        GO TO EDIT2.
            ⋮
IF ACCOUNT-NUMBER > TABLE-ENTRY-8 AND BRANCH = 9
        GO TO EDIT-2.
```

EXAMPLE 3

Suppose we have an Accounts Payable record with the format indicated in Figure 15.5.

Concepts of Computer Programming

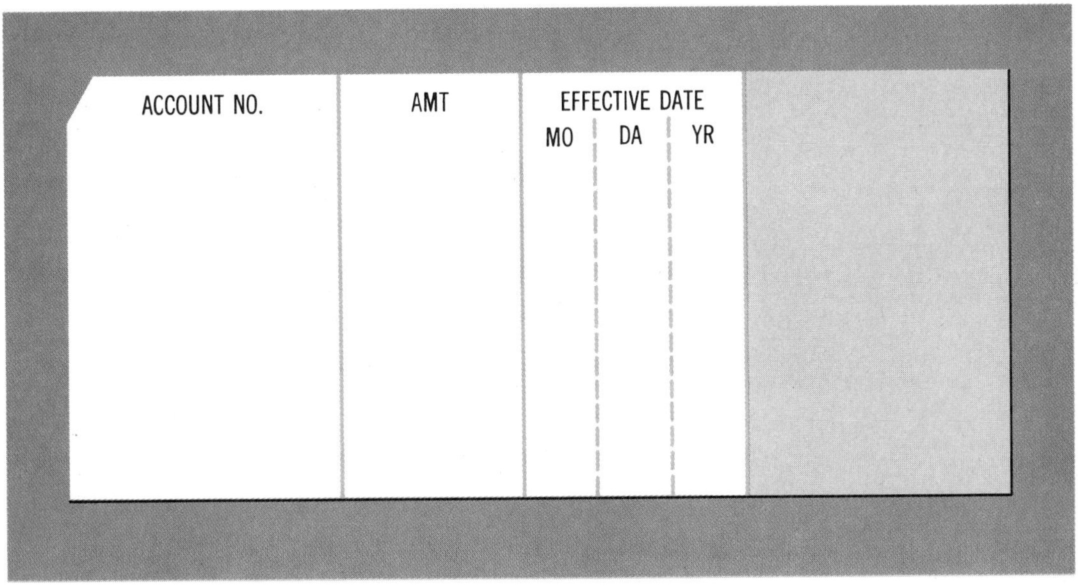

Figure 15.5
Example of Accounts Payable record.

When the company receives merchandise, the invoice data is keyed into the record described. EFFECTIVE DATE is the date on which the merchandise was received.

Each week we run an edit to determine if EFFECTIVE DATE contains a valid month, day, and year. This field in an Accounts Payable System is critical, since it is used to determine whether a discount can be taken if the company pays the bill within a specific period of time.

Often the edit routine incorporates a procedure for determining, for example, if EFFECTIVE DATE is relatively current. That is, we can determine if EFFECTIVE DATE is within one month of the run date. If the EFFECTIVE DATE is not relatively current, this may denote an error; that is, the field may have been erroneously coded as 12/01/70 instead of 12/01/73.

The computer operator prepares a card with the month, date, and year of the current run. If the EFFECTIVE DATE is any date *more recent than the previous month* (month before RUN MONTH), but not any date beyond the present month, it is considered valid. That is, if current run date is 12/30/73, then any date more recent than 11/30/73 is considered valid.

The following procedure in COBOL may help to illustrate the point (see Figure 15.6).

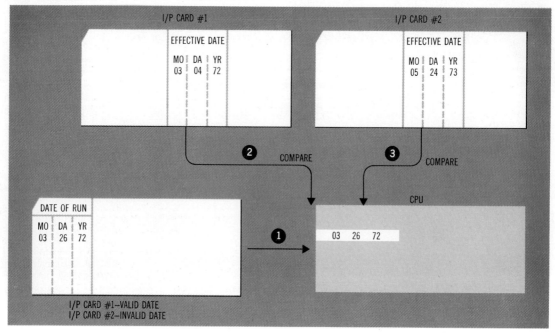

Figure 15.6
The use of an edit routine to determine if a date is relatively current.

IF YEAR-OF-CURRENT-RUN = YEAR-OF-EFFECTIVE-DATE NEXT SENTENCE ELSE GO TO STEP-2.
IF MONTH-OF-CURRENT RUN > MONTH-OF-EFFECTIVE-DATE GO TO ERROR-DATE.
IF MONTH-OF-CURRENT-RUN = MONTH-OF-EFFECTIVE-DATE OR
   DAY-OF-CURRENT-RUN < DAY-OF-EFFECTIVE-DATE GO TO NEXT-EDIT ELSE GO
   TO ERROR-DATE.

If the year on both dates is the same, we merely test the month. If the month is valid, we proceed to the next test, otherwise we branch to an error-routine. If the year on both dates is not the same (e.g., EFFECTIVE DATE is 12/01/73 and CURRENT RUN DATE is 01/01/74), then a more complex logic operation is required at STEP-2. For simplicity sake, we have omitted that routine.

3. Sequence Test

In many cases it is imperative that data be entered into a system in a specific sequence. In the case where *detail cards,* for example, will be used to update a *master tape,* the cards must be in a specific sequence, since tape updates require sequential processing.

If a sequence error is found, we can:

450   *Concepts of Computer Programming*

a. Reject the record in error. Rejected data will be entered in the data flow for the next cycle, where it must be sorted again.

b. Reject the record in error, but if a predetermined number of errors occurs, the run will be terminated. We can reject out-of-sequence data, but if the data has been missorted, we can conceivably have more rejected records than correct ones. Thus, to insure that only a small number of out-of-sequence records exist, we can incorporate a routine where each time an out-of-sequence condition occurs, we add one to a counter; if the counter should exceed a pre-determined number, then the run will be aborted and reexecuted after the data has been resorted. In COBOL, the routine, within a program, may appear as follows.

```
ADD 1 TO CTR.
IF CTR IS GREATER THAN 10 DISPLAY
'RECORDS MUST BE RESEQUENCED  JOB ABORTED'
UPON CONSOLE,
STOP RUN.
```

This will permit 10 out-of-sequence errors to occur. If any more appear, then an error message is printed and the run is terminated.

c. Abort the run if any sequence errors occur. The data is initially arranged in a specified sequence. Therefore *no* errors should occur. Rather than reject any record, it is sometimes more advisable to stop the run, resequence the erroneous records and insure that the remainder of the file is in correct order.

4. Missing Data Test

For most records, key data fields are required for processing. For example, a Payroll record *must* contain a social security number and annual salary. If either of these fields are missing, then the record must be rejected since it would not be serviceable in any Payroll file maintenance. Similarly, an Accounts Receivable record with a missing ACCOUNT NUMBER or AMOUNT is equally useless.

In summary, if a key field is missing data, then the edit program usually rejects the entire record. For data fields that are not critical, missing information may be merely noted or else filled with some compensating data. For example, an EFFECTIVE DATE field on a card that is erroneously blank may be filled with the date of the run, as supplied by the computer operator. Again, changes to an input file are only made if a validated file is created as output. If the input file is merely checked, then errors can only be rejected and not corrected.

5. Check Digit Test

Many numbers such as charge account numbers, inventory numbers, and identification numbers can easily cause errors in file maintenance routines if they are incorrectly written or keypunched. For example, if a customer buys an item on credit and his account number is written on the sales slip or keypunched on a card as 123 456 instead of 123 546, this can result in the wrong customer getting billed. The most common type of numeric error is in transposition of digits, as above. One way to minimize this type of error is to incorporate an extra digit called the *check digit,* in the number. A typical procedure is as follows:

a. Assign the number, such as 123 546.

b. Beginning with the first digit take every other digit and multiply by two:

$$1 \times 2 = 2$$
$$3 \times 2 = 6$$
$$4 \times 2 = 8$$

c. Add these numbers together and then add the digits that have not been multiplied by 2, obtaining a single total:

$$(2 + 6 + 8) + (2 + 5 + 6) = 29$$

d. Subtract the low-order or units digit of this sum from 10:
$$10 - 9 = 1$$

The low-order digit that results is the *check digit,* which is then added onto the original number (see Figure 15.7). Usually, although not necessarily, the check digit is tacked on at the right of the number. (Note that when the sum obtained in Step 3 is a multiple of 10 the check digit is zero: $10 - 0 = 0$). Therefore, for the above example, the full account number assigned is 123 546 1.

Thus the account number is originally assigned to the customer *with* the included check digit. The edit program must include a routine

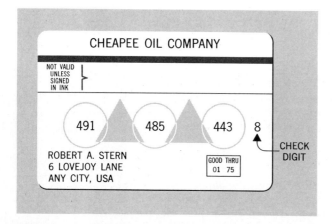

Figure 15.7
Credit card with check digit.

with the above arithmetic operations to determine if the account number on a card punched from a charge slip is valid; that is, if the digit calculated by the computer is the same as that in the input then the charge account number is considered valid. If not, then the input number probably contains a transposition of digits and the record must be rejected. If the number were entered as 123 456 1 instead of 123 546 1, this would be detected as an error. When the computer performs the calculations to produce the check digit, a digit of zero would result. When compared against the check digit of 1 that was entered as input, an error condition would be noted.

Note that this technique is not foolproof, since 123 645 1 could be an incorrectly coded version of 123 546 1 and yet the check digit routine would *not* indicate an error. In general, where a *single* transposition of digits in coding occurs, a check digit routine is extremely useful. Where more than one transposition exists, which is not as likely, then the error may not be recognized until the incorrectly billed customer complains. Note also that the above check digit routine is not the *only* one commonly used.

6. Limit Test

This test determines that specific fields do not exceed reasonable limits. Perhaps a weekly salary at a company, for example, should never exceed $700.00. If the coded salary on the input record is greater than this amount, the record must be rejected for containing an erroneous field.

At this point, the business and data processing students should be cognizant of the overwhelming need for precise and thorough edit routines on input data to insure, where possible, that errors do not appear in the record. Errors in key data fields of input can cause serious problems in File Maintenance Routines resulting in inaccuracies in the master file, erroneous reports, and so on.

The programmer who takes great care in specifying precise error conditions will ultimately save the company much time, effort, and expense. The businessman must insure that all input is edited as precisely as possible, and that seriously inaccurate records are not used to update files.

Remember that the above edits represent only a few of the possible tests. The number of edit tests performed is directly proportional to the input form. If input is on tape or cards, for example, it may require more editing than if it is on source documents entered on an optical scanner. The cards or tape data may have two types of errors: original errors on source documents and encoding (keypunching or key-to-tape) errors. The source documents used as input to an optical scanner may contain only the former type and, thus, theoretically, are not as prone to inaccuracies, assuming that the optical scanner itself does not make errors in transmission.

In general, terminal data requires the most precise edit control for several reasons: (a) Source documents may be coded improperly.

(b) The terminal keying may be inaccurate. (c) There is no verification (other than visual) of terminal typing as there is with card or tape encoding. (d) The equipment itself is prone to transmission problems because of the distance the data must travel.

II. *Updates or File Maintenance Routines*

A. TYPES OF UPDATES

We have seen that an update or file maintenance procedure is the process of making a master file of data current (see Figure 15.8).
File Maintenance procedures can be performed:

1. Online
When data that is used to update a file is entered via a terminal and through immediate access to the computer alters corresponding records, online processing is required.

File Maintenance routines are performed online only when the master file *must* be current at all times, to optimize the answering of customer inquiries or to optimize management's decision-making process. That is, for example, systems that utilize a master reservation file to answer customer inquiries or to make flight reservations, require the master file to be updated online. To wait for periodic update cycles would invalidate much of the data on the file, since it would not be current.

INPUTS
  MASTER FILE—Contains *all* pertinent data for a specific system and serves as a frame of reference and a source for compiling output data.
  DETAIL or TRANSACTION FILE—Contains all current activity that is not yet part of the master file—changes to existing master records, new entries to master file, and so on.

OUTPUTS
  UPDATED MASTER FILE—Contains all previous master data together with all current changes.
  ERROR LISTS—Contains any errors that have appeared during processing: unmatched records, inconsistent records, and so on.
  TOTAL LISTS—Contains totals of all updated records, all errors, all new entries. Such totals are used mainly for control purposes.

Figure 15.8
Files used in update routines.

454

Concepts of Computer Programming

2. In a Batch-Processing Environment

When data on a file need not be current or timely at any given moment, it is far more economical to batch or group all changes to the file and thus perform a single update, at periodic intervals. In this way, the computer is processing data more efficiently than it would online, where data is entered sporadically from terminals.

The vigorous process of updating a sequential file has been discussed in depth in Chapter 8, on Flowcharting. Figure 15.9 illustrates a sample update.

B. TYPES OF FILES UTILIZED IN FILE MAINTENANCE ROUTINES

1. Master File

Contains all relevant information for a particular system that is used to provide output data.

2. Detail File

Contains current information only; usually used to update master files.

3. History File

Contains information that is *not* currently used for inquiries or some output reports. Rather than maintaining a large, cumbersome Master file, some noncurrent master data can be switched to a history file that can be used for periodic reference. History file data includes, for example:

a. Payroll History File
   For each employee, all departments where he was previously assigned and the corresponding level he reached and salary he received.
b. Accounts Receivable History File
   For each account, all transactions that were recorded *prior* to the present year.
c. Inventory History File
   For inventory files, all items that are no longer maintained by the company.

These history records generally do not have relevance for present processing but may be required for special studies or statistical reports. For example, the Payroll Department may desire a special report indicating all employees who were, at some time, assigned to the Purchasing Department.

Rather than maintaining massive master files, file cleanup procedures are performed periodically to transfer data from master to history files.

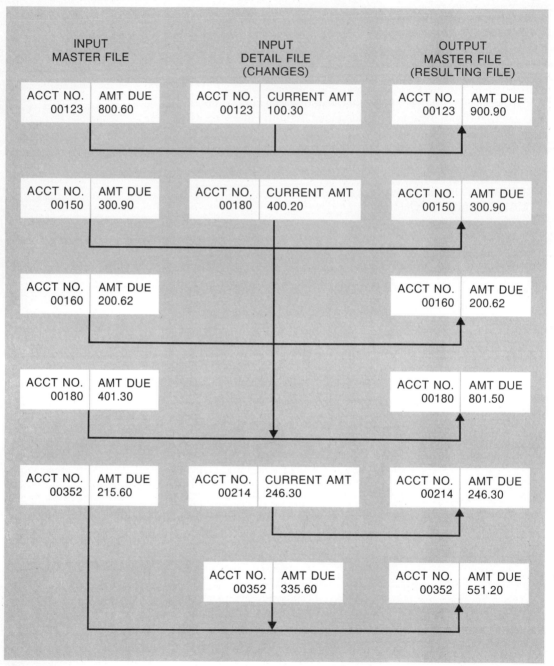

Figure 15.9
Sample update.

Concepts of Computer Programming

4. Table File

Contains information that is needed for reference purposes during some file maintenance routine. Such files usually include data that is variable. Examples of such files include:

a. Payroll Tables indicating for each net salary range, state, local, and federal income taxes. These tables are employed in Payroll updates and/or the preparation of payroll checks. Since these figures change rather frequently, they must be entered on a table file as variable data.
b. Inventory Tables, denoting for each item, the name of the vendor or supplier. These tables are used for computer preparation of Purchase Orders. Since vendors or suppliers are frequently shifted, this data must be entered on a table file.
c. Inventory Tables, denoting for each item, the amount in stock at each warehouse location. The purpose of such a table is to ship the items sold from the *nearest* warehouse.

III. File Cleanups

A file cleanup or "purge" is the process of deleting all unused or obsolete records from a file, typically a master file.

Because of its nature, this sort of file maintenance is performed less often than other runs. Once or twice a year are typical file cleanup cycles.

Any records deemed obsolete or no longer in use are removed from the file. Such records may no longer enter the processing flow or they may be placed on a "dead" or history file for possible inclusion in historical reports. Such records would include, as noted previously:

a. Accounts Receivable customer records that have not shown any activity for a specific period (3 years, for example).
b. Payroll records that indicate an employee has been permanently terminated.
c. Inventory records for parts that are no longer used by the company.

Output from a file cleanup is a "purged" or "clean" file and, sometimes, a listing of records that have been eliminated. In this way, a manual check can be made to insure that current records were not inadvertently deleted.

Keep in mind that these represent only a few of the basic procedures common to most business applications. The following procedures are also common to business, but are normally performed by utility programs and thus require no complex logic.

IV. Utility Programs

A. SORTING OF FILES

A master file may be in one specific sequence for ease of updating, for example, and require a different sequence prior to output reporting. Thus the master file must be sorted or resequenced during each cycle. This is true when the master file is stored on sequenced media, such as cards or tape. For disk processing, it is often not necessary to sort the file, since the ability to access records directly or randomly can be utilized. A *sort program* might, for example, be required prior to step 5, CREATION OF OUTPUT, in Figure 15.1.

B. MERGING OF FILES

Several data files from different offices or branches may require a merging operation to produce one inclusive master file.

C. CARD-TO-TAPE OR CARD-TO-DISK PROGRAMS

For ease of processing the detail data, for example, may first be keypunched on cards and then converted to a high-speed tape for future editing and updating.

Since these operations include standardized procedures that do not vary substantially from one system to another, *utility* programs are almost always employed. You will recall that a utility program is a prewritten program that performs specialized tasks. The programmer need only supply parameters or specifications such as sort field, ascending or descending sequence, and so on.

Note that there are utility and application programs that may be used to handle each of the above routines (EDIT, UPDATE, FILE, CLEANUP) as well. They include the most commonly used routines for the specific application. If standardized procedures with no distinctive or extraordinary operations are all that is required, then the programmer can employ a utility program, supply the necessary parameters or specifications, and thereby eliminate much programming and debugging effort. If, however, several nonstandard routines are required that are not provided in a prepackaged standard utility program, he would do better to write his own program than to attempt to revise or alter the utility program.

Note, too, that there are utility packages which contain design and programming specifications for total systems, such as Accounts Receivable, Inventory, and Payroll. These, also, utilize basic techniques and logic common to most systems. For systems that use a standard approach, such utility packages are ideal. For those systems that require some distinctive processing, these packages are often unadaptable.

Concepts of Computer Programming

In short, the above-mentioned techniques and programming concepts are those that are commonly utilized in business applications. It is important that the businessman, as well as the computer specialist, be aware of these so that he can better communicate his needs to the analyst and programmer and, in addition, be cognizant of what he can reasonably expect from computer applications.

SELF-EVALUATING QUIZ

1. The process of testing data to determine if it is valid is called an _____ .
2. Edit procedures are usually performed prior to _____ and prior to _____ .
3. An update procedure is the process of _____ .
4. A file cleanup is the process of _____ .
5. A UTILITY program is a _____ .
6. Output from an Edit run includes _____ and _____ .
7. A FIELD TEST determines _____ .
8. If input data is to enter the flow in a specified order, then an Edit routine should perform a _____ test.
9. CHECK DIGITS are often employed to detect the erroneous _____ of digits.
10. In general, five types of edit tests that may be performed include _____ , _____ , _____ , _____ , and _____ .
11. Input to an update program includes _____ and _____ .
12. The major form of output from an update is a _____ .
13. The two types of file maintenance procedures are performed _____ or in a(n) _____ environment.
14. Utility programs may be used for _____ , _____ , or _____ .

SOLUTIONS

1. Edit
2. Master File creation; Updating a Master File
3. making a master file of data current
4. purging all obsolete, unused, or invalid records from a file
5. "packaged" or prewritten program usually supplied by the manufacturer to accomplish a given task
6. validated data; an error list
7. if the classification of the field is valid (e.g., if a numeric field contains numeric data)
8. sequence
9. transposition
10. FIELD TEST; SEQUENCE TEST; MISSING DATA TEST; LIMIT TEST; CODE TEST; CHECK DIGIT TEST
11. a detail file; a master file
12. current or updated master file
13. online; batch-processing
14. sorts; merges; card-to-tape runs

Section Three *Systems Analysis and Design*

Chapter 16 *The Interaction Between the Analyst and the Businessman: Systems Analysis*

We have now reached the point where we can appreciate not only what a computer system is, but what is involved when typical business applications are programmed for the computer. However, several questions may have occurred to you.

1. How is an *integrated* business system, consisting of many related elements, computerized?
2. How long does it take to convert to a computerized system?
3. How much will it cost to convert to a computerized system? Or, alternately,
4. How much will be saved by the new system?

The answers to these questions will become clearer in this chapter and subsequent ones, as we explore the activities of a systems analyst and see how he works with the businessman to computerize a specific application. In addition, we will discuss some of the recent advances in systems techniques, such as Management Information Systems, simulation, and linear programming. These concepts have been developed to give the businessman new dimensions in information processing that are simply not possible without computers because of the volume of information involved. It is thus hoped that the businessman will appreciate why he cannot get his application computerized overnight. In addition, it will show him why, once a computerized system is operational, it is not always an easy task to make "minor" modifications to the system. In other words, we will attempt to illustrate why it is so important for the businessman to work closely with the systems analyst during the design of a computerized system.

Note that we will first consider the basic phases of the analyst's job: (1) analysis of a current system in order to evaluate its problem areas (this chapter); and (2) design of a new system (next chapter) that will alleviate these problems and make the system run more efficiently. After these discussions, we will present two case studies to illustrate how typical business systems are designed for computer processing. Finally, we will discuss Management Information Systems and other advanced decision-making tools.

I. Basic Elements of any Business System

Before we proceed further, it is important that we recollect what is meant by a system. In Chapter 1, we indicated that a system basically refers to any organized method for accomplishing some goal or objective. Below are some brief objectives of typical business systems.

System	Basic Objectives
PAYROLL	To provide periodic paychecks to employees and to maintain payroll information on each employee for processing of tax reports, etc.
ACCOUNTS RECEIVABLE	To maintain records on money owed by customers and to send out monthly statements to each customer.
ACCOUNTS PAYABLE	To maintain records on money owed to various suppliers.
INVENTORY	To maintain records on the various types of merchandise, and the quantities that are on hand for each.
PERSONNEL	To maintain records on all personnel working for the company so that various "profile" reports can readily be prepared for management's review.

The way in which these objectives are met constitutes the *system* for carrying out the particular business application or function. Thus an analyst must evaluate the manner in which a current system meets its objective and attempt to revise the operations so that the objectives are more efficiently met.

It will enhance your appreciation of what a systems analyst does and why his tasks require much time, if we realize that regardless of the specific system that is to be evaluated there are seven elements or building blocks that must always be considered. These elements are shown in the diagram in Figure 16.1.

An understanding of each of these elements will give the student a clear perspective on the amount of detail that the businessman must supply the analyst who is trying to computerize the specific system.

We will discuss each of these elements below and will illustrate the discussions with an Accounts Receivable system and a Payroll system.

Note that we cannot overemphasize the importance of proper communications between the analyst and the businessman. More systems are rendered inadequate because of communication problems than for any other reason.

The businessman who understands the nature of the analyst's job and the type of information that must be supplied will work closely with the analyst to provide a proper perspective on the present system, so that a more efficient and useful design, with automated procedures, will be created.

A. OBJECTIVES

The systems analyst must be aware of exactly what the businessman requires from a specific system. That is, management's goals or objectives must be fully known and understood. For example, one of a company's objectives for a new design might be to establish a computerized Accounts Receivable system so that a customer can walk into any branch store and have a clerk tell him immediately what his balance is at that time, based on computer records.

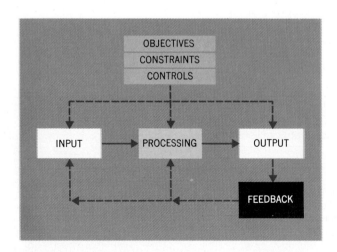

Figure 16.1
Basic structure of a business system.

Systems Analysis and Design

After reviewing the objectives of a current system with the businessman, it is quite possible that the systems analyst will recommend a modification to those objectives. The analyst has specialized expertise in data processing. Consequently, he may be aware of computer capabilities that can be utilized to give outstanding performance or to attain broader objectives for some systems.

B. CONSTRAINTS

The analyst *and* the businessman must both recognize any limitations or constraints that may be imposed when the analyst is designing a computerized system. There are several common constraints that usually affect most systems being computerized. These are legal constraints, budgetary constraints, and equipment constraints, as discussed below.

1. Legal

Depending on the specific system, there are certain legal requirements to which the system must adhere. For example, in a Payroll system, the company must withhold various taxes such as federal, state, social security, and local. In addition, a W-2 withholding form must be sent to each employee at the end of the year. The analyst may feel, for example, that the design of the W-2 form is inefficient. He may, in fact, have a better design. However, there is little that the analyst can do. In this instance, the federal and local governments have dictated what the form should look like, how many copies there should be, and when they must be sent to employees. The businessman must thus make the analyst aware of all legal constraints under which the system is to operate.

2. Budgetary

Often the management of a company imposes a budgetary constraint on the analyst, limiting him to the time, and hence money that he can expend in analyzing and designing a new system. Management may say, for example, that the new computerized Accounts Receivable system must be operational within one year. The analyst must therefore work with the businessman to achieve a functional system within the alloted time. However, because of the budgetary constraint, the result may be a system that is not as ultrasophisticated as that which the analyst and/or the businessman might have ideally desired, but it is still one that satisfies the basic needs.

3. Equipment

Computer equipment or hardware devices that are employed within the company represent another type of constraint. Systems analysts generally attempt to utilize the computer configuration that is currently available at the company. Additional equipment not presently utilized in the company that the analyst considers an asset to his system must be justified from a cost standpoint. In this case, the analyst must perform a *feasibility study* to determine the economic feasibility of acquiring such equipment.

For companies with no existing computer facilities, the analyst must perform a feasibility study prior to *any* design work. The computer system that is deemed feasible from a company-wide standpoint then becomes the equipment constraint for the new design of each business system. The feasibility study is discussed, in depth, as an appendix to this chapter.

C. OUTPUT

The analyst must ascertain from the businessman just exactly what is currently produced as output under the current system. In a payroll system, for example, some of the common outputs are paychecks and W-2 withholding statements. However, there are other outputs, such as Internal Revenue Service Form 941—Employer's Quarterly Federal Tax Return. This form is a detailed breakdown by employee of wages earned during a specific quarter and federal income taxes and social security taxes withheld. This form accompanies the check issued by the company to the government for taxes withheld.

It is the businessman's job to be cognizant of *all* output forms so that he can describe them to the analyst.

Based on his experience and on a complete comprehension of how the particular system functions, the analyst should be able to recommend to the businessman new or revised reports, for example, that can be readily obtained from a computerized system.

Output, however, constitutes more than just reports. For example, it is usually necessary to save information in the form of updated files that can be used for producing reports in the future. The businessman must therefore make the analyst aware of how output information is currently stored for future processing.

D. PROCESSING

Now that the analyst is aware of the output that is produced under the current system, he must recognize what processing, or types of operations, are currently performed in order to achieve the desired results. He must be made aware of all procedures that are followed and the way in which various computations are made. For example, in an Accounts Receivable system, the company may include a finance charge for late payment. The computation may be as follows: $1\frac{1}{2}$% charge on the first $500 overdue, and 1% charge on the excess over $500, with a minimum charge of $0.50. It is imperative that the businessman relay *all* processing steps, in detail, to the analyst. Any omission or misunderstanding can result in expensive redesign and reprogramming effort, once the new system has been implemented.

E. INPUT

The businessman must make the analyst aware of all input information that serves as the basis for desired outputs. The analyst will typically seek answers to questions such as the following, to insure that he obtains the desired information about inputs from the businessman:

1. Can the analyst determine where all information used for processing originates?
2. How often is each type of input generated?
3. If there are codes or abbreviations used for input, does the analyst have complete lists of these?
4. What happens to input documents after they have been processed?

In a Payroll system, for example, we might expect to find time cards as an input form. In addition, we must consider, as input, various forms filled out by a new employee. These would include such items as a W-4 form (Internal Revenue Service)—Employee's Withholding Exemption Certificate. On this form, the number of exemptions for tax purposes is indicated.

F. CONTROLS

The businessman must familiarize the analyst with the ways in which errors are minimized under the current system. That is, the methods used to control or check errors must be specified. With knowledge of these controls, the analyst can then incorporate them in the computerized system, and perhaps suggest some controls with which the businessman may not be familiar. The following is a brief sample of some of the common controls that have been utilized in many business systems.

1. Batch Total

If a group of inputs is to be processed, a total figure is taken of a specific input field prior to processing. After processing, this *batch* total is compared to the input total to confirm that all input was, in fact, processed. For example, suppose that in a department store at the end of each day, each sales clerk takes all of the charge slips from his department and adds up the total of charge sales for that day. He then sends the slips to the Accounts Receivable department, where posting is made to each customer's account and various reports are prepared. After all posting is done for that day, a report is prepared that shows the total of the charge sales that were posted from each department. If one of these totals disagrees with the batch total obtained by a particular sales clerk, then that information has been incorrectly processed. Appropriate measures must then be taken to ascertain the reason for the discrepancy and then to take corrective action.

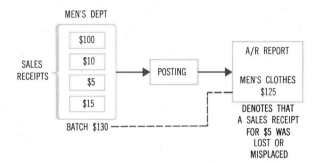

Figure 16.2
The use of a batch total.

2. Item Count
In addition to using a batch total, another control is to count the number of items both before and after processing. In this manner, if any items are lost during processing, an error in the item count will occur.

3. Limit Check
A limit check is a test that is performed to make certain that figures being processed are reasonable. If a particular figure is found to be unreasonable, then the specific item must be investigated. For example, in a particular Payroll system, a reasonable limit check for weekly payroll checks might be $2000. If any check that is processed exceeds a gross of $2000, then we must ascertain if an error has occurred. In this case, we might not issue the check until it has been verified.

4. Trial Balances
A trial balance is a report that is prepared to insure the accuracy of all posting to account ledgers. If the transactions for the specific time period are properly posted, the total of debits shown on the report will equal the total of credits, as shown in Figure 16.3.

G. FEEDBACK

It is essential that the analyst be made aware of how errors in the current system are handled, once they are discovered.

Even with the use of many controls, it is still possible for errors to occur. The businessman must therefore explain all current procedures for adjustments and corrections when feedback procedures indicate that errors have occurred.

For example, in a Payroll system, what happens when a paycheck is issued for an incorrect amount? Suppose, for example, that the check is in excess of the correct amount. The procedure may call for the check to be voided and a new one issued. In addition, however,

Systems Analysis and Design

ACCOUNTS RECEIVABLE TRIAL BALANCE

AS OF 9-30-72

ACCOUNT NO.	DEBITS	CREDITS
01025	50.25	
01026	27.65	
01030	35.10	
01035		27.15
01037	26.07	
01038		
TOTALS	557,233.10	385,957.15
DEBITS–CREDITS	171,275.95	

Figure 16.3
Trial balance.

appropriate adjustments must be made to the employee's year-to-date figures for earnings, federal tax withheld, social security tax deducted, etc. Similarly, in an Accounts Receivable system suppose that a customer complains that a charged item has incorrectly appeared on his monthly statement. The procedures might call for the Accounts Receivable department to investigate the claim, and if it proves valid, to issue a credit to the customer's account. In addition, appropriate adjustments to various sales figures must be made.

From the previous section, we have seen that a systems analyst must work closely with the businessman in order to achieve effective analysis of the basic elements in a system. Next, we will explore in more depth exactly how the analyst collects data on a system.

II. Methods of Collecting Data

The collection of accurate data by the analyst is essential for thorough analysis of the system. All aspects of the system must be evaluated in depth. The careless omission of a single factor could drastically alter the analyst's interpretation of the present system. Similarly, the smallest fact, misunderstood, could change the interpretation of the system.

Data can be collected by the following means:

1. Study of procedures manuals
2. Evaluation of forms
3. Interviews with the businessman and other personnel who work on the current system

Most companies have formalized written manuals containing the procedures and operations for each system. These manuals provide a general idea of how a system *should* function. Unfortunately, they are often out-of-date and the procedures indicated are sometimes not followed. The analyst can, however, utilize them to obtain background information about the system without expending valuable time of the businessman to obtain this information.

Similarly, the analyst should familiarize himself with all the forms used within the current system, thus minimizing the need to ask the businessman superfluous questions. The analyst must know the exact nature of the data presented on the forms. He must also know the *distribution* of forms. The analyst will often draw form distribution charts, such as the one shown in Figure 16.4. He will then review these with the businessman to ascertain that he clearly understands the current distribution of forms.

In analyzing forms, the analyst will be evaluating such things as:

1. Are there any unnecessary items of information on particular forms?
2. Is there any unnecessary distribution of forms?
3. Are there manually prepared forms that could be more efficiently prepared by computer?
4. Are there some forms that could be combined into a single, comprehensive report?

The most important tool for the collection of data is the *interview* with the businessman. The analyst can learn all the details on the system from the interview. What he has learned from procedures manuals is how the system, if functioning as originally constituted, would operate; what he hopes to learn from the interview is how the system *actually* operates. In addition, the analyst will be asking the businessman questions, such as those in the checklist below, to assist him in evaluating existing forms and their distribution.

1. Who uses the report or form?
2. How often is it used?
3. How much of the information on it is used?
4. Is the data on this report necessary for:

Systems Analysis and Design

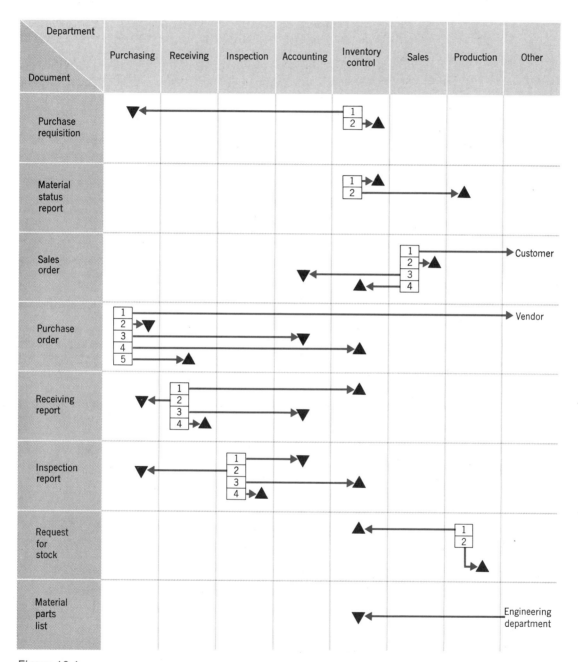

Figure 16.4

Forms distribution chart for inventory system: $\boxed{n}$ *n*th copy of report (shown where form originates); ▽ permanently filed; △ temporarily filed and then destroyed; → sent to.

a. Making decisions on some form of action?

b. Keeping the department informed of current conditions?

c. Checking the accuracy of other matters?

d. Establishing control of other matters?

5. What would be the effect on each employee's job if he:

a. Did not receive the report at all?

b. Received less information than at present?

c. Received more information than at present?

6. What other reports or records are prepared from data on this report?

7. Can the data on this report be obtained from any other source?

8. Is this report easy to read and use?

9. How long is each copy maintained?

10. How and where is it filed?

11. How often is it referred to after its original use?

The following is a checklist of *general* items that represent the type of information that the analyst will be seeking from interviews with the businessman.

1. Can a monetary savings possibly be realized with new or revised operations?

2. Do the present procedures and operations utilize too much time and effort of the employees?

3. Does inaccurate reporting result in duplication of effort? Similarly, is the output data reliable enough for decision-making purposes?

4. Is the present system so rigid and inflexible that minor changes require major revamping?

5. Can the present system handle larger volumes which would result from normal growth?

Note that the businessman working within a current system is in the best position to evaluate its problem areas and to make recommendations on revisions that will result in more efficient processing. The businessman with knowledge of data processing requirements and capabilities is the single greatest asset in assisting computer specialists to realize the most effective designs possible.

III. Analysis of Current System Costs

While the analyst is studying a particular system, he will be collecting data on the cost of operating the system. This information will be useful later for comparing present costs to costs of a revised design. Management often will not approve a proposed system unless it can show a savings in operating costs over the current way of doing things. Another reason for analyzing current costs is that many systems have subsystems, or specific facets, that are disproportionately expensive. The analyst must determine when these costly operations are inefficient and when they should be maintained.

The analyst will probably want to compare the system costs to expenditures in previous years. In this way, he can determine how well growth factors have been accommodated in the system.

The businessman may thus be called on to supply appropriate cost data to the analyst. The major costs that must be considered are labor, equipment, material, supplies, and overhead associated with the current system. The resource sheet in Figure 16.5 is an example of a typical form completed by an analyst when he is collecting cost data on a particular system.

Name and description	Amount	Cost	Resource Sheet Notes
Typewriters	30	600 per month	
Teletype	(1)	175 per month	(1) 5 units
			1 sending
			4 receiving
			Each is 3 ft. x 3 ft.
Main office—161 Front Street	44 ft. x 37 ft.	200 per month	
Sales offices	4 offices	880 per month	
73 Clover Street	Each 24 ft. x 58 ft.		
7476 Jones Avenue			
35 Myrtle Street			
1 River Street			
Sales records, monthly for last 10 years	1200	15 per year	Monthly sales report includes 8 fields
			Repeated 120 times plus totals
Stock certificates	850	25 per unit	Each certificate is registered and insured

11/21/73	N. Stern	Life policy	Life insurance	2
Date	Analyst	Activity	Study	Page

Figure 16.5
Resource sheet.

Keep in mind that the purpose of collecting data and cost figures on the present system is *not* to find fault with the businessmen responsible for its design. Existing systems often become obsolete because of growth factors or changes in company policy or other variables over which the businessman has no control. The analyst studies the existing system to learn more about it in order to prepare a proper design. Thus the businessman should not attempt to favorably impress the analyst or otherwise distort data or figures. In the end, an honest presentation of present procedures will be most effective in formulating an efficient analysis and design.

IV. Problem Definition

Before the analyst can design a new system, he must thoroughly evaluate the current system. Many revised systems become inadequate because of poor evaluation of the present system.

The ultimate objective of the analytic phase of the analyst's work is thus to determine, in essence:

1. The goals and objectives of the particular system.
2. How the system strives to meet these goals and objectives.
3. What aspects of the present system hamper the fulfillment of these goals and objectives.

There are basically five major problem areas that the analyst will explore with the businessman: (a) policies, (b) output forms, (c) processing, (d) inputs, and (e) controls and feedback. These items will be discussed below to provide the student with a perspective on what types of questions the businessman can expect from the analyst. The analyst must evaluate all amassed data on the system before making judgments concerning its problem areas.

The executive *policies* and directives of the company, in so far as they affect the system, must be evaluated in depth. Too often these are treated as "sacred cows," too holy to be questioned. If the analyst or businessman determines that specific company policies require revision, they should work together to indicate this. Following is a sample checklist of typical policies that are generally analyzed when investigating a system.

1. Is the leadership of the department in which the system functions overburdened? Perhaps a separation of the system into two unique units might enhance the achievement of the company's goals and objectives.
2. Is the leadership of the system divided between two or more individuals to the detriment of the company? Often, for example, there are ambiguous lines of responsibility.
3. Can the objectives of the company best be served by combining the system with another one?

4. Is responsibility clearly defined and, if so, is it properly delegated?

5. Is the work flow adversely affected by the necessity to coordinate operations with other systems?

With regard to the preparation of *forms,* we have previously discussed the types of questions that the analyst will be asking in order to properly evaluate existing forms and their distribution. The design of better forms will be discussed in the next chapter.

The *processing* of data requires employees to perform activities or operations. In addition to learning the specific activities performed by employees, the analyst will want to evaluate the employee work force to determine: (1) if changes in personnel might be beneficial for the system, or (2) if changes in the system are required to meet growing dissatisfaction or resistance on the part of employees.

Cumbersome or inefficient *input* documents can make processing difficult and the resultant output inadequate. It is therefore necessary for the analyst to analyze the input forms after he has determined any problem areas in both output and processing.

The following is a checklist of items that may be considered when evaluating input:

1. Is the input data considered reliable and accurate? Sometimes input data must be completely edited and even revised before it is considered acceptable.

2. Does the input data enter the system on time? Sometimes late input reporting substantially thwarts productivity.

3. Is the input data readable? Sometimes the sixth carbon copy, for example, which enters the system is too blurred to be useful.

4. Is the input document really necessary at all? Sometimes a department can obtain the same data from another input document.

An analysis of the *controls and feedback* of the system gives the analyst a general idea of the reliability of the system as a whole. That is, if the system maintains adequate controls, then the output data will probably be considered reliable and generally contain few errors. Sometimes, however, growth of the system has made previously used controls inadequate and even unworkable.

The above discussion has presented the primary areas in which analysis occurs. When this is completed, the analyst must formalize his impressions, ideas, and criticism of the system.

The *PROBLEM DEFINITION* is the formal document prepared by the analyst, which defines in the utmost detail all aspects of the current system (including cost) and its basic inadequacies. It ferrets out the fundamental flaws in the system that impede the achievement of its stated objectives. In essence, it highlights those areas that the analyst will improve in a new design for the system.

Generally, the analyst will show the completed Problem Definition to the businessman who has responsibility for the specific system and who has worked closely with the analyst to provide all relevant information.

The businessman might have some pertinent suggestions or comments on items overlooked or misrepresented in the document. It is possible that the analyst has misunderstood various facets of the current system.

Thus the Problem Definition contains the analysis of the present system. This document is used to provide management and the businessman in a specific department with the analyst's understanding of the system and its basic problem areas. All data obtained in this Problem Definition represents a joint effort of both the analyst and the businessman.

The next chapter will illustrate how businessmen and analysts work closely to produce the design of a new system.

SELF-EVALUATING QUIZ

1. Before an analyst can design a new system that will alleviate system flaws, he must _____ .
2. The seven basic elements of any system are _____ , _____ , _____ , _____ , _____ , _____ , and _____ .
3. (T or F) After analyzing a system's objectives, it is quite possible that these objectives could be more efficiently met with the use of computers.
4. A constraint is a(n) _____ imposed on a system.
5. Two common types of constraints are _____ and _____ .
6. To determine the economic possibility of acquiring new equipment to handle business tasks, a(n) _____ study must be performed by the analyst.
7. (T or F) Control procedures are built into systems to minimize errors.
8. A batch total is _____ .
9. A(n) _____ is a test that is performed to make certain that figures being processed are reasonable.
10. A(n) _____ is a report that is prepared to insure the accuracy of all posting to account ledgers.
11. The three basic methods for collecting data are _____ , _____ , and _____ .
12. Procedures Manuals generally indicate how a system _____ .
13. The single most effective method of collecting data is the _____ .
14. (T or F) When an analyst attempts to determine current system costs, the businessman should favorably impress him by minimizing these figures.
15. The _____ is the formal document prepared by the analyst which defines in the utmost detail all aspects of the current system.

SOLUTIONS

1. study the present system in depth
2. objectives; constraints; outputs; processing; input; control; feedback
3. T
4. limitation or restriction
5. legal; budgetary; equipment
6. feasibility
7. T
8. a total figure of specific input fields to be used for comparison purposes to confirm that all input has been processed
9. limit check
10. Trial Balance
11. study of procedures manuals; evaluation of forms; interview
12. *should* function
13. interview
14. F
15. Problem Definition

Appendix to Chapter 16 *Feasibility Studies*

I. ANALYZE CURRENT COMPANY OPERATIONS

II. DETERMINE JUSTIFICATION FOR COMPUTER

III. DERIVE A LIST OF REQUIREMENTS AND CRITERIA FOR THE PROSPECTIVE COMPUTER

IV. ANALYZE BIDS FROM COMPUTER MANUFACTURERS

V. DEVISE A PLAN TO PREPARE FOR THE COMPUTER

Many companies do not have their own computer facility. They process information in one of the following ways: (1) manually, (2) by electronic accounting machines, usually in conjunction with manual operations, (3) through the use of service bureaus, which are companies that design computer systems and then program and operate them for a fixed fee or (4) through the use of time-sharing.

When company processing expands greatly, the management will generally request that a study be conducted to determine if a data processing facility could be justified; that is, a group is appointed to determine if it is feasible to acquire, maintain, and profit from a computer system. This type of study is called a *feasibility study*.

A special committee within the company is generally formed with

480   *Systems Analysis and Design*

the authority to conduct the feasibility study. The typical committee consists of the following employees.

1. One member of each department in the company, who can best convey his department's need for a computer.
2. A member of the executive committee of the company, who is most concerned with the company's policies and monetary limitations.
3. Senior systems analysts who are best suited, because of training and background, to determine a company's need for a computer.
4. An outside consultant, who is considered an expert in designing alternative computer systems.

The importance of each of these members is discussed below.

1. It is important to have each department represented on the committee for several reasons. Each representative is aware of the particular needs within his area. He can often indicate any special requirements that could be handled by a computer system. In addition, once management decides to obtain a computer, it needs the operational support of all departments within the company. Since each department takes part in computer selection through its representative on the feasibility committee, the possibility of resistance to the computer from independent areas is reduced.
2. A member of the executive committee of the company is needed on the feasibility committee to act as chairman. Since a feasibility study involves much time and effort and extensive paperwork, a chairman is required to coordinate the committee's efforts. In addition to serving as chairman, this member's high position in the management echelon lends great prestige and support to the committee. It is always advantageous for a committee of this kind to have management's explicit support so that any barriers to its endeavors can be easily handled. For example, the committee generally spends much time in collecting information, interviewing employees, and in meeting in conferences. These disruptions in normal daily activities are more readily tolerated by department managers, when a committee has the explicit endorsement of the management. An executive is an added advantage on this committee because of his familiarity with company policies and monetary limitations. He can save the committee much time and effort by channeling its proposals to insure its future acceptance.
3. The senior systems analyst is needed on the committee because of his expertise in computer hardware and software. By synthesizing and analyzing the requirements of all departments in the company, the analyst can determine the size and specifications of the computer system that should be installed. He can also determine the type of system that would be most suitable. For example, he might suggest that a computer system incorporating data communications through a terminal network be adopted. Or, he

might recommend a much smaller system that would be adequate. The analyst, then, must possess specific knowledge of various computer configurations so that he can assist management in determining the most practical one for the company.

4. An outside consultant is often needed to act as a kind of catalyst on this committee. Note that he, like the senior systems analysts, has specialized knowledge in computer hardware and software. Unlike the analysts, however, he can be completely objective, since his responsibilities are independent of any company or department ties. An analyst who reports to the Comptroller of the company, may recommend computer systems that are most conducive to handling accounting procedures, since this is the area with which he is most familiar. A consultant, however, can maintain his objectivity and can often make valid recommendations.

The basic functions of the feasibility committee can be segmented into several phases:

1. Analyze the current operations of the company.
2. Determine if the implementation of a computer system can be justified. It is possible that an overhaul of the current operations might eliminate the need for a computer installation. If not, a further investigation would be required.
3. Assuming that a computer system is still feasible, it would now be necessary to devise a list of requirements and criteria to be fulfilled by the prospective computer. This list of specifications would then be submitted to several computer manufacturers. They would evaluate the data and make bids to supply specific computer configurations to fulfill the requirements.
4. Evaluate carefully the bids received by the feasibility committee. The computer manufacturer that can best meet the company's needs is then recommended to management.
5. Devise a plan for the company to prepare for the installation of the computer system, if management gives its approval.

The above steps are not unlike the systems analyst's tasks in analysis and design. All areas must be scrutinized carefully, a design recommended and, if approved, a plan must be indicated for implementing the system.

It is important to examine each of the above functions in more depth so that the scope of a feasibility study can be fully appreciated.

I. Analyze Current Company Operations

This is generally regarded as a major systems analysis, where the company itself is evaluated in depth. Each department must be individually considered, as well as their relation to each other.

482   *Systems Analysis and Design*

Documents must be evaluated and costs must be compiled. Each department is *not* evaluated with regard to its flaws but, instead, with regard to how a computer system could improve its productivity.

II. Determine Justification for Computer

It is conceivable that, after analysis of the company's operations, a computer installation may not be justifiable from a cost standpoint. Perhaps a redesign effort of various forms and procedures can lead to a more efficient utilization of the company's manpower. Even with this type of redesign effort, the feasibility committee may feel that a computer is still warranted.

Notice, however, that a computer installation must pay for itself in the end in order to be considered profitable. This implies that the cost of acquiring and of maintaining a computer system must be approximated at this time to determine if further investigation should be conducted. These costs would include the following items.

1. The cost of designing computerized systems.
2. The cost of programming effort.
3. The rental and/or purchase costs of computer hardware and software.
4. The cost of training company personnel to use computer inputs and outputs.
5. The cost of supplies.
6. The costs of operating a computer facility.
7. The cost associated with "housing" the computer, that is, the construction of an air-conditioned room for the computer.

The current cost of processing information must be compiled and then compared to the projected computer costs. Note that often it is necessary to project present costs into the future to determine what the costs would be under the present system, but with normal growth trends. Very often, an existing system, if continued indefinitely, would require extensive revision anyway. These revision costs should be included in present system costs so that a fair comparison to a computerized system can be made.

If, after cost comparison is completed, there appears to be a savings in the end, by installing a computer, then the company can proceed to derive a list of requirements and criteria to be fulfilled by a computer system. Observe that the savings need not be in the near future. Sometimes, the savings obtained by installing a computer system takes many years to be realized.

If a computer system cannot be justified, the committee may recommend a redesign of forms or procedures. Or, a service bureau that can perform company operations on a computer for a fee could be investigated. The distinct advantage of contracting a service bureau is that the initial cost is greatly reduced. Note, however, that the company would have no computer systems of its own; everything is owned and operated by the service bureau. If the company decides to install a computer at a future date, it must buy or rent the programs and procedures from the service bureau, or must develop them on its own.

III. Derive a List of Requirements and Criteria for the Prospective Computer

This represents the set of specifications of what is desired from the computer. The various computer manufacturers will use this as a basis for preparing bids to supply specific computer configurations. The type of information required would be as follows.

1. A review of the company's objectives and goals.
2. The sample input and output forms currently used and the frequency with which they are generated.
3. The descriptions of the type of processing done, including types of arithmetic operations performed.
4. The statements of the major controls currently used.
5. The description of the information that is on file, including the length of time it is maintained.
6. A list of any special capabilities desired under a computer system, such as terminal inputs, specific processing requirements, etc.
7. The description of the company's physical structure, including locations of branch offices, warehouses, etc.

IV. Analyze Bids from Computer Manufacturers

Once the bids are received from the manufacturers, they must be carefully evaluated by the feasibility committee. The cost of operating each computer system proposed is the most important factor in rating competitive bids. However, intangible benefits must be considered as well. The following items must be considered prior to rendering any decision:

1. The cost of renting the computer system.
2. The programming languages available with the system.
3. The multiprogramming and data communications capability.
4. The ability to expand storage as required at a later date.
5. The specifications of input-output devices included in the configuration.
6. The availability of educational materials and their corresponding charges.
7. The availability and cost of service in case of computer malfunction.
8. The compatibility with larger models in case a future conversion is deemed necessary.

Once the committee has reviewed all the bids, it should make its recommendations to management, in writing. The recommendation should highlight the reasons that this particular system was chosen over the others considered.

V. Devise a Plan to Prepare for the Computer

When a company finally signs a contract with a computer manufacturer, it may have to wait a year or longer before delivery is made. The feasibility committee should map out a plan that would insure a smooth transition from current operations to a computer system. A typical plan includes these items:

1. Establish a Data Processing Department. This necessitates the hiring of computer and keypunch operators, programmers, systems analysts, and managers. Some members may be transferred from other departments and may be trained for new positions in the Data Processing Department.
2. Design systems for the new computer.
3. Program the new systems. Even though the computer has not yet arrived, it is possible to write programs and have them tested. Often a computer manufacturer has test centers available for running programs for a company which has not yet received its computer. If this is not available, programs can usually be tested by renting computer time from other companies. If systems work and programming effort for specified systems is completed when a new computer arrives, there need be no delay before the implementation occurs. Often, these phases are not even begun until the computer is delivered and, as a result, the equipment is rarely used for many months.
4. Test the new system. It is possible to have people simulate their projected tasks until the computer comes, by using sample forms and data. In this manner, "bugs" in the system can often be detected. In addition, the personnel who are required to use the system will become familiar with its operations and procedures.

From the foregoing discussion, one can easily realize why feasibility studies sometime take two or more man-years to complete. These studies are the foundation for tremendous change within a company.

SELF-EVALUATING QUIZ

1. The typical feasibility committee consists of a _____ , _____ , _____ , and _____ .
2. (T or F) The tasks involved in a feasibility study are similar to those in system analysis and design.
3. (T or F) Analysis of current company operations are required for a feasibility study.
4. (T or F) Cost evaluations are not required in a feasibility study.
5. Bids from _____ must be compared during a feasibility study.
6. (T or F) A feasibility study may indicate that it is cheaper, in the long run, to use a service bureau rather than establishing a computer center.

SOLUTIONS

1. businessman; executive; systems analyst; consultant
2. T
3. T
4. F
5. computer manufacturers
6. T

Chapter 17 *The Interaction Between the Analyst and the Businessman: Systems Design*

The previous chapter has outlined the steps involved for a thorough analysis of systems. We have stressed the importance of proper communication between the businessman and the analyst to achieve an interaction of ideas and to determine the major problem areas within the current system.

This chapter will outline the steps involved for proper systems design. Here again, it is the systems analyst, the trained computer specialist, who has the ultimate responsibility to design a revised system that will more effectively and efficiently perform the required operations and procedures.

Note, however, that he cannot independently or solely design a new system. The analyst must again interact with the businessman to obtain a proper perspective on what is specifically required from an "ideal" or more appropriate system.

A new design must ultimately be approved by both management and businessmen, who are the supervisors within the specific department. The management in many companies, as well as other businessmen, are unfamiliar with data processing techniques and terminology and thus are not in a proper position to judge the effectiveness of a new design. It is the analyst's task to "sell" the system; it is the business leaders' task to attempt to understand its elements so that they can make appropriate decisions as to whether the new design warrants implementation. In short, the communication

Systems Analysis and Design

lines between these two groups must be open, at all times, in order for
a new system to be successfully implemented.

I. *A Step-by-Step Approach to Systems Design*

A. OVERVIEW

You will recall that analysis of business systems follows a step-by-step
approach. The ultimate aim of this analysis is an understanding of the
current operations and an insight into their major problem areas.

The design phase of an analyst's job also follows a step-by-step
approach, similar to the one previously mentioned. Figure 17.1
represents a sample flowchart illustrating *all* the steps involved in the
design phase, from designing the specific elements to implementing
the new system.

B. ELEMENTS INVOLVED IN SYSTEMS DESIGN

This section will discuss the elements indicated in the first processing
symbol and how they are integrated.

The illustration in Figure 17.2 is a graphic representation of these
elements.

Note that Figure 17.2 represents all the elements that must be
integrated to obtain a proper and efficient design. The order in which
the above steps are evaluated and redesigned by the analyst is noted
by the numbers included within each element.

Let us discuss each independently, in the sequence indicated,
keeping in mind that all elements must be integrated before a
meaningful design can be produced.

1. Objectives and Constraints

The management of a company or perhaps the business supervisors
who manage the specific departments are responsible for determining
the revised objectives and constraints for a new system.

As was indicated, in many companies business leaders are often
unfamiliar with data processing capabilities and thus are either
short-sighted in their objectives, underestimating computer capabilities,
or are too far-reaching in their requirements, necessitating extremely
expensive design work. Similarly, they may impose constraints that are
unrealistic and severely limiting. The systems analyst must work closely
with these policy-makers who determine objectives and constraints so
that he may guide them by suggesting realistic requirements within
appropriate limits.

The constraints imposed upon the analyst that are legally binding
cannot generally be revised. Hardware and monetary limitations,
however, must be realistic, or an effective design cannot be realized.

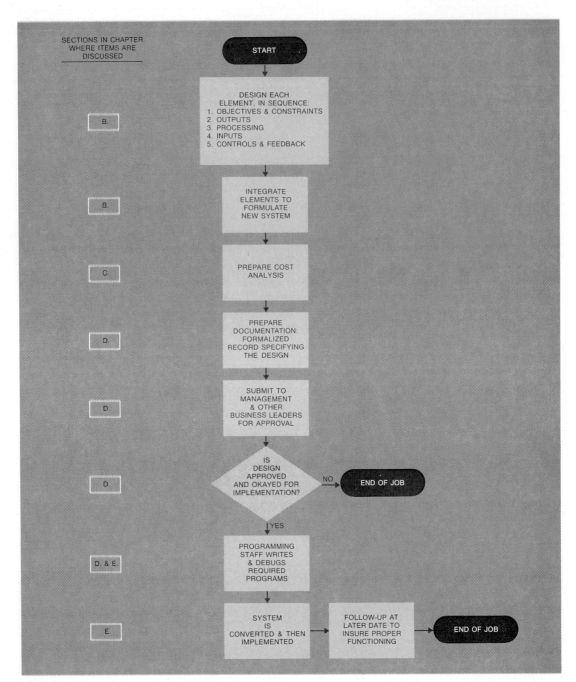

Figure 17.1
Flowchart of the steps involved in systems design.

Systems Analysis and Design

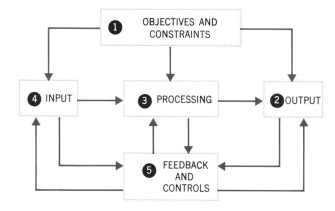

Figure 17.2
Steps involved in systems design.

The analyst must coordinate his effort with these policy-makers to produce objectives that fulfill the department's needs without costing too much. If the analyst thinks that additional computer hardware can fulfill the objectives within monetary limitations, for example, he will have to justify this claim, in a feasibility study.

The following represents possible revised objectives, for a new design, that are within the constraints imposed, and that may be suggested by an analyst.

a. The distribution of sales by product line will be made available to management each day for decision-making purposes.
b. A Banking system will be equipped with terminals in each branch office to facilitate personal check cashing. The teller will dial the computer via touch-tone telephone, enter the account number and amount of check, and receive an audio response which indicates central office approval.
c. An Inventory system will utilize the computer to automatically generate purchase orders whenever the stock level for an item reaches its predetermined reorder point.

2. Outputs
Here, again, the analyst suggests revisions in output, based on his understanding of the present system and the requirements of the revised one. These revisions are generally in the following areas.

a. New reports that provide more meaningful information.
b. Revised distribution or frequency of reports that results in an improved information flow.
c. New types of output forms that better serve the department's needs. These include specialized forms, multiple-carbon types, and so on.

The analyst will suggest changes to existing output that he deems appropriate. Keep in mind, however, that he is a member of the *staff* organization and, as such, his role is one of advising, not dictating. No one knows better than the businessman what serves his interests best. Thus, suggestions by the analyst may be appropriate ones or they may be based on misconceptions or misunderstandings of the system's requirements. Perhaps a given output form can be condensed so that it is more efficient from the analyst's point of view. Ultimately, however, the businessman must judge whether it would satisfactorily fulfill his requirements.

The design of output is perhaps the single most important element of systems design. It is, after all, this output with which the businessman will be required to work long after all elements have been integrated. Thus, when new reports are recommended, the analyst should provide:

a. A sample form with representative data on it; and,
b. (if multiple copy forms are suggested) all copies—with the different color schemes and notations that will be used in the new design to designate each copy.

3. Processing

Once the outputs for the new system have been prepared, the analyst designs the processing steps that will be needed to produce them. At this point he has a *general* idea of the types of inputs that will be employed in the new system, based on his familiarity with current inputs. These will provide a general frame of reference for processing requirements even though the inputs may be modified later on in the new design.

An experienced and thorough analyst designs a *total* system, utilizing computer equipment, that does not necessarily follow the present way of performing operations. The use of a computer affords the analyst a greater degree of flexibility than is feasible in a manual system.

Thus it is possible that the analyst may recommend *online* (or immediate-update) processing to replace *batch* (or group) processing in a particular system, if such online capabilities will enhance productivity or increase profits.

For example, a small department store may currently utilize an Accounts Receivable system that manually updates customer records once a week. That is, weekly, all charge slips are *batch* processed to update the file. The analyst may suggest a new design that utilizes terminals at sales counters within the store. These devices are keyed with customer charge account data, at the time of purchase, to immediately update the specific record.

Here, again, the businessman is far more informed on the department's needs and operations than the analyst. Thus the businessman must work closely with the analyst so that the processing adequately serves the department.

A common tool used by the analyst for communicating his ideas on the new design's processing is the *SYSTEMS FLOWCHART*. The systems flowchart, like its more detailed counterpart, the program flowchart, depicts the relationships between inputs, processing and outputs, in terms of the system as a whole. It is a general representation of the information flow within the total system.

The businessman who is familiar with the organization of a systems flowchart can understand the analyst's new design far more quickly and completely than if he had to wade through numerous pages of narrative describing the system.

Figure 17.3 illustrates the symbols used in a systems flowchart. The representation of a systems flowchart is very similar to that of a program flowchart.

a. Each symbol indicates a type of function.
b. A notation appears inside each symbol, indicating the specific operations.
c. The flowchart is normally read from top to bottom.

EXAMPLE 1

Figure 17.4 illustrates a sample systems flowchart for a new Payroll system. Payroll forms indicating new employees and changes in position are punched into cards, sorted, and used to update a master payroll tape. In addition to the updated payroll tape, the payroll checks and a payroll report are generated by the computer.

Note that it is relatively easy for trained businessmen to understand the processing involved by reading a systems flowchart.

EXAMPLE 2

Figure 17.5 illustrates the procedure for the updating of an Accounts Receivable File with credit and sales information.

In short, a businessman with the ability to read flowcharts has the advantage of understanding clearly and distinctly the processing of data by computers in the new design. He can then determine if this processing realistically serves the needs of the department.

4. Inputs
The source documents such as time sheets, sales slips, and credit slips that are entered into the present system represent the initial input forms. You will recall that usually these source documents are converted into a machine readable form, unless they have previously been designed for machine acceptance (for example, a time card as input to a card reader). Often, these are not redesigned by the analyst since: (a) they may be utilized by more than one department, (b) they may be required in a specific format; or (c) they will

The Systems Flowchart is a *standard* diagram. That is, the symbols conform to those established by the United States of America Standards Institute (USASI). Let us discuss the most widely used symbols:

SYMBOL	NAME	DESCRIPTION
	INPUT/OUTPUT (I/O)	This is a generalized I/O symbol used to denote data entering the system or information that is generated as output. It is most often used when the medium of input or output is not specifically designated. i.e.  INVENTORY ERROR CORRECTIONS where such corrections may enter the system by cards, slips of paper or even telephone messages.
	PUNCHED CARD	This symbol is used when the data entered into the system or coming out of the system is in the form of a punched card.
	MAGNETIC TAPE	Magnetic tape is either the input or output medium.
	DOCUMENT	The input or output is a printed document or report.
	ONLINE STORAGE	Data is stored on all online or direct-access device such as a magnetic disk or drum.

Table title: INPUT/OUTPUT SYMBOLS

Figure 17.3
Systems flowchart symbols.

Systems Analysis and Design

INPUT/OUTPUT SYMBOLS		
SYMBOL	NAME	DESCRIPTION
	DISPLAY	*Output* information is displayed on console typewriters, displays, online terminals, plotters, etc.
	MANUAL INPUT	*Input* Information is supplied manually at the time of processing from an online device such as a console typewriter.
	COMMUNICATION LINK	Information is transmitted automatically from one location to another via communication lines.
	OFFLINE STORAGE	Data is stored on an offline medium; that is, data stored is not immediately accessible by the computer. An online device, such as a magnetic disk may always be available for immediate processing. A magnetic tape, however, is generally stored offline in a tape library and cannot be accessed immediately.
	PUNCHED TAPE	Data is stored on a punched paper tape as either input or output. This medium is often used as the initial data form, before conversion to magnetic tape. i.e. 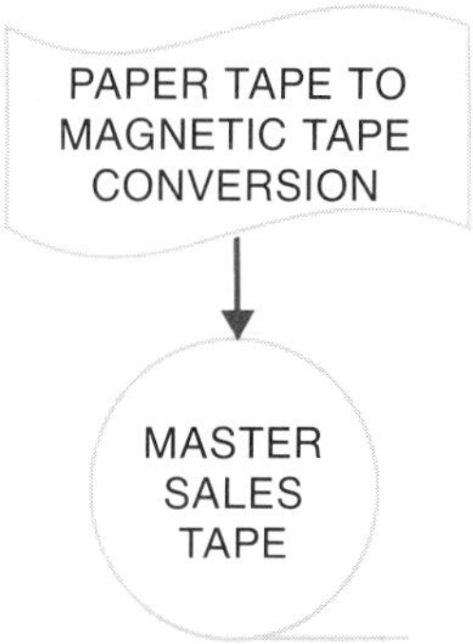

PAPER TAPE TO MAGNETIC TAPE CONVERSION

MASTER SALES TAPE

Figure 17.3 (*cont.*)
Systems flowchart symbols.

	PROCESSING SYMBOLS	
SYMBOL	NAME	DESCRIPTION
	PROCESSING	This symbol represents the performing of an operation or a group of operations, generally by a computer or accounting machine, where the processing is a major function of the system. i.e. CARD TO TAPE PROGRAM REPRODUCE INPUT CARDS
	MANUAL OPERATION	This symbol represents a manual operation or one which requires an operator. Keypunching and verifying are examples of manual operations.
	ANNOTATION	This symbol is used when explanatory notes are required to clarify another symbol. This symbol is not in the main flow of the diagram. i.e. CONSOLE SWITCH MUST BE OFF COMPUTER RUN # 107
	AUXILIARY OPERATION	Offline equipment is used to perform such functions as sorting, merging, collating, etc.
	CONNECTOR	This symbol is used to alter or terminate the flow of data. i.e. 2-B Go to page 2, symbol labelled B

Figure 17.3 (*cont.*)
Systems flowchart symbols.

Systems Analysis and Design

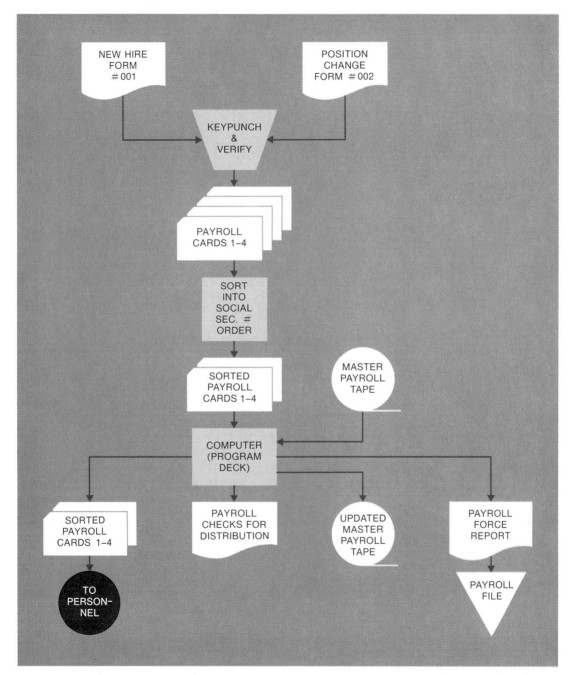

Figure 17.4
Sample systems flowchart for payroll application.

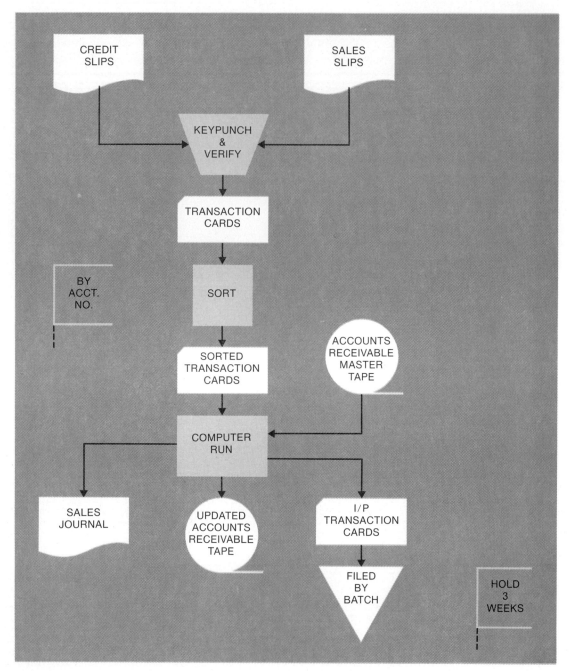

Figure 17.5
Updating procedure of an accounts receivable system in a department store.

Systems Analysis and Design

```
1. Selection of file type
2. Design of the files with respect
   to
   a. Field size
   b. Coded fields
   c. Positioning of data within a
      record
```

Figure 17.6
Elements of input design.

satisfactorily serve the new system. If the analyst does think they need revision, however, he must alter them to provide data in a more meaningful and efficient manner.

Thus the input design that the analyst produces is the one that will be used by the computer for processing.

The elements of input design include (see Figure 17.6):

a. Selection of file type

Cards, tape, or disk are traditional file types that are selected by the analyst as input. He bases his selection of file type on:

1. Cost
2. Speed of device
3. Volume
4. Projected future growth
5. Current hardware
6. Type of processing

The relative merits of each file type have been outlined in Chapters 3 and 5. Figure 17.7 reviews the major characteristics of each. (Note that for terminal processing the input file type is generally the source document itself keyed into the device and transmitted across communication lines.)

The businessman should be aware of the file types selected by the analyst for the input files. He should also be advised as to the reasons why the analyst chose the specific types. In this way, the businessman who possesses some familiarity with data processing equipment can perhaps make suggestions for alternative file types based on his expertise in the business area.

b. Design of the files

Once the file type has been chosen, the analyst must structure, organize, and design the file as efficiently as possible.

Generally, the analyst will exhibit his file design with the use of a Card Layout Sheet (Figure 17.8) for card files, or a Tape or Disk Layout Sheet (called a STORAGE LAYOUT SHEET; Figure 17.9) for tape or disk files.

These sheets serve the same purpose as Print Layout Sheets. They

File Type	Characteristics	Advantages	Disadvantages
Punched card	80 columns; data recorded by keypunch and card punch of computer	utilized by electronic accounting machines to supplement computer use; relatively inexpensive in small volume jobs, can be maintained by operator because data is visual	warp easily; easily mishandled; very inefficient for large volume of jobs because of relatively slow I/O
Magnetic tape	data represented as magnetized bits on an iron oxide coating; data recorded by computer or a keytape converter	efficient for large volume jobs; any size record can be stored; store millions of characters on a single tape;	information not visible with the naked eye; strictly sequential processing; cannot read and write from same tape during a single operation
Direct access files	includes magnetic disk, drum and data cell; addresses of disk records may be "looked up" on an index— data recorded by computer via disk drive	efficient for large volume jobs; any size record can be stored; stores millions of characters on a single disk; random and sequential processing; can read and write from one disk during a single operation	data usually recorded by computer only— there is no inexpensive keying device; relatively expensive; requires much software; restrictions must often be placed on number of drives in an installation

Figure 17.7
Characteristics of the three major file types.

indicate the positioning of data within a record so that the record format can be exhibited.

The businessman who must work with the analyst should pay particular attention to the following file design items that will directly affect processing:

1. Field Size.

Each field must be long enough to accommodate the largest data item. A NAME field, in a Payroll file for example, must generally be large enough to accommodate the employee with the longest name.

The analyst determines the field size, but the businessman must ascertain that it is adequate.

2. Coded Fields.

To conserve space on a file and to facilitate the processing of data, the analyst often uses coded fields of information. ACCOUNT NUMBER, for example, in place of CUSTOMER NAME, may become a new design item in a file. It is more appropriate for computer processing to use integer fields (ACCOUNT NUMBERS), as key items, rather than alphanumeric fields (CUSTOMER NAME). Similarly, it is easier to sort on such numeric fields.

If coded fields are employed by the analyst in the file design, the businessman must make certain that they are adequate and will be used effectively. It should be ascertained that the length of the coded field is adequate enough to handle all items—both for the present and in the future. For example, an Accounts Receivable Department which currently has 986 customers should use an ACCOUNT NUMBER field of at least four positions (0001–9999) to assure that it is large enough to allow for future growth.

Also, the analyst should provide an implementation or training

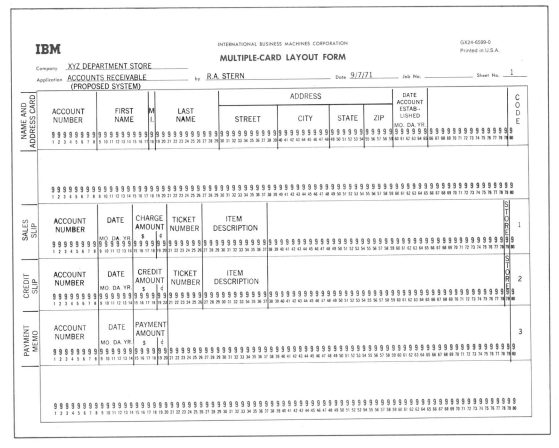

Figure 17.8
Card layout form. Courtesy IBM.

The Interaction Between the Analyst and the Businessman: Systems Design

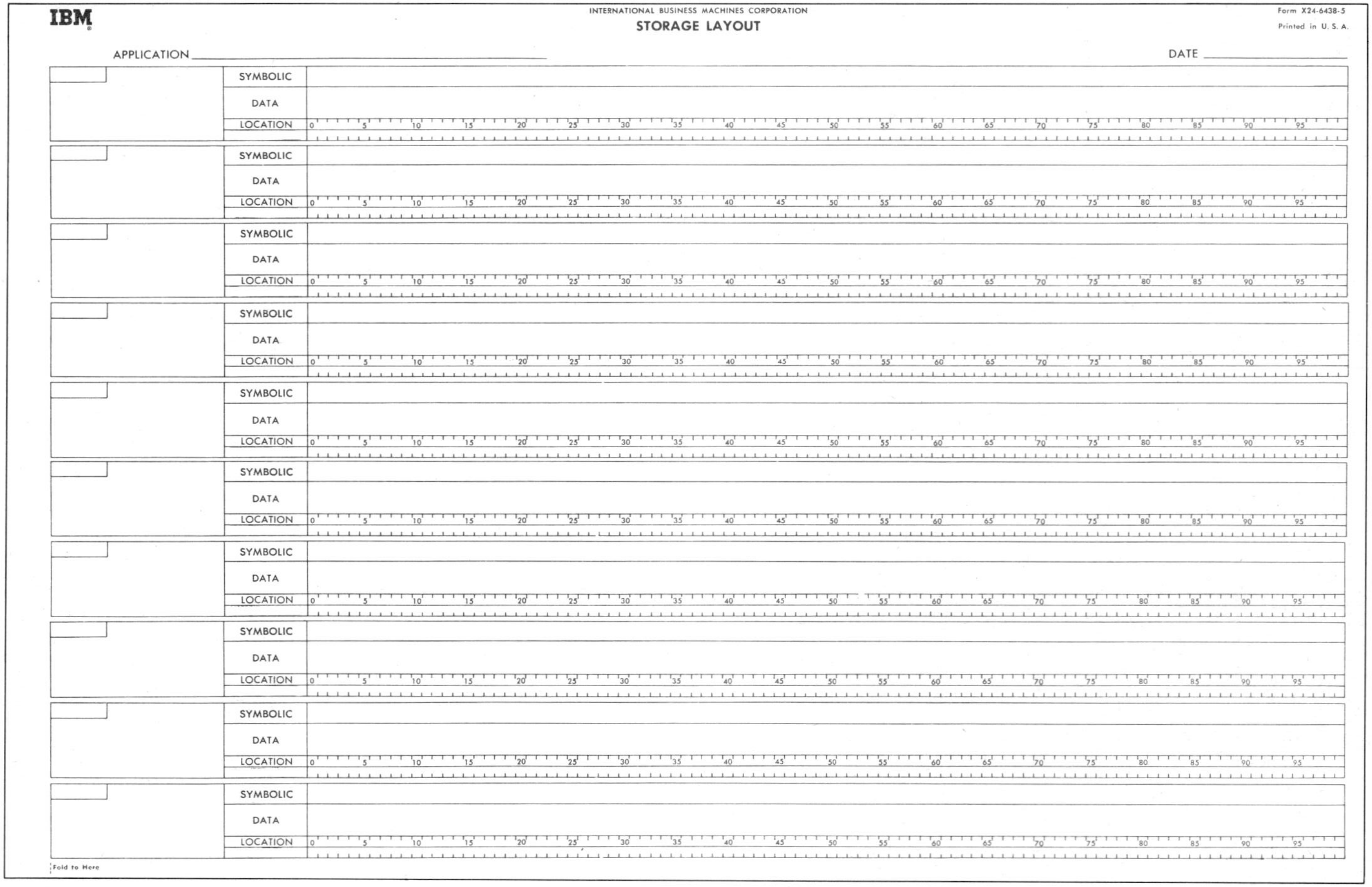

Figure 17.9
Storage layout sheet. Courtesy IBM.

schedule, as required, that familiarizes the current staff with those coded fields with which they will be required to work. If new output reports will contain these ACCOUNT NUMBERS in place of CUSTOMER NAMES, then those who utilize these reports must be familiarized with the codes used.

3. Positioning of Data Within a Record.

Generally, the analyst arranges a record format so that the encoding operations are facilitated. For tape or disk files, it matters little to the business staff how fields are arranged. If, however, card files are to be used by the business staff, then data should be arranged in a meaningful way so that any manual operations, which use the cards, are simplified. Key fields such as ACCOUNT NUMBER, SOCIAL SECURITY NUMBER, and INVENTORY NUMBER should be easily identifiable at the *beginning* of the record.

5. Control and Feedback

Control and feedback procedures must be integrated in the design to insure that the new system is functioning properly and to spot any minor flaws so that they may be corrected before they become major ones.

All the above elements (constraints and objectives, outputs, processing, inputs, controls, and feedback) must be organized and integrated by the analyst in such a manner that a meaningful design evolves.

C. COST ANALYSIS

Once all the elements for the new design have been prepared and integrated, the analyst must prepare a cost analysis of the proposed system, as it compares with the present one. (See the flowchart in Figure 17.1.)

1. Justification of the New Design from a Cost Standpoint

Note that the new design must be approved by management and the business leaders of the related department before it can be implemented. In most companies management will study the cost figures on the proposed system for justification of the new design.

The chief reason, in most cases, for converting to a new design is that it *eventually* will save the company money. Thus a proposed system, in such cases, must clearly indicate a monetary savings. In other cases, a proposed system, while not resulting in a monetary savings, may mean increased productivity or profits for the company as a whole. Initially, we will limit our discussion to those proposed systems that are designed to result in a monetary savings over present operations.

Costs of the present system cannot, however, be compared *directly* to the costs of a proposed system without some economic analysis.

Initially, costs of the proposed system will include programming and implementation expenses. Often it takes many years to assimilate these expenses. Thus the new system cannot usually show a savings before several years have passed.

The graphic representation of cost analysis often utilized in accounting called BREAK-EVEN ANALYSIS is employed by many systems analysts.

The basic concept of this type of cost study is to illustrate graphically the point in time at which the system begins to break even; that is, the point at which revenue equals costs or where profits are no longer negative or indicating a loss. Figure 17.10 illustrates a sample BREAK-EVEN graph.

In summary, many new designs are approved by management mainly because they will eventually save the company money. Often, however, business leaders seek new systems because of intangible cost factors. A new system may not directly result in a monetary savings but may result in the following intangible benefits, which will improve a company's profits:

a. By providing better service, a new system may attract more customers. This is often justification for utilizing terminals at key locations in an online or real-time environment to answer customer inquiries and to update customer files.
b. By improving production planning, the businessman may have tighter control over production scheduling and material requirements.
c. By reducing the work loads of clerical staffs with the use of

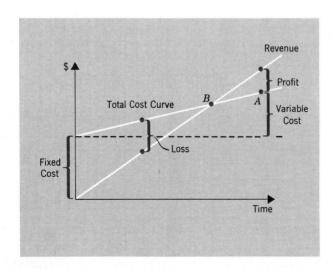

Figure 17.10
Sample break-even graph.

Systems Analysis and Design

computers, a new system may stabilize manpower requirements and reduce extensive overtime.

d. By providing for future growth with the use of computer processing, a new system needs less revisions and less increases in labor and equipment.

Thus, the monetary factors associated with a new design must be outlined and justified before management or business supervisors, in the respective departments, will give approval. These factors may mean a monetary savings to the company within a few years after initial design and programming expenditures have been assimilated. Or they may mean an intangible benefit or savings to the company. In either case, the analyst must justify, from a cost standpoint, his new design to help "sell" it to those businessmen who will be required to work within it.

2. Basic Cost Factors
The costs of the proposed system fall into two basic categories.

a. *DESIGN COSTS*
SYSTEMS DESIGN
PROGRAMMING
TRAINING OF DATA PROCESSING AND BUSINESS STAFF
    TO EFFECTIVELY WORK WITH THE SYSTEM
CONVERSION AND TESTING

b. *RECURRING COSTS*
PERSONNEL
EQUIPMENT RENTALS
SUPPLIES
OVERHEAD

Cost figures for a proposed system should be projected at least three years into the future to adequately allow for projected growth. After three years, cost estimates tend to become inaccurate due to alterations within the system and changes in the economy.

Figure 17.11 illustrates a sample cost breakdown for a new design. Note that it is projected for five years, since the first two years are used exclusively for development of the system.

These figures can then be compared to the current cost figures that are prepared by businessmen working within the present system. For those new systems that are designed to effect a cost savings, a break-even analysis may be performed. For those new systems that result in intangible savings, the analyst must indicate its advantages.

3. Cost Factors for Alternative Systems
The businessman must be aware of the fact that a new design is not unique in its ability to alleviate problem areas in a current system. Any system designed by an analyst should accomplish its required

	Year 1	Year 2	Year 3	Year 4	Year 5
Study Cost					
System design	$ 80,000	$ 10,000			
Programming	65,000	10,000			
Training	6,000				
Physical planning	4,000				
Conversion and test	5,000	8,000			
Recurring Costs					
Personnel		30,000	35,000	40,000	46,000
Rentals		30,000	34,000	38,000	40,000
Overhead		16,000	18,000	20,000	20,000
Supplies		20,000	20,000	20,000	20,000
	$160,000	$124,000	$107,000	$118,000	$126,000
Savings	$(50,000)	$ 7,000	$ 45,000	$ 54,000	$ 75,000
Net annual saving	$(50,000)	$(43,000)	$ 2,000	$ 56,000	$131,000

Note that figures in parentheses denote a loss.

Figure 17.11
Cost breakdown for new design.

objectives and eliminate problem areas. However, each analyst will offer his own solutions that will, no doubt, differ from another analyst's design.

An experienced systems analyst should offer the businessman *alternative* designs, each with its own completion timetable, equipment and personnel requirements and, most importantly, costs. By providing varied systems designs, with different perspectives, management, together with the businessmen in the related fields, are able to select an alternative.

	Initial Costs	Monthly Operating Costs	Time	System Type
SYSTEM 1	$105,000	$2,600	9 mos	Unit Record Equipment, Card System
SYSTEM 2	$187,000	$3,400	14 mos	Computer Oriented, Card System, Growth Potential
SYSTEM 3	$314,000	$8,700	36 mos	Real-time Computer System, Terminals

Figure 17.12
Table of alternative system designs.

Let us consider an example. Suppose an analyst has been assigned to design an Accounts Receivable system. He may provide the alternatives noted in Figure 17.12.

The initial costs associated with each system are broken down on a separate form. Each system offers a specific solution. The analyst should indicate that:

a. System 1 is least costly initially, but does not provide for adequate growth capabilities. Eventually, its personnel operating costs would become quite extensive.

b. System 3 provides the most accurate and up-to-date Accounts Receivable system. Even though it is the costliest and requires the most time to implement, it could result in increased company profits by attracting more customers and allowing for maximum growth.

c. System 2 offers a compromise and provides a realistic, workable system.

With the above alternatives, management and businessmen in the specific area can determine which is best suited to the department's needs. The recommendation by the analyst to select System 2 will probably result in its selection, but management should at least be cognizant of possible alternatives.

D. DOCUMENTATION

Once the analyst has fully designed a system by integrating all of the above elements, he must prepare a formalized, detailed record called the DOCUMENTATION package which describes that design. (See the flowchart in Figure 17.1.) This DOCUMENTATION serves many functions.

1. It is a businessman's tool for evaluating the design.

The DOCUMENTATION is utilized by business representatives, within a department, and management. Together they determine if the new design satisfies the objectives of the company within the established constraints and if it is justifiable from a cost standpoint. That is, the documentation provides a record that is used by management to assess the new design.

2. It provides a frame of reference on the new system.

The department in which the new system will function needs formalized procedures by which the staff can be guided. Similarly, the programming and operations personnel assigned to implement the new design will need a standard from which an understanding of the system as a whole can be derived and from which a detailed picture of the program specifications can be obtained.

Basically, the DOCUMENTATION contains the following.

1. Cover Letter

This defines the objectives and constraints of the new system and indicates briefly how the new design will meet these. It is an introduction to the revised system and is an attempt to "sell" it or to convince management of its feasibility and advantages. Keep in mind that unless business leaders approve the new design effort, then a new system cannot be implemented.

2. Narrative

This is a brief outline, in narrative form, of the workings of the new system.

3. Systems Flowcharts

4. File Specifications

In addition to the required layout sheets, each file must be described with respect to:

- **a.** Purpose
- **b.** Programs that will utilize the file
- **c.** Volume
- **d.** Frequency of use
- **e.** Source from which file is obtained
- **f.** Description of fields
- **g.** Layout and samples

5. Specifications of Each Program Necessary Within the System

6. Costs of the Proposed System and Economic Justification of the New Design

E. CONVERSION AND IMPLEMENTATION

The analyst must prepare a conversion procedure to insure a smooth transition from the old system to the new, once the new design has been approved and programming effort has been completed.

Typically, the new system is used in a *parallel run,* together with the old, to ascertain that the same results are achieved. If output data is not the same, then the causes of the inaccuracies must be found and eliminated before the new system can be implemented. Once the new design has been proven error-free, all procedures and operations can be systematically transferred.

The steps involved in most system conversions that must be prepared by the analyst include the need to:

1. Establish schedules for the transfer of operations to the computer. An estimate must be included indicating the time required to completely convert or cut over to the new system.

2. Assist in the creation of master files that will be required for most operations. The data for these master files must be amassed from manual files, edited, and converted to a machine-readable form.
3. Supervise a pilot operation.
4. Train and reorient clerical and business staffs.

Clerical staffs will often be given new assignments after conversion has been completed. They must receive proper training from the analyst on their new tasks. Similarly, businessmen who receive the output must be advised of all changes in forms or forms distribution.

After a system has been cut over, the analyst still has the responsibility to follow up and insure that it is functioning properly. Approximately three months after the new system is fully operational, the analyst should check back to see if the system is working properly. He may find, for example, that some employees are no longer following the procedure exactly. They may have found a better way of performing some aspect, or new personnel may have been misinformed on some procedure. The analyst might also discover some flaws in his design, during the follow-up. Note that it is much easier to correct a flaw after a short time has elapsed than to wait and attempt to patch it after a considerable duration.

In summary, the systems analyst's design tasks involve many major responsibilities. In each phase, however, he must work closely with the businessman to insure a proper understanding of the system's requirements. Similarly, the businessmen must become familiar with aspects of the new design so that successful implementation can be achieved.

SELF-EVALUATING QUIZ

1. The business leaders and the _____ must work together to create a new systems design.
2. First, the _____ and the _____ must be revised so that they provide realistic requirements of the new system within appropriate limitations.
3. Next the _____ of the system are revised to provide business leaders with more meaningful reports.
4. The processing steps involved in a new design are best illustrated by a _____ .
5. The revised inputs must be redesigned with respect to _____ .
6. The new files are best illustrated by _____ sheets.
7. Once all the elements for a new design have been prepared and integrated, the analyst must prepare a _____ of the proposed system.
8. The chief reason for converting to a new design, in most cases, is that it eventually will _____ .
9. Initially, costs of the proposed system will include _____ , _____ , and _____ , expenses that must be assimilated before a comparison between present and proposed system costs can be evaluated.
10. The graphic representation of cost analysis often utilized in accounting and employed by many systems analysts is called _____ .
11. The basic concept of this type of cost study is to illustrate, graphically, the point in time at which _____ .
12. In addition to saving the company money, a new design may have _____ cost benefits.
13. An example of an intangible cost benefit is _____ .
14. Elements included within *DESIGN COSTS* are _____ , _____ , _____ , and _____ .
15. Elements included within *RECURRING COSTS* are _____ , _____ , _____ , and _____ .
16. Because many systems designs can satisfy objectives and alleviate problem areas, a systems analyst should provide businessmen with _____ designs, each with cost figures and justifications, from which a choice can be made.
17. Once the analyst has fully designed a system by integrating all of the above elements, he must prepare a formalized, detailed record called _____ describing that design.
18. After the system has been designed and approved, and programming effort has been completed, the analyst must have a _____ procedure to insure a smooth transition from the old system to the new.
19. A parallel run is _____ .
20. The follow-up is a procedure where _____ .

510

SOLUTIONS

1. systems analyst
2. objectives; constraints
3. outputs
4. systems flowchart
5. file type used and design of the file
6. layout
7. cost analysis
8. save the company money
9. design; programming; conversion
10. break-even analysis
11. the system breaks even, or the revenue equals the costs
12. intangible
13. improved production planning; better customer service
14. systems design costs; programming costs; training costs; conversion costs
15. personnel costs; overhead costs; equipment costs; supply costs
16. alternative
17. the Documentation
18. conversion
19. a procedure where the current and the new system are run together, in parallel, to insure that the new system operates properly
20. the analyst checks the system, after a three-month interval, for example, to insure that it is functioning properly

Chapter 18 *Case Study I— Accounts Receivable*

513

The purpose of this and the following chapter is to present the student with examples of how typical business systems are designed for computer processing. These illustrations will demonstrate several important facets of computerized systems.

1. How the techniques and approaches described in the previous chapters are integrated to achieve the best design for a particular business application.
2. How typical business systems in a data processing environment operate.
3. How well-designed business data processing systems can operate more efficiently, accurately, and quickly than noncomputerized systems.
4. How the presentation of a proposed computerized system for management's approval can be made understandable and yet thorough, without the need for a technical and verbose approach. That is, these case studies will illustrate what the student should expect to find in a typical documentation package.

The first business system to be presented is that of a typical Accounts Receivable System. The company portrayed is a department store which, at the present time, has approximately 15,000 charge account customers. The Accounts Receivable system is currently

Systems Analysis and Design

being run with the use of Electronic Accounting Machines. However, with the rapid growth of charge accounts that the company has been experiencing, the current system is proving inadequate to handle the volume of activity.

It is becoming increasingly difficult to maintain schedules for processing and to insure the accuracy of information processed. For these reasons, the following proposal for a computerized Accounts Receivable System has been prepared for management's consideration. If accepted, the new system will save the company approximately $15,480 a year (after an initial write-off of 28 months for design costs). It will not only provide management with information that is more quickly and accurately processed, but it will incorporate computer features that will provide new capability heretofore unattainable in the Accounts Receivable System. The following represents a sample documentation package which is written by the systems analyst to provide management with a detailed presentation of the new design.

I. Proposal for a Computerized Accounts Receivable System at Nanbeth's Department Store

A. OBJECTIVES AND CONSTRAINTS

The major *objectives* of this Accounts Receivable System are as follows:

1. To establish and maintain accounts for each charge customer.
2. To send monthly statements to each customer.
3. To suspend charge account privileges for customers who are delinquent in payment for more than three months.
4. To provide sales personnel with the ability to quickly retrieve information from the computer in response to customer inquiries concerning their accounts.
5. To provide management with accurate reports for decision-making and planning purposes.

The system will be processed on a third-generation computer that is already operating in the company. The basic constraint is the computer system which consists of:

1 CPU with storage capacity of approximately 130,000 characters
4 tape drives
2 disk drives
1 card reader-punch
1 printer
6 display terminals

B. THE BASIC OUTPUTS OBTAINED FROM THE COMPUTERIZED SYSTEM

1. Monthly Statement—for Transmittal to the Customer—Figure 18.1

The Monthly Statements are prepared on preprinted forms on a rotating basis. That is, the accounts are subdivided into groups by account number, and statements are rendered to each group on different dates. This eliminates peak loads for the computer, which would occur if all statements were produced at the same time.

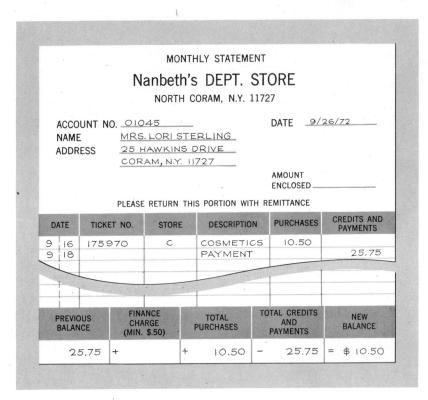

Figure 18.1
Monthly statement.

2. Trial Balance—for Accounts Receivable Use (prepared monthly)—Figure 18.2

The Trial Balance for Accounts Receivable is prepared on stock paper and is used to insure the accuracy of all debits (e.g., charge sales) and credits (e.g., returns of merchandise) posted by the computer to the Accounts Receivable file during the current accounting period. Account balances are determined by adding the debit and credit amounts for each account. These balances are then listed in the trial balance. The resultant balances are then added and checked against totals obtained from the Accounts Receivable Summary Report, below.

ACCOUNTS RECEIVABLE TRIAL BALANCE

AS OF   9-30-72

ACCOUNT NO.	DEBITS	CREDITS
01025	50.25	
01026	27.65	
01030	35.10	
01035		27.15
01037	26.07	
01038		

TOTALS	557,233.10	385,957.15
DEBITS—CREDITS	171,275.95	

Figure 18.2
Trial balance.

3. Accounts Receivable Summary Report—for Accounts
   Receivable Use (prepared weekly)—Figure 18.3

This report is prepared weekly on stock paper. Each month the four weekly reports are used collectively.

These Accounts Receivable Summary Reports (4 per month) serve three basic purposes:

a. All four reports for the month are used by the Accounts Receivable Department for checking *totals* in the Trial Balance for Accounts Receivable. This total is compared against the cumulative *totals* in the four summary reports.

b. These four reports, each month, may be used by management to determine which store or stores might benefit from having special sales for charge account customers only.

Case Study I—Accounts Receivable   517

c. These reports are used by Sales personnel to confirm batch totals taken on inputs sent for processing, as discussed under Source Documents below.

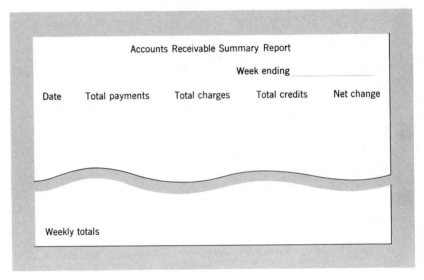

Figure 18.3
Summary report.

4. Changes in Customer Information—for Accounts Receivable Use (prepared monthly)—Figure 18.4

This report, prepared on stock paper, is used by the Accounts Receivable Department as a "double" check to insure that information transmitted to Data Processing pertaining to additions, deletions, and corrections of customer accounts has been correctly incorporated. The codes are as follows:

1 New Account
2 Account Deleted
3 Change of Name
4 Change of Address
5 Change of Name and Address

The report is also used by the Sales Department for determining whether the number of charge account customers are on the rise or decline.

Systems Analysis and Design

```
                CHANGES IN CUSTOMER INFORMATION
                         AS OF 9-15-72

            ————NAME————    —————ADDRESS——————
ACCOUNT NO.  LAST    FIRST  M.I.  STREET        CITY        STATE  ZIP    CODE

   02057    BAKER   JOHN     A   16A MAIN ST.  HUNTINGTON,  N.Y.  11746    1
   02169    CARROL  NANCY    B   20 E. 101 ST. BROOKLYN,    N.Y.  11224    3
   05217    ADAMS   STERLING     5 NORTH AVE.  CORAM,       N.Y.  11727    4


NEW ACCOUNTS:    362              ACCOUNTS CHANGED:   36

ACCOUNTS DELETED:  57
```

Figure 18.4
Changes in customer information.

5. Delinquent Account Report Used for Suspending Accounts (prepared monthly)—Figure 18.5

This report, prepared on stock paper, is normally produced once a month. It is used by the Accounts Receivable Department to suspend charge privileges for customers who are delinquent in payment for more than three months. The report is also available upon request by management for special use. As an example, prior to special sales for charge account customers only, management might want the most

```
               DELINQUENT ACCOUNT REPORT          AS OF 10-25-72

ACCOUNT CURRENT   DATE OF    ——NAME———      ————ADDRESS—————
NUMBER  BALANCE LAST PAYMENT LAST   FIRST   STREET         CITY      STATE  ZIP

 05073  350.22   5-28-72   CRIMSON JOHN   112 NORTH ST.  SELDON,    N.Y.  11728
 06092   87.20   4-20-72   ABRAMS  JOAN   5827B JERSEY ST. CORAM,   N.Y.  11727
 06095  469.10   8-07-72   WATERS ROBERT 11-05 E. 5 ST.  BROOKLYN,  N.Y.  11223
```

Figure 18.5
Delinquent account report.

current report to determine whether special consideration is to be given to these delinquent-account customers (e.g. suspension of charge privileges).

The Master Accounts Receivable File, which is stored on magnetic disk, is the major file that is used in processing information to produce all output files. All information pertaining to each customer is maintained here, as depicted in Figure 18.6.

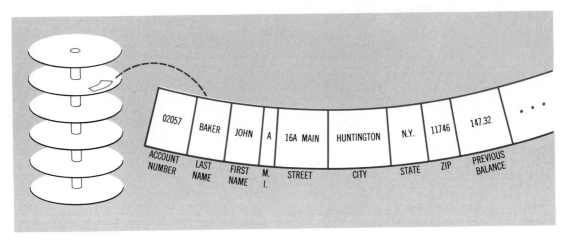

Figure 18.6
Master accounts receivable disk file.

An online disk file has been chosen so that customer inquiries can be easily handled from terminals located on the sales floor.

There are six terminals at specified sales counters linked electronically to the CPU and to the disk file, at the computer center. The *online* feature of this system allows sales personnel to make inquiries of customer accounts at the specified sales counters via the terminals.

The random access feature of this type of file was the primary factor in choosing a disk file over a strictly sequential file such as tape or cards.

C. THE BASIC SOURCE DOCUMENTS USED IN THE SYSTEM

1. Application for a Charge Account—Figure 18.7
A customer desiring charge privileges must fill out an Application for a Charge Account. This document, once approved, supplies the information that is used for establishing a new account in the Master Accounts Receivable File on disk.

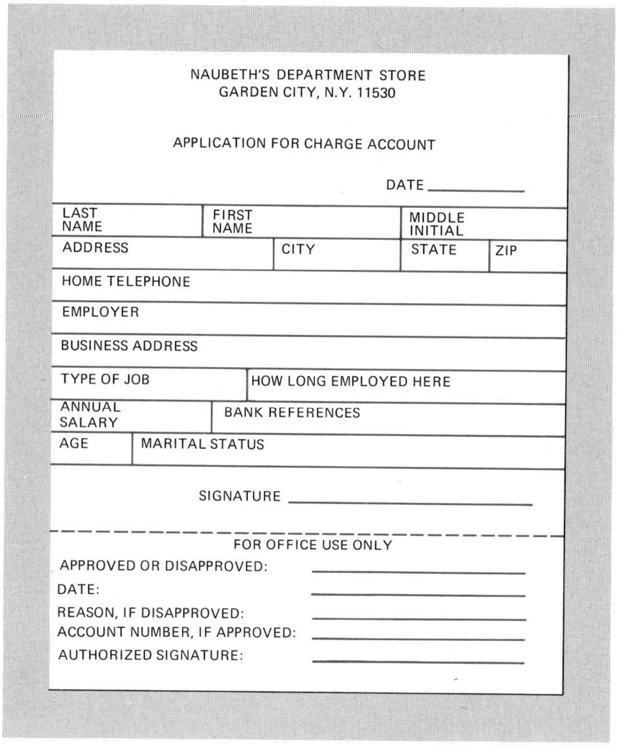

```
            NAUBETH'S DEPARTMENT STORE
            GARDEN CITY, N.Y. 11530


            APPLICATION FOR CHARGE ACCOUNT

                              DATE _____

  LAST          | FIRST         |  MIDDLE
  NAME          | NAME          |  INITIAL
  ADDRESS             | CITY     |  STATE  | ZIP
  HOME TELEPHONE
  EMPLOYER
  BUSINESS ADDRESS
  TYPE OF JOB         | HOW LONG EMPLOYED HERE
  ANNUAL   | BANK REFERENCES
  SALARY
  AGE    | MARITAL STATUS

            SIGNATURE _____

  - - - - - - - - - - - - - - - - - - - - - - - -
                FOR OFFICE USE ONLY
  APPROVED OR DISAPPROVED:      _____
  DATE:                         _____
  REASON, IF DISAPPROVED:       _____
  ACCOUNT NUMBER, IF APPROVED:  _____
  AUTHORIZED SIGNATURE:         _____
```

Figure 18.7
Application for charge account.

2. Charge Slip—Figure 18.8

The charge slip is a prenumbered, white form that is filled out for all sales that are charged. The customer's account number, name, and address are imprinted on the slip from the charge card.

The sales clerk fills out the charge slip, imprints the account number, name and address from the charge card, signs the slip and has the customer sign it.

There are three copies of the charge slip:

Copy 1 is transmitted to the Data Processing Department.
Copy 2 is given to the customer.
Copy 3 is filed by the Sales Department for determining batch totals, as explained below, and for future reference.

At the end of each day, each sales person takes the charge slips for his department and totals them on an adding machine before sending the batch to Data Processing. The weekly totals are checked against the totals in the Accounts Receivable Summary Report, produced weekly by the computer. If a discrepancy exists, then it is likely that one or more charge slips have been misplaced.

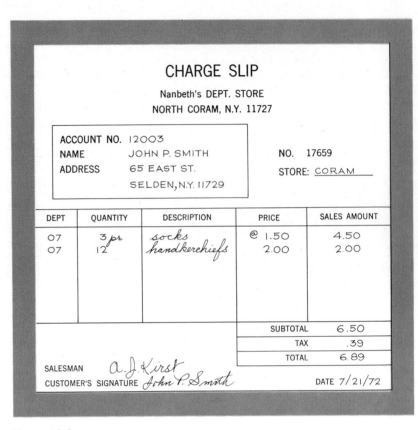

CHARGE SLIP

Nanbeth's DEPT. STORE
NORTH CORAM, N.Y. 11727

ACCOUNT NO. 12003
NAME   JOHN P. SMITH   NO.   17659
ADDRESS   65 EAST ST.   STORE: CORAM
    SELDEN, N.Y. 11729

DEPT	QUANTITY	DESCRIPTION	PRICE	SALES AMOUNT
07	3 pr	socks	@ 1.50	4.50
07	12	handkerchiefs	2.00	2.00

	SUBTOTAL	6.50
	TAX	.39
	TOTAL	6.89

SALESMAN   a. J. Kirst
CUSTOMER'S SIGNATURE   John P. Smith   DATE 7/21/72

Figure 18.8
Charge slip.

3. Credit Memo—Figure 18.9
The credit memo is used when:

a. Merchandise is returned for credit.
b. The customer is given an allowance for damaged merchandise, which he will accept.
c. An adjustment is necessary to the account, to compensate for an improperly recorded transaction.

    The memo is a prenumbered *pink* form to clearly distinguish it from the charge slip (which is white). Customer identification (account number, name, and address) is imprinted on the form from the charge card. The three copies of the credit memo are distributed as follows.

Copy 1 is transmitted to the Data Processing Department.
Copy 2 is given to the customer.
Copy 3 is filed by the Sales Department for determining batch totals and also for future reference. The process of determining batch totals is identical to that discussed above for the charge slips.

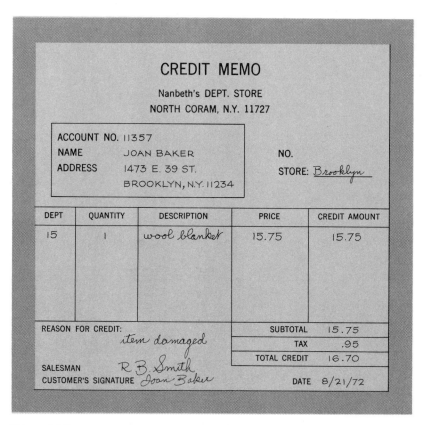

CREDIT MEMO

Nanbeth's DEPT. STORE

NORTH CORAM, N.Y. 11727

ACCOUNT NO. 11357

NAME   JOAN BAKER

ADDRESS   1473 E. 39 ST.

              BROOKLYN, N.Y. 11234

NO.

STORE: *Brooklyn*

DEPT	QUANTITY	DESCRIPTION	PRICE	CREDIT AMOUNT
15	1	*wool blanket*	15.75	15.75

REASON FOR CREDIT: *item damaged*

SALESMAN *R. B. Smith*

CUSTOMER'S SIGNATURE *Joan Baker*

SUBTOTAL	15.75
TAX	.95
TOTAL CREDIT	16.70

DATE 8/21/72

Figure 18.9
Credit memo.

4. Payment Memo—Figure 18.10

The payment memo is generally completed by the credit office upon receipt of the customer's remittance and the remittance stub from the monthly statement. A copy is sent to Data Processing so that the customer's account can be properly credited.

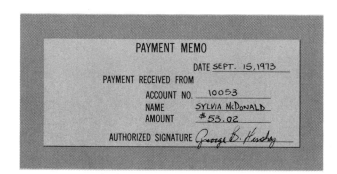

PAYMENT MEMO

DATE SEPT. 15, 1973

PAYMENT RECEIVED FROM

ACCOUNT NO. 10053

NAME SYLVIA McDONALD

AMOUNT $53.02

AUTHORIZED SIGNATURE *George B. Hershey*

Figure 18.10
Payment memo.

```
                    CORRECTION MEMO
ACCOUNT NO._____

CHANGE ☐ NAME FROM _____|__|_____  TO _____|__|_____
                        FIRST  INIT.  LAST          FIRST  INIT.  LAST
        ☐ ADDRESS FROM                   TO
            STREET  _____        _____
            CITY    _____        _____
            STATE   _____        _____
            ZIP     _____        _____

AUTHORIZED SIGNATURE _____  DATE _____
```

Figure 18.11
Correction memo.

5. Name and Address Correction Memo—Figure 18.11

Each month customers notify the Accounts Receivable Department of changes to their accounts pertaining to name and/or address corrections.

This memo is prepared by the Accounts Receivable Department to record changes in a customer's name and/or address. A copy is sent to Data Processing so that this customer information can be correctly recorded on the Master Accounts Receivable Disk File.

D. THE BASIC PROCESSING

The basic processing in the proposed system involves:

1. The processing of Approved Applications for Charge Accounts, and Name and Address Correction Memos (see Figure A).
2. The updating of accounts with information from charge slips, credit memos, and payment memos (see Figure B).
3. The processing required to obtain specific outputs from the Master Accounts Receivable Disk File (see Figure C).

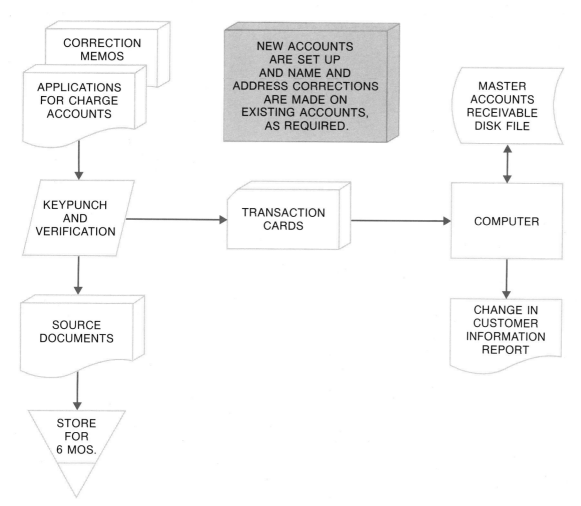

Figure A
Processing of approved applications for charge accounts, and name and address correction memos.

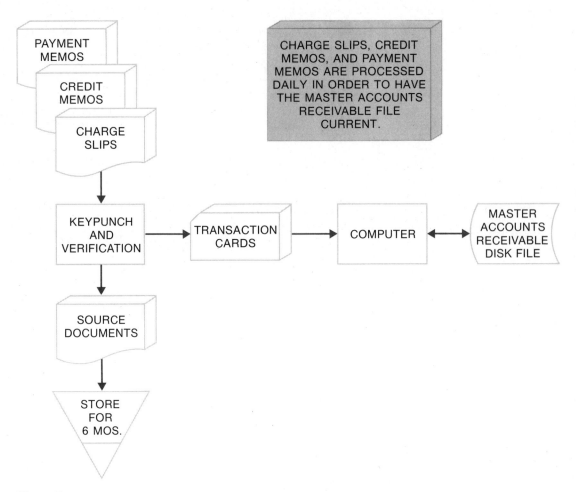

Figure B
Updating accounts with information from charge slips, credit memos, and payment memos.

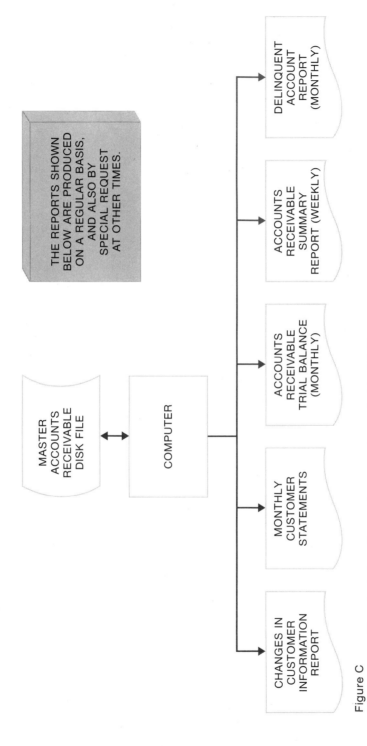

THE REPORTS SHOWN BELOW ARE PRODUCED ON A REGULAR BASIS, AND ALSO BY SPECIAL REQUEST AT OTHER TIMES.

MASTER ACCOUNTS RECEIVABLE DISK FILE

COMPUTER

CHANGES IN CUSTOMER INFORMATION REPORT

MONTHLY CUSTOMER STATEMENTS

ACCOUNTS RECEIVABLE TRIAL BALANCE (MONTHLY)

ACCOUNTS RECEIVABLE SUMMARY REPORT (WEEKLY)

DELINQUENT ACCOUNT REPORT (MONTHLY)

Figure C
Obtaining specific outputs from the master accounts receivable disk file.

Table 18.1

Monthly Costs for Current System—Adjusted for Growth		Monthly Costs for Proposed System	
PERSONNEL			
Manager of Accounts Receivable	$ 1,500	Manager of Accounts Receivable	$1,500
9 Accounts Receivable clerks	3,450	2 Accounts Receivable clerks	770
3 typists	1,425	1 typist	475
3 keypunch operators	1,200	3 keypunch operators	1,200
1.5 unit record operators	750	.5 computer operators	300
EQUIPMENT			
.6 sorter	90	Computer system, including	
.3 collator	45	keypunch machines and	
.9 accounting machine	225	verifiers—an allocation of	
3 keypunch machines	255	25% of the total antici-	
3 verifiers	300	pated company-wide	
(*Note*. Times allocated to each device were esti- mated by Operations Manager.)		monthly cost of $14,620 has been determined by management to apply to this system.	3,655
SUPPLIES			
120,000 punched cards	135	120,000 punched cards	135
60 boxes of preprinted forms[a]	600	60 boxes of preprinted forms[a]	600
30 boxes of stock paper[a]	150	40 boxes of stock paper[a]	200
TOTAL COST	$10,125		$8,835

[a] Primarily 2-ply paper, 1,600 sheets to a box.

E. COST ANALYSIS

Table 18.1 shows a detailed cost comparison between the current Accounts Receivable system and the proposed computerized one.

As can be seen from the comparison, the proposed system will cost $8835 per month to operate as compared to the adjusted figure of $10,125 for the current system. (The current system has been adjusted for growth for comparison purposes.) Therefore, the proposed system will save the company approximately $1290 per month once it is operational. Since the design of the new system plus implementation will cost $36,100, it will take 28 months to write off the developmental costs of the proposed system.

II. Appendix—Sample Layout Forms

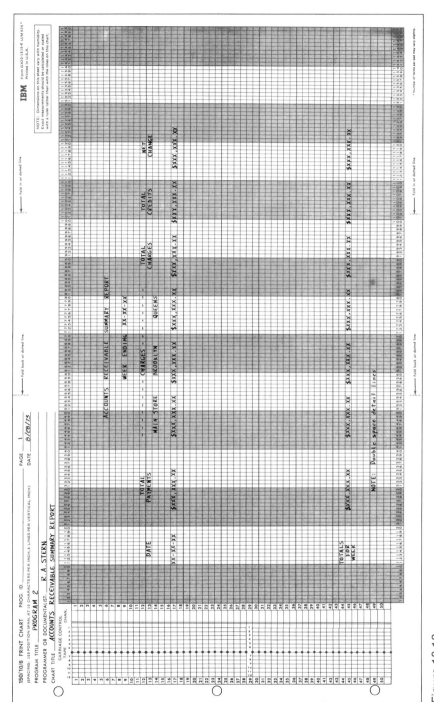

Figure 18.12
Accounts Receivable summary report.

529

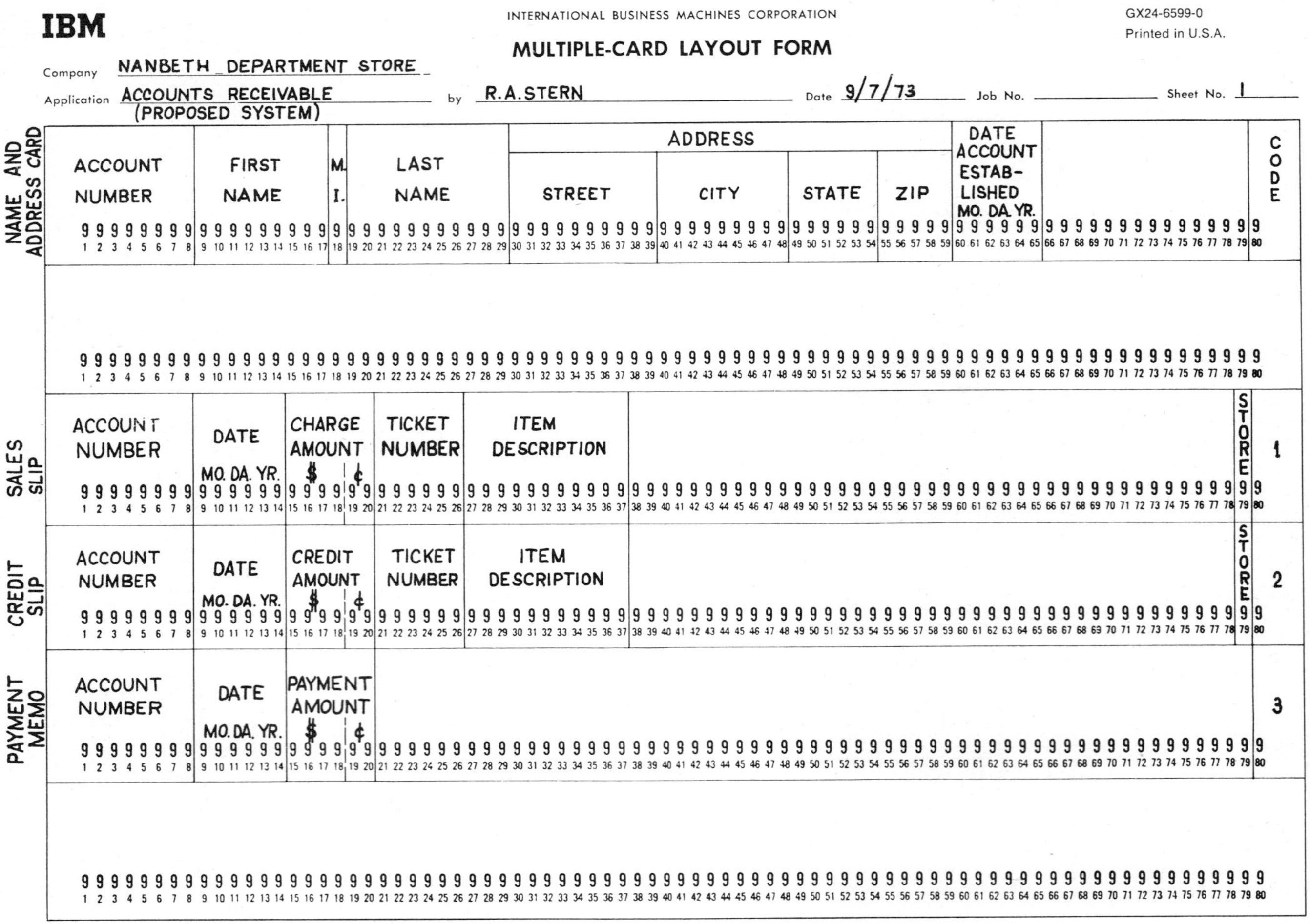

IBM

INTERNATIONAL BUSINESS MACHINES CORPORATION

MULTIPLE-CARD LAYOUT FORM

GX24-6599-0
Printed in U.S.A.

Company __NANBETH DEPARTMENT STORE__

Application __ACCOUNTS RECEIVABLE__
(PROPOSED SYSTEM)

by __R.A.STERN__ Date __9/7/73__ Job No. ____ Sheet No. __1__

NAME AND ADDRESS CARD

| ACCOUNT NUMBER | FIRST NAME | M. I. | LAST NAME | ADDRESS | | | | | DATE ACCOUNT ESTAB-LISHED MO.DA.YR. | CODE |
| | | | | STREET | CITY | STATE | ZIP | | |

SALES SLIP

| ACCOUNT NUMBER | DATE MO.DA.YR. | CHARGE AMOUNT $ ¢ | TICKET NUMBER | ITEM DESCRIPTION | STORE | 1 |

CREDIT SLIP

| ACCOUNT NUMBER | DATE MO.DA.YR. | CREDIT AMOUNT $ ¢ | TICKET NUMBER | ITEM DESCRIPTION | STORE | 2 |

PAYMENT MEMO

| ACCOUNT NUMBER | DATE MO.DA.YR. | PAYMENT AMOUNT $ ¢ | | | | 3 |

Figure 18.13
Accounts Receivable card formats.

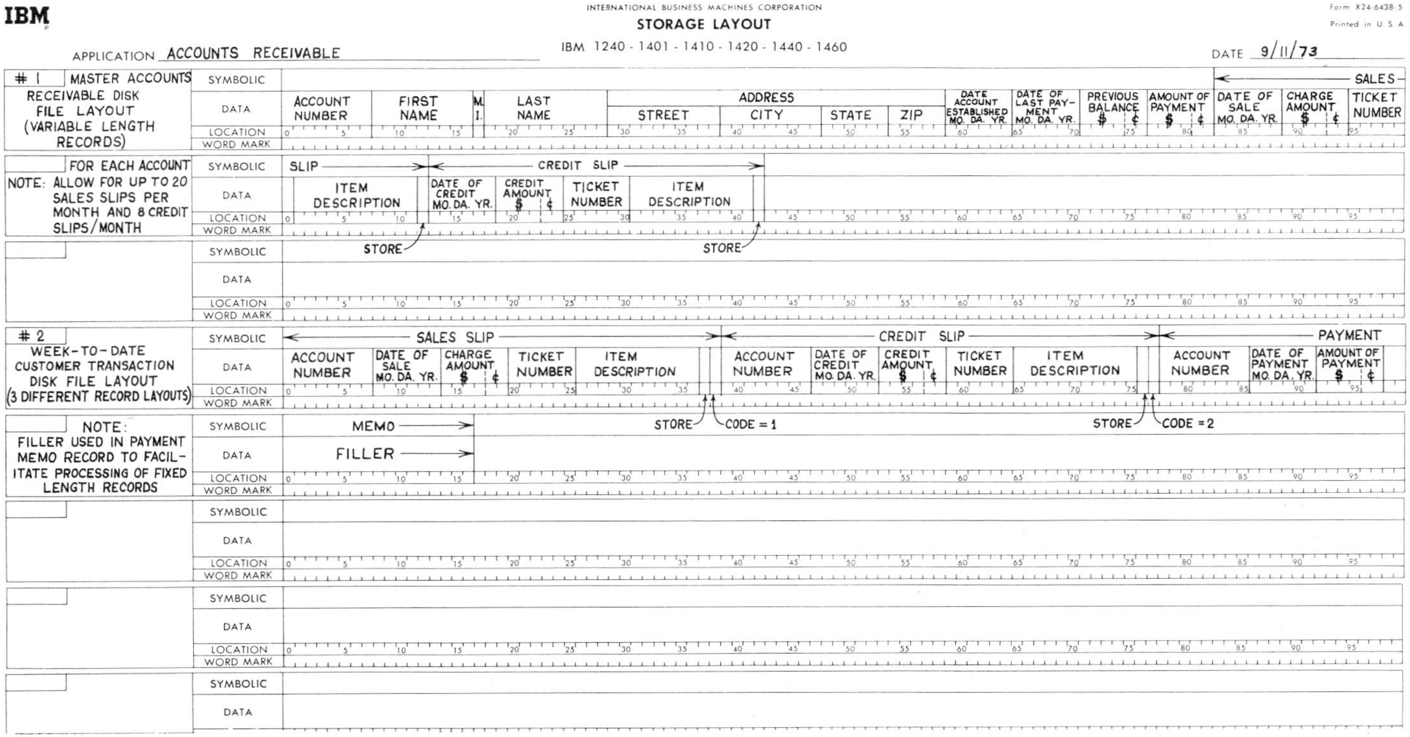

Figure 18.14
Accounts Receivable disk layouts.

1. (T or F) An Accounts Receivable System is concerned with the accounting of charge account customers.
2. (T or F) The proposed system described in this chapter will eventually result in a monetary savings to the company.
3. To indicate that the write-off of design costs is 28 months means that _____ .
4. The constraint on the proposed system is a(n) _____ constraint.
5. The monthly statements are prepared on _____ forms.
6. Monthly statements are rotated, which means _____ .
7. The purpose of rotating monthly statements is _____ .
8. The purpose of the Trial Balance is to _____ .
9. The _____ report is used by management to determine which store or stores might benefit from special sales to charge account customers.
10. The master file in the sample system is stored on _____ .
11. An online file was chosen so that _____ .
12. (T or F) The master file is a standard sequential file.
13. A customer desiring charge privileges must fill out an

_____ .

14. A credit memo is used for _____ .

SOLUTIONS

1. T
2. T
3. in 28 months the system will begin to break even; that is, there will be no losses associated with it.
4. equipment
5. preprinted
6. they are not all prepared simultaneously, but are prepared in groups or shifts.
7. to eliminate peak work loads
8. insure the accuracy of all debits and credits posted to the Accounts Receivable File
9. Accounts Receivable Summary
10. disk
11. sales personnel can inquire about customer accounts through the use of a terminal
12. F
13. Application for a Charge Account
14. returns or adjustments

Chapter 19 *Case Study II— Inventory System*

This chapter will show the design of a computerized inventory system for the ABC Manufacturing Company. The company's main product line is small appliances such as toasters, broilers, and coffeepots. Currently, the inventory system is being performed manually, as described below. Inventory Control Management has requested that a systems analyst design a new system to take advantage of computer capability. There are approximately 475 different part numbers stocked in the warehouse, which is managed by the Inventory Control Department.

I. Analysis of Current System

A. OBJECTIVES

1. To maintain information for each part such as the quantity in the warehouse, the quantity on order, the quantity in the receiving and inspection departments, and the quantity that is needed by the production line but which is not available.
2. To requisition material when it is found that stock levels of particular items are inadequate.
3. To provide management with reports for planning purposes.

Systems Analysis and Design

B. CONSTRAINTS

The analysis of the current system and the design of the new one must be completed within nine months. The new computer system is scheduled to arrive at that time.

C. OUTPUTS

The basic documents generated by the Inventory Control Department are shown below.

1. Purchase Requisition

This form is sent to the Purchasing Department when it becomes necessary to order additional material. The Purchasing Department is responsible for contacting vendors and ordering the items needed (see Figure 19.1).

2. Material Status Report

This report is prepared biweekly to show the status for each part; that is, the quantities in the warehouse, on order, in inspection, in receiving, and backordered. Quantity backordered means the quantity

```
                    PURCHASE REQUISITION

                           NUMBER _____

        DATE _____

        ISSUED BY _____  DELIVERY REQUIRED BY _____

  | QUANTITY | PART NUMBER |        DESCRIPTION         |
  |          |             |                            |
  |          |             |                            |
  |          |             |                            |

            TO BE FILLED OUT BY PURCHASING

     VENDOR SELECTED _____

     APPROVED BY _____   DATE _____

     PURCHASE ORDER NUMBER _____
```

Figure 19.1
Purchase requisition.

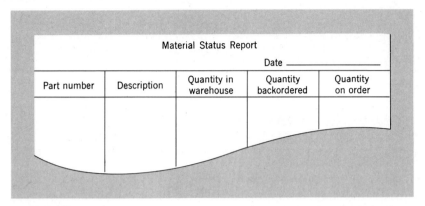

Figure 19.2
Material status report.

of a part requested by the production line but not in the warehouse. It is owed to production as soon as it comes in. This report consists of mimeograph sheets that are preprinted with each part number and its description listed. The clerk prepares this report by simply copying the appropriate quantities from each stock status card. While it is preparing the report, the Inventory Control Department is alerted to critical part shortages. Appropriate requisitions are then issued. In addition, the report is used by the production department for their planning and scheduling of work (see Figure 19.2).

3. Updated Stock Status Card

A 5 in. by 8 in. index card in Figure 19.3 is maintained for each part. These cards serve as the basis for information found in the Material Status Report (see Figure 19.2).

STOCK STATUS CARD

PART DESCRIPTION _____   PART NUMBER _____

DATE	QUANTITY					
	ON REQUISITION	ON ORDER	IN RECEIVING	IN INSPECTION	IN WARE-HOUSE	BACKORDERED

Figure 19.3
Stock status card.

D. PROCESSING

Posting to the Stock Status Cards is done at the time that any of the following forms, shown on the following pages, are received or generated by the Inventory Control Department: Purchase Requisition, Purchase Order, Receiving Report, Inspection Report, and Request for Stock.

The system functions in the following manner. When a Sales Order is written by the Sales Department, a copy of the order is sent to Inventory Control. The Inventory Control Department has on file Material Parts Lists for each product that the company manufactures. This list shows the quantity and description of every part number needed to produce one unit of the given product number. Inventory Control computes how much it needs of each part, based on the Sales Order, and checks the Stock Status Cards to determine how much must be requisitioned.

Requisitions, or requests to buy material, are then forwarded to the Purchasing Department. A copy of the Requisition is kept in Inventory Control for follow-up purposes. Once a copy of the Purchase Order is received by the department, the Requisition is destroyed.

The Purchasing Department contacts vendors and places Purchase Orders with them. The Purchase Order indicates what items are needed, when they are needed, and their prices.

The material from the vendors is received by the Receiving Department, which issues Receiving Reports. This report indicates the quantity of each part number that has just been received. A copy is sent to Inventory Control.

From the receiving dock, the material goes to the Inspection Department, where it is accepted or rejected. If rejected, the material is returned to the vendor. If accepted, the stock is sent to the warehouse. In either event, Inventory Control receives a copy of the Inspection Report which shows the disposition of the material.

When the production line needs parts, it fills out Requests for Stock and forwards them to Inventory Control. If material is not available in the warehouse, Inventory Control contacts the Purchasing Department to request that vendor deliveries be expedited.

The forms distribution chart shown in Figure 19.4 will clarify the distribution of the basic forms involved in the inventory system.

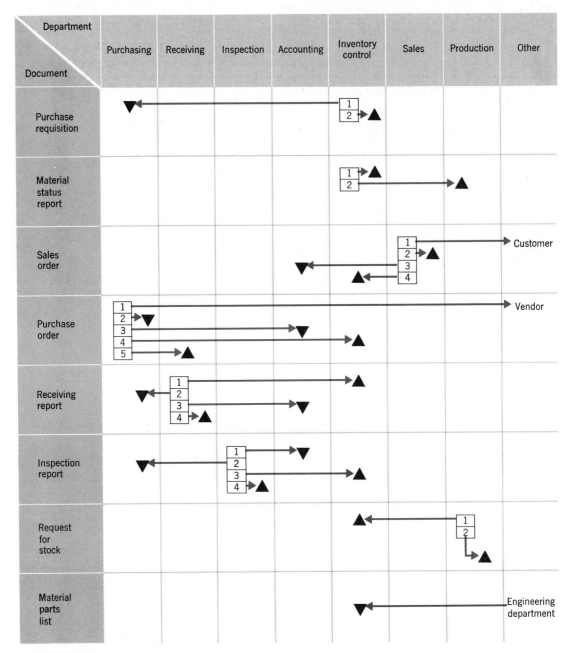

Figure 19.4

Forms distribution chart for inventory system: $\boxed{n}$ nth copy of report (shown where form originates); ∇ permanently filed; $\triangle$ temporarily filed and then destroyed; → sent to.

E. INPUTS

The basic inputs used in the current system are shown below.

1. Sales Order

ABC Manufacturing Company
187 West Avenue
Garden City, N.Y. 11530

Sales Order

Sold to _____   Number _____

Date _____

Salesman _____

Quantity	Production number	Delivery date	Price	Total

Subtotal _____

Tax _____

Total _____

Figure 19.5
Sales order.

2. Purchase Order

Figure 19.6
Purchase order.

Systems Analysis and Design

3. Receiving Report

RECEIVING REPORT

RECEIVED BY ______________ NUMBER ______________

PURCHASE ORDER NO. ______________ DATE ______________

VENDOR NAME ______________ INVOICE NO. ______________

QUANTITY	PART NUMBER	DESCRIPTION

Figure 19.7
Receiving report.

4. Inspection Report

INSPECTION REPORT

VENDOR NAME ______________ NUMBER ______________

INSPECTED BY ______________ DATE ______________

QUANTITY	PART NUMBER	DESCRIPTION	QUANTITY ACCEPTED	QUANTITY REJECTED	REASON FOR REJECTION

Figure 19.8
Inspection report.

5. Request for Stock

REQUEST FOR STOCK

REQUESTED BY ______________ NUMBER ______

FOR ORDER NO. ______________ DATE ______

PART NUMBER	QUANTITY NEEDED	QUANTITY ISSUED	QUANTITY BACKORDERED	DATE ISSUED	ISSUED BY

Figure 19.9
Request for stock.

6. Material Parts List

Material Parts List for Product Number ______

Date ______

Part Number	Description	Unit of measure (feet, inches, pieces)	Quantity needed

Figure 19.10
Material parts list for product number.

F. CONTROLS

The primary controls that exist in the current system are for follow-up purposes. When a Requisition is forwarded to Purchasing, a copy is kept in a folder in the Inventory Control office. When a copy of the Purchase Order is received by Inventory Control, the corresponding Requisition is pulled out. The Purchase Order is then filed in a permanent file and the Requisition is discarded. By checking the Requisition folder (containing Requisitions for which Purchase Orders have not yet been generated) periodically, Inventory Control can ascertain when Purchasing must be called to follow up on outstanding Requisitions. This procedure also serves as a control to detect Requisitions that may have been lost either in transit to Purchasing, or in Purchasing itself.

Another control is used by the warehouse to insure that back-ordered material is supplied immediately to production once it is received in the warehouse. Before material is put into stock, the warehouse clerk checks a back-order list to see if there is an outstanding demand for it. If there is, the parts are sent directly to production instead of putting them into the warehouse.

G. FEEDBACK

Once every three months a physical inventory is taken. This means that every part in the warehouse is counted. Any necessary adjustments are made to the Stock Status Cards to reflect the actual quantity found in the warehouse.

H. COST

The current monthly cost of operating the Inventory System is shown below. This information was obtained from conversations with the manager of the Inventory Control Department.

Manager of Inventory Control	$1650
2 typists	900
8 clerks	4160
Supplies	65
Miscellaneous	85
TOTAL	$6860

II. Problem Definition

A. INTERVIEW

Interviews with members of the Inventory Control Department have revealed the fact that Material Status Reports are virtually useless because of inaccuracies. By the time the clerks are able to post information to the Stock Status Cards and to prepare the biweekly Material Status Report, the information is obsolete. Transactions not yet posted often alter key figures such as the balance in the warehouse. As a result, frequent errors are made regarding decisions to requisition material. This situation is dramatized every time a physical inventory is taken and extensive adjustments must be made to the Stock Status Cards.

B. OBSERVATION

Observation of the Inventory Control clerks shows that much effort is expended by them to manually analyze Sales Orders, prepare Requisitions, to post all transactions that affect the material, and to prepare Material Status Reports.

C. FORMS ANALYSIS

Analysis of the forms distribution chart shows that several departments keep permanent files of the same documents, as enumerated below. This situation has resulted in the duplication of filing costs.

Document	Department Where Permanently Filed
Sales Order	Sales, Accounting
Purchase Order	Purchasing, Accounting
Receiving Report	Purchasing, Accounting
Inspection Report	Purchasing, Accounting

III. Design of a New Inventory Control System

A. OBJECTIVES

1. To have the computer maintain the status of all material used for production in the company.
2. To have the computer generate all reports needed by management for decision making purposes.
3. To have Purchase Requisitions prepared by the computer when it calculates the need to order more material.

B. CONSTRAINTS

1. Since $1\frac{1}{2}$ months have already elapsed in analyzing the current system, this leaves only $7\frac{1}{2}$ months to design the new system in time for the arrival of the computer system.

544   *Systems Analysis and Design*

2. The computer system on order has the following configuration:
   a. 1 Central Processing Unit with storage capacity of approximately 131,000 characters
   b. 4 magnetic tape drives
   c. 2 magnetic disk drives
   d. 1 printer
   e. 1 card reader-punch
   f. 1 console typewriter
   In addition, three key-tape machines are on order.

C. OUTPUTS

Changes from current outputs are noted below to facilitate the review of the proposed system.

1. Material Status Report (Figure 19.11)

The format of the report remains unchanged. However, instead of being generated automatically on a biweekly basis, it will only be produced upon request.

2. Purchase Requisition (Figure 19.12)

The form is unchanged from the current design, except that it will be generated by the computer on stock paper instead of being prepared on preprinted pads. The computer will prepare a Requisition whenever the stock level for a particular item falls below a predetermined level. The Requisition will also be generated manually by Inventory Control when vendor delays necessitate additional procurement to supply critical parts to production. A preprinted form is deemed unnecessary and excessively costly for this system. A Purchase Requisition on stock paper was determined to be just as clear and efficient, but much less costly.

3. Vendor Expediting Report

This is a new report, shown in Figure 19.13, which will be produced every other day by the computer and forwarded to Purchasing. It will list all parts that should have already been received by the company but have not yet come in. Parts listed will be alphabetically arranged by vendor name. The expeditor in Purchasing will use this report as a basis for determining which vendors must be called because orders have not yet been delivered. If, on calling a vendor, the expeditor discovers a change in the delivery schedule, he will then notify Inventory Control. They, in turn, may choose to issue a special Requisition for additional procurement from another vendor.

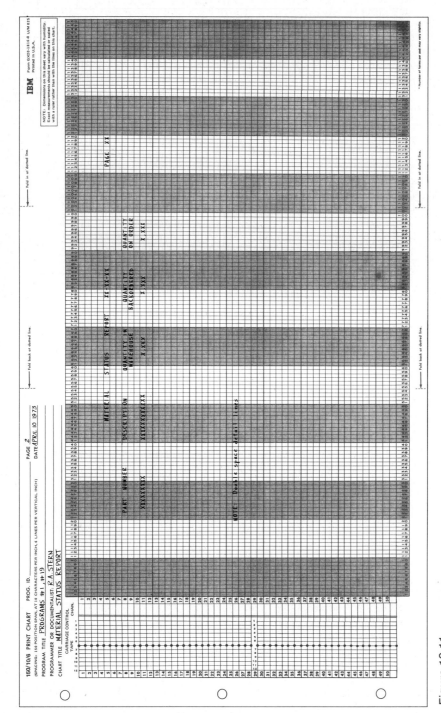

Figure 19.11
Material status report.

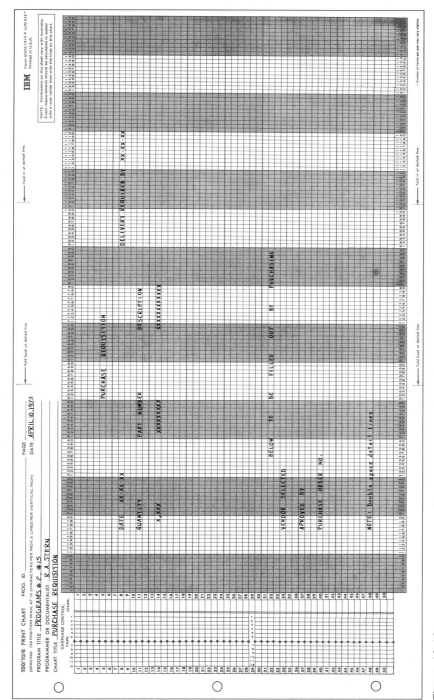

Figure 19.12
Purchase requisition.

547

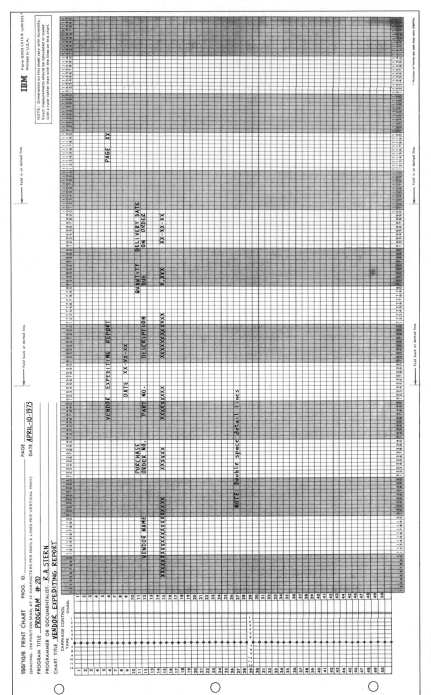

Figure 19.13
Vendor expediting report.

D. PROCESSING

The requirements of this system can easily be met by establishing sequential tape files, as will be shown below. There is no immediate need for the random access feature of disk files.

1. Creation of Master Inventory File

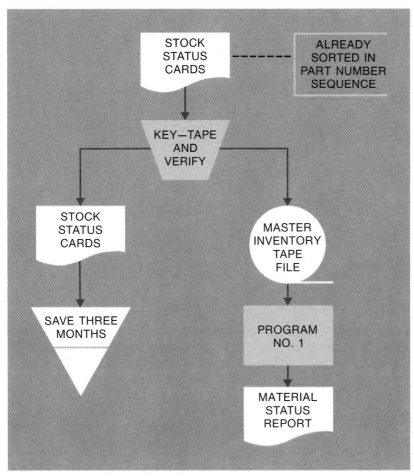

Figure 19.14
Creation of master inventory file.

2. Creation of Material Parts File
This file shows, for each product that the company makes, the quantity and description of every part needed to produce each assembly.

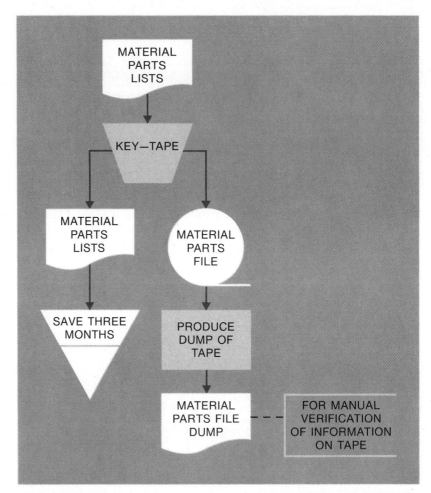

Figure 19.15
Creation of material parts file.

3. Daily Updating of Master Inventory File

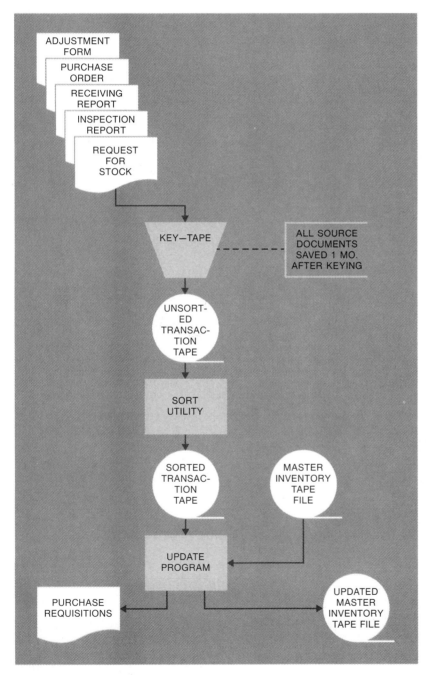

Figure 19.16
Daily updating of master inventory file.

4. Updating of the Material Parts File
This file is updated when there are changes to be made to parts lists.

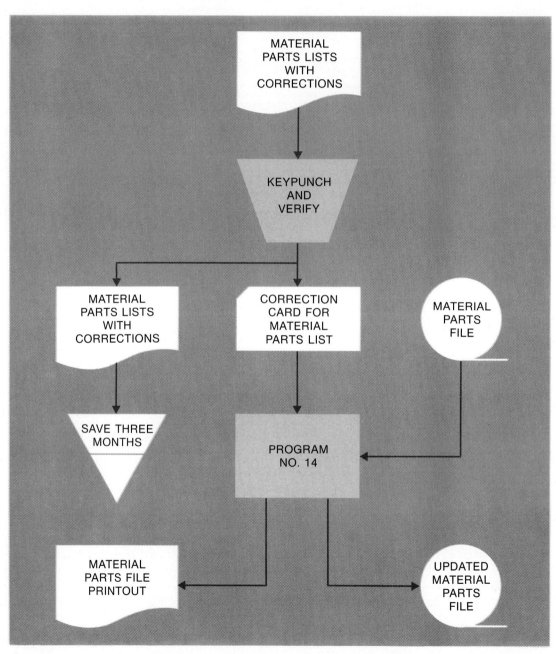

Figure 19.17
Updating of material parts file.

5. Sales Order Analysis for Stock Requirements

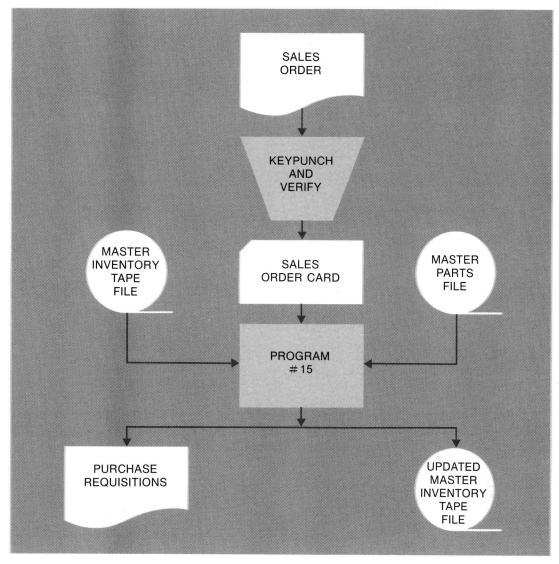

Figure 19.18
Sales order analysis for stock requirements.

6. Processing of Material Status Report
This report is run on request only.

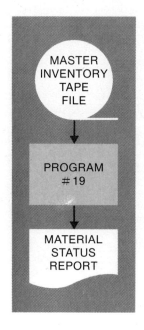

Figure 19.19
Processing of material status report.

7. Processing of Vendor Expediting Report

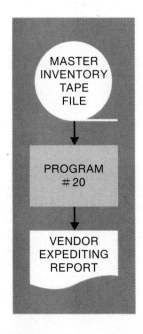

Figure 19.20
Processing of vendor expediting report.

E. INPUTS

Most of the inputs in the proposed system remain unchanged from the current system. These include the following forms: Purchase Orders, Receiving Reports, Inspection Reports, Requests for Stock, Material Parts Lists, and Sales Orders. The inputs listed below are new to the system.

1. Master Inventory Tape File

This file is in part number sequence. For each part number, it is possible that there may be up to three unfilled Purchase Orders at one time. The storage layout in Figure 19.21 shows the fields that appear for each record.

2. Master Parts Tape File

This file consists of the descriptions and quantities of each component part that make up each product that the company manufactures. The file is in product number sequence. It is possible that up to 75 component part numbers are needed in order to build a given product. The storage layout is shown in Figure 19.21. Note that the Master Parts Tape File has variable length records with a maximum record size large enough to accommodate 75 component parts.

3. Transaction Tape for Updating Master Inventory Tape File (see Figure 19.21)

Source documents are recorded daily on tape in any order in which they are received by the Data Processing Department. The tape is sorted in part number sequence before being used to update the Master Inventory Tape File. In order to allow for processing of fixed length records, fillers have been added, as necessary, to make each record 47 positions long. Note that a code in the 47th position of each record indicates the type of record, according to the following table.

Code	Type of Record
1	Purchase Order
2	Adjustment Form
3	Inspection Report
4	Receiving Report
5	Request for Stock

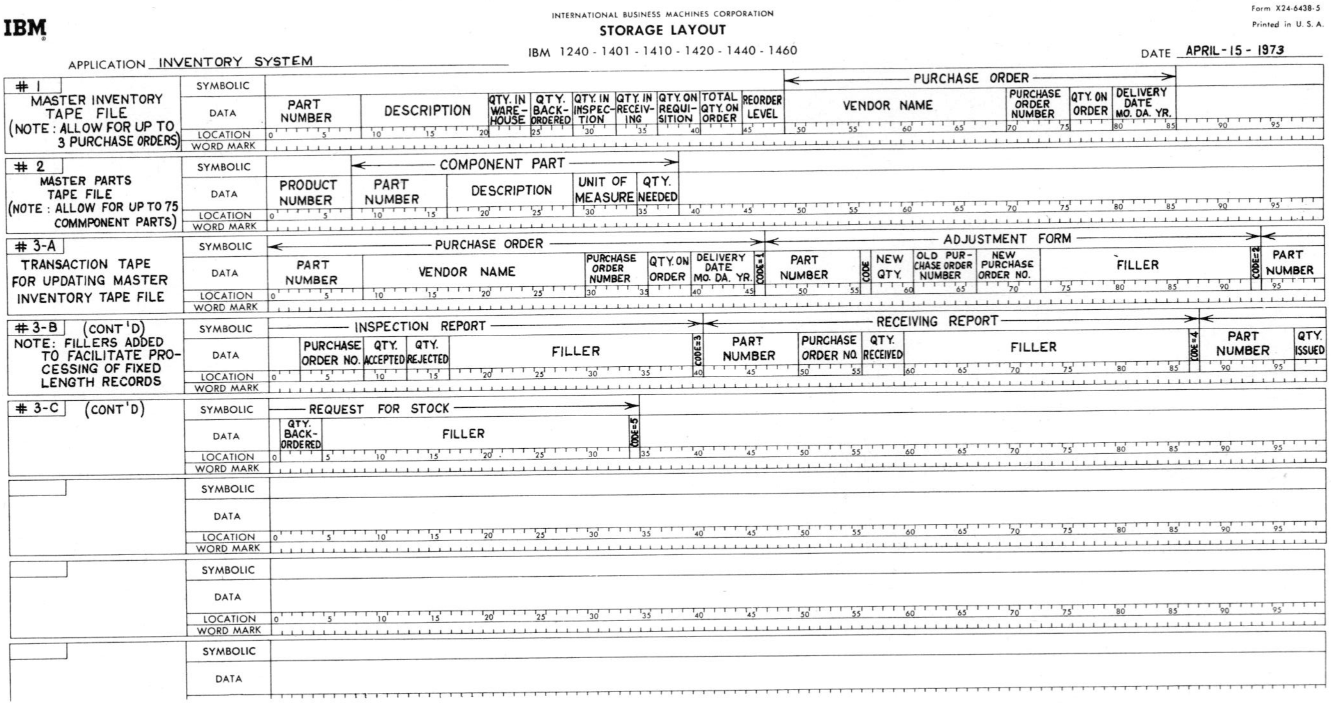

Figure 19.21
Inventory tape layouts.

4. Adjustments to Master Inventory File

```
          ADJUSTMENTS TO MASTER INVENTORY FILE
   AUTHORIZED BY _____   DATE _____

   PART NUMBER _____

 □ DELETE PART NUMBER FROM FILE

 □ CHANGE THE FOLLOWING ITEMS TO REFLECT INFORMATION SHOWN:

            ITEM              CORRECT INFO
     □ QTY ON REQUISITION    _____
     □ QTY ON ORDER          _____
     □ QTY IN RECEIVING      _____
     □ QTY IN INSPECTION     _____
     □ QTY IN WAREHOUSE      _____
     □ QTY BACKORDERED       _____
     □ PURCHASE ORDER NO.    _____
            ON FILE_____    SHOULD BE._____
```

Figure 19.22
Adjustments to master inventory file.

5. Correction Card for Material Parts List

The card layout is shown in Figure 19.23. The code in column 9 is as follows:

Code	Explanation
1	Delete part number shown.
2	Delete product number.
3	Change items shown to reflect information indicated. A blank field means that there is no change to that particular field.

The codes for unit of measure in columns 31 to 36 are as follows:

FT = feet
IN = inches
PCS = pieces
ASREQD = as required

6. Sales Order Card

The card layout is shown in Figure 19.23.

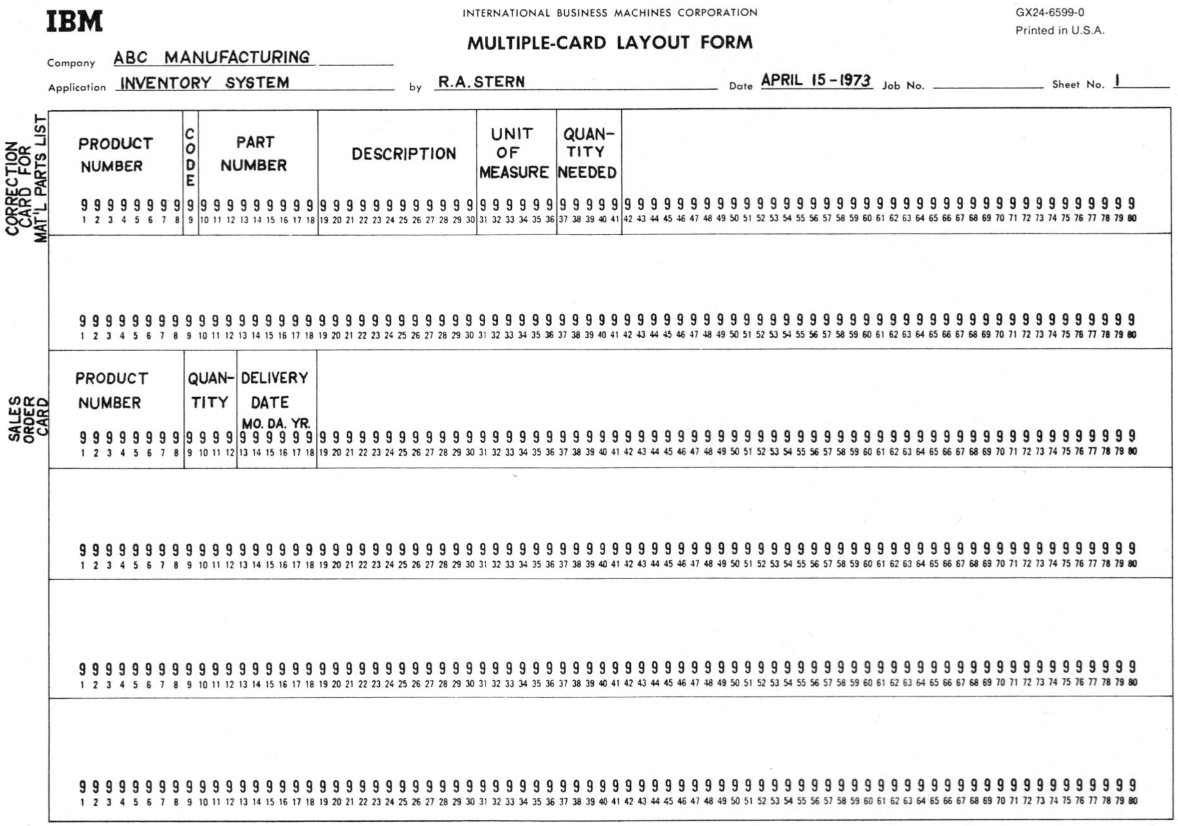

IBM

INTERNATIONAL BUSINESS MACHINES CORPORATION

MULTIPLE-CARD LAYOUT FORM

GX24-6599-0
Printed in U.S.A.

Company ABC MANUFACTURING

Application INVENTORY SYSTEM by R.A. STERN Date APRIL 15-1973 Job No. ______ Sheet No. 1

CORRECTION CARD FOR MAT'L PARTS LIST: PRODUCT NUMBER (1–8) | CODE (9) | PART NUMBER (10–18) | DESCRIPTION (19–30) | UNIT OF MEASURE (31–36) | QUANTITY NEEDED (37–41) | (42–80)

SALES ORDER CARD: PRODUCT NUMBER (1–8) | QUANTITY (9–12) | DELIVERY DATE MO. DA. YR. (13–18) | (19–80)

Figure 19.23
Inventory card layouts.

F. CONTROLS

Back-up information is saved in order to regenerate the master files on tape in case they are inadvertently lost or destroyed. Most source documents are saved one month after being processed. Every time a tape file is updated, the old tape file is saved at least one month. Material Parts Lists with corrections are saved for three months.

G. FEEDBACK

Changes to the Master Inventory Tape File can be made by completing an Adjustment Form for this purpose. Changes to the Material Parts File can be made by entering corrections to the appropriate Material Parts List and forwarding it to Data Processing.

Vendor Expediting Reports are generated every other day by the computer and forwarded to the expeditor in Purchasing. It is his responsibility to contact the vendors on the list to find out why delivery of material is behind schedule. This information is then forwarded to Inventory Control for appropriate action.

H. COST ANALYSIS

The costs for the proposed system are shown below.

Manager of Inventory Control	$1650
3 clerks	1560
Computer Equipment and Personnel	
(An allocation of 10% of the computer's monthly anticipated cost of $28,280 has been allotted to the Inventory Department by management.)	2828
Supplies	
20,000 punched cards	20
Computer paper—4 boxes	
(primarily 2-ply, 1600 sheets per box)	25
Miscellaneous	20
	$6103

The proposed system will cost approximately $6103 per month to operate. The design and implementation costs of the new system are $25,000. Therefore, it will take 33 months to write off these costs, since the current system costs $6860 per month to operate. This was determined as follows:

$ 6,860	Current system cost per month
− 6,103	Proposed system cost per month
$ 757	Savings per month

$$\frac{\$25,000}{\$757} = 33.$$

SELF-EVALUATING QUIZ

1. The Inventory System's basic objectives include _____ .
2. In its daily functions, operations of the Inventory Department relate closely to those of _____ , _____ , _____ , and _____ Departments.
3. One of the major problems in the current system is the number of inaccuracies in the _____ Reports.
4. The constraints on the proposed system include a(n) _____ constraint.
5. The proposed system will include a new report called a _____ .
6. The master file in the proposed system will be stored on _____ .
7. The new system will begin to break even in _____ .

SOLUTIONS

1. maintaining information for each part stored in the warehouses
2. Purchasing; Receiving; Inspection; Sales; Production; Accounting
3. Material Status
4. equipment; time
5. Vendor Expediting Report
6. tape
7. 33 months

Systems Analysis and Design

Chapter 20 *Management Information Systems and Other Decision-Making Techniques*

I. *Management Information Systems*

As a company expands and departments become more and more autonomous, it becomes increasingly difficult for management to effectively perceive the company's total position. That is, although management may know, from a weekly report, the status of the Accounts Receivable and the Accounts Payable Departments, for example, data on the company's total liabilities and assets is not readily available.

Computers have been effectively employed in most companies to maximize the efficiency of each individual department so that management can obtain status reports on a timely basis. The utilization of a computer, however, to reflect the interaction between departments, in order to produce meaningful data on the company *as a whole,* reflects an entirely new orientation and application *not* employed in many companies. Generally, to obtain such data, management must compile the information from various departmental reports using manual methods. By the time the data is obtained, the resultant report is usually obsolete.

A Management Information System (MIS) is a recent advance in computer technology designed to provide management with an integrated, all-encompassing approach to the total company in order to facilitate the decision-making process. Thus, management can receive up-to-date, pertinent computer-produced information that is needed to plan, control, and manage the company's entire position.

The use of MIS represents a new computerized approach. Previously, each system within a company was designed and implemented by computer, but almost always independently. Little or no interrelation between systems resulted. Management Information Systems strive to eliminate this piecemeal effort and to effect a totally integrated entity.

The use of MIS has greatly facilitated the decision-making process for management. With the use of terminals management can obtain from the computer, at any given moment, profit and loss statements, a statement of total assets and liabilities, sales distribution charts, daily work force figures, and so on. In addition, sales and marketing forecasts can be charted at any time. MIS provides management with current information that is obtained from computerizing the *interaction* of the various organizational departments.

A. REQUIREMENTS

When utilizing MIS in a company, each department has computerized *subsystems* that are subordinate to an overall company-wide system. That is, we no longer refer to departmental systems that function autonomously, but, rather, we consider that each *subsystem* will interact to result in a more efficient total company system.

1. Common Data Base

One of the prominent features of the MIS concept revolves around a *COMMON DATA BASE*. In lieu of each subsystem within the company having its own unique file, all subsystems can access data from the same vast storage medium through a computer system. This storage medium contains data required by *all* subsystems. In this manner data does not have to be duplicated by each system requiring it. It can be retained in one place, and then accessed by each subsystem that utilizes it. Figure 20.1 presents a comparison that shows how data is conventionally stored on a system-by-system basis and then how it can be stored utilizing a common data base. For the purpose of demonstrating the fundamental concept, only two systems (Payroll and Personnel) are used for illustrative purposes.

In this illustration we can see immediately one of the many features of a Management Information System—the savings of storage space. Suppose this illustration pertains to an automobile manufacturer that employs approximately 100,000 people. With the conventional manner of designing systems (the system-by-system approach), 100,000 records would be required in the Payroll File. Similarly, 100,000 records would be required in a Personnel File. A common data base incorporating all Personnel and Payroll information in a *single* Employee Record would save much storage space.

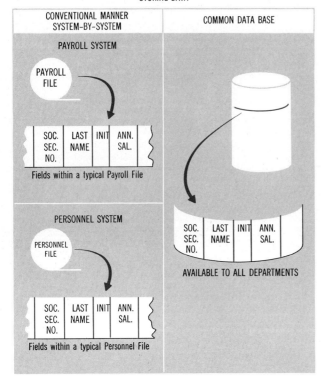

Figure 20.1
Comparison of methods for storing data.

Another obvious advantage of the common data base is the elimination of duplication of effort. For example, it is not necessary to update two separate files (such as Payroll and Personnel) with the same data, since all data is maintained in one massive file. In short, MIS can effectively increase profits by optimizing customer service and can decrease the production and distribution time of individual items. In addition, MIS projects help to standardize the decision-making process by utilizing the computer to produce results that are calculated using a standard technique.

Notwithstanding the oversimplication of this example, by extrapolation, we can begin to see how a Management Information System strives to effect a totally integrated entity.

In addition to a Common Data Base, there are other characteristics of the MIS concept that are typical of this type of system, as enumerated below.

2. Online Real-Time Capability
All data must not only be current but also immediately accessible in order to provide management with reliable and timely information

needed for planning and for decision-making purposes. As a result of this requirement, an online system with real-time capability is an essential feature.

3. Data Communications Equipment to Provide the Online Real-Time Capability

In order to employ the online real-time feature, it is essential that Data Communications equipment be utilized. Remote terminals using telephone lines, for example, can transmit data instantaneously to the computer so that information in the Common Data Base can be updated immediately. Likewise, inquiries by management, requesting either specific reports or isolated items of information, can be transmitted directly to the computer, with responses being returned over the Data Communications equipment.

4. A Large Central Processing Unit (CPU)

To adequately process data in an MIS environment, a CPU of considerable size (usually 100,000 positions or more) is required for the sophisticated supervisor which is needed. The control system provides the computer with the capability to handle an online real-time system, incorporating the use of Data Communications equipment. In addition, this sophisticated supervisor usually provides the ability for the computer to operate in a multiprogramming environment. As an example, this feature can be used to process two different inquiries from managers using separate terminals at the same time.

5. Extensive Time for Development

A Management Information System typically takes 3 to 5 years of systems design and programming effort to implement. Much effort must be expended to thoroughly interrelate all subsystems and tie them together to produce an integrated information system.

6. High Costs for Development

The cost of developing an MIS environment is, for many companies, a prohibiting factor. The expense involved often runs into millions of dollars. Because of the number of analysts and programmers required, the equipment needed, and the time involved, an MIS project is not undertaken by every company.

Note, however, that MIS projects are becoming increasingly popular. As the cost of hardware and software packages become cheaper to operate and implement, the cost of MIS becomes correspondingly less.

In summary, we have seen that some of the basic characteristics of a Management Information System include:

1. A Common Data Base
2. Online Real-Time (OLRT) Capability
3. Data Communications Equipment

4. A Large Central Processing Unit
5. Extensive Time for Development
6. High Costs for Development

B. LIMITATIONS OF MIS

Management Information Systems have extensive potential and capability for the decision- and policy-makers in a large company. Note, however, that not all MIS projects undertaken have met with success.

Some of the reasons for failure of MIS projects to provide management with the type of information it requires follow.

1. The task of planning, designing, and implementing an information system to be used by management was left to the computer specialist, a technician often not skilled in the area of management and thus poorly equipped to guess at the requirements of such a system.

As one expert states:[1]

Many companies rushed to obtain the new generation computer equipment, justifying the cost with vague notions of the potential services it would provide. How much of this was a result of effective computer selling, the data processing manager's enthusiasm, or management's pride in having the biggest and the newest, could easily be the subject of many books. Computer hardware and software expenditures mounted, and companies suddenly discovered that they had large investments in equipment whose overall use had never been defined. They had a horse, but no wagon for it to pull. They had complex, costly, and sophisticated data processing equipment, but no idea of how to use its data output.

Management then asked: How can we use this equipment? Answers to this question had to revolve around the computer, and a computer-oriented management information system developed. This approach usually allowed the computer technicians to set the goals for the information system. The technicians' goals, however, were frequently geared to maximum computer operating efficiency rather than to the usefulness of its output. Since computers are very efficient by human standards—particularly in terms of the speed with which they can manipulate data—the effort would have been better spent by restricting information input and output to that necessary to manage the business.

More appropriate questions would have been: What information do we require to control and manage our business,

[1] *"Why Management Information Systems Fail," by John R. Gale, FINANCIAL EXECUTIVE, August 1968.*

Systems Analysis and Design

and what is the most economical way of getting it? To answer these questions, the users' information needs must be determined, evaluated, and if feasible, used as the objectives of the system. Only after determining users' needs should the company consider what sort of computer equipment to procure.

2. The task of planning, designing, and implementing this vast and complex system was often underestimated. Management was often inaccurately briefed as to the time and cost estimates of such a system by computer specialists who were very enthusiastic to undertake such a project.

Here, again, management has not been properly trained to make evaluations on data processing functions:

> Because of the difficulties encountered during implementation phases, few management information systems are now functioning as originally conceived. This results from failure to realize that the systems are complex and require the same—if not more—top-management involvement as any other major company effort.[2]

3. It was difficult to establish priorities so that the most critical departments' executives who are the prime users of the system obtain information first. In with a priority schedule, critical factors can be decided upon by the major departments.

Unfortunately, when priorities are to be established, power politics become a major factor. Thus it is often the most powerful executive, and not the prime user, who has the priorities within the system.

> The successful management information system has a clearly defined set of priorities and related implementation objectives. For example, a company operating in a highly competitive low-margin consumer market should give top priority to elements of marketing and distribution information, with production and financial information to follow.[3]

4. Company personnel have often been inadequately trained as to the nature and purpose of the system. Thus personnel are too eager to satisfy their own immediate needs, often sacrificing the total company's requirements.

In short:

> A management information system should be a continually changing and evolving activity as long as the company exists. To compete in today's market place, a company must have

[2] *Ibid.*
[3] *Ibid.*

available information for planning, decision, and control. The company that obtains effective data upon which to base decisions, at a reasonable cost, will be better able to compete and improve profits.[4]

C. TYPICAL COMPANIES USING MIS[5]

1. Westinghouse Electric Corporation

Westinghouse chose to implement a Management Information System in a middle-management area that dealt with large amounts of data and required judgment and computation in decision making. This area is monthly sales forecasting and production scheduling for one of their major appliance products—the Laundry Division. In the Westinghouse application, for example, all parameters of the problem are initially presented to the manager in the form of a light pen menu. By pointing the light pen at the information on a cathode ray tube, the manager can choose the information content and form he wants displayed. The display data can be manipulated by light pen and keyboard, and in this way, the manager conveniently moves back and forth within the data base, asking, "what if?", and making decisions. Although the data is computer generated, it is presented in a form with which the manager is intimately familiar. He need not learn a new language in order to communicate with the computer. And the response from the computer is fast enough so that he does not forget the original "what if?" question.

The market managers can access any report. The user selects information desired with a light pen by pointing to the appropriate places on the cathode ray tube and indicating (a) whether he wants the data to be shown in cumulative or noncumulative form, (b) which product he wants to display, (c) whether he wants the plot to be compensated for seasonal variation, (d) the month and year over which he wants to start the plot, and (e) the month and year over which he wants to end the plot.

This results in a plot like that shown in Figure 20.2, which includes both numeric and graphic data describing the conditions the operator selected. Notice that to the right of the presentation are additional light pen functions so the manager can continue to interact with his data base.

In the Westinghouse application, the planners move through approximately 20 presentations in order to complete their monthly schedule. Westinghouse concludes that the system is a practical tool and the prototype of future manager-computer interactive systems for planning and control activities.

[4] *Ibid.*
[5] *Information in Section D is supplied through the courtesy of Information Displays, Inc.*

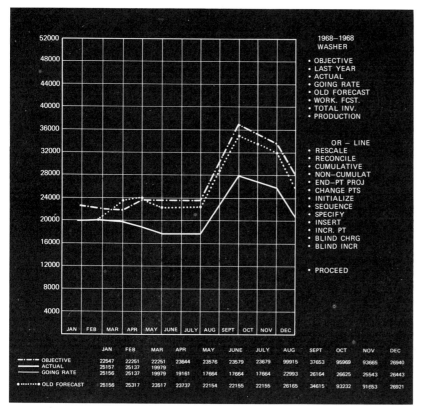

Figure 20.2
Sample light pen menu. By placing light pen on desired item at right,
the appropriate graph is produced. Courtesy Information Displays, Inc.

2. Boeing Company

In conjunction with the SCRAM missile program, Boeing Company was
required by their customer (the Air Force) to maintain an MIS that
would give their customer access to the same planning data that
Boeing was using to make decisions. Boeing chose to implement this
requirement by establishing a computer-based MIS in which all of the
appropriate information describing program status was kept in a central
file and could be retrieved by Boeing managers through a series of
light pen interrogated displays. In all, about 8000 different reports and
presentations could be reviewed. In order to satisfy the customer's
requirement for access to the same data base, the central computer
was connected by telephone line to an identical installation at the
customer's facility in Dayton, Ohio, and the customer had the same
information retrieval capability as did Boeing.

3. Chemical Bank of New York

Chemical Bank of New York requires a way for money managers to jointly view timely economic information. Chemical Bank of New York has just contracted for a display system that automatically presents computer generated data in four colors on screens up to theater size. Chemical Bank's initial use of the system will be to produce economic charts on a 5-foot by 6-foot screen. The Bank will be able to call up computer stored data and have it displayed within seconds on a large four-color chart. Initially, Chemical Bank will tie into a cooperative economic data bank shared by several large New York companies and financial institutions. The output of the computer will produce graphs of economic international time series. Later, as part of the Bank's information system, data can also be quickly relayed from computers to a display projector in the Banks main office. Closed circuit television could then relay the information to several remote offices.

II. CPM and PERT Charts

The MIS project discussed previously is a fully integrated approach to aiding management in the decision-making process.

There are, in addition, several individual techniques that can be used, as either part of an MIS project by large companies or as independent methods for producing more standardized and effective decisions.

The creation of CPM and PERT charts are techniques that assist management in obtaining realistic time estimates of when projects will be completed.

A CPM chart is a CRITICAL PATH METHOD and the PERT chart is a Program Evaluation and Review Technique. These two charts are very similar. They show, fundamentally, the relationships among activities within a proposed system and indicate where critical problem areas may occur and possibly cause delays during implementation.

A. CPM

A CPM chart drawn at the onset of a project informs management, prior to implementation, of the magnitude of the job and of possible problem areas that may cause delays. A CPM chart drawn or updated while a system is being implemented informs management of the progress made to date.

Thus CPM can help management to observe the time estimates of a new system. In this way, management is kept constantly abreast of progress made.

Construction of CPM charts is performed by analysts who have training in this area. This section will briefly explain to the student, in a general way, how these charts are designed.

CPM charts illustrate the relationships among activities so that:

Systems Analysis and Design

1. Schedules can be determined on the entire project.
2. Problem areas, due to difficulties within certain activities, can be evaluated.

Thus relationships among activities within a system must be clearly understood by the analyst. For example, suppose that Activity 2 can be performed *at the same time* as Activity 3, while both activities must be completed prior to Activity 4. In addition to establishing these relationships, an estimate of the time required to perform each must be determined. The estimate is a reasonable guess as to how long it will take to accomplish each part of the project or system, based on the anticipated availability of resources. Resources include items such as manpower, material, and money. Thus, to alter the schedules of activities, management can alter the allocation of resources.

After the list of activities is prepared, and time estimates and relationships are clearly understood, a chart is drawn to reflect this information so that management can obtain estimates of when the project will be completed.

CPM charts are used to determine the *critical* or *longest* path. It is this path, or sequence of activities, that must be reduced in order to make maximum use of company resources. Because of the complex calculations required to prepare a CPM chart, computers are often utilized to produce one.

Consider the chart in Figure 20.3. The dashed line indicates that the next activity connected by this line cannot be started until the previous activity has been completed. For example, Activity 4 cannot commence until Activity 1 has finished, and Activity 8 cannot start until Activities 3, 4, and 5 have all been completed.

It is useful for management to recognize which series of events will take the longest, since that "critical path" will determine when the project can be completed. Observe that it is possible for a CPM chart to have more than one critical path. The critical path is usually indicated on the chart by a heavy line running parallel to the activities that comprise this path. The determination of the longest path for the illustration in Figure 20.3 is shown in Table 20.1.

Table 20.1

Path Number	Activities that Comprise the Path	Total Time for Completion of Path
1	1,4,8	5 + 3 + 8 = 16 weeks
2	1,3,8	5 + 6 + 8 = 19 weeks
3	1,5,8	5 + 4 + 8 = 17 weeks
4	1,5,9	5 + 4 + 5 = 14 weeks
5	2,6,9	7 + 9 + 5 = 21 weeks
6	2,7	7 + 6 = 13 weeks

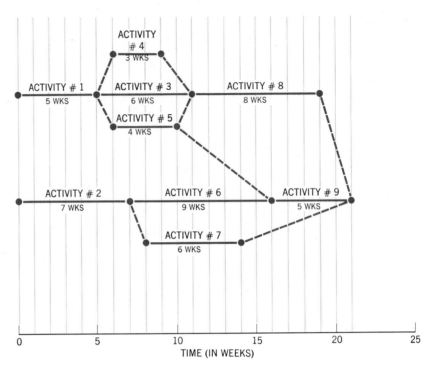

Figure 20.3
CPM Chart.

Path number 5 is thus the critical path, requiring 21 weeks for completion. Knowing this fact, management may decide to reallocate its resources in order to achieve its goal in a shorter time period.

A CPM chart drawn at the outset of a project alerts management immediately to the magnitude of the job ahead. Once the project has begun, the chart is updated periodically to reflect the progress to date. It may also become evident, for example, that some of the original time estimates were incorrect. A reevaluation of all of the paths at this point in time may produce new critical paths.

The process of *updating* a CPM chart involves the following:

1. Observe which activities have been completed since the last time the chart was updated. This can be accomplished by crosshatching the circle at the end of the activity.
2. Reevaluate the times required to finish each activity currently in progress. Previous times should be crossed out, not erased, and the new times should be added to the chart.
3. Reevaluate the estimated times for activities not yet started, and correct them as required.

Systems Analysis and Design

4. Add or delete activities from the chart if there has been a change in the approach to achieving the particular goal.

It should be noted that it sometimes becomes desirable to use a computer to generate and to maintain CPM charts. This is especially true when a given goal has several hundred activities, and the chart is to be updated on a weekly basis. The determination of critical paths in this situation becomes rather tedious.

B. PERT

A PERT chart (Program Evaluation and Review Technique) is similar in construction to the CPM chart. However, essentially three time estimates are associated with each activity, as described below.

1. A *most likely* time for completion of the activity is determined.

2. The earliest expected time for completion, or an *optimistic* estimate for the activity is derived.

3. The latest expected time for completion, or a *pessimistic* estimate for the activity is also determined.

The "most likely time" is the best guess as to the duration of the activity under normal operating conditions. The "optimistic estimate" is the best possible time for completion of the activity. This would occur if ideal conditions existed and if all resources were operating at an optimum level. The "pessimistic estimate" indicates the time required under the worst possible circumstances. With these three estimates for each activity, it is then possible to determine three corresponding times for the overall completion of the project. These times would be: the most likely time for completion, an optimistic time, and a pessimistic time. Management can then review these results to determine how it might want to reallocate its resources and, perhaps, to restructure its priorities. That is, if more resources are allocated, the "optimistic estimate" is more likely to become a reality. If, however, management decides to allocate less resources because of changes in company priorities, then the "pessimistic estimate" is more appropriate.

As with CPM, when many calculations are required, a computer is ideally suited for preparing a PERT chart.

In short, both CPM and PERT are methods of determining and evaluating the progress being made to achieve specified goals or projects. The computer is often used for preparing both. There are prepackaged programs available that will produce both CPM and PERT charts after the computer specialist has supplied specifications appropriate to the individual system. Often, the engineering staff of a large company utilizes PERT and CPM for its time studies.

III. Simulation

A. BASIC CONCEPTS

Simulation is an operations research[6] technique that refers to some representation or model of a system which can be manipulated and studied in order to understand the behavior of the actual system itself.

There are, in essence, two basic kinds of models used. There is the *physical model,* such as a model airplane which is flown in a wind tunnel to simulate actual flight conditions. The other kind of model is the one of primary interest to the businessman, the conceptual or *mathematical model,* which can be described by an analyst and then programmed by a programmer.

The technique of simulation affords the manager the opportunity to ask the computer "What would happen if I were to do this?" thus allowing him to test the effectiveness of decisions without actually implementing them. In this manner, the computer can *simulate* the conditions the manager *intends* to impose on a system and can then project the corresponding results. Listed below are some typical applications to which simulation can be applied for the businessman.

1. How much should the sales force in a department store be increased in order to adequately handle customer demands at peak times?
2. By how much will the addition of a specific number of new machines in a manufacturing plant alleviate production backlogs?
3. How will a specific change in policy of the Inventory Control Department reduce inventory investment and, at the same time, maintain adequate availability of merchandise to meet consumer demands?
4. How will the company's profit picture be affected by specific proposed capital expenditures?
5. How will a change in the store's policy affect sales?
6. How will the addition of a new branch office affect the company's total profits?

Simulation is an extremely powerful technique that is becoming more widespread for several reasons:

1. It uses the computer to *simulate* time so that the effect is the representation of time, in minutes on a computer, of events that would take an actual time span of days, months, or years. Thus, a manager can see immediately what the effects of a particular policy might be over an extended period of time.
2. It is often prohibitively costly, especially in terms of financial risk, time spent, and manpower, for management to implement a

---

[6] *Operations research (O.R.) basically refers to the use of mathematics to solve business problems.*

particular decision on the gamble that it *may* be successful. The use of simulation can increase the likelihood that a simulated decision which is found to be successful will, in actual practice, be a wise one.

3. In many business structures, the interrelationships among the various systems are extremely complex. As a result, it is not possible to determine simple relationships.

   If management varies some facet of one system, for example, the effects on all other systems may not be precisely known. Thus, using simulation, the possible effect of a major policy decision can be more precisely defined.

4. Special high-level programming languages have been developed specifically to facilitate the programmer's task of writing a program to perform simulation experiments. These languages, to mention a few of the more common ones, include:

   a. GPSS—General Purpose Systems Simulator
   b. DYNAMO
   c. GASP—General Activity Simulation Program
   d. SIMSCRIPT

   With the use of these programming tools, the programmer or analyst need only supply a series of system specifications in order for the machine to perform a simulation. Thus, simulation, today, has become more widespread because of software assistance.

5. Simulation is used in many companies as a training tool for management, to enable them to enhance their decision-making skills. Managers can thus participate in *management games,* a technique whereby business leaders can experiment with a hypothetical company to see if they can pinpoint problem areas and to see whether the various decisions made by them to alleviate the *problems* would be effective if implemented. With the use of management games, it is hoped that these business leaders would become more effective in their decision-making role.

B. AN EXAMPLE OF A MANAGEMENT GAME

As was mentioned above, management games as a simulation technique are used in many companies as a training aid for management. There have been many management games developed for this purpose. We will now briefly describe how one of these, the IBM Management Decision-Making Game, operates. The following illustration has been oversimplified in order to present the major concepts of the game, without dwelling on the intricate details.

Let us assume that there are three hypothetical firms in a particular marketing area that produce just one product for sale. At the beginning of the game, all firms start with the same cash, inventory, and plant facilities. The net worth of each firm, in this game, is equal to the total assets of the firm, since none of the firms is allowed to incur debts.

Management personnel are asked to make executive level decisions

Firm 1 Report

SALES ANALYSIS

Orders	253
Sales	253
Unit price	$40
Sales revenue	$10,119
Marketing expenses	$600

PRODUCTION

	Inventory	Plant Capacity	Current Production
Quantity	9	260	216
Unit cost	$35.49	$34.44	$35.49
Total cost	$304	$8,955	$7,650

PROFIT and LOSS STATEMENT

Total Revenue		$10,119
Cost of goods sold	$8,881	
Marketing	$600	
Research and development	$100	
Depreciation	$104	
Total expenses		$9,685
Profit before taxes		$434
Taxes		$217
Net profit		$217

CASH STATEMENT

Old balance		$8,500
Total revenue		$10,119
Production cost	$7,650	
Marketing	$600	
Research and development	$100	
Plant Improvement	$104	
Taxes	$217	
Total outlay		$8,671
New cash balance		$9,948

BALANCE SHEET

Cash balance		$9,948
Current Inventory		$304
Old Plant	$5,200	
Depreciation	$104	
Plant Improvement	$104	
New plant		$5,200
Total assets		$15,452
Net worth		$15,452

Figure 20.4
Simulation models.

576

for each of these hypothetical firms. In this way, the business leaders can observe the effects of any decisions and, depending on which firm produces the greatest profit, the best decision maker for this specific type of firm can be determined.

At the beginning of each operating period, each of the firms makes its own decisions regarding:

1. Price
2. Marketing expenditures
3. Plant improvement expenditures
4. Production expenditures
5. Research and development expenditures

The decisions are punched into cards and fed into a computer. The computer then simulates the behavior of each firm and produces reports, as shown in Figures 20.4 and 20.5, showing the results of the activity in the period. This process can be repeated as many times as desired in order for the manager to see the results of his decisions and what kind of improvement he is making.

Industry Report

Firm 1 Balance Sheet
Cash	$9,948
Inventory	304
Plant	5,200
Total assets	$15,452

Firm 2 Balance Sheet
Cash	$9,948
Inventory	304
Plant	5,200
Total assets	$15,452

Firm 3 Balance Sheet
Cash	$9,948
Inventory	304
Plant	5,200
Total assets	$15,452

Total Market Survey
Total orders	759
Total sales	759
Total marketing expenditure	$1,800
Firm 1 price	$40
Firm 2 price	$40
Firm 3 price	$40

Figure 20.5
Simulation of economic systems.

IV. Linear Programming

Linear programming, like simulation, is an operations research tool that can be used to find the best way of performing a particular activity. That is, linear programming determines the optimal method for performing a task. The term "programming," in this case, refers to the planning of economic activities rather than to the activity of a computer programmer. The term "linear" refers to the fact that this mathematical technique is applicable only if the economic activities being investigated are related in a straight line, or in a linear way. That is, if it costs $1.00 to produce one item, a linear relationship exists if it costs approximately $2.00 to produce two items, $4.00 to produce four items, and so on.

Linear programming problems are most often solved by a computer where a program, often supplied by the computer manufacturer, is used to incorporate the appropriate mathematics.

Fortunately, many business activities that can be analyzed using linear programming usually have a reasonably close linear relationship. The two main types of linear programming problems concern: (1) the allocation of resources, and (2) the transportation problem, as discussed below.

The allocation of resources involves a situation where there are numerous activities that can be performed in many ways, but since the necessary resources are limited not all activities can be carried out in the best way at the same time. The basic idea of the linear programming technique is to allocate the available resources in such a way as to optimize some objective, such as maximization of profits, or minimization of costs, depending on the nature of the problem. As an example, management might want to determine the best way of assigning work to its employees in a factory or, the best way of scheduling jobs on machines. Management might also want to determine the best way to allocate corporate financial resources. Since there are so many variables, a simple problem-solving set of equations cannot be used. Instead, the computer is employed to maximize the desired result. In this way, necessary changes to the variables are listed by the computer to effect maximization of profits, for example.

The transportation problem is a common type of problem solved by the linear programming technique. As an example, a company may have several warehouses located throughout the country which supply various items of merchandise to different stores. The question arises as to the best way to stock merchandise in the warehouses so as to minimize the cost of distribution. Here again, the use of linear programming can help the manager to determine the best decision to make.

We have thus seen some of the sophisticated tools, such as MIS, PERT, CPM, simulation, and linear programming, that can provide the businessman with the information he needs for decision-making and planning purposes. It should be clear to the businessman that these tools can be a great benefit to him in the decision-making process. He must keep in mind, however, that such benefits are sometimes extremely costly. Management Information Systems, in particular, take many years to implement, require the staffing of highly skilled computer specialists, and necessitate the use of extremely sophisticated computer equipment. Many business leaders have undertaken these projects with misinformation as to their cost and requirements. For this reason, the businessman must be cognizant of what he can reasonably expect from such projects *in addition* to being aware of their cost. He should also be familiar with the less costly tools of PERT, CPM, linear programming and simulation, which are often employed as alternatives to costly MIS projects.

1. MIS is an abbreviation for _____ .
2. MIS is a recent advance in computer technology that _____ .
3. A common data base of an MIS system is _____ .
4. Data communications must be used with MIS systems to provide _____ .
5. (T or F) MIS systems are very costly.
6. MIS systems have sometimes failed because of _____ .
7. (T or F) MIS systems are generally used by large companies.
8. CPM is an abbreviation for _____ .
9. PERT is an abbreviation for _____ .
10. CPM and PERT charts are used to _____ .
11. CPM charts drawn at the onset of a project inform management, prior to implementation, of _____ .
12. The three time estimates obtained from a PERT chart are _____ , _____ , _____ .
13. _____ are used to prepare PERT and CPM charts.
14. _____ is a technique that uses a model of a system which can be manipulated and studied in order to understand the behavior of the actual system itself.
15. A computer is used with simulation studies to simulate _____ .
16. (T or F) There are programming languages in use today that can facilitate simulation techniques.
17. The use of management games is a technique whereby business leaders _____ .
18. Linear programming determines the _____ method for performing a task.

SOLUTIONS

1. Management Information Systems
2. provides management with an integrated, all-encompassing approach to the total company in order to facilitate the decision-making process
3. a storage medium containing data required of all subsystems
4. online real-time capability
5. T
6. (a) management's misunderstanding of the system's capability
   (b) computer specialist's lack of understanding of management's requirements

7. T
8. Critical Path Method
9. Program Evaluation and Review Technique
10. assist management in obtaining realistic time estimates of when projects will be completed
11. the magnitude of the job and of possible problem areas that may cause delays
12. most likely completion time; earliest expected completion time; latest expected completion time
13. Computers
14. Simulation

15. time

16. T

17. experiment with a hypothetical company to see if they can pinpoint problem areas and to see whether the various decisions made by them to alleviate the problems would be effective if implemented

18. optimal

Appendix *Numbering Systems and Their Significance in Computer Processing*

I. BINARY NUMBERS

    A. REPRESENTING NUMERIC DATA WITH BINARY NUMBERS
    B. DETERMINING THE DECIMAL EQUIVALENT OF
       A BINARY NUMBER
    C. DETERMINING THE BINARY EQUIVALENT OF
       A DECIMAL NUMBER
    D. ADDITION AND SUBTRACTION OF BINARY NUMBERS

II. OCTAL NUMBERS

    A. REPRESENTING NUMBERIC DATA WITH OCTAL NUMBERS
    B. DETERMINING THE DECIMAL EQUIVALENT OF
       AN OCTAL NUMBER
    C. DETERMINING THE OCTAL EQUIVALENT OF
       A DECIMAL NUMBER
    D. CONVERTING OCTAL TO BINARY AND BINARY TO OCTAL
    E. ADDITION AND SUBTRACTION OF OCTAL NUMBERS

III. HEXADECIMAL NUMBERS

    A. REPRESENTING NUMERIC DATA WITH HEXADECIMAL
       NUMBERS
    B. DETERMINING THE DECIMAL EQUIVALENT OF
       A HEXADECIMAL NUMBER
    C. DETERMINING THE HEXADECIMAL EQUIVALENT OF
       A DECIMAL NUMBER
    D. ADDITION AND SUBTRACTION OF HEXADECIMAL
       NUMBERS
    E. CONVERTING FROM HEXADECIMAL TO BINARY AND FROM
       BINARY TO HEXADECIMAL

IV. REPRESENTATION OF CHARACTERS IN STORAGE

    A. REPRESENTATION OF ZONED DECIMAL CHARACTERS IN
       STORAGE
    B. REPRESENTATION OF DATA IN PACKED FORMAT
    C. OTHER METHODS OF REPRESENTATION

I. Binary Numbers

A. REPRESENTING NUMERIC DATA WITH BINARY NUMBERS

Thus far, we have discussed the use of circuits to represent data in storage. Each core position is represented as "on," when the circuit is complete, or "off" when it is not. We call this a *binary* or two-possibility state.

We shall see in this section that the BINARY NUMBERING SYSTEM, where each digital position can store a 0, denoting "off," or a 1, denoting "on," is ideally suited to representing data in computer storage. (See Figure A.1.)

Keep in mind that all characters such as letters, digits, and special symbols are entered into a computer system as input in a normal alphanumeric form. All printed output from the computer is in a similar readable or alphanumeric form. However, the data is converted internally by the computer to a machine-readable code that is used for processing.

For a complete understanding of computer operations, it is important to know this computer code. It is indeed helpful for the student, since it will give him further insight into computer processing. This can assist him in further understanding and evaluating the tasks of computer specialists and in making judgments about specific computers and their capabilities.

Systems Analysis and Design

BINARY STATE REPRESENTATION

	"0"-STATE	"1"-STATE
CIRCUIT	—o⁄ o—	—o—o—
ELECTRICAL IMPULSE	———————	⎍
MAGNETIC CORE	(DEMAGNETIZED)	MAGNETIZED

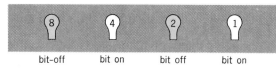

8	4	2	1
bit-off	bit on	bit off	bit on

REPRESENTING A DECIMAL-5

Figure A.1
Binary state representation.

Let us first review some features of our own Decimal Numbering System that apply to the Binary Numbering System as well.

The term *Decimal* denotes 10. That is, there are 10 unique digits, indicated as 0 to 9, that can be used in this numbering system. We say that this system has a *base* of 10.

The Decimal Numbering System is also a *positional* numbering system. This implies that the position or relative location of each digit is significant. The following is a schematic of the Decimal System.

Positional Values

...	10^3	10^2	10^1	10^0	Exponential Value of Position
	1000	100	10	1	Integer Value of Position

That is, the first position has unit or 10^0 value. (Any number with exponent[1] of zero is equal to 1). The second position has value 10, or 10 raised to the first power. The third position has value 100, or 10 raised to the second power or 10×10. The fourth position has value 1000 or 10 raised to the third power or $10 \times 10 \times 10$.

[1] *The term exponent is used to denote a number raised to a specified power. That is, an exponent of 2 indicates a number raised to the second power, or a number multiplied by itself twice. Thus $5^2 = 5 \times 5 = 25$, and $4^3 = 4 \times 4 \times 4 = 64$.*

Thus the number 384 is really:

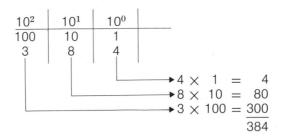

To obtain the rather obvious value three hundred and eighty and four from the three digits 384, we multiply each digit by its positional value. This results in a product, which can be determined in other numbering systems, where the results are not so obvious.

The Decimal Numbering System, as indicated, has 10 unique digits, 0 to 9. To represent the numbers 0 to 9 we merely use the digits 0 to 9. To represent the next number, however, we cannot use an additional digit, since there is not any. Instead, we proceed with the next position (10's position) by putting a 1 there and initializing the units position at zero. Thus we have:

    0
    1
    2
    ⋮
    9
    10
    11
    ⋮
    19

With 1 more than 19, we initialize the units position at zero again and add 1 to the tens position. Thus we have:

    19
    20
    ⋮
    29
    30
    ⋮
    99
    100

When we have utilized all digits in the units and tens positions (99) we proceed to the next position, the hundreds, and begin again by initializing units and tens at zero: 100.

While this entire introduction may seem trite and obvious, we shall

Systems Analysis and Design

see that the basic elements are similar in all positional numbering systems.

The Binary Numbering System is a *base 2* system where only the digits 0 and 1 are used. This is ideally suited to computer processing, where 0 is used to represent an off-state and 1 is used to represent an on-state.

With only 2 digits, we can only represent the numbers 0 and 1 using a single digit. To represent a 2 we must use the next position and initialize the units position at 0. Thus 10 in binary, or base 2, is a 2 in decimal. A 3 would be 11; to represent a 4 we must initialize these two positions and place a 1 in the third position. Thus 100 in binary is a 4 in decimal. A 5 would be 101. Notice that the sequence is 0,1, then proceed to the next position and initialize (10,11,100, and so on).

Binary	Decimal
0	0
1	1
10	2
11	3
100	4
101	5
110	6
111	7
1000	8
⋮	⋮

Let us now consider the *positional* attribute of binary numbers. You will recall that the decimal or base 10 system has the following positional values.

	10^3	10^2	10^1	10^0	Exponential Value of Position
...	1000	100	10	1	Integer Value of Position

That is, a 1 in the second position and a 0 in the units position (10) is the number after 9. When there are no more single digits, we proceed to the next position, initializing the first position with zero.

Since this system has a base 10, each position has a value that is a factor of 10. The first position is 10^0 or 1, the second is 10^1 or 10, ... , the seventh position would be 10^6 or 1,000,000.

The binary numbering system has a base of 2. Thus each position has a value that is a factor of 2. We have then:

	2^4	2^3	2^2	2^1	2^0	Exponential Value of Position
. . .	16	8	4	2	1	Integer Value of Position

You will recall that any number raised to the zero power is 1; 2^1 is 2; 2^2 is 2×2 or 4; 2^3 is $2 \times 2 \times 2$ or 8, and so on. This is logical from our previous discussion: 0 and 1 are the two binary digits. To represent the number 2 we must use the next position. Thus 10 in binary is two in decimal. That is:

2	1	← Integer Value of Position
1	0	← Binary Number

$$0 \times 1 = 0$$
$$1 \times 2 = \underline{2}$$
$$2 \quad \text{Decimal Equivalent}$$

We say, then, $10_2 = 2_{10}$ (10 in base 2 = 2 in base 10).

B. DETERMINING THE DECIMAL EQUIVALENT OF A BINARY NUMBER

Thus all positional numbering systems are similar. To obtain the decimal equivalent of a number in any base, multiply the digits by their positional values and add the results.

EXAMPLE 1

Find the decimal equivalent of 1001 in binary (represented as 1001_2, where the subscript denotes the base).

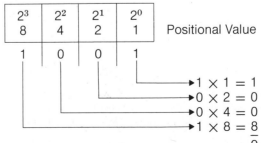

2^3	2^2	2^1	2^0	
8	4	2	1	Positional Value
1	0	0	1	

$$1 \times 1 = 1$$
$$0 \times 2 = 0$$
$$0 \times 4 = 0$$
$$1 \times 8 = \underline{8}$$
$$9 \quad \text{Decimal Equivalent}$$

Thus $1001_2 = 9_{10}$. We can simplify this calculation by eliminating all multiplications where 0 is a factor. Thus we have

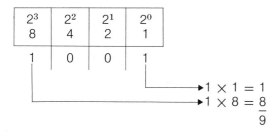

In short, the binary digit 8 and the binary digit 1 are "on," the others are "off." That is, the 8-bit and the 1-bit are on, where bit is an abbreviation for *binary dig*it.

EXAMPLE 2

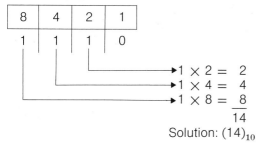

Solution: $(14)_{10}$

EXAMPLE 3

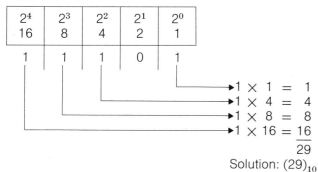

Solution: $(29)_{10}$

Thus, given any binary number we can find its decimal equivalent by the following technique.

```
┌─────────────────────────────────────────────────────────┐
│                  GIVEN BINARY NUMBER—                    │
│                FIND DECIMAL EQUIVALENT                    │
│                                                           │
│   1. Determine positional value of each digit.           │
│   2. Add the positional values for all positions that    │
│      contain a 1.                                         │
└─────────────────────────────────────────────────────────┘
```

C. DETERMINING THE BINARY EQUIVALENT OF A DECIMAL NUMBER

Suppose we are given a decimal number and we wish to determine its binary equivalent.

This is a relatively simple task when small numbers are used. We merely employ the positional values of binary numbers to find the right combination of digits.

EXAMPLE 1

$$(10)_{10} = (?)_2$$

Let us use the positional values of binary numbers:

8	4	2	1
1	0	1	0

We need not use more than 4 binary digits since the next position has value of 16, which exceeds the number we are seeking.

Thus, we must find some combination of 8,4,2,1 that will produce 10. There is, in fact, only one such combination: 8 and 2; that is, the 8- and 2-bits (*binary digits*) are on while the others are off.

This is represented as:

	8	4	2	1
$(1010)_2 =$	1	0	1	0

Thus $(10)_{10} = (1010)_2$.

EXAMPLE 2

$$(14)_{10} = (?)_2$$

Here, again, we use four binary digits since the next position has value 16, which exceeds the required quantity. Again, we must determine what combination of 8,4,2,1 will produce 14.

There is only one such combination: 8,4,2 bits are on $(8 + 4 + 2 = 14)$, while the 1-bit is off.

Thus $(14)_{10} = (1110)_2$.

EXAMPLE 3

$(23)_{10} = (?)_2$

Here, we must use a combination of the numbers 16,8,4,2,1 which will produce 23. We must determine which bits are "on." The 16-bit must be on, since 8,4,2,1 bits can produce a maximum decimal number of 15. Thus the 16-bit must be on to obtain a number larger than 15. The 8-bit is off since 16-8 produces 24 which exceeds the required number. Thus the 16-4-2-1 bits are on and only the 8-bit is off. We have, then,

$(23)_{10} = (10111)_2$

This method of determining the combination of positional values that produces the required number is useful only with small numbers. Consider the task of finding the combination for the decimal number 1087, for example. The above method is too cumbersome for larger decimal numbers.

There is a technique called the REMAINDER METHOD which may be used to convert a decimal number to any other numbering system. The technique is as follows:

REMAINDER METHOD FOR CONVERTING
DECIMAL NUMBERS INTO ANY OTHER BASE

1. Divide the decimal number by the base (for a binary equivalent, we divide by 2).
2. Indicate the remainder.
3. Continue dividing into each dividend (result of previous division) until the divide operation produces a zero result or dividend.
4. The equivalent number in the base desired is the numeric remainders reading from the last division to the first.

EXAMPLE 1

$(38)_{10} = (?)_2$

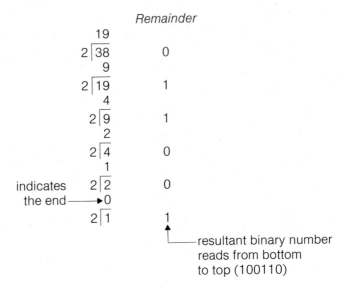

Remainder

When the divide operation produces a dividend or result of zero, then the process is terminated. The binary equivalent, reading from the last division to the first is:

$(38)_{10} = (100110)_2$

We should check our result to insure its accuracy:

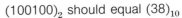

$(100100)_2$ should equal $(38)_{10}$

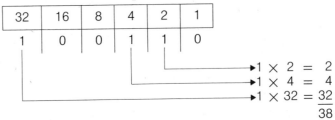

Using the REMAINDER METHOD for converting from decimal to binary, it is a more efficient procedure to perform the first divide operation at the bottom of the work sheet and work up:

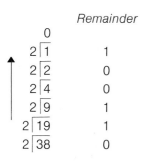

Remainder

$$
\begin{array}{c|c}
 & 0 \\
2\,|\,1 & 1 \\
2\,|\,2 & 0 \\
2\,|\,4 & 0 \\
2\,|\,9 & 1 \\
2\,|\,19 & 1 \\
2\,|\,38 & 0 \\
\end{array}
$$

In this way, the result is read from top to bottom: $(100110)_2$.

EXAMPLE 2

$(67)_{10} = (?)_2$

To find the binary equivalent by determining the combination of positional values can be a long and arduous procedure where the numbers are large. Instead we may use the REMAINDER METHOD:

Remainder

$$
\begin{array}{c|c}
 & 0 \\
2\,|\,1 & 1 \\
2\,|\,2 & 0 \\
2\,|\,4 & 0 \\
2\,|\,8 & 0 \\
2\,|\,16 & 0 \\
2\,|\,33 & 1 \\
2\,|\,67 & 1 \\
\end{array}
$$

Thus the result, reading from top to bottom is: $(1000011)_2 = (67)_{10}$. All operations should be checked for accuracy. Let us make certain that $(1000011)_2$ is indeed equivalent to $(67)_{10}$.

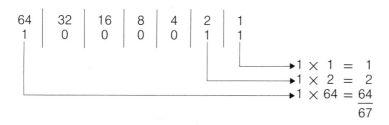

64	32	16	8	4	2	1
1	0	0	0	0	1	1

$$1 \times 1 = 1$$
$$1 \times 2 = 2$$
$$1 \times 64 = 64$$
$$\overline{67}$$

SELF-EVALUATING QUIZ

1. The binary numbering system uses _____ digits.
2. The digits used in the binary numbering system are _____ and _____ .
3. The binary numbering system is ideally suited to computer processing because the digit _____ represents the _____ state and the digit _____ represents the _____ state.
4. The term bit is an abbreviation for _____ _____ .
5. The decimal and binary numbering systems are called _____ numbering system since the location or position of each digit is significant.
6. The binary numbering system has a base of _____ .
7. The binary number 1011 is equivalent to the decimal number _____ .
8. The binary number 110110 is equivalent to the decimal number _____ .
9. The binary number 11101 is equivalent to the decimal number _____ .
10. The largest decimal number that can be represented by 4 binary digits is _____ .
11. The binary equivalent of the decimal number 86 is _____ .
12. The binary equivalent of the decimal number 101 is _____ .
13. The method used to convert a decimal number to a number in another system is called the _____ _____ .

SOLUTIONS

1. two
2. 0;1
3. 0-"off"
  1-"on"

4. *binary digit*
5. positional
6. 2

7. 11

8	4	2	1
1	0	1	1

$1 \times 1 = 1$
$1 \times 2 = 2$
$1 \times 8 = 8$
$\overline{11}$

8. 54

32	16	8	4	2	1
1	1	0	1	1	0

$1 \times 2 = 2$
$1 \times 4 = 4$
$1 \times 16 = 16$
$1 \times 32 = 32$
$\overline{54}$

594

9. 29

16	8	4	2	1
1	1	1	0	1

$$16 + 8 + 4 + 1 = 29$$

10. 15

11. $(1010110)_2$

		Remainder
	0	
2	1	1
2	2	0
2	5	1
2	10	0
2	21	1
2	43	1
2	86	0

12. $(1100101)_2$

		Remainder
	0	
2	1	1
2	3	1
2	6	0
2	12	0
2	25	1
2	50	0
2	101	1

13. REMAINDER METHOD

D. ADDITION AND SUBTRACTION OF BINARY NUMBERS

Thus far, we have seen that binary numbers are ideally suited to computer processing since they can be used to represent the on-off state of circuits. An ''on'' condition in a core of storage can be indicated by a 1; an ''off'' condition by a 0.

We have learned how to convert numbers from binary to decimal by utilizing the positional values and how to convert from decimal to binary by using the REMAINDER METHOD.

This section shall discuss the addition and subtraction of binary numbers as they are handled by the computer.

The addition of binary numbers follows a simple schematic:

ADDITION OF BINARY NUMBERS

For Each Position:

1. $1 + 0 = 1$
2. $0 + 1 = 1$
3. $0 + 0 = 0$
4. $1 + 1 = 0$ with a carry of 1 to the next position.

EXAMPLE 1

BINARY	DECIMAL
10	2
+ 11	+3
101	5

Units Position: $0 + 1 = 1$
Two's Position: $1 + 1 = 0$ with carry of 1
Four's Position: carry of $1 +$ zero (nothing) $= 1$

Thus, we have 101, as the sum.

EXAMPLE 2

BINARY	DECIMAL
1101	13
1010	10
10111	23

EXAMPLE 3

	BINARY					DECIMAL
+	1	1	1	0	1	29
	1	0	1	1	1	23
1	1	0	1	0	0	52

   Notice that in each example, we checked our solution by converting the binary numbers to decimal and then determining if the decimal sum was equal to the binary total. If not, then an error was made in the binary addition.

   The process of binary subtraction is somewhat more complicated than addition. Note that a computer does not perform simple subtraction in the manner that we customarily perform it. It performs subtraction by a series of negative additions:

SUBTRACTION OF BINARY NUMBERS

1. *Complement* the Subtrahend (number to be subtracted) by converting all 1's to 0's and all 0's to 1's.
2. Proceed as in addition.
3. Cross off the high-order or leftmost digit (a 1 when the number is Positive) and add a 1 to the Total (called End-Around-Carry).

EXAMPLE 1

	BINARY	DECIMAL
	1101	13
	−1000	− 8
		5

1. Complement the subtrahend or number to be subtracted:

   Complement of 1000 = 0111

2. Proceed as in addition:

   ```
       1101
   +   0111
     10100
   ```

3. Cross off high-order 1 and add it to result:

   ```
       ̸10100
   +  └───▶1
       ̷0101
   ```

   0 unnecessary: 0101 = 101
   (just as 038 = 38)

Since $101_2 = 5_{10}$, the binary subtraction solution is correct.

EXAMPLE 2

	BINARY	DECIMAL
	11101	29
	−11000	−24
		5

1. Complement the subtrahend:

   Complement of (11000) = 00111

2. Proceed as in addition:

   ```
       11101
   +   00111
     100100
   ```

3. End-Around-Carry:

   ```
       ̸100100
   +  └───▶1
        101
   ```

This procedure for subtraction, which is the method used by the computer, is called COMPLEMENTATION AND END-AROUND-CARRY.

SELF-EVALUATING QUIZ

1. The addition of 1 + 0 or 0 + 1, in binary, results in _____ .
2. The addition of 1 + 1, in binary, results in _____ .
3. The method used by the computer for subtraction of binary numbers is called _____ .
4. 11011
   +10011
   _____

5. 11111   7. 11011
   +11011   −10011
   _____   _____

6. 111   8. 111011
   +101   −110001
   110   _____
   _____

SOLUTIONS

1. 1
2. 0 with a carry of 1
3. COMPLEMENTATION AND END-AROUND-CARRY
4. 101110 (27 + 19 = 46)
5. 111010 (31 + 27 = 58)
6. 10010 (7 + 5 + 6 = 18)

7. 11011
    +01100   (27 − 19) = 8
    ‾‾‾‾‾‾
    ̷100111
    └──→1
    ‾‾‾‾‾‾
    1000

8. 111011
    +001110   59 − 49 = 10
    ‾‾‾‾‾‾‾
    ̷001001
    └──→1
    ‾‾‾‾‾‾‾
    1010

II. *Octal Numbers*

Only on specially constructed engineering or scientific computers are pure binary codes utilized. On these computers, alphanumeric input is automatically converted by the computer to binary, all operations are performed and the data is then converted back to alphanumeric form as output. All displays of core storage images and addresses are in binary.

Pure binary representation has, however, one distinct disadvantage. It requires many more positions for data than any other numbering system. To represent the two-digit decimal number 86, for example, we must use 7 binary digits (1010110). Thus most commercial computers *group* binary numbers in an effort to conserve storage. IBM, specifically, utilizes the hexadecimal or base 16 system that groups four binary digits to form one hexadecimal digit. This system will be discussed in the next section.

Here we will discuss the OCTAL numbering system, or base 8 system, used by other computer manufacturers. We will see that this numbering system can be used to represent *three* binary digits as a single octal number. In this way, we can significantly reduce the number of digits required to represent any number and still maintain the binary concept. That is, we can still utilize the on-off electrical impulse concept of binary numbers to represent numbers:

impulse on: impulse off:
2-bit on ⟋ 1   0 ⟍ 1-bit off

It should be noted here that while some computer specialists and businessmen are unfamiliar with binary, octal and hexadecimal numbering systems, knowledge of these concepts can be very helpful in debugging programs, understanding how a computer operates and selecting computer equipment.

A. REPRESENTING NUMERIC DATA WITH OCTAL NUMBERS

The OCTAL Numbering System uses the 8 digits 0 to 7 to represent any number. The decimal numbers 0 to 7, respectively, are represented by the corresponding OCTAL numbers 0 to 7. The decimal number 8 is represented by a 10 in the OCTAL code. Since 7 is the largest octal number the next octal number (8 in decimal) requires the next position, 10

$$
\left(
\begin{array}{c|c}
\text{Position} \quad 8 & 1 \\
\hline
\text{Value} \quad\quad 1 & 0 \\
\end{array}
\right)
$$

Thus we can begin to see a pattern. In the octal numbering system, as in the binary and decimal systems, we write numbers in sequence until all digits in a specific position are exhausted:

DECIMAL	OCTAL
0	0
1	1
2	2
3	3
4	4
5	5
6	6
7	7
8	10
9	11
⋮	⋮

Thus, we continue with ascending digits, in one position, and in sequence until all digits in the numbering system have been exhausted. Then we initialize the given position with 0 and add 1 to the next position. Consider the following pattern in the OCTAL numbering system:

$$
\begin{array}{ll}
0 & \\
1 & \\
2 & \\
\vdots & \\
\underline{7} & 7 + 1 = 10 \\
10 & \\
11 & \\
\vdots & \\
\underline{17} & 17 + 1 = 20 \\
20 & \\
\vdots & \\
\underline{27} & 27 + 1 = 30 \\
30 & \\
\vdots & \\
\underline{77} & 77 + 1 = 100 \\
100 & \\
101 & \\
\vdots & \\
\underline{107} & 107 + 1 = 110 \\
110 &
\end{array}
$$

B. DETERMINING THE DECIMAL EQUIVALENT OF AN OCTAL NUMBER

Let us analyze the octal numbering system in another way. The decimal, or base 10, numbering system gives value to each position in factors of 10:

...	10^3	10^2	10^1	10^0	Exponential Value
...	1000	100	10	1	Positional Value

The binary, or base 2, numbering system gives value to each position in factors of 2:

...	2^3	2^2	2^1	2^0	Exponential Value
...	8	4	2	1	Positional Value

The octal, or base 8, numbering system gives value to each position in factors of 8:

...	8^3	8^2	8^1	8^0	Exponential Value
...	512	64	8	1	Positional Value

Thus we can determine the decimal equivalent of an octal number by multiplying the positional values by the corresponding digits and adding the results, as illustrated in the following examples.

EXAMPLE 1 $(725)_8 = (?)_{10}$

8^2	8^1	8^0
64	8	1
7	2	5

$$5 \times 1 = 5$$
$$2 \times 8 = 16$$
$$7 \times 64 = 448$$
$$\overline{469}$$ ANS. $(469)_{10}$

EXAMPLE 2 $(707)_8 = (?)_{10}$

8^2	8^1	8^0
64	8	1
7	0	7

$$7 \times 1 = 7$$
$$0 \times 8 = 0$$
$$7 \times 64 = 448$$
$$\overline{455}$$ ANS. $(455)_{10}$

EXAMPLE 3 $(1436)_8 = (?)_{10}$

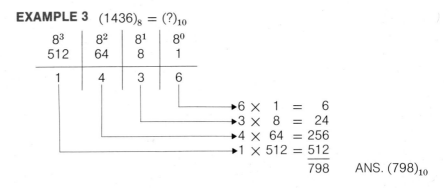

In summary, to find the decimal equivalent of an octal number, we multiply each digit by its positional value.

C. DETERMINING THE OCTAL EQUIVALENT OF A DECIMAL NUMBER

To find the *binary* equivalent of a *decimal* number, we use the *REMAINDER METHOD,* dividing by the base number, 2:

$(15)_{10} = (?)_2$

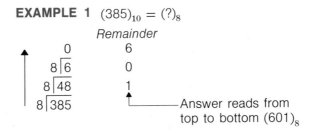

To find the *octal* equivalent of a *decimal* number, we again use the REMAINDER METHOD, this time dividing by the base 8:

EXAMPLE 1 $(385)_{10} = (?)_8$

Remainder

```
        0          6
      8⌐6          0
      8⌐48         1
      8⌐385        
```
Answer reads from top to bottom $(601)_8$

To check our work we should determine if our octal number 601 is equal to the decimal 385:

Systems Analysis and Design

Check:

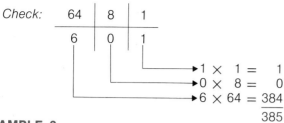

$$1 \times 1 = 1$$
$$0 \times 8 = 0$$
$$6 \times 64 = 384$$
$$\overline{385}$$

EXAMPLE 2

$(1326)_{10} = (?)_8$

	Remainder
0	2
8⟌2	4
8⟌20	5
8⟌165	6
8⟌1326	

Answer reads from top to bottom

ANS. $(2456)_8$

EXAMPLE 3

$(496)_{10} = (?)_8$

	Remainder
0	7
8⟌7	6
8⟌62	0
8⟌496	

ANS. $(760)_8$

Thus, to convert from the decimal numbering system to any other system, we may use the REMAINDER METHOD, using the base of the latter as a divisor. To convert a decimal number to an octal number, we divide by 8, using the remainder of each division to produce a solution.

D. CONVERTING OCTAL TO BINARY AND BINARY TO OCTAL

At the beginning of this section, we learned that octal numbers are used to represent data on many computers in place of binary numbers. Binary numbers are uniquely suited for computers since each position can be represented as a 1 or 0, that is, an on or off state of an electrical impulse. Such numbers, however, are often cumbersome to deal with, since it requires many binary numbers to represent relatively small decimal numbers. To represent 26, for example, we must use 5 binary digits, 11010. To make more efficient use of computer storage, we can group binary numbers in some pattern. The OCTAL NUMBERING SYSTEM can be represented as a group of 3 binary digits, or bits. That is, any three binary digits can be represented as a single octal number.

EXAMPLE 1

$(100111)_2 = (?)_8$

4	2	1	4	2	1
1	0	0	1	1	1
	4			7	

ANS. $(47)_8$

In short, we subdivide binary numbers into groups of threes, with the positional value of each group represented as 4 2 1. We then determine the octal equivalent.

EXAMPLE 2

$(11011)_2 = (?)_8$

This number does not contain two complete groups of three. You will recall, however, that 11011 is the same as 011011, since high-order or leading zeros have no significant value. 011011 does contain two complete groups:

4	2	1	4	2	1
0	1	1	0	1	1
	3			3	

ANS. $(33)_8$

Note that a computer usually uses the binary numbering system since each core of storage can be represented as on or off depending on whether an electrical current or impulse is present. Data on many such computers can be represented for display purposes on core image printouts in the *octal system*. In this way, the computer can easily print out data by combining binary numbers into groups of

Systems Analysis and Design

threes. This is a relatively simple conversion and requires far less circuitry than converting binary numbers into *decimal* numbers for display purposes. Thus if a storage position contained 11111110, and the computer were asked to display this position, it would be a simple task to display it in the OCTAL system:

011   111   110
 3   7   6

In short, many computers utilize the octal numbering system for displaying core image printouts to programmers and operators. That is, data that is currently in the computer can be accessed by a programmer or operator if he can read the octal code. Such core images are usually required when a program has an error and requires correction.

These computers accept normal alphanumeric or decimal codes and print reports or write other forms of output in decimal, as well. But instead of converting binary numbers to *decimal,* which can be very cumbersome because of the number of digits, they convert to *octal* first and then to decimal.

EXAMPLE 1

$(110111110011011)_2 = (?)_{10}$

To use the normal method of multiplying the digit by its positional value is, indeed, cumbersome:

16384	8192	4096	2048	1024	512	256	128	64	32	16	8	4	2	1
1	1	0	1	1	1	1	1	0	0	1	1	0	1	1

$$
\begin{array}{r}
1 \\
2 \\
8 \\
16 \\
128 \\
256 \\
512 \\
1024 \\
2048 \\
8192 \\
16384 \\
\hline
(28571)_{10} \quad \text{ANS.}
\end{array}
$$

It would be far simpler to determine the octal equivalent of the above and then to determine the decimal number.

I. Convert to octal

110	111	110	011	011
6	7	6	3	3

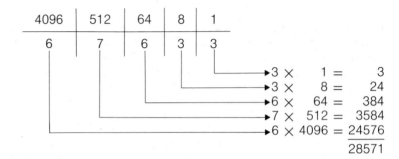

4096	512	64	8	1
6	7	6	3	3

$$3 \times 1 = 3$$
$$3 \times 8 = 24$$
$$6 \times 64 = 384$$
$$7 \times 512 = 3584$$
$$6 \times 4096 = 24576$$
$$28571$$

ANS. $(28571)_{10}$

Thus, to simplify conversions, many computers utilize the octal numbering system. In fact, most operations could be performed in the octal system, to further simplify computer procedures.

It is just as simple as the above to convert from octal back into binary. Thus a computer can convert a number from binary to octal, perform the required operations, and convert back again into binary. To convert from an octal number to a binary number, we merely represent each octal number as three binary numbers, as shown below.

EXAMPLE 1

$$(725)_8 = (?)_2$$

7	2	5
(421)	(421)	(421)
111	010	101

ANS. $(111010101)_2$

EXAMPLE 2

$$(302)_8 = (?)_2$$

3	0	2
011	000	010

ANS. $(011000010)_2$ or $(11000010)_2$ since the high-order zero has no significance.

E. ADDITION AND SUBTRACTION OF OCTAL NUMBERS

Thus far we have seen the conversions required from any octal, binary, or decimal number to any of the other systems. Let us now see how to perform the arithmetic operations of addition and subtraction of octal numbers.

To add two octal numbers, we proceed as we do in the decimal system, keeping in mind, however, that if any addition produces an octal number in excess of 7, we must utilize the next position: $8_{10} = 10_8$, $9_{10} = 11_8$, and so on.

EXAMPLE 1

$(73)_8 + (24)_8 = (?)_8$

```
   73
+  24
-----
  117
```

ANS. $(117)_8$

EXAMPLE 2

$(243)_8 + (745)_8 = (?)_8$

```
   243
+  745
------
  1210
```

ANS. $(1210)_8$

We should check our work by converting each of the octal numbers into the decimal system and determine if, in fact, the addition is correct.

To subtract in the octal numbering system, we may use the complementation and end-around-carry method used in the subtraction of binary numbers: $(715)_8 - (603)_8 = (?)_8$

```
   715
 - 603
```

1. COMPLEMENT THE SUBTRAHEND: 174
603 + (ITS COMPLEMENT) = 777
(*ANY NO.*) + (ITS COMPLEMENT) = 777

2. PROCEED AS IN ADDITION

$$
\begin{array}{r}
715 \\
+\ 174 \\
\hline
1111
\end{array}
$$

3. END-AROUND-CARRY

① 111
   └──▶1
   ────
   112   ANS. $(112)_8$

It is very useful to be able to perform arithmetic operations in the octal numbering system when utilizing a machine that employs this code. Suppose, for example, that a computer program has a "bug" or error in it. While the program is running, a computer display indicates the following:

PROGRAM CHECK INTERRUPTION 5721.

This implies that at core storage position 5721 there is an error.

It is possible to find this error on a program listing which indicates core storage positions of each instruction. The address of the instruction often cannot, however, be determined directly. In many cases, the program listing indicates each instruction address in relative terms; that is, relative to the loading point of the program. The computer must relocate each program at the time of execution to allow room for the supervisor and any other necessary programs or subroutines. Thus while the program listing may denote instructions from storage positions 0000 to 3653, which are the available numbers at compile time, the computer may actually place the program in storage positions 3012–6665. For many computers, these addresses are noted on program listings and displayed in the octal numbering system. Thus to find the instruction at 5721, we must first subtract the starting address of the program, 3012. Since the program *listing* begins at 0000 we must find the *absolute* error point, which is determined by subtracting the actual or relocated starting address from the actual program error point.

$$
\begin{array}{r}
5721 \\
-\ 3012 \\
\hline
\end{array}
$$

1. COMPLEMENT THE SUBTRAHEND: 4765

2. PROCEED AS IN ADDITION

$$
\begin{array}{r}
5721 \\
4765 \\
\hline
12706
\end{array}
$$

Systems Analysis and Design

3. END-AROUND-CARRY

①2706
└──→1   ANS. 2707

Thus 2707 on the program listing would be the error point, where the error may be found.

In short, for computer purposes, we can think of the octal numbering system as a shorthand method for representing binary numbers. Since each group of three binary numbers can be used to represent a single octal number, a computer can eliminate much of the cumbersome qualities of binary numbers by representing some of its internal computer codes in the octal system.

SELF-EVALUATING QUIZ

1. The octal numbering system has a base of _____, using numbers _____ .
2. The major advantage of octal numbers for computers is

   _____ .
3. The use of binary numbers by computers is advantageous because _____ .
4. Binary numbers, for display purposes, however, are often

   _____ .
5. Three binary numbers may be used to represent _____ .
6. One octal number may be used to represent ___(no.)___ binary digits or bits.
7. $(8975)_{10} = (?)_8$

8. $(7099)_{10} = (?)_8$

9. $(7576)_8 = (?)_{10}$

10. $(6607)_8 = (?)_{10}$

11. $(111011111)_2 = (?)_8$

12. $(11110000110)_2 = (?)_8$

13. $(7552)_8 = (?)_2$

14. $(66051)_8 = (?)_2$

15. $(11111111011111111)_2 = (?)_{10}$
    HINT. Convert first to the octal system.
16. Suppose you are helping to debug a program that has an error at storage location 7562. The program listing has instructions that have absolute addresses beginning at 0000. The program has been relocated to start at 3300. Find the absolute error point that can then be found on the program listing.

SOLUTIONS

1. 8; 0–7

2. it may be used to represent binary numbers by combining them into groups of threes

3. each binary digit or bit can be used to represent the on (1) or off (0) state of a circuit

4. cumbersome because many digits are required to represent relatively small decimal numbers

5. a single octal number

6. three

7. $(8975)_{10} = (?)_8$

	0	*Remainder*
	8 ⎴2	2
	8 ⎴17	1
	8 ⎴140	4
	8 ⎴1121	1
	8 ⎴8975	7

ANS. $(21417)_8$

8. $(7099)_{10} = (?)_8$

	Remainder
0	
8 ⎴1	1
8 ⎴13	5
8 ⎴110	6
8 ⎴887	7
8 ⎴7099	3

ANS. $(15673)_8$

9. $(7576)_8 = (?)_{10}$

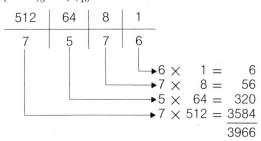

512	64	8	1
7	5	7	6

$$6 \times 1 = 6$$
$$7 \times 8 = 56$$
$$5 \times 64 = 320$$
$$7 \times 512 = 3584$$
$$\overline{3966}$$

ANS. $(3966)_{10}$

Systems Analysis and Design

10. $(6607)_8 = (?)_{10}$

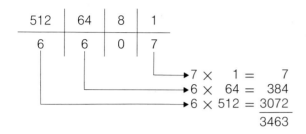

512	64	8	1
6	6	0	7

$$7 \times 1 = 7$$
$$6 \times 64 = 384$$
$$6 \times 512 = 3072$$
$$3463$$

ANS. $(3463)_{10}$

11. $(111011111)_2 = (?)_8$

111	011	111
7	3	7

ANS. $(737)_8$

12. $(11110000110)_2 = (?)_8$

011	110	000	110
3	6	0	6

ANS. $(3606)_8$

13. $(7552)_8 = (?)_2$

7	5	5	2
111	101	101	010

ANS. $(111101101010)_2$

14. $(66051)_8 = (?)_2$

6	6	0	5	1
110	110	000	101	001

ANS. $(110110000101001)_2$

15. $(111111111011111111)_2 = (?)_{10}$
I. CONVERT TO OCTAL

011	111	111	011	111	111
3	7	7	3	7	7

$(377377)_8$

II. CONVERT FROM OCTAL TO DECIMAL

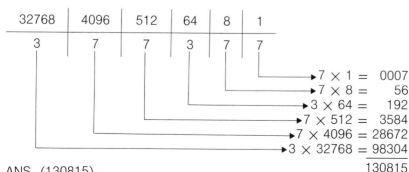

32768	4096	512	64	8	1
3	7	7	3	7	7

$$7 \times 1 = 0007$$
$$7 \times 8 = 56$$
$$3 \times 64 = 192$$
$$7 \times 512 = 3584$$
$$7 \times 4096 = 28672$$
$$3 \times 32768 = 98304$$
$$130815$$

ANS. $(130815)_{10}$

611

16.

```
  7562
 −3300
  4262
```

OR USING COMPLEMENTATION AND
END-AROUND-CARRY:
I. COMPLEMENT SUBTRAHEND 4477
II. ADD 4477 + 7562 = 14261

III. END-AROUND-CARRY ① 4261
└──▶1
4262

III. *Hexadecimal Numbers*

A. REPRESENTING NUMERIC DATA WITH HEXADECIMAL NUMBERS

We have seen that a computer uses binary numbers rather than decimal numbers to perform arithmetic operations. This is because the two binary numbers 1 and 0 can be made to correspond to the on-off state of computer circuits.

Note however that it is not feasible for the computer to utilize an entire storage position to represent one binary digit. Binary numbers utilize many positions to represent relatively small numbers. While the decimal number 23 would use two storage positions, one for the 2 and one for the 3, its binary equivalent 10111 would utilize *5* storage positions. Thus to have the computer store a single binary digit in one storage position would make inefficient use of large core storage capability.

Instead, the computer can group together *four* binary digits to produce a single digit in the hexadecimal numbering system. In this way, each storage position can be used to store a hexadecimal digit, where the digit corresponds to four binary digits.

The Hexadecimal Numbering System has a base of 16. That is, there are 16 individual digits corresponding to decimal numbers 0 to 15 as follows:

Hexadecimal	Decimal
0	0
⋮	⋮
9	9
A	10
B	11
C	12
D	13
E	14
F	15

Systems Analysis and Design

B. DETERMINING THE DECIMAL EQUIVALENT OF A HEXADECIMAL NUMBER

Note that while the decimal numbering system has only *10* digits 0 to 9, the hexadecimal numbering system requires 6 more individual characters to represent numbers 10 to 15. Arbitrarily, the letters A to F were selected to represent these numbers.

To determine the next number after F in the hexadecimal system (or 15 in decimal) we must utilize the next position. That is, $(10)_{16} = (16)_{10}$. Since the hexadecimal numbering system has a base of 16, each positional value can be expressed as a factor of 16:

. . .	16^3	16^2	16^1	16^0
. . .	4096	256	16	1

To determine, then, $(10)_{16}$ in base 10 we have:

16	1
1	0

$$0 \times 1 = 0$$
$$1 \times 16 = 16 \qquad \text{ANS. } (16)_{10}$$

We use the same method as previously discussed to convert from any numbering system to the decimal system: multiply each digit by its positional value and then obtain the sum or total. Do not become disoriented by the use of hexadecimal digits A to F. When performing any arithmetic operation, merely convert them to their decimal counterpart (10 to 15, respectively).

EXAMPLE 1

$$(AF)_{16} = (?)_{10}$$

16	1
A	F

$$15 \times 1 = 15$$
$$10 \times 16 = \underline{160}$$
$$175 \qquad \text{ANS. } (175)_{10}$$

EXAMPLE 2

$(B6A)_{16} = (?)_{10}$

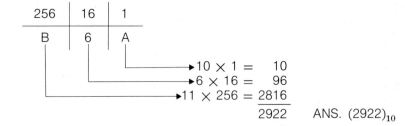

256	16	1
B	6	A

$$10 \times 1 = 10$$
$$6 \times 16 = 96$$
$$11 \times 256 = \underline{2816}$$
$$2922 \qquad \text{ANS. } (2922)_{10}$$

C. DETERMINING THE HEXADECIMAL EQUIVALENT OF A DECIMAL NUMBER

To convert from the hexadecimal numbering system to the decimal system we use the Remainder Method, by dividing by 16.

EXAMPLE 1

$(382)_{10} = (?)_{16}$

Remainder in Hex.

```
        0          1
     16⌐1          7
     16⌐23         E
     16⌐382
```

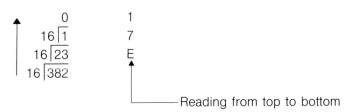

———— Reading from top to bottom

ANS. $(17E)_{16}$

EXAMPLE 2

$(1583)_{10} = (?)_{16}$

Remainder in Hex.

```
        0          6
     16⌐6          2
     16⌐98         F
     16⌐1583
```

ANS. $(62F)_{16}$

Systems Analysis and Design

D. ADDITION AND SUBTRACTION OF HEXADECIMAL NUMBERS

Arithmetic Operations in hexadecimal are similar to those in other numbering systems. Perform the operation on each column decimally, convert the decimal number to hexadecimal, and proceed.

EXAMPLE 1

$(BAD)_{16} + (431)_{16} = (?)_{16}$

$$
\begin{array}{ccc}
B & A & D \\
4 & 3 & 1 \\
\hline
F & D & E
\end{array}
$$

$11 + 4 = 15$
$= F$ $10 + 3 = 13$ $13 + 1 = 14$
$= D$ $= E$ ANS. $(FDE)_{16}$

EXAMPLE 2

$$
\begin{array}{cccc}
 & C & B & A \\
+ & 6 & 2 & 7 \\
\hline
1 & 2 & E & 1
\end{array}
$$

$12 + 6 = 18_{10}$
$= 12_{16}$ $10 + 7 = 17_{10} = 11_{16}$ (carry 1)

ANS. $(12E1)_{16}$

Keep in mind that the carrying of hexadecimal numbers to the next position is performed in exactly the same manner as in the decimal numbering system. A sum of 16 results in a carry of 1 ($10_{16} = 16_{10}$).

EXAMPLE 3

$$
\begin{array}{cccc}
 & 8 & 3 & E \\
 & F & 6 & F \\
\hline
1 & 7 & A & D
\end{array}
$$

$14 + 15 = (29)_{10} = (1D)_{16}$ (carry 1)

ANS. 17AD

We can subtract hexadecimal numbers by again converting each digit to decimal for each position and then converting the difference obtained back to hexadecimal. Note that the system of borrowing from or exchanging with the next position results in an exchange of 16 rather than 10.

EXAMPLE 1

$$(26)_{16} - (7)_{16} = (?)_{16}$$

$$\begin{array}{ccc} 26 & 1 & (16+6) \\ -7 = - & & 7 \\ \hline 1 & F & \end{array} \quad \text{ANS. 1F}$$

On some computers, specifically the IBM line, computer printouts *of storage locations* and their contents are specified in hexadecimal. While the normal program output is printed decimally, any program specifications are indicated in hexadecimal. Thus programmers are required to understand positional numbering theory to assist in computer processing.

When errors or "bugs" exist in a program or when programmers wish to pinpoint the contents of specific storage locations for testing purposes, they must be able to perform hexadecimal arithmetic.

Core Dumps, or displays of storage contents, are given in hexadecimal. Thus a programmer may be advised that his program began at hexadecimal location 28E6 and that an error occurred at location 3EF2. His program listing has the address of each instruction, but only in relative terms, that is, from address 0000 on with no relation to where the program began. Thus to obtain the absolute error point and to find the corresponding instruction he must subtract the starting point, 28E6, from 3EF2 to obtain the absolute error point.

In order to extract items from core storage, then, the average programmer must understand hexadecimal arithmetic:

$$\begin{array}{l} 3EF\,2 \\ -28E\,6 \\ \hline 160C \quad \text{ABSOLUTE ERROR POINT} \end{array}$$

E. CONVERTING FROM HEXADECIMAL TO BINARY AND FROM BINARY TO HEXADECIMAL

At the start of this section, we indicated that hexadecimal numbers are used by some computers because they effectively reduce 4 binary digits to a single digit.

That is, we can represent any four binary digits by a single hexadecimal digit.

Given any binary number, regardless of its size, we can convert it to a hexadecimal number by dividing it into groups of four digits and representing each group with a single hexadecimal digit.

EXAMPLE 1

$$(1101001101110111)_2 = (?)_{16}$$

8421	8421	8421	8421
1101	0011	0111	0111
D	3	7	7

ANS. $(D377)_{16}$

616

EXAMPLE 2

$(101101111)_2 = (?)_{16}$

0001	0110	1111	
1	6	F	ANS. 16F

Note that when the binary number does not consist of a multiple of four digits, it can be enlarged by using high-order or insignificant zeros. That is, 11 is the same as 0011, which has 4 digits. Because of the simple relation between binary and hexadecimal digits, the computer can represent data in hexadecimal, by still maintaining the binary (on-off state) configuration.

Notice also that it is sometimes easier to determine the *decimal* equivalent of a *binary* number by first finding its hexadecimal equivalent. A large binary number requires numerous calculations to determine the positional values, and then to convert to decimal. The conversion process is simplified from hexadecimal to decimal and since we can easily represent binary numbers as hexadecimal numbers, the double conversion often simplifies the operations.

Let us consider the binary number in Example 2 directly above.

$(101101111)_2$

Suppose we wish to find its decimal equivalent. We can use the standard method by determining each positional value and then adding all "on" positions. Or we can convert the number to hexadecimal and obtain 16F as in the example. Then we can convert:

256	16	1
1	6	F

$$15 \times 1 = 15$$
$$6 \times 16 = 96$$
$$1 \times 256 = \underline{256}$$
$$377$$

ANS. $(377)_{10}$

Often we find that the time it takes to convert large binary numbers to the decimal numbering system is significantly reduced by performing the intermediate conversion to hexadecimal.

SELF-EVALUATING QUIZ

1. $(8E6)_{16} = (?)_{10}$

2. $(9FC)_{16} = (?)_{10}$

3. $(1387)_{10} = (?)_{16}$

4. $(8365)_{10} = (?)_{16}$

5.   8EC
   +DE2

6.   9CC
   +DEE

7.   9CE
   −8DF

8.   AEC
   −932

9. $(11011111110111)_2 = (?)_{16}$

10. $(111111101111)_2 = (?)_{16}$

SOLUTIONS

1. $(8E6)_{16} = (?)_{10}$

256	16	1
8	E	6

$6 \times 1 = \quad 6$
$14 \times 16 = \quad 224$
$8 \times 256 = \underline{2048}$
$ 2278 \qquad$ ANS. 2278

      Systems Analysis and Design

2. $(9FC)_{16} = (?)_{10}$

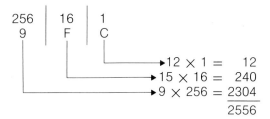

256	16	1
9	F	C

$$12 \times 1 = 12$$
$$15 \times 16 = 240$$
$$9 \times 256 = \underline{2304}$$
$$\overline{2556} \qquad \text{ANS. 2556}$$

3. $(1387)_{10} = (?)_{16}$

        Remainder in Hex.

$$
\begin{array}{ll}
\phantom{16\overline{)}}0 & 5 \\
16\overline{)5} & 6 \\
16\overline{)86} & B \\
16\overline{)1387} &
\end{array}
$$

ANS. 56B

4. $(8365)_{10} = (?)_{16}$

        Remainder in Hex.

$$
\begin{array}{ll}
\phantom{16\overline{)}}0 & 2 \\
16\overline{)2} & 0 \\
16\overline{)32} & A \\
16\overline{)522} & D \\
16\overline{)8365} &
\end{array}
$$

ANS. 20AD

5.
$$
\begin{array}{r}
8EC \\
DE2 \\
\hline
16CE
\end{array}
$$

6.
$$
\begin{array}{r}
9CC \\
DEE \\
\hline
18BA
\end{array}
$$

7.
$$
\begin{array}{r}
9CE \\
8DF \\
\hline
0EF
\end{array}
$$

8.
$$
\begin{array}{r}
AEC \\
-932 \\
\hline
1BA
\end{array}
$$

9. $(11011111110111)_2 = (?)_{16}$

0011	0111	1111	0111
3	7	F	7

ANS. $(37F7)_{16}$

10. $(111111101111)_2 = (?)_{16}$

1111	1110	1111
F	E	F

ANS. $(FEF)_{16}$

IV. *Representation of Characters in Storage*

We shall discuss a common method for representing data in storage. Although this method is not universal, it is applicable to many computers.

Each storage position consists of 8 cores which may be used to represent 8 bits or binary digits. Each storage position, or group of 8 bits, is called a *byte*.

A. REPRESENTATION OF ZONED DECIMAL CHARACTERS IN STORAGE

As we have seen, the computer utilizes its own code for representing data in storage. Through a combination of on-off bits in each storage position or byte, we can represent all possible characters.

Each byte is often divided into 2 groups of 4 bits:

The high-order four bits, numbered bits 0 to 3, represent the *zone* and the low-order four bits, numbered bits 4 to 7, represent the *digit* portion.

You will recall that letters and special characters in the Hollerith code utilize a zone (12,11 or 0-zone) in conjunction with a digit.

The chart in Figure A.2 illustrates the computer code that corresponds to the Hollerith code.

Each zone is converted to a binary equivalent in the high-order 4 bits of a byte. The digit portion 0 to 9 corresponds to the binary equivalent of digits 0 to 9. Thus the letter A in Hollerith, a 12-zone and a 1 punch, is:

Zone				Digit			
8	4	2	1	8	4	2	1	Positional Value
1	1	0	0	0	0	0	1	Bits

BYTE

The 12-zone corresponds to 1100, a 12 in binary and the 1 is a 0001. A hexadecimal printout of this byte would be: C1(8 + 4 in the hexadecimal system is a C). That is, the zone and digit portions are treated independently for printout purposes.

The letter T corresponding to 0–3 punches is represented as:

Systems Analysis and Design

Character	EBCDIC Zone	Digit	Hollerith
A	1100	0001	12-1
B	1100	0010	12-2
C	1100	0011	12-3
D	1100	0100	12-4
E	1100	0101	12-5
F	1100	0110	12-6
G	1100	0111	12-7
H	1100	1000	12-8
I	1100	1001	12-9
J	1101	0001	11-1
K	1101	0010	11-2
L	1101	0011	11-3
M	1101	0100	11-4
N	1101	0101	11-5
O	1101	0110	11-6
P	1101	0111	11-7
Q	1101	1000	11-8
R	1101	1001	11-9
S	1110	0010	0-2
T	1110	0011	0-3
U	1110	0100	0-4
V	1110	0101	0-5
W	1110	0110	0-6
X	1110	0111	0-7
Y	1110	1000	0-8
Z	1110	1001	0-9
1	1111	0001	1
2	1111	0010	2
3	1111	0011	3
4	1111	0100	4
5	1111	0101	5
6	1111	0110	6
7	1111	0111	7
8	1111	1000	8
9	1111	1001	9

Figure A.2
EBCDIC and Hollerith Codes for representation of characters.

Zone				Digit			
8	4	2	1	8	4	2	1
1	1	1	0	0	0	1	1

0-ZONE   3-DIGIT

In a hexadecimal printout, the T would be represented as E3. All numeric characters are represented in this form, by a sign and a digit. For unsigned numbers, all zone bits are on. Thus we have 1111 as the zone portion of all numbers. The number 8 then is represented in a byte as:

Zone				Digit			
8	4	2	1	8	4	2	1
1	1	1	1	1	0	0	0

+   8

The 1111 in the zone portion of a byte is used to represent an unsigned number which is assumed to be positive. The selection of 1111 was based on the fact that it would make unsigned numbers the highest in the collating or sorting sequence. Note that an unsigned 5 in a hexadecimal printout of core storage would read as F5.

A definitive positive sign is denoted by 1100 and a minus sign by 1101.

This particular computer code is called EBCDIC an abbreviation for *Extended Binary Coded Decimal Interchange Code*. The original BCD (Binary Coded Decimal) code was used on second-generation computers.

Note that, as indicated in the previous section, each group of 4 bits or binary digits can be used to represent a single hexadecimal digit. Thus a shorthand method for representing characters in EBCDIC is to represent them as *two* hexadecimal digits. Since each hexadecimal digit is used to represent 4 binary digits, two hexadecimal digits are needed to represent 1 byte or 8 bits.

E6 in hexadecimal represents the EBCDIC code for W:

Zone				Digit			
1	1	1	0	0	1	1	0

0-Zone   6-Digit

This is equivalent to 0–6 in Hollerith or the letter W (see Figure A.2).
F5 in hexadecimal represents the Zoned Decimal Format in EBCDIC for a positive 5:

Zone	Digit
F	5
1111	0101

All unsigned numbers in zoned decimal format are represented hexadecimally with an F followed by a digit.

In addition to the 8 bits, a P-bit (parity bit) is used to insure that there is always an odd number of bits on. Hence EBCDIC is a 9-bit code.

B. REPRESENTATION OF DATA IN PACKED FORMAT

Thus far, we have seen how data may be represented in Zoned Decimal Format using one byte of storage for each character.

For numeric items, we have seen how a byte can store one digit, where the zone portion is equivalent to all bits on, a hexadecimal F, and the digit portion is the binary equivalent of decimal numbers 0 to 9.

Consider the number 68254. Using zoned decimal format, it would take 5 bytes to represent this number in storage, one for each digit. The zone portion of each byte would indicate all bits on, as in Figure A.3.

It really is unnecessary to represent a zone for each digit within the number. That is, one zone for the entire field to indicate that the number is signed positive, would suffice. There is a method that can be employed so that the computer eliminates or strips the zone of all digits except one to indicate the sign. Thus the zone portion of each byte can be employed to represent *another digit*. In this way, *two* digits can be represented by a single byte. This technique is called *PACKING* (see Figure A.3).

It operates as follows:

1. The zone and digit portions of the *low-order* digit are reversed.

ZONED DECIMAL REPRESENTATION OF THE NUMBER 68254:

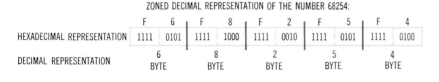

PACKED REPRESENTATION OF THE NUMBER 68254:

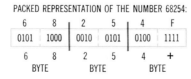

Figure A.3

Representation of zoned decimal and packed formats

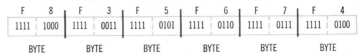

REPRESENTATION OF 835674 IN ZONED DECIMAL FORMAT

F	8	F	3	F	5	F	6	F	7	F	4
1111	1000	1111	0011	1111	0101	1111	0110	1111	0111	1111	0100

BYTE BYTE BYTE BYTE BYTE BYTE

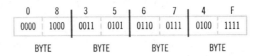

REPRESENTATION OF 835674 IN PACKED FORMAT

0	8	3	5	6	7	4	F
0000	1000	0011	0101	0110	0111	0100	1111

BYTE BYTE BYTE BYTE

Figure A.4

Thus all 1's or a hexadecimal F, in the low order 4 bits of a byte, indicates that the byte contains a packed number. (All 1's could not be used to represent any single digit.)

2. All other zones are stripped and 2 digits are *packed* into 1 byte.

Thus 68254 in packed format is indicated as in Figure A.3.

Note that the number in zoned decimal format utilizes 5 bytes while in packed format it utilizes only 3 bytes. A major advantage of packing numbers is to conserve storage.

Figure A.4 illustrates the number 835674 in both zoned decimal and packed format.

To complete or "fillup" the high-order byte, we add four zero bits at the beginning of the field.

Thus, for numeric fields, we can save considerable storage space by using the packed format. In addition the computer *requires* numeric fields to be packed in order to perform arithmetic operations. To print out or display numeric fields, however, they must be in zoned decimal format.

In most programming languages such as COBOL, FORTRAN, or PI/1 the programmer need not instruct the computer to pack prior to any arithmetic instruction. The computer will generate the pack instruction prior to an arithmetic operation, generate the arithmetic command, and then unpack the field so that it is in zoned decimal format for any printing or displaying.

C. OTHER METHODS OF REPRESENTATION

EBCDIC is a common method of representing data in storage. BCD, Binary Coded Decimal, is the method from which EBCDIC has been devised. BCD is still in use today.

The BCD code consists of a check bit (C) and B A 8 4 2 1 bits. Including the check bit, it is considered a 7-bit code. It is used as an internal computer code predominantly for second-generation computers.

To represent a digit, we use any combination of the digit bits
8 4 2 1. That is, to represent a 2 we use the 2 bit; to represent a 7 we
use the 4 2 1 bits.

To represent a zone we use the following bit configuration:

BA   12-zone
B   11-zone
A   0-zone

Thus, to represent the letter A, corresponding to the Hollerith code of
12 and 1 punches, in the BCD code is BA1; to represent the letter M
(11–4), we have C B 4. The C-bit is a check bit which is automatically
turned on to insure that there is always an *odd* number of bits on in
one storage position.

SELF-EVALUATING QUIZ

1. Numeric data can be represented in storage in _____ format or in _____ format.
2. The term _____ is used to represent a single core storage position.
3. The high-order ____(no.)____ bits of a byte is the _____ portion.
4. The low-order ____(no.)____ bits of a byte is the _____ portion.
5. The zone portion of a byte that is used for unsigned numbers is _____ .
6. EBCDIC is an abbreviation for _____ .
7. The letter G represented in EBCDIC is _____ .
8. The letter M represented in EBCDIC is _____ .
9. To conserve storage, numbers are represented in _____ format.
10. The number 63872 in zoned decimal format, represented hexadecimally is _____ and uses ____(no.)____ bytes.
11. The above number in packed format, represented hexadecimally is _____ and uses ____(no.)____ bytes.

SOLUTIONS

1. zoned decimal; packed
2. byte
3. 4; zone
4. 4; digit
5. 1111 (F in hexadecimal notation)
6. *Extended Binary Coded Decimal Interchange Code*

7. | 1100 | 0111 |
|---|---|

8. | 1101 | 0100 |
|---|---|

9. packed

10. | F6 | F3 | F8 | F7 | F2 |
|---|---|---|---|---|
; 5

11. | 63 | 87 | 2F |
|---|---|---|
; 3

Index

630   *Index*